BROKEN
LANDSCAPES

BROKEN LANDSCAPES

SELECTED LETTERS *of* ERNIE O'MALLEY

1924–1957

Edited by CORMAC K.H. O'MALLEY and NICHOLAS ALLEN

AFTERWORD BY DAVID LLOYD

THE LILLIPUT PRESS
DUBLIN

First published 2011 by
THE LILLIPUT PRESS
62–63 Sitric Road, Arbour Hill,
Dublin 7, Ireland
www.lilliputpress.ie

A CIP record for this title is available from
The British Library.

1 3 5 7 9 10 8 6 4 2

ISBN 978 1 84351 195 3

Set in 9.5 on 12.5 pt Sabon by Marsha Swan
Printed in England by MPG Books Ltd, Cornwall

Contents

Illustrations   VI

Acknowledgments   IX

Introduction: Nicholas Allen, *Ernie O'Malley's Afterlife*   XI

Personal Note: Cormac K.H. O'Malley, *Searching for Ernie*   XXVII

Prologue: *A Volunteer's Experience*   I

PART I: European Travel, 1924–1926, and Ireland, 1926–1928   7

PART II: Travel in the United States and Mexico, 1928–1935   45

PART III: Dublin and the West of Ireland, 1935–1944   121

PART IV: Post-Emergency Life, 1945–1950   215

PART V: Decline, 1950–1957   277

Afterword: David Lloyd, *On Republican Reading*   375

Appendix I: Critical Works   389

Appendix II: Malley and Hooker Family Relationships   431

Appendix III: List of Works by or about Ernie O'Malley   432

Abbreviations   433

Notes   435

Index   499

Illustrations

The following plates are between pages 258 and 259.

Ernie O'Malley climbing in the Pyrenees, winter 1926

Ernie O'Malley driving Helen Golden's car from California to New Mexico, September 1929

Ernie O'Malley in Carmel, California, May 1929

Helen Hooker with her sculpted fawn, New York City, July 1930

Ella Young, Eithne Gold and Marianna Howe at Ranchos de Taos, New Mexico, 1934

Helen Hooker, New York City, 1930

Ernie O'Malley at Acoma Indian pueblo, New Mexico, 1930

Ernie O'Malley in the Yaddo Foundation Class of September 1932, Saratoga Springs, New York

Helen Hooker and Ernie O'Malley, New York City, 1934

Helen H. O'Malley, 1937

Ernie O'Malley and his brother, Dr Kevin Malley, at Kilteel, Co. Kilkenny, 1937

Catherine (Bobs) and Harry Walston, Burrishoole Lodge, March 1939

Ernie O'Malley at gravestones of Diarmuid and Grania, Louisburgh, Co. Mayo, 1938

Cathal O'Malley, nurse and Ernie O'Malley, Burrishoole Lodge, 1939

Ernie O'Malley in beekeeping gear, Burrishoole Lodge, during the Emergency, 1942

Leased lands, overlooking Burrishooole Abbey, Burrishoole Lodge, 1942

Threshing of wheat, Burrishoole Lodge, 1942

Etain, Cathal and Cormac O'Malley, Burrishoole Lodge, 1945

Cathal, Etain, Helen, Ernie and Cormac O'Malley, Clonskeagh, Dublin, 1946

Jack B. Yeats and Ernie O'Malley, at an art exhibition in Dublin, 1947

During the filming of *The Quiet Man*, June 1951: Ernie O'Malley, Maureen O'Hara, Tom Maguire, John Wayne, Metta Stern, John Ford

Ernie and Cormac O'Malley, Burrishoole Lodge, with guard dog,
    August 1951

Cormac and Ernie O'Malley, Galway Races, July 1954

Ernie and Cormac O'Malley, Kilmurvey, Inishmore, Aran Islands, August 1954

John Ford and Ernie O'Malley, after filming, Co. Clare, May 1956

John Ford and Ernie O'Malley on location in Co. Clare, May 1956

Cabinet ministers Seán Lemass, Eamon de Valera and Frank Aiken attending
    Ernie O'Malley's state funeral procession in Howth, Co. Dublin,
    27 March 1957

Funeral oration by Sean Moylan, TD, at Ernie O'Malley's graveside,
    Glasnevin Cemetery, Dublin, 27 March 1957

Acknowledgments

Many of my father's friends have helped me over the past forty years in assembling elements of this publication. I hope that I have not overlooked any and offer my apologies if I have. Many original letters, some photocopies of letters, and much anecdotal information used in footnotes or otherwise, were given or told to me by his friends, their children, grandchildren or custodians. I am grateful to all who have helped, including the families of Frank Aiken, Anthony Behan, James Brady and Andy Cooney, Sighle Breathnach-Lynch, Martin Brennan, Dorothy Brett, Mrs Rose Byrnes, Seamus Cashman, Rebecca Citkowitz (Liber), Madge Clifford and Jack Comer, Eamon de Valera, Luke Duffy, John Ford, Frank Gallagher, Eithne Golden, Helen Merriman Golden, Sigle Humphreys (O'Donoghue), Spud Johnson, Una Joyce, John V. Kelleher, P.J. Kelly, Thomas J. Kieran and Delia Murphy, Emmet Larkin, Mary Lavin, Michael MacEvilly, Jean McGrail, Des MacHale, Roger and Patricia McHugh, Bryan McMahon, Tom Maguire, my father's family, Desmond O'Malley, Ita (Mrs Patrick) Malley, Kathleen Malley Hogan, Liam Manahan, Maighread and Seamus Murphy, Michael Noyk, Frank O'Connor, Matthew O'Connor, Peadar O'Donnell, Sean O'Faolain, Liam O'Flaherty, Aodghain and Maureen O'Rahilly, Tommy O'Reilly, Johnny and Bea Raleigh, Liam and Barbara Redmond, Michael Sheehy, Sammy Sommerville-Large, Jack Sweeney, James Johnson and Laura Sweeney, Sean Sweeney, executor of the estate of James Johnson Sweeney, Catherine and Harry Walston, Tony Woods. My brother, Cathal, and sister, Etain, were supportive of this enterprise as was my late mother, Helen Hooker O'Malley Roelofs, who kept finding letters for me in the 1980s. Needless to say this effort could never have been accomplished but for the backing in so many ways, including research, transcription and moral support, of my wife, Moira Kennedy O'Malley and our children, Bergin O'Malley Boyle and Conor O'Malley, as well as my son-in-law David Boyle.

Fortunately, many original letters and records are now held in institutional archives from which I have received photocopies, and their staffs have been most helpful to me over the years. They include Susan Charlas, Registrar, Paul Strand Archive, Aperture Foundation, Amy Rule and Tammy Carter, Center for Creative Photography, University of Arizona (Paul Strand and Eward Weston Archives, posthumous digital reproduction from original negative, Edward Weston Archive, Center for Creative Photography, © 1981 Arizona Board of Regents), Indiana University-Bloomington (Lilly Library, John Ford Archives), Irish College Rome (Vera Orschel), Limerick City Gallery, the Military Archives including the Bureau of Military History (Commandant Victor Laing), the National Archives, the Yeats Archives of the National Gallery of Ireland (Roisin Kennedy), the National Library of Ireland (Noel Kissane, Gerald Lyne), the New York Public Library, Radio Telefís Éireann Archives (Brian Lynch), the Tate Gallery Archives (Adrian Glew), Trinity College Library (Bernard Meehan, Keeper of Manuscripts), University College Dublin Archives (Seamus Helferty), University of Chicago (*Poetry* Magazine Archives), and Yaddo Foundation. My archive of Ernie O'Malley Papers relating to his life after 1924 were presented in 2010 to the Archives of Irish America, Tamiment Library, Bobst Library, New York University in New York City.

Some special recognition is due to those individuals who have helped me at various points in this long journey, including transcription, well above the normal collegial level of support, including Frances-Mary Blake, Marion Casey, Mabis Chase, Mary Cosgrove, Riann Coulter, Anne Dolan, Richard English, J.J. Lee, Padraic MacKernan, Deirdre McMahon, Niamh O'Sullivan at Kilmainham Gaol Museum, Susan Schreibman, Matt Thomas and Liam Webb. Seamus Helferty and his staff at UCDA have been most helpful in allowing access to the Ernie O'Malley Papers over the years.

Antony Farrell of The Lilliput Press encouraged me for the last decade to persevere and to bring this project to completion. My original manuscript of typed letters had no real form until the talents of my co-editor Nicholas Allen turned a mere manuscript into an interesting book, and for this I am deeply indebted.

Cormac K.H. O'Malley, 2011

Introduction
Ernie O'Malley's Afterlife

NICHOLAS ALLEN

Ernie O'Malley was born in Castlebar, Co. Mayo, in May 1897. He died in Dublin aged fifty-nine, long weakened by wounds sustained during the Irish revolution. This book is a collection of his letters in the period after his involvement in the Anglo-Irish and civil wars. The period previous has been covered in two documentary volumes, *Prisoners: The Civil War Letters of Ernie O'Malley*, and *'No Surrender Here!' The Civil War Papers of Ernie O'Malley*. These are in addition to Richard English's biography, *Ernie O'Malley: IRA Intellectual*, and the various books that O'Malley published or brought to manuscript form in his own lifetime. A hidden hand in this activity is Cormac O'Malley, Ernie's youngest son by marriage to Helen Hooker, the American heiress whose presence makes for much of the drama in the later pages of this book. Cormac has spent a lifetime in pursuit of his father, who died when he was a boy. This pursuit, as Cormac describes it, follows a sense of Ernie O'Malley as an unknown figure. The letters show a caring, considerate and occasionally fierce father of Cormac and his two siblings, Cathal and Etain. But the domestic presence bumped continually against the public profile, Ernie O'Malley a controversial figure into his late life, losing a libel case for his representation of one Volunteer action during the War of Independence and representative to some of an unforgiving republicanism.

Cormac's desire to fill out the picture of his father is well rewarded here. The one-dimensional portrait of the revolutionary with an ambition to write is given depth by the following letters. These confirm O'Malley's interest in the cultural life of not only Ireland but also America, Mexico and Europe during the great period of transition from representative art to modernism in the first half of the twentieth century. Further, they show his equal rooting in the practical life of family and farm. Having married Helen Hooker, O'Malley moved to Burrishoole, Co. Mayo, where the two struggled to keep a family in the damp extremes of the western climate. Their mostly separate excursions to Dublin and its nightlife of pubs and theatres show a city still alive after the excitements of the pre-independence period. Through it all O'Malley kept a correspondence with a set of friends and associates that is published now in a record of his less well-known life after release from internment in 1924. When Cormac asked if I might help him with this book I had no idea of its promise. Like most readers I knew O'Malley from *On Another Man's Wound*, an imaginative memoir that John McGahern considered among the best works of Irish prose. I remember reading the book for the first time in appreciation of its landscape as much as its action. *On Another Man's Wound* is an account of coming to a sense of one's self through engagement with the natural world as much as it is a reflection on the traumas, experienced and inflicted, of an active life (which reminds me of J.J. Lee's acute observation of O'Malley's portrait of the artist as revolutionary, not the other way round). These letters detail and deepen the mental cartography of O'Malley's work and life. They offer insight into the progress of a life through many trying situations, from spoiled crops to a failing marriage. Ever the strategist, O'Malley met these challenges with a persistent imagination, his insistent independence a personal metaphor for the social collective that he espoused once so violently.

In the following pages, I offer a reading of O'Malley's cultural presence, rather than repeat details of his life, which are to be found in Richard English's indispensable biography. Similarly, the contributions of Anne Dolan and J.J. Lee to *'No Surrender Here!'* have upholstered fully O'Malley's involvement in the revolutionary period. Rather than give an overview of the materials to follow here, I direct the reader to the short essays that introduce each section for particular details of O'Malley's life as it progressed. If this introduction gives a setting for O'Malley's achievement, it speaks also to David Lloyd's afterword, which builds a broader context for O'Malley's writing. As Lloyd argues, O'Malley lived an idea of the republic as much as he articulated its ideals. Given this, I have taken latitude to range widely across O'Malley's creative life, and perhaps to the reader abruptly, in order to give some sense of what I understand to be his unique achievement. O'Malley is remembered now as an insurgent and a writer. He was a leading organizer and activist during the War of Independence. Violently against the Anglo-Irish Treaty, he was party to the republican surrender at Dublin's Four Courts in late June 1922. This period is memorialized in one of the great prose works of twentieth-century Irish literature, *On Another Man's Wound*, which was published in 1936. O'Malley's transition from activist to writer has been a transition that many of his readers have found difficult to negotiate. Historians have looked to the memoir as a material account of his specific involvement in particular actions. The licence taken by the work of art has registered in many of their readings as evidence of laxity, or worse.[1] Literary scholars have been unsure where to place O'Malley (which has meant frequently that he has no place at all). He has retained a passionate place among many readers. But there is no sign to date of his entrance to the canon of twentieth-century writing, despite the skill, composition and reflection of his prose. The clipped lyric of O'Malley's writing owes its various origins to his time in the Americas, his experience as a senior officer in the revolutionary movement and his voracious reading in literatures of many traditions. This heterodox formation challenges many local assumptions; that republicanism and republicans are bound to single-frame versions of politics and the past; that literature is by definition antipathetic to the actuality of violence. These assumptions lead to curious disfigurements, suitably dissected by J.J. Lee in his introductory essay to the earlier volume of O'Malley's civil war papers, 'No Surrender Here!', and amplified in David Lloyd's afterword to this book.

Put simply, Ernie O'Malley's anomalous condition reflects our history, not his. The inability to situate the complexity of his life in any vital sense of combined activity is a challenge to Richard English's *Ernie O'Malley: IRA Intellectual*.[2] Similarly Ann Dolan's introduction to 'No Surrender Here!' misplaces O'Malley as 'little more than a literary figure'.[3] The answer might be that for all his activity in the War of Independence and civil war, O'Malley's enduring importance might be exactly here, in the literature. More than this, it might be argued further that culture was the presiding sphere of intellectual dissidence in the decades post-independence. Given the state's tortuous acquaintance with words in the form of treaties and constitutions, it is no surprise to think that words in the form of novels and newspapers, magazines and manifestoes, might have operated as a continuing republic of letters. Certainly O'Malley's former comrades thought so. He found himself in America first as a fundraiser for *The Irish Press* and on his return to Ireland was enticed into the set of former republicans who formed *The Bell*.[4] Typically, O'Malley took this activity one step further. An autodidact of relentless energy, he pursued an interest in the visual arts that took him from the sodden fields of the west of Ireland to the dry baked murals of Mexico. To read the letters, diaries and fragments that follow is to enter into more than a testimonial to one person's genius. It is to think how, when and, less frequently, why Ireland entered into global conversation even in the years of its most apparent separation. It did so through the movement of its people, their contacts and their chance relationships. A great gift of these letters is the revelation of the subterranean networks that most of us cultivate, but few preserve. O'Malley's correspondence across Europe and the Americas throws light on an Ireland that often sits in darkness. The skills of improvisation, once learnt in war, persist in a straitened economy, O'Malley chasing up contacts to cadge petrol coupons, whiskey, places to stay.

The O'Malley of the following pages is, then, a character that few of his readers, friendly or otherwise, will recognize. Partly this problem is our own, partly it is inherited. Elements of O'Malley's archive have been available to scholars for decades. Besides their biographical and contextual use, little has been made of their importance as a rebuke to the limitations of our theories of the past. The cold exterior of a young man burdened with mortal responsibility over his soldiers begins to

thaw in the walking tour he set himself through France, Spain and Italy on release
from prison in 1924. Certain habits of his war experience remained throughout
his life; an attachment to brusque orders to even his closest relations; a careful,
sometimes miserly, account of stores and possessions; a physical stubbornness
that kept him moving even as the doctors ordered rest. Other elements flowered,
particularly his study of art, literature and history. O'Malley's dissociation from
his siblings has been read as evidence of his fanatical republicanism; the letter that
marks D.H. Lawrence's death with reflection on O'Malley's dead brother and
friends places his psychological response in more human context.[5] His feeling for
children is evident. O'Malley's papers are full of books his girl and two boys might
read. One letter jumps to life with the rhythm of a boisterous band played out by
the children on tree stumps.

The farm at Burrishoole was run on model lines. A small holding, its fences
ran up against long-established locals who did not always welcome the blow-ins,
O'Malley and his American wife. The farm buzzed with the activity of bee hives
and cattle, but there is a sense always of a darker future only just kept at bay.
Two photographs in Cormac O'Malley's possession show this in vivid detail. One
pictures Ernie O'Malley in good health, the garden well attended, the flowers in
bloom. The next shows him in worse health and older, the lawn now weedy and
long. The O'Malleys hung on in Mayo, as did many others. The privileged packages of cheese and fine foods from Dublin were not enough to make a livable life
on the edge of the Atlantic. It is hard not to think of their many neighbours who
had to make do with less. The liminal landscape between earth and sea around
Clew Bay offered a welcome escape. Through it all there are the family troubles
that marked his private life, O'Malley's marriage to Helen Hooker eventually a
difficulty for them both. The unveiling of this private world in letters offers a
glimpse into the lived past of an Ireland that we know more frequently from statis-
tics and encyclicals. For O'Malley the flame kept singing, if lit from a different fire.
These letters present a revised figure whose focus is less the revolutionary war than
the revolution in art. The year 1922 saw the publication of *Ulysses* as well as Irish
independence. *On Another Man's Wound* took its place in this modernist tradition
with its Joycean composition in Europe and the Americas. O'Malley knew Beckett,
was a friend of Jack Yeats and an encouragement to Louis le Brocquy.

A suggestion might be again that O'Malley's investment in this cultural world
of mid-century Ireland was the result of a near unique set of circumstances. His
marriage into money and the liberty of his military pension afforded him the rare
advantage of resources and time with which to develop his interests. Once again,
O'Malley is the exception. The letters and diaries collected in this volume suggest
otherwise. There was a deeper dimension to the practice of literature, art and criticism than we allow. A reason for our contemporary ignorance of this fact is that
such activity took place in unlikely venues, in pubs, branch libraries and commercial galleries. O'Malley seems the exception, in part because of the paucity of our
contemporary historical account. The late nights, theatre shows, ballet productions
and cinema all form the basis of an underworld whose tips we see in those other

great singular characters of the period, Patrick Kavanagh and Brendan Behan, both of whom make brief appearance in O'Malley's correspondence. Dublin, in addition, reveals itself as an international transit point for scholars, diplomats and intellectuals. Whatever their individual projects, these people invariably ended up on Dublin's dinner and drinks circuit. If O'Malley was in their company he noted their names and so we have a newly rich source by which to map the social networks of a steadying state that was beginning to find form after the terrors of the twenties. This source suggests some of the darkness that made for Ireland's edges. Helen Hooker O'Malley's suffering during and after the delivery of her first child Cathal points to the professional unaccountability that still persists. And the suggested violence of disaffected neighbours suggests that the land hunger that attended, and perhaps impelled, the revolutionary war, continued decades afterwards. O'Malley played many roles in this society. In Mayo he was a farmer, an oddity, and a hero of the independence war. In Dublin he was a writer, drinker and sometime dissident. In between he could be found taking photographs of medieval church monuments, collecting folklore and, later in his life, conducting an epic set of interviews with republicans whose memories offer counterpoint to the official mechanism of the Bureau of Military History.

O'Malley's standing in this volume proceeds from his ability as a writer. To date, the primary document of his achievement has been *On Another Man's Wound*, which is set between the year of O'Malley's birth and the Truce of 1921. Its chronological order gives careful account of O'Malley's involvement in key moments of the Anglo-Irish conflict, particularly in his attacks on police barracks and the raid for guns that led to the burning by way of reprisal of Mallow, Co. Cork. This well-inscribed Ireland of intimate violence and local knowledge is shrouded with other, less immediately visible, layers of experience. An archival recovery of O'Malley's writing life asks us to rethink the ways in which experimental art and literature registered dissidence from a post-imperial state. This dissidence has disappeared largely from the cultural account, smothered by the familiar intimacies of constitutional argument and high political history. O'Malley's letters, diaries, photographs and paintings create an alternate critical panorama in which it is possible to imagine art in coincidence with republican cultures that were modernist in their impulse to look at the local globally. Mid-century Irish culture was made of images found to hand. Patrick Kavanagh's long poem *The Great Hunger* is perhaps the best example. Later, John McGahern trod his familiar ground with increasing ambition. This literature shows little of the improvisational techniques of more familiar experimenters like Beckett and Joyce. Suggestive in O'Malley's archive, and the letters from it that appear here, is the possibility of a lost bridge from the townlands of Ireland to the still pressing contemporary questions of social and cultural responsibility. In the ruins of our present island it is possible to see in O'Malley's writing a correspondence between the familiar and the unknown, which is rendered from Kavanagh to McGahern in images of spiritual frustration. There is less space in O'Malley for reflection since time so rarely stood still. Just as in his near and late contemporaries, O'Malley's engagement with an unwritten republic helped shape a new set of questions for Ireland after empire, of how intellectuals imagined a world beyond the immediate in images of the partial and the unfinished. O'Malley's place in this shifting world was registered early. He was kept a prisoner in Jameson's Distillery with Seán Lemass after the Four Courts surrender. Since no one had locked the door they walked out.[6] O'Malley spent the next fugitive months moving between hiding places. His last redoubt was a windowless hidden room in the home of the Humphreys family, from which he slipped occasionally for tennis in the garden or a cycle to his other fugitive colleagues. An army raiding party stormed the house and in the confusion O'Malley shot and grazed a housemate before shooting dead a soldier, Peter McCartney. Running for cover as he tried to escape, O'Malley was shot several times and was captured, as reported in *The Irish Times* of Monday 6 November. These wounds added to the crushed feet suffered in torture by British soldiers in Dublin castle in late 1920. Refusing to reveal his real identity O'Malley was then beaten by interrogators who disbelieved he was Bernard Stewart of Kilkenny. A medical student at University College Dublin before his involvement in the Volunteer movement from 1916, O'Malley later gave a clinical account of his injuries to the Irish pension board: 'Seven wounds in back, two on left high up below lung wound and in towards spine; five on right side, scattered, but between a middle line halving the lung and the spine.'[7]

In 1924 O'Malley was one of the two last prisoners to be released from internment in the Curragh Camp. He left jail weakened physically and mentally drained after a prolonged hunger strike (and one letter to Erskine Childers' widow Molly asks for art catalogues to read even as his arms were too weak to hold them).[8] Penniless and without profession O'Malley joined the post-civil-war exodus of republican prisoners from Ireland. Most went to Boston or New York, but O'Malley struck off for the Pyrenees where he discovered a love for climbing. There he continued his habits of intrigue by pairing up with Basque separatists. The landmarks of his journey were the churches and museums of Italy, passing through Florence, Rome and Sicily. O'Malley felt later that the 'years abroad taught me to use my eyes in a new way'.[9] He had carried art books throughout his military campaigns but here, for the first time, were Giotto, Michelangelo, Fra Lippi. This grand tour ended with O'Malley's return to Ireland by October 1926. The subsequent extension of his visual vocabulary was the foundation of O'Malley's later enthusiasm for many of the century's key Irish painters. He could not settle back in Dublin (and it is ironic to read this insurgent general worrying about his parents' reaction to his inattentive scholarship). Failing his second-year medicine exam in 1928, O'Malley was recruited by Eamon de Valera to travel to New York with Frank Aiken and raise money for the proposed publication of *The Irish Press*, a newspaper in support of constitutional republicanism.

O'Malley spent the next months grimacing through his hosts' bloodthirsty introductions to evening speeches. At the Waldorf Astoria in October 1928, the 'chairman introduced me, said that I had fired the first shot in 1916, that I had once after blowing up a rifle range flung gelignite at a party of soldiers and rescued prisoners, that I had left school at 17'.[10] He watched Gaelic football at Innis-fail Park and ran into old Volunteer associates. In all he had few friends and the grind of sourcing contacts for fundraising told on his patience. The work took him from one coast to the other and by 1929 he was released from his duties. Left at a loose end he travelled to New Mexico, making his way there in pursuit of a meeting with Ella Young, the Celticist and poet who made a career for herself in the University of California at Berkeley. It seems to have been during a trip to Carmel, California, that the idea of spending time in Taos, New Mexico, came to him. Having arrived there he entered a social set that included the actress Helen Merriam Golden and the painter and author Dorothy Brett. He lived in a cabin on the grounds of Golden's property and taught her children in exchange for food and lodging. As O'Malley described to Golden, 'I took my "Kick in the Pants Tribe" into the hills "for training".'[11]

> When the imagination and communal sense is stimulated, it is easier to talk about an attitude to nature, people and life than if one did it in class in a 'preachy' way. That is how I trained my Fianna Company and my young brothers. I have some bronze woodpecker feathers for the tribe but they'll keep.[12]

In the same period, O'Malley wrote of D.H. Lawrence. A letter to Brett of March 1930 registers his surprise at the writer's death.

> I did not know that he had been so ill. I had finished *Sons and Lovers* and am re-reading *The Plumed Serpent*. I'm sure it must have been a shock to you, expecting and looking forward to meeting him again in Spring. I do not know whether you like me to write as a grief is often so personal that one does not want anybody to intrude.[13]

There follows an upset reflection on his own experience.

> I have seen so many of my comrades die that death seems as much a part of life as life itself. Yet I know that there were some deaths that I never recovered from. They left a strange void which has always remained, a gap, yet a communion as well for I can feel the dead, nor would I be surprised to find someday that they walked in to resume an interrupted conversation. I found it easier to get over the losses in my own family than I did those of my friends ... I think I understand how you feel and though I feel for you myself, sympathy somehow can never be properly expressed in writing. Often the gaps in conversation mean more than the lucid, placid flow of words. I send you a piece of sage from Taos Mountain.[14]

This letter establishes many of the themes of O'Malley's life. Grief and fam-ily trouble are measured in writing and landscape, the physical and emotional trouble of life compensated for with a persistent, near-obsessive, fascination with the forms of art. There was good reason as to why he felt the dead near him in New Mexico since O'Malley spent what time he could writing of his past. He read as he worked, particularly in Coleridge, De Quincy, Swift and Sterne. With three chapters composed he began to send drafts to New York for circulation among publishers. December 1930 brought the opportunity to drive south to Mexico with the artist Dorothy Stewart. He later recalled to Harriet Monroe, the editor of *Poetry* magazine in Chicago, his attendant friendship with Hart Crane, the poet in Mexico City on a Guggenheim Fellowship.

> We became friends and remained friends to the end despite clashes from my sense of personal discipline and his lack of it. Inspired by our memories of poetry and stimulated by rum toddies we wrote long letters to many people, amongst them Wallace Stephens, E.E. Cummings, and yourself whom Hart always referred to as Aunt Harriet. Unfortunately we afterwards burnt the letters ... I liked him a great deal. He was generous, enthusiastic and spoke the most amazing rhetoric, good rhetoric. He believed in America, in its creative ability and had a dislike for the nostalgia of induced foreign culture as a standard.[15]

This friendship is an intriguing foundation for O'Malley's own writing. As he drank cognac in Mexico City he sent letters to friends trying to trace his posted drafts ('I am missing four chapters and if they're lost to hell with the book').[16] This American light reflects through *On Another Man's Wound*. First, the lyrical landscapes echo on occasion the abundance of Crane's *The Bridge*.[17] Second, and related to this, given the intersection in Mexico new and old between writing and painting, there is a visual aspect to his work that comes to connect O'Malley's memories of the War of Independence to the writing of literature. One passage describes O'Malley and his orderly Jerry Kiely caught in an ambush in the Blackwater Valley in Cork. Just before a ferocious firefight the two halt by the river bank.

> I had heard a starling mimic a disgruntled sparrow and then the clear whistle call of a blackbird. As we watched him feed on purple elder-berries there was an orange blue-green flash and a petulant screech as a kingfisher slipped into yellow flags amongst the reeds at the bottom of the slope.[18]

The bright panorama of radical activity found its Mexican correlative in the public frescoes of Diego Rivera and Jose Clemente Orozco. O'Malley appreciated Rivera's use of colour but thought his art decorative. Orozco was magnificent (though interestingly, and perhaps self-revealingly, O'Malley felt Orozco slipped to propaganda in his representation of the bourgeoisie). O'Malley registered a quality of hopelessness in the Orozco paintings that spoke to his civil-war experience. O'Malley experienced Mexico as a new beginning. He had established friendships outside the Anglo community in Taos and Santa Fe, and was aware acutely of the colonial disfigurement of Mexican society. As with Ireland, that disfigurement had long and complex historical roots. The Catholic churches that he visited caught his attention in this regard, the formality of their architecture in juxtaposition with their sometimes gaudy interiors. Catholicism and the invader were nothing new to O'Malley. More unusual was the sympathy he maintained with the people he encountered, a fellow feeling that suggests a social ethic not usually associated with a die-hard republican. Perhaps in Mexico, as later with Burrishoole and his family, O'Malley found a social ideal in existence only in a personal relationship to broken places. And Ireland was never far away, even in Mexico City. He wrote to Merriam Golden at the time.

An ex-British officer wants to get in touch with me. He said he had to resign during the Tan War as he refused to do dirty work, and he talks in terms of a high rank which an unfortunate individual was supposed to have held there. Did you ever smell a Secret Service man. The poor British, they still (pardon me, senora) think they are like their own backsides; they can't be licked![19]

O'Malley's interest in Mexico extended to his work in training schools for rural teachers. He used his spare time for archaeological research in the Academy of Fine Arts, work that surfaced a decade later in a broadcast on Mexican art for the BBC's *Third Programme*.[20] On returning to New Mexico in late 1931, O'Malley decided to travel east in pursuit of a book contract. He ended up in New York, working briefly for a state park on Long Island and staying at Hartford House, a respite for the indigent. One break was his receipt of a residential fellowship at the Yaddo Foundation for writers and artists in Saratoga Springs. By this time he had written eighteen chapters of *On Another Man's Wound*. He was still unsure of its final form, as a memoir or as a collection of short stories (and this tension can be read in the book's final section, which deals with an execution of captured British officers in a motif very similar to Frank O'Connor's 'Guests of the Nation', published in the *Atlantic Monthly* in 1931 and shot by Denis Johnston as a film in 1933 and 1934. Silent, it was first shown at the Gate Theatre to a soundtrack of Holst's *The Planets*).[21] Moving on the margins of New York's literary circles O'Malley was invited to the home of Elon Hooker, a successful industrialist, in June 1933. Hooker's daughters were artistic and travelled. Helen Hooker had spent a year painting in Russia, learning dance in Greece and was a sculptress. Her sister Adelaide later married the bestselling novelist John Marquand; Blanchette married John D. Rockefeller III. Helen's father argued with O'Malley over 'American Indians' and the 'negro question';[22] O'Malley was banned from the house as a dangerous revolutionary. As the two grew close the Hooker family sent a family friend to Ireland to scout O'Malley's family history. Wryly, he remarked later:

I had a cousin, Sir Gilbert Laithwaite, who had been private secretary to Curzon, or whoever tried to settle the Indian question at the expense of the Indians. Sir Gilbert evidently showed some sign of respectability. He was interested in Ming Ware, a good judge of claret and I expect he wore a silk hat in bed.[23]

The two continued to correspond as O'Malley travelled. One letter has him jobbing at the Irish Free State exhibition at the World's Fair in Chicago in July 1933, tongue in cheek, as he put it. In his spare time he visited the Newberry Library and the Field Museum, looking at 'a Basque head that reminded me of Scipio Africanus, whom I have always admired as a soldier, and some strange faces from Kashmir'.[24] The Hooker family's solution was for the mother to take Helen and Adelaide on a tour of Japan in 1935. Helen, however, continued the trip around the globe, arriving in London where they were married in September 1935. O'Malley's only financial prospect besides his pension was the publication of his book. He was offered the opportunity to run for a Fianna Fáil Dáil seat for South Dublin the same year, which he refused, wanting to 'be free to settle my own affairs and look for a job independent of a government'.[25] His book did not promise much. It was rejected by fifteen American publishers, one because it lacked sexual interest. Then the London company of Rich & Cowan's reader stayed up all night to finish it. The birth of Cathal, the first of three children, followed.

On Another Man's Wound was serialized before publication in *The Irish Press*. Trouble followed immediately in the figure of Joseph O'Doherty, a Donegal Volunteer. O'Malley had described plans for a raid in Donegal from which O'Doherty had excused himself because he was married. O'Doherty countered that his reason for not taking part was his election as a Dáil representative. If he was arrested, he argued, the political cause might suffer. O'Doherty pleaded his case against O'Malley and his publishers in Ireland. The courtroom was crowded. Frank Aiken, now minister for defence, was there, as was Eoin O'Duffy. The opposition counsel Fitzgerald began by describing the book as 'very extravagant and over-coloured', 'a glorification' of O'Malley's 'exploits', 'Mr O'Malley ... a typical example of the amateur soldier'.[26] In response, counsel for *The Irish Press* argued that no charge of cowardice had been made and asked for an honorable agreement outside the law. This was not forthcoming. Counsel voiced his frustration.

> Mr O'Malley risked his life for years in an uneven fight against the force of an Empire, which was waged by a handful of courageous men, most of them ill-armed, but he was described as a 'Robinson Crusoe' who fired buckshot from behind a hedge.[27]

The jury found for O'Doherty, with a combined judgment of £550 against the defendants. The defeat signalled early trouble in the O'Malley's marriage as Helen's father offered to pay the costs. O'Malley refused. Ultimately the family removed from Dublin to Mayo in mid 1938 and settled into Burrishoole Lodge near Newport in November 1938.

This Mayo landscape was to frame the next decade of O'Malley's life. His move west sets a new range of questions for our understanding of the cultural life of post-independence Ireland. With a world war looming he set himself to creating a self-sufficient farm from rented land adjacent. His letters from this time are full of instructions to Dublin merchants to supply books and equipment for bee-keeping, seed-sewing and the keeping of hens. The O'Malleys had the first tuberculin-tested herd of cattle west of the Shannon and ran a model farm. The work exhausted and eventually defeated them. O'Malley's reputation as a military commander was based on his preparation and discipline. He was unable to shed these habits in his domestic life and it is occasionally upsetting to read his lists of orders to domestic staff who are forbidden to eat his rashers. The minute precision of community life in such a physically isolated space was difficult for Helen to take, used as she was to New York society. One revelation of the letters is the degree to which this lack of external association was compensated for by a rich interior decoration (and it is no surprise that one of Helen's later achievements was to design the inside of several Dublin libraries). The two collected classical records on their trips to Dublin, London, Paris and New York. Bach, Mozart,

Debussy, Tchaikovsky, Mussorgsky, Stravinsky and Franck were favorites. They listened to the concert broadcasts of Radio Éireann. O'Malley read voraciously, even if his habits occasionally caused his departure to a downstairs bed, O'Malley staying up all night with a bottle of stout to read Flann O'Brien's *At Swim-Two-Birds*. He liked Forster's *A Passage to India* and letters request copies of Proust, Edmund Wilson and William Carlos Williams. He read Philip Horton's study of Hart Crane, I.A. Richards' *Principles of Literary Criticism*, the *Yale Review* and *Art News*. He collected the catalogues of the London bookshops Foyle's and Bumpers. And the O'Malleys even arranged bog oak in local imitation of Hans Arp's 'Concretion Humane' (and the medium for his knowledge of modern art was perhaps *transition*, copies of which he requested sent to him from James Johnson Sweeney in New York).

The occasional journeys abroad also allowed a further indulgence, the purchase of paintings, part funded by his pension and her dress allowance. O'Malley had always frequented galleries. He was addicted to picture postcards and was a devoted student of art history, taking a diploma on the subject at University College Dublin (one letter records a visit to 'the National Gallery tripping over English people feeding pigeons in Trafalgar Square. That's their emotional outlet. Burnt frontier towns in North West India and compensate by being sappy to pigeons in Trafalgar Square. The Gallery was a joy so I remained as long as I could').[28] The O'Malleys saw a Cézanne exhibition in 1936 in Paris, Ernie moved by his own memories of the countryside from Aix to Estaques and Marseilles. By 1938 the two had bought widely in then-contemporary continental art. They had a Kisling, a De La Serra, a Marchand, a Roualt, a Vlaminck, a Lurcat and a Modigliani, all hung in the living room and the study. Paul Henry visited Mayo in the company of Sean O'Faolain, who introduced O'Malley as the gunman. The two painters O'Malley valued most were Jack Yeats and Louis le Brocquy. He met Yeats in the late 1930s and they remained friends, as registered in Cormac's painted Christmas cards in the National Gallery of Ireland. The third co-ordinate between O'Malley and Yeats was Thomas MacGreevy, who O'Malley had first met in Lennox Robinson's flat on the night of Bloody Sunday, O'Malley in hiding from military raids.[29] In May 1939 O'Malley wrote to MacGreevy.

> I spent a few days in the National Library, came back with my material, as I had no time to see a tailor. I saw Jack Yeats, fell clear in love with a picture and felt I must have it. I was able to arrange payments over a long period. We had a very nice afternoon with him, he spoke of you kindly. He is very fine and we came away in a glow. Then I began to think of my commitment and had a shiver at the knees for some time, but I am very glad of my rashness.[30]

The painting was *Death for Only One*, which was first exhibited the year before at the Dublin Royal Hibernian Academy. Perhaps O'Malley recognized the sense of loss associated with the image as Yeats described it, 'a dead tramp lying on a headland with another tramp standing by – and a dark sea and dark sky'.[31] The artist kept a pen-and-ink sketch of the painting after he sold it, thinking it one of his important pictures; and the two men maintained their friendship, Louis MacNeice once finding O'Malley in Yeats' studio, drinking a Malaga. O'Malley's interest in Yeats extended to his involvement in the National Loan Exhibition of Yeats' work held at the National College of Art in Dublin in June and July 1945. O'Malley wrote the catalogue introduction to a Jack Yeats moulded by his western background.

> Great roaring winds sweep in from the Atlantic to drench the land with spray, soften the intention, weaken the will and perseverance. Cloud forms drift slowly in threat or, when storm has ceased, model to a painter's delight land forms below. Sky bulks large to give a sense of infinite distance and mystery mixed with tragic desolation. This spaciousness of sky is the most noticeable feature of the Western scene; it is, at times, as if the land were a prelude to the atmosphere above.[32]

To O'Malley, 'The new Ireland, still fluid politically and socially, has found in Jack Yeats a painter of major rank'.[33] His insight was to see the work that Yeats put in to make his art seem improvisation. O'Malley saw this feature particularly in *Low Tide*, which hung in the Municipal Gallery in a room of contemporary European painting. He had an equally familiar relationship with Louis le Brocquy. The young painter stayed for periods at Burrishoole in the mid 1940s and produced a number of watercolours. O'Malley inscribed this friendship in an essay on the artist in *Horizon* magazine of July 1946, O'Malley attentive to the particular textures of le Brocquy's material practice, the painter's watercolours made from layers of colour and wax in the manner of Henry Moore.

> This creates a superimposed movement within a small area, and adds to the total impression of vitality. Monotonous surface is broken up, and colour subtlety is increased. By these means the artist aims at a strength of texture which he opposes in counterpoint to what might otherwise become a hard isolation of line.[34]

O'Malley then traced le Brocquy's sense of the local geography as a symptom of the Emergency, Ireland driven back on itself for the period of the war. O'Malley singled out *Famine Cottages, Connemara* and *Condemned Man* to show le Brocquy's 'feeling for this land as an emotional concept of colour and form'.[35] O'Malley retained this sense of form in his own experience of the land and seascape. He was a practised sailor and escaped frequently down the estuary from Burrishoole to the islands of Clew Bay. The sea seeps into his private writing from the practical application of sails and oars to the changing light on the water as the seasons changed. O'Malley's compositional sense of the western coastline extended to his travels through the countryside. He had a longstanding interest in photography and maintained a lifelong correspondence with Paul Strand, who he met in New Mexico and brought to Ireland. He particularly admired Strand's photographs of Mexican saints. This appreciation fed into O'Malley's Irish life. Frequent letters describe the difficulty of photography in the Irish landscape, the unavailability of plates, the breaking of a lamp globe in Kilfenora, the endless rain and bad light. O'Malley's interest was the medieval sculpture of the Irish churches, photographs of which were intended for a never-published book. He caught something in this visual world of the trace of an Ireland that did not register in the deeds of statehood. O'Malley's obsession with landscape can be easily equated with a romantic nationalism, except that his descriptive attention was drawn reiteratively to Ireland's ephemeral human geography. Just as he carried a notebook everywhere to take down scraps of folklore, he thought of the country through which he moved as aesthetic, not essential. *On Another Man's Wound* is in this sense a cultural reprise of the civil war in its disturbance of the image of Ireland as a given territory. One of its central passages records O'Malley's passing through the four seasons of 1920 on his bicycle. The physical discomfort of wet trench coats, sodden boots and bad food frame word pictures of the counties he moves through.

> Orange berries of the blackthorn, dark purple elm flowers, silver willow catkins and the tiny crimson flowering of hazel stood out against masses of bluish willow thickets, darkened boles and leafless branches. Kestrels struck at tiny finches and small wrens made thin points of sound in the furze.[36]

Cultural historiography in Ireland has neglected the experience of objects. O'Malley's unique rendition of this visual sensorium transforms Ireland into a modern landscape of vivid colour and sharp edges. It does so directly. The refusal of sentiment mirrors another Irish writer of the 1930s fascinated with painting, Samuel Beckett. Both writers had a practical interest in art criticism and both found themselves in disaffection from Ireland. O'Malley stages years on the run in a compact chronology of turf smells and nature sounds, a hint of threat throughout.

> Mountains rounded or irregular, bare of wood, showing a recession of curve or a chain mass thrusting out, in a drizzling rain, separate echelons of its blended strength; hills, hazy, purple, mauve and lavender in the distance, changing colour as the day advanced; aloof or personal. Clouds forming, reforming, hanging still, drifting leisurely or moving swiftly with darkened menace; bog water with seemingly unfathomable depths, quiet, mysterious, the bare black wall of clean-cut turf overhanging.[37]

This landscape is informed by practice and study, O'Malley's correlation of visual art and literature a recurring concern of post-civil-war Irish modernism. In this mode the experiment of modernism is not registered in the malformation of signs. Its innovation depends on the register of a particular historical deficit imaginable in the reader between the Ireland fought for and the Ireland won. O'Malley's assembly of the written landscape as a procession of visual images inaugurates a dreamtime rooted in the memory of a republic. This I think speaks to O'Malley's overall arrangement of *On Another Man's Wound* into three sections, Flamboyant, which goes from 1897 to 1917, Gothic, which goes from 1918 to 1920, and Romanesque, which goes from 1920 to 1921. In art history this is reverse chronology. Romanesque describes an architectural style between the classical period and the Gothic, which followed. Flamboyant is a descriptive term for waved lines that appeared in mid-fifteenth-century French building. In O'Malley's work, going forward is going backwards, the art image drawing the imagination back to a source obscured by the new state's forward march. O'Malley's sense of Ireland's historical geography continued in the other project he set himself, a solo attempt to record interviews with republicans who may not have given their accounts of the War of Independence and civil war to Free State archivists, interviews that extend to more than four million handwritten words. There is a hidden Ireland in O'Malley's chance observations as he travelled. A letter of May 1938 mentions his visit to Wexford for the beginning of the 1798 commemorations at the Place Boulavogue where that rebellion began. He described

> Men on white horses wearing green sashes, not the horses, four or five bands (we call an orchestra a band), one piper in saffron kilts, men with great banners, wooden and curve pikes, then an acting of incidents of '98 in the open. All very simple, awkward and very moving.[38]

A long, intimate letter of 1948 to John Kelleher gives some sense of O'Malley's style of travel. Kelleher was a pioneer of interdisciplinary study with regard to Ireland at Harvard University. He consulted O'Malley on questions of literature and history and the two formed an important information conduit across the Atlantic, many of O'Malley's book recommendations ending up on Kelleher's class reading lists (as did *On Another Man's Wound*). In the period of his work as book editor of *The Bell* from 1947 to 1948, O'Malley asked Kelleher for his information on scholarly studies, an example being Clarence Haring's *The Spanish Empire in America*. One letter describes O'Malley's adventures in a car fuelled by unrationed petrol from a Volunteer friend who ran a garage. In company of his eldest son Cathal he drove to Limerick to see the new City Library Gallery run by Robert Herbert. Its highlight was 'a rotten portrait painted by Sean Keating from a photograph'.[39] After this,

> Bob and I drank for three days: and in between times we talked of books working in the Library. Bob, Cathal and I equipped with one camera and six bottles of whiskey, purloined by me in the noble city of Limerick, set off on Good Friday for Burrishoole. We went to Ennis Friary, Dysert O'Dea, Kilmaboy, Kilfenora, Kilcreely on the sea shore near Lahinch ... Later up along the edge of the Burren mountains up the pass to Corcomroe in its valley of limestone. There we photographed, waited for light to swing on the figures on capitals and drank. The drink was good as was the sun ... [40]

By the late 1940s O'Malley's family life was in crisis. Helen had left for the United States, taking Cathal and Etain with her. There followed bitter negotiation over the status of Burrishoole, which Helen had bought solely in her own name to protect the family from any consequences of further libels. O'Malley's health declined rapidly. Unable to maintain the regular rhythm of farm work he began to spend more time in Dublin while Cormac attended school at Willow Park. From his rented apartment on Sussex Road O'Malley entered a newly emergent social world. And O'Malley's habitual addiction to note taking and diary keeping offers a near-unique record of the social networks that made for bohemian life. The clubs that he subscribed to are a snapshot of post-war cultural associations. He was a member of the United Arts Club, the Royal Dublin Society, the Royal Society of Antiquaries of Ireland, the Irish Academy of Letters, the Irish Historical Society, the Shorthorn Breeders' Association and, best of all, the Country Women's

Association. He put together a radio show for the BBC's Country Magazine that featured Seamus Ennis playing 'Will you come with me over the mountain' on the tin whistle. A pocket diary from 1948 maps this world in allusive detail.

February 1948
21 Sat.   In bed. Went to see Jack Yeats in a snow storm. Tom McGreevy turned up.
22 Sun.   Snow. Children went out to see Jimme O'Dea ...

March 1948
14 Fri.   8.50 pm. Cathal arrives. Drink Pearl 7–8.30. Saw Kevin with Cathal. Met Donagh, Paddy Kavanagh ... at Pearl adjourned Tommy's until 1.0. Downstairs were the Plunketts.[41]

Back in Mayo O'Malley went to a production of *Hamlet* in Castlebar produced by touring Dublin actors and acted as host to a succession of writers and painters. He drove to Achill to be bored by Liam O'Flaherty's endless complaints: 'That morning before we left he was charming but then he was flat in bed.'[42] And he visited his family home in Castlebar where he remembered the room where as a young child he had held a guest at pistol point, in imitation of a scene from Thomas Malory's *Morte D'Arthur*. There was persistent stress concerning Helen's refusal to pay rates on her Irish property, which led to threats from the Mayo County Council to take his property. The last years before O'Malley's death are a catalogue of uncertainty. One late friendship in Ireland was with John Ford, who O'Malley helped in the production of *The Quiet Man* and *The Rising of the Moon*. The two had a close, occasional correspondence and it seems that Ford helped financially with Cormac's schooling. O'Malley began to spend more time in England, partly recovering his broken health in Newton Hall, the Cambridge house of the Walston family, who he knew originally through the Hookers. When able to get out of bed he helped Harry Walston's unsuccessful campaign as a Labour candidate in the 1955 General Election. Walston's ambitions could not have been helped by O'Malley's interventions with local Tories if the following conversation from a late letter is anything to go by.

'Good morning. I am canvassing. Did you vote last time?'
'Yes.'
'Will you vote this time?'
'Most certainly.'
'Then I hope you'll vote for Walston as he is a good farmer.'
'Who I vote for is no business of yours ... Where are you from?'
'I'm from Ireland ... Now will you vote for Walston?'
'No I will not, but I'll see you to the gate, and good luck.'[43]

He was frequently bedridden, with barely the strength to read (a favourite for recuperation was *Cosmopolitan*). Newton Hall was quiet as the family travelled frequently, leaving O'Malley alone with the domestic staff. O'Malley returned to Dublin where he died on 25 March 1957. He was honoured with a state funeral presided over by the president Seán T. O'Kelly, de Valera, Lemass and Aiken.[44]

Now more than fifty years later, what are we to make of this enigma, this Volunteer who killed and collected modern art, who was commandant of the defence of the Four Courts and partly responsible for the destruction of the public records even as he spent the rest of his life keeping diaries, clippings, postcards, letters, art catalogues and the rest? There is a case for the revision of a cultural account to include not only O'Malley's intervention in the Anglo-Irish and civil wars (which was crucial) but also his involvement in the aesthetic subcultures of the independent state, subcultures that sustained ideas of liberty that were excluded from the bureaucracy's foundational rhetoric. But this is only part of the picture, and the claim for the recovery of neglected figures is now so common as to have become a common symptom of the problems that caused exclusion in the first place.[45] These problems may be characterized bluntly as the representation of Ireland's experience of modernity through the prism of empire and its aftermath. In this context, Ernie O'Malley's case is an exemplary rebuke. He had active experience of revolution (and disillusion), and evolved a theory of life in response. The following letters are important as objects in themselves, speaking as they do to the immediate needs of an individual and then a family life. Their collection together shows the ways in which a direct engagement with the problems of a moment, from guerilla war to farming during the Emergency, might knit together into radical praxis. O'Malley's mixed social life of leisure and activity suggests his strategic significance to the present. Yes, his book lists and farm techniques fill out our picture of Ireland in the post-independence decades. More than this, however, the literal correspondence of these practices with a lifelong scheme of writing and reading in letters and books suggests how a miniature republic of one's self might survive the decimation of the republic as reality or ideal.

If O'Malley rarely declares his hand in the following pages with regard to the particular events of Irish politics as they occurred around him, it can be said that his own philosophy of self-reliance exceeded the initial ambitions of advanced nationalism. In the millions of words that he wrote and collected in his prose, poetry and military interviews, O'Malley placed himself in the future, not the past. His dispersal of memory and event in this literary explosion points to a wider spread of his archive among private and institutional collections in Ireland, Europe and America. Major parts of O'Malley's collection of notes, drafts and cuttings are stored now in University College Dublin and New York University. There remains a sense, however, in which O'Malley never quite came home. This is as it should be. The volume of his work still exceeds in capacity and optimism the place from which it was created. This excess is a final defence of a republic in letters that O'Malley continued to create. His experience of the wide world redirects the progress of dissident thinking in Ireland from a fatal embrace with the British question. Thinking of Mayo in New Mexico, O'Malley gives the revolution a modern afterlife.

Personal Note
Searching for Ernie

CORMAC K.H. O'MALLEY

As the gunshots by the honour guard rang out over my father's Glasnevin grave while my brother, sister and I stood there watching the solemn occasion of his burial in March 1957, I began to ask just who was this man? I knew I missed him terribly and realized that the security blanket he had provided me for seven years since 1950 had now completely disappeared. I was to be whisked away by my mother from my stable, if solitary, life in England and Ireland, and thrust at fourteen into an entirely new life in America.

It was not until six years later at university that I began thinking about Ireland, its history and the roles my father played. Years later I picked up the threads of my search to document my father, who he was, what he stood for, what he was like as a person, and what he had accomplished. I found some of his unpublished manuscripts and arranged for their publication. They covered the young militant, nationalist Ernie. The autobiographical sketch of *On Another Man's Wound* was extended by *The Singing Flame* through the end of the civil war and *Raids and Rallies* added other glimpses of the man of action. Both memoirs suggest a personality and an intellect quite different to the dedicated guerilla who wrote memoranda on the tactics of warfare. I started to pursue the older, more mature Ernie. I discovered in his files, packed away in boxes in my attic for many years, traces of the traveller, art observer, mountain climber, poet, husband, father, sailor, art collector, essayist, art critic, folklorist, book editor, military historian and friend of artists, poets and writers. I had only an inkling of these various dimensions of his character, but I wanted to learn more. In 1982 I heard that Padraic O'Farrell of Mullingar wanted to write about him, and I offered to help. He published *The Ernie O'Malley Story* in 1983. I felt his telling was only the start of the journey.

For several years I tried to get people interested in writing a full-length biography. Ulick O'Connor and I chatted after I read his biography of Oliver St John Gogarty. The alignment was excellent as it was Ulick's father, Dr Matthew O'Connor, who, as a Free State Medical Officer, had helped save Ernie from a court martial by not signing a certificate stating that he was well enough to stand trial. Late one evening we agreed that I should first publish Ernie's letters and then he would write the biography as his letters would provide insight for a biographer. I remember well waking up next morning and realizing that I actually had none of my father's letters as he had mailed them all without keeping copies. As a result I knew that I had to start to collect these documents, to get in touch with his friends and to record their memories before they died. I wrote to many people and asked the obvious questions, and they, in turn, wrote to me of the stories about him. So I started to compile a compendium of fragments of information to assemble for that fuller biography and for my own fund of knowledge. The quest for letters had many twists and turns. I found that several people before me had collected original letters, or copies thereof, from father's friends. Colbert Martin and Frances-Mary Blake had talked to many people in the 1970s, and they generously shared their resources with me. The hunt for letters was an exciting one but it had to be merged in between my business trips to faraway places and would take over twenty-five years to accomplish, with diligence, persistence and a great deal of luck. Along the way there were several incidents that are worth retelling.

At the start of the quest, I wrote to the editors of several Irish national daily newspapers asking for correspondence. Several people responded and all had to be pursued by letter from my then home in Brussels. One such response was by Brigid FitzSimon who invited me to visit her house on Bushy Park Road, a Dublin address that meant nothing to me. As we had tea and chatted, she produced a long scroll of black paper and with excitement we unwrapped it on the floor. Therein were letters Ernie had written from Kilmainham Gaol in 1923 to Molly Childers, the widow of Erskine Childers. Ernie had visited their home. She had carefully wrapped his letters in paper, surrounded them with newspaper clippings of his capture and stored them under the stairs. Mrs FitzSimon had only discovered the documents when the stairway was refurbished in the 1980s. Mrs Childers had been crippled and I could see her strained handwriting on her notes about 'Poor Ernie'. What a treasure to find and be given. These letters, along with an earlier collection given to Mrs Childers' son, Erskine Childers, then president of Ireland, and subsequently given to Trinity College, formed the basis of *Prisoners: The Civil War Letters of Ernie O'Malley*, which I edited with Richard English for publication in 1991. Those letters disclosed Ernie's acceptance of the physical defeat of the republican position, but also documented his effort to educate himself in the arts, languages and literature through his extensive reading, before, during and after his 41-day hunger strike.

At the outset of this letter venture in the 1980s, and with trepidation, I asked my mother if she had kept any of Ernie's correspondence. She was thrilled as she had never thrown out anything written by 'the love of her life', and over the course of the next several years she continued to locate his letters to her from their first meeting in 1933 through 1956 as well as many letters to my brother and sister. How she had kept all these letters with her many household moves is a mystery, but we are fortunate to have them. She was pleased to think his letters would be published, and I was also able to share with her letters from her that Ernie had kept. In fact, there are over ninety letters to her, and many of them illustrate the softer side of the military man, the concerned husband, the music lover, the bibliophile, the farmer, as well as the kindness and concern for my siblings and myself. Within a few years I had also received letters from Eithne Golden and Jean McGrail, both of whom I was able to visit in New York City, as well as copies from the Paul Strand, Edward Weston and John Ford archives. I was now starting to get a more accurate impression of the mature Ernie. Fortunately for me (and for Ernie), Richard English came forward in 1988 and asked if he could write a full biography of Ernie. Richard spent time in my archives and did his own extensive research, interviewing many of Ernie's comrades and friends. Richard was partially sidetracked by editing *Prisoners* with me but preparing those letters for publication also helped him get a better feel of the man he was dealing with. Ultimately his *Ernie O'Malley: IRA Intellectual* was published in 1998 and gave a detailed perspective of his military, intellectual and personal lives. As a result of Richard's intense interrogatories I gained many insights into both the background and nature of Ernie as well as myself.

Another constant source of knowledge of Ernie has come about as a result of authors, researchers and a composer asking to include Ernie in some manner in their articles, website, musical composition or television documentaries. In 1999 Mary Cosgrove received a grant from the Irish American Cultural Institute to research Ernie's interest in the visual arts. She discovered in Ernie's files his interview notes with Irish artists in the 1945 period and was able to decipher his lecture on the origins of modern art. In their 2003 RTÉ *Hidden Ireland* documentary Ruan and Manchan Magan shed light on Ernie's dramatic capture at the home of their grandmother, Sighle Humphreys, and her O'Rahilly family. A 2004 RTÉ *Hidden History* documentary told of Ernie's role in fundraising in the United States in 1928 to 1929 with Frank Aiken for the establishment of Eamon de Valera's *Irish Press*. Susan Schreibman pursued the online publication of the exchange of correspondence between Ernie and Tomás MacGreevy in the MacGreevy Archive that she created. At the same time Micheál Ó Súilleabháin composed his *Country Cycle*, performed first in 2006 in Wesport, and based in part on Ernie's reference to the use of his bicycle as a mode of transport during the revolution. In making his exciting documentary on Ernie's life, *On Another Man's Wound, Scéal Ernie O'Malley*, shown on TG4 in 2008, Jerry O'Callaghan discovered materials in my archives that I had never noticed before, including Ernie's notes from the Four Courts, poems, and extensive diaries he wrote in New York, San Francisco, New Mexico and Mexico.

As I started doing research in 2001 for *'No Surrender Here!' The Civil War Papers of Ernie O'Malley, 1922–1924*, I found myself trawling through diverse resources for correspondence among those in command of the anti-Treaty IRA activities, and in the course of that search came across post-1924 correspondence and references. During the same period I was starting to consider what could be done with Ernie's military notebooks with 430 interviews located at UCD Archives. In tandem with sons and grandsons of the comrades he had interviewed, we typed up some of these interviews and that in turn led to the discovery of further correspondence. At this time I also rediscovered an unpublished manuscript that came out with UCD Press in 2007 as *Rising-Out: Sean Connolly of Longford, 1890–1921*. That memoir helped connect the extensive military interviews with how such interviews could be used to support further publications on a local hero, such as Sean Connolly on whom almost nothing had been written. By word of encouragement to other researchers I would endorse the principle that one should reach out to all possible sources and not to leave the library just because the first warning bell has sounded. On so many occasions I found something of importance during those last five minutes while others were getting ready to leave.

Recently I was checking a footnote regarding Ernie's relationship with John Hagan, Rector of the Irish College, Rome. From another source I had received copies of some letters he had written from Rome, but their chronology was confusing. With a simple internet search I discovered late one Sunday night a website for the Irish College. On Monday the archivist, Vera Orschel, responded, noting that she had been working on the Hagan files for over three years, was leaving in four days and was familiar with Ernie's name as well as his alias, Cecil Smyth-Howard, which was news to me. After further exchanges, within one week I had on my desk a series of Ernie's letters to Hagan in the 1925–8 period that caused me to reorganize significantly the work I had already completed for those years.

The last phase of the search, preparing the footnotes of the persons mentioned, has been one of the most rewarding. The discipline of locating information on the referenced individuals, books, events or locations has caused me to dig deeper into the hidden recesses of my files and other archives, as well as to contact more people with specific questions, and the result has been an enormous amount of collateral information, far more than was needed for that particular footnote.

So the search for Ernie has been meaningful to me in more ways than one. There was the relatively narrow process, and the ever-expanding results. I hope that this volume of letters and limited diaries gives the reader a fuller image of my father, as they have for me. Finally, there is still an abundance of unpublished materials, including poetry, translations, folklore, songs from the War of Independence and civil war period, short stories, numerous diaries and essays (some of which can be viewed at www.ernieomalley.com), not to mention four million words of military-history interviews recording the 1912–24 period. In this edition we have striven to make minimal changes to the original text, some of which was in poor handwriting and with some spelling errors and unusual phrases.

Prologue
A Volunteer's Experience

After the Fianna Fáil party came to power in 1932, the de Valera government was sympathetic to providing pensions to previously excluded republicans who had fought in any part of the Easter Rising, the War of Independence or the civil war. In 1934, while in America, Ernie O'Malley (EOM) applied for a service pension and disability allowance due to wounds. Within ten months he was advised that he would receive both pensions, but that it would be best to return to Dublin to finalize the paperwork. His two letters (14 May 1934 and June 1934) are included below out of chronological sequence so that the reader can better appreciate them as a brief description of EOM's military experiences and wounds from 1916 through his time in jail under the British army, and then under the Irish army until he got out in July 1924.

Draft application to Irish Pension Board[1]

[New York]
14 May 1934

To: Markham, Runai:

As other forms whose purport I do not as yet know may be forwarded to me, I wish to give this summary of experience. I am on the move and it is not easy for me to get in touch with this address of mine in New York.

In March, 1918, I was sent to report to Mulcahy, D/C/S[2] in Tyrone. I organised the Coal Island district of the Irish Volunteers. Attached as Second Lieutenant to the Organisation staff under Collins[3] I organised Offaly, South and North Roscommon Brigades, went to England as a British officer to obtain arms,[4] and organised East Donegal Brigade. This in the year 1918.

As a Lieutenant I organised West Donegal, Mid and West Clare, North Tipperary Brigades. I did special work in Inishowen[5] and served as a Captain at GHQ Dublin on the Adjutant General's and the Director of Organisation's departments. This in 1919.

I organised South County Dublin Brigade, Monaghan, South Tipperary, East Limerick Brigades, trained the nucleus of a column in South Tipp. and the first column in North Cork Brigade. Mulcahy, C/S appointed me to command the Martial Law area,[6] but first sent me to Kilkenny Brigade to attack the Auxiliary headquarters at Inistiogue. I was captured, condemned to death, imprisoned in Kilkenny barracks, Dublin Castle and Kilmainham Gaol. I escaped from Kilmainham as Bernard Stewart in February, 1921.[7]

I was appointed to command the Second Southern Division in March; in April I took command of Mid and South Tipperary, Kilkenny, East and Mid Limerick Brigades. I held this command until March, 1922. I was appointed Director of Organisation by Liam Lynch, C/S. I was in charge of the garrison of the Four Courts on its surrender in June, 1922. I escaped, organised the South and East Command in South Dublin, Wicklow, Carlow and Wexford Brigades. I was appointed Assistant Chief of Staff by Liam Lynch,[8] C/S with authority to direct the Divisions and independent Brigades in the provinces of Ulster and Leinster.

In November of 1922 I was surrounded by Free State troops and was wounded.[9] I was in bed through wounds in hospitals and jail until September, 1923. I went on hunger strike in Mountjoy gaol in October, 1923 and lasted 41 days. In bed as a result in Bricin's Hospital[10] until May or June of 1924, transferred to the Curragh Command and released in August or September, 1924.[11]

I remained two years abroad, the White Cross[12] advanced me one hundred pounds. I was two hundred pounds in debt when I returned. The White Cross could not see its way to advance me any money to pay my debts. I may add that I gave the White Cross, through the Adjutant General, G.O. Sullivan,[13] eighty pounds between March and November of 1920, so I count their advance to me as twenty pounds, perhaps unjustly.

To amplify the Form M.S.P. 34/1

In Easter Week 1916 I fought for 3 nights: Wednesday, Thursday and Friday with another boy, now a captain in the British navy. We harried outposts from Cross Guns Bridge to Charlemont Bridge crawling up close to them, using a rifle. I was not attached to any unit then and discovered my real feelings only during that week's fighting. I do not know if my brothers, Paddy and Cecil, can verify my absence; my people did not know I fought. I cannot give the naval officer's name without his consent.

1916. I joined 'F' Co., 1st Battalion, Dublin Brigade of the Irish Volunteers in August or so of 1916. I served as a Volunteer and then as an NCO attached to Signals until February of 1918 when I left for East Tyrone and acted in an organising capacity to the instructions of Dick Mulcahy, Assistant Chief of Staff, as a second lieutenant. Active service as such in this period might be dressing in officer's uniform to get an arms permit in Dublin Castle[14] and taking part under Diarmuid Lynch,[15] Sinn Fein Director of Food Control, to seize and slaughter pigs at Drumcondra bridge, the latter in October of 1917.

1918. In April I went to *Offaly* acting to the instructions of Michael Collins then Director of Organisation and Adjutant-General. I worked in Queen's County,[16] West Meath and Longford as well during the time the British attempted to threaten us with conscription. I had several clashes with police who made attempts to arrest me. In June I organised South Roscommon brigade. I was wounded twice at Ballymoe on the Galway border when I ran into a police trap.[17] I organised North Roscommon brigade and clashed with police there. In August I was sent to London by Collins; dressed as a captain I attempted to buy arms.[18] I remained in London for a month.

I went to Donegal in September, organised and trained the East and West Donegal Brigades and part of Tyrone.

1919. In January I was sent to Clare by Cathal Brugha,[19] Minister of Defence. There was trouble in Clare due to the Brennans[20] who wanted to force their views on GHQ. I had to inspect all companies in Mid and West Clare brigades, talk to the officers and then train and prepare them for operations. I worked a little in East Clare brigade. I had a fight with police near Inagh (mid Clare) and Kilkee (West Clare).

I organised, held officers classes and manoeuvers in North Tipperary brigade in May, went to Inishowen on a special raid for arms in September, but it was abortive. On my return to Inishowen I had to fight my way through police at Omagh. In October I worked at General Headquarters then in a deserted room at St Ita's School.[21] I did staff work with the Adjutant-General, Quartermaster General, with organisation and communications. In December, tired of paperwork I asked to be sent out to the country. Collins ordered me to a thoroughly bad area, North County Dublin.

1920. In February I was sent to Monaghan brigade. I fought police at Ardee and was in the Ballytrain attack.[22] The barracks was captured. In May or June I went to the South Tipperary brigade. For the first time I had officers with me who were really interested in their work and who understood it: Sean Tracey[23] and

Seumas [*sic*] Robinson.[24] I was badly burnt in the attack on Hollyford barracks,[25] burnt in the attack on Drangan,[26] present at an abortive attack in East Clare and at the destruction of the Cahir rifle range. I went to East Limerick and trained the brigade from July to the beginning of September. I was wounded when surrounded and alone, near Oola[27], wounded by hand grenade in an attack on Rearcross[28] in North Tipperary. I was slightly wounded in September when Jerry Kiely,[29] my orderly, and I were surrounded by troops when on our way to North Cork; we fought our way through. I trained the first officers' column in North Cork brigade, took part in the capture of Mallow barracks and an ambush near Newmarket.

In November I worked at GHQ. I was given command of Munster by the Chief of Staff. I was to build up my own staff as I went around but first I was sent to capture Auxiliary headquarters in Inistogue. I was captured close to the buildings in December and was manhandled there and in the Intelligence Room, Dublin Castle, I was sent to Kilmainham under the name of Bernard Stewart. I was to have been hanged for the Kilmichael ambush[30] in which I had no part but in February escaped with Frank Teeling,[31] then under sentence of death, and Simon Donnelly.[32]

1921. I was given command of the Second Southern Division, Mid and East Limerick brigades, Mid and South Tipperary brigades and Kilkenny brigade. I was sent to Cork to appoint Liam Lynch as Officer Commanding the First Southern Division. I was on active service until the Truce of July 11th.

From July to December I was busy on administration and training in the division. I broke away from GHQ in February of 1922; in March I occupied Limerick and forced the so-called I.R.A., really Provisional Government troops, to vacate the city which was in my area.

1922. When other divisions in May broke away from GHQ, a new Executive was elected.[33] I was a member of it and was appointed Director of Organisation by Liam Lynch, then Chief of Staff. In June our Headquarters in the Four Courts was attacked by troops of the Provisional Government.[34] I was given command of the GHQ section which consisted of the Staff and general staff officers; 3 days later I was appointed to command the garrison. I surrendered to the Provisional Government,[35] escaped four hours later with Sean Lemass.[36] I waited for men from South Tipperary who were to advance on Dublin but by the time we were within 3 miles of the city, we found that our men of the Dublin brigade had evacuated their positions. I organised a South and East Command in Wexford, Carlow, Wicklow and South Dublin, captured Enniscorthy, Ferns and Borris-in-Ossory and was moving on Carlow when I was appointed Assistant Chief of Staff with command of all divisions and independent brigades in Ulster and Leinster, and was ordered to Dublin. I remained in Dublin save for inspections until November. I was surrounded and wounded about 5 times; it was thought I would die of wounds. I had the satisfaction of reading of my own death in a Dublin paper. I was removed on a stretcher from Portobello barracks to Mountjoy Gaol.

1923. The Free State wanted to execute me but I was too weak to be court martialled. I was not able to walk until after the Cease Fire order when hostilities ceased.[37] In October conditions were bad in Mountjoy. Senior officers decided to hunger strike. I was opposed to their decision but went on strike. After 41 days our officers called off the strike. There wasn't much left of me by the time the strike was over. I was brought to St Bricin's Hospital, removed in March to the Curragh internment camp. In August or September[38] we were released two by two; Sean Russell[39] and I had the mixed pleasure of being the last to be released.

It is hard for me to give the names of officers commanding in all the areas I served in. Generally when on inspection or training, I was myself in charge of the area I happened to be in from April 1918 to May 1920.

NO. 2 EOM PAPERS NYU
Application to Irish Pension Board[40]

[New York]
[c. June 1934]

To: Markham, Runai:
In reply to your Ref No I/RB/3572 of 30/5/1934.
1. May, 1918. Right wrist wound, left ankle wound.
2. Held up by RIC who had warrants for my arrest at the village of Ballymoe, Co. Galway. I refused to halt, used my revolver, police reinforced from the barracks.
3. Grenade wounds in right shoulder in June 1920. During a stage in the attack on Rearcross barracks, Sean Tracey and I were in the open throwing bottles filled with an incendiary mixture at an unburnt portion of the roof. Our snipers, appointed by me to cover us, withdrew without orders. Police used grenades. I was wounded in front of right shoulder through Deltoid and behind through Latissimus.[41]
4. Right hip wound, July 1920. English of Templebraiden, Co. Limerick was captured with a despatch of mine which he had carefully kept for a day in his pocket. The despatch instructed him to remove my bag to a house near Oola. That night the house I was in near Oola was surrounded by police and military, and my two armed sentries ran without firing. By virtue of bad enemy shooting I got through them with one wound.
5. Slight face wound, right cheek; I forgot to mention this. Jerry Kieley my orderly, from South Tipp. and I were surrounded by military on the Limerick-Cork border, south of Mitchelstown, as we were on our way to a Brigade Council of North Cork. We fought them off; they had nine casualties.
5. Bullet through piece of clavicle emerging about two inches lower in rear. Lung wound.
6. Seven wounds in back, two on left high up below lung wound and in towards spine; five on right side, scattered, but between a middle line halving the lung and the spine, November 1922. I was surrounded by Free State troops in Humphreys, Aylesbury Road; I drove attackers out of the house twice and then fought in the open as there were three women in the house, one of them wounded. I would not surrender as I thought I should wipe out the disgraceful surrender of the Four Courts.

PART I

European Travel, 1924–1926, and Ireland, 1926–1928

EOM was captured with serious wounds on 4 November 1922 in the Dublin suburb of Donnybrook. His injuries were treated although his recovery was slow, and he was soon released from military hospital to Mountjoy Prison and then Kilmainham Gaol. In March 1924 he was transferred to Hare Park Internment Camp in the Curragh from which he was released as one of the last of the republican prisoners in mid July 1924. EOM returned to Dublin and met old friends and comrades. Though he was in poor health and the immediate military effort had been defeated, it is clear that he had not given up his republican commitment. He was still an elected member of the Dáil, though as an absentionist republican he would not take his seat.

After his release EOM started to fraternize with his former comrades. On 10–11 August 1924 he attended the meeting of the executive committee of the IRA, called by the chief of staff, Frank Aiken. At the meeting he agreed to serve on a sub-committee to the Executive for consultative purposes, the other members being Comdt Gen. Tom Derrig, Major General Andy Cooney (quartermaster general), Col Comdt Peadar O'Donnell, and Major General P.A. Murphy (adjutant general). He proposed a resolution that was passed unanimously, 'that Volunteers be instructed not to recognize the Free State and Six County Courts when charged with any authorized acts committed during the war ...'. Austin Stack wrote to EOM on 24 October asking him to be nominated as vice-president and honorary secretary of Sinn Féin, and it appears that he accepted as he signed Sinn Féin membership cards in that capacity. As the cold and damp Irish winter of late

1924 set in, EOM prepared to go abroad in search of the warmth that would restore his health.

In February 1925 he left on an eighteen-month European sojourn, heading to London, Paris and down to the sunshine of Barcelona. After a few months there during which he met some of the members of the Catalan independence movement but failed to get work, he moved to the French side of the Pyrenees. By late spring he decided to wander across the south of France and travel down through Italy to Rome, where he would visit John Hagan, Rector of the Irish College. Members of the James Brady family from Belfast were visiting Rome for the ordination of a family member. EOM struck up a correspondence with the two daughters, Frances (Frank) and Kathleen (Kay), some of which is included here.

Letter to Madge Clifford[1]

[*Dublin*]
28 *July* 1924

[*Madge Clifford,*
Dublin]

Dear Madge,

I got your nice note and did not reply as I did not like to use Communications; now I find I can. How are you? Please write and say exactly how you feel. I heard that you have not been feeling well and I don't wonder at that. I thought I should see you at the C/S's[2] when I was out there, but I did not like to call out to the A/P[3] when I had not any business to transact. Do you remember how annoyed I used to be, internally, when John Long Tall and often Lemmy[4] called out when they had no reason to do so. I was with Miss O'Rahilly[5] all day on Sunday. Also I was out there for tea on Friday. I was nearly killed for not going out before that. I heard she was out of town, and of course, I received a great telling off when I did go out there. Are you going to get holidays? Could you, please, definitely tell me that as I want to take the matter up before I do anything. I know in some small way what 'the Shack'[6] has done, what he has suffered and what a brick he has been right through, but I do not think he should have kept you without holidays. Did you see Tom?[7] He has gone home now also. I saw ½" but refused to have any row as it exhausts me too much. Beyond Miss O'R, ½" and Eileen McGrane[8] I have not seen anyone. Sheila and Mrs Humphries[9] are still in Kerry. I would like to see them. The house has been repainted. Miss O'R was very nice to me and I felt at home there at once. It was a great place really and it was the one opportunity I had had of getting fit. I wonder could you come for a spin on Sunday? Dick[10] said he would bring Miss O'R and I and if you could at all come in. I'm at 36[11] some time on Sunday, say at 11a.m., even if the day was wet we could have a good chat together. I wish I could get hold of a car. I feel inclined to commandeer a few as it is not so easy to go round when one's feet are bad.

Recently I met a lad who had been in Tullow and he said the Tullow people always spoke well of me and wished to be remembered to me. Can you beat it? Please reply. It was very mean of me not to have written to you before this.

Ever yours,
Ernie[12]

Letter to John Raleigh[13]

[Barcelona, Spain]
c. March 1925

[John Raleigh,
St Joseph's Street, Limerick]

Dear Johnny,

I suppose you will be surprised to hear from me; at last I am away, but I have not as yet met with a streak of good luck as owing to my peculiar circumstances I have not any friends here and doubt if I can find work. The weather may improve soon, and then I will get a chance to build up; the money question is, however, somewhat in the way. Could you please let me have £30 as I would like to have it to fall back on for travelling if I had to leave and go home; if you are hard up anything less would do but, please, tell me so. You may guess that I do not like to ask you, but you are a good old sort, and I do not mind so much asking you. The address money is to be sent is enclosed; please send it as if you were writing to the address as to myself and if writing please write as if you were writing to the girl direct; do not put your own address on it save that it is different from the one I put on your letter. By the way, I owe Mrs Crowe[14] one pound, will you, please, give it to her and say that I would have written to thank her for her kindness to me before this but that I wanted to have the money when writing. You will, please, forget where I am as I am supposed to be in Italy. I hope you are well and that you are busy collecting stamps for me. Please remember me to Madge Daly,[15] she was very nice and kind. I may not be able to write again for a long time so you will please understand.

Ever yours,
Ernie

This is the address: Mdlle C. O'Sullivan, Aragon, 249, 1 Piso, 2a, Barcelona, Spain

Letter to John Hagan[16]

c/o Mdlle C. O'Sullivan,
Aragón 249, 1°, 2ª,
Barcelona, Spain
3 April 1925

[Monsignor John Hagan,
Rector, Irish College, Rome, Via Nazzarino,
Rome, Italy]

Dear Monsignor,

Perhaps you remember meeting me at my home address in Drumcondra in August or September 1922.[17] I was released from Camp last July and was then ordered abroad by the doctor. I was unable to leave til February and now have to remain at least a year abroad before the surgeons can operate on me, as I have still eight pieces of lead in me. My funds are rather limited and I thought I might be able to supplement them by teaching or by some such work. My passport is made out in the name of Cecil Smyth-Howard and it rather handicaps me. I intend to remain in Spain til about July; practically I do not know any one here now. I have been endeavouring to get some work to do even to exchange English for Spanish free but so far have failed. The people here speak Catalan and I have small opportunity of learning Spanish. An Irish girl here has been endeavouring to get me away to the country where I would be boarded and where the climate is good and also where living with a family though they spoke Catalan, yet would speak Spanish to me. If I go to the country I will probably remain there for six weeks or so then I intend to go to Majorca or into Spain proper, preferably some place on the sea coast.

Perhaps you might be able to help me by giving me introductions to some one you know in Barcelona. The Balearic Isles or some place in Southern Spain not far from the sea. At the end of July I intend going to Italy – Rome, perhaps first. Could you please tell me if you know of any digs I could go to there as I do not wish to stay in an hotel, even for a few days, as I would have to register there, also do you know of any position I could get in Italy which would help supplement what money I have, as I doubt if it will last me beyond the month of August. I do not know what I am fit for. I am a medical student. I know a little about English literature, could teach English and perhaps make some kind of a "shot" at Spanish. Anyhow this may not be necessary as I may be able to get more money, but I should like at any rate to have something to put in my time at as teaching or exchanging languages.

I feel I am wasting my time here as I am not learning Spanish, save what work I do myself at a text book. Some of the Catalan institutions are interesting, and I feel that I could do some work here if I had the language which might be of some [help] to my country. I know you are busy and feel very mean for troubling you, but the people at home cannot help me in any way. If you have not the time, please, tell me so and just send on the name of some 'digs' or place to which I could go if I did happen to arrive in Italy. Are there any specific regulations about registering there; I am anxious to know this as the Spanish agents are on to me at present, the British must have passed me on but I could always "slip" them if I want to leave the country. By the way I am supposed to be in Italy so will you please not mention the fact that you have heard from me. When on hunger-strike I met a friend of yours, Father Morrissey,[18] a great old saint whom we liked well; he often spoke of you. I enclose a covering address in case you wish to write at any time. When replying please do so as if writing to the lady in question. The initial "C" on the letter means that it is for me and it will be sent to me accordingly.

Yours very sincerely,
Ernie O'Malley

NO. 6 HAG 1/1925/316(1) IRISH COLLEGE ROME ARCHIVES
Letter from Cecil E. Smyth-Howard (EOM) to John Hagan

Hotel du Commerce,
Bourg-Madame (Pyr-Or), France
19 June 1925

[Monsignor John Hagan,
Rector, Irish College, Rome, Via Nazzarino,
Rome, Italy]

Dear Monsigneur,

I received your letter of June 8th on June 18th. As you see I have changed my ground. Also I received the money which you so kindly sent, and though I do not like to use it, yet if occasion arises I will do so. I have not had a pleasant time down South, I had no friends and the climate was not suitable, but here it is quite healthy and, as I have been able to make up for the months I spent further South, I feel somewhat more healthy than I did when I left home which is, at best, somewhat a negative statement of fitness.

I have not heard any news of how things are at home for five months. This address will get me til about the 21st July, then I will move off. I may be able to stay with a friend in the North of France for August, as I wish to learn French and justify my existence; if so I probably would not go to Italy til October. If you correspond with Frank Brady,[19] when abroad,[20] please ask her to send me her address or, perhaps, you may be able to do it. As you have my name already it will not be necessary to glorify my letters with it. I will write again as soon as I heard that you have received this one. I have been 'laid up' for a month here, but, as I carry a good book reserve, it has not been too unpleasant. I will have a friend visit your friend in Barcelona in case I have to go there again, anyhow I will let you know what I propose to do when I receive your correct address as at present I do not have it.

Thanking you again for your kindness and help,

Yours very sincerely,
Cecil

Letter to John Hagan

Florence, [Italy]
22 October 1925

[Monsignor John Hagan,
Rector, Irish College, Rome, Via Nazzarino,
Rome, Italy]

Dear Monsignor,

I received your letter of October 16th today. After writing to Father Magennis[21] I met a lady, an aunt of Bob Barton,[22] who rescued me from my hotel; as she had to visit a friend in the country, who was sick, I went to Siena from which I have just returned, so will you, please, excuse me for not replying before this. Just now I have consulted Miss Priestly as to the manner in which I should address you and she has given me a very lengthy title in Italian; she is rather horrified at the manner in which I have begun the letter, but, I am, I must confess, very ignorant about the matter.

I am glad that I was not in Rome as there are some people whom I would not have wished to have know I was there. I had expected that things would not mend; indeed I think they will be a little word in the near future as the "spring" has gone out of life for many people there. I am sorry to give you trouble, knowing you are so busy, and I think it very good of you to bother about my affairs.

Yours very sincerely,
Cecil Smyth-Howard

NO. 8 PRIVATE COLLECTION (DUBLIN)
Letter to Kay Brady[23]

[Rome, Italy]
27 December 1925

[Kathleen Brady,
Menton, France]

Dear Kay,

I have just received Frank's letter, so I know that you reached your destination alright, without any mishap, whatever about adventures, but they were not included. Please excuse this paper. I have none other and as it is a holiday I cannot, so I think as I'm too lazy to leave my room, obtain any more. For a whole day I thought I had lost my fountain pen and wandered round in a forlorn fashion, but luckily it turned up again. It always does. I shudder to think of using a new pen because this one, of itself, is quite fluent. I suppose you celebrated Christmas in a riotous manner and are now sadder and wiser.

I have been thinking how delicate I am since I left you with this result:

25th Rose at 9.30 a.m. Slept in the evening.
26th Rose at 12.30 p.m.
27th Rose at 9.30 p.m. Slept all the evening.

On the 26th I did not remember that it was a holiday of obligation, so you will have a heavy bill to account for. The woman always pays, you know. I have been endeavouring since Christmas Eve to obtain some information about the closing of the Holy Door, but everyone was busy, so I do not know what to do about it at present. The Rector[24] helpfully advised me to buy a book on the Holy Year, but did not say what it was or where it might be obtained. He suggested getting me a typewriter, but I suggested that an introduction to a civilian who could tell me something about a function before it came off would be much more to the point. Anyhow things are at or in an impasse.

I'm glad to hear Eileen has had a baby. I hope she will teach it to make tea and to wash up. I went over to the Irish College to send a telegram to her, but I could not locate anybody. I met three lovely young ladies in a tram today. I was quite struck and quite forgot the other one who shared my affections. They consisted of twins and another. The twins had lovely melting brown eyes, the other had very fine blue ones. The twins should be about 4 or 5 and blue eyes could not be more than 4. They got friendly with me and then got off the tram with their pa. The other young lady aged 6 comes to visit the landlady, and though shy at first, now talks to me in Italian and confides all her secrets. It's terrible not to know the language. Kiddies are terribly fond of their mothers in Italy; that is why there is such reverence for the Madonna. Families usually fast on Saturday in her honour, and it is strange to know that the Saturday fast is kept better than is the Friday one.

There are many functions on these days if I could find any information about them. In Aracoeli I have just learned that there is a function at 3 p.m. at which the children deliver sermons. Yesterday I visited a church which was entirely controlled by kiddies. A little girl regulated the crowd and her word was law. The Italians, who always try to squeeze past any barrier, moved back at a wave of her hand and waited patiently.

Recently I saw that Raphael's 'Transfiguration' was left unfinished at his death and completed by Guilio Romano. The lower part was completed by the latter. Do you remember the two figures on the left on the mountain top? They represent St Julian and St Laurence, personified by Guilio and Lorenzo di Medici. I think it would be useful if I made up notes on good pictures for myself anyway as it is hard to obtain information save one buys a book by a good critic on a particular artist. Now I find I might have saved myself the trouble if I had at first consulted *Baedeker*.[25]

I have not seen Father Ronayne[26] since the day I returned. I evidently 'fluttered the dovecots' I hear, by my absence, more than I did by my presence. I find it hard to settle down again here. You people have disturbed my equilibrium. I debated to myself if I should return to my own country and at once, not the first time to do so, but the fact of not being fit prevents. Once it was a very near thing: I was just off when I sat down and fought with myself and remained on. I am much 'fitter' than I was when I left, but, generally, after 5 in the evening I am useless for anything and very often up to 12 noon, so I must fight hard to beat that. Those months I spent in my country before leaving were really terrible. You did not realize it. Mrs Childers[27] did and only for her peculiar insight, through suffering, I don't suppose I would have become anyway normal, not that I am normal now.

I saw the Vice Rector[28] the other day. He was busy, but I had time to borrow a book on sculpture. It sounds interesting as it gives each statue in detail; perhaps I may locate such a work on painting also.

Please tell Frank I called over for her relics to-day and as they were all out of doors left her address with instructions. Also I wrote to a friend of mine about her eyes. There was a very wonderful oculist in Nice. He is now dead, but he had pupils and, perhaps, this lady who lived in Nice may be able to supply some information.

This is disjointed and I'm sorry, but this has been a bad day for me and I cannot connect up my ideas on account of my head. I did not know to-day was Sunday, only this evening I found it was so, luckily I had been to a High Mass as St John Latern's. A peculiar function in which the Cardinal sat facing the audience and only moved up to the altar a few times. I will write to you again to make up for this. When are you going away? I will enclose this letter in a very special envelope, which I brought with me from Spain. Please kindly remember me to all.

Yours very sincerely,

Cecil[29]

This is to wish you all a Happy New Year. I hope you will be able to get something which will make you feel more settled, but I think you should continue Medicine, but I suppose it is Andy who must decide that.

NO. 9 PRIVATE COLLECTION (DUBLIN)
Letter to Kay Brady

[Rome, Italy]
29 December 1925

[Kathleen Brady,
Menton, France]

Dear Kay,

I received your letter of 24th on the 29th; it was delayed, so am dutifully replying at once. I was worrying over that blessed article on the Holy Door and felt very strongly tempted to write another one, 'How I did not see it' and send it to a paper. Again yesterday I smoked one of the Rector's cigars, daring the inevitable headache as he seemed pleased at my effusion in print. Then again he wanted to get me a typewriter, but as diplomatically as I could, like a bull in a china shop,

I insinuated again that if I knew a civilian who would 'put me wise' to a function before it came off, I would make some attempt at writing it. He said once he would see about my writing a weekly letter for that rag and, perhaps even now he means me to do so, but he has not said anything. I can only state what crystallized philosophy I once issued regularly to harassed troops. 'A slovenly order begets a more than haphazard execution'. However I will steer clear of him for a week and see what happens.

I'm deep in work now trying to 'do' the Roman Churches. They require a deal of time, the light is bad, but there are many good tombs. At present I am sidetracked after Renaissance Tombs. Today in the Sistine Chapel I was getting a new light on Michael's[30] sybils, when I met a priest and with him were Mrs Murphy and Honor and, that's the sort of me, though I loved going and 'doing' the rest of the Vatican, still I would have had preferred to remain. I map out a programme and wish to see it through, very selfish indeed, and though interruptions may leave me with no vain regrets, still this sightseeing for me is work, and I like to be able to get through so much each day. A delightful lady with the Murphys could not remember if she had 'done' the Raphael Stanza, on returning there we found she had. Shades of Ruskin and other prigs, like myself! Fancy Ruskin and I together!

I'm afraid the timing is not wearing off, save for letter writing. Is it too late now to apologise for not answering your last note for I have duly let the year go by without replying or have I? I think not though for you wrote after Christmas and my last letter should reach you before the end of the year. As I am penitent for that I must also apologise for not turning up that morning at 9:30 a.m. I had a previous engagement – with a person – and as the time was definite, I found I would be 10 or 15 minutes late. I was waiting til I got you both together til I explained, but Frank took the offensive, not giving me credit for some good intentions, and then, as usual, I made matters worse – so there. I forget if there is any other reason for examining my conscience. My head is full of the Sistine Chapel just now. Michael's work is rather uneven there. I think his Jonah very good, every whit as good as anything I might attempt myself.

I was over in Aracoeli this evening to hear the kiddies preach sermons. It was very interesting. Kids of all ages spoke and, though a little bashful, none of them are shy. Yesterday, to digress, a girl, an Italian, fell into my arms in a train, and she actually blushed; I felt like rendering First Aid. Anyhow the kiddies, prompted often, spoke their little piece, made as a general rule a beautiful bow before beginning. The last thing was a dialogue between two little girls, one answering the other questions about an imaginary Nativity. And the gestures, the expression and the inflection were, as a lady beside me, with whom I was on smiling terms, said 'They were simply too cute; weren't they cunning?' she remarked. They certainly were, so was she.

I have tried to recover from the shock of your handing back my letter; perhaps after all you are an autograph hunter and wished me to sign the souvenirs of the 'trip', nice word that. I hate it, so I suppose my devil of perversity, which helps me to erect my own barriers, tempted me to insert it. I am overwhelmed with your gifts, but the autograph only confirms my suspicions.

I'm glad you like your Honolulu. I can both dance and play bridge. We three eldest were well brought up by unfortunate governesses, who never remained long: the experiment has never been attempted for the remainder; two of the three are dead,[31] so I, the last of the tradition, have unlearned everything from dancing, and its interludes, to manners. Cards required time so they too 'went by the board'. It's hard to serve as we have had to, not hard to serve but to survive the serving. Anyhow, 'Cheer up, we'll all soon be dead' as we used to say in Camp.[32]

I'm glad you sent such a long letter. I'm a very bad correspondent especially here. I'm going all day and at evening I'm tired and then I do not know but that letter writing gives vent to egotism, whether you consciously or unconsciously polish up one's good points in one's writing is difficult to say. Anyhow it all looks as if I were trying to make excuses for not writing in future. I would like to do so to both Frank and you, but if I'm on the move I generally walk til I drop and then I cannot write as I move off again next day, but if I am stationary I have little or no excuse much save that I keep putting it off til I feel it would be an insult to write and then I have an evil conscience, but generally try to create a mental atmosphere of telepathy. I really did feel quite miserable when the train steamed out almost as much as the day you all left for Naples when I wandered round like a lost soul, more by reason of the fact that we had not begun in the least to know you both, now that I feel I do a wee bit, it is not so bad. I am sending the address back with M. who leaves in a day or so; you need not deliver it to Mrs C,[33] but I wish you would go to see her and give her all my love. I don't belong anywhere, but I am at home there. I know her manner is too sweet but she was reared in that Bostonian set and she does not realize that we are not used to it, but beneath it she is very wonderful and of all things, brave. I know you will be afraid she will kiss you, but that's that manner again breaking out.

I wish I had your background to hang my stray scraps of knowledge on: I really don't know anything except handling of men and I wish I had had to go through the home tuition work which one must to get a degree. I suppose I will have to muddle along somehow, but I know I waste my time. I could write a lot more but I won't. I'll keep it for my next. I think I wished you and all a very Happy New Year in my last so I now wish it again with every good result to what you most wish for.

Ever your friend,
Cecil

I'm sorry to enclose two letters; please forgive the rudeness. By the way 30 December could not get this off. I am moving to a new place, this is too dear, to a kind of hostel for University Students and others, both sexes; all round 600 lira a month: a good place so if either of you want, or both, to 'do' Rome for two weeks or a month don't say I did not tell you.

Letter to Kay Brady

[Rome, Italy]
6 January 1926

[Kathleen Brady,
Menton, France]

Dear Kay,

I received your second note of 29 December on 5 January. This is my third to you, also to Frank, so I would like very much to know if you received the others, especially after the indecent display of my soul. I like the phrase. One of my Americans[34] said it to me because I passed some remark about Art, which she thought learned – an indecent display of intellect she called it, so for a while I was very careful and filtered, or rather, unfiltered my remarks. My Americans are really fairy godmothers, or 'aunts', as they themselves say they are, to me. The Christmas night invitation was very welcome and then on the New Year they invited me to lunch. I had said goodbye to Honor[35] and her mother the night before and I hate so much to say goodbye to anyone, who for the time being represents my country to me. The next day we went to see Ostia and had quite a nice day there.

Well, so far my Americans have occupied the page. They have designs on my meeting nice girls, so they say, and I have had to 'steer clear' for a few days as I know they have some Americans 'up their sleeve' for me. How goes it with you in your Oriental atmosphere? Any paladins, camels, arras, harem, lotus flower, oasis or any of those Oriental creatures near you to give local colour. I would feel lonely when you mention the sea, but the Mediterranean (only one 't' I think) is never such to me, but bathing! I have not had one for nearly three years and before then for about four, and I was once a good swimmer; pretty 'tough', eh? Hardly have room for this address.

I wrote to my Florence friend about an oculist in Nice, but though she acknowledged my letter she did not mention the subject; the mother of her old servant is dying, and she is night and day nursing her. Father Ronayne[36] has been very busy since you left, trying to drown his sorrows in work: one day I brought him out to tea in a very dull affair, and told him stories, one of which was the best he had ever heard, so he said, and I rather think it was. Yesterday we went with two Australians to visit a maestro and they sang for his criticism: it was quite interesting and Father Ronayne was delighted. He is very fond of music. I was at a concert on Sunday in the Augusteo and felt bad at not having been there before now. I'm hunting up advertisements of other concerts, so I think I should be able to hear four or three a week. All this of myself, sorry, but I have already warned you of the effects of letter writing. I have moved into a new place as you will see from the address and at table, this university one. I sit near to a Spaniard, and we talk a little in broken French and Spanish adding a few words of English and Italian to show what gay dogs we are. There is a billiard room here also and I feel a 'churl'; it has been so long since I have played billiards, so long since I had my year a dance [*sic*] that I'm sure it will be hard to get back to it, not the dance exactly, but to young student mentality, more difficulty now as I cannot talk to them. I note your address. Please ask her sister for the stamps if you see her and give her my kind regards, if she has collected any, but that's mean, give them, anyhow. Also don't you forget stamps for me.

You had no mountains around to climb. You'll never feel properly alive til you spend a week or so in high mountains. For deep sea, or dangerous sea coast water, or high mountains you had best, I think, be by yourself: unless your friend is a chum, it may spoil things. I lived at over 6,000 feet for some months, and it was glorious, very healthy and bracing, and one's lungs become accustomed to the clear atmosphere. You should 'hike' off sometime for a week or so. I'd map a tour in Europe for you only I would not like 'to impose my will'.

Why limit your pen when writing? I think it unfair; one should write what one wants when the pen is in the hand. It seems kind of mean to write a letter because the other person does not or will not write much, unsound tactics also if only for the reason that one should always put the other person on the defensive. I don't know when you intend to leave, but I will see Bobby[37] before I post this and if you receive this and my others, please send a wire to me, if you don't mind, as I would like to be sure that my letters have reached you and Frank, also you did not test the address I gave, and it would be better to do so before official stuff might be sent to it.

Weather cold again. I was down in the Piazza Navona the other evening. There was a kind of kiddies fair in progress. The whole square was lighted up with the multi-coloured electric lights of the booths. Every imaginable make and shape of toy could be seen there from the ragged man who sold the run away mouse to the gramophone stall. The gramophones were of pure tin, though another metal had been evidently employed as their voice was brazen. I saw a curé haggling over paying for two wooden, not well brought up, figures who, with long arms, smacked alternatively each others' faces, actually, not figuratively, as well brought up people do. Monkeys who climbed ropes when one pulled a string and descended with equal rapidity. Balloons of all shapes, colours and sizes, the noisy ones predominated, for the gamut ranging from a thin female shriek to that of a disused Klaxon horn with a bad cold and a worse temper. The side shows were the most interesting. With corks one shot at miniature figures, with small shot one aimed at groups of figures, some with musical instruments, one a curé with a shawl hat, as in the Barber of Seville, mounted on an ass. If one got a bird's eye in the musical ones, they begin to play. I wonder what would have happened to the curé. Mainly a Roman crowd save for myself, therefore the 'mainly'. Please remember me to your mother, father and Frank.

Ever yours,
Cecil

I have not at all written what I intended to write, and I must dash for the post when I have seen Bobby first, but one needs ample business to write what one wants to say and not to write against time as I am at present. Cheerio (I know you'll like that word). Hope you can read this. It's rather a test I admit.

Letter to Kay Brady

[Rome, Italy]
6 January 1926

[Kathleen Brady,
Menton, France]

Dear Kay,

I have just seen Bobby. He was at a Concert in the College[38] and would not allow me in save I sang, and though I offered to sing small he still refused. I had been chatting with Doctors, Bishops and mere Monsignors, been smoking a cigar, which has always dire results, and felt like doing a dance on the littered table to show I could do something other than listen to people talking about the various diseases Cardinals suffer from. Anyhow, to get back, I found that you had left Menton on the 1st[39] or so, and my pile of letters is wandering round and will be delivered to your old address, and now I wonder what did I say in them. I understood that you would not leave Menton til the 11th or 12th, and if I had thought you would have done so I would hardly have written. My thoughts now would fill volumes. We will just have a two minutes silence and leave a space here for things

1.

2.

May your son – no, may the twins … one of them a Bishop, the other a Cardinal Secretary of State or a Cardinal in England! Now I feel better.

However I discovered something to-day a real masterpiece unknown and perhaps unforgotten and I feel ready to blazon it forth to the world. It is produced only on very State occasions and I had the good luck to see it twice. The first time I had not my *Baedeker* with me, so of course it could not be a work of art, now however I had an opportunity of studying it at close range. The colour is wonderful; something of Raphael, something of Mantegna, and subdued Titian, and the line! I talk of Florentine line; it is the quintessence of such. I'm really fearful excited. Composition I did not study so closely but grouping, chiaroscuro, movement, expression – everything perfect. The decorative work is Mimo[40] at his best, rather an odd combination, this of schools of sculpture and of painting but there it is. The subject is classical, the cornucopia which reposes on the Rector's table when anyone above the rank of a Msgr. drops in. I would have loved a cross section through its delicate rose setting. It has been restored. There are some baroque ornaments which clash a little, but still they fail to impair this wonderful work. I shall sketch it for you if you wish and perhaps I may be able to study composition if I am left alone with it – and whisper it – a knife.

I have finished my supper, chatting with a final medical, who sat beside me and offered to settle my matric[41] for 30 liras, and who also said I might be able to see Rustionelli's work. I explained my hiatus in studies by my Salonika campaign; you know I am rather shy about telling people of my foreign service,[42] but if you ever get me in a good humour, which is doubtful, I will tell you some queer tales.

I am afraid to write to Frank. Her relic has now been entrusted to me, and I am waiting til I get someone going back, but I suppose if she puts me on the defensive; I cannot excuse myself. People here never keep their word. That is rather terrible I think, even of the most trifling things it is quite as important. I have not the faintest recollection of ever inviting you out to dine, otherwise I should have had a bad conscience, til I explained it away to suit myself or carried it out faith-fully. Yesterday I nearly said things. I had arranged with a young priest to bring him out to tea with a friend and then on to Piazza Navona. I had to refuse Father R's[43] insistent invitation for the musical tea, later as he importuned me so much I went round in rather a bad state of mind to apologise to the priest and to ask him to excuse me, telling him where I was going. He was going elsewhere also, had not thought of it when he made my 'app' and had not the slightest intention of telling me of his new arrangement. No more 'apps' for me with that gent. Talking of 'apps' reminds me of a pretty girl I met in the French mountains, who said proudly that she spoke English and said, 'Happy – kiss me – good night'. I added a few more words to her vocabulary, having first explained what they were.

Please 'abort' the telegram now as it is not necessary, and you need not remember the address. If I had a month of sun tramping round I would feel fit; winter is hard on me, and I only shine in summer time, then I feel fit for anything from pitch-and-toss to manslaughter, not that I could not fill that gap now. I like Rome but I'm a little tired of it. It's comfortable, and I want to 'hike' off and do something even if it's only to risk breaking my neck on a mountain.

Now I have to buy a needle. I have been humming that haunting refrain:

'Do you remember long ago Kathleen,
That time you first did bid me sow,
And made my life so full of woe, Kathleen!'

The buttons insist on coming off my waterproof; it is made of some rubber composition, and it is very difficult to make them keep on. Also I have now one pair of socks. All my others I have worn to 'flitters', as I cannot darn well and bad darning hurts my feet which are still tender, so I just wear out my socks now til they are just a collection of highly strung holes to match the nervous temperament of my feet.

You seem pretty keen on driving me into a monastery. If I had either religion or courage I would try, but nothing doing that I can foresee. If my early Mass impressed you it is only an effort to keep somewhat straight, hard enough at all times, harder still when one is so much alone. It's not good for either body or soul and I have had 8 years of it now since 1918 by myself, for one is often far lonelier in crowds than one ever is by oneself. People don't make allowances at home. You know the work for some of us was a kind of Crusade in which first you left your home, then your real friends, then your social environmental and the amenities. One had to stop one's reading of literature, prevent oneself from making friends as that meant obligations, and more important – time, and then you are suddenly landed not into your old circle, but into the new people whom you have met as you travelled in your narrow circle. It is difficult to readjust oneself, more difficult to attune to the circle which you never really knew and then to have physical and mental complications as well. It's what I call 'tough'! This is in a way an apologia for my rudeness for my silence which was often, I felt, much more offensive than any very cutting remarks I might have passed on the company present. I lost my manners for, I felt, it best in our crowd, after careful consideration, not to do things which would come natural to me as I had been thus brought–up, as it might seem to emphasize their lack of politeness or form though, not lack either, but lack of training in such. And, perhaps, it was a quite wrong line of policy; anyhow I won't again pursue it.

Miss O'Rahilly[44] said to me once last December that I was a very 'uncomfortable' fellow because I did not wish to smoke or play cards; if she took me for granted as Mrs H[45] did it would be alright, but it's not the way to put people at ease. I feel then often that I do like to fill Emmett[46] who is a fine (old fashioned) boy, full of good whiskey, whisk a piece of frilly fluff beside him, put both into a Rolls Royce, clap on the accelerator and leave him. It would do him good, I feel. That's often what I think in places where I say nothing. People could say the same of me, but I don't suppose I would need the whiskey or the Rolls Royce. It's hard to keep a broken lid on Vesuvius and even in the lid there must be a vent hole and when something goes wrong there's generally trouble. I think mostly our people have no knowledge much of life, even to sum it up from a distance and consequently little grasp of the complexities of human nature.

Sorry for all this for the I, I, I, but if I seize on a point in a letter of yours, I can eliminate that portion of mine. I wish I was quite fit for although I do not like it as an end or a means, still soldiering is good work. Men are rotters indeed on the moral plain, but they are truly great companions and much more thoughtful and courteous to each other than they are to women. And they put up with hardships, often ignorant hardships, so well that it's good to be with them. Their vision is broader, I think, but more liable to compromise probably because they have more responsibility. I often think that if above a certain position of responsibility, it is very nearly impossible to see and hold on to a quite straight issue. Whether the larger horizon weakens your will or whether added responsibility means that you cannot see one issue and one only I do not know, but I always feel that if a man rises beyond a certain mark he changes somehow. I often wish people who talk were confronted with responsibility! This may lead to new companionship. I have never yet met a complete rotter. You think you have a man 'sized up' only to find in a crisis that this degenerate spineless person puts everyone to shame by his disregard of self, his courage or his momentary sincerity. Anyhow humans are mighty queer fishes; don't know about the women side of it.

They always say their sex for us is impossible to understand and that they know us inside out. Well someone does anyhow for we don't know ourselves and the fact that we don't grow up disarms the opposite sex and gives them that know – all atmosphere. What trite and unsound logic! Anyhow it does not matter.

How you will read this writing I do not know: I find some letters together, and it must be passing difficult to read the writing. Anyhow don't you ever complain that I did not write to? you, even if you don't receive this, perhaps whoever does open it will feel better for it, as I do not know if it will make him feel worse. And if you and Frank have time, you might someday get some blank sheets of paper and amuse yourself by seeing if you could fill them, for me. If an indecent exposure of soul is not possible you have at least no apologia to write. The mystic letters on the address means that I have decided not to enclose it as I do not see that it can be of any earthly use. The best of bad writing is that if you do make a mistake you can generally change it into anything you like. The other letters perhaps prepared you for the shock. I would like to write to Eileen and will one day, but it must come gradually and perhaps her health is none too good just now.

Yours very sincerely,
Cecil

(I am preparing a budget for Frank. My speling gets worser and worser as I rite so pleese exkuse me and put it down to geniral igorance.)

NO. 12 PRIVATE COLLECTION (DUBLIN)
Letter to Kay Brady

[Rome, Italy]
24 January 1926

[Kathleen Brady,
46 Lower Leeson Street, Dublin]

Dear Kay,

> 'He smoked cigarettes like a woman who detests them but feels that it is the correct thing to do. Stan Bride who bore no resemblance to anything virginal. Bertie's father was rich beyond the dreams of actresses. For he had a skin beside which an elephant's was gossamer silk.'[47]

The above from a book I had been reading; wish I could get a really humorous book; do you know any; in default I'll have to write short stories. This between gasps as I am trying to read a volume of Symonds' *Renaissance*[48] and my hand is bad so I'm going to get into bed. I am too lazy to get out to root up your letter, but I will try and answer some things from memory. The seemingly cryptic sentence means that if I reply to points in, or arising from, a letter of yours, I need not bore you with my reflections which are not or would not be relative to the points in question. 'Hence I could eliminate that portion of mine', is that how it runs? Also I'm afraid you misread some words of mine. 'Stuff' should be 'fluff',[49] quite another thing indeed. One presupposes that one has already quite a quantity of 'stuff' on board before adventuring with a piece of 'fluff'. Have you seen where something happened to the real Vesuvius? Shall I tell you that it was a duet and, not a solo, and if so would you believe me? The Italians say 'Queér sat',[50] sounds like it, and shrug their shoulders, and once I knew a girl who had at times a most annoying cant 'Well one never knows does one?'

This writing is the line of least resistance, therefore it is something to fight against. I know if I get into the habit I would write every night, but it's one of the luxuries of modern life and as such I must fight against it, and I prefer if possible to run counter to the line of least resistance. About a photo: no thanks very much. I have 'no use' much for photos; every now and then I tear up any I happen to have and I take them only because people think I should like to have them and not to offend; even on very rare occasions to ask for one, but save they are of scenery I never look at them again, tear them up in my very periodical 'spring cleans'; I have found them dangerous and it's quite enough to be responsible for my own funeral. First I thought I would ignore the point leaving you to do what your wished, then thinking that was not honest I decided to write what I thought. Photos are as egotistical as letter writing.

27 January 1926

'And he reflected, as all men reflect from time to time, that women are strange and incomprehensible, a device invented by Providence to keep the wit of man well sharpened by constant employment.'

'But then, when a woman loves a man – she sees in him a radiance shed from her Own soul, and it changes him.'

'Yet, with a cold and penetrating insight which women have.'

'In common with many English and other girls they were capable of displaying brazenly, for a man they had scarcely seen, an affection the tenth part of which certain males with whom they were intimately acquainted would have been delighted to receive.'

I shall continue to plague you, so you can guess what book I have been reading. Yesterday I watched horses exercising on the Pincio. There is a magnificent ring there about 3/4 quarters of a mile in circumference. I thought these people here might be some good to get me a mount, but now of course knowing them from the point of view of what I cannot expect I know that is impossible. My knee grip is very bad and weak after my last spell in bed, and I would need pretty constant practice and for long spells. Still it was nice to watch them. Then I went to the Baths of Caracalla – the nearest approach I have been to a bath for a long time. This is the most terrible thing in Latin countries. It seems that if you do bathe daily your skin gets to need it more and though I invent contrivances yet they are never the real thing. Today I was out a little on the Appian Way. I sat on a stone seat, always stone in these countries, talked to two tramps and went to sleep and woke up to sit opposite there rings of little girls seated on the grass clothed in white who were singing softly. I rubbed my eyes and found it was not a dream: Thursday is a school holiday so I suppose the teachers utilized it by bringing the kiddies for a walk and then a sing-song on the grass. Then I went into a church accompanied by a flock of kiddies who wanted soldi,[51] but as the spell would be broken if I gave them anything I refused, so they introduced themselves and a little one called Zita, held on to my hand and seemed quite 'struck'; I was anyhow, so reluctantly I left them.

I read a paper today which gave a nice description of your Kemel Pasha (can't spell) the first, advisedly I say first, as you seem to have the male equivalent of a harem. It was a paper to which you probably at one time contributed when you were 'little Katy Brady' as the General said. I chat every evening with a Monsignor now. He wants to learn English, and I give him all the delicate shades of meaning I can for the same word. He has a good memory, poor dear. It is very good for my English. To-day I told a person that the past of 'do' was 'dud' and that fiancé was pronounced 'fiasco'; I intend to enlarge his now peculiar vocabulary.

30 January 1926

Today is mild. My window is open and I am writing early in the morning. Indeed I find it very hard to get up now; I expect I could put a certain amount of the blame on you two for that, but I won't; that sounds magnanimous, but it is not. I was just at 'the end of my tether' when I received a letter from a chum of mine so I can now exist for another month, but it's only postponing things I know. This winter has been exceptionally severe for Rome. I feel the cold here much more than I do in my own country. It cuts one more and the houses are so uncomfortable that one can never get warm save one goes to bed or gets so absorbed in one's work that it does not matter. I get very much 'fed up' with Rome at times. Days are too cold to remain out; galleries are very cold; if the Florentine Galleries were here, it would be lovely as then I could spend all my time in them. They tell me that February is a cold month here and counters the idea of my starting off to tramp. My feet are not good.[52] They always give trouble for even a short distance, but on trying their paces lately I find I cannot do more than five or six miles and that's no earthly use, so I have to begin again; not so bad as it was last week, really bad, when I had to sit down often and say, excuse the vernacular, 'you have bloody well got to go on my son, see' – and so I would carry on for another short spell and kick myself forward again, but I more or less won through in the end.

This is a rambling disconnected letter. I had ideas in my head the first time I began to write, since they have disappeared. I keep myself busy now so that I don't have, or won't have, time to think. But some remarks in your letter need explanation. My detachment is not like your defensive armour, as a defensive purpose, as I don't voluntarily use it; I have built it up, so that it is not a pose to prevent myself from flinging myself in reckless abandon on the neck of the first female I see (lovely word 'female' – it always sounds like a third sex) but is now part of myself and Republican society has helped it to develop. Really one needs an armour for Republicans, why? Are they a sex to themselves? The women I fear are females. Why are they different from normal people. And why do they haul in their own, or other people's ideals, on the walks of everyday life. Perhaps I'm putting you too many questions.

I'm glad to hear you intend to keep some stamps, but what if the other lady will become so interested that she will make a collection for herself alone. I fear it. To my mind it is difficult realizing how attractive stamps can be, to avoid doing so. The situation is embarrassing. If you had not said some things I might write and thank her as I really should do. Certainly if ever I see her with a collection and for me I shall have difficulty in restraining myself from falling on her neck. This place is 'dud' for stamps and I had such hopes. It's rather a nuisance not to have anyone to talk to about the things I'm interested in; ordinarily 'tripe talk' is so futile, why should I resurrect the past when I meet John,[53] and why sit thinking near him when my head is bursting with things to tell him of what I have seen that day or since I have seen him last. If I did enthuse, he might send for a doctor. (Sorry to say ordinary 'tripe' talk, but I mean that for the little English I do talk I would like to talk of things which would keep my train of thought from being bottled up; it sounds priggish, I know, but I don't mean it so). I am getting like Qusil. I think that is the name of the book. To-day I tried to use a tube of vaseline instead of my toothpaste. Could you find out for me please if my brother[54] received about five letters, which I sent him between last July and October, five boxes of books, and *L'Illustration*[55] for three months. I have not had any reply and I just want an acknowledgment as now I have nothing to write to him about. And my books are my best friends and it is so terrible to lose them, yet I always expect to. I had lost them steadily by fire, sword and rapine up to 1923, when I tried again to build up; luckily in 1924 finding the remnants of my art library which I had left with a friend for safety. I had a good Anglo-Irish library once, collected 1915–18, left it when I departed to see the world in 1918 with a friend, removed it with my notes to the country to a friend's place so that now and again I might drop in to look at it; in 1921 the whole house was burnt by my friends the enemy.

Tuesday, 1 February 1926

I have rather a grudge against Germans. So far as I can see, they have few pretty women and I don't like the nation for that. I can invariably tell them now. They do not dress well, they wear a peculiar kind of hat, all look plain, methodical, and not very exciting. Are they all the same and why did God inflict such a punishment on their race? If I could have tea in the evenings I would be supremely happy, but not by myself. Tea is a social meal, one for light chatter and a sense of humour. And if I could 'trot' someone out to tea every day, it would be good, not the same one, of course, as I'm too much of a tramp for that. However always we want something. My Monsignor, if different individually from anyone mentioned before, is turning out to be a treat. When young he travelled through the Umbrian hilltowns, knows Rome well, artistically, is very interested in music and, for a Monsignor, quite intelligent. To-night I hummed some bars from the Tannhaüser Overture, and he continued to finish it, quite excitedly. Also he heard the Catalan Orfeo when it came to Rome, and I loved it so much in Catalonia. The andando was a treat; he conducted with the hair of his head, with his moustache, with his legs and he was so very very proud of his orfeo (choir). Now if he knew anything about Ballistics or Strategical Geography, it would be too lovely, or even stamps. Perhaps he does it all; he is a mountaineer, at least he was once, so he is saved. He is a keen photographer; that's a branch I want to know and I miss quite a lot by reason of not having a camera with me. The other day on the Pincio I was leaning over the balustrade watching the hill outlines prior to sunset when a man, not five feet away, took an interest in my profile. I moved a little whereupon he continued to stare, then I put myself in such a position as to study his face without him being able to watch mine. He had a fine face, a humorous chin; have you ever seen a humorous chin? When I had mentally filed his profile and full face, he turned round deliberately and looked hard at me and we continued to stare at each other in a fascinated way. It was too much for me, even if he were a 'spotter', so I smiled and he smiled back, then I clicked my back and bowed and he did likewise and I walked away for fear I'd spoil a perfect moment.

6 February 1926

I must get this off now or it will never go.

Good bye or Cheerio, as you like it best,
C.

NO. 13 PRIVATE COLLECTION (DUBLIN)
Letter to Kay Brady

[Rome, Italy]
5 February 1926

[Kathleen Brady,
46 Lower Leeson Street, Dublin]

Dear Kay,

To-day's great thought: 'His way was like other people's; he mounted no high horse; he was just a man and a citizen. He indulged in no Socratic irony. But his discourse was full of Attic Grace; those who heard it went away neither disgusted by servility nor repelled by ill-tempered censure, but on the contrary lifted out of themselves by charity and encouraged to more orderly, contented hopeful lives'.[56] Today I missed it. I was invited to Tivoli, but as I had bought a ticket for the Augusteum, I could not forgo it, and also I thought I would be more or less a bird alone as the students have their own chums and generally do not go out of their way to talk to a stray like myself. Anyhow I was seated at dinner with the Monsig, when they all came in gloriously tight, covered with confetti and the Monsig said to me 'They are silly' and words failed me to answer him. I just glowered and said 'I'm so sorry now I did not go'. They 'kicked up' a frightful row, and I had to talk English to him whilst he deplored the din. The old cucumber: he should have been glad of it. However the music was good: a Mozart overture, some Beethoven, Vivaldi (an 18th cent. Italian), Sibelius (a Scandinavian I think) and a little César Franck. I was interested at the end in the audience. Godowsky[57] the pianist was applauded when the concert was over, the 'gods' wanted him to play again: he appeared five times but only played on the sixth appearance, and played a very beautiful thing at that, but the audience 'kicked up' a most unearthly din until he did play; in fact began to hiss him at the fifth appearance. They hardly applauded him when he played; if he had appeared the sixth time without playing, I'm sure he would have been hissed and booed off the stage. An interesting sidelight on these people.

11 February 1926

Tonight I have made a speech; if you knew the amount of bad champagne that contributed to it, you would have some sympathy. People spoke in Spanish, Hindustani, English and French, Italian and dialect. I had said to myself to-day I would make time to-night so I am keeping my promise, though I think this is sufficient as such an auspicious occasion is not a time for letter-writing. To-morrow I go to Frascati and on Sunday we go on a right good 'bend'; if I write that night you will know that my Muse is inspired, so 'Try and cheer up, you'll soon be dead'!

This is late. I have returned from Tivoli. We had a good day; water water everywhere and only wine to drink! I saw quite a number of places including the Villa D'Este ...

I want to maintain a high standard of excellence, sounds like an ad for a superior Girls High School. I have proved to my complete satisfaction that the earth is round. I remember an old fellow in the National Library always ensconced behind a barricade of bulky volumes and was told that he was endeavouring to prove that the earth was not round. Poor flat as Mutt would say, or is it Jeff? I feel like writing an essay, but refrain, so write it mentally; it would be good fun to write some, some day. Have you ever tried?

Now I am going to read Charlotte Young's *Book of Golden Deeds*; a great old book I think because I can don a corselet and helm or ruffs and a rapier for a few hours and do daughty deeds all by myself. Always as a kid I loved Greek fairy tales and those of Arthur and his table round; unfortunately I never had Irish hero stories, though I do remember Seamus McManus' *Donegal Fairy Tales* which annoyed me then by their reiteration. It's all right to listen to an old man in the nook of a turf fire spinning such, but in print it is hard to catch the atmosphere. And I do remember the fight at the ford and how we cried because our hero, Ferdiah[58] (is that right?) who was from Erris and a Connaught man of ours was beaten by a man from the North; even then we were antagonistic to Ulster influence. And I remember a book of stories called *The Lost Cause*, but I had best stop or I shall feel like Compton McKenzie with his reminiscences of what happened a few years ago, yet I'm sure if people did put on paper their seemingly uneventful memories how interesting they would be, even for themselves.

Well, I have been to Tivoli again with the bunch, a tame one. Their lack of organised effort nearly made me weep. If they attempted to carry out my suggestions we could have had a good 'rag' but then one's ideas are always the best, aren't they? In the tail of the evening I commandeered a waiter and we went off and celebrated by ourselves. This is the 16th or 17th the last day of Carnival here, a very quiet affair and I'm feeling just as one feels at the age of 14 when one returns to school after the Summer holidays only worse at what happened to me today or at least what I failed, by reason of cowardice, to make happen; however, I suppose in three days' time I will be able to see it from another angle but I doubt it.

NO. 14 PRIVATE COLLECTION (DUBLIN)
Letter to Kay Brady

[Tuscany, Italy]
4 March–26 April 1926

[Kathleen Brady,
46 Lower Leeson Street, Dublin]

Dear Kay,

I received your letter of 24 February just before I moved off. I have not yet finished the one I began on 5 February and goodness knows when this will be finished. I have saved some things from the general haulocost (spelt wrong I fear) of your letters and Frank's, amongst others, so now I will be able to read them again and see if I have omitted to answer much. Sorry you did not take my being honest and thought I mean to be otherwise; such is life! Once Miss O'Rahilly said that I must tell her some story of my past career, this in 1922 of glorious memory, so I began a story stripped of all ornament not particularly unexciting either and she would not believe me; the first story I had ever told her or anyone else – for years. Then again in Florence I told the maid a few Spanish customs, and she said 'it's impossible', whereupon I related the story of the returned sailor who when asked by his mother what things wonderful he had seen on the trip said: 'Aaron's rod what had been picked up from the bottom of the Red Sea and some peculiarly coloured flying fish.' Whereupon, his mother said, 'It's alright about Aaron's rod, but flying fish – you can't fool me.' Whereupon the maid laughed all the more and said that there is no such thing as flying fish and thought he more than ever an untruther. So there. Not so bad as the recent display of new engineless aeroplane by a Spaniard. A cruel representative who had watched its manoeuvres closely said when asked by an excited group what he thought, said 'I saw it alright, but I don't believe it.'

When I say writing is easy I mean purely the act of writing not the getting myself to do it. That may take months; in fact in some cases it has taken years and I have yet to write. I'm in a monastery. It's miserably cold and I have no pyjamas and I'm trying to keep warm by writing to you so don't boast overmuch now of having kept me warm one night. Instead of pyjamas I have silk undies, a remnant of prosperity, which I refused to wear til quite recently; I have worn the vest already but to-day is the first time for the shorts portion. So you have all my tender secrets now.

To-day was quite a lovely day, but it is terribly cold here at night. I wrote you a mental letter to-day lying up on the hill on my back in the lapses of reading Xenophon's *Anabasis*, good stuff it is too. I see Cyrus fought just as I always like to with bare head: I wish I had my copy of the *Peloponnesian Wars* – chock full of names as it is yet there are interesting bits, and it helps to supplement one's Plutarch. Herodotus is much more interesting and readable. It's a pity that the *Anabasis* episode is so remote; it would make Cortes' note book very 'small beer' if diaries dealing with it could be unearthed. I wish if it would not bore you, you would write of books. Of what you are reading or books generally I do not know if you feel about them as I do. A few days ago I asked the lady in Wilson's if she would let me unwrap some few humdrum books that had arrived, but she would not as she thought I was not serious, and I would have gladly paid to have been allowed to give her help there in the shop. It would be so very nice, I think, to be in a good book shop.

To-day I wrote mentally on country as I was trying to describe this particular country round here, but I had to drag in names of other places which perhaps you had not seen so I refrain from writing. Then I described local colour as it struck me. Last night I made a speech in *Italian* to the university section; I had brought them to a wine shop and I spoke of your country and explained things to them and made them stop relating their sexual experiences for I wanted them to think on my last night, and they did.

Somehow when I feel a thing very intensely I can make myself understood. I did it twice in Spanish, once in French and now once in Italian. And to-day I can hardly ask my way in Italian. The boys have been quite nice to me latterly, somehow, and I feel very much of them though I hardly ever speak a word. They may develop physically here quicker than we do but mentally no. They are more childish than we are; of course you will say as girls always do 'all men are children' – yet that's their only saving grace, for few women are girls. Anyhow they nearly all fell on my neck, asked me all kinds of questions from 'had you any relations with women in Rome', to 'how old is you sweetheart' and 'have you any sisters' and so on. Good night now I'm warm, but I have not answered points in your last letter. You see I read it and generally have not it by me when I write.

Well again I take up my pen at you. I don't know what date it is, probably the 10th or 11th, and anyhow it does not matter. I have dined wisely and well. Here I have unearthed two nice restaurants and a nice hotel; the first night I came I fought with the cabby and with the hotel keeper and cleared out next day as I found a cheaper place. To-day I performed mental gymnastics in the Museum trying to find who the pictures are by; the numbers are carefully hidden for fear you might learn something, and they dare not offer the names as the pictures are generally not by the people whom they state they are by. The attendants are a pestiferous breed, very importunate, obvious (in their statements) and inaccurate.

I like Lorenzo di Credi (does anyone else I wonder?), and I find two by him, one of which is certainly his. Mis-interpretation of devotion is fine, I think. He also was influenced by Savonorala. What a pity Fra Bart burned his pictures. I'm sure he destroyed some very fine ones at the general bonfire and he could ill afford to as his later work is stiff and cold, the draperies wooden, and the aping of Michael very detrimental. Also there is a Botti, seems very like a Fra Filippo, especially the Madonna. Then I could have sworn to a Crivelli but it was a Vivarini; I had a stiff fight to decide between Lotto, Palma Vecchio and Veronese for one – it was a little of each but finally I decided for Palma as only the Madonna could be by Lotto. The Raphael here is not his. I like some of the bronzes well especially the Herculaneum ones as the earth has given them a pleasant colour.

I am worn off my feet walking the streets; to-night I located this street by chance; I had been 'doing' the Via Roma, always chock full of life and movement, as was the other street or series of streets but here one could see pretty dresses and faces and catch people's eyes and feel as if one was in a long-drawn out Grafton St. I have smoked the last but one of my cigars, only after a good dinner can I smoke one and then it is a blessing. I am trying to economise but have given it up. In Rome I missed much of the life as I did not dine out, indeed it is not a city to walk round in after 7, save perhaps the Corso, but it is a homely place, and small. You will say I have not answered your letters so now I consult them – to answer briefly:

(1) The monogram followed the pen, no serious intention.

(2) I see you say you find it too easy to write, in your first whilst in your last you say you wish you could be as fluent as I was with the pen (as I said I was when I got started). Why the inconsistency?

(3) Why consult anyone on what you intend doing as a career? You have always held advanced feminist views, now your seeming lack of desire to follow a definite career upsets any little belief I may have in a feminist outlook.

(4) The walking tour – Have not my maps by me to do it now. Anyhow you don't want it.

(5) For goodness sake get coup out of your mind. Our people could not carry it off: I doubt if they could properly carry off that portion of it that generally goes with killing.[59]

(6) Re the good story I told R.[60] It is kind of writeable (can't spell), but such with me are for men only.

(7) About the hunters. I think you could order two, one for Frank and your-self, though they would be really mine and you two could exercise them for me. You might purchase them on the overdraft at the bank I once had (2 parentheses as well as brackets: what do you think I am?) (I know that country well and the people there, to their cost, though years may tone down feeling and they might sometimes think not so badly).

I cannot find your letter which came between the one of 16 January and 24 February so I must have burned it. I am again cleaning up to-night. I left before I could look up the humanists for you, and I am sorry as I would have had liked to have done so. I saw both tombs in Santa Croce. In the Uffizi there is a Madonna and Child by Filipino, child on right, Our Lady in blue robe clasped hands kneeling. I'm glad to hear about the circle, mine is non-existent, worse than ever at times now. I expect I won't be able to forward you an address for quite a long time now. Thanks for the notes on books.

Here's at you again whether you will or no. I am a glorious tramp and feel at ease which I never do in the clothes I generally wear, for though made by a good tailor gent, as I had asked him to allow for the supposed expansion of my weak shoulder and back muscles, he did not make them to fit properly and they annoy me. Now in a very old suit, the trousers reinforced, a pearl grey sweater with a roll collar and a pair of heavy boots and a battered hat, the only portion of the *ensemble* that I do not like and my trusty now well worn haversack I strut round. The best of such clothes is that one can go anywhere; if you want to enter a low joint to eat or drink no one takes it amiss and even if you want to eat with the 'best people', you can also do so. The roll collar is a great idea. At first I did not like it as I wanted one that would support a tie but at night this one is very fine and you can cover up as far as your mouth. It's a very important point to keep one portion of your body really warm. Generally on very cold nights your waist needs to be kept warm, but I feel quite content with my sweater, and for sleeping out it is more than serviceable so if ever you tramp wear a roll collar. They are fashionable now I believe; I suppose they want to copy me!

I think previously I asked you if I should write of country but as you did not comment I won't. I could mentally, but when I come to do so on a paper I am too lazy. I was somewhat hungry to-day and am still, where there are not good pictures I move round all day getting to know the town or city walking til I can just crawl to my digs.

Well here's my expenditure to-day so far you will see that I am becoming a coffee fiend, oh for a tasty tea. Coffee, a kind of bread and a sweet cake at 9 a.m., this after a 12 hours voyage and I had not eaten since lunch time (1.70 lira), tips to see things (3 lira), ½ kilo of figs (1.50 lira can you believe it – dried figs), nice fish, ½ bottle bad wine, coffee (10.10 lira), Museum 3 lira, a drink, grenadana, 1 lira, coffee 0.80 tip 1 lira (rash!), pictures jolly good (good sound – sly – 17th century stuff) 3.20 lira, coffee and cake 1.25 lira. Total = 1.70 + 3.00 + 3.00 + 1.50 + 10.10 + 2.80 + 3.20 + 1.25 = 26.55 and I have to pay 12 lira for my room. The lunch was rotten and I fought hard for a good dinner as I wanted a half bottle of good wine and I only drink the latter when I eat but, nothing doing. I held out good and strong as I had considerably exceeded my 30 lira. That's a kind of typical day. I think it's rather fun especially when you fight yourself and defeat your own very plausible arguments. I had to keep away from bookshops though. I've made a resolution against books and postcards yesterday.

20 March 1926

I notice I have not kept the latter resolution. I seem to be in a kind of haze travelling most of the day and staying up at night. I have some photos of temples for you two. I hope you will not be bored thereat, especially as the reproductions were not good ones. You see I feel interested in certain things and that interest carries me through; it needed it for the past week, for it was active service conditions with a vengeance, but always an achievement, as one thinks, is something to look back on and to think kindly of as time goes by. I would like very much to know what has actually happened in the old country, but am quite content to wait 'til I do know. I don't know what I am going to do next, the necessity for what I thought I would have had to do has not yet arisen so that I take life easily in the interim too easily. I should have a long letter ready for Frank by this but I cannot write just now and I write this because I have to stay up all night. I had quite a number of things to write about but at the last moment they seem like an indecent exposure, so I will content myself, to save you, to write about the usual things I do write about. I was surprised to hear that Sean MacB[61] was married. A very nice girl with a good sense of humor. I chuckle when I think of the time they both belonged to that (awfully!!) important branch – Organisation – and what the Assistant D/O used to say of the typists.[62] I have been reading Knox on women and of course don't agree with him, though from my point of view they would be the line of least resistance, taking one from the things that count and making life too soft!! (This will give you time to breathe. How is Eileen doing and her baby girl and what is the latter's name?) I'm afraid I have not read anything much or strange; travelling I read Shakespeare as best I can. He certainly justifies his weight in my sack, one strap of which is now ready to snap, so I will have to carry it on one shoulder; rather a nuisance as it's too heavy.

   Please remember me to your mother, Pa and Frank and the others.

Yours very sincerely,
Cecil

26 April 1926

Some gap in between. I feel this letter will never be posted so I will post it as soon as possible. I hope you are all well.

———

NO. 15 EOM PAPERS NYU
Letter to John Raleigh[63]

[Barcelona, Spain]
15 April 1926

[John Raleigh,
St Joseph's Street, Limerick]

Dear Johnny,

   At last I have an opportunity of writing you so I hope you will, please, forgive me for not having done so before this. How are things with you? I would have written, but it was so difficult to get a reply through that I was unable to forward you an address. My health has improved now, and I feel in good form and if my old feet were alright, I would be as good as ever. I have been trying to find work, but it is very difficult and so far has not materialised, nor do I see any chance of my getting any. I do not speak the language and that is a big drawback. The next time I write I hope to be able to forward you an address and if so please reply to the name at the bottom of the letter and to the address at the top. I hope you are in good health and that your work is progressing.

> With kind thoughts,
> Yours very sincerely,
> Ernie.

NO. 16 HAG 1/1926/152 IRISH COLLEGE ROME ARCHIVES
Letter to John Hagan

> *Paris, [France]*
> *18 April 1926*

[Monsignor John Hagan,
Rector, Irish College, Rome, Via Nazzarino,
Rome, Italy]

Dear Monsignor,

I am very sorry not to have seen you when you passed through Paris. I was at the Gare de Lyons some time before the train was due to arrive and waited til a train did arrive and 'hung round' for some time but failed to see you so then I thought that you had arrived. Later I was informed, by Mr Kearney,[64] that you had passed through and I inferred that you were considerably annoyed at not having had anyone to meet you. Mr Kearney was ill and had asked me to give you his regards so that only makes the matter worse. I hope you will understand, please, that it was due to my ignorance of Paris and not to any forgetfulness on my part.

I hope the weather is better with you than it is here; it has been quite bad for some days past and I see no prospect of it improving. I went first to Rimini and Ravenna then to Ferrara and Bologna and eventually arrived at Venice. The weather was fine all through and it was not til I reached Milan that I met rain again. There I met an American student and we went to Switzerland together, but after a few days we left as it is a country for millionaires only. I hope all are well at Rome. Thanks awfully for bringing my bags to Paris; it was very good of you to do so. I hope you will enjoy your visit to Ireland and that you will find things improved.

> Yours very sincerely,
> Cecil

Letter to John Hagan

Hotel Leroy,
35 Rue Franklin, Place de Trocadéro,
Paris 16, France
25 May 1926

[Monsignor John Hagan,
Rector, Irish College, Rome, Via Nazzarino,
Rome, Italy]

Dear Monsignor,

I hope you are quite well and that the Italian weather is somewhat better than the French. Dr Lynch[65] asked me to write and tell you that your hotel is the Perry, Cité Retro near the Fog. St Honoré[66] and the Rue Boissy D'Anglais. You are, I understand, to arrive by the 2.30 p.m. on the 2nd so that I will meet you at the station; in the meantime if you have to make any alteration could you please let Dr Lynch, 20 Rue de la Paix (Paris 2) know. Will you, please, remember me to the General,[67] Father Ronayne and Bobby Brady.

Yours very sincerely,
Cecil S-Howard

After his letter of May, EOM travelled through northern France, Belgium, Holland and part of Germany, before making his way back to Dublin via Paris and London. He decided to live at home and to resume his medical studies at UCD. He had to pass his second-year exams following his abrupt removal from student life in March 1918 to go on the run with the Irish Volunteers. It was difficult to concentrate on his medical studies after all his experiences and he found himself dabbling in the arts, writing poems in his notebooks and reflecting on his past. He was especially interested in drama. With his fellow students Denis Devlin, a future diplomat and poet, William Fay, also a future diplomat, and Roger McHugh, later a distinguished academic and literary critic, he formed the Dramatic Society at UCD under the aegis of the Literary and Historical Society. It was such a success in its first year that the president of UCD allowed it to be an independent group in its second year, 1927–8.

NO. 18 HAG 1/1926/511(2) IRISH COLLEGE ROME ARCHIVES
Letter to John Hagan

Medical School,
Cecilia Street, Dublin
1 November 1926

[Monsignor John Hagan,
Rector, Irish College, Rome, Via del Santi Quattro 1,
Rome, Italy]

Dear Doctor O'Hagan,

I hope you are quite well and that the weather is good. As you see I have resumed Medicine, beginning again at my second lectures and, so far, I have not settled down to work, but it will come in time. There has been some talk of an Election pending some say at Christmas, but so far there is nothing definite.[68]

I expect you are in the new College now, the envy of all the others. How are the General and Father Roynaye and Monsignor Curran?[69] I met Dr Quinn and his wife[70] just before they left Paris so I suppose they are still with you. Sean and his wife[71] are still in Paris. Con Little is staying outside Paris or at least he was daily planning to leave for Italy. He is a confirmed optimist. I hope his operation was really successful but as I have not heard from him, I do not know.

The weather is quite cold now and the coal and fuel is scarce. The people will suffer much this winter, I fear. We will know definitely that an Election is pending when the Staters begin to seriously consider the position of the poor with regard to fuel. I have not much news for you as I am only beginning to pick up the threads. Later I will write when I get a fountain pen. With Analist regards to all in Rome and more especially to yourself, who were so very good and kind to me. I feel I can never in any way express or return it.

Go Deo,
Ernie[72]

NO. 19 NLI MS 18353(14)
Letter to Frank Gallagher[73]

University College Dublin Medical School,
Cecilia Street, [Dublin]
2 November 1926

[Frank Gallagher,
Raheny House,
Raheny, Co. Dublin]

Dear Frank,

I received your note thanks. I have bought a pen and it's quite unintelligible. I despair of training it. I will be glad to hike off on Sunday. I do not know what time would suit you, but I will turn up at 11 am or at any time you wish. I think it would be very nice to meet Estella Solomons.[74] How is Cecilia?[75]

Trying to work hard just now so goodbye.

Ever yours,
Ernie

———————

NO. 20 NLI MS 18353(14)
Letter to Frank Gallagher

[St Kevin's,
7 Iona Drive, Glasnevin, Dublin]
Friday, 12 November 1926

[Frank Gallagher,
Raheny House,
Raheny, Co. Dublin]

Dear Frank,

I am very sorry that I was unable to see you yesterday so you will please, in your bounty, excuse me. I had intended going out to you about 3 p.m. to tell you that I could not go out later but I had cakes to buy as Eileen McGilligan and Maureen Buckley were to come out to tea, and after that, the cake buying, not the tea, I 'did' Grafton St looking at the Poppy wearers and feeling sympathy for them for many had relatives killed I'm sure,[76] and then I dropped into a flat to find a nice kid sick in bed so I remained to talk to her and the dog and so it was close on 6 before I knew where I was. And the guests could not turn up so we ate the cakes with joy.

And I went up to my study and patted my books and wished I could work but failed. I could not read even. I have just been drifting since I came back here. Everything is in a kind of haze but I expect I will get over it; I hope so and before Christmas at that. I was reading a book *Here's Ireland* by Harold Speakman.[77] I liked it though some few points on the question of taste I did not. He must be a rather fine fellow as I picture him. It would be nice to be able to write like that even if one did store it away in a drawer. And then I listened to the radio, Clarke Barry's band and foxtrots. I was trying to analyse them, to take the bars and snatches from foxtrots I know. I wonder are they synthesised or is there such a thing as a composite foxtrot which plays on a gramophone record whilst the composer works.

And then (too many ands, mister!) I dreamt of Florence, of pictures and houses there and felt that Dublin is good to live in. It grips one somehow in some strange way for it is a friendly town and friendly towns are few and far between. I could not locate Paddy Fleming's pamphlet[78] to forward to Seamus O'Sullivan,[79] but I consoled myself with the thought that in all good libraries one should lose manuscripts and books which will be located in several hundred years' time to create mild excitement amongst grubby bookworms.

I was not down town in the morning as I cut a very nice piece out of my toe by wearing Paddy's[80] shoes. I attempted to decorate my bedroom with a few photos of the works of Florentines – Luca della Robbia, Desidero de Settignano, Mino da Fiesole, Michelangelo's 'Dead Christ', a very lovely thing, and a woodcut of Rheims Cathedral. Mother, I'm sure, would prefer the weirdly coloured first Communion certificates which decorated the walls, painful souvenirs of our one time innocense (thus Kevin[81] spells it). I really must decorate the study but here I will have to manufacture frames. I was thinking of writing something on Radio voices as one often forms a mental picture when we hear the voice over the phone. Even in a tram one visualises the voices behind and the contrast with the reality is often funny.

Goodbye now for the present. I hope Cecilia is well and that she has recovered from her orgy of clams. I owe her five pence.

Ever yours,
Ernie

A very funny thing happened last week. I discovered a magic pocket in my waistcoat. Every time I dipped my hand in I found silver with the result that I smoked many Churchills, brought a girl to the pictures and tea and generally had a wild riot. Two days ago I found that the money comprised subs for the Republican Club[82] amounting to over 10/0 so that's the story of the 'The Magic Pocket' about which I was very elated but was afraid to interfere with the spell by attempting the account for it.

Letter to John Raleigh

[UCD] *Medical School,*
Cecilia St, Dublin
21 November 1926

[John Raleigh,
St Joseph's Street, Limerick]

Dear Johnny,

I hope you are very well. Any chance of your coming to Dublin; if so don't forget to give me due notice. I met Mae and Eva[83] in London before I came over and told them to go to Limerick specially to see you so I hope they have done so, if not there will be a row. I am a very bad correspondent as you will know, it has taken me over three weeks to write this, but that does not mean that I forget. You were a real brick to forward that money when I so badly needed it, and I don't see how I can ever thank you, and I'm afraid you'll have to wait a long time til I wipe out the debt. I'm a second medical now trying to settle down but it's extremely difficult.

How are all in Limerick: Bob de Courcy[84] and the Misses Daly's and the sister in the Blue Nuns.[85] I don't know if there's anyone else I would bother much about. Mr Geary of course who showed me through the factory.[86] I am waiting to write to Gertie Crowe, now married, and to Mae King who is engaged, but times are hard as I'm back home again and honestly have to postpone writing letters often because I have not got a stamp. Please drop a line and say how you are.

Ever yours,
Earnán[87]

———————

Letter to John Raleigh

[St Kevin's,
7 Iona Drive, Glasnevin, Dublin]
Sunday 20 [December 1926]

[John Raleigh,
St Joseph's Street, Limerick]

Dear Johnny,

I wonder if I could trouble you again. If I arrive at 9 or 9.30 on Christmas Eve I will have an escort of two ladies who need to go to Newcastle with me that night. Do you know anyone friendly who has a car who could drive us out? I do not know if the Crowe's have a car, anyhow Gertie[88] is not at home. If you cannot get anyone please tell me, and don't forget to write and let me know your arrangements for Christmas Eve.

Ever your friend,
Ernie

Letter to John Hagan

7 Iona Drive, Glasnevin, Dublin
20 December 1926

[Monsignor John Hagan,
Rector, Irish College, Rome, Via del Santi Quattro 1,
Rome, Italy]

Dear Dr O'Hagan,

I hope you are well and that the new College agrees with you. I hear that your number have increased so Maynooth will soon become jealous. I have my holidays now as my lectures are over. I have been trying to settle down to work but I think I will be able to do so next term. Distractions are not so formidible as they once were and really to settle down to hard work would be a relief and keep me from thinking too much. It is a changed country with the gleam of hope there, however, but everywhere, particularly at the University, one notices the lack of serious thought, on any subject.

Now for news. Sean McBride's wife[89] had a daughter. Seoirse Plunkett[90] was married to Mary McCarthy last week. Madge Clifford was married to Dr Comer[91] some months ago. Stella Solomons, the artist, was married to Seamus O'Sullivan. I do not know if you know them, and there are various engagements and other such happenings. Dr Lynch[92] is here in Ireland, but one is, I think, more in touch with home affairs when one is on the Continent. Mother returned from Nice last Saturday and in considerably improved in health.

How are all the visitors to the College and the inmates. Monsignor Curran, Dr McGrath and the many others whom I met there from time to time. I'm sure you are very busy with the new College and have no time to reply to letters. I have not met any of the church dignatories I met in Rome since my return. I thought I should have quite an amount of news and now I find I have nothing to write about. Please kindly remember me to all my friends in Rome.

With every good wish for Christmas was the New Year and my thanks always for your very great kindness to me.

Ever Yours,
Ernie

Please don't forget to write prior to your next visit.

Letter to Frank Gallagher

[St Kevin's,
7 Iona Drive, Glasnevin, Dublin]
2 February 1927

[Frank Gallagher,
Raheny House, Raheny, Co. Dublin]

Dear Frank,

The 'At Home' will not be 'til Friday week as the Committee[93] did not think that I had given them sufficient time so I hope you will be then able to attend. I wonder would you be at home on Sunday evening. If so I will drop over perhaps before six. I am going out to lunch with a decent Carmelite.

I have not been doing anything much since I saw you save attend lectures, exist and try to work. In fact trying to justify myself at a weekly exam of conscience I find I have no justification for existence. I wrote a little not much, even a poem I attempted and some limericks inspired by the names of the girls in my class Ita, Monica and Jenny.[94] Presently I am reading Galsworthy's plays and Oscar Wilde. I read *Caligula* and liked it. I must read *Storm* to see what it is all about. Now I'll stop before you say 'damn, he's hard up for something to write about'.

Love to you and Cecilia,
Ernie

NO. 25 EOM PAPERS NYU
Letter to John Raleigh

[St Kevin's,
7 Iona Road, Glasnevin, Dublin]
21 March 1927

[John Raleigh,
St Joseph's Street, Limerick]

Dear Johnny,

My exam is nearly over. I know I am down in Physiology so there will be a large row at home; possibly I will clear out.

Would you mind if I went down to your place next Monday as want to start work for the June exam. I will let you know by wire before I go down as to when you may expect me.

With love to both of you,
Ernie[95]

Letter to Sheila Humphreys[96]

[St Kevin's,
7 Iona Drive, Glasnevin, Dublin]
5 January 1928

[Sheila Humphreys,
36 Ailesbury Road, Donnybrook, Dublin]

Dear Sheila,

Thanks for your letter. I did not recognize your handwriting; it has become so good, especially the Irish portion of it. The translations, unfortunately, more than ever convince me that we have no literature save a certain amount of very good early poetry. I tried to read O'Rahilly's poems, with a translation alongside, but a year ago I lent them (loaned?), and since I have cured myself. Really since you stopped sending me the booklets you once did I have not done any Irish.

I write every now and then though your typing nearly cured me of that vice. It relieves my mind and as I throw my papers into drawers, which are periodically cleared and emptied, I save myself the trouble of correcting and other people of reading. What I would write would not suit you for I have the bad and disagreeable habit of writing the truth as I see it, and not as other people (including yourself) realize it, in which we are a race of spiritualised idealists with a world idea of freedom, having nothing to learn for we have made no mistakes and whose mission in life is to broaden the outlook of folks who do not quite see that point of view.

Why don't you people publish selections from Irish literature in small booklets? They would help to popularize authors unknown to us and perhaps would interest the heathen. And when you recline (I will leave this line a blank).

You might even do it with the people who write though the medium of English. But perhaps that is heresy.

Anyhow, Sheila, I think that often more harm is done by the extremists (not using the term in the generally accepted sense) in organisations than we realize. The spiritualistic interpretation of nationality is the only thing that matters and that no one save the '16 group ever seriously considered. Present organisations ignore it. Result eventual disintegration for their aims are not based on it.[97]

So I would bore you if I continued.

I am trying to work at present.

Ever yours,
Ernie

Letter to John Raleigh

[*Kilkee, Co. Clare*]
19 July 1928

[*John Raleigh,*
St Joseph's Street, Limerick]

Dear Johnny,

Thanks very much for the parcels. I was expecting you down last week and went over to the Stella[98] on Friday evening. The landlady tried to pump me for information, but I doubt that she got much though I remained an hour. Are you coming down this weekend? If you do I'll go back with you. How is B.[99] and her cooking? I was coming back to see you off that evening but found when I reached the lodge that I had dropped my 'togs' on the rocks so went back for them, thus I missed seeing you off.

Look here. You had best stop inviting the family down. If they come I'll clear off to the West. They do not trouble themselves to invite any of my friends to stay at the house and I think one of us is enough to plague you with. I'm serious about this so beware. Please kindly remember me to B. I have had three new skins[100] since I last saw you.

> With love to all,
> Ernie

PART II

Travel in the United States and Mexico, 1928–1935

In the late summer of 1928 EOM was facing yet another resit of his medical exams. At this time Eamon de Valera asked him if he would accompany Frank Aiken on a tour of the United States to raise funds for the founding of an independent newspaper to be called The Irish Press. *Many republicans felt they had no public voice in the media in support of their position and ambitions. EOM was delegated to spend October 1928 to February 1929 on the East Coast, moving from March to July to the West Coast. He decided, then, not to return to Ireland at that time. In a telling interview in Seattle in March 1929, he was reported as saying, 'I cannot decide whether to continue my medical training … My soul lies with the arts. In them lies happiness. I hope to be able to restore Ireland's interest in them. If I could it would be a far greater reward than becoming the most famous surgeon.'*

EOM's Diary
First Impressions of New York, 12–16 October 1928

Friday, 12 October 1928

Landed on Columbus Day,[1] awakened at 4.30 to find that the ship had cast anchor at 2. There was a general muster on deck at 5.30. It was sunrise, a mist over the river but Long Island was visible.

Chewing gum was the first sign that caught my eye on the off shore, further up an American flag flew from an old fort evidently obsolete, astern was the *Mauritania* with tugs fussing round. We[2] watched the haze lift slowly and the building and wooded shore become distinct. Boats passed up and down as we waited for the doctor and the passport people. Eventually they arrived, the doc clipped a piece out of my ticket, the passport man who continuously smoked a cigarette even whilst he interrogated the ladies stamped my passport. We had moved up the river and after an hour reached Hoboken. The sun was warm, very warm, people exchanged addresses and talked of the little happenings on board. Ferries crossed our bow and canal boats and square nosed vessels carrying bricks and coal. A United States destroyer passed, a small fishing punt hauled at its baskets possibly lobster ones, small motor boats cut through the water. From the higher deck two bottles hit the water with a splash, an angry splash. I thought one was gin the other whisky, Scotch Whisky, the last drink before landing.[3]

There was a little delay on landing waiting for my bags, but a Customs official who talked of Ireland made a cursory examination and we were free. Our taxi man stated his fare was $5.50. My companions assured him we did not want to buy the taxi. An official summoned a taxi, so we walked to the tube, from henceforth subway. It was hot, a close heat below, but after a few stations the fans proceeded to work and the air cooled. You can imagine what it's like in Summer, my companion Healy[4] said, when it's 30+ degrees warmer. I watched the people. The men wore rather striking ties, but they did not seem to be good ones. The women had close fitting hats such as one has been led to associate with them, not many chewed, about 6%. On other subways one finds 90% chewing. Smoking was forbidden in the underground and the fine for spitting was $500.

The MacAlpine Hotel was our location, on 6th Avenue,[5] and in our room we were able to unclothe and walk at ease in our shirt sleeves. The room was warm, very warm, a damp heat. Unusual for this time of year I was told. Indeed, I've found that it had been the warmest October day for 42 years. We walked up 6th Avenue. The women used bright red on their lips, a fairly large percentage, some of them wore brilliant blues, velvet browns, skirts shorter at the back than ours but few above the knee. To-day being a general holiday, there are a good number of such in the year I was told, most of the shops were closed and people were taking life more leisurely. We strolled, took buses, saw the editor of 'The Irish World',[6] took an open street car, walked, then took a bus again. One does not receive tickets; a ticket is inserted in a slot and a bell rings; that is all. Our conductor was

Irish, from Dublin, he had not been there since '82. In the subways one inserts a nickel in a slot and the gate opens. A nickel is a valuable coin and one wants a supply for there is a regulation bus and subway fare. The sky scrapers did not seem so gigantic perhaps because the smaller buildings were 10 to 20 stories high. Some sky scrapers looking like houses of cards built up at random, others bare raw looking, others more rectangular, but had some ornamentation, few were beautiful. The Gridiron, the Times and others in Madison Square were beautiful. The shop fronts on Fifth Avenue were good to look at.

The traffic is controlled by red and green lights. The Avenues run North & South and the Streets East & West. The green light shows on the Avenues and red lights simultaneously appear on the Streets. Traffic stops in the latter; then after some minutes the procedure is reversed. Fire engines passed, bell ringing loudly, small red cars first, then a long motor ladder carries with steering front and aft. Many times during the day I heard the fire gong and on Broadway we saw the remains of a fire. Police walked along jauntily, swinging batons were ever in their hands. Broadway, the milk-white way, was a revelation in coloured-electric signs. We called to see Paddy Quinn and Tom Daly. The latter had been in the Adirondacks in the bad weather amidst six feet of snow and is now getting ready to go to New Mexico. He has tuberculosis and talked much in professional strain, too much I thought. He has had bad luck. Crofton evidently saved him at first by drawing off fluid from the lung and injecting it into his hip joint, then he went to the South of France where he walked 12 to 15 miles a day, then to America to the Canadian border when he nearly died of cold. He looked better than when I last saw him. Miss Frances Steloff has started a book shop.[7] It is a week old and we went to see it. There is a dollar edition of Lawrence.[8] I did not know it could have been issued cheaper than 30/–. I saw a copy of Lewis' *Francois Villon* for $5, but I could not afford it. We visited Dr Quinn later and discussed books. Those imported have to bear a tax of 75%, I think so no wonder books are dear here. The wrappers are very striking.

Saturday, 13 October 1928

Yesterday was 83 in the shade, the hottest day known in New York for this time of year. So I arrive on the 'George Washington' on Columbus Day and it is 83 in the shade. Is this an omen. We went to Liberty St where I saw some of the original Republican bonds.[9] The winding up process will last until next February. I left in my watch to be overhauled and cleaned, have a new second hand inserted and have a new strap. $8.00. It would have been cheaper to buy a new one.

The photographs arrived. I had been taken in every possible attitude save standing on my head. Some of them were good but nothing could compensate for the distress of sitting for them. We went up town by the overground and from it I saw many beautifully proportioned buildings at the back of Liberty St. I was told by Frank that I should have to speak to-night at a meeting to be held in the Waldorf Astoria, I was told quite casually as if it accompanied supper so I sat down to write a few notes, but thought it might read as a newspaper article; it would not read as a speech. At 8.30 Frank and I went to the hotel. The first person I met was Brian Shanahan who had been engaged in various jobs and is now part owner of a motor van. Then I met Nally[10] lastly, a newspaper reporter. I told him I did not know what I was going to talk about so Frank told him. The chairman introduced me, said that I had fired the first shot in 1916, that I had once after blowing up a rifle range flung gelignite at a party of soldiers and rescued prisoners, that I had left school at 17. Luckily he had just scanned a few pages of notes that Frank had given him otherwise if he had read the entire document heavens knows what he might have said. The audience stand up to welcome people I notice. A Congressman spoke after Frank. I spoke first in a dream. Then later we finished by shaking hands with anyone who cared to shake hands with us. So that ordeal was over.

Sunday, 14 October 1928

We went to Cathedral,[11] but as the last Mass began at 11 and finished about 12.30, we went to the Franciscan Church.[12] The congregation sang hymns, at the elevation organ notes sounded and around the Church were electric fans. Seating was 10 cents there was a collection as well. A friar asked for funds for a new ciborium. He wanted jewellry, gold or silver which would be melted down and utilized. It was a warm day so we walked around watching people and things. I saw a double deck bus shaped so the underneath portion for luggage. Men's trousers are loose and cover their boots; they take good care of their clothes. Last night we rang for the valet and this morning our suits were returned folded and pressed. The Mass we attended was the 12.30 one and even at that there were Communicants. We lunched at a restaurant near by, one run by a Sean Cripps, quite good. Frank decided to go to Pennsylvania alone so rang up enquiries and booked a reservation whilst I accompanied Jerry to Innisfail Park[13] to see Gaelic matches. I met Ryan, the president of the GAA,[14] Dwane, the Tipperary trainer, the Cavan trainer, Dwyer of Bansha, who invited me to a smoker of the Tipp crowd on Saturday night, Father Devine and others including Bell, who said there would be no difficulty in my getting a job here. Tipp played first and beat Mayo. There was one little fight, as there was also in the next match between Cavan and Kerry. The first match commenced 1½ hrs after schedule. Afterwards Jerry and I took an overhead.[15] We met Scanlan, who had gone over with the team for the Tailteann Games.[16] Seldom does a man stand up to give his seat to a lady though in the lifts men doff their hats when a lady enters, but they do not remove the cigarettes from their mouths. We went to Riverside Drive where I saw the Nallys. They were very kind. Mr Bell spoke as if translating from a foreign language. Six years ago he had had a stroke of paralysis and recovery was slow. He had completely lost his memory and had to begin to learn the alphabet by means of a card. He first learned to say 'water' and then 'very well' for he had to say something to people who asked him how did he feel. When blessing himself he used to say 'In the name of the Father and of the Son very well Amen!' 'Very well' was meant to fill in any sentence as he thought it meant different things. A kindly, grey haired man, prematurely grey I should think. The others talked of people, Mayo folk, full of my relatives whom I scarcely knew, of this person from such a place, a typical Mayo conversation and though they were all kindly, I was glad when Mr Bell produced a fiddle and played Irish and Scotch airs. I was told that their station was an express one, that the express ran in the centre track and that the next stop would be, I think, Times Square, then Penn. Mr Bell came to the hotel with me. He knew the history of New York well and told me the story of Washington Heights in terms of existing streets. It seems the States' Government wished to reconstruct Washington's old fort, but could not locate records. They got in touch with the British and from them obtained a sketch of the position drawn by a British officer before the attack. The Govt. intend to reconstruct the fort, in a park on the heights.[17] The forward pass has been instituted in Ball Game,[18] 9 men have been killed already in this season which has lasted but 3 weeks. He came to the States when he was 20, and the presence of a history of the United States in his trunk insured a speedy transit through the customs. In any other place but New York one feels one is camping out he said.

Monday, 15 October 1928

The usual routine of trying to make work. The streets looked dirty as we walked along, and there was no evidence of the American hurry: indeed I thought that I was the only one who rushed about. In the subways one enters by placing a nickel in a slot and a turnstile, which serves as exit and entrance. I have not as yet found the 'rush hour', when I am told one could not even scratch one's nose, if so desired. I found that as well as the $500 for spitting one can also be imprisoned for a year. Frank came down with a squelch on a mass of what I took to be tar, but was really chewing gum.

At lunch in Swartz's a vegetable dish, cabbage and boiled potatoe and turnip, my two abominations. Baked potatoe is the only variety of the plant to be eaten here. Afterwards we visited Transportation Building[19] and from the 39th floor, we viewed the city. A magnificent view. It is only from on high that one can appreciate New York. Near us was the Woolworth building with cathedral lines and a beautiful roof. They are most all too narrow for their height, but from the 40th storey one can see the ornamentation near the roof, which is difficult to appreciate from the ground. The river, the East and West rivers,[20] could be seen on either side and the suburbs across the water. The weather was fine, a very pleasant day and though the air was not very clear yet we had a good view. From the buildings near at hand white steam or smoke emerged; only from the river was there black smoke drifting from the tugs and steamers passing up and down. Below one could see the traffic crawl, so it seemed and the traffic control was evidenced by the disciplined stops. Here though the side streets are clear and one could avail of the halt to push on without danger, not everyone halts up to after midnight after which one crosses at one's own risk. Transportation Building is severe on the outside; inside however each floor has walls of shining marble, the doors are beautiful and the offices, judging from the one I visited, are luxurious. Near the office table was a dictaphone with records. It was quiet up there, no noise of the city and though Frank said he felt the vibration of the building I could not do so. Ryan, who had been working for us in Germany, said that owing to a legal decision the Free State bonds had to be withdrawn from open market and retained by the banks.[21] Seemingly there is an organised silent opposition to the new Irish daily news. In many parts of town the fire escapes on the outside of buildings look ugly; in the larger ones the escapes are on the inside. An anti-fire campaign has been organized here to show the people how best to prevent fires. In most of the scrapers only one room at a time would burn as save for the furniture there is nothing flammable. Frequently during the day one hears the fire bell going and the small red car can be seen dashing around.

At about 3.30 the sirens in the harbour gave tongue and from the windows of the 11th floor we saw aeroplanes going down the river; then they reappeared on their way up. The top of the buildings, which are all flat when they are low, was soon crowded, as was every window. Papers and streamers rained down whilst the boats continued to siren. A silvery gray cigar body[22] floated over the Woolworth building and soon after returned going down the river towards New Jersey. We saw Frank P. Walsh[23] in the evening in the General Motors building. He was working for Smith[24] and working hard, the first contest he had entered for 12 years more on account of tolerance than for any other reason. The opposition endeavour to make it a religious question: they always do so when a Catholic runs for the higher offices. The prospects of success are pretty fair but anyhow he thought that Smith would succeed the next time. In the evening we found that the Eugene O'Neill play[25] began at 5.30, there being a dinner interval from 7.30 to 9.00. Frank suggested the military display in Madison Gardens so we walked slowly up Broadway. There was an election meeting in progress, a dictaphone and a cinema machine operating. After the speeches a song was dictaphoned and the audience joined in but somewhat feebly.

Tuesday, 16 October 1928

On a trolley car I saw 'Live Long' as a safety first motto. As we walked up Wall St, we saw some armoured cars transferring money, the engines are not armoured, however. We crossed a wooden street beneath which a subway was being built. The bank's interior was beautiful; a man who was in charge of the guard in plain clothes conducted us around. The banks keep a man who controls detectives, a kind of gun man, who knows customers and directs newcomers. The ties of the men in this locality were not so bright. Itinerant vendors seem to do a good trade and they sell a varied assortment of eatables. I took a pineapple drink last night for 10 cents and found it cool and refreshing. Many people wore Al Smith's button. They are given away free at meetings. On our way down from Wall St we passed another armoured car. Recently, in Chicago one was blown up, and the hold up men or blow-up men got away with the money. We bought a bag, a rather good one for carrying papers etc and when the boy in the shop heard me that we worked in the building across the street he gave us a reduction and presented us with a reduction card for further purchases. The office was warm, nearly 80 in the shade. At intervals I read the *Saturday Review of Literature*, tried to review it but had not sufficient time to finish the article. This is the 12th number of the paper and I cannot locate where it is printed as I would like to purchase the previous issue. Peadar O'Donnell's book[26] has received a favourable review. It has been taken up by the Catholic Book of the Month Club.

——————————

NO. 29 UCDA P104/2626(2–4)
Letter to Frank Aiken

[New York][27]
Wednesday, 24 October 1928

Frank Aiken, TD,
[Los Angeles, California][28]

Dear Frank,

Could you, please, forward me a covering address for Dev[29] and forward me what impressions you now have of the places I have to visit. I cannot report much progress here, though I see some possibilities. I am afraid there is a great slackness in the method of circularising members about meetings; in some cases, in one anyhow, the president of the branch did not know a meeting was to have been called; in another case only one of the members had been notified, although the president of the branch had had a hand-bill printed with 'Mass Meeting' on top, the meeting comprised twenty people.

I did not know that M.J. O'Connor's car was at my disposal, and since I did, I have used it a little. Scanlon of No. 1 Unit[30] and another man, Ganley, I think his name is, the best worker I have met is willing to lend and drive his car after seven o'clock in the evening; he will lend his car if he can get anyone to drive it. I find that a personal canvas is best though if one has a good chairman, like M.J. O'Connor or Major Kelly,[31] it makes all the difference. This is a rough summary.

Friday, 19th

Meeting of
    Old Glory
    Chris Farrell Councils in Brooklyn
    Patrick Nally
    Old Glory decided to raise $500 and appointed a committee to organise canvas. I received some pledges.

Promotion Committee, Waldorf Astoria, 9 p.m.

About 25/30 people present.

It was decided to hold a weekly meeting of the committee. A few names and some subscriptions handed in.

Tipperary Men's Club 1 am

I addressed the Club. They gave me a good reception but did not offer to take any shares; the majority present was not in a position to discuss finances at that hour judging by their quiet. The secretary promised to discuss the matter at a finance meeting and I had some literature forwarded to him.

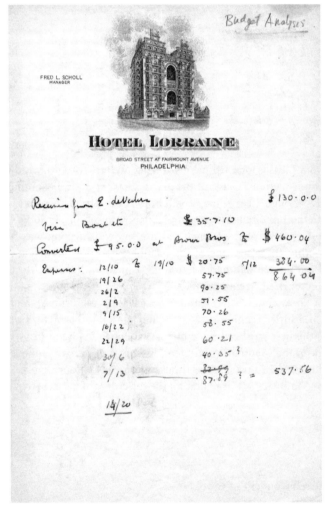

EOM's accounting for funds received (£130-0-0) from Eamon de Valera for his Irish Press Ltd expenses, 12 October to 13 December 1928. Source: *EOM Papers NYU*

Sunday, 21st

I spent most of the day losing myself round the town, but I managed to see a few people. Scanlon of No. 1 Unit and his friend gave me their car and we canvassed til 10 p.m.

10.30 p.m. AAIR[32] Dance. I addressed the meeting; some small sums received, about $40, and some promises.

Monday, 22nd

Canvassed Yonkers. Some promises.

Canvassed New York with Scanlon.

Addressed the 'Mass Meeting' of four councils of the AAIR. I received $140 and many promises.

Tuesday, 23rd

Canvassed by myself – little result.

Meeting in Newark at 8.30 p.m. 9 people present, $300 promised.

I am trying to get M.J. O'Connor's car this evening to canvas and I will ask to have it all day tomorrow.

On Saturday last I suggested the formation of a Publicity Committee not knowing that such had already been formed. Anyhow extra names were added to the list. The Committee is to consider all forms of advertising and is to suggest the matter for leaflets. I think that the present Committee thinks in terms of the Irish American papers only. Canvassing committees are slack, in some cases the councils have not formed any. My general impression of New York is that the Promotion Committee thinks of the Irish Press Ltd at their weekly meetings, that it is not a part of their daily lives after office hours and hence the driving force is lacking. I will ask Garth Healy when he is advising people of my coming to ask if cars could be placed at my disposal for certain portions of the day and evening and that people volunteer to accompany me when canvassing. I feel that I have wasted considerable time in New York as I did not know my way around (I do now to some extent) and did not know the people. Please write to Boston and give me some information about the places you have already visited.[33]

I want

(a) a covering address
(b) a list of expenses up thru the date you left New York
(c) a rough idea of the workers in the places you have visited
(d) any suggestions or 'brain waves' you have since last we met
(e) an address or addresses to which I can write you.

> Ever yours,
> Ernie

Letter to Editor of The Irish World

Boston, Mass.
10 November 1928

Editor, The Irish World,
[New York]

I noticed in a recent issue of your paper that I am referred to as General O'Maille. I wish again to stress the fact that I do not now hold any military title. May I ask you, therefore, that in future issues in which reference is made to the work I have undertaken in the country, I may be spoken of as Ernie O'Maille.

I am not a member of Dail Eireann. Neither am I am member of the Fianna Fail party, not have I ever given it political assistance or adherence.

I have come to America anxious and willing to do whatever I can to help the establishment of the new Irish Daily Newspaper, because I see clearly the necessity that a paper to be read by the Irish people should be owned by people who are genuinely Irish and edited and written by people who are genuinely Irish. Such a paper can present to the Irish people and to the world outside of Ireland the truth about the present economic situation in Ireland. It can discuss and invite discussion of methods by which the present terrible economic conditions can be remedied. It can spread among the farmers the latest scientific information in regard to the methods of farming, and give them advice and assistance in regard to marketing. It can hold up before the nation the picture of the irreparable loss to Ireland of Irish manhood and Irish womanhood through emigration, and unceasingly agitate for the removal of conditions which cause this emigration, and for the establishment of conditions which will put a stop to it. It can arouse the nation's concern at the depopulation of the Gaelic speaking districts not only as a terrible loss of men and women but as the crumbling of the last defences against the destruction of the Irish language and the complete Anglicisation of the Irish people. It can oppose the payment of $25,000,000 yearly to the British Empire. It can see to it that proper scrutiny is exercised with reference to public undertakings, such as the Shannon Scheme and the Carlow Beat Factory. It can give to all parties in Ireland whose program is Irish nationalism and Irish independence a national medium for the expression of their views and methods. It can give to the people of Ireland the truth with regard to all current events in the world seen through Irish eyes and not through the eyes of English imperialists. Finally it can give to the world outside Ireland and to all the other newspapers of the world the truth abut Ireland, about the aims and aspiration of the Irish people, their thoughts and their purposes, instead of a misrepresentation of all these things by a press whose first purpose is to serve the interest of the British Empire.

Sincerely yours,
Ernie O'Malley

Letter to Frank Aiken

Chicago, [Illinois][34]
10 December 1928

[Frank Aiken, TD,
Los Angeles, California]

Dear Frank,

I received your two letters, thanks. There is little to write about. I have been considerably held up by mistakes and confusion. I would suggest:

(1) that there be a paid whole time secretary.
(2) that a plan for further operations be drawn up at once.
(3) that there be more co-operation with the AAIR office in Chicago, diplomatically.
(4) that a Press Committee consider the situation as a whole.

Mass: Was good. I could have remained two weeks longer but I did not get in touch with the neighboring cities.
R. Island: Bad. Little can be done here.
Conn: Considerable organisation needed, have yet to get in touch with New Haven.
Penn: Bad. Philadelphia put me in touch with very few individuals.
Pittsburgh: Shows some promise if there is more co-operation there.
Ohio: Bad. Lacked organisation but much can be done in Cleveland.
Detroit: Very bad. I sat down and waited and people did not visit me or phone. I waited over until Tuesday, Dec 11th (I arrived there Dec 8th) for a meeting which did not materialise.
Chicago: Mr Lyndon told me that I would not have sufficient work to keep me 'til Tuesday, Dec 18. Now I think I could with profit remain here 'til Christmas, but this is a bad time to call meetings. People will not subscribe at Christmas time. So far I have been promised $2,100 and $1,200 at two meetings. I am going to Cincinnati on Thursday 20th, will visit Washington on the 22nd and will arrive in New York on Christmas Day.
Suggestions: That we sit down in New York and organise this campaign, even if we spend a week at it. We will be amply repaid. The drive so far has been disorganised and conducted in a haphazard fashion. I suggested that we get in touch with all the states we have visited for definite dates in advance, urge them to organise their districts, point out exactly what co-operation we want and await a reply before we begin.

I would suggest that I visit the following places again:
Mass: 12–14 days visiting Rhode Island, Worcester and the outlying cities in Mass
Conn: 3 days. Hartford, Bridgeport, New Haven
New York: 1 day

Penn: Philadelphia 2 days Pittsburgh 2 days
Cleveland and district: 7 days
Detroit: 3/4 days
Chicago: 7 days
Total: 40 days

If I can do this beginning some time in the New Year then I could have covered this area by February 10th or 12th.

I hear you have been ill. I hope you are better by this as I am sure you must be worried. I hope to meet you in New York. If not, if you give me permission I will, myself, organise this programme and carry it through.

Ever your friend,
Affectionately,
Ernie

American Irish Republican League, Detroit, Mich
Eugene McCartan, President, 738 Waterman Ave.
Miss Mary T. Sweeney, Cor-Sec., 5814 Second Ave.
Thomas P. Monaghan, Vice-Pres., 617 Harmon Ave.
M.J. Kavanagh, Rec-Sec., 6638 Frederick Ave.
Thomas P. Barry, Treas., 262 Navahoe Ave.
Joseph Carey, Fin-Sec., 3721 14th Ave.

NO. 32 UCDA P104/2628
Letter to Frank Aiken

c/o John T. Hughes, Boston[35]
Thursday, 31 January, 1929

*[Frank Aiken, TD,
New York]*

Dear Frank,

I received Garth's telegram. I have had a bad abscess on my face. It was opened by a doctor and I remained in bed for ten days. Then I went to Providence, RI, and canvassed a little for four days, but the opening was still discharging. I saw the doctor again, had a few X-rays taken, and found that I would then have to see a dentist. He again opened my face and proceeded to drain the contents of the swelling. I have an abscess on two teeth and both will have to be extracted, but not until all the pus has been drained away. I am to see the dentist to-morrow and do not know what report he will make. Personally I would like to go to New York on Friday evening, but I think it would be silly as I am very much run down and it would perhaps be best to have the cavities thoroughly drained otherwise the infection may spread or at any rate continue.

I cannot then decide until Friday. I have been unable to do much work here.

The condition was aggravated by my trying to go round when I should have been away from the cold. Have you any programme outlined now? I cannot make any arrangements presently as I do not know if I can fulfill any. I hope you are in good form yourself. I was sorry to hear you had been ill in California. I am really 'fed up to the teeth', realizing how bad conditions are and unable to do the work I should.[36] Mr Hughes sends his kindest regards.

Yours affectionately,
Ernie

NO. 33 NLI MS 18353(14)
Letter to Frank Gallagher

[Reply address]
c/o Garth Healy, Irish Bonds Office,
117 Liberty Street, New York.
Boston
4 February 1929

[Frank Gallagher,
Raheny House, Raheny, Co. Dublin]

Dear Frank,

I hope Cecilia and you are very well. I have just read your book.[37] I think it is very good. It was thrilling for me to recapture the spirit of those years and to get that for the first time the world at large is going to know something of our thoughts and ideals through you. There are many beautiful passages, and I feel very proud. I viewed it impartially first, and I do not know how much my judgment was prejudiced by my own feelings only I know it spelt utter sincerity and after all, that is the test of any writer. I am sure it will sell well in America. Are you writing anything at present?

How's the garden? I suppose it is now covered in exotic orchids and rare plants, that there is a small Japanese garden with oaks one foot high and a tiny pool with gold fish. I was going to say carp, but I thought of a palace in France where they lay so thick that one could walk upon them. I expect you speak of cabbage in the past tense. I can hardly mention potatoes.[38] I was expecting to hear that Cecilia and you had left for the South of France or for the Lido and that you wear a velvet jacket and chew bhang,[39] that is not how it's spelt though I know, it's now g.u.m.

Will you please give my love to Molly[40] when you see her. I hear that Stella Solomons has illustrated a book of Kelleher's.[41] How are Seamus O'Sullivan and she? I often meet people who talk of him. I will write again some other time. I am trying to write with little success. Please give my love to Cecilia.

With love,
Ernie

Letter to Frank Aiken

c/o John T. Hughes, [Boston]

15 February, 1929

[Frank Aiken, TD,
New York]

Dear Frank,

I received your two letters thanks that of Feb 4th and Feb 13th enclosing checks for $100 and $484.50.[42]

My face is practically alright now but it is still discharging and will continue to do so for some time; the dentist attends to it every second day. I asked him to give me ether and have the jaw scraped, but he said it would not hurry matters. I am tired of Boston. Everyone here has been very kind to me, but there is really very little work for me and it is annoying to say the least of it.

I cannot speak at the meeting not because I am not feeling sufficiently fit, but because the meeting is political[43] and though it raises a larger issue that a man should be permitted to go where he likes in his own country, yet I could attend and speak for that reason, but not for the other. I have to see the dentist on Monday, and I will be ready to leave on Wednesday next. I have visited Worcester, Lynn, Norwood, Providence, with very little result. Worcester, as you know, has already subscribed $1,500, $500 from Harrigan, the remainder raised on loan is being paid off by holding card-parties. Harrigan said nothing could be done until the money was paid off. Lynn is bad so far, no result save a promise of $25. In Norwood, I arranged with two people to form a committee and placed their quota at $500. Providence is hopeless. New Bedford has promised $200 and will pay it in time. I am endeavoring to locate Ryan of New Bedford as he has promised $500 but is difficult to see. Privately I am endeavouring to obtain some three thousand dollars outstanding.

I think that Boston is very nearly 'played out' on account of faulty organisation. If I had been continuously at work I could have kept up pressure, but intermittent work does not achieve results. If I had remained for a further two weeks or more, when I was last in Boston, more money could have been raised as some enthusiasm had been aroused and Mr Hughes was free, at times, to accompany me. He has not had a free day since I have been here, and I am convinced that if he is not available that little can be done in Boston. When I was in Chicago I asked Lyndon how long I could remain there. He said four or five days. I, however, arranged to remain a week and then felt though Christmas was approaching that I could have, with profit, remained another week. I would suggest that if I am to go West that I proceed first so some big city, say San Francisco, arrange good publicity in advance and work in that city until such time as enthusiasm develops, that is if one feels it can be developed, otherwise as in Philadelphia, one would waste time. It is difficult to work to time as I have mentioned in the case of Boston. What do you propose to do? New York can be worked up. There are a few good workers there like Gillespie and some of the boys attached to M.J. O'Connor's unit. By the way Dr Gallagher of Boston has organized such a unit. What does he propose to do and is he interested in the newspaper? This letter rambles on I am afraid. I was so much out of action and doing so little here that I was going to resign. If Wednesday next is not too late, please say so. I will have to have my teeth seen to every two days for the present, but I cannot stand this enforced idleness any longer, though I find many ways of availing of time. Please kindly remember me to Garth.

Yours affectionately,
Ernie

NO. 35 EOM PAPERS NYU; UCDA P17B/168
Excerpts from EOM's Diary, San Francisco and Berkeley, California,
29 March–1 April 1929

San Francisco, 29 March 1929

Miss Hilbert, Preston,[44] Tucker and I on the 28th went to dinner at Miss Hilbert's house. She is from Hamburg. The North Germans are slow to make friends, but when they do they are for life. Her description of Switzerland and of food shops after her family had starved probably during the war. She gave us a North German supper. Vegetable soup, fish (hake or finnin), cheese, toast, celery, nuts, bananas, apples and very good coffee.

Her best friends are mostly Irish in SF. After a while Sediz(g) entered. He's a poet evidently as he could not work out the theme of a poem in L.A. so came up further to do so.

He knew Ella Young,[45] John O. Varian,[46] whom, he said knew an immense amount about mythology and was a good Republican, Arthur Olman of Dublin. He told us of Los A., the cults whose free life is there, how natural the case of a migration en masse to a country with the same climate, as Italy, where individuals – Shelly, Goethe, Byron, Browning etc. – get their inspiration. Freedom Hill. One can do what one likes and live as one likes. The man who toured America to test the hospitality of different American states, then he became converted to different cults and lasted for a considerable time before he quite disappeared. Life is rich there and very individual so Miss Hilbert said. Sediz says that this culture will ultimately defeat American standardisation as the latter cannot fight it, not understanding it.

A discussion of Kaiserling's work. Hatred grown of envy will increase in Europe as the U.S. gets more wealth.

Berkeley, 1 April 1929

Saw Sam Hume,[47] whom Mrs Kincaid reported as having passed out, a tall, spare, energetic man with great vitality and an interesting manner. He started 'Theater Art', he said, whilst in Detroit and then he proceeded to set me right about the theatrical movement along the Coast. When I told him of Mrs Kincaid and that she had said that he 'passed out', he became serious and took a note of the fact. He has worked in the Little Theatre, Detroit – since burnt down. Considers Chicago the best Museum as do I …

NO. 36 UCDA P104/2633(1–6)
Letter to Frank Aiken

Hotel Whitcomb, Room 723,
Market Street, Civic Center,
San Francisco, Calif.
3 April 1929

[Frank Aiken,
TD, New York]

Dear Frank,

I received your letters of March 23rd and enclosures, for which thanks.

Butte City was good. I was promised $1000 dollars. Seattle was unsatisfactory. There were many complaints of a technical nature. The committee did not like the sudden change from $100 to $25.[48] They said that you did not wait for authority from Dublin to lessen the amount that might be subscribed. They seemed to think it unbusinesslike. Then they wished to have a local bank of their own to handle the money. They wrote to de Valera and obtained such permission.

I phoned Father Lanigan when I arrived. He said he would meet me in two days' time at the hotel. I waited, but he did not appear. I phoned again, and he said he would call next day; he did not do so. I phoned Father O'Callaghan and asked him if I could call out to see him. He said he would call to see me. I phoned again; no result. I went to a meeting at Michael O'Brien's. Father Lanigan was to have been there, but did not attend. Father O'Callaghan said he rang up the hotel, found out I was out, but did not leave any word at the office. It all seemed strange and I thought that they had reconsidered their promises. I held a badly attended meeting[49] and saw people, but Mr Griffin was awaiting the new prospectus which did not arrive whilst I was in Seattle. He promised to work with Mr Cohan. I have heard from him since, but, so far, the committee does not seem to have accomplished anything.

I went to Tacoma to attend a meeting, but it consisted of meeting seven people in an hotel. Mr Prendergast is good but his wife is seriously ill and he was worried. I saw the younger priests, and they promised to help and forward their subscriptions.

Portland was bad, no meeting. Rooney said he could not get more than five people together. The people whom you met there seem to have reconsidered their promises and it seems to me that little or nothing can be accomplished there.

I wrote to Sacramento and told them to wire me if and when they could arrange a meeting but they did not reply so I went on to San Francisco. I had informed Quinlan that I was due to arrive and I had written to Doran. Quinlan was out of town. Doran was in Balboa building. I located him. He had not made any arrangements for St Patrick's Day for me. I went to Oakland on the eve of St Patrick's Day and spoke to the Auditorium on St Patrick's Day. I was told that it would be impossible to hold meetings, that people would not attend not even a committee meeting. I visited some Hibernian[50] meetings and spoke. Father Hunt suggested I see the people on your list, but did not know who could accompany me. O'Looney proffered the same suggestion, but I did not have any one to accompany me. Monsignor Rogers promised to get a young priest to accompany me, but so far his list of prospects is 'dwindling'; he is very kind to me.

Doran is secretary of the Father York Memorial[51] and is interested in some play in which his sister acts so he has no time to devote to the paper. I gave him an idea of the publicity I wanted before I arrived. He promised to see to it, and after repeated demands I did obtain some publicity but along Doran's lines showing how interested I was in the play. I have attended some other Hibernian meetings and generally enjoy myself in such fashion. O'Looney has given me some help and has brought me around a little. I will be able to get some assistance from him.

I saw Father Samson of Oakland and am going out there to-morrow to visit a number of priests. Last week I asked Doran to arrange a Committee meeting. On Sunday he told me that he had not sent out any notices as he did not think Tuesday a suitable day, and he stated the reason. I asked him to arrange a meeting for Friday; he promised to do so. I met him to-night and found that he was going to send out notices tomorrow morning, Thursday, for a meeting on Friday and was going to notify all members of the AARIR about one hundred and fifty though I had asked him to call a small number, about fifteen. I have seen some people personally about the meeting, and they have promised to attend.

The situation is bad, but is improving. If I could develop a paunch, a loud voice and was able to persuade these people that I could be of use to them in the next mayoral election, I feel I might get them interested as I might be of use as an object of exploitation. Unfortunately the paunch will not develop, and I will try the other two requisites.

There remains the priests and some other people, and they are the only field. I feel useless here wasting good money and not having any result. I was going to leave the city last week for I feel like a lost soul. Minnie McCarthy has suggested some people, but they were of no use to me, really does not know anybody. I attended a meeting of the Veterans and spoke at a dance. To show you how desperate I was I tossed up a coin to see whether I would go to Mexico or not meaning to join some side there, the side to be determined when I arrived and obtained some information. I lost the toss so remained here.

There is a little sun here so that is not so bad. Perhaps I am a pessimist but the situation has not been good: the next few days should determine something. I have written to Sacramento and intimated that I would go there on Wednesday, the 10th. I am replying to your enclosure and to your challenge. I was very sorry to hear that you had had an operation. I hope you have quite recovered now and that you are taking some care of yourself. This work, or, rather this lack of it, would kill a Kerry cow or make a mountain ewe more like a DMP man[52] on night duty.

Please kindly remember me to Garth and all the others.

Yours affectionately,
Ernie

I have not reread this for fear I would have to re-write it owing to errors.

NO. 37 UCDA P104/2633(7)
Letter to Frank Aiken

Hotel Whitcomb,
Market Street, Civic Center,
San Francisco, Calif.
8 April 1929

[Frank Aiken, TD,
New York]

Dear Frank,

I hope your health is good. I am glad to be able to report that things are beginning to improve.[53] The meeting on Friday 5th was poorly attended, but some work was done. Since then I have obtained over $200 in cash. Enclosed please find $100, forwarded by Mart Killalea, Providence, on behalf of Miss Margaret Dunne, 99 Plain Street, Providence.

Martin says that J. O'Connor, 64 Meeting St, Providence states that he sent his $500 to his brother in Kerry and that he has had a letter from Dev thanking him. Killalea has his doubts, however, and wishes to 'check up' on him.

In a hurry,
Ernie

Unlike Frank Aiken, EOM decided not to return to Ireland at the end of his Irish Press *mission*. Instead he stayed on in America to write poetry and a memoir of his Irish military experience. While in California he visited San Francisco, Carmel, Los Angeles and San Diego. Apart from his Irish and Irish American contacts, he met many people in the artistic and literary world, and he had heard of the artistic community in Taos, New Mexico, that Ella Young, the Irish scholar and poet, was visiting. In Los Angeles it is thought that he met John Ford, the film director, who at that time was filming Liam O'Flaherty's novel, The Informer. When he went to Pasadena to visit Helen Merriam Golden, widow of the Irish nationalist and actor Peter Golden, she wanted to show her children and a close friend, Mariana Howe, the Grand Canyon in Arizona. EOM agreed to help drive them there.

Once underway in September, they forged on to Taos where they knew Ella Young was staying. Golden knew her well as she had visited with Young in the Theosophical Society community of Halcyon, California. Golden and EOM both liked the community they found in Taos. Mabel Dodge Luhan, with her Native American husband, Tony, held forth in her grand house, Los Gallos, surrounded by her bevy of guests. That summer these included Georgia O'Keefe, Ella Young, Rebecca Strand, Miriam Hapgood and her mother, Neith Boyce Hapgood, and John Marin.

There were also local characters such as Dr Gertrude Light and Ernest Blumsenschein. Dorothy Brett ventured in occasionally from the D.H. Lawrence ranch that Luhan had given the novelist in 1924. Golden returned to Los Angeles and brought her family to Taos in November to look for a house. In February the Goldens returned to Pasadena and then made the move to Taos. EOM stayed on in Taos and house-sat for Spud Johnson that winter, while he was in Carmel, and for Dorothy Brett, while she was in New York. The Wall Street Crash occurred in October 1929, but it had limited impact on EOM as he was already living on the margin.

EOM's pencil sketch of Mount Lobo, near Taos, winter, 1930. Source: COM Papers.

Excerpts from EOM's Diary, Carmel, California,
20–2 April 1929

Carmel, 20 April 1929

… Walked along the beach and sat down under a tree trying to shelter from the wind. The sand is very fine and deep. This is a fishing village with many boats inside and outside the harbour.

Back to the Indian Craft Shop where Preston[54] had been doing the weaving: some people who had been in Santa Fe dropped in for a few moments. The Unitan[55] and his wife were there very much absorbed in each other. There are Mexican and Indian workmanship in the shop: baskets, rugs, 'throws', chairs like our sugán ones only the backs are painted, bowls, cups in the shape of jugs, gourds, rugs, toys, pictures painted about 100 years ago looking like primitives etc …

Carmel, 21 April 1929

… Down to the sand dunes passing the gates of the 17 mile drive where one had to pay to enter in an automobile. It was warm lying on the sand which was white and heaped up 20 feet high, below was the sea, a faint blue in the distance, the shore line studded with trees. I went to Mass in the old Mission Church; a girl in riding breeches Spanish looking on my left reading a book during the service but she knew the order of the ceremony – others did not and just sat there. The priest protested against late comers and had the door blocked after the gospel. Ran down the coast. Lupines grow in clumps on the hillside giving a delicate forget-me-not blue shade to the green fields of mustard flower and patches of moss with a pleasant pink-red colour. Many wild flowers and trees near the wood bridge over a canyon. The coast road was narrow and we had to halt for cars to pass. Then trees became fewer and fewer and when we reach a line of birds running at right angles to our course there were no trees.

Looked up Mr Weston.[56] He was out so I had a chicken waffle lunch and later located him in his studio. Medium height, head slightly bald on top, brown eyes, quite pleasant contours. We sat and talked of Mexico. He had been there 3 years and liked it.

> *Jose Clemente Orozco*[57] was, he thought, greater than Rivera.[58]
> *Jean Charlot:*[59] French and Mexican.
> *Masimo Pacheko:*[60] young, shows much promise.
> *Tina Modotti:*[61] photographer an assistant of his.
> *Pintao:*[62] sculptor and wood carver has lived 40 years in Mexico
> *Luzano:*[63] painter
> *Goitia.*[64]

The influence of the frescoes on the population at large, Scholars build their own school. His son has a broken leg and has to live in bed so he cannot move out at present.[65] He showed me work from his studio studies of desert, rock, trees, pottery, cloud effects, female form, photographs, shells. The photos show the texture of the material. The shells have a lustrous look on certain curves, the stones have a full of sand formation, the faces show the pores of the skin and all the lines especially on men's faces.

He played Mexican music for me whilst I ate nuts and looked at the photos. Later I went to see his son – 16 – who had broken his leg in five places and had been five weeks in bed. His leg was encased in Plaster of Paris. He had been reading a book on Lawrence and I recommended Lawrence's *Wanderings in Arabia* and Doughty's *Arabian Deserts* …

Met Preston[66] and Mrs and one of the kiddies on the way, sister, so we walked up home, picked a bunch of clementines. Brother and Bumps were there so I had my hands full. Mr and Mrs Langton Howard and baby arrived. Between them they studied all ten arts, the truth being idleness. He was a nice boy, very devoted to her; they had been married recently. She is clean cut, camel like, too hard perhaps and does not want children. They left after a while so P's mother and the rest of us sat down and ate.

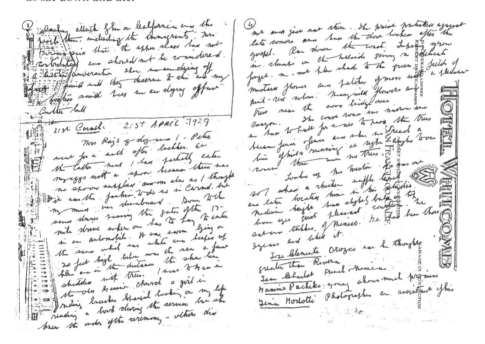

Excerpt from EOM's April 1929 diary in Carmel, California, upon meeting the photographer, Edward Weston. Source: EOM Papers NYU.

We discussed books. *Moby Dick*, *The Way of all Flesh*, R. Erickson, *The Knickerbocker History of New York*, Jeffers,[67] which Mrs Ray[68] thinks stark and elemental thus seeming in extremes from pretty lyrical poetry. This country does things by extremes. (Restlessness and moving inspired by the Indians?) *Jean Christope*. We studied a book on symbolic movements in the Burmese and Siamese

Dancers. I had seen them dance in Boston. Isadora Duncan,[69] her personality. She was a real dancer, Mrs McCrossan thought. Ambrose Bierce[70] we did not approve of. We went over to see Mrs Ray, calling at the Greens on the way over. Mr Blackmore and wife were at R's so after desultory conversation I told them of our country beginning at the beginning and giving my own story. It was the general opinion that the British were stupid and did not know how to govern. Mrs Sheridan wanted me to write for tomorrow's issue of her paper but she did not give me any specific directions or state the length of the article. I tried a few articles, tore them up, wrote one, a bad one and went to bed. On the discussion that arose afterwards it was thought that a friendly Ireland would be of more value to England, that a disturbed Ireland would always be hostile and willing to help England's enemies.

Carmel, 22 April 1929

Mrs Sheridan called for me, took me out to the Beach School in her car with her son. Mrs Dougals i/c school was interested in I.[71] as some of her best friends were I. and she had a glorified idea of the nation. It was poetic and spiritual, splendid horsemen, good friends and people who did not know how to surrender. Mrs S. is a pacifist and she is training her son to be one. We were fighting pacifists, I explained. Drove me back. Talked of the colour in my life, of the mediaeval attitude in Ireland and invited me to lunch. Drove to Monterey, waited for lunch as there were strawberries so we ate strawberries, raisins, cream and milk. We called to see Ray[72] and watched him make frames then wandered out the road to Del Monte to Mack's ranch. Much pink moss and many live oaks and pine trees at the ranch. Radiators at the back of fireplaces in C.[73] The fire-places are real ones and one sees iron and irons. In Monterey, Patterson makes much iron work. We met Maximo Allno, a girl dressed in corduroys and a hat who was doing fresco work on the walls (white) of the new guest house. Mack is a Catholic so the subjects are saints. Miss Allno talked of her method. As far as I could gather she was going to use milk and also white of eggs. The colours were not strong – that modern tinge of white. She traced her drawing on to the wet mortar then worked on it whilst it was wet. She brought us through the creamery and upstairs to a small study decorated in tempera. The virgin of Monte Louis, a nice piece of work, a copy from an Aztec drawing of the conversation of the natives on a side wall and two angels on another wall. The smoke from the fireplace will blacken the tempera, but a screen will be arranged there. The house will take another year to build. We examined a fresco in a niche on the way out and found that it had begun to rack. The ride that should have been forthcoming was not offered and so we walked back going through the beautiful grounds of the Del Monte Hotel. There was an exhibition of pictures above stairs and also some permanent. Piazzoni[74] – decorative tendency – Ray Boynton. Armand Hanson[75] – dashes of colour not straight drawing and in the temporary collects were Stanley Wood[76] (water c. landscape, good); Ray Boynton drawing, Arthur Hill Gilbert;[77] W. Ritschel,[78] 'Sail Boats', 'Cloudy Day'. Watts[79] (bad) and many other very bad but the bad ones had been sold …

Letter to Edward Weston[80]

c/o Peter Murray,
640 E. 37th Str,
Los Angeles, [California]
16 June 1929

[Edward Weston,
Carmel, California]

Dear Edward,

I hope you are very well and that Brett's leg is now much better. I am in Santa Barbara, house keeping for a friend of mine who has been invalided out from Ireland. I am hardly able to move as I lay out on the bench yesterday and my back is raw and sore now. The weather is fine here, much warmer than the Carmel variety.

I meant to write to Chandler (is that how he spells his name) but did not do so as I left Los Angeles after a few days. I did not like the look of it; it does not compare favorably with San Francisco, to my mind. I will return there on Thursday, to Los Angeles, I mean.

How is Sonia?[81] Did she make the photo for my locket yet? I miss Carmel, the talks there. I have been invited by a friend of mine to McDowell Colony, somewhere near Boston, but I do not know if I will go there. I may go to Mexico, so if you have any spare time, please send me a few introductions. I would like to go to Santa Fe, however, before I decide on anything else.

I hope you have had some wealthy visitors recently. I have Chandler's description of how to get to his house and a map which he drew, but I have no address so, perhaps, you might give him my address in Los Angeles. I want to thank you for your kindness to me. You have been very good and kind and I felt very much at home there. Sophisticated people with their quasi-intellectual notions make life appear so difficult that it is often like a Chinese puzzle, so it is good to meet people like yourself who restore one's confidence in human nature. I am sorry I was unable to say goodbye to Sonia; she is very charming and sweet. Please remember me to Jimmy Hopper[82] and to the Beckholts[83] if and when you meet them. I will write to the latter.

Very affectionately yours,
Sean[84]

Excerpt from Letter to Miss Sheila Humphreys[85]

Los Angeles, California,
24 July 1929

[Sheila Humphreys,
36 Ailesbury Road,
Donnybrook, Dublin]

... I have grown to like New York. It is intellectually alive and I think one can see angles on modern movements there, but I never got 'beneath its skin' and had not sufficient time. I liked Cleveland and Chicago, Butte City, San Francisco, not Boston, I thought it 'dead'. I have a fairly good idea of certain portions of the United States, but I know nothing about the South ...

The climate is warm here and I melt as I move around, everybody else seems cold and calm, so I suppose my blood has not been sufficiently thinned yet. The Pacific is warm and one can remain in the water for some time, so that is good as I love my swim especially as I am forbidden to swim.[86] It's fashionable to be brown here amongst the girls, and from what one can see of them, and that's a lot, they have had quite a lot of sun. They spend the summer getting tanned and the winter getting rid of it, so a priest told me, but he was Irish and homesick.

I have said nothing about the Irish here. My remarks on cities do not include them. That is a story in itself so I will be silent. I have met few people I knew since I came out, some Tipp men in New York and Chicago, some Claremen there also. I met Mick Sheehan in San Francisco; he had just arrived from Australia, but I really know very few and as I did not make many personal friends during the 'Troubles' there are few that I like to visit. The fibre of many does not seem to be sufficiently virile to stand the atmosphere of the States and a few years record of carrying a gun may be sufficient to live on but it does not compensate many for their lack of a spiritual tradition of nationality.

What most appealed to me in Tone[87] was his very obvious humanity, not one of those stern commanding figures who seem full of fierce directing energy and who seem born to be placed on a pedestal. These people are evidently human, though one does not regard them as such; they make few real friends and their ascetic sense of duty makes them a landmark when human effort and endeavour are lacking. Tone may have been all this, but he was evidently a good companion and was well loved, not so much for his sterling honesty of principle as for his personality. I liked to hear the human note in his diary: 'drunk last night'. To me it doesn't in the least take away from him. It makes me think he was a human being. I like Tone, for he was the first person I read in a huge first edition, 1825, with leaves, which had been in the house for goodness knows how long. I suppose he may have influenced me when I thought for myself.

NO. 41 EOM PAPERS NYU
Letter to Dorothy Brett[88]

*[c/o Dorothy Brett's Cabin,
Mount Lobo, Taos, New Mexico]
11 March 1930*

*[Dorothy Brett, Shelton Hotel,
Lexington Avenue, New York]*

Dear Brett,

Today I am over with Dr Light[89] and she told me of Lawrence's death. I did not know that he had been so ill. I had finished *Sons and Lovers* and am re-reading *The Plumed Serpent*. I'm sure it must have been a shock to you, expecting and looking forward to meeting him again in Spring. I do not know whether you like me to write as a grief is often so personal that one does not want anybody to intrude. Yet I know you are direct and you can either say 'Alright' or 'Go to hell'; I do not know how it affects you as far as the ranch is concerned.[90] I'm sure you must now be very pleased that Frieda[91] sent you a peace offering. It will be hard for her to go back on that now when Lawrence is dead.

I have seen so many of my comrades die that death seems as much a part of life as life itself. Yet I know that there were some deaths that I never recovered from. They left a strange void which has always remained, a gap, yet a communion as well for I can feel the dead, nor would I be surprised to find someday that they walked in to resume an interrupted conversation. I found it easier to get over the losses in my own family[92] than I did those of my friends. Somehow a family makes some kind of barrier and the members of it often live in little compartments of their own. Their very intimacy in adolescence seems to prevent a fusion when growth has been reached. I think I understand how you feel and though I feel for you myself, sympathy somehow can never be properly expressed in writing. Often the gaps in conversation mean more than the lucid, placid flow of words. I send you a piece of sage from Taos Mountain.

Ever your friend,
Ernie

Dr Light sends her affectionate regards to you. Any date I expect to hear of Tony smashing Barnes' head.

Letter to Merriam Golden[93]

> *[c/o Dorothy Brett's Cabin,*
> *Mount Lobo, Taos, New Mexico]*
> *Wednesday morning [early May 1930]*

[Mrs Helen Golden,
Adms Auto Camp, Hut 25,
Taos, New Mexico]

Dear Merriam,

Thanks very much for the oranges – they were a blessing, the nuts, tea, writing pad, the shirt. The shirt is too good to wear up in this country. I will hold out until I get the other khaki one. I was sorry to miss you all and not to see Miss Doherty.[94] I'm sure she enjoyed her stay. She was nice but a little knowledge is a dangerous thing. Somehow I suspect archaeologists and philologists; it's a kind of escape from life. Seldom they pound it up with modern art, poetry, drama, writing history. It's really extraordinary how few people really understand the basis of design which opens up the history of art. That is to my mind the jumping-off place for modern work after one has read the classics. If one gets too much of modern work, one is inclined too much to take a part for the whole. From Joe[95] to modern art – a long step.

I am reading a good book by Orage,[96] a really good book which shakes one up again. *On Reading* is the name. Excerpts from his weekly reading in an English journal. One does not agree with all his opinions, but most of them hit hard. He sends one back to think. Coleridge, De Quincy, Swift, L. Sterne, Barton, all of whom I have now read thoroughly. I have reserved them with the King James Bible, Shakespeare, Doughty, Bunyan, Tomlinson. Defoe for a special year, but the year never comes so I am starting Doughty and Bunyan again.

I am too tired of wordy books. Powys to me is wordy; a lot of wind. Mentally I am redoing his book. There seems to me too much labouring to produce a theme: phallacusian in land mood, people, incise, introversion, adultery, fornication, a harp of many strings all striking the same note. Did you ever read Tomlinson's *Old Junk*? It is word perfect. He describes wind at sea not in a short pithy paragraph, but in a long one. Longer than one would think positive, yet no words could be left out. Tomlinson will last I think. I would like to have a good sea library with me. At home I have Esqueleling[97] on the pirates, 10 volumes of Hakluyt's *Voyages*[98] (even the Spanish expeditions to Hopi Land and Zuni are related), *Moby Dick*, some naval records, Dana Smith's *The Saicha*, *The Daunted* and many others beginning with *Ulysses*. Have you ever read any of de Coster, a Belgian? He's good. He rewrote *The Owlglass* in the legends of the Dutch wars of independence.[99]

I am sending down 3 chapters;[100] could you ever post them, register them, to Mae McKernin, Apt 3D, 1145 Woodycrest Ave, The Bronx, New York. The enclosed 'Mac' is for her also. Two envelopes, one inside the other. I do not know if the drug store has them, perhaps Cordova. If I had known you were going to Santa Fe I would have asked you to bring back a dozen.

How are the kids?[101] I had hoped to bring them in turn up the hills for training. That is the idea behind the Kick in the Pants Tribe. When the imagination and communal sense is stimulated, it is easier to talk about an attitude to nature, people and life than if one did it in class in a 'preachy' way. That is how I trained my Fianna Company[102] and my young brothers. I have some bronze woodpecker feathers for the tribe but they'll keep. Eithne has improved, the solitude was too much for her the last time. Kids can learn to be aloof in a crowd of their own age.

I got on very well with the Indians. I am their amigo now. We talk Spanish. An additional relish to them as the carpenter does not understand. They drop into Indian when there are things I should not hear in Spanish. I do not know how the carpenter will work out. If he is satisfactory it is well to have him in mind as a builder, plasterer, carpenter, but so far I have not seen any of his woodwork. I smoked a cigar – headache – so I gave them to the Indians.

I had a letter from Spud.[103] He will come at the end of the month. Thus I will need a load of wood, if I can trap Bright Eyes. There was about a dollar's worth in the wood-house and I will have to buy a lock. The old key I lost. I placed the key under the adobe under the black triangle. In fact a piece was broken off. Your pillow slips are with my clothes any that I have in one of the soft bundles. One I had used as a sack to keep shirts in; the other was folded up, and I expect you have the third as I used only one.

I hope Terence is alright now, and Deirdre. I have been reading the Deirdre story in the *Táin*, also Synge's *Deirdre*, and I found Stephens' *Deirdre* which I think one of his most beautiful poems. How is Eithne? She has more colour than Fat Pants. Norah's letter was fine.[104] I enclose it. I am writing her a letter slowly. If I can I will send it down by the wooden prophet Elijah.

With love to all,
Ernie

Is Mariana[105] carpentering? I will share some experience of (a) pulling nails, (b) smashing houses, (c) hauling wood, (d) laying foundations, (e) making adobe (my house work I hope to add other things to my half day's work).

Bring the kids – the tribe – up the hills for training – training in Fianna.

Letter to Merriam Golden

> *[c/o Dorothy Brett's Cabin,*
> *Mount Lobo, Taos, New Mexico]*
> *Saturday [mid May 1930]*

[Mrs Helen Golden,
Adams Auto Camp, Hut 25,
Taos, New Mexico]

Dear Merriam,

I hope all are well. Weather bad: I got a few good wettings. The carpenter goes today so ends a minor war.[106] Very fine clouds for the past three days and fearsome sunsets. This morning Taos was covered in a low row of jagged clouds drifting slowly our way, in two layers. Last evening there were many varieties of clouds, dark woven silver high behind dark rugged edges in the distance pink clouds standing by themselves over the high mountains – the Goden Mountains[107] will be those from your canyon or to Hoffman's[108] and the Pass. There are canaries in these woods. One of the boys said so; I heard a noise but have not seen one as yet.

Rotten weather taking it as a whole, cannot write which is worse. I will go down next Saturday. If convenient could you or Mariana[109] drive up on Saturday evening and please tell me if you can. I hope Spud[110] thought the house satisfactory. The stove was a bit knockkneed; however perhaps he will not mind – and perhaps he will.

This for Deirdre:[111]

Biscuit-shootin' Susie –

She's got us roped and tied;
Sober men or woozy
Look on her with pride
Susie's strong and able
And not a one gits rash
When she waits on the table
And superintends the hash.

Brett will be down on Monday; could you please leave my leather grip bag (attaché case in old English) into Chapman's.[112] Martin Peck wanted to paint me. I said I would let him do so when I got down. Nobody would probably recognize me anyhow; all he wants is the beard!

> Love to all,
> Ernie

Letter to Merriam Golden

[c/o Dorothy Brett's Cabin,
Mount Lobo, Taos, New Mexico]
Saturday, 17 May 1930

Mrs Helen Golden,
Adams Auto Camp, Hut 25,
[Taos, New Mexico]

Dear Merriam,

Will you please empty out these. Did a bundle of MSS come? It should be here by this. The carpenter will return tomorrow night. I will go down with him next Saturday. I don't know where you will be then. I will stay at Spud's if he is not there, and if he is I will trot out to Talpa. I will probably return on Sunday evening, but most likely I will stop over on Monday to clean up the place, get in wood. Spud is due to arrive at the end of the month. I had intended to write a letter but I was rushed trying to take some notes on the *Táin* before returning it. I am sending back whatever books I read to have them out of the way. I have no time for *The Bits* now. I have nearly finished Orage's book. He's very good. Slow, pithy paragraphs on everything. He disliked Shaw, Wilde, Baudelaire, Pater, Le Gallienne, Swinburne, Yeats, Stephens, Tagore, Maeterlinck, Flaubert. I underline the ones I myself dislike. It's a pity he did not write of painters. I could imagine what he would say of Rossetti and his band. His other book, *Readers and Writers*, must be good. I'm sorry I can't let you have the copy of *Reading* – it's a dedication copy to Brett, not a dedication, an autographed copy.

When you leave please send anything for me to the Chapmans'. I hope all are well. A heavy storm last night, but growly not City kind of thunder.

Love to all,
Ernie.

[Santa Fe, New Mexico]
27 May/6 June 1930

[Frank Gallagher,
Raheny House, Raheny, Co. Dublin]

Dear Frank,

I received your two letters within the past three weeks, one of March 27th, the other of a later date. I have not written because I could not. I have had fever for the past six weeks off and on and now I walk in a haze of it trying to fight on my feet. I was very glad indeed to get the first letter: it was nice to hear from you. I miss the talks we used to have, here where I have nobody to talk to. It has begun to rain at last, and it drums straight down like spear blades. Eileen McCarvill suggested what I should apply for.[113] I laughed at 'Social Editor' thinking that I would be sent to a Horse Show Ball[114] or to a christening breakfast for one of Dick Mulcahy's scions. I would be at once surrounded by CID,[115] tanks would patrol his lawn, then he would find that I was an interviewer and talk baby talk for the rest of the meal.

I will drum up some articles when my head is clear. One can't say what one thinks about this country. I fear for a daily paper: one has to suit readers so it has the limitations of a sonnet form of restricted matter. I have wandered a good bit since with and against my will at times. New Mexico I love, but my body cracks too much now and I would be glad to leave but can't for the present. I have striven to study it, but I must confess failure. The deeper one goes the less one knows: perhaps that means one gets closer to reality or to one's own futility.

Some time ago Kevin, who is in New Jersey, wrote to me and said that my work for the paper had been very unsatisfactory.[116] I expect that it is true, but certainly not 'til I reached the West Coast in March 1929. Then the cheap political bums who could afford to insult Dev's representative but who in public made use of their knowledge of him to win votes knocked me flat. On the other hand I did not draw a salary so I expect that might even up the matter. I do not know if Eileen McCarvill showed you my letter ...

6 June 1930

I don't know what 'the fact that' related to. I have been sick again. I really don't understand why Eileen McC did not acknowledge my letter as you say you read some poems I had sent. Then, I was desperately hard up, as now, but now I have learned to adjust, and I sent her a registered letter asking her to get somebody to criticize them so that I might know if they would ever be of monetary advantage, but I never to this day received an *acknowledgment* of them. You know however, as a friend what I think about efficiency so I want the best people you can get to help you not those who might live on a one-time reputation. Why don't you get Frank O'Connor[117] as Literary Editor. His translations and poems in The *Irish States-*

man[118] were fine. I read a good story of his in *The Atlantic Monthly*[119] or Peter McBrien who was once on *The Independent*: he, if he keeps sober, is excellent.

I will write you again when I am out of this whirl. One gets a detached outlook abroad in the places I have been in the deserts and in the mountains – but cities kill me. I have been in one for months past. I met Ella Young once, and we talked and discussed things for a good long month. I hope Cecilia is well: I had even forgotten her name, not herself, but names go somehow. I began on all the saints in the calendar but failed to find her. I don't know what I did at C, so I had to call her Mrs G. How are the Murphys now: very well I hope?

With best love to you both

I hope you have time to read now and again.

Frank, Please *don't* ever put *my name* on a letter: insert my letter inside as in the old days. I have many difficulties,[120] and they have been increased by the last letters. The Santa Fe address is now the only one left.

To Frank and Cecilia with love,[121]

I wrote this yesterday so send it before I tear it up which would otherwise be its fate.

'Cromlech'

In glen-side minds their memory can endure
Stronger than stone, grey splitting in the frost,
There gravured deep composite pictures lie
Of lovers who with love were storm tossed.

Monolithic bulks of angled weight
Shoulder dull age and fill the heart with sight
As no tooled story can; nor roof the hill,
While death's hound, Time, bells loud of their delight.

Diarmuid and Grannia's bed of muscled stone.
Here in the snow their loves have burst to flame.
Around the lonely fang of black bog turf
They glow again in speech that cries their name.

O'Malley to Read
Joyce on Tuesday

Last week's talk by Ernest O'Melley at the house of Mr. and Mrs. Raymond Otis on the subject of Irish poetry, was attended by a number of interested listeners, in spite of the blizzard. Mr. O'Malley read first from the works of the earliest Irish bards, beginning with a vigorous and beautiful poem of the fifth century. He told of a thousand poets who roamed the country side until, upon the production of a certain number of lines, they obtained the rank of Bards. As bards they had entree everywhere, and if they were not satisfied with what they received, they were said to be able, by their words, to blister the skin of their hosts.

In the course of the centuries this fellowship, with its annual conventions, became entirely too much of a good thing, and had to be supressed, but the impetus toward poetry-making has remained among the Irish people to this day, ample proof of which is found on any research into Irish literature. Among the modern poets, Mr. O'Malley read from Synge, Stephens, Padraic Collum, a Douglas Hyde translation of the Gaelic of Raferty; and among earlier poets from which he read were Hugh O'Dennell and O'Rahilly; emphasizing the charm and virility of Irish verse, continuing through the centuries, not built upon literature, but springing from the soil.

At the final talk of the series, tomorrow evening, at the Raymond Otis house, Mr. O'Malley will discuss modern Irish novels and novelists, and has promised a reading from the much talked of Ulysses, of James Joyce.

Newspaper clip of EOM's Santa Fe lectures, November 1930.
Source: New Mexican, *Santa Fe, NM; COM Papers.*

BROKEN LANDSCAPES

In 1931 EOM spent an intense seven months wandering around Mexico, initially with two artists, Dorothy Stewart and Theodora Goddard, and later by himself. He filled up many notebooks with details of costumes and architectural details, as well as research notes and diaries. While there he tried and failed to secure work teaching English. He met up with Hart Crane and when Crane returned to Chagrin Falls, Ohio, EOM took care of Crane's house in Mexico City. While travelling he met two Russians, Sergei Eisenstein and Eduard Tissé, who were working on the film Thunder over Mexico *in Teflafaque and Yucatan. In the summer of 1931, EOM returned to New Mexico with Stewart.*

Pen and ink sketch of EOM by American artist Dorothy Stewart included in EOM's letter to Helen Golden of 6 January 1931, just after they had driven from New Mexico to Mexico City. Source: EOM Papers NYU.

Russian film director, Sergei Eisenstein (right), *and film photographer, Eduard Tissé, whom EOM met in Mexico, spring 1931.*
Source: COM *Papers, photographer unknown.*

Hart Crane, American poet, sent his photo to EOM, spring 1931, with greetings: 'for Ernest O'Malley with much affection and devotion from Hart Crane'.
Source: COM *Papers, photographer unknown.*

Letter to Merriam Golden[122]

Guanajuato, [Mexico]
6 January 1931

[Mrs Helen Golden,
Rio Chiquito, Talpa,
Ranchos de Taos, New Mexico]

Dear Helen,
I hope Mariana, Eithne, Deirdre, Terence and you are very well. So far so good. My escorts[123] have protected me in a wonderful way: which is the escort is the question. For me they most decidedly are. Dorothy's gaiety, as usual, makes friends of everyone she meets. It's warm here and I am getting my usual red skin. I hope the weather is nice in Talpa, but I doubt that you have roses as we have here. I am a traveler again. New Mexico seems very far away in space and time. I doubt that I will see it again, that's a hunch, but it's time for me to move elsewhere. It's no use writing you a long letter as you cannot read it and I'm not going to type one. A letter should be spontaneous not a slow deliberate, curseful, nervous hitting of keys! I expect your winter building is over by this. Please remember me to Tony Mirabel, Manuel,[124] Louis, Mrs Margo,[125] Lucinda's sister, Lucinda,[126] Dr Light.

Love to all,
Ernie

Love to Dr Light. I hope she is very well. It's hard to get real information about Mexico, about the position of the people and the land.

Alvaro Obregon 74, Mexico City, DF
18 January 1931

Do you want an elaborate log of the way we went and of the other roads to Mexico City? If so I'll prepare one, but perhaps Dorothy has sent you one. There's some talk of the road to Laredo being finished in two months, but the talk is in Mexico City. Men with wheel-barrows were working near Saltillo; I think the road might be finished in six years with luck. The best way to use the roads here is by avion – consult your dic[127] – you can't laugh that off!
Could you please root amongst my packages as I am missing four chapters and if they're lost to hell with the book:

Chap 4 Roscommon, Donegal, England in 1918
5 Tyrone and Offaly in 1918
6 A resumé dealing with the country and the people
9 North Cork Aug–Sept–Oct 1920

If you find these could you please tell Sylvia[128] and myself. In the meantime I take to drink a bottle of cognac, 4 pesetas, but wine is dear enough.

Mexico City
19 January 1931

Received your note tonight thanks.

We had lunch with Mabel and Toni[129] yesterday and wine. I ate enough to keep me going for 2 days as I cannot cook for myself here and I cannot eat cookies in your kitchen or dried apples. I hope you are better by this. How are kids? Sylvia sent me some photographs, Deirdre on her steed and Eithne (hope she doesn't erupt at this) on her bronco.

I saw a man telephoning, talking vigorously with his free hand as in this sketch.

I have drawings of saints in niches. Dorothy says they're good. They should be as they are primitives. The Diego frescoes are not a patch on Orozco. In places Diego almost looked like Bonotzo Gozoli (If you have ever seen the latter you will know what I mean). Diego has colour, a grand sense of design, but design as design not as result, more decorative than formful. Orozco has form, paints in greys, has a steel-like quality and when he deals with the Indians, he is magnificent but when he introduces the bourgeoisie or the best people it is pure caricature and his colours get high and one feels an atmosphere of propaganda. I don't think I have ever seen a more moving picture than the one of his showing 3 soldiers and two women bending away towards the hills followed by a woman carrying a baby on her back. I will sketch it for you. It shows the hopelessness and weariness of man, the part the soldiers play and the dreadful agony and cheerlessness of continued warfare; those people are going to be beaten, one feels the drawing is equal to the emotion so bet your shirt and one of mine on Orozco. He's *the* Mexican painter. Diego was disappointing to me but still wonderful in what he has done here. What are you reading? You see I can't write a damned telegram. The very best love to Marianna and to you all; you are such grand people that I wish you were here.

Ernie.

I had a good laugh whenever I think of you being in a hurry to go by road to Mexico before the tourists over do it. Mexico swallows them up, the half of them are afraid anyhow of the country. I saw a lovely sketch the other night in a theatre, a girl dressed as a tourist talking to a Mexican in *charro* costume. She wore glasses, a tweed suit with a tie, very severe, spoke execrable Spanish and bore a huge camera, and the girls wearing costume as the successive sketches dealt with southern Mexico. They danced and tried hard to wear the clothes but in some dances their frocks parted, showed a foot and a half of belly and they always swung vigorously so as to show their tiny little thighs. It was very hard on them as in Mexico they generally parade with a wee loin cloth.

Carleton Beals[130] was held up, where I don't know, outside the city. They took all he had including his clothes. His watch was bad, they said, but he replied that it

---

BROKEN LANDSCAPES

was a cheap one and that he had much pleasure in thinking that his good one was in his room. Eventually as a great favour, as he objected to walking bare-footed, they gave him his socks. He said he had influence, that he knew the President and that he would have him pay special attention to that district. 'The President, do see him, why he is our chief,' and they swept their hats. Exit Beals walking back in socks only. Can you imagine Dorothy, Theodora and I marching in wistfully in socks to some town or Marianna, yourself, Deirdre, Eithne and Mullingar.[131] It's a good country to grow wool in.

Mrs Eastman[132] at Vera Cruz waiting in her carriage, the train to start at 8 – 'It won't start till 11, Senora, for we heard there's another train to come in with many tourists,' so the trains will suit the last-comers (that's some consolation to you too).

Dorothy in San Luis Potosi asked for a cloudburst instead of a shower, but still they showed her to the bathroom.

I had trouble finding the WC in a hotel. The manager showed me a wash-basin in the dining room, but there were too many people present; then the kitchen sink but the cooks were Indian and a little shy; finally he shouted, 'Excusado'! and escorted me to a lavatory. He was so polite that I thought he would remain to pull the string. Any country that calls them things excusado is certainly genteel, but I think the name explains this country.

Mabel in the market refusing to buy some little thing a woman wanted her to, some little affair of coloured straw, finally the woman shoved the toy into Mabel's bag. 'It's yours, senora, free!' Brett is writing her memoirs[133] in New York City (probably knocking spots off Mabel).

Barnes is about to descend on the South West. A big earthquake is due here for the 23rd. An ex-British officer wants to get in touch with me. He said he had to resign during the Tan War as he refused to do dirty work, and he talks in terms of a high rank which an unfortunate individual was supposed to have held there. Did you ever smell a Secret Service man. The poor British, they still (pardon me, senora) think they are like their own backsides; they can't be licked!

This ends my telegram. It's a pity I haven't a paper to write to.

Excerpt from EOM's Mexican Diary, February 1931

Mexico City
Thursday, 5 February 1931

... I sat in the Alameda against one of the tiled seats in the centre ... I even tried to write a poem but poetry does not come now. My mind is a blank about everything. Poetry seems to need a crisis of some sort for me – to be in love or badly out of it, to live near mountains or desert. Here the city is alright as a city. There is movement and life even but I would prefer to live outside in the outskirts or away where there is Mexican life. This is a city, again on the side streets it is Mexican; in the centre of the well built *colonias*, it is cosmopolitan as much as Mexico can be that way. I tried to write some of the MMS; the 2nd chapter is a devil. I think Mae has one I have already written. It has not turned out to be a blessing after all. She should have returned the MMS when she found herself unable to type it ...

EOM's sketches in his February 1931 Mexican diary. Source: *EOM Papers NYU.*

Letter to Edward Weston

Alvaro Obregon 74, Mexico, DF

15 February 1931

[Edward Weston, Carmel, California]

Dear Edward,

How are you and Brett? I was talking about you the other day to Frances Goor. She said she had played around with you two and Sonia last February. I heard accounts of you from time to time, that at last you were doing well, so I suppose you can have coconuts for breakfast now. I am after my weekly of *mole* so I feel at peace with the world.

Often I was gong to write to you and to Frederick Beckdolt. You were both so very kind to me, but somehow the fact of my not having accomplished anything kept me from writing. I have nearly finished a book, when it will be typed goodness knows, as I hit one key slowly, then search around, becoming more and more annoyed with myself. I wrote some poems: that is about all. I liked New Mexico very much, I had a little hut, of late, up in the Chimayo Valley amongst the Mexican people – Northern New Mexico is fine. I'm sure you would like it, the people are somewhat of the frontier type, the Indians are fine, the Mexicans are very little understood, much more Mexican than the Mexicans here, but more remote, living close to the soil, a hard life.

I have had a hard time trying to find work. I helped to build a house, gave lectures, even on James Joyce, leaving a group behind me who were to read *Ulysses* aloud! I was a housepainter and did odds and ends, just enough to keep my belly from hitting too hard on my backbone. Rene Dinny, we expected out to Santa Fe last September, but she was not able to come. The McCrossens, whom you probably knew in Monterey, are there weaving, trying to foster Spanish Arts in the State.

I like Mexico very much though I am indeed on the outside as I do not know people. I'm fed up being a tourist. I made an offer to the ex-Minister of Education[134] to teach English free in one of the Rural School training centres, but I have not heard from him. I would like to do something like that to help as I have enough money, with a very tightened belt indeed, to last for about 2 months.

S.[135] is in Russia now so your introduction could not help. I wonder could you introduce me to some people here as I am anxious to get below the surface and to do anything I can, but if you think I am a damned nuisance to ask you, please don't bother. How have you been doing since I saw you last; it's nearly two years now. How are Brett's legs? Is he able to walk alright now or does he ever have any trouble? And how is Sonia? Is she an expert photographer now? I read an article of yours on D.H. Lawrence which I agreed with thoroughly: it was issued as a supplement to the *Carmelite*.[136] There was so much tripe being written about him at the time by people who did not help him when they could have done so that I was glad to read what you had to say. Mrs Luhan is here, also Toni: he's in Tepic at present visiting the Indians there with his drum. I like Toni, the real Taos Toni not

---

the travelling Toni. Please give my kindest regards to Mrs and Mr Beckdolt. I felt mean after about not writing to them but as I said I was waiting for a result. Sometime or other I will have to visit Carmel again. My love to Brett, Sonia and yourself and please write to me sometime, when you have leisure. As I'm not supposed to be here, please don't mention me save to the Beckdolts.

With love,
Sean O'Malley

NO. 49 EOM PAPERS NYU; UCDA P106/1616(20–21, 26–27)
Excerpt from Letter to Sheila Humphreys[137]

[Mexico City,] Mexico
13 March 1931

[Sheila Humphreys,
6 Ailesbury Road,
Donnybrook, Dublin]

... It's terribly hard to get work anywhere especially here. I even offered my services free to teach in one of the rural schools here, but I have been turned down.[138] This is an interesting country, and I'm trying to get under its skin; some of the experiments are fine, but many are not real revolutionists, only one country is and I'm glad you have at last discovered it. So many at home work without any ultimate idea as to what is to happen, leaving the future running to people who will become reactionary. Always this is a truism, and may seem trite, one set bring about freedom and are then knocked on the head by the second group who always take advantage of their efforts, simply because the first group was not long sighted enough to know exactly what they were going to do, how much they could enforce and how much of a thorough groundwork they had laid; and even if they had done so, there would always be the second group.

I suppose you can't try housepainting! It's a grand job, only my partner was such a mean thing I might be still at it and sure of a meal. The hunger strike has proved of good service to me;[139] I know that hunger is not so bad as one thinks ...

So far I've been lucky, have managed to avoid typhoid, and the hundred and one diseases here: smallpox is pretty bad and there is much of it, and water is seldom safe but somehow I stumble through. At times I've a kind of an escort against bandits. The country is really a chance. There are no fixed rules. Bandits have a merry habit of stripping you naked not even leaving your shoes.

I was going to climb a mountain 3 weeks ago: Popo is its short name, I won't trouble you with the long one.[140] I then heard 30 climbers have been held up on its slopes and sent back naked to the nearest village. They could only take my clothes anyhow as I had intended to go alone.

There's a lot to write about but my pen is bad. At last after being 6 months without one I invested in a fountain pen, a really horrible extravagance – it writes when I dip it in the ink well. This unfortunate country has been so cut up and maltreated that it is hard to see any permanent day light. The clergy have been sat upon anyhow and they richly deserved it. At one time they owned 1/3 of all the land here. This is of course an Indian country though it has been mostly ruled by whites and maztitos; it's the problem of mixing Gaelic and Anglo-Irish and solving the problem of both ...

NO. 50 NLI MS 11376(7)
Letter to Countess Plunkett

[Mexico City, Mexico]
15 March 1931

[Countess Plunkett,[141]
40 Elgin Road,
Ballsbridge, Dublin]

Dear Countess Plunkett,

I hope you are very well. In the few letters I sent Kevin I asked him to see you to give you all my love but as he has not mentioned you in his last letter written from America I expect he has not seen you. How are you anyhow and all the family? I have not written, why I don't know. My letters are very rarely answered so rarely indeed from Ireland that I have given up writing there, but I send you mental letters if you ever get them and think of you and your many kindnesses very often.

How is Miss O'Daly? Are there any of her friends I could see whilst I'm here – if so I would be glad to do so or do you know anybody here? I expect to remain for another 2 months – after that quien sabe?[142] I thought I might get some work on archaeology, but they don't want foreigners and I lack letters after my name and an income.[143] I came here on the promise of newspaper work but people had talked much and meant nothing so I found when I arrived. How is the Count;[144] is his health good? I miss indeed the talks I used to have with him: all too few indeed. This country is in many ways like home and I like it very much. The United States seems pale and anemic compared to it, yet I did like parts of the States, especially the South West which is still farmed in small holdings and where 'efficiency' has not too much penetrated. How is Owen: has he by this got together an aeroplane? And Seoirse and Mary and baby or babies and Fiona?[145] I will write again if you get this letter. Anyhow please remember that I never forget you all and say an odd prayer for me. How is your motor car? Beyond the family you needn't say I'm here.

With love to all,
Ernie

Letter to Eamon de Valera

Return address
c/o Miss S. Laithwaite,[146]
Librarian, Santa Fe, New Mexico
18 June 1931

Eamon de Valera,
Dublin, Ireland

Dear Sir,

I received your letter this week but as it is not by me[147] I cannot record its date.

I have been away from the city and my letters take very circuitous routes. Over a year ago Garth Healy advised me that there was money in Brown Brothers[148] but was not quite sure that it was mine; hence I could not withdraw it. However, I did draw my fare to New York. Then I felt that if I reached New York, where I have no friends, it would be nearly impossible to find work. So since I used the train fare as a base, feeling unsure in my mind as to how legitimate that was, and making vain attempts to restore the original sum whenever I could find work.

When I left Ireland there was, I understood, a tentative arrangement about salary for my work which was to end about the middle of December. In fact it lasted until July. I used whatever money I had for current expenses: eventually when I ceased I had no money on hand.

I would like to know for what service the money standing to my credit in Brown Brothers should be given to me as I have not been hitherto notified that a salary is due to me.

My accounts, in detail, sent to Garth Healy have never been acknowledged from the home office. That I submit may probably be due to the fact that my address has been difficult to find. I would like that these accounts be now considered. Also I have been informed, indirectly, that my work in North America had been adjudged unsatisfactory. There is reason in that judgment. I would suggest that the money standing in my name be transferred to Garth Healy's account. I am far away from a financial adviser so do not know if it can be so arranged without my interference.

I hope you are feeling fit. Has Frank Aiken yet built his house on the Dublin mountains? When replying, please, do so to my cousin's address, and under cover, as there are reasons.

Sincerely yours,
Ernie O'Malley

In late summer 1931 EOM returned to New Mexico with Dorothy Stewart, and then lived again in Chimayo. Since the New Mexican school system had been closed down for financial reasons, Helen Golden asked EOM if he would tutor her children, and so he returned to the Taos area. While Golden was hospitalized in the winter of 1932, EOM effectively ran the Golden household for several months, in a brusque military manner. That spring Paul Strand returned to Taos and befriended EOM and took photographs of him. EOM had almost completed his memoir and wanted to return to New York to see if he could get it published. He drove Stewart's car all the way to New York. His friendship with Strand was most fortunate as Strand was able to provide him with many introductions to his artistic circle of friends in New York and through them he got admitted to Yaddo Foundation to help finish up his memoir.

NO. 52 PAUL STRAND ARCHIVE, CCP, UNIVERSITY OF ARIZONA
Letter to Paul Strand[149]

[New York]
Tuesday 13 July 1932

Paul Strand, Box 461,
Taos, NM

Dear Paul,

I had a letter half written when yours came,[150] now I begin another. It was nice of you to write. I have been slightly dazed after the journey, leading a very normal sort of existence, losing keys, straying money and generally being utterly incompetent. To-day however I have got hold of myself.

I was dead tired out when I reached Indianapolis. I rang up Hapgood,[151] but he was not at home, this at 7:30 p.m., and I could not find his factory. I would have been incapable of talk anyhow. That day something went wrong with the radiator, no one seemed to be able to find the trouble so I was feeling pretty desperate, and when I reached Indianapolis on Saturday evening I felt it more important to sleep out on the road. I am more than sorry now as I was looking forward to Hapgood.

I went to Yaddo[152] by the Delaware and was very well received. Ted S.[153] was very kind. We had dinner at one of the tables, but I did not sleep there. Mrs Ames[154] pressed my hand on leaving and said that she would have liked to have heard more of me (I talked out our table) and said to be sure and send her my address. Ted S. said that was a good sign, she had rarely been so nice to anyone. He was looking well and had been working hard and was very interested in Hapgood, whom he intends to visit on his way back to Santa Fe.

Next the Group.[155] I remained 2 days. I felt very much at home. They had a fine spirit, great comradeship and what impressed me most was that the sex side seemed to be pure good comradeship. It was like the schools I worked with in Old Mexico. I watched Lee Strasberg[156] work at his classes. I liked the cool impersonal deliberateness of his judgments and comments. His talks were of the group spirit and the stress on creation. I would have wished to have heard more. Harold Clurman[157] had fine poise, an easy, informal, very friendly working ability, apart from what we understand as organization, but reaching its objective all the time. Gerald Sykes[158] I saw most of. I read all his reviews which he had pasted in a book. They were refreshingly honest and real. I liked him very much. We talked of Joyce and that in itself was a bond. The cooks were fine, joyous and giving, 2 brothers like some fine type of lay brothers in monasteries who mean as much to the place if not more than the monks. All the small parts seemed to fit in which is the real test, I think.

I mean to go back. I thought if I should get a job I would have money enough to pay my way there for a week or more. That's what I would like. It seemed unfair to me to go back on any other basis as the living costs fall on the group.

My job has not turned up. I have waited a week. There is some hitch. Now I have an offer to go to the Catskills to stay as guest with a lady whom I don't yet know, but she says I can work there and remain a month. That I don't know. She is working, I presume, and I don't know how I will fit in. From there I will write to Ted S. and find out about Yadoo and also to Gerald Sykes.

Thanks very much for putting me in touch with Yadoo and the Group. Ted S. seems to fit into there also. It was fine to leave you at one end and shake hands with Harold Clurman, Ted S. and Gerald Sykes at the other. It was like meeting an extension of yourself in them.

I have heard your show[159] praised by two very discerning people and I am very glad. If you didn't have sales you certainly left an impression.

I had a fine time on the trip. West Kansas was beautiful, lush olive sheens and tints along river valleys, infinite shades of green in the landscape. Ohio was a surprise, beautiful at dawn, the switchback country when I got off the main road. I had the advantage of being in the open all the time of rising with the dawn. I was eaten with mosquitoes twice, slept 2 nights wet through, got stuck in a woody culvert and after 4 hours of early morning work remembered chains and so pulled out. A double complete spin on a wet road in New York State, but I did not injure the car, and I was not going fast – 35 – that was lucky. I never had more than half a spin before, a skid on sking car tracks and a wallow for 20 feet before I could control the car; somehow I did not hit the parked cars on the curb. In Columbus I was so interested in watching a man stop traffic with an orange flag that I did not notice it was a train crossing until the locomotive was nearly on top of me. But why a yellow/orange flag? I drove through the New York traffic – twice since. It's easy enough to get through it. That's my story. I picked up a hobo who told me remarkable stories of an almost purposefully aimless life which left me with a sense of pity.

I heard the reading of a new play with the Group. The play was very good, neat but a little 'canned', I thought, no lift. Harold C. said it was a mule kick and it had to be put over as such. Anyhow the Group is the only unit that can create something of it, and it will be a severe test on them. I met a number of the people there whose names I do not even know, many spoke of you, and it was your name that made them accept me.

I am sorry that I had not met you long before I did. It would have meant a different Taos. Taos seems far away now as I am being drawn into New York. To me there is stylization but no style in the sense that full form often gives. If you see Ella Young please give her my love. She needs a long rest. I will write again when I have an address. I found 2 gold sovereigns in a bag which I had left in New York 3 years ago and that has saved the financial situation.

Very affectionately,

Ernie

NO. 53 EOM PAPERS NYU
Letter to Merriam Golden

c/o Joe McKiernan,
Apt 10, 444 East 10th Street,
[New York]
24 July 1932[160]

Mrs Merriam Golden,
[Rio Chiquito, Talpa,]
Ranchos de Taos, New Mexico

Dear Merriam,

I have been trying to pull myself together after the journey, but the heat hit me so I am now a thoroughly sucked orange. It's hard to realize New York; presently it's like a bad headache and one waits for bits of oneself to come back and get together again. I had a good journey and I drove through New York traffic 3 times, so as they say here, 'It's not so hot'!

I expect Terence is up at the ranch now with Brett. Deirdre must have looked well when she came down. Her pants didn't fit her, I bet. I was laid off a job the day I was to have started to work so I am still one of the unemployed. Luckily I found 2 gold sovereigns which I had left in a house here years ago so getting back to the gold standard saved the situation. I have no address as I am moving around. For the present Joe McKiernan, Apt 10, 444 East 10th Street will serve. Apartments are quite cheap now I'm told, so is food. I shop on 1st Avenue when I can. I hope you are taking things easy, if you can, and that Marianna[161] has started in on the loom. Please kindly remember me to Mrs Lopez?[162] I can't think of her name. Lopez, Margo, Felinici, Anita, Lucinda, Flavio, Aurora, Andres and the others. Please give my love to all in the house and to Ella.[163] Thanks very much for being so very kind to me and putting up with so much.

Affectionately,

Ernie

Letter to Elizabeth Ames[164]

444 *E 10th St, Apt. 10,*
New York
[c.2 August 1932]

[Mrs Elizabeth Ames,
Yaddo Foundation,
Saratoga Springs, New York]

Dear Mrs Ames,

I'm sure Ted Stevenson expressed my thanks to you for being so kind to me that evening at Yaddo. I was in a hazy condition after the long drive and it was a week before I could realize something of New York.

I have been trying to work on my book and to look for work at the same time. New York with its heat and the uncertainly owing to the great difficulty of finding anything to do just now keeps me from writing. I was to work in one of the State Parks on Long Island, but when I went out to begin I was told that I was laid off. Indeed I would be glad of any work.

Writing seems to me at times to take one away from reality. In New Mexico I was able to work on the land, teach the local Mexican children, whose school had closed through lack of funds, and tutor some American children whom I liked. That was necessary I thought then, but it left me without money when I decided to come East to finish the book and see about its publication.[165]

I am using material from my own experience. Reared in an Imperialistic setting I became an Irish separatist and fought there. I have written eighteen chapters out of a proposed twenty-three. I have to rewrite about six or seven chapters. That would take a month I should think. Writing has helped me to work certain prejudices out of my system, to clarify experience. Until the book is completely finished I will not know what exactly to do with it; leave it as autobiography or work detached episodes into short stories. I do not know if it would be possible to remain at Yaddo for three weeks or a month. There are many people who would like to go there I expect. But if it were possible, I would like to know. I wish to thank you for being so kind to me that evening.

Very sincerely yours,
Ernie O'Malley

Letter to Mrs Elizabeth Ames

444 E 10th St, Apt. 10,
New York
12 August 1932

[*Mrs Elizabeth Ames,*
Yaddo Foundation,
Saratoga Springs, New York]

Dear Mrs Ames,

I received your letter today.[166] Thank you very much for your invitation. I will only be too glad to go. It has been a worry not to be able to be quiet myself sufficiently to write. I have appointments to keep on Monday as I am trying to get rid of some poems of mine. I will take an early train on Tuesday. I don't know how when I have looked forward as much for a month's work: this evening in relief I was able to plan a short story.

Thanking you for your kindness.

Sincerely yours,
Ernie O'Malley

Letter to Paul Strand

Yaddo [Foundation,]
Saratoga Springs, New York
Wednesday 19 August 1932

Paul Strand,
PO Box 461, Taos, New Mexico

Dear Paul,

Here I am at Yaddo. And was I glad? I did not know where I was when I awoke in the palatial bed this morning: if a discrete butler had gently said 'What do you desire for breakfast, my Lord,' I would have believed it all. I was waiting until I had settled down to write to you, but I did not get settled down. New York was tough. It left me in a strange ferment, holding on looking for a job, yet unable to write in between. Three jobs I had been promised fell through or there was a deliberate butt in; this happened in 2 cases where I was practically certain of a job. Anyhow I'm here, and I'm going to work like hell. Ted Stevenson is next door to me in the 'Oratory' (I'm in the 'Den'). His book has been sent off to the publisher; he is very happy and content, says that he has never done so much work before as he has been able to get through here.

When I crossed the Mississippi I was appalled by the senseless waste and extravagance, living in New York down and out myself. I think I'm not awake when I reach 42nd Street. Movies, shows, bookshops, drug stores. How can anyone afford to go to a show or buy a book or live up to American advertisements! I had been used to the life East of Broadway and South of 14th Street. Men walking up, 'Have you a penny, buddy?' 'Can you give me 5 cents for a meal?' 'Spare a cigarette, mister?' Some faces tough and lined, others, but few, with pathetic gentleness, many shifty and cunning. It's hard to live there and not be affected by the terrible want. Street corner meetings every night, men talking in clichés. It's stupid, a shirted crowd mostly, waiting eagerly for a few honest, direct words; instead they get isms. It's brutal and selfish. Why the hell aren't some men trained to talk now, speak out of their hearts? All the crowd needs is a formulation of their desires, a knowledge that they are not alone in misery, that so-called 'white-collar' people suffer with them. In shops I find much sympathy with the Bonus Army,[167] the general impression seemed to be 'tear gas and tanks', that's the way to settle unemployment. I talk to all kinds of people. What strikes me most is the aimlessness of their thinking. I find something beautiful in many faces, something I don't associate with Americans, a kind of tenderness, but perhaps it's wistfulness or that quality men have in comradeship in misfortune.

I have seen nobody attached to any ism and I'm glad of that. It's better to talk to barbers, bootblacks, newsboys, and all who meet casual people. They know how serious the unemployment is. But there's no direction, no trust and no guts. That's my opinion. I heard some of the people in Yaddo talk last night; they had been to New York, but they had met organisations. The Amalgamated is on strike;[168] their pickets lay on the street the other day when trucks of strike breakers approached their factories. 'Let them drive over them,' they said, but the trucks turned away.

I hope you are working. There seems nothing else to be done just now; it's no use making a mess of one's mind trying to solve a problem; perhaps if I could talk things over or out with people of simplicity or good will I would not feel in a ferment, but I know I must get back serenity through work, then see the 'ism' people. That's my programme. I can't tell you how grateful I am about you suggesting and helping me about Yaddo. I had sold a good number of the books I cared for when Mrs Ames arrived to say she would make a place for me at once in view of my circumstances.

Now this is all about myself, but I thought you might like to know what I thought of things from the point of view of an aimless one like myself. I wrote a rotten little news story for a Hearst sub-ed. I think he'll pay me for it this week. Also I feel that when I return to New York, I'll be able to get a job, but I'm not sure. Time is queer in New York. It rushes. I don't understand it. It's like living in a subway. I'd like to photograph the hands strap-hanging in a subway during the rush hour as seen from a platform, or boots and shoes on the Third Avenue 'El'.[169] I don't believe there's such a place as Taos.

I hope Beck[170] and you are working. Please tell me how you both feel about it. I have not written to any of the Group but I write today; they'll think I am very rude, I know, and I don't know if they'll understand. Dynamic Symmetry.[171] Theosophy. Taos. Artists. Indians: is all that true? One thing I envied you, the trip to the Navajo country; always I had wanted to spend some time there.

With love to you both,
Ernie

By October EOM had a sufficient amount of his memoir complete to send it to friends for comment. To keep afloat financially, he worked on odd jobs such as housepainting or house-sitting. Whenever possible he would accept people's hospitality and continue to write and do research. He spent a lot of time in the New York Public Library reading Irish history, literaure and poetry, translated some early Irish poems, and continued to write, now including short stories and essays, none of which were published. At Yaddo and afterwards EOM met a new circle of people, including Aron Copeland, Israel Citkowitz and his sister, Rebecca, who helped type much of EOM's writings, Gerard Sykes, Georgia O'Keefe, Alfred Stieglitz, James Johnson Sweeney and Mariquita Villard. The latter introduced EOM to the Elon and Blanche Ferry Hooker family of Greenwich, Connecticut. There he met three of their four daughters, including the sculptor, Helen, who asked him if she could do his head in sculpture, which began their lifelong relationship.

NO. 57 UCDA P104/2687(1)
Letter to Frank Aiken, Minister of Defence

[New York]
6 October 1932

[Frank Aiken, TD,
Dún Gaoithe, Sandyford, Co. Dublin]

Dear Frank,

I heard, 4th hand, that you said there was work for me in a library. Today Oct. 5th that was half-confirmed by a boy who had seen Conor Neehan.[172] I heard the same about the paper[173] over a year ago, but nothing came of it. Now if there is something could you, please, tell me of it, what I am expected to do, what salary I could expect and whether you think you are under any obligation to do it. It's no good beating about the bush in such a case. I am here. I manage to live somehow, and I think I'm content enough when I'm not too hungry, but at least, I have a certain ease of mind. I am not torn in two by a political situation, and I don't read the papers and I have not talked to Irish people for years so that I do not know of cross-currents here or at home.

This seems abrupt, I expect, but I am trying to see things as I see them. I heard your home was finished; it must be fine out there on the mountains. I expect you are overworked anyhow so I won't prolong this. This is a covering address, the same old game:

John Keane,
269 Jewelt Avenue,
Jersey City, NJ.

Ever yours,
Ernie

Draft Letter to HH[174]

[*New York,*
c. May 1933]

Dear Miss Hooker,

I enjoyed Sunday in the country and the people I met; it was fine to feel trees
for New York is like a bad dream again. I would like to meet if you do come to
New York; perhaps we could eat together and I could show you my photographs
of the South West and some of Laguna which I might give you (maybe). Perhaps
I romanced, Maraquita[175] thought I did; anyhow if there was romancing, it was
rather nice. Talking to you was like talking to my friends at home. Enclosed poem,
I meant to give you but forgot about it, may be of interest. If you were really
serious about going to Ireland I could give you some introductions.

Very sincerely,
Ernie O'Malley

NO. 59 EOM PAPERS NYU
Letter to HH

4442 *University Ave,*
Chicago, Ill
9 July 1933

[*Helen Hooker,*
Zacheus Mead Road,
Greenwich, Connecticut]

Dear Helen Hooker,

I wanted to meet you again in New York, but I had not had the sense to ask
you for your address that Sunday. I wrote to Quita[176] for it, but she was in the
silences for weeks, and when she replied I had left New York for Woodstock to
paint (housepaint) and later for Chicago. I had a heap of photographs which I
wanted you to see; there were some of Laguna and a good one of the church.

Presently I am in the Irish Free State exhibit[177] giving information with my
tongue in my cheek. If you come to Chicago, and I wish you would, please look
up that exhibit. I had a very pleasant day in Greenwich and New York was more
liveable for a time after I had seen real trees again. I would have liked to have
talked more to your sister[178] but she disappeared. I hope you are working to your
satisfaction; I liked best your statue figure. Do you really intend to go to Ireland or
were you making conversation?

Very sincerely,
Ernie O'Malley

Letter to Merriam Golden

> *4442 Union Avenue,*
> *Chicago, IL*
> *August, 1933*

Mrs Helen Golden,
Ranchos de Taos, New Mexico

Dear Merriam,

This letter has been long in the process of being written. I was collecting stuff from as many exhibits as I could get to for the kids but at times I am oppressed by the thought that the kids are now grown up and sophisticated and I stopped the collection, and again the heat and the general inanity of the Fair has kept me from writing any thing for the past 3 months.

On Sunday, Brett, Edward and Miriam came in here and yesterday we had a whole day together at the Art Institute, Planetarium and Aquarium; we met Fechin[179] and the Blumenscheins[180] and it was more than ever a Taos day. I feel lost today now that they are gone.

My letters are contingent on events and nothing has happened much so I have not written. America seems such a good country when I think of Ireland and Ireland such a pleasant place when I think of America that it is hard to resolve my doubts. Anyhow I never had my passage back, or food money much for that matter, but the lilies exist and so do I, without their justification.

News of New Mexico seemed to come all together: Virginia, Mary Hamlin,[181] Brett and a letter from Sylvia,[182] She had looked for me at the Fair but in the Mexican and Indian Exhibits; she did not expect to find me in the F/S nor would I myself save that the Consul[183] is alright, but everything else, I found, all wrong. I expect Sylvia will be as happy inside as she would be on the outside, but a girl should have a love affair before she goes into a convent, and I don't know whether Sylvia has had one. The Irish are so damned aloof about their personal life.

I went to see Joe Campbell[184] once. It was a shock. Fat, gross and cushioned living, I thought, on an Irish background; sentimental in retrospective and untrue to what might have been himself. I talked with him until 4 one morning giving him as far as I could a chance to be real and then as he didn't I have never gone back to see him. It does not seem of much use to meet a person who really speaks another language. He had very kindly memories of you and that almost thawed me; he talked of the twins and in going back he was alright but he has fallen between the armchairs and he looked for sympathy as a father and husband so I did not give him any. I have not met any one else whom you know. Once I was out on an island after a swim, the island being in the Sound and I heard someone call 'Paul, come here', so I said that's Dorsha and Paul Hayes,[185] though I did not know either of them by sight. They were waiting for a rowboat to bring them out to an island, but I did not act on the impulse to speak so I saw them being rowed away. That's as near as I came to speaking to Dorsha and Paul. Mary Vorse[186] I met at Saratoga

Springs, Provincetown and New York. I stayed in Woodstock, housepainting, so that's completed my round of American 'art' colonies.

There's less than nothing to write when you have too much. If you see Dr Light, please kindly remember me to her. I met a very fine girl at the Fair the other day who was in Taos once and was very enthusiastic about Dr Light, so we had a Light chat for some hours – Helen Hooker and her sister Adelaide. They had both been in Russia much to the distress of their money-producing father.

How is Marianna; has she gone on with wood work or has she got hold of another house to improve? I heard you rented the canyon house, so Campbell said and that must have been a great relief. Did you put up jams and jellies again; (oh for pea chips) and was the market continued[187] and how are the horses and now I fear dignified Ruairi.[188] Is Lucinda fatter (out of purity) or not or is Clara still as gentle as ever and Andie as definite. Terence I hear is going to art school. I hope the dynamic symmetry is not too engrained by this. The kids talk as much as ever, so I am told. Maybe my kicks in their pants have now – faint from distance – been worn to a pat as my barkings to unfortunate Volunteers became pleasant with the years, to them. Dorothy Stewart I nearly wrote to several times. Please give her my love. I found 2 long unfinished letters in my bag to her; a long one to you and Mariana and I to Eithne but writing is hopeless. You write, I mean, I do and then fail to say what you began would need a volume or a chapter length so that I think a postcard is better and as I hate sending an open letter I don't send it. How are the McCrossens? Please give my love to Mariana, Terence, Eithne and Deirdre and please believe even if you don't hear from me that I bear you all in mind very affectionately.

Best of love,
Ernie

NO. 61 EOM PAPERS NYU
Letter to HH

c/o McGlynn Travel Bureau,
Victoria Hotel,
51st St and Broadway,
[New York]
17 December 1933

[Helen Hooker,
Zacheus Mead Road,
Greenwich, Connecticut]

Dear Helen Hooker,

What have you been doing; working, which I presume means sculpting, or orthopedic nursing? Anyhow I hope you have done something to your satisfaction. I had a great quotation from *Poor Splendid Things* about a sculptor's lot, but I forget it. I visited the Field a good deal; I tried to see that lady's bronzes in an unobjective way, but I failed save in the Abyssinian girl.[189] There was a Basque head that reminded me of Scipio Africanus,[190] whom I have always admired as a soldier, and some strange faces from Kashmir.

I gave some lectures, one of them good for I got a lift myself, then I went to the Newberry Library to look up a place I knew little of, and after close on a month's work I found I knew less than ever.

Could you, please, when in town, and have time, meet me some place and time; I would like to see you again. At present I am wandering around but I may be able to find a place to stay in. I had a book for you on Ireland, but now I don't know if I have it. I lost all my good books and note books last week, and I am in deep mourning. Please kindly remember me to your nice sister, Adelaide.

Ever yours,
Ernie O'Malley

NO. 62 EOM PAPERS NYU
Letter to Eithne Golden

McGlynn Travel Bureau,
Hotel Victoria,
51st Street & Broadway, NY
21 January 1934

[Eithne Golden,
Rio Chiquito, Talpa,
Rancho de Taos, New Mexico]

Dear Eithne,

Thanks for your long letter; it was a good talk. I lost the habit of writing letters now and the more I think of writing the less I have to say. I left Chicago by bus, a bus is bad enough at any time but when a woman with 2 fat greasy women and a baby insist on keeping windows closed for babba's health one feels inclined to launch a nudist colony on the seat or to kill said babba by spells and incantations; neither of which I did but I opened the window saying 'to hell with the baby'. Better a baby to die than 10 grown-ups. Chi, as hobos say, was a city without any center, a good symphony orchestra and a really good collection of French paintings. A friend of Sylvia's was librarian there. She could not understand Sylvia becoming a nun, but that was her own business, I thought, and if she wanted why shouldn't she, but her friend thought of her new profession in terms of waste. If you know your geography you know that there's a lake and that has saved what was left of my sanity in the heat. I could swim before I went to work and that cooled me for at least 2 hours, then the temperature went up as people began to ask questions. It seems that the most extraordinary thing that can happen to one is to have been born in Ireland and with people speculating audibly as to whether I was or not or then gazing in admiration and astonishment when they heard I was, or asking me to pronounce words to test my brogue or those from Ireland who doubted I was from Ireland, or superior people who thought that Ireland never did anything like that. I felt like a cross between a polar bear and an armadillo. The best thing about Chicago was the Newberry Library where I worked for 3 weeks when the Fair was over.

I thought to see the Station Wagon held together by Marianna's joinery and Sylvia's prayers roll up one day. But maybe you all wait for the next Fair in June. Brett blew in on a cold day with Edward and Miriam and all continued to look colder than each other, but we did see part of the exhibits. In the Art Institute we saw Blumenschein and Fechin family and looked at O'Higgins' painting[191] and a canvas by a boy who later committed suicide. I had hoped to show Brett the flea circus because there was a flea there named Pat who carried a green flag in his or her and perhaps bisexual hand. I had already as the daughter of an old Fenian written a letter to the Free State Consul to complain about such a derogatory inference especially as said flea was picked up in a Dublin hotel, and the idiot had written a letter to the Fair management but before he posted it some interfering reporter hold him it must be a joke. I heard of you through Jenny Noggle whom I met several times at the Fair, then there was Mary Hamlin, quieter, subdued and more directed, quite a new Mary whom I liked, but only saw for a short time before her train left. I did not hear from her so I expect she intends to use her house for the winter.

Last Christmas I had saved up money intending to send you 3 some decent books (a limited edition of the *Wind on the Prairie*[192]) but being hard up I spent it and felt as if I had robbed the kids' savings banks. Then this Christmas also, but life being reduced as to what I should next eat, or where outside of bus stations, I should next sleep, made me again unable to send the books. I had the pile of stuff from the Fair, but I thought it might sound too stupid. I missed Dorothy Stuart[193] who was in New York busy at chasing a man all evening and when I turned up she, Dorothy, had gone and next day left for the home of the Ladies of Philadelphia. Since then I have seen her bouncing with energy as usual visiting museums, galleries, and what New York has to give with her friend Maria,[194] a nice girl. Now Dorothy has gone to Boston. I met a friend of Dr Light's the other night; he had been in Russia for 4 years, and when he heard I knew her he was very pleased. It was at some boiled shirt affair to which I contributed a herring bone brown suit once belonging to a Chicago rotund millionaire and given me by his Irish cook. I'm sorry I can't think of his name but he was nice.

I have been weeks trying to sit down to finish this letter, but I am unsettled, my papers and things scattered in 5 places, and I postpone writing always until I can settle down in one definite place. Maybe with luck that will happen next week. I had Theo Goddard's place for Christmas, but I was sick in bed and just as I had begun to work she returned and I cleared out. New York's alright though. I like it. You're up against it so much and it's such a sad headache. Now this letter had best go while it can. I won't now be able to wish you a Happy Christmas or New Year but that's alright. I'm glad to hear you continue to write and that you like it. How is Ella? Please give her my love. Brett is somewhere, but not in New York.

I think Deirdre I owe a letter to. That will come also later. Please kindly remember me to the Lopez – one and all, Andie and anyone I know. How's Marianna? The station wagon is a great old bus to still go; it must be like an Irish car now. Our cars become part of the family and grow up with us. My love to you all and Dr Light, and I will write when I clear this jam.

With my love,
Ernie

NO. 63 EOM PAPERS NYU
Letter to Helen Merriam Golden

c/o John Keane,
Apt 26, 25 St Nicholas Terrace,
New York, NY
30 June 1934

Mrs Helen Golden,
Ranchos de Taos, New Mexico

Dear Merriam,

I hope you are all very well. Eithne's letters pulled me up and made me realize I was a cur for not writing but it's hard to explain until you are East again and try to live interiorly in this maze. I had intended to see Helen Crowe[195] before I wrote you. I called many a time but she was always out and then came a letter from Theo, received late, which gave me her address in the library. I looked her up and found her in the Print Room. She is seldom at home, she says, being busily engaged at meetings. I went to dinner. I had looked her up so often thinking she might be hungry, but when I went to her place to eat it was I who was hungry. She had been in a CWA[196] protest and had been beaten up by police and so was jumpy and nervous due to the psychological effect of such a beating. She did not seem, as far as her body went, to think that life was worth living and had been contemplating suicide. Her stay in Paris had been bitterly hard, but as we compared notes not as bad as mine in New York. Now she has a job, food, and a room. I liked her a great deal.

I had for 3 months been working steadily in the 42nd Street Library[197] on Irish, old and middle, and had got through a vast amount of stuff in Irish, German and French. The German by proxy, unfortunately, and was most interested in certain Greek affinities in Irish lit. and so we had a long chat on that and as a result I think she will do some work on Irish and Greek. She had translated poems and so had I, so we have to swap. That was fine because I was working towards a given end and felt a fool for sticking it out and there were no immediate gains that I could see but a far ahead value and she more or less restored a certain idiotic faith I had in what I was doing.

I intend to see her again, but presently I dot not feel like anything much. About 5 weeks ago I went into the woods and lived for 2 weeks sleeping out, living on the country rabbits and odd hens whose owners I had not been introduced to and some fresh vegetables which belonged, I presumed, partly to the earth, partly to myself and perhaps, to an owner. Then I decided to become a Transient on Federal Relief as I knew of a house in New York, a YMCA,[198] they had taken over, so I filled up forms and entered. Since then I am a painter, decorating the place and mixing paints in an underground dungeon, the boiler room, so it's not a cool job. I have my bed, food and 2 dollars a week. This week was bad when I painted floors, my last meal came up on the floor so I hope it will show eventually. Now today I am fit enough again and will stick it for another week. It's really an extraordinary place, one for white collar men, and when I talk to these men here and feel the dignity of some and the broken spirit and boot licking tactics of the others I feel thank God for Ireland. Whatever the hell they may be there, they're primarily men and they would never do the sopping up and in genteel language, arse licking, that the majority do here. I don't give a damn for anyone and strange to say, get on well with all. Some day when I'm out of it, I may write you about it all. It's like Dante's *Inferno* and Gilbert and Sullivan rolled into one, but the whole scheme seems like bailing out a boat in mid-seas which is full of holes.

I lectured at New York U[199] this spring, 4 lectures but was not paid. That did not seem to matter, actually it did, but the people were very interested, and I would have been given a Summer Course if the U had had any money, but its lecturers have been cut 33 1/3 %. Many from the English Department said they at least realized the futility of Anglo-Saxon research. So that's something.

I met Colum[200] for the first time. And I was very disappointed in him. He resurrected Collins and Griffith[201] 'til I was ready to clap down his green hat on his elfish face and use my boot. And there were other unaccountable aspects, a little snobbery, a Fascist outlook given to or taken from Mary Colum[202] whose articles in the *Forum*, one that I had read, so I presume others, were definitely reactionary. The whole meeting was a good short story, there was so much cross purpose. I was trying to find out about my 'script'[203] refused at Macmillan which he, the previous week, had told a girl at some big dinner, was on his table. Also he told the girl what he thought of me, she being wealthy and respectable. And she being a friend of mine drew him out and said nothing. So that's that. Campbell has out a new mag,[204] but I don't think it will last. I was asked to contribute but refused without being paid. It is maintained by voluntary contributions, and I think such a mag will deteriorate and deserves to because it should have the dignity of self-support. This comes well from me. But I do believe that if you are in the writing game you should try and make a publication self-supporting and not 'for fools do some stuff to save the Irish name.'

There's no one else you know that I know here so I have no news to give you about your friends. Perhaps Helen Crowe has written to you and if so she would have oceans to my bucket. I hope Marianna is very well. What is she doing now? Your house finished, what carpentry is needed? I'm hoping to get a job in an A & P[205] or to become a 'bus boy'[206] in a restaurant. I have been able to save my eyes lately and that has been good. I am reading John Donne steadily, and Shakespeare's *Sonnets*. I am now 2 years at the *Sonnets* and lately have got hold of a book that works them out pretty well into seven books or so and after much testing I am inclined to agree with that hypothesis, but the arrangement of precedence of poems in order in any book must be arbitrary. Read much of Stephen Spender and Auden, two young English poets, both Left and good especially Spender, have tried to translate Rimbaud but have decided after 2 months application that I must get them off by heart in French and let time take its course. Meier-Graefe has done a fine piece of work on Van Gogh,[207] but it's not as good as Vincent's letters to his brother, Theo. Cramer aptly named, and others have begun a drive against contemporary artists and some of the articles seem to me mean. More and more writers are declaring themselves – that is interesting to watch, but for the past few months, I have not seen periodicals. Do you know Ramon Fernandez? I read a letter of his recently to Andre Gide.[208]

However, this is far from a satisfying look at a desert, a sunset and the smell of piñon, but the memories of all such help and well up every now and then. I don't know now if this letter means anything and am inclined to tear it up, but maybe I won't. I was very glad to get Eithne's letter and will reply faithfully to her and also Deirdre and I have some poems for Ella. Please give my very kind regards to Dr Light. I hope her clinic is going well and I'm glad of it. My love to yourself, Marianna, Terence, Deirdre, and poor little Eithne (last because she's nearest) and my affectionate regards to Mrs Lopez, Andie, Felinici, Margo, Ernesto and Lucinda. Actually by time and distance except Dorothy and the MacCrossens, other people are vague to me. I yet have the feeling of not justifying my existence when I don't write something; maybe I'll get rid of that, but it seems to me an ethical code and perhaps my only one. Looking this over I know it will be hard to read, but my hand is pretty jumpy. I fell off a ladder this week and crashed through a skylight and got hung up on another skylight of decorated glass further down, but no damage much to shout about save the penmanship.

With love,

Ernie

Letter to Paul Strand

c/o Martin Kyne,
Pickwick Arms Hotel,
230 East 51[st Street], NY
12 July 1934

Paul Strand, Alvarado,
Vera Cruz, Mexico

Dear Paul,

It was a very pleasant surprise, your letter, as I had my doubts about your being located. And so again I had a long read and felt a great deal better. I have not heard from Ella since last November or so, maybe later, but then I have not written her. The winter had been hard. I was trying to exist all the time and had no place in which to write and had to read in the Library.[209] I read steadily in Old and Middle Irish and that reading kept my mind free and saved my nerves; as I had to hunt for places in which to sleep. I could never do anything after the Library closed at 10. I had a room of my own for 2 weeks and in relief wrote 5 poems. For the past month I have been what is known as a Transient on Federal Relief. There is a house here for such; it's said to be the best house in the USA. I undertook the work of mixing paint and of painting and now I'm finished. I had to mix paints in a boiler room without ventilation and the heat spell was terrible, but I again had contact with men, and I liked the work. The paint began to affect my eyes and do something to my nerves so I left yesterday with the noble sum of $5.70 for my month's work, but I had a good bed, food, and for 2 weeks, privacy as the other beds in my room were not slept in. Now I am sorting out a few clothes to go to Boston to see the 'Atlantic Monthly' about my book.[210]

That accounts for winter and spring; from July of last year to November I worked in the World's Fair, but it was not real work, not enough to do and pay too small to save anything.

I was very glad to hear you have been working steadily, and I'm sure your film[211] will be a fine one as you can introduce something new into that kind of photography. I don't know what the subject matter is, maybe the life of a community but so long as you can direct the spirit of the whole I know it will be sensitive and will get the 'feel' of your actors and workers. I am jealous when I hear of your work, I who seemed to have wasted a year biting my nails but yet never sinking. I don't know anything about scenario writing, but I'll look the matter up, and I would work for my food, and peanuts on the side.

I did not look up any of the Group nor could I afford to see *Men in White*,[212] which is now available in the movies. When I come back from Boston I will look up Gerald[213] because I want to have a long talk with him. Somehow this being up against it too much drove me in on myself. Also I was keen on a girl but found when spring was over that she was living vicariously through me in the memory of a man with whom she was really in love.[214] That hurt a great deal, the shock of it. A very fine girl indeed, but it seems unfair to presume or let another think your heart is whole when it is not. I am very inexperienced in the ways of women; that hurt I am beginning to get over.

The Transient House was strange. The man in charge had been a missionary in Burma. He has a fine sensitive face. I hope you can take a photograph of him some time. The handling of men was good; the staff was not hide bound and all were easy to approach and to talk to. All transients are allowed 90 cents a week and in return do 30 hours work. Special work, as painting, was to be paid at the rate of $5 a week but there was a cut the week I arrived, to $1. The house is being reconstructed and that gives a kind of cooperative sense as transients do all the work, but I found there was a great difference between the idealism of men who were being well paid and that of the men who were actually working with their hands. The organisation I found faulty in that there was not sufficient contact between the staff and the transients. Fundamentally I thought this patch up system wrong, but I was interested in the men and in the human qualities of the staff.

Last winter I met Paul Rosenfeld.[215] He and I went over to visit Israel Citkovitz,[216] a young composer, and we three talked of you and of Hart Crane.

I have looked through my things for the long letter I wrote to you, but I cannot find it. I have moved so often and have shifted my books and notes and spread them out over much territory. Now, out of the habit of writing, I don't find it easy. During the winter I attended chest clinics as a 'doctor'. I worked under a man whom I knew at the University in Dublin. That also gave me a contact with people and was a help. I lectured 4 times at NYU, but was not paid. Anyhow I had a good time and it helped me to get my notes and thoughts in order.

I would like if you could send me one of your stills of Mexico or of New Mexico. Sometime or other I might be able to hang it on the wall of my study in Ireland. Not that anything objective is necessary to remind me of you, but there was a spirit in the New Mexican photographs that was close to what I thought of that land. Now that I have your address I can write you again. My pen is sluggard this hot evening. Things are drifting here. It will be a bad winter. Strikes should be on the increase. The human equation in this Administration is covering many a hole, but everything being done seems 'hostages to fortune'. I was very much surprised at the number of men amongst the transients who were willing to suck up to authority. Was there such a thing as sturdy independence? But then the men once wore white collars. Workers are more robust. The handling of material seems to give them a different sense of reality. I know your film will be a fine one.

Very affectionately,
Ernie

Letter to HH

[New York]
28 July 1934

[Helen Hooker,]
220 East 73[rd Street], Apt. 11C,
New York

Dear Helen of Paint Pots,[217]

How are you? On the third floor now or higher? Perhaps in the boiler room; if so add some red in my memory. And when will you be finished; but perhaps you are? You see all my sentences are??

Please give Amburino, that's not it I know, nor is it Ottorino, but that's what I remember her as, a hug for me. She was very sweet before I left and kind. I felt rather rotten because I wouldn't promise her to return, but we say *Is fiuc' tsa gelltar* – a promise is a debt,[218] and so I couldn't. Anyhow I, feeling thankful, nearly kissed her when I was saying goodbye, and in the reading room at that. Perhaps she would have understood had I done it for I'm sure nobody else would have had.

Are you going away in August you said you were? ... Well ... What can I write anyway or what can I say that you would understand.

Ernie

NO. 66 UNIVERSITY OF CHICAGO POETRY MAGAZINE ARCHIVE
Letter to Harriet Monroe[219]

c/o J. Hughes,
122 Englewood Ave,
Brookline, Boston
7 August 1934

[Harriet Monroe, Editor,
Poetry *magazine,*
Chicago, Illinois]

Dear Miss Monroe,

I received your letter of the eighth of August. I have very little information to give as my life has not been a literary one.

Born: Mayo, Ireland
Residence: Anywhere from Morocco to Mexico, but my people live in Dublin, Ireland
Occupation: Uncertain
Publications: None

I studied medicine in University College, Dublin, attached to Staff or fought, 1918–1922, prisoner 1922–1924, recovered from wounds by tramping, climbing and studying in Western Europe and North Africa. I have lived in the South West of this country and in Mexico.

I met a friend of yours and former helper in Santa Fe, Alice Corbin Henderson.[220] She wanted to send on poems I had written on the South West. In Mexico City I met another friend of yours, Hart Crane. He spoke kindly of you and had intended to review some books for *Poetry*.

Sincerely yours,
Ernie O'Malley

NO. 67 PAUL STRAND ARCHIVE, CCP, UNIVERSITY OF ARIZONA
Letter to Paul Strand

[Boston]
22 October 1934

Paul Strand, Lista de Correos,
Alvarado, Vera Cruz, Mexico

Dear Paul,

I hope you are very well and that your film works out to your satisfaction. I did not hear from you when I wrote in early July so I expect you must have been busy or did not get my letter. Last week I was leaving the 42nd Street Library when I met Gerald Sykes. He took me up to his apartment, and we talked till well into the morning. He showed me a snap of yourself which you had sent in the last letter.

Gerald is working hard on a book which he expects to have finished by the end of November. His girl is in Boston with the Group. He has been out West and North and says that the trip has changed every idea he has had about America. He met Ted Stevenson in Santa Fe.

I saw Flaherty.[221] I gave him the letter which you had written me in Taos. And I saw the film 'Man of Aran'. It was prefaced by a stupid introduction. An Irish girl, an intelligent fool, whom I know spoke, then three of the actors came on the stage, the mother of the film singing a cradle song and rushing it to a *caoine*, the death song, whilst off stage is Henry Lowell playing some banshee air while the wailing of wind presumes that the banshee is there. Very bad I thought. The woman's singing was fine; it was like oriental music but Lowell!!

The film was too highly keyed; mainly it resolved around the breaking of limestone rock to make tillage, the capture of a shark, and a storm. To me there was a certain distortion in the life as cut by F. The shark capture is very exciting. The storm intensely so, but to me it seemed that the material had got hold of Flaherty. In between was needed normal life: spinning, gathering seaweed for kelp, the burning of it, baking a cake, ordinary fishing and the quiet life of the island. And through the storm with its howling wind, men's courage and the lash of sea completely carries one away in a mood of beauty and apprehension and a very definite sense of unfocussed beauty much like that of good music, yet the leaving out of the simple normal tempo of existence was I thought a distinct drawback. The material fascinated F. too much. Perhaps I'm wrong. Anyhow I actually heard the Irish waves again and Irish wind and I was very happy sitting there in the theatre.

Have you heard from Ella? I wrote and sent her some poems but I expect she is busy. I am leaving New York this week. My head is going round the wrong way. I have a place to sleep in now but none to write in, and so I can read in the Library and look out for odd jobs. The 'Atlantic Monthly' saw the book last and suggested changes which I could not see my way to agree to. Now today it goes to the Viking.[222] It has been a regular Old Man of the Sea up to this.

If you have time please tell me how you are and how the work goes on. Gerald said that you expected to be in New York in December. I hope you will write to me before you come up as I would very much like to see you.

Affectionately,
Ernie

Hughes will know where I am.

NO. 68 PAUL STRAND ARCHIVE, CCP, UNIVERSITY OF ARIZONA
Letter to Paul Strand

[Return address]
McGlynn Travel Bureau,
Hotel Victoria,
51st & Broadway, NY
28 December 1934

Paul Strand, Abraham Gonzalez,
66, Mexico, DF

Dear Paul,

Thanks for your letter which I received when I came to New York last week. I think it's terrible that your work has been destroyed in the sense that it is unfinished for I think you do need to see the results of that year's work in its definite form. If there's any compensation it's in the work itself. You know I do believe there is a law which I call the balance of compensation. Once I mountain climbed in Europe for close on a year to restore muscular tone after surgeons had told me I would never be able to walk again. I carried a few things when I lived and slept in the Pyrenées. You sweat, ache and curse on a long climb, you think you're the biggest fool working for six hours and then you reach your objective. Suddenly all the weariness goes; you have ease, the peace of height and complete serenity. All that long bloody climb disappears and for the rest of the day you have that peace which is apart from mind, for mind seldom functions above a certain height. In life the same as far as I know it. Only we don't see the objective as in mountain climbing where we can suddenly understand the sweat, but it comes every now and then. So I feel you have done good work. I don't even want to see it to know. This last year I went through several kinds of hell, and only last month was I able to realize that I was above defeat. That may sound presumptuous, but it's true. I touched bottom and found that at any rate.

I wish you could come to New York. Harold and Gerald[223] would love to see you and myself most of all. They talk of you whenever we meet. And to tell you the truth if I can do that I'm afraid of your going to New Mexico. You may hurt yourself again and now need the strength that the year's work, whatever about the unfinished result, has given you. You, however, are your own best judge.

I wish I could see some of your stills some time. You must have learned a great deal in Mexico. I learned about betrayal, how a people is sold by spurious politicians and the futility of super names like 'revolution' and 'republic'.

In Boston I wrote seven short stories. I don't know how good they are and I don't care. It was fine to be able to write again. The Viking have my book, have been considering it for some time past, and I should hear from them any day now, but I don't think they'll take it. A poetry magazine has accepted four of my poems but will not pay till they publish.[224] Harold is trying to get me a grant from a foundation here, then I can be sure of two months to find if I have anything else to say. Also I have been given a pension of £120 a year; I am due to receive it in a month or more and can apply for another pension for services from 1916–1924 which should bring me in about £300 a year. That means I can go back to Ireland. I may go back in a few months' time, and I would like very much to see you before I go. If you are in New Mexico soon I will take a run out if I feel I cannot settle down to writing something definite. Harold is lecturing on drama, and he has asked me to attend his classes which I will very gladly do. He is thinking of going to Russia and said you might go also. If so be sure and find out what equipment you had best bring. They are very short of technical equipment, cameras, lenses and above all film: Tissé,[225] Sergei M. Eisenstein's[226] camera man, told me that Russian film is rotten. So you had best get in touch with someone in Russia before you go, Tissé, if necessary, and mention that I met him at the Hacienda in Hidalgo and I'm sure he will give you technical information, but you will, of course, have your own contacts if you decide to go.

Gerald has written a play. I have not seen it. I met him in Boston and the last night before the play, *Gold Eagle Guy*,[227] opened. The play has greatly improved since yet it's not a good play. I have not heard from Ella Young but I heard of her about five months ago; then she was, I think, in Berkeley, Cal. I hope things will improve. The unexpected always seems to happen in Mexico and maybe there will be a swing the other way for you. It was fine to hear from you.

Affectionately,
Ernie

c/o Israel Citkowitz,
100 Van Cortland Park Sth,
New York, NY
10 January 1935

[*Harriet Monroe, Editor,*
Poetry *magazine,*
Chicago, Illinois]

Dear Harriet Monroe,

It was a welcome New Year surprise to see my poems in *Poetry*,[228] and I take it as a good omen for the year. I had written to you from Boston, but my movements are uncertain at their best.

In the Southwest I first met Alice Corbin Henderson after a lecture of mine on the continuity of Gaelic thought in Irish poetry. She was, I found, the A.C.H. whom Tom MacDonagh, executed after the Dublin Rising of 1916, had referred to in his book on Irish literature.[229] She knew the work of the Anglo-Irish school and we spent many pleasant evenings together. Later she read the poems I had written on the South West and suggested that I send them on to you, but I was too uncertain of my work then; since that time I have lost the greater part of them.

In old Mexico I met Hart Crane. We became friends and remained friends to the end despite clashes from my sense of personal discipline and his lack of it. Inspired by our memories of poetry and stimulated by rum toddies we wrote long letters to many people, amongst them Wallace Stephens, E.E. Cummings, and yourself whom Hart always referred to as Aunt Harriet. Unfortunately we afterwards burnt the letters. Hart had books from you to review. We each wrote reviews but I don't know what happened to them. I liked him a great deal. He was generous, enthusiastic and spoke the most amazing rhetoric, good rhetoric. He believed in America, in its creative ability and had a dislike for the nostalgia of induced foreign culture as a standard. He was kind to his friends, irritable and pugnacious, but Mexico with its criss-cross racial clashes and its general effect on unrest of mind was no place for a stranger to solve personal or creative problems. He always spoke of you affectionately. You may like to know that. I did not like some of the articles that appeared after his death and I meant to write of him as I had known him, but did not. He gave me some poems which he had written in Mexico and which have not published. He said they were for myself as I had stood by him in trouble. I sent them back to Ireland with some of my books but since I have heard that they have been lost.

Two weeks ago I met Vassos and Tanagra Kanellos.[230] They are working in Hartford House on mural decorations in the great hall. I had worked there last summer as a 'house painter'. Last evening we talked of Greece, and they both sent their affectionate regards. We are to get together soon to exchange Greek and Gaelic poetry. I have lectured on Gaelic poetry from the 8th to the 18th century and so have a deal of material for them. I have been working on the earlier Gaelic stories and epics to access their sidelights on the old Gaelic mind and character and am interested in their heroic temper and the aspects of life uniting them with the Greek heroic Age. I have made translations from old poetry but will have to wait until I really understand the language.

I have a book now with the Viking Press. It is called *On Another Man's Wound* from a Gaelic proverb 'it is easy to sleep on another man's wound'. It deals particularly with the period 1916–1921, as seen through my eyes. I was in a small way connected with the fighting in 1916 from which the new Ireland emerged. I was then attached to the Irish Volunteers whilst I studied medicine at the National University. I had to leave the University, became a captain on Headquarter's Staff; later the Volunteers became the Irish Republican Army in 1919 under our own government, Dáil Éireann. Before the end of the Tan War, as we call it, I was in charge of a division of 5 brigades in the counties of Kilkenny, Tipperary and Limerick in the Martial Law area. I was captured by the British, was to have been hanged but escaped.

Later, after the treaty of 1921 I remained with the IRA, became Director of Organisation and when the civil war began was made Assistant Chief of Staff. Badly wounded and captured I read of my own death in a Dublin paper and a brief account of my career. I was to have been executed by the Free State Government but they hesitated to shoot me on a stretcher. I was elected a Member of Parliament for North City Dublin whilst a prisoner. I was in jails and internment camps for close on two years; when released I was considered a hopeless invalid.[231]

I went to Catalonia to help the Catalan movement for independence;[232] I studied their folklore and cultural institutions. I learned to walk again in the Pyrénées. I became a good mountain climber, covered the frontier from San Sebastian to Perpignan, lived in the Basque country. I walked through a part of Spain, southern and South East France and most of Italy. I did some mediaeval history at Grenoble. I walked through Italy slowly, worked at archeology in Sicily and lived in Rome and Florence for a time. I walked through Germany to Holland and through Belgium and then to North Africa.[233] After some years I returned to the National University to again take up medicine but I did not get my exams. The years abroad taught me to use my eyes in a new way.

In America I have lived in New York, Boston, Chicago, Pasedena, San Francisco, Taos, Chimayo and Santa Fe. I have been in most states except those of the South. I have lived in Carmel, Woodstock and Provincetown, have written at the Yaddo Foundation at Saratoga Springs. In the southwest I lectured on Gaelic and Anglo-Irish literature from our first poet to James Joyce. I learned something about the Indian way of life and that neglected people, the Mexicans of New Mexico. In old Mexico I spent a year. I worked in the training schools for rural teachers in two states; that work brought me in touch with Indians from twelve or more states and mestitos. I stayed some months with the local people, lived as they lived and found out something about their life and feeling. In Mexico City I studied archaeology in the Academy of Fine Arts. (I have a rough idea of the physical nature of this country now.)

From the above you will see that this sketch of the physical nature of my life has been mainly action. Here in America I have been cut away from my own country where I found I was developing into a symbol. This country has helped me to live my life apart from all the associative memories that intrude too much at home; its impersonality and detachment have helped me to find something of myself.

I am enclosing some poems. I would be grateful if you could find time to comment on some of these poems. This address will find me as I have no address of my own. The Viking have now had the book for close on three months and are considering it. I would like to forward it if they accept and publish it. Israel Citkovitz who is working on songs and a ballet wishes to be kindly remembered to you.

Very sincerely,
Ernie O'Malley

NO. 70 EOM PAPERS NYU
Letter to Eithne Golden

[New York]
28 March 1935

[Eithne Golden,
Ranchos de Taos, New Mexico]

Dear Eithne,

I hope you are very well. I have been sick most of this year so far. The weather changed a great deal, now hot, now cold, and it seems impossible to adjust to the variations. Paul Strand I met here a number of times but he had no time to go to see anyone of you in Rio Chiquito although he wanted to go there. I'm glad you saw Ted Stevenson for he's a fine fellow.

I saw Georgia O'Keefe[234] and had a long chat with her once in the Stieglitz Gallery but though I was to call on her I have not seen her since. She does not go near Taos now but lives down the river somewhere. I met another lady from down the river from somewhere near Alcalde, Mary Wheelwright,[235] I think she was. I had been told about her, the work she did collecting Navajo creation myths and her intention to build a temple in the Navajo country. Anyhow at dinner I was telling the company something about a Yeibishi[236] when she said 'I am the greatest living authority on the Navajos', and I was not impressed. I had intended to say, 'Well what about their medicine men, do you think they are authorities too?' I'm a little fed up with the usual type of wealthy person who goes out there to escape humanity or to become interested in ceremonies, dance or legend of the Indians and who does not care a damn for the actual spoliation of Indians or Mexicans there. It's too much of a damned escape from reality ... so beware ... beware.

What have you been writing? Still on short stories ... or have you attempted biography? Anyhow the main thing is to write and only show your stuff to writers otherwise you'll become a 'tea hound' reading stories to people who think you're wonderful and a writer instead of keeping quiet suffering as if you were trying to give birth to an elephant and feeling the silliest idiot under the sun. Which are you going to be – a tea hound or the silliest fool? That's an important question to settle. Do you know of the American Poetry Society?[237] Well, it consists I think of 95% women who read poems every now and then and feel they have justified their delicate existences. So beware!

I don't seem to have been reading anything for a long time. The best short stories I have read have been Liam O'Flaherty, *The Mountain Tavern*[238] and Gogol and Dostoevski. Gogol is published in one volume but Dost. takes 5 volumes. He's hard to read but somehow or other you should make up your mind to read him later on. Some of the short stories you could read, I think. They will upset all your views if you have any on writing, but his fundamental understanding of people is the best I know. I'll look up a book of his and send it to you.

Mary Sinclair: *The Three Sisters*. That's a really good book.
Malroux: *Man's Fate* is the best novel I have read for years.
Franz Kafka: *The Castle*, an imaginary true story, the best of its kind I have ever read. Difficult to get. He's dead now, Kafka.
Virginia Wolff: *Orlando*, imaginative.
Meier-Graefe *Vincent Van Gogh*: based on Vincent's letter to Theo on which Meier-Graefe saturated himself but if you can somehow get the letters and read them you will find them the best approach to creative work of any I know. They show you what creative work means, the sweat and blood in it, and not the tea side.

I might go on like this but what's the use; you'll be bored or may have your own standards of judgment. Can you speak Spanish now fluently and have you done any more work on their vocabulary there as compared with Spanish in Spain? That could be of interest to you, to quietly study the conservative element in a colony of Spain for always in a colony the older forms of language are preserved.

How's Mary … Mary I can't think of her name, Mary Hamlin that's it, anyhow it doesn't matter about the tail end. Is she still hefty and strong and nice. She was a comfort to look at when one viewed some of the 'arty' types in the valley.

New York is alright in its way. If you want to see any plays or movies or if anything has to be arranged about publishers or assignments then one has to be in the city. But otherwise, just a big mess unless one lives quietly to oneself. Have you heard from Ella Young or do you know her address; if so I would like to have it as I want to send her some poems. I was going to send you a long letter, but I have to stop now. Please tell your mother I have a letter under way but am too distracted to write.

With love,
Ernie

Georgia O'Keefe has been operated on; but I saw Stieglitz the other day.

[New York]
9 April 1935

Mrs Helen Golden,
Rio Chiquito, Ranchos de Taos, New Mexico

Dear Merriam,

Thanks very much for your letter and the enclosed letter. It had been sent in triplicate to all my once addresses and for all its importance and urgency, it was neither.

I have been sick with pneumonia and am going on to John T. to lead a quiet life for a few weeks. I really only see him when I am a hospital case, and it is really mean but he likes me to be in the house to talk to, so I don't feel as if I was in his way. I intend to return to Ireland soon but don't mention the fact for it is very important that I get into the country without being met at the boat by officials from the Ministry. If I can arrange about my pension I'll stay at home from some years.

Writing has been very bad. I'm fed up with it. The book is now at the 9th publisher, but I have had a few decent letters from publishers; however, that is no consolation as I have a great contempt for them because they won't adhere to their protestations. If a book is bad they keep it for months. And so I am going to rewrite the book in Ireland for myself and forget about it. I have written 7 short stories, but they're bad, I know, and so do editors; so I have no ill feelings there. Of the poems I had 6 accepted by *Poetry* but selling things is a difficulty. You have, if unknown, to pave the way with introductions, 5 introductions to pass a fairly bad poem and that upset me. So that's another reason to get back, sit down for a year or more and forget about writing.

I haven't been doing any reading for a long time except poetry. I was making an anthology of my own from contemporary Irish, British, and American poets, and it meant a lot of work. It saves referring to books and being too much bored by reading bad stuff. I also have made an anthology of Irish poetry, a rather large one from Old, Middle and Modern Irish with some translations of my own, but I will have to go to Connemara and tackle the language before I can continue the translations.

I have been seeing a number of plays so you might like to know what the city is doing. The Group Theater are working almost as a party group; they help the Theatre of Action,[239] the Artef[240] and the 14th Street Group. It seems to me that only these groups are alive now. The Group is presently on 44th Street Belasco and the Longacre, the Artef is on West 48th St and the 14th Street Group is as you know Eva Le Gallienne[241] or at least was. That means that revolutionary plays command audiences and indeed they are the most worthwhile plays in the city. They are able to carry on in competition with Broadway.

Of the 14th Street Group I have seen three plays:

Stevedore[242] (negro workers problems)
Sailor of Kathare (attempted revolution in 1917 in Austrian Navy)
Black Pit (worker who turns stool-pigeon due to economic forces)

All were good and moving. The last seemed to me to be one of the best. Starts well, high emotional tension and a good study of company monopoly in the South.

Of the Group's work I have seen:

1. *Success Story*, J. Lawson, story of a radical seduced by power.

2. *Gold Eagle Legacy*, Levi, dealt with the sanctimonious development of a man who gets rich in the California gold rush and wins his way to power.

3. *Awake and Sing* (Odets), study of a Jewish family in Bronx; one of the younger generation decides that he is going to fight to change conditions.

4. *Waiting for Lefty* (Odets), the best of them, study of taxi drivers' strike in New York of last year and the machinations of the AF of L and the resolution of the members to adopt direct action.

5. *Until The Day I Die* (Odets), Nazi Germany: a communist arrested is made to seem a traitor by being brought round by his captors well dressed in lorries – his comrades believe these stories (Nazi stories) and the worker has to shoot himself to save his name.

Cliff Odets is a Group Actor and if he doesn't write too many plays will be good. I have heard last Friday a new play of his read, *Paradise Lost*. He will have to work on it and have it ready for next year. He is really good but as there is a big demand for his plays he may have to turn out stuff such as (5) written in 4 days which is loose and really bad but has excellent points and situations.

ARTEF: *Recruits*[243] is Yiddish. The best play in town. Theatre seats about 400. Stylised play.

Noah: fair, a very good French actor. I saw the Moscow Art[244] (they're not the Moscow Art but Chekhov their leading player is) in *The Inspector General* and *Marriage* both of Gogol and both to me fine. Chekhov is amazingly good.

The Green Pastures:[245] interesting with a background of negro songs.

Saw Katherine Cornell[246] in *Romeo and Juliet* – she was fine but the others were bad. She had no one to play up to her simple sturdiness and it was all wrong focus, save in the last act. Mac Runty,[247] Aherne,[248] an Irishman in hose, seemed to be trying to prove he wasn't a fairy by displaying his sex as much as he could.

MOVIES

Life is Beautiful[249] (Russian) one of the best. Photography poor but the approach to everything interesting. It compares with *The Road to Life*[250] which is up to now the best picture I have seen.

Chapayev[251] (Russian) story of a guerilla leader in civil war: good, much action but human.

Moscow Laugh (Russian comic) not so good but fresh and light. Contrasts well with the Hollywood idea of humour.

I saw Paul Strand's Mexican photos. They are his best, I think. He gives all that deep sorrow and endurance of the Mex. mestitos and Indians and in the women at times a hope of resurgence. He has taken people who did not know they were being taken at markets, in doorways and so they do not pose; also they sit so quietly that they are easy to concentrate on. He has done strange things with sky in relation to white adobe. Best of all are his studies of Mexican images of saints selected for what they tell of the people who pray through them. He has chosen random Christs and groups but the pictures tell more of the Mexican point of view than anything I know that explains a religious sense.

I would like if you could dig up a series of notebooks in which I took notes when in Mexico;[252] about 5 or 6 of them in the form of a rough objective diary and my copies of the *Dial*.[253] It is hard to get and I would like to have it with some copies of *The Arts*. I will send you on some money for postage and an address to which they can be sent.

It has been very upsetting deciding to go and waiting for publishers' decisions so for the past 3 months I have been mostly sick and irresolute. Last year being so hard I organised New York so that I could be invited out to dinners about 4 nights a week, but they became too hectic and they were mostly society or semi-society functions and in the end I decided it was much better to be hungry.

This is a hurried letter as you can see but the best I can do under the circumstances. I will write again when I get to Boston and try to make it a letter that means something.

Love to all,
Ernie

NO. 72 EOM PAPERS NYU
Letter to HH (on way to Japan)

[c/o John T. Hughes,
122 Englewood Ave,
Boston, Massachusetts]
23 April 1935

[Helen Hooker,
San Francisco, California][254]

Dear Helen,

Thanks for your long letter and photographs.[255] I liked the one where I sat down for then I could see my beloved shoes in direct relation to the rest of my body. Thanks also for getting rid of some of my stuff.

I'm just back from Harvard and am trying to get this off in time as I was too screwed up about the lecture to reply to your letter.[256] As usual I worked so much on it that I nearly wrote a book of notes on Sunday and Monday and had enough material for 8 lectures. I really should write out lectures fully for then I would have a series of small booklets. The boys took it very well and liked it, so the professors said. Anyway they gave me a very warm send off. But I was nervous enough and was thinking in terms of what I might have done and worrying about time, looking at a professor's watch. And I'm glad that's over. I tried to compare writing in English by Irishmen, with the Anglo-Irish school that began in 1890, and with Gaelic literature of 7th to 10th centuries, to construct from all 3 what would help the literature the future has to make. (Where's your notebook?)

Somehow you don't seem to have really gone yet. I suppose I don't believe it. Anyhow I don't want to. This place is so quiet and pastoral save for the dinners Mr Hughes has tried to make me attend until I struck because I wanted to sit down quietly and read. Lectures, however, are good because they make me work in terms of a definite theme and then resolve the information into some form; but they're pretty bad for me until they're over.

When you have finished this trip you'll be a rotarian and will want to start Garden Clubs all over Ireland. I can't see you much as a clubwoman but I'm afraid that's what will happen.

I'll have to go and see Weeks soon. He was rather nice to reply to me at length but there's nothing we can do together on the book now.

I'm glad Blanchette liked the photos because I liked her. She was simple, in the good sense, and easy to talk to. I liked her a great deal, and since have been worried about her.

Oh dear, but its hard to write a letter in a hurry. My head is in a whirl after that talk today and I don't seem to have anything to say much, not about ordinary things anyhow. Are you supposed to remember the names of all the ladies on the trip and will they tell you all about their sons and their enthusiasms? Some people get confidential on the ocean and spill whole cartloads of emotion on one's head.

I think things seem to have worked out as reasonably well as we might have expected. I don't know what false moves we made or how the situation might have been improved. It seems alright as I look at it now and if you think so also there is nothing much to worry about. I regret that Miss O'Brien[257] has to go into the furniture removing business, for that's what my books mean. That mass of books has stopped me from writing so I look on them with a mixture of pleasure and enmity. The next time I always say I'll bring the Bible and Shakespeare, but though I've read the latter often enough I've never got down to the former. Possessions come too much between one and the sense of reality, even books do that, so I'll have to reform. You'll be allowed one sketch pad in Connemara and myself one book.

How is Adelaide bearing up and are there any people of your ages with you? I hope your mother is very well and that you are all enjoying San Francisco. It's a lovely city, I think, and I like its people. They have a friendly and a spacious sense (Due to mixture of Spanish and Irish?). If you meet Ray Boynton, a fresco painter there, you might give him my regards. When do you reach Tokyo? I won't hear from you for another month or so then, maybe. It will be best to enclose your letter for me in the one you send to Paddy. I expect things will be smooth, but I'd better be certain first. Your postcards from Omaha have just arrived. I like the station.

I hope you are feeling settled and somewhat happy. There's nothing either of us can do now except adjust ourselves to two very different series of conditions and keep as physically fit as we can. It's hard that you should be away when the buds are about to come out and there's a sense of spring. I feel quite warm inside whenever I think of you but there's so much I would like to talk to you about that it seems hard to have you so far away. Please adjust your mind anyhow as I will, to absence and be kind to your mother.

> With my love always,
> Ernie

NO. 73 EOM PAPERS NYU
Letter to HH

[Return address] J.P. Malley,
Hibernian Bank, College Green,
Dublin, Ireland
[Sent from New York]
8 May 1935

Helen Hooker,
c/o Garden Club of America,
SS Tatsuta Maru, Japan Tourist Bureau,
Kyoto, Japan

Dear Pussy Cat,
(Please seal your envelope: all I received were open except one. It may be accident but it seems strange)

Monday (29th) was a good day with me for I received your letter when I reached Brookline and outside the door on the top wooden step was a large envelope with photos and another letter. I seem to begin a letter backways. On Saturday 27th I went with the Chanlers, Maria and Teddy, up to their place at Harvard,[258] up about 40 miles from Boston. It was warm and springy. Their son, Ig, was engaged to be married to a Protestant and she for the past month is becoming a Catholic getting ready for her wedding in June. Maples looked apple-red in the distance and it wasn't until next day that I found maples had a furry deep red-brown blossom. There were daffy-down-dillies,[259] crocus, blue and yellow, hyacinth, and best of all, three Irish larch trees in bloom. The trees had a soft green spikey, fur and then a brown knob and the green against the slender stem was more a sign of spring to me than the pink-red maples. Also there were two kinds of birches, one dark looking without leaves, very handsome, like a girl with dark eyebrows or Paddy, my brother, and a white satiny bark with very soft olive-green leaves. By this you'll think I belong to a garden club but I can't help it. I was there for two days and just sat down looking at the near hills, indigo and blue, and the flowers. There were six Japanese plum trees, Maria (Mrs Chanler) said eventually they were Chinese but then she knew I don't like Japanese and she likes Ireland. Two of the trees bloomed whilst we were there. The pink petals open out into a white or slightly pink leaf, and they open in 24 hours; then the petals are blown away in an hour. But they opened when I was there. Maria said it was the oriental custom to wish when they opened. Well, I wished you were there with me, then I knew that was really impossible to have you really there, so I wished that you might feel the peace I felt during those two days in the country. I feel rested now and much nearer to you now that I have really touched earth again. This morning Ig, who has a monoplane, took me into Boston in the early morning. Do you think you would like to use a plane? It's very exciting to me. Ig, like Lindbergh,[260] has a 'bird' sense, feels insecure on the ground but really lives in the air. He can only appreciate country from on high. That's the trouble about your being away. When I really feel anything most I miss you most, but I'm glad I have been able to tank up on the countryside. That will do me until I smell the sea on the way over.

I saw the Russian players in Boston during a Chechov evening. You remember we had intended to go and didn't. There was a one act play by Anton Chechov, at least it's down as a one-act, but it's really the dramatisation of a story. A study in temperament which oozed all over the place, eventually most of the principal characters were in a state of coma due to overuse of temperament. A *Jubilee* was the name of the one act. The funniest thing was a stiff Boston lady in front of me who would not unbend – looked around in surprise-astonishment at my prolonged applause.

Part of my lecture was a study of the Irish understanding of actuality. Living is so fantastic and strange and un-understandable that they accept the supernatural or that which cannot be explained as the actual, and with the actual they reverse the effect. The dead are almost closer to us at home than the living and things called 'miracles' seem to fit into life like toast and cream. Modigliani felt that as did a number of distortionists, but why'd I draw it in here I don't know.

I went down to Providence to see a very fine priest, an Irish Franciscan. I asked him about a marriage ceremony. He was very understanding. The Franciscans you know really believe in the spirit of the church and not its organised form so they are mostly always rebels. He said that a marriage between Catholic and non-Catholic can take place in a Catholic church only when the non-Catholic agrees to sign that the children will be brought up Catholics. Even then it is not a full ceremony, that can only take place between professing Catholics. If I marry you in any other circumstances it means I am outlawed from the Church. It would mean a civil marriage. So at last I am clear on that.

I am back in New York now. I phoned Miss O'Brien. Barbara's pouch has arrived and I must get it. I tried to see if I could get away to-morrow but couldn't so I have to wait a few days. I have it all now: a small trunk, 6 boxes, a typewriter, 2 bags, 2 grips and a pile of rugs, not including 3 bags at Theodora's which Miss O'Brien couldn't get as I wasn't there to identify them and no one in the building knew which were mine and which were not. I was going to take a boat to-morrow morning and say to hell with the books, I'll get on without them.

A bus is a strange thing to travel in.[261] I came over last night. It was very wet. Behind me a woman who had met a friend by accident. He, it seems, was connected with some choir in New York and she was very vivacious and intelligent and had been his pupil once. They discovered a member of the Boston symphony in the bus. And I gathered a great deal of their lives through their almost uninterrupted talk. I thought of you so much all that journey that it hurt. In the morning I could see the trees in fine spring colours, very beautiful against the soft morning light, and we had only one trip into the country together,[262] and here was I coming back over the same road, for a time. So many things I have striven for have never had any physical realization that I began to think even, that something would come between to upset our eventual reunion in the flesh. I was trying to prepare my mind for it, but I could find no consolation. I have had to spread certain ideas and upset others, whereas a person like your father has built up something tangible to tower his pride and his sense of pride and to compensate for work done. However, we'll fight it in our own way. A bus gives you a strange feeling of people asleep, half-asleep, half-conscious, grunty and somewhat ugly, and yet an intimate feeling as if you felt a little about their lives.

I received all the photos, thanks. It was nice of you to send me the snaps from Carmel. I have had a canvas envelope so that I can carry 3 of yours in my pocket. Of the ones you took by the river I like best the one of me sitting down because I can see my shoes, but I think I told you that before, and of yours I'm not sure. I like them all.

You took the key of the trunk with you! I don't seem to like New York any longer, perhaps that's because you are away from it. For the past 3 weeks I have been in a strange world. I'm not in America and I'm not in Ireland and so I sit and try to think with one fourth of what used to be my head: and it doesn't seem to matter whether I try to do something or not, so the sooner I find myself on the other side the better for myself. I'm not going to see Eunice[263] or anyone. I did think of calling Blanchette by phone to say goodbye, but I know I won't do that. You did not tell me your plans, I mean dates of leaving and sailing and when to get you by mail. Will you please do so as otherwise I won't know when to get you. Until to-day I had not thought of air mail. Miss O'Brien says this will get to Japan in 48 hours. I don't quite believe it. I expect to be in Ireland by the 19th so please let me know details so that I won't miss you by letter. It's hard enough to miss you as much as I do and I regret I advised you go but it can't be helped now. I went through the Chinese collection in the Boston Museum to keep in touch with you. Please kindly remember me to your mother and Adelaide. I know it isn't as bad for you as it is for me not to be able to see you now that I am in New York again.

With all my love,
Ernie

Letter to HH

> *[Return address: J.P. Malley,*
> *Hibernia Bank, College Green,*
> *Dublin, Ireland]*
> *[Sent from New York]*
> *Thursday night [10 May 1935]*

[Helen Hooker,
c/o Garden Club of America,
SS Tatsuta Maru, *Japan Tourist Bureau,*
Kyoto, Japan]

Dear Helen,

Just before I go I hope you are having a nice time with the garden girls. The enclosed may open up research work for them.[264] I saw Miss O'Brien to-day and thanked her for packing my things, and, through her, sent my regards to Blanchette. I got a very fine tobacco pouch from Barbara. I hope I don't lose it. Yesterday I lost my pipe. To-day I lost one of my gloves. It's well I haven't a hat, but the losses are symbols because I know I can leave all my possessions behind and not really care a rap. Are you a possession; you mustn't be because I couldn't think of leaving you behind.

I saw Ben and Vivian. They had their apartment furnished and were very happy looking. It has helped Ben a great deal and has made him more tender. Both attend classes in the Worker's School.[265] Also I saw Theodora. She's trying to make up her mind to be married and I advised her to stop thinking of herself as important, take a train and get married. She said she would. She also is attending classes at the Worker's School for her boy is a Communist. This is not official, so please forget about it, but I thought you might like to know. She is really different these times and much nicer. I phoned Maraquita to take her to lunch but she's in Washington so I can't see her, and I wanted to. She has been nice to me in a very genuine way, and also I met you through her.

That is all the news I can give you except to tell you how much I love you. Is that news? As at school I am ticking off days until I see you again but at school holidays ended on a definite date and we have no definite date, which is distressing. I went to that Italian restaurant on 48th St with Dr Murray, he of the paintings, and drank Chianti, but I didn't enjoy it at all: the other associations of the place were so missing that I could hardly eat there. I expect this sounds, as we used to say if anyone complained in our family, like a long moan, but I don't complain to anyone else and I wish I were away from New York, but I can't see it when you're away. I hope you are keeping fit and that you are not in any way worried. It will be so nice to have a note, perhaps, from you when I reach the other side. I wish we were starting off together. Please kindly remember me to your mother and to Barbara.

> With all my love,
> Ernie

PART III

Dublin and the West of Ireland, 1935–1944

EOM and HH fell in love in New York, but since he wished to leave America and return home, he would not marry her until she had seen Ireland. He knew in 1935 that he would receive sufficient pension for his 1916–24 military service to marry, settle down, and plan to return to his medical studies. He also wanted to secure the publication of his now completed memoir that had not been well received by American publishers. He had published some poems and thought he could write and publish some more but ultimately did not pursue this. He felt the few short stories and essays he had written in America were not publishable. And so EOM and HH planned that she would go on a garden tour to Japan with her mother and sister, Adelaide, and then continue on through Korea, China, Mongolia and across Russia to meet EOM in London and go on to Dublin. Meanwhile EOM had returned to Ireland in May 1935 and was exploring other possibilities for his livelihood, while living at his family home in Dublin.

Letter to John Raleigh

[St Kevin's,
7 Iona Drive, Glasnevin, Dublin]
4 June 1935

[John Raleigh,
St Joseph's Street, Limerick]

Dear Johnny,

I hope you and Bea and the Four Evangelists are well.[1] Did the swelling go down in the children's hands? I expect they should have orange juice or tomato juice. Kevin says it's a run down condition so perhaps their food should be changed a little.

I delayed in replying because there was nothing much to report on. I saw Aiken but he remarked 'You're pretty well fixed now' and did not discuss anything specific though he did mention a certain line of work. I remained over night at his place near the mountains. I met de Valera. At first he wanted me to run for South Dublin and so did most of his Cabinet who were with him, but I put them off and acted, for me, very diplomatically. Next day I saw him, discussed a line of work which it was proposed I might take up when I felt fit. That I said would be in three months' time, no salary mentioned so I don't know if it is confirmed or not, but I know I can definitely start in on that work whenever I feel fit. Dev was really nice and considerate. I'll tell you what he suggested when I see you. He was in a hurry, but I told him I really wanted the pension fixed up as I owed money in the USA and needed some to go on with to get back my health. He said he would see Aiken about it. It may take a month, he said, or more. I don't intend to be confirmed in any work until the pension is settled. Then I can be free to settle my own affairs and look for a job independent of a government, if necessary.

That's all I have to say and that explains the delay. I will go down on next Tuesday or Wednesday to Limerick, and then go on to Connemara. Could you please find out from the Stewarts about the Hotel of the Isles. How much per week and per month or the possibility of learning Irish there.[2] I really would like to spend a month or 6 weeks there and then go on to Kilkee for a few weeks.

Will you please thank Bea for her kindness to me. I felt very much at home and I liked the children very much, especially my girl Peggie. Please don't mention the proposed job to anyone. For the past few days I'm trying to clear the dust off my books in the study, but I do have to get in a man for a few days as every book had to be dusted individually. Are you thinking of coming to town?

I am keeping out of the way of everyone save for a few old friends whom I knew apart from the movement. I seem to be thoroughly suspect by every side. If that will suit you I'll go down on Tuesday or Wednesday and then later to Galway. Please give my love to Bea and the children. Is there anything I can do for you here?

Affectionately,
Ernie

Letter to John Raleigh

[St Kevin's,
7 Iona Drive, Glasnevin, Dublin]
Tuesday [c.12 June 1935]

[John Raleigh,
St Joseph's Street, Limerick]

Dear Johnnie,

I had to see some kind of a commission on Saturday and will have to remain until next Saturday to see them again.³ They wanted to know if I could tell them anything about Con Moloney⁴ as to when he was appointed Adjutant General. Do you know? It must have been on the 4th or 5th of July 1922 or later. Do you know when Sean Moylan⁵ was appointed Director of Operations or Deputy Chief of Staff? They seem to think the Moylan appointment more important in relation to me. I hope the process won't take any longer. I expect I will be able to go down on next Monday. You did not reply to the questions I asked about the hotel. Could you please find out, otherwise I'll hike off to Donegal or Kerry.

I hope Bea and all the children are very well; are their fingers any better and has Peggy got rid of the cough. Kevin and I were down in Galway this weekend near the Shannon. We saw the Tobins.⁶

Affectionately,
Ernie

NO. 77 EOM PAPERS NYU
Letter to HH

[St Kevin's,
7 Iona Drive, Glasnevin, Dublin]
1 July 1935

[Helen Hooker,
c/o Garden Club of America, Japan]

Dear Helen,

Thanks for your long letter which you sent May 29th on train from Kyoto and for the others forwarded before you reached Japan. They, by the way, were frittered badly as the outside envelope became undone and was reclosed in the Post Office here and so the use of a covering letter exists no longer.

I got your telegram but couldn't make it out, save that you would stay at Peking. No date added. I wrote to Miss O'Brien asking her for your definite itinerary with dates but in the meantime your letter came from Kyoto and I now know. Also I could not find the typewriter at Keanes'.⁷ It had been left there with my things by Miss O'Brien in the trunk room. I looked at the heap of packages and boxes when I reached New York and thought the typewriter was in a box. I had to leave in a hurry four days later and the night before sailing could not find the typewriter. Mrs Keane suggested that it was in one of the nailed-up boxes. The janitor next morning before I sailed said he had never seen a typewriter and so I was convinced, having no time to phone Miss O'Brien, that the t-w was in a nailed box. However, when I arrived in Cobh[8] I declared a t-w but none could be found. I wrote then to Keane and Miss O'Brien, that must be nearly 5 weeks ago, but have not received a reply. I told Miss O'Brien to tell me the price and I would forward the money because it is yours, but given by your mother and so I must replace it.

I became acclimatized in a few weeks. June was a wet month and so I could not go to the sea and mountains to learn Irish. Icebergs have come very far South this year and have upset our weather. They have upset me also as it means I have to stay in cities. I had thought by the end of July that I would have had two months of warm weather and then would have been ready to settle down to work at a job offered to me, but now it's the first week in July and I'm trying to cut the book for a prospective publisher.[9] I have already cut the first 5 chapters, 7,000 words and feel very proud whenever my score mounts up in cutting. That may mean another week or more of indecision.

Everything so far has gone very well. I had a satisfactory interview about pension; indeed the judge suggested I apply for service which I was entitled to but was leaving out. Then two jobs were suggested. I wish you had been here as you would have been more interested in the one I did not accept. The other I accepted tentatively to begin work in August, but I know I can leave it to October or November if I wish.

Now if I begin work soon I'll have to rent a house and if I rent it it'll have to be for a year I expect. If I was thinking of myself it would be easy as I could think of a few places I would like and then look for a house there, or have one built. A contractor friend of mine in the S/W[10] says he will build free for me within a decent radius of his home.

I do wish you were here however for many reasons besides the very personal one that it seems impossible to live happily without you. The weather breaks usually in October and then becomes chilly. I don't know how you can become acclimatized if you come late in the year. I found it difficult even in May but I adjust quickly. The long twilights now are beautiful but are closing in; however there is fine light up to 10:45 at night. In June there was light till 11:30 or 12 midnight. If the weather does not clear up here I'll go to Spain for a month or six weeks and climb, say from middle of July to end of August. If it clears I'll spend a month or more in the islands[11] and mountains here and then begin work or I walk abroad for another month. That would bring me to September. I would like to be free if I knew very definitely what time you intend to come here, but now I see no chance of getting a reply quickly. Peking is in some danger it seems, and I don't even know if you'll go on there now; and if you don't go on I don't know what you intend to do. This distance and the fact that I did not know definitely your itinerary has made things uncertain for me. If I go abroad it will be the devil to find me as I will have no fixed address in the mountains. So I expect I'll rent a house within a month or more and leave my things there; then I can come back to it whenever I want to.

Anyhow I'll send this letter on chance. You may go on to Peking after all. I asked you for two months' grace and that will end on the 20th of this month July, but indeed things were so easy to again adjust to that 3 weeks grace would have been sufficient. Anyhow you have I hope cleared off your debt; that after all was one of the deciding factors in your going away so I hope you are clear of this. I can let you have some money any time you need it, up to £100; if you were in a corner you could wire direct to my brother at the bank[12] and I will arrange that he forward it to you.

Japan seems far away and what you have been doing so far little related to the realities of life here, but please come as soon as you can, but I don't want you to upset any plans you both have made. It would be well for you, on coming here to know customs regulations. I don't know whether you will go on to Peking now and so I am writing a detached letter. Please read between the lines how much I miss you ...

This new pen writes very fine; it makes my letter harder than ever to read I fear. I have not read a book since I came back but I have done a certain amount of work on archaeology. A friend of mine is in charge of a section in the Museum. I have visited counties to look up certain Romanesque 12th century details, but I am putting off another inspection until you come. I am very content to be back and to feel definitely related to something that is of your blood and bones. I am trying to prepare an archaeological map for you in periods for each county then I can later hand it over to the Irish Tourist Association.[13] The trouble at present is for a place to put my books in. My study shelves at home, the study about the size of my room in the village, all lined two deep so that I cannot get at anything without deep digging. Thanks very much for the shirt; will I have to wear a silk hat with the black kimono?

I'm glad you saw some good sculpture. That is always fine to see. I wish you could have been with me when I went to the sculptured doorway of Clonfert Cathedral;[14] the door was practically intact although most of the rest of the church has been burned innumerable times. Even to study sculpture here one needs to be a bit of an archaeologist. I'm stopping now. Please wire as soon as you get this and tell me what you intend to do for I want to you here. The country is amazingly beautiful I think, but I don't know if I confuse my aesthetics with my actual love of every square inch of it. I hope you'll be able to give a detached opinion. I hope Adelaide is well and that her articles and movie camera are working to her satisfaction.

With all my love (and excuses for a short letter – the uncertainty of this reaching you),

Ernie

I like your snap. The others being large were hard to fit in my pocket book. If there's anything you can get on Japanese or Chinese poetry, please bring along some.

In August 1935 Paul Strand visited EOM in Dublin as he was travelling to New York from Russia, but he never returned to compile a book of photographs of Ireland as EOM had hoped he would. HH's older sister, Adelaide Hooker, had accompanied her on her round-the-world trip to Japan and thence London. HH ventured on to Dublin and after visiting there agreed to marry EOM. The couple married in London and in attendance were Adelaide and Mrs Belinda Sheridan, as well as EOM's siblings, Cecil and Kathleen. Knowing that there would have been difficulty in seeking HH's father's approval of the proposed marriage, they decided to proceed without prior official family approval. Thereafter they returned to Dublin, settling into Rathmines, while EOM restarted his medical studies and HH, now HHOM, became pregnant.

NO. 78 EOM PAPERS NYU
Telegram to HH

Dublin, Ireland
[Early September 1935]

HELEN HOOKER
GRAND HOTEL MOSCOW
WILL SEE YOU IN LONDON IF YOU FORWARD YOUR LONDON ADDRESS
ERNIE

NO. 79 EOM PAPERS NYU
Letter to Elon H Hooker[15]

Swiss Hotel,
34 Fitzwilliam Square, Dublin
13 October 1935

Mr Elon H. Hooker,
Hooker Electro-Chemical Co.,
Lincoln Building, 42nd Street,
New York City, USA

Dear Mr Hooker,
    We were both pleased to receive your cable in London. I know how trying the circumstances have been for you, but I hope you will realize that owing to the fact that I had to begin medicine at my University and to our desire to have at least one member of your family present,[16] it seemed wiser to get married quietly, so that we might be able to settle down to a fixed programme of work in Dublin this winter. We expect to move into our home[17] in a week's time. I hope I will have the pleasure of meeting you on your next visit to Europe, and that you will stay with us in Dublin.
                    Sincerely yours,
                    Ernest O'Malley

Letter to Military Pensions Bureau, Dublin, regarding Jim Moloney[18]

> *229 Upper Rathmines Rd, [Rathmines, Dublin]*
> *15 March 1936*

To Whom It May Concern:

I first met Jim Moloney in August, 1919. I was then attached to GHQ Staff and had come down from North Tipperary Brigade to meet some of the brigade staff of South Tipperary. He gave me an idea of the strengths of posts in and around Tipperary.

In May, 1920, I was working in the South Tipperary Brigade area. Moloney was then in charge of Intelligence in the Tipperary Battalion. He helped the Brigade Staff and myself in our attempts to organise Intelligence. During June of 1920, and at subsequent dates, I held officers' classes in Tipperary. Intelligence was then so organised that I was able to hold classes without enemy interference.

He supplied information which helped us in the attack we made on Hollyford Barracks (May, 1920?). He supplied information about the barracks at Limerick Junction, which it was proposed to attack. He gave me information about the movements of a convoy from Lisvernane to Tipperary. I waited for the convoy but it did not appear that day.

Later, in July, he forwarded information to me about the movements of enemy troops between Tipperary and East Limerick, but my proposed ambush did not materialize.

In May, 1921, I was in the Tipperary (4th) Battalion of South Tipperary. Moloney, who had been battalion Quartermaster, was now Adjutant. He took part, with members of the Divisional Staff, in an attack on police at Bansha. A few nights later I organized an attack on Tipperary town; about sixty men were co-operating. Moloney was selected for one of the bombing squads that night. The attack was called off at the last moment.

At that time I was in charge of the Second Southern Division; our Headquarters was in his battalion area, and rather close to Tipperary town.[19] I was in constant touch with the battalion officers. Their team work was good and the Division made extra calls on their time.

I was in touch with Moloney during the Truce when he helped to organise classes in his battalion, and he contributed to our advance on Limerick in March of 1921, and I was able to see the results of staff work in his area until I left the Division in April of 1922.

Later, after hostilities broke out between the IRA and troops of the Provisional Government, he was GHQ Director of Communications.

He was a good intelligence officer, painstaking and methodical. He was energetic and conscientious in the other positions he held. He was level-headed at Battalion Councils, and always eager for fight. Next to the Commandant, I considered him the best officer in his battalion.

> Signed,
> Ernie O'Malley

Letter to John and Bea Raleigh

229 Upper Rathmines Rd, [Dublin]
26 April 1936

[Mr and Mrs John Raleigh,
St Joseph's Street, Limerick]

Dear Johnny and Bea,

We both reached Dublin alive a few days ago. We had a fine time, and Helen is in good form after it, despite what you think. Our main trouble was plates for the big camera. We went on to Dysert O'Dea, Kilfenora, Termona, Kilmacduagh, Athenry, Tuam, Sligo, Drumcliff, Enniskillen, Devenish Island, Donaghmore, Arboe (on Lough Nenagh), Donaghmore, near Newry, and then home.

Some of the photos are good. We broke the lamp globe[20] in Kilfenora and that was a bit of a loss. An old man beyond Sligo sat beside Helen and showed her the country. 'Do you see that big house. Well that belongs to the landlord, a fellow called – and if he came back here the people i'd eat him and they wouldn't wait 'til they were hungry either.'

All the family are in good from. Kevin was sick for a week or so but is alright again now. We were down in Glendalough on Sunday but the rain came down hot and heavy on us. When are you both coming to Dublin? Why don't you bring Bea up for the Spring Show.[21] It's vastly better than the Horse Show and more thoroughly Irish.

I have written to Frank Aiken and will let you know the result. Please give my love to Peggy, Sheila, Mary and Oona.

Thanks very much for being so kind to us. We enjoyed that run around the South. I hope you weren't utterly laid out for a week after it. Please remember me to Frank Geary, McGlynn or Glynn and Dave Duncan and Johnnie Grant.[22]

Affectionately,
Ernie

By October 1936 EOM had returned to yet another year of medical school. He was also on the verge of publishing On Another Man's Wound *in serial form with* The Irish Press *and in hardback with Rich & Cowan of London. An American edition with Houghton Mifflin under the title* Army Without Banners *was scheduled for 1937. The book covered only the War of Independence and stopped at the 1921 Truce. It was a great success, but that was only one of several distractions in EOM's life. The first child of his marriage to HHOM, Cathal, had been born in July. Meanwhile, the Spanish Civil War was raging, and EOM chaired a public panel to discuss the destruction of the Spanish Republic in early November 1936.*

THURSDAY, **Irish Independent** NOVEMBER 5, 1936.

" Irish Independent " And Spain

In view of the success of the "Irish Independent's" drive to organise, under cover of a ramp against the Spanish Government, the anti-Republican forces in Ireland, and the danger of its propaganda actually attaching to its campaign bewildered sections of Republican opinion unless some exposure of its role is attempted, a number of Republican people are arranging to meet at the ENGINEERS HALL, DAWSON STREET, on THURSDAY, NOVEMBER 5, at 8 p.m.

The Basque Government will send a Representative with a message to the meeting.

Please bring the enclosed card, which will secure, admission for yourself and two others only.

ERNIE O'MALLEY WILL PRESIDE.

Irish Independent notice, signed by Owen Sheehy-Skeffington and George Gilmore, 5 November 1936, of public meeting on Spanish Civil War to be chaired by EOM. Source: Irish Independent; EOM Papers NYU.

Letter to Eithne Golden[23]

229 *Upper Rathmines Road, Dublin,*[24]
Calvi,
[Corsica, France]
4 October 1936

Eithne Golden,
Rio de Chiquita,
Ranchos [de Taos], New Mexico, USA

Dear Eithne,

Thanks very much for your two letters.[25] I was very pleased indeed to get them with your branch of sage which flavoured the medical notes in my study drawer for many a day. Of course, I should have written but indeed I don't now write at all. I'm completely inhibited, especially to anyone in the USA.

However, as my new course[26] begins in a week or so I am full of new resolutions and one of them is to answer letters promptly, and another is to write a big number of people.

I'm writing this in a restaurant (I can't spell it) cave in Calvi, island of Corsica, a kind of sailor's dive where I'm having breakfast with Helen on a wet morning. We are leaving for Marseilles this morning and are hoping that the rain will hold off until we can bath. This is a dour, swarthy, bare country. Yesterday in the train coming down from Comte, the hills were like New Mexico, and I was suddenly homesick, but as the carriages hung at an angle over precipices I had again to think of my stomach. Have you ever been at a game of pelota? They play it in the Basque country and Mexico. You become so worn out by watching the men play that at the end of the game you are physically tired. And so yesterday, we were so tired watching the valley far below and the steep twisting curves that we were worn out when we reached Calvi.

You know that I was married, to my own surprise, that of her parents, and mine *and* herself. Now she has a baby, Cathal,[27] and had a bad time having him so we came away looking for sun and we found the sun elusive. We chased him from Cobh, outside of Cork, by sea to Havre, then to Paris, where we became broke buying books and clothes, then to Avignon. The country North by East of Avignon is very like Arizona, coloured mountains, sage, cedars in thick rows as a hedge along the roadside and cactus. I'm going to go back there someday but the mosquitos are bad. If I had lifted you with a magic hand and set you down there, you would have thought that you weren't very far from Taos.

Already I know the country below Avignon, Provence, very well. We had seen a Cézanne show in Paris,[28] the best one of his I had ever seen and here below was the country he painted from above Aix until you reach Estaques near Marseilles. I am glad I have seen that show because I could trace Cézanne's complete development ending with a huge canvas 12' by 18' of 'The Bathers' – nudes, standing and sitting under arched trees.

To get back to facts. I started medicine again last October in the National but was perturbed by publishers. An English publisher took the book at once.[29] His agent in Dublin sat up all night to finish it and then made out a contract. I stipulated that the price of the book would be 8/6 and that it be printed in Ireland. Then my troubles began as the English firm objected to many passages and were afraid of libel. Eventually I consented to the suppression of certain pages on ill-treatment, but the book kept being hung up until eventually it was published after a delay of a year and four months, in October, and I am only too glad to be rid of it. Correcting and re-correcting proofs and trying to cut down parts of it ate up my time so that I couldn't sit for my second[30] as I had intended.

I put by a copy before I sailed for your mother, but as I was in a hurry to pack I had to rush off. I had been away walking through Clare and Mayo, from close to Ennis up through Corrafin to Lisdoonvarna, up through the hills to Ballyvarney and by Corcomroe Abbey at the far end of the Burren to Galway. I took a boat to Aran, found a newly wedded couple,[31] the girl a daughter of Tommy MacDonagh executed by the English in 1916. They invited me to stay in a huge house, an empty hotel which they had rented from the local doctor for 7/6 a week. There was a ghost thrown in for the 7/6, but a polite ghost who only opened doors downstairs and never came upstairs.

The weather had been bad on the mainland but it changed suddenly and became very hot. Aran is of limestone and can be very warm. I walked all through the big island, studied the forts and crosses, climbed the cliffs and then visited the other two islands. I found a legend about myself there. The people remembered the time I landed there in 1918 and had built stories around Peadar O'Loughlin and myself.[32] Then back to the mainland walking up through Headford by lakes across the mountains to Leenane and by the mountains and Clew Bay to Westport. I went out on the islands then and sailed a lugsail again by myself and got wrecked on a very rough day, but made land eventually. And so when I returned to Dublin I saw the tail end of Helen's sister and mother who had come over to see what strange animals the Irish were.[33] I decided then we must pack one morning and look for sun, so here we are in the rain.

During the winter and spring Helen, Kevin and I worked on early Irish sculpture.[34] It has been approached from the view point of archaeology, but never from that of aesthetics. The nearest to that approach is Kingsley Porter[35] from Harvard, now dead. Kevin is my brother, now a specialist.[36] We intend to work until we have covered the field, perhaps for 4 or 5 years more. This time in France I was not as much impressed with French mediaeval sculpture. Chartres had only one good door which was perfect, and a few figures here and there in the others. Irish sculpture had changed my point of view. Only round Arles in Provence did I meet with interesting sculpture again.

There's not much left to tell you. Medicine takes up all my time, and I am eternally tempted by books and reading but this year I'll have to eliminate everything, and won't read or write anything, so I say, until I get my second in March.

Ireland is the best place after all, but next comes New Mexico. Do you think you might ever come to Ireland? There's always a bed in my study for you when you come, all ringed around with books. Do you want any books specially? If so could you please send me a list and I'll get them and forward them to you.

How is Brett? There is a rage for D.H. Lawrence in France now. I saw her book in French. How is Terence doing? Have his studies advanced well and how is Deirdre? I bought two books for her, monographs, when I was last in London, but I didn't send them to her as yet.

You asked me about Helen. Well, she has neither bow legs or a squint. She is not platinum blonde nor does she talk through her nose. She is not smaller than 4' 1½". And she likes Ireland and the people like her. Now I think I have described her perfectly. Cathal looks like four million other babies and I am getting in a sound-proof door to my study, which juts out from the house.

How is Theodora? She was to live out West. If you see her will you please give her my every affectionate regards [*sic*]. She was a good skin and a good friend. And Dorothy Stewart. I sent two of her New Mexico wood blocks to be framed and they caused a sensation. One I have in my study, a man turning a plough. If she is still interested in niches,[37] Arles and some of the towns of Provence are her meat! I have seen some very fine niches there; here also there are some, in the church are models of all kinds of boats from schooners to warships hanging up beside the side altars.

How is Mabel? Is she writing and Tony? Manuel and Antonio in the pueblo? I hope they are still alive and well. Spud, Marion, the fair Mary (now married), Preston and Helen, Harold Nash and wife. I'd better stop or I'll keep on with names, but please remember me to all whom I once knew there.

Do you hear from Ella? And do you know her address? Is there anything you think she might want from here because she might not ask for it herself.

How is Marianna's carpentry doing, and have you learned to use your hands or are you as hopeless as myself. I'm sure she had had all kinds of ideas since, from the interior decoration of Kiowa to rivaling the coffee room of the White Sisters. All notes of interrogation. And what is your mother up to? Has she ever done anything better than pear chips and that green tomato pickle? And does she take life any the more easily?

Again to thank you for being so kind as to write and to ask you to excuse me for not replying. I am full of good intentions until Sunday each week, but that day I spend out in the open and put off writing until the following Sunday which I again spend in the open. My love to your Mother, Marianna, Deirdre and Terence and to Dorothy Stewart. How is old fuss-pot; I hope she is still going strong and as gallant as ever in her outlook. She's a good skin. And if you see Ella, please give her my special love. Now please tell me what books you want and how you are doing yourself and here's a special hug for you.

Love,
Ernie

Letter to John Raleigh

229 *Upr Rathmines Rd, [Rathmines, Dublin]*
24 *November 1936*

[John Raleigh,
St Joseph's Street, Limerick]

Dear Johnny,

I hope Bea is doing well,[38] and that she is not having too bad a time, and I hope the children are in good health. I am dug into work[39] and though I don't seem to get any result from it, I am kept busy plodding. Helen is in good form and the baby is blooming. Give my love to Bea.

Ever yours,
Ernie

EOM's life was enmeshed in several activities at this point. He pursued his medical studies, but less and less enthusiastically. He was sued for libel – defamation – over his newly published book that had taken so long to write. He was helping to run the household in the absence of HHOM, who returned to Greenwich to visit her family with her first child. EOM kept a detailed diary of his reading, the music he listened to on the radio, the plays he attended, and the people he met, including Jack B. Yeats at Con Curran's in August 1937. Some of his Irish poems were published in The Dublin Magazine *that spring, and he was elected to The Irish Academy of Letters. By late 1937 EOM had lost the libel suit and had decided to stop his medical studies but pursued a Diploma in European Paintings at UCD. The O'Malleys had decided to rent a house in the west for the summer of 1938, but HHOM's father died suddenly that spring, and she had to return to America for a period. The house in Louisburgh was a great success. They continued to roam the countryside on photographic expeditions, documenting the early Irish Christian monuments and rural life.*

In late 1938 they found a permanent home in Burrishoole Lodge, near Newport, Co. Mayo, which they rented and later purchased. For the duration of the world war, they became farmers, leased additional acreage for tillage and established an almost self-sufficient operation. They found Mayo life socially and intellectually isolated and made regular visits to Dublin. Their daughter, Etain, was born in 1940 and Cormac in 1942. Cathal was effectively home-tutored. HHOM pursued her sculpture, interior decorating and domestic design but also decided to expand the outbuildings of Burrishoole to make it a modern farm. EOM enjoyed his sailing in Clew Bay, taking down folklore stories and meeting some of his former comrades, who relayed to him their own stories of the struggle for independence.

The O'Malleys kept their own moneys carefully segregated. HHOM ran and paid for the household and construction. EOM, out of his pension and royalties, paid for his boats, paintings and personal matters such as liquor, cigarettes and books. Though the world war was fought in Europe, there was little impact on the O'Malley household and few references are made to those events in his letters. Both EOM and HHOM got to know socially the German Ambassador, Dr Eduard Hempel, and his wife. EOM volunteered to lecture to the Irish Civil Defence Forces in Cork at the start of the Emergency in 1939. In his 1946–7 article, 'Renaissance', published in La France Libre, *he wrote of the rebirth that had been engendered in Ireland as a result of the Emergency, with the coming together of former comrades from both sides of the civil war and even descendants of the landed gentry to help defend Ireland.*

Letter to Madge Clifford Comer[40]

229 Upr Rathmines Rd, [Rathmines, Dublin]
18 December 1936

[Mrs Jack Comer,
Rathdowney, Co. Laois]

Dear Madge,

Greetings. I hope you are well. I'm deep in physiology and feel sorry for myself. You know I would like to see you both whenever you are in town, so if you come up before January 12th please write and come out here. After the 12th I wouldn't see the ghost of Pearse[41] even until March 5th.

This letter was really written because Sean MacGuiness asked me information about his brother Jim, now in Portumna Mental Hospital, poor fellow. The risks such as he ran weren't worthy of the little use people like myself made of his information.

His brother wants:

Position Jim held in Gearóid O'Sullivan's department.
Nature of work done for IRA Hd Qrs.
Cause of arrest by O'Sullivan.
Trial, conviction and anything else.

I have written to John Dowling and I am writing to Tod.[42]

Evidently Jim is applying for Disability Pension for him so I want to help all I can. How are the children and can my child say anything yet?[43] The baby[44] here doesn't even know me. He cries when he looks at me. That, at least, shows good judgment.

Now Madge if you and Jack do come up before the fatal date of Jan 12th, let me know.

Affectionately,
Ernie

Letter to Desmond Ryan[45]

229 Upr Rathmines Rd, Dublin
22 December 1936

[Desmond Ryan,
35 Burlington Avenue, Kew Gardens,
Surrey, England]

Dear Desmond Ryan,

Thanks for your letter.[46] Over in New York a girl told me that you would like to hear from me. This was in 1934 or 1933. She was to send me on your address, but I never heard from her since so it remains a mystery.

I don't mind being called a gunman; we were, I suppose, though we didn't use that term ourselves. And as you are a pacifist, and I respect you for your beliefs, I don't see why you shouldn't use the term.

I read *Remembering Sion* and liked it very much. Your approach was a very interesting way to telescope or capture memory. I have your other book but as I am working for my second year medical exam in March, I have to keep my fingers away from books. Frank O'Connor is working on a life of Collins.[47] I am sure it will be interesting as he has a very human person to present. I brought my story to the end of the civil war, to 1924, in fact, and the whole book should have gone together, but it was too long.

If you are ever in Dublin, I hope you will drop in to see us. And a happy Christmas now and best wishes for whatever book you will tackle next.

Sincerely yours,
Ernie O'Malley

Letter to HHOM

229 Upr Rathmines Rd, Rathmines, Dublin
February 1937

Helen O'Malley,
620 Park Avenue,
New York, NY, USA

Dearest Helen,

Everything is alright so far as I can see. I ate chicken, dutifully took my tea and later on went to bed; then I got up and ate my breakfast and so to College. Nothing very strange as you can see in all that. I played a Beethoven concerto and tried to keep warm. I discovered that the bird sings at times to attract attention.

I am sending you on a list of your records in case you are not quite sure of what you have. Anyhow we're not constrained to buy unless we like, but I expect you can test certain records which later we might order through Dublin like Symphonies of Bach or Schubert and Mozart.

I have to dash for a lecture now so I'll cease. I had a chat with Mlle Henri today. She's talking on Tuesday; the Society[48] wanted to know what she was going to say and advised her on her talk so that it would be understandable. You may consider yourself lucky that I didn't send you on more books to look up.

With my love,

Ernie

I don't know if you have the complete list of your records:

Bach	Concerto E Major
	B Minor Mass Kyrie (Christie). Are there other records of the B Minor?
	Passagaglia in C Minor 2 Records.
	Bits of Bach on back of other records
	Sarabande Partita in B Minor
	Andante Sonata No. 2 in A Major
Mozart	*D Major Concerto* violin
	A Major Concerto
Debussy	*Prelude in l'Apres Midi* 1 record
Tschaikovsky	*1812 Overture*
Stravinsky	*Dance of the Fire Bird* 1 side of 1 record
Mussorgsky	*Farewell and Death of Boris* 1 Record
Franck	*Prelude, Chorale and Fugue* 2 Records

Bathing togs[49]

Hunting Knife

Camera

Post Cards in Museum Galleries

Modern Library: Anything in this of Proust, except *Swann's Way* and *The Captive*. List of Modern Library to be sent to me

The Art News: Vol. XXXVI No. 60 March Section I Venetians; is there a Section II?

Yale Review Spring, 28, review of *Army Without Banners*

Catalogue from new private museum opened in New York

Edmund Wilson: The Triple Thinkers Harcourt Brace $2.75

Mary Colum: From these Roots Scribner $2.50

H.S. Cunnly: *The Works of Thoreau* H. Mifflin $5

Carleton Beals: *America South* $3.50

The Case of Leon Trotsky Preliminary Commission Report Harpers $3.00

W. Carlos Williams: *Life Along the Potomac River* (New Directions) $1.75
        Middletown in Transition (Harcourt Brace) $5

Philip Horton: *Hart Crane* Norton $3.0

Modern Library
Gertrude Stein: 3 Lives
Franz Boas: I have *The Mind of Primitive Man* and would like information forwarded of the rest of his work.
List of Modern Age Books, 155 E 44 send me them; I will tell you what I want.
Rebecca,[50] 100 Van Cortland Park South
Clurman[51]
Hughes, 122 Englewood Ave., 1 Brookline, Boston
F De Laurentis: History of Italian Literature
Giovanni Bellini Bassano (Jacopo)
V. Cappuccini
Giorgione	Cina da Conegliano
Titian	Bonifacio
Lorenzo Lotto	Cutena
Tintoretto	Paris Bordone
Veronese	Basaiti
Palan Vecchio	Bart Montagna

That's all for the 16th century – there are others – pupils but that's enough.

Please have a look at Philip L. Hale's *Vermeer* (Cushman & Clint $5). You don't like Vermeer, but I do.

I'm sure I'll have you all mixed up about books, so I'll postpone sending on a list I have. On 6th Avenue above 42nd near Bryant Park are shops which sell second hand magazines; you may be able to get copies of *Fortune* which had the Chicago exhibition of 1934 or 1933,[52] or whenever it was; they then had coloured illustrations of pictures in Chicago.

I told you the name of the new Collection, and I don't now remember it, given to New York by now by some millionaire lately. It had a good catalogue, I believe.

NO. 87 EOM PAPERS NYU
Letter to HHOM

229 Upr Rathmines Rd, [Rathmines, Dublin]
28 February 1937

[Helen O'Malley,
London, England]

Dearest Helen,

I hope you reached London alright. It was so cold that motors found it hard to go through many of the streets and the sides of Grafton St were lined with people wanting to see motors go through plate glass windows or smash into each other.

I have the bird for company. I find he sings to attract attention, for when I placed a piece of raisin on the top tier, he stood on his toes, and failing to reach it he sang for over an hour to attract my attention.

The name of the man in Rich & Cowan[53] who signs letters to me is D.S. Duncan, and I think I may have met him. Someone tried to act as a buffer between myself and the lawyer in 1935.[54]

You have a greater friend in Beethoven than you think. He could never keep accounts and when he had to multiply 13 by 24 he put down 13 twenty-four times, and then added the total. Mathematicians are supposed to know and understand music, but it doesn't seem to work the reverse way.

I've been thinking over records as you may suspect, and I'm inclined to keep the Bach and Beethoven with a Mozart or a Brahms to break the camel's back.

Definitely I want the 3rd and 7th Symphonies then a good specimen of (a) a piano sonata, (b) 2 String Quartets and (c) a trio.

Piano sonatas: 1. E Flat Major opus 31 No. 3

2. F Sharp Major opus 78

3. E Minor opus 90

4. F Minor opus 57

5. C Major opus 53

The last two are brilliant and the first charming so possibly your choice will be between F Sharp Major and E Minor.

There's a sonata in A Major opus 69 for violin, cello and piano which is very good but I can't have everything.

Trios: 1. B Flat opus 97

2. D Flat Major No. 1 opus 70 (neither recorded in USA)

3. E Flat Major No. 2

Probably the 1st in B Flat

Are you worn out yet? I have always liked the quartets. I have seldom heard them played.

Definitely I would like:

1) C Sharp opus 131

Then I would be torn between

2) F Minor opus 95 which is short

3) E Flat opus 127 also short (not recorded in USA)

4) the First Rasoumovsky F Major No. 1 opus 59

A Minor opus 132

So in all that amounts to 2 symphonies of Beethoven (the 9th is fine also despite the chorale), and 4 others of his, and if you feel like being rash, be rash as far as his quartets are concerned for symphonies can be tried out even in Dublin.

I played with the baby and he now knows somehow what to expect from me – nobody else does I'm sure. It's been snowing hard all day, in between terrific wind gusts, and it's really cold indoors.

If you run across Roisin's friend of the book supply store you might look out for: *Robert Schauffler's Beethoven* published 1936 by Doubleday Doran and J.W. Sullivan's *Beethoven: His Spiritual Development* you may find second hand or buy new. It's a fairly good book.

All are recorded in USA save the ones I have marked.

My last letter from R & C was Jan 20th to say that some would be included in next edition and also corrections I sent over. You might find out from Duncan how sales went in England and in Ireland.

I hope you won't rush around too much now. It looks to me as if you would have to attend at least 5 full-length concerts or more of your own choosing. Please kindly remember me to Cecil, Kathleen, your friend Winnie[55] and Mrs Emily and husband. You should look up whatever clothes you want and have a really good restock in shoes and other things. Now, I'm off to bed.

With all my love,
Ernie

And rest yourself whatever rush you may want to be in. The baby has another tooth and is looking very well. I told the nurse about reducing the bottle so I hope I understood your message, but you did not confirm it by writing.

Weather has been very snowy and slushy but to-day was fine. I have letters for you. I did not send them as I did not know of your intentions so now they can wait until you arrive. Please kindly remember me to all your friends Dr Bordan and wife and the girl who teaches history of art and whom you let down about a visit, Cecil, Kathleen. I'm trying to become a philosophical bachelor but it doesn't work any more, because I miss you a great deal.

Now be sensible and do not rush around like a bat in a belfry and take your time over your purchases. My order in records runs to £16 or £18 which I'll forward you if you need it, but that much of it is my buy.

With my love,
Ernie

Is *Portugal, a book of Folk Ways* by Rodney Gallop, Cambridge U. Press 15/ any good? You have at home:

Beethoven:	5 and 6 Symphonies
Mozart:	Symphony in G Minor
	Concerto in D Major
	Concerto in A Major
Beethoven:	Concerto No. 4 in G Major
	Concerto in D Major violin
	Concerto No. 5 in E Flat piano
Bach:	Passagaglia in C Minor
	Concerto in E Major
	B Minor Mass. Kyrie Christie No. 3, 4
Sibelius:	Symphony No. 2 in D Major
César Franck:	Prelude, chorale and Fugue
Richard Strauss:	Op. 40. Ein Heldenleben
Shostakovich	Symphony No. 1
Chopin	Op. 28 24 Prelude 4 Records
	Op. 23 Studies 3 Records

To Look Up

Bach	3 Chorale – Preludes
	Try the 3rd 'Wacher auf … ' and the other two.
	Brandenburg Concerto 6th in B Flat. Try it
	Orchestral suites
	Try 2nd in B Major for flutes and strings
	3rd in D Major
Mozart	Try Symphony in C Major [Jupiter]
	Symphony in E Flat
Beethoven:	Symphony No. 3 E Flat Major Eroica
	No. 7 A Major
	Try 4th and 8th Symphonies
	Try String Quartet
Rasumovsky	7th opus 59 in F Major
3 of these	Try 7th Sonata opus 30 No. 2 in C Minor violin and piano
	Try *17th Sonata* Opus 31 No. 2 in D Minor for Piano
Brahms	Symphony No. 4 in E Minor
	Try No. 2 in D Major Symphony very lyrical and No. 3 in F Major
Caesar Franck:	Symphony in D Minor.
Jean Sibelius	Try Symphony No. 4 in A Minor
Schubert	Try No. 7 in C Major
Von Weber	Overture to Der Freischutz

If not worn out by this try Tchaikovsky's Symphony No. 6 in B Minor
Finish with Debussy or Stravinsky

3 Nocturnes for Orchestra
La Mer Trois Esquisses Symphoniques
Iberia. Images for orchestra No. 2

Letter to HHOM

[229 Upper Rathmines Road, Rathmines, Dublin]
1 March 1937

Helen O'Malley,
c/o Dr Cecil Malley,
24 Harcourt Terrace, Earls Court,
London, England

Dear Helen,

Thanks very much for tweed. I meant to have a suit made for rough wear as all my suits made recently are too good for county wear but I need a coat and I didn't know when I'll be up here again.

Enclosed catalogue of an exhibition open until end of month

The following good:

1, 4, 5, 14, 16, 17, 27, 35[56] Nearly all interesting
Two good Norah McGuinness (19/20).[57]

I hope you are well and that Cathal is not wearing you down.

Love,
Ernie

Letter to HHOM

[229 Upper Rathmines Road, Rathmines, Dublin]
16 March 1937

Helen O'Malley
24 Harcourt Terrace, Earls Court,
London, England

Dear Helen,

Thanks for letter. So far I haven't address from Solomon's, but your rush tactics don't give one much time.

If you haven't bought the records I ask for don't buy them now.

Thanks for information about R & Cowan. No wonder they didn't advertise as the editions were very small. I'm writing this in a tram to catch post.

Paddy sent on £40 and I expect to Cecil's address as I didn't give him your new address. I didn't send any more. You'll need the money for the U.S.A.

Love,
Ernie

Letter to HHOM

[229 Upper Rathmines Road, Rathmines, Dublin]
Tuesday morning [20 March 1937]

Mrs Helen O'Malley,
Red Court Hotel,
17 Bedford Place, Russell Sq,
London, England

Dear Helen,

Thanks for your long letters. I think London will do you a lot of good by reason of meeting people, seeing some theatres; it's a pity it's not the ballet season.

I'm writing this in Roisin's office.[58] She's off on inspection with the city architect whom I congratulated on the new libraries he has built – 2 new ones now to be opened. It's a proof that live work is shown often by external results. The work done by Roisin is reflected in good architecture.

Please thank Dr B and wife for me.[59] I think records about the nicest present just now. And if you have time to spare hear as many as you can so that we can check on the information for future use. It's a pity Dublin is so slack about music as I would like to hear Brahms' symphonies again, some of his quartets and piano music and also Beethoven's.

Have you seen any painting, or are there any exhibitions?

I have slacked off for the past two weeks or more and am now going to start in again to work for June. I had a kind of an orgy reading for the past week and I will mix it up on Thursday and settle down to work properly.

If you get any of the books I wanted will you please send them on by post, also I want *Life and Letters To-day* for Dec. – Spring 2/6 each. They're slow here about ordering things.

I find it hard to write as I seem to have forgotten all about holding a pen again and when I finally set myself down I haven't an idea except to look like a catalogue in my lists.

The baby is doing well and will soon be able to stand up. The yellow jersey seems to suit him well. I have taken him into my room a few times and now he is almost used to it.

Kevin came out for dinner the other night. I sent Nancy down to Dunn's for a lobster for which I made a dressing with garlic against all purist theories of subtle tastes being allowed to strike the palate, then a boiled chicken with white sauce and cauliflower. Nancy did quite well. I have a campaign on about slamming doors. I have threatened to take off her door if she slams it but I expect I'll end by nailing all downstairs doors to a piece of wood. I have a report to present to you on the general situation. It's not yet written.

Weather has been bad. Much soft mushy snow. On one hard day of snow there was none up to Portobello bridge and none beyond O'Connell bridge but snow fell heavily in between.

Now take your ease. It's time for you to get away from the house for a while and to feel free of it. Please kindly remember me to all I know there. How is Cecil doing, and has his operation been quite successful? The house is very lonely without you. The fact that you are in the house even though I don't see you means a lot.

With my love
Ernie

NO. 91 EOM PAPERS NYU
Letter to HHOM

229 Upper Rathmines Road, Rathmines, Dublin
22 March 1937

Helen O'Malley,
Red Court Hotel,
17 Bedford Place, Russell Sq,
London, England

Dear Helen,

The address you want is Heppellys and Paris Pessaries.

The baby has another tooth.

I don't know when you'll be back, not when you say, I think, as I'm taking the car away to-morrow to wander about the country.

Love,
Ernie

NO. 92 EOM PAPERS NYU
Letter to HHOM

[229 Upper Rathmines Road, Rathmines, Dublin]
Tuesday morning [6 April 1937]

[Helen O'Malley,
Red Court Hotel,
17 Bedford Place, Russell Square,
London, England]

Dear Helen,

I'm going away for a while. I have left a file of bills and letters in the table drawer of the Library, also key of radio. Will you also if you leave again take the keys of your closets and any other keys that lock your things with you.

As my holidays officially began last Friday I began by demanding bills. Now I found that Nancy was not keeping the stubs, about 10 missing from Free[60] over a three week period.

Order 1

Nancy to be responsible for all stubs. No parcel to be taken without a stub. If so whoever takes them will be charged with their cost. I did not find the bills excessive, but I ate out most of the time to lighten the load. However there were two items of Butter and Rashers which I thought too high. I asked Nancy why rashers expressly ordered for me were being eaten by the house. She told me that no one else eats rashers during lent except myself.

Order 2

Every morning Nancy will present a list of groceries to be bought to me, or if I'm not at home, to you. She will keep a notebook entering separate items and they will be checked off by me according to her entry every morning. Yesterday I sent her out for bills and I want to pay them every Monday evening.

Order 3

Nancy to instruct the shops to send their bills in by the Monday following current week. Where bills are too small Nancy will pay them in cash on Mondays. Tea as usual came along from Bewleys for me 1 lb a week not until I mentioned the fact at the end of the 3rd week did anyone think it strange that tea should be cut down. I sent word to Bewleys that tea not be sent until a definite order be given. There should be some pounds on hand but I have not checked.

Milk: I did not check account but you have been away and I drink my usual complement with cream amounting to less than ¼ of a cup. Find out from Nurse the change in baby's diet then deduct all unnecessary milk leaving Nancy and Nurse an ample quota. Any extra milk for puddings etc. to be bought from the outside.

Laundry: Please check list and find if handkerchiefs could be washed in this house.

Cream: Order for me stands 1 carton a day i.e. 7 a week. No extra carton even without express order.

I have cut out salads.

Lilly: Lilly not to do any work such as washing up, making beds etc. except when ordered by you. She will leave when she has had her meals and has finished work.

Gas: Gas bill absolutely excessive. I ordered that fires be relit and that the gas jet for water in kitchen be not used (please put wire on it). No cooking to be done on gas range *save morning breakfast* and emergency meals. Tea for instance not to be prepared on gas stove. (This rule has been broken about tea, but you can do that check.)

Nurse not to wash her stuff in the bathroom using the jet there. She can have kettles boiled in the kitchen.

Nancy to hang up in kitchen a list of coal; the amount and when bought.

That's all I seem to be able to think of.

This kind of crisis was bound to come and I want to have supervision fixed.

When you go away I am thinking of giving Nurse and Nancy holidays with pay, of leaving the baby with mother. I can look after myself.

Now don't get into a whirlwind about the house. If these few details are put into practise and enforced it would soon become a matter of routine, but the house is like a ship on fire and no one has any responsibility here. Nancy is competent but needs great supervision. She is kindly and really looks for assistance to us.

Love,
Ernie

Please settle up all outstanding bills.

NO. 93 EOM PAPERS NYU
Letter to Elon H. Hooker

229 Upr Rathmines Rd, Dublin
5 July 1937

Mr Elon Huntington Hooker
c/o American Express, 11 Rue Scribe,
Paris 11, France[61]

Dear Mr Hooker,

I hope you are having better weather than we have here just now. Helen received your letter when we came back from a visit to the West and this is an acknowledgment of it.

We would be both very much pleased if you could spend some time at our house. The only international event of any importance which might interest you is the Horse Show which lasts from the third to the seventh of August. The American army team is for the first time represented this year. My brother,[62] who is a golfer, can arrange that you play with him in the evenings at some of the clubs near Dublin.

There is an aeroplane service between London and Dublin. Instead of returning to England to go to Scotland, you may prefer to reach Scotland through Belfast.

Helen is especially anxious that you see the baby.[63] He can now crawl and stand up.

We have suggested to Mrs Hooker that she sail on the *Caledonia* which arrives at Dublin on the first of August, but if she is unable to make the trip, we would enjoy very much entertaining you alone. If, however, you are unable to be here for the Horse Show, we will leave you to select the dates for a visit which best fit in with your plans.

Looking forward to meeting you in Ireland.

Sincerely yours,
Ernie O'Malley

Letter to Madge Clifford Comer

229 *Upr Rathmines Rd, [Rathmines, Dublin]*
28 September 1937

[Madge Comer,
Rathdowney, Co. Laois]

Dear Madge,

I got back alright about two weeks ago and ever since have been putting off the thought of writing a letter.

I had a very nice time with you and Jack, and I enjoyed it thoroughly. The sun left me almost as soon as I left your house, and I saw little else but broken weather after that. We went on through Ennis, Ennistymon and Ballyvaughan by slow stages to Galway. I met Conroy there, Isaac (why Isaac?), Padraic O'Connair's[64] brother, in the street as I was trying to photograph an armorial bearing over a door. In Westport I became tired of rain and left Helen to go on to Achill by herself whilst I came back to Dublin by train.

I thought you might be up for the Kerry match on last Sunday. I was going to go there, but I found it crowded out and I went off to the mountains for the day.

I haven't any news for you. I haven't met anyone since I came back here. Dave Nelligan is writing an autobiography. It is a strict secret so I am letting you know before anybody else does. I believe he writes well, but I suppose he'll avoid certain incidents in Kerry.[65]

I suppose you have your hands full now with all the children. Give my love to Eilis[66] and now give us warning before you start out next for town and come here to stay. We have a cook at last. Please thank Jack for the loan of his books. They were a great help. Please remember me to your sister and to the children. Tell them I have the goat here still.

Affectionately,
Ernie

Letter to Eithne Golden

229 *Upper Rathmines Rd, [Rathmines, Dublin]*
13 December 1937

[Eithne Golden,
c/o Mrs Victor Shoepperle,
Hobart Ave, Short Hills,
New Jersey, USA]

Dear Eithne,

And after your grand long letter not a word. The truth is that since I came back here with medicine around my neck for the first year making me miserable and a libel action[67] around my neck for another year I was more so. Now I have stopped medicine for a while, the libel action is over and I have been defeated, and I am a little more at peace. I'm in bed at present laid up for some time and just able to write today. It's the last day for US post before Christmas so I hope you get this in time.

I will reply to your letter in the New Year, that's a New Year resolution. How are Deirdre and Terence, Marianna and your mother? I had a letter from Dorothy Stewart from France saying she might be coming to Ireland in the Spring. I asked her and Maria over for Christmas and so far I haven't heard. Maybe they'll come. It would be nice to see anyone from New Mexico again.

How is your reading going? I have read more for the past few days than I have read for months but it's hard to hold books in bed and I'll have to get Helen to make a rest for me. Did Helen send you a photo of the baby or not; I must get one from her if she comes in before this goes to post.

Winter is hard here and runs one down but we have had a glorious autumn. The beeches were gold, Ghirlandajo [*sic*][68] yellow, and saffron almost, the heather almost wine (Helen says I'm mad when I say heather can be wine) and the bracken dun and russet. The hills in Wicklow now tawny russet and painting shades in between and the lakes ultramarine. We have never had an autumn like this before within living memory. Please give my love to your mother; Marianna, Deirdre, Terence and to yourself. How is Brett, Dr Light, Andy and all near you?

Love,
Ernie

Letter to HHOM

24 Harcourt Terrace
[London,] S.W. 10, [England]
6 April 1938

Helen O'Malley,
229 Upr Rathmines Rd,
Dublin, Ireland

Dear Helen,

Here I am footsore trying to find my way around subways. The boat[69] was nice; the cabin clean but somewhat hot at night even with the door on latch. There were nice gadgets for putting both glasses in, a velvet hot water bottle and a kind of strong tissue paper for wiping razor blades in to save the towel. The train got in to London at 11.15 a.m. You can get a call at 6.30, leave at 7.15 from the dock by company's bus arrive at station at 7.30 and stop, platform 6 for London. The train goes right through to Euston.

Cecil and Sweetie met me thinking I was you, and they both cursed me for making them put in an appearance just to see myself.

I sent Rich & Cowan a note through a solicitor[70] and made for the National Gallery tripping over English people feeding pigeons in Trafalgar Square. That's their emotional outlet. Burnt frontier towns in North West India and compensate by being sappy to pigeons in Trafalgar Square. The Gallery was a joy so I remained as long as I could. I tried to get some photographs of certain pictures a little out of the ordinary[71] but evidently only popular pictures are photographed.

I hope you found the passport, and include a towel for me please.

I have had a fine day stalking around cocking an eye at the girls. I saw a great number I liked but they weren't up to yourself when your nerves are alright. I'm going to look up Helen Lowenthal to-morrow if she's in town as I want to visit the Institute.[72]

Take things easy now and don't get rushed. Drive out to the mountains for two days running and let the rest of the world chase itself.

My love to you and the baby,
Ernie

I feel tempted to go with Cecil for 5 days on the yacht at Easter. Enclosed please post to Andie McDonnell address *outlined in telephone book.*[73]

Letter to Eithne Golden

229 Upper Rathmines Rd, Dublin
29 May 1938

Via SS Queen Mary, *Southampton*
Miss Eithne Golden,
c/o Mrs Victor Schoepperle,
Hobart Avenue, Short Hills, New Jersey, USA[74]

Dear Eithne,

Thank you very much for your letter. I feel miserable not have written you but I have had a great deal of trouble over the libel action. I left the country for a while and very nearly left for good. I had to raise money and that was another complication. The photos were very interesting. Terence looks like a movie hero. You look very well and Deirdre is as romantic as ever.

I was planning to have you over here with us for a while and I had put some money for your passage. That is gone now so I may as well tell you about it, but I would like to have you over here for a year, if you would like to come and even I could manage it now. We intend to live in France for a year or more and save some money. This is 1938. 1939 – 1940 in France. 1941 you over here. Do you think that would suit you? I had meant to have you over here in 1939. So if that fits in with your plans you could think ahead, or if not, you could let me know what you think about it. We might even go to New Mexico in 1939.

Helen and Cathal are either in New York, 620 Park Avenue, or in Greenwich, Connectt. (can't spell). Will you please write Helen as she left in a hurry and I had no time to give her addresses. I am writing her today and am sending on your address.

Please select a book for your mother, one she would really like, and a good one for Marianna, perhaps something with designs, then a few for yourself. I will ask Helen to settle up for me.

I was down in Wexford for the beginning of the 1798 commemorations at the Place Boulavogue[75] where the rebellion began. Men on white horses wearing green sashes, not the horses, four or five bands (we call an orchestra a band), one piper in saffron kilts, men with great banners, wooden and curve pikes, then an acting of incidents of '98 in the open. All very simple, awkward and very moving.

I'm sure you must miss New Mexico. I miss it myself even though in Ireland, the sun and the colour. In Ireland you must become accustomed to being out in the open in all weathers. If you go out any day you enjoy it, but you must go out or you would be miserable in damp cold or in rain, inside.

No matter when I go out here I am heart-stung with the beauty of it. New Mexico is vast, spacious but there is absent the haunting, lyric, unexpected glimpses that you get all the time here.

I hope your mother, Marianna and Deirdre liked Mexico. I know they should have and I expect they had plenty of adventure. I will write your mother before the end of the month.

I think you should do some *work* when you read. Early English prose writers, then it will be easier to understand good contemporary writers.

In the United States it's so easy to be fashionable when you read and to read the latest because it is in the public eye or because people talk about it. The hard reading is what you read now, some Elizabethan or post-Elizabethan, who nobody will talk about to you perhaps, but will give you a sense of neat, lean prose; and then go on to another who will give you a sense of rhythm, balance and style. I'll send you a list later. Otherwise, if you don't read such people, you will neglect a basic vocabulary. A little translation is a great help. Translate good Spanish into English, so much each week, and you will find from the use of a dictionary shades of meaning in a word.

American writers use larger conundrums, I know, to help them choose a shade of meaning, but if you sit down and think out of your own head all the different words which you might use in a particular instance it is better practice and throws you back on your own personal vocabulary. As soon as you have gathered such a word supply, you had best forget the source and revisit the words for yourself.

Did Brett go to England? I thought you said she was on her way. If you have her address please forward it as I should very much like to see her.

Please kindly remember me to Helen Crowe. She's a great girl. Helen would like her also. My love to your mother, Marianna, Deirdre, Terence and all my friends in Rio Chiquito, Taos and Santa Fe when you write.

Best love,
Ernie

I heard from Dorothy Stewart, two lines. I think she's in England now but no address.

NO. 98 EOM PAPERS NYU
Letter to HHOM

229 Upr Rathmines Rd, [Rathmines, Dublin]
30 May 1938

via SS Queen Mary,
Southampton, England
Helen O'Malley,
c/o Mrs Elon Hooker,
620 Park Avenue,
New York, NY, USA

Dearest Helen,

I hope everything went well for you on the voyage,[76] yet I had some misgivings about Annie's[77] efficiency; if in addition she was sea-sick you must have had a bad time, indeed. I hope you will take things easy now as there is no rush about doing anything in a hurry over there; but I expect you will have to invent a crisis.

Your American cheque came for $550.00; the Hib Bank[78] manager wrote to say he lodged your $350.00 which realized £70.11.4 and your credit to date is £97.2.8.

Letters came some of which I opened as I thought I might be able to reply (1) from Adelaide, (2) Gladys Virgile, (3) Helen M.[79] I will forward them to you in a separate letter.

About the Virgiles. There is no legal adoption in Ireland. The parents could later claim the child as one would have to deal through convents, and nuns, being women, are human and talk so there is no such thing as a dead secret. In England there are adoption societies which deal with the parent and with the adopter, but none allow adopter correspond with parent. Children's parents are interviewed by the society and certificates of blood tests etc. given to the adopter. Irish children can be obtained in England. I will forward that information to Mde Virgile with 3 addresses of adoption societies in England. I will also get in touch with Father Murphy[80] and find out if he could help me. I would advise the Virgiles to adopt peasant stock from Ireland as it has more good blood in it than either middle or upper middle class, but I cannot write them this as they probably have preconceived ideas about classes.

Miss Guinness back from Greece asked you and I out to tea, so did Mainie Jellett, also Mrs Sean Keating.[81]

The Ganesco[82] etc has not arrived from France, nor have any of the books, nor even the 2 magazines for which I paid a year's subscription. I cannot find the Tinteretto's photographs which you left some where or other. I have searched all files but yet they are missing. However I found El Greco's and a miscellaneous assortment of photographs from Madrid.

I would ask you to forward any art books that you can get that I ask of you at once and postcards as I want to have them before the exam. The exam is a hard one.[83] I looked at some papers and received an unpleasant shock.

I have rehung some pictures.

In Hall
Kisling
De La Serra
Boynton Pastel

In Drawing Room
Theo Goddard
Marchand
Vlaminck, water colour
Roualt
Dyf
Modigliani

They look fairly well, I think.

My Study
Vlaminck, Bridge
Lurcat

Rebecca Citz's[84] address is 100 Van Courtland Park South. Be sure and bring the baby to see both herself, her father and her mother. Eithne Golden's address is c/o Mrs Victor Schoepperle, Short Hills, New Jersey.

I received your flowers; thanks very much for sending them: had I not dropped in to Byrnes[85] by accident I might never have known as Mary did not mention the fact of their arrival, and I was not eating in the house so might never have known.

Writing is such an effort now. I expect it's because I tried to write to your mother five or six times in the past two weeks and was unable to write a decent letter of sympathy and so I did not write to you. Now, I know that if I don't get this off first you won't hear from me, at all. (That's the intensive Irish ending as you know.)

Do you remember that moron who invited you to lunch in Paris – Cummins? – well, Niall Sheridan and a friend of his were in here last night drinking porter out of very large bottles. Niall told me that Cummins had been with his wife to dinner in this house when you were in hospital. He had been in Greece, was very interested in archeology and was a great friend of Dennis Devlin. So that fixes that item. I remember him now but I would only know him by his face.

To-day Frank Aiken called. He wanted me to stand for a constituency, then when I declined he wanted me to work in the general election, also which I declined.[86]

I have written to Eithne Golden. I told her that if I am able to save up enough money I will have her over here for a year in 1941. It might be of use to her to come down to earth in relation to Ireland, if it does not interfere with her other work. I also said that you would select a book for her mother and for Marianna who lives with them; and a few books for herself. I would prefer that Eithne scouts around the second hand shops in 125th Street, in the village below 14th, or West side near Wannemakers;[87] and get some English classics or translations rather than that she should buy the latest compendium or spurious philosophy, or some other ephemeral contemporary work. Rebecca could help her in this. Also I would like you to buy Rebecca a good book. I will ask her to tell you but she may not. She is a very good reader. I might suggest a book on Giorgione.

Helen could you please forward me at once

The *Art News Annual* on Venetian Painting, Knoeldler's April 17th 2 parts, I believe also George Martin Richter, *Giorgio de Castlefranco* (Univ of Chicago Press); Duncan Phillips, *The Leadership of Giorgione* (American Federation of Arts), and if you get a good book on Tintoretto, let me have it. These I want at once by return so that I can have a read before the exam. (Perchance I brought over the Tintoretto photographs to the study in No. 7. I will look them up there to-night.) Any postcards you can find of the Venetian School in the Metropolitan (particularly colour reproductions) or in any other museum. I'm supposed to know the 16th century Venetians. That concludes following page.

The Queen Mary sails on Wednesday so I am trying to rush this letter.

Please give my best love and sympathy to your mother. It must be very hard for her to reshape her whole world when she had adjusted so long to another person like Mr Hooker. I hope you will be able to comfort her and to leave things you might want to do undone as her need of comfort is greater than whatever we may want. I hope Cathal is adjusting to food and climate.

I am working so there is no hurry about returning. Please remain as long as you wish and bring your mother back with you if she would like to come over here for a while. She could remain in the house during July if she would like to be in Dublin.[88]

Please kindly remember me to Anna (I never sent her the whiskey), to Bobby, Adelaide and Blanchette. Please congratulate Blanchette on the baby for me.

This is not the kind of letter I meant to write. Looking at it is like looking at an account book.

With my best love,
Ernie

NO. 99 EOM PAPERS NYU
Letter to HHOM

229 Upr Rathmines Rd, Dublin
7–11 June 1938

via SS Georgia,
Southampton, England
Helen O'Malley,
c/o Mrs Elon Hooker,
620 Park Avenue,
New York, NY, USA

Dearest Helen,

I have received three letters from you so far, one from the boat, and two together yesterday. It was very good of you to write as I'm sure you must be very busy. You don't say anything about Nurse so I hope she is keeping her end up. I think, however, that Cathal has outgrown her. She has been very good for him, her placidity offset all our jumping-bean spurts, but now I think he has been able to sum up her essential character and perhaps take advantage of it to domineer and bully. That may happen with an adult, but it has to be stopped with a baby. So I was thinking of giving nurse a trial for a while to see if she really can dominate Cathal and if not she will have to go, or he will become a terrible little pup.

Wet slashing rain here, day after day. I cannot find the keys of the garage; my old key seemingly will not open it so I have had to leave the car out. Now it leaks after rain. You drive for 10 minutes then a small shower bath falls incriminatingly on your pants. The garage owner has been dogging me for the rent. He came five times one day, the day on which it was due, and so I haven't paid him yet.

A gardener comes and looks after the garden. It looks neat in front but what it looks like at the back I don't know. He wants some kind of rings for sweet pea, which I must get for him. Mary, I find, has never lighted a fire in a room when she washes out the room. She complains of pains in her side. I am sending her to a young doctor in the Mater[89] to-morrow who is a good man and will give her an overhaul. She is a good girl, but has no sense of taking charge.

I saw Eileen's mansion.[90] It's very big, but the afternoon was sunny and so it looked pleasant nicely undulating the ground; and the small lake, though stagnant, is attractive, but I wouldn't like to live in such a place. Too dull, cold, inhuman. Painters have done pretty well, I think, and she will move in in a week or so.

A recent note from your bank in America to tell you how you stand. $1,861.20 at present in bank.

I haven't Gladys's name so I cannot send on the address to her. It's Vigil, I think, but I don't want to make a mistake in spelling. And I haven't seen Fr Murphy yet to question him.

Letter from Marvin from 455 E. 57th on your father's death asking for information about your drawings.

Card from old Mrs Curtis[91] from New York May 30th. She is now in Tuxedo. Programme from Vassos with X[92] in it.

Note from Bobs to you in London, dated April 20th, a few lines. Probably kept by Cecil and forgotten until later.

I wrote to the International bookshop,[93] but the books arrived this month; he had not sent the magazines we had paid him for and he had not, evidently, paid the carriage. I wrote asking that the magazines paid for be sent on monthly. To-day yours have arrived for past 2 months. The pictures came to Dublin, but for past week I have been trying to get them, not having your prices of the frames. Yesterday, I pulled some strings, and so, on paying about 7/6, and carriage, which is about £2.10.0, heavy enough, I think, I will probably have the pictures to-morrow. I have brought up all your stuff from below and have dried it out in the upper study. I then had an exhibition of your work on the walls. I think you should frame at least 6 when you get back and hang some up decently.

Francoise came for lunch. She has gone away to Iniskean, off Blacksod Bay, to live on an island and to 'dig' there for a month. I hope she finds something extremely important to bring her name before this unworthy public. She is going to France in the autumn to take charge of the St Germaine Museum,[94] for her lectures on painting have to be renewed year by year and are uncertain; the new lectureship she was to have been given on Irish manuscripts material has been turned down. She is sad and somewhat disheartened as she does not like the idea of becoming a fossil in a museum. Her book should be out by Christmas, and will have about 110 photographs.[95]

Kevin is working very hard. His exam comes in a week or so now. I hope he gets it as he has lost a great deal of time at his study, but I expect it will freshen him up on some things in which he is rusty. Kathleen is in England and the Boss[96] is at home. I saw him; he was looking well. I have not as yet written to the Ma. Kathleen was to have given me her new address before she sailed but did not come out to the house.[97]

The long evenings are here again but not so pleasant on account of the rain. I hope it holds off for a few days as I want to run out some evening to the hills for the long twilight. I saw the O'Faolains[98] at their new home, Dr Hayes[99] at his. He wrote a very good book of the French invasion of Mayo and the West in 98.[100] I have been officially informed that I am a member of the Academy and also of their Council of Five.[101] It doesn't interest me, I must say, so I shall resign the Council at the first meeting because I will not be available. O'Faolain has a new book on O'Connell.[102] Sound enough; it keeps me up late at night when I should be asleep.

I didn't find the Tintoretto photos yet, but I'll have a look for them. I have rearranged all reproduction so it is now time to do some work.

I hope you will have your back seen to thoroughly and take whatever treatment is necessary. I'm sure also that your teeth might want an American overhaul. Please tell me the result of the examination, and if treatment is necessary you may have to remain longer for as you know there's not much treatment here.

The brown camel hair sweater can't be found. Newells[103] returned a little green coat which they said did not belong to them. You had left it in there as a return when you were fitting out Cathal.

It's strange about your father not leaving a will. That will mean endless complication I'm sure for your mother and worry. The Hooker thorough method gets you there, I expect, but it wears you out completely in the process. Bobbie means another worry for her. That elephant of a house is another problem in itself and needs energy to run. I don't think it too good for your mother to have the responsibility of Bobbie, of the house, of Mr Hooker's estate, and of her own together. Combined, they will make a nervous wreck of her.

I hope you can see Paul Strand. Please tell him that I hope he could come over this August or September while we have a place in the West. Next year will be uncertain if we go to France and so we would have to wait until 1940 to see him. Also I hope you can see Maraquita and send my affectionate greetings through her to Theo Goddard, Rebecca and Israel, Harold Clurman and if you drop into an American Place, Stieglitz and Georgia O'Keefe.

I find that the fastest boat is the *Queen Mary* leaving on the 10th, arriving 15th. The minor boats are less certain about mail, I believe.

Your pictures should arrive in the house on Monday next if all goes well so I have just been told.

Do you know when you might be back? You might fix a rough date if possible. For I will move off when the exam is over and walk for 3 weeks or so. I am having a new pair of heavy shoes made. The old man is anxious for you to come in and say exactly what you think about the shoes to him. If I go off I will send Mary home and leave the key with the boss. I'll come back just before we move to Westport.[104] I expect we need not bring much stuff with us; bed clothes, drink, and books. If the nurse takes Cathal by train there will be a certain amount of room for things in the car.

Mary put the camphor in all of your things except the big press to right of mantelpiece which is against the dividing wall. I took the key out for safety and have been unable to find it since.

11 June. Sunday night

Your case of pictures comes tomorrow. Waiting for them has kept this letter off for ten days. I'll send you another letter in a few days. It has been raining hard for nearly three weeks and it can wear you down. Finally, last week I bought some whiskey so the staying in doesn't matter so much.

I miss you very much, and the baby. It makes you feel as if you had lost something in some room and you keep on searching for it. Anyhow I love you very much and wish you were here if only to fight with you. Mary saw a doctor and reported all well.

With all my love, and to your mother also,
Ernie

Please give Georgia O'Keefe my warm regards. Mabel[105] kept us apart once, but I have always admired her at a discreet distance.

NO. 100 EOM PAPERS NYU
Letter to HHOM

229 Upr Rathmines Rd, [Rathmines, Dublin]
20 June 1938

via SS Normandie,
Southampton, England
Helen O'Malley,
c/o Mrs Elon Hooker,
620 Park Avenue,
New York, NY, USA

Dearest Helen,

I hope you and Cathal are in good form, and that the nurse is still alive. How does she manage to survive America?

There doesn't seem to be any news for you. I haven't seen anyone you know. Yesterday I went down to Mullingar and took Frankie O'Shaughnessy as far as Loch Reagh where we ate our lunch. The day was cloudy in spots with rain but we were on the shore of the lake opposite the island where Queen Maeve of Connaught was killed by a sling shot from our shore. Frankie has always been very kind to me. I used to eat and work in her flat once. So when you come back, would you write to her c/o Mrs Gallagher near the Hibernia Bank, Main St, Mullingar and ask her up for a day. She is free on Sundays but could come up by bus on

Saturday and you could leave her down on Sunday. Mullingar the land of heifers.

Mullingar people say that 'Mayo men have no intelligence and Mayo women no morals', whilst we say 'Beef to the heels like a Mullingar heifer' when describing their women.

Kevin is away. He had a break-down the night before his exam as he had been working too hard. He went off to London. He had worked up till four in the morning. Now he'll have to start again when he comes back. I won't be sitting for my exam. I don't know enough about it so I'm liable to wander off any time, but I have to do some reference work in the RSAI first.[106]

I began this letter this morning then began one to your mother which I found hard to write. I gave up both letters and went to the library[107] feeling sure I would finish them and be home by six. I continued making a bibliography of Connaught as I want to do some work on that province. After 2 and a half hours' work and rooting amidst the catalogue I was tired standing on my feet. Sat down and worked on *Carew's Manuscripts* and a few others trying to tabulate some information about the O'Malleys. Then thought that the Annals of the Four Masters would give some dates. Found a little information. Then decided that the *Annals of the Four Masters* was a standard Irish authority from Adam onwards to about 1600 so began at the A's to find out information about Connaught. My Irish vocabulary on place names is weak so I'm sure I skipped many a Connaught name of a place in the A's. However I finished the A's. Then I thought of Lewis's *Topographical Dictionary* which is in 2 volumes and deals with places in Ireland giving notes on each. I checked it on the A's by the *Four Masters*, beat it by about 30 to 1. Then I thought that I might go through Lewis and arrange a list of Connaught place names when we are in the West this year as luckily I have Lewis myself. Then came across on the shelves 2 volumes dealing with Irish monasteries. Found the last volume which dealt with Mayo was missing. I was looking for Annaghdown because a Thomas O'Malley was bishop there before the time of Henry I. Then thought about it and educed that Annaughdown was in Galway. Looked up Galway in Vol 2, but no mention of Annaghdown.

Were you with me when I was at Annaghdown on the shores of Lough Corrib. Yes you were, I remember. There were 5 heads like Kilteel plastered together with unbreakable cement. That happened 50 years ago and they are stuck flush up against a wall so that they can't be photographed.

Took down by chance the *Calendar of Judiciary Rolls* for 1305–1360 and found an archbishop of Tuam up before the Chief Justice for grabbing abbey and attaching it to his own of Tuam. So that's how you look for information. Anyhow I finished at 8.45 and felt very hungry and tired. Came home, ate salad, cold ham and tea. Then decided to finish your letter and have it posted before midnight as SS *Normandie* leaves Southampton on 22 and is due to arrive on 28, so with any luck you should get this.

I found books from you and from Boston. I expect you have seen John T.[108] I hope he is very well and that you have a good talk with him. I meant to tell you to look up books in The Old Corner Book Store on Ireland as books were published in Boston between 1830–1860 by Irishmen, and they have not been reprinted on this side of the water. Also I wanted you to get from John T some of the books, duplicates of his which he had put aside for me, but never sent. He gave you some last year ones I mentioned by name. I badly want Roderic O'Flaherty's *Chronographical Description of West or H-Iar Connaught*, edited in 1846 by James Hardiman. But if you have been there I can do nothing about it.

Weather has been fair enough. To-day was dry. Cold at times and warm, I believe, when I was in the library.

I haven't seen Roisin for a month nearly. She told me that her sister said it was a shame for me not to have gone with you to help you on the journey, that you would need me. So I told her to tell her sister both of us were inclined to mind our own businesses, that we didn't order other people's lives or comment on their way of life and that as long as we agreed among ourselves we didn't consider the outside world. Roisin asked me for dinner at her place but I couldn't face the brood of sisters.

The enclosed cutting to remind you of home.[109]

I have to dash for the post now.

With all best love,
Ernie

NO. 101 EOM PAPERS NYU
Letter to HHOM

[229 Upper Rathmines Road, Rathmines, Dublin]
1 July 1938

Per SS Europa, *Southampton*
Helen O'Malley,
c/o Mrs Elon Ferry Hooker,
620 Park Avenue,
New York, NY, USA

Dearest Helen,

I received your last long and involved letter but I don't know if I was able to piece it together. You didn't number pages and so it is more like a cross-word puzzle than anything else. I received the list of books: *Life along Passaic*; *Triple Thinkers*; *Life of Leon Trotsky*; *Life of Hart Crane*; *Spring Yale*.

I would suggest that you give the order to the place you gave it last year. It is cheaper and we would have one shop which might be interested to reply if either of us wrote. As it is now we are held up, at least I am at times for having no such place which knows me, to write to.

I'm probably leaving in a day or two to walk. My shoes are ready and I'm anxious to test them. The weather has been very bad so far but if it lifts in a few days I'll start off and stay out for 3 weeks or so.

I found the key of the garage by rooting through your keys. I have lost the key of your main press, the one where wine was stored, to my loss. I have left all your keys in the 2nd drawer from top of the bunch of drawers outside of your room. I have left your letters and bills in 3rd drawer left of your own writing desk. I am leaving key with Kathleen in case you haven't the other key. I have paid all bills so far except B and F, which didn't send theirs, Byrnes and Frees. Frees sent theirs a week after you left so I told them they could wait for money until you return. Please don't forget to give them notice about leaving the house.

I went down to see Frank O'Connor and his lady. Garden, rhododendrons, a river, a great number of rooms for £50 per year including rates; and they saw it by chance.

I don't know whether this will reach you in time so I won't write anything else. Please kindly remember me to Barbara whom I never seem to ask for but remember well – I have her pouch yet[110] – to Miss O'Brien, Anna, Blanchette, Johnnie, Adelaide and John.[111] Please give my love to your mother. She must find it very hard now to adjust her life all of a sudden. How is Mrs Sheridan[112] and my love to her.

My best love,
Ernie

NO. 102 EOM PAPERS NYU
Letter to Peggy Raleigh[113]

*[Old Head Lodge, Louisburgh, Co. Mayo,
November 1938]*

*[Peggy Raleigh,
St Joseph's Street, Limerick]*

Dear Peggy,

I was sorry to hear we took away your mother and father on your birthday and that you had to put it off until this week. I didn't know it was your birthday or I wouldn't have asked your father and mother to come up here. I hope you will have a very happy birthday and that your doll will reach you in time.

We thought you would be able to come down to see us, but maybe we'll see you before long. Young John seems to have as many words as Cathal so we'll have to teach Cathal some more quickly. He can remember the last words of some lines of songs and when the song is sung he comes in with the last word as a chorus.

What book are you in now? And can you speak any Irish? Do you remember the time the pup frightened Una[114] at Kilkee; perhaps you don't as it was nearly three years ago. You weren't speaking to me then so I married Helen.

Cathal and Kathleen and Helen have been out all day and I am waiting for them to come in for their tea but it doesn't look as if they would come as they are over an hour late now. Please tell your father that we expect to have the house by the sea.[115] Helen was to sign the lease but I cannot say now as she has not yet returned. Please give my love to your mother and father, to Sheila, Peggy,[116] and Una, a pat to the Major and my best love to you; and a very happy birthday.

Love,
Ernie

NO. 103 EOM PAPERS NYU
Letter to HHOM

Burrishoole Lodge,
[Newport, Co. Mayo]
27 February 1939

[Helen O'Malley,
London, England]

Dearest Helen,

Thank you for your letter. I hope you had a good crossing for there was a mild wind here that night and the next day. The weather has been cold. Much snow on the mountains and little sun. I hope you are having better health.

Cathal is looking well. I brought him to Newport one day with the laundry and to Westport the following day. He inspected sheep, pigs, a donkey and a bullock in McCormack's yard, pulled the pig's ears when he saw me pull them and held on to the sheep's wool. He made up to a small girl, followed her up the street and when I found him he had his arm round her waist and was calling 'come', trying to get her to the car. Then I brought him across the street to talk to another young lass, one Maureen MacKenna with crinkly blue eyes, but when I left he tried to wrestle with her and frightened her. Evidently the O'Ms are tough to their women. On the way home I stopped at a steam-roller and placed him standing near the driving wheel. He was frightened enough but since talks of it with great gusto as if he had driven the steam-roller himself.

Have you seen any decent paintings, or is this not the exhibition season? I read that there's to be an Italian exhibition in London this week[117] so I suppose you will see it.

I hope Bobby is improving and that you have been able to have a good chat with her. How is Mrs Sheridan; she bears up wonderfully though I suppose she finds it trying enough at times to be away from America? Tremors due to writing late at night and to the nib, I think. Please remember me affectionately to Bobs and Harry; perhaps they'll come back with you.

A few daffodils very nearly out; I expect a few will bloom to-morrow but the sleet is against them. Brennan has been out for the past few days. I do not know if he caught anything, he didn't the first two days for the weather was then very cold.

I hope you will take as much time as you want. Everything is going on well here. I am going to let nurse off the first fine day as she refused so far.

With best love,
Ernie

Letter to HHOM

Burrishoole Lodge,
[Newport, Co. Mayo]
28 February 1939

[Helen O'Malley,
London, England]

Dearest Helen,

Your second letter came this morning (Monday) but as the post-man had not come up to 11 a.m. I went out with the dog to find when I returned that he had called at 11.15. The morning was very wet and I thought he would not come.

That is bad news about Bobby,[118] but it is better to know of it definitely than to be juggling on for years, when, in the meantime she might do something foolish. I'm sure your mother will be hurt and upset, but the main thing in such cases is to forget one's pride and to remember the patient as a medical case.

I am enclosing Violet Woods' letter to you. The girl you saw did not call, and had no intention of doing so.

Could you please get me some wooden gramophone needles, charts of Newport Bay and Westport Bay; there are two – one for each side. They may be sold at the Stationary Office, the maps of the surroundings of this house which you can buy in College Green Dublin. If you go near Longmans Green + Co. Ltd, 39 Paternoster Row, London E.C. 4 give them a sub for me for *The Bulletin of Historical Research*, Univ of London, 7/6 yearly, ask for any articles on the period 1550–1612 in Ireland and buy No. 32 (2/6).

Martin bought two carts of manure, had planted one row of peas and put up 50 yards of wire but the base of the wire was above ground so I will have him take out the staples and sink the wire 6' in the ground. He is changing the soil in the boxes and the potatoes, late for them, are sprouting slowly under the stairs. They won't be ready for St Patrick's Day, I think.

No boating since you left as there has been no good day. Sun comes for a while then rain follows. The only bit of sun I met with was in Achill. It was warm at Keel and along the strand where great breakers were smashing although the sea was calm, but over the other side of Achill towards the Sound and along one part, it was very cold as there was snow on the mountains.

I hope you will have a good holiday and see all your friends. You might price some French pictures in London until we compare prices with ours.

With best love,
Ernie

If you see Cecil, tell him to sail his boat over if he can and ask him to tell you the name of a good book on how to sail a small boat.

Have you seen the Venetian exhibition? Perhaps there may be some interesting things there. The World's Fair is preparing a very good exhibition. I suppose it will

---

be much superior to Chicago which was a very good exhibition indeed.

I send you by wire the address of the sister of the girl who you saw before you left. The other girl married after the mission in Achill and the mother was not too pleased. She walked over to see you last Saturday as she felt you should know the daughter's decision; the other girl whose address you have is good also as a cook, but I expect you will make your own enquiries.

If you have time will you please drop into Foyle's,[119] Charing Cross or J. & E. Bumpers,[120] 477 Oxford St (his best for select books) and find if he has any second hand or cheap copies of E.M. Forster's work. The only one I have is *Passage to India*. If they are cheap buy a few; if not obtain his quotations, but please get me his *Aspects of the Novel* anyhow.

Looking over my Yeats I find I am missing the *Trembling of the Veil* and *The Cutting of an Agate*, both of which I want.

You might get a quotation for I.A. Richards *Principles of Literary Criticism* and *Practical Criticism* and for Benedetto Croce's works. Bumpers can send his own quotations direct to me.

I have to leave now to go up the lake before the evening becomes bad. Then I will go into Westport to post this. This evening may hold, but I doubt it. Andie McDonald[121] came here for tea one evening but could not stay the night as he was on his way home. Please kindly remember me to Bobs and Harry, Bobbie and Mrs Sheridan.

> With my best love,
> Ernie

NO. 105 TRINITY COLLEGE DUBLIN MS 8117/1: LETTER 1/5
Letter to Thomas MacGreevy[122]

> *Burrishoole House,*
> *Newport, Co. Mayo*
> *6 March 1939*

[Thomas MacGreevy,
London, England]

Dear Tomás,

I hope you are bearing up this weather in London but I hope you have less of rain than we have: a steady three weeks of it. I am not sure of your address now. I can't find my pocket book so I'm sending this on to Eileen[123] to address it for me. I wrote to you in the Summer but did not hear from you. I have another letter written but I want to be sure first that you are alive as I want you over for Easter. You were to have been invited for Christmas but that is another story, hence the second letter.

I read that there was a good Pissaro show recently.[124] I dream of pictures down here and read of them: seeing them is another matter.

> Ever yours,
> Ernie O'Malley

Letter to Thomas MacGreevy

Bernis Café,
54 Lower O'Connell Street, Dublin
5 April 1939

[Thomas MacGreevy,
London, England]

Dear Tomás,

I rushed up to Dublin to help Helen drive the car as the dirt road was long. I was hoping that any letter of yours would have been forwarded to me from Burrishoole but the post is a slow one there and is held up for a day or so just to show that the Kingdom of Connaught has been reached. I am enclosing the fare so that there is no excuse.

To-day Jack Yeats and I talked about you. He is a good soul, wise, human, kind and we spoke of poetry and paint, that which there is no better combination.

Helen sends her very kindest regards. She is worried at present about the heading to this paper but my other letter to you is in the Library with my notebooks and if I have to tear it off I would feel I was writing to the wrong person.

Come on over and you'll write a few poems afterwards.

Affectionately,
Earnán

Letter to James Johnson Sweeney[125]

Burrishoole House,
Newport, Co. Mayo
22 April 1939

SS President Harding, Cobh,
Mr James J. Sweeney,
120 East End Avenue,
New York, NY, USA

Dear Mr Sweeney,

Will you please let me know what numbers of 'Transition' have been published recently and the price. I have No. 24 but none later; others I have loaned; an Irish loan is gone with the wind.

Don MacDonagh, who recently has been staying here, tells me that you have some old Irish gramophone records. Will you please tell me who has published them? I hope that if at any time you are near here you will call in to see me.

Sincerely yours,
Ernie O'Malley

Letter to Thomas MacGreevy

> *Burrishoole Lodge,*
> *Newport, Co. Mayo*
> *1 May 1939*

[Thomas MacGreevy,
London, England]

Dear Tomás,

Thanks for your letter. We drank your health at Easter and I was in a unique position for conversation as I injured my back on Easter Sunday and had to remain in bed for two weeks. My brother, Cecil, who had come from London, happens to be a surgeon and so was able to improvise a pulley arrangement so that I could move in the bed. It's rowing does it. Yesterday was a glorious day here. I started off to explore the islands in my boat, the *Walruss*, visited old friends on Island Mór who had known me as a friend but on the way back the wind and tide were in my teeth and I reached home at midnight as if I had been just through a mangle.

I have succeeded in breaking the gramophone spring half an hour ago and I am derelict as I will have to wait until someone goes to Dublin for a restoration. Music means a great deal here. We have no wireless, the country ride their high and rather wooden horse, and our daily hour of records may begin or end a day.

To-day was again very warm. I have been burnt brick-red. I went up the river under the old bridge, then under another bridge where there are rapids to a wide lake beyond. The mountains soft with a line one finds in Greek or in Japanese prints. Now it is late, the mountains have disappeared and the birds are lazily singing for bed: it is another world to the cockpit of Europe.

Helen persuaded me to go to Dublin as I had bought some material in Galway for a suit, and I went. I spent a few days in the National Library, came back with my material, as I had no time to see a tailor. I saw Jack Yeats, fell clear in love with a picture and felt I must have it.[126] I was able to arrange payments over a long period. We had a very nice afternoon with him, he spoke of you kindly. He is very fine and we came away in a glow. Then I began to think of my commitment and had a shiver at the knees for some time, but I am very glad of my rashness. When I think of money I had saved up to build a small house or a place of my own now going to pay off a form of blackmail, generally spoken of as libel, I have less qualms.

I hope you hear some favourable news about your Yeats monograph.[127] It would do you a great deal of good to have it definitely accepted. Could you please give me an idea of its length as I am writing soon to Houghton Mifflin[128] in Boston and they, if not interested, may be able to suggest a publisher. Personally I don't think they publish such material but they are kindly, I find.

How did the Cezanne exhibition turn out? I saw an exhibition of his two years ago, 1936, at the Musée de l'Orangerie. 'Les grands baigneurs' has since gone to the United States from the Pellerin Collection. The Pellerin has, I think, some of his best.

When in Dublin I called out to see Eileen McGrane, who is now in the country.

Helen had designed some rooms and their fabrics for her. They look very well, and Eileen who has not much certitude on such matters is beginning to like them very much now. My pen is acting in bad faith just now but it results from yesterday's excessive galley work.

I have been translating Rainer-Maria Rilke's *Letter to a Young Poet* from the French, but recently Donagh MacDonagh, who has returned from America, told me that Auden is translating it for an American publisher. My book has been translated into German since November last but the English publishers had not told me about it. Only when a German officer wrote for my autograph did I find out! I suppose any stick is good enough to beat a comic with.

My brother has joined or is to join the Navy as a surgeon in case of war.[129] I'm sure your ARP work[130] is interesting as it has to do with storage and protection. Periodic debates come under way here as to whether glass should or should not be on pictures. In this rather damp climate I do not know if moisture collects behind the glass, but our paintings are in rooms where coal and turf is burned. Perhaps you could advise me.

This German technique of tension is a new psychological factor. This war fought in peace conditions has some slight resemblance to old Chinese warfare where generals maneuvered without coming to grips until a conference was called at which one general explained to his opponent that he was irreparably checkmated: whereupon the opponent surrendered.

Helen has had a slight operation and is now in Dublin. Cathal has a pet lamb two weeks old. He was out with me to shoot the rapids to the lake to-day. Have you written any poetry of late?

Affectionately,
Earnán

NO. 109 EOM PAPERS NYU
Letter to John Raleigh

Burrishoole [Lodge,]
Newport, Co. Mayo
1 May 1939

[John Raleigh,
St Joseph's Street, Limerick]

Dear Johnny,

How are yourself and Bea and the children. I haven't heard from you, but I expect you are busy. Why don't Bea and you run up for a few days. The weather is beautiful now. Couldn't you come up this week and then maybe I'll go back with you.

This is a different place in the sunshine. The winter was cold, frosty and the house damp enough but these days it is lovely. Helen has been working hard in the garden and is now ready to plant tomatoes; possible this week. She has lettuce, peas, beans, potatoes, onions, cress, mustard down, has made five or six frames covered with a kind of imitation wired glass but nothing is so dear as real glass. If you come across a greenhouse cheap you can let me know.

I have the boat and have had a few long pulls out to sea, consequently I have spent a while in bed as a result, but I have enjoyed it. The nurse is good and capable and Cathal is in good health. He has a pet lamb now aged ten days and that is great excitement for him. Your dog disappeared about three days ago, and I have not seen him since. If he doesn't turn up I'll have to ask you to look out for another, if you don't mind, as it's good to have a dog around here that can swim. Helen bought two police dog pups. They're about three weeks old and will grow up quickly I think.

I hope Bea is in good health and that she can come up for a holiday. Perhaps this warm weather will continue but the wind is rising to-night. I was thinking of going to the auction at Cong and look at boats if there are any: perhaps I may go to Limerick to look at a boat if there are any down there.

Please give my love to Bea and to young John and the girls.

Love,
Ernie

NO. 110 EOM PAPERS NYU
Letter to HHOM

Burrishoole [Lodge,
Newport, Co. Mayo]
2 May 1939

Helen O'Malley,
Swiss Hotel,
34 Fitzwilliam Sq, Dublin

Dearest Helen,

Thanks very much for the book which you kindly sent. I sat up on Saturday night fortified with six bottles of stout and a little brandy to read. I read until four or five o'clock with great interest and amusement. I'm writing to Flann O'Brien[131] as a result.

I was out in the boat with Cathal to-day up to the lake. It's hard at times to keep him quiet in a boat when he is by himself as he wants something to fiddle with, and I had to talk severely to him, but I expect the best way is to keep repeating your instructions in a mild voice. The weather is beautiful and the mountains are a dream.

Everyone is well here, the house running smoothly. I cooked rashers for Bridie one morning and gave her a talk on tea and so far she has carried out instructions. She is very kind and good. Kathleen wrote to ask for three aprons which you were to have forwarded to her. Do you know where they are to be found?

A man called Joyce near Newport has some good tomato plants for sale. You left no instructions with me about routine in the garden so I expect the two lads carry out your own instructions as I do not interfere with them.

I hope the operation won't be painful. And I hope it's not a periodic operation on a person who can be milked regularly. Can you give me any exact date as to when Helen Landreth comes? I promised a book to a little girl on Island Mór aged 3; if there are any notebooks in Woolworths this size can you please bring six (6).

Brid is waiting for the car to go to Newport for food. High wind last night and a rather cold morning now. Cathal talks of going to see 'Nammu', but he is wrapped up in the 'Mummy non-nous' and the lamb and Nanna.

With best love,
Ernie

NO. 111 EOM PAPERS NYU
Letter to HHOM

Burrishoole [Lodge,
Newport, Co. Mayo]
Thursday [4 May 1939]

Helen O'Malley,
Swiss Hotel Hotel,[132]
34 Fitzwilliam Sq., Dublin

Dear Helen,

I hope you reached Dublin alright.

Enclosed please find auction cutting. I wonder if you could find at what price the McGuinness goes, maybe getting it if cheap and very good.

Also could you buy the catalogue of the Iveagh Sale to take place at Cong in May 10 or so, price 4/.

Dublin for boots (Properts, Dublin, Brown, prepared by B. Beddow & Sons Ltd, Battersea, London), several tins required.

Enclosed list of Irish records[133] so that you won't duplicate and Mozart suggestions to help you pass the time. Any more Mozart sonatas available and literature on same.

Enclosed for translation please. If you drop into Hodges Figgis see if they have a copy of *Suibhne Geilt* (Irish Texts Translations)[134] and a copy of their catalogue.

E.

Letter to Thomas MacGreevy

> Burrishoole Lodge,
> Newport, Co. Mayo
> 27 June 1939

[Thomas MacGreevy,
London, England]

Dear Tomás,

The rain has come at last and I have been definitely driven indoors. A long time now since I heard from you without a reply on my part, but my replies are not, unfortunately, governed by manners, feelings or duty. I find it hard to write and I'll have to get down to some regular system before this year is over.

The original query about pictures arose I think as to whether glass should be put on the frames or not. Glass takes from the visibility of much painting but I expect it does preserve a work from dust. I had intended to glue paper over the backs of frames to keep out the dust; if I use such a backing can I then use glass in front? The works are not too good in winter. Helen is in trouble about her ikons[135] as some have flaked a little, and, in a few, small worm holes have suddenly appeared. I read a book by (can't think of his name) last year on antidotes for worm holes. Now I forget all about it. Is there anyone in Dublin she could bring her ikons to?

There has been a spell of fine warm weather during which there was a hole in my boat and State Papers to be read quickly: as a result I did not reap enough sun. But a few days of it burned the skin of my face, arms and neck and I have to lay low. May is, I think, the best month here. The light is more gentle, softer on mountain and land structure. June light is hard, flat and the evenings from 7 o'clock onwards are magical for then light slants low filling out the forms in a tender way. The land is then like a half-dream. Helen and I made a collection recently of bog-wood forms in the upper lake. We intend to mount some of them. They do not attain the sophisticated sublimity of Hans Arp's 'Concretion Humane', but they please us.

I haven't heard from Houghton Mifflin as yet. I didn't ever remember seeing a collection of illustrations of Jack Yeats' pictures. *Life in the West of Ireland* I have but they are gentle, more interesting at times for character than for intrinsic merit. Between broadsides and ballad illustrations he could have another book. I expect you have photographs.

2 July 1939

A boat came in from the islands while I was writing your letter and off I went to sail a lug sail and to visit people on five or six islands, to return yesterday.

Helen told me that you were writing about W.B. I do not know if she confused W.B. with Jack. If you had a book on W.B. ready it would sell well here and especially in America. Hone is to do the official biography. He gets £1000 and Mrs Yeats gets the royalties. Lennox Robinson[136] is also writing a short memoir.

Last night Sean O'Faolain and Dr Collins called here. Sean is writing a guide book to Ireland. His stay in Connaught was two days: however, he knows the craft well enough to be able to write about anything. They talked about a paper to carry on the work of 'The New Statesman'.[137] I did not ask what was the idea behind it but F. Packingham[138] (spelt wrongly, I fear) is behind it and is ready to put up some money. I'm sure you could do weekly art critiques. I'll suggest your name, if you wish as soon as I hear from O'Faolain. Evidently the people concerned are going about the venture in a rather thorough way, slowly covering the ground. We need a paper here badly but I do not know the real reason behind it, the motive or its direction: a purely literary paper does not appeal to me now.

Helen has worked hard at the garden. Flowers have come out to her satisfaction, and vegetables. Also a chicken house has been imported and some fowl. Here we find that we must produce our own food as far as possible otherwise food is worse than in the city. Cows and pigs are the next items but we have no land.[139] In case of war we will have to be self-producing here or will be hungry.

News again warlike. I'm sure England is in a complete frimble about it all. O'Faolain tells me that many publishing houses in England will close down shortly and that American houses will follow. So you had best come over before the deluge. Helen and I send affectionate regards.

Ernie

NO. 113 EOM PAPERS NYU
Letter to HHOM

[Dublin]
4 October 1939

Helen O'Malley,
Burrishoole Lodge,
Newport, Co. Mayo

Dear Helen,

Thanks for clothes which you kindly forwarded. I saw Gantley.[140] He said the shoes had not come in, but when I called to-day he said that last Saturday the shoes had been sent back from the PO as you had not put his right name or address. GANTLEY, 45 York St, Shoemaker. He will send them on to-morrow evening. I am getting a pair of heavy shoes made as leather will be hard to find. Do you want a pair as well?

I bought some dubbin from Aungier St from Central Leather Co. as we need a supply.

I hope you have done what I suggested about cinders and manure as you will find it very difficult to obtain fertiliser as there is a great scarcity of it. You might try Westport and buy your supply now and not in the Spring when it will not be available.

I was looking up paraffin as I thought of getting a barrel at 10/9 per gallon so it would then save journeys to Westport in case petrol is further restricted. If you have any samples of heavy coating material for me would you please send them on as I might get a coat made if I find any good stuff, a warm one for winter.

Is there anything you want here? I have been delayed and will probably be another week or so. I sent on some rope, oil skins etc. from Vernon of the Quays.[141] If the parcel arrives please notify me. Do you want any more notepaper etc as it will go up very much I think?

I hope Cathal is well.

Ernie

NO. 114 EOM PAPERS NYU
Letter to Cathal O'Malley[142]

[Dublin]
4 October 1939

[Cathal O'Malley,
Burrishoole Lodge,
Newport, Co. Mayo]

Dear Cathal,

I hope you are very well. Here is my [boat with no sail] and your boat [boat with full sail] and the [cow] and the [two] little [rabbits]. These are rabbits not lobsters. And do you see any [fish] in the river or [swan]s. Do you read you [*sic*]? [two books, entitled 'Tale of a Little Boy' and 'Cathal's adventures with Moo Cow in the Moon']. And how is the [moon] at night and the [three stars]'s. What would you like for a present? A book, a train or a small boat? Please take a [two ladles] and bail out my [boat at anchor] and see how big the anker [*sic*] that Eoghain O'Rahilly sent me? Is it in a parcel? [a rabbit, a fat fish and a bird]

Love,
Daddy

EOM's letter to his son, Cathal O'Malley, dated 4 October 1939.
Source: EOM Papers NYU.

NO. 115 EOM PAPERS NYU
Letter to HHOM

[Dublin]
5 October 1939

[Helen O'Malley,
Burrishoole Lodge,
Newport, Co. Mayo]

Dear Helen,

I hope shoes have arrived. I'll go around and look up Gantley now. I have just seen Maurice McGonigal. I had seen a very interesting piece of work of his in Waddingtons,[143] 2 girls standing on a street corner. Saturday there is to be an exhibition of contemporary work and borrowed works of contemporary continental painters organised by the new Contemporary Art Shop;[144] I hope they will have something new that I have not seen.

I was speaking to Jack Yeats last evening. He showed me some of the paintings which had come back from Farrel[145] in America. Interesting the few I saw, one very good. 24 in all returned to his surprise.

Could you please look up my oar locks and find the narrowest width across here as I want to buy a few pairs and can't do so until I am sure the oars will fit. It might be better still to measure the distance of the two pairs of oars as I want to buy oar locks which will not be jumped by oars. Nothing else strange.

Ernie

NO. 116 EOM PAPERS NYU
Letter to HHOM

[Inishmore, Co. Galway]
9 October 1939

Helen O'Malley,
Burrishoole House,
Newport, Co. Mayo

Dearest Helen,

I'm away to the islands as Josey Gill came in here at 12 noon. I'll be at West-port Quay to-morrow morning at 10 or 10.30 am. Could you please have the car meet me and bring my brown bag of photo equipment as I might stay on for the day. I can't bring it in boat for fear of rough weather.

Love,
Ernie

NO. 117 EOM PAPERS NYU
Letter to HHOM

Dublin
23 October 1939

Helen O'Malley,
Burrishoole House,
Newport, Co. Mayo

Dear Helen,

I hope you are in good form by this and that Kathleen is having a rest. The following were asking for you:

Evie Hone
Da Barton
Dr Solomons and wife[146]
Mainie Jellett

Stella Frost
Con Curran
German Ambassador and wife[147]
Dr and Mrs Kiernan[148]
Mr Byrnes and wife and staff
Don McDonagh
Miss Guinness of the primrose house
Cecil Salkeld[149]
Norah McGuinness
Henehan of the Museum[150]

I have not seen Roisin as yet though I met her on the street one day. Nor 'Dear Dark Head',[151] I called but she was out.

Could you please open a parcel from Vernon or Verdons and see if they sent on rope and oil skins as I have no way of checking. Also please find if Graham Bros sent on shirts and underclothes. I owe them £3.3.0 extra if they have sent on shirts so I would ask you to open the parcel and remove 2 shirts keeping the reddish one, and remove 2 sets of the heavy underclothes and bring them up with you as I can't afford the extra £3.3.0 just now. Measurement of oar needed again for row locks and weight of anchor sent by young O'Rahilly. It may not hold the boat and if so I could have it returned and buy a larger one. Could you have Michael bring in my old anchor to Newport and weigh it as well as the small new one, as I need a folding anchor but I want to know the weight of the old one.

Nothing strange here. I haven't been doing anything save go to parties for close on a week and it's time to stop that. Mother is looking well. I hope Cathal is very well.

Love,
Ernie

The weather has been very strange here foggy, rather dark, but the few times I went out into the country I found it gloriously fresh and sunny.

Letter to Desmond Ryan

12 Herbert Park, [Dublin]
1 November 1939

[Desmond Ryan,
35 Burlington Avenue,
Kew Gardens, Surrey, England]

Dear Desmond Ryan,
 There is to be a meeting in a room in the Mansion House at 8 pm this Friday to discuss the formation of an Irish Culture League.[152] The idea is sound enough, the working out can be made sound. I would so like very much if you could be there. Perhaps you could ring Mrs Kiernan[153] and she could explain further.
       Very sincerely yours,
       Ernie O'Malley

Local Security Force

14 / 10 / 1940.

A CHARA,

There will be a {parade / meeting} of L.S.F. Making of Declarations and Nomination of Group Section and Squad Leaders after Declarations are made;

at *Newport Boys School,*

on *Friday 18th Oct* at *9* p.m.

You are particularly requested to attend.

Mise le meas,

EOM's Local Security Force parade notice for meeting in Newport, 18 October 1940.
Source: EOM Papers NYU.

Letter to HHOM

[Burrishoole Lodge,
Newport, Co. Mayo]
6 December 1939

[Helen O'Malley,
Swiss Hotel,
34 Fitzwilliam Square, Dublin]

Dear Helen,

Parcel from Rowans, Browne & Nolan, Maguire & Co.[154] and my clothes arrived alright. Thanks very much for sending on the clothes.

I think you should be careful about helping people like Breckinridge as the contacts made with friendly people may be, and have very often been, abused by other people when they subsequently send over to the same sources. I help only people who are liberal and emotionally friendly to Ireland; the others can look after their own interests for it is in their own interests they come ...

I am enclosing my permit for .22 stuff. I bought my last amount when I bought the gun at a shop on the Quays, the O'Connell bridge side of the Four Courts ...

When in Dublin I had a box compass which I brought out in Mrs Kiernan's car to Halligans. I searched for it before I left and then thought I had left it with Kevin; now I remember that I left it in the back of Mrs Kiernan's car. Could you please 'phone her and get it from her, leaving it with Kevin, so that he can bring it down at Christmas. Mrs Kiernan 32 Elgin Rd, 64001.

It's rained here until yesterday; rain so heavy at times that it's like a light curtain but today is quiet and very still. All the edge of bluffs reflected in the water in a more interesting way than they appear on land, a haze on the water from sun. No oar locks when I went to take out the boat; later I found a pair of tulip oar locks. Speaking of boats I really want a heavy anchor up to 20 pounds of the folding type. This will cost about 36/1 or £2.0.0 and could be sent by rail. It is safer than the big one when I have a sail up in bad weather and move about the boat.

Fr O'Malley is evidently well again as he spoke to Cathal in Newport the other day. I am trying to catch the post by sending Michael into Newport with this letter. Kathleen cannot find the cheese knife and said you must have locked it away. If that is not the case, perhaps you could buy another and save the situation.

I don't believe you're coming home this week-end anyhow. You'll find plenty of other things to do at the last minute. I hope you can send the chocs to Jenny and one to Georgette Kerrigan,[155] from me also. I'll settle up with you later, so please keep an account.

Love,
Ernie

Letter to HHOM

[Burrishoole Lodge,
Newport, Co. Mayo]
9 December 1939

[Helen O'Malley,
Swiss Hotel,
34 Fitzwilliam Square, Dublin]

Dear Helen,
    Cathal received his letter and I mine. I hope your work is turning out to your satisfaction and that the figure is now completed. Raining here all the time save one fine day.

    1) We will need some good stout picture rings especially for the 5 very heavy new frames and for the other frames Johnny sent on.
    2) Tips for billiard cues, some billiard chalk.
    3) Remnants from Lehane and the heavy coat with the pattern in it in light brown.
    4) Please look at a table tennis table in Healy's so that we can think about it later.
    5) If you visit J. Yeats could you please copy down a ballad *To General Monroe* in one of his Irish boxes; it's on the top of one, I think.

    This seems to be a list of things to do I find, as are all my letters but it can't be helped.
    It has rained steadily, practically since I came here. Cathal is well and sends you a letter. I'm glad you were pleased about the McGuinness picture. Did you see the tennis player, and what are his prices like? He seems to have movement and vigour. I would like to know something of his training. What price are turkeys per pound as I placed an order locally for turkeys for Christmas. In a hurry to get to town for post.

                            Love,
                            Ernie

Burrishoole House,
Newport, Co. Mayo
11 December 1939

Helen O'Malley,
Swiss Hotel,
34 Fitzwilliam Sq., Dublin

Dear Helen,

I'm very glad about your news. I hope now you'll take life a little more easily, if you can. There's no hurry about you coming back, the house is easy enough to run, Kathleen is doing pretty well, and my demands on them are few enough.

Cathal is looking well, very busy as usual when there's anything to be done, rushing around to help and get in everyone's way. I have made up a new set of stories for him about two small foxes as Redhead and Blackhead, 'Reddy' and 'Blacky'. I find he likes to hear the same story repeated with the details stressed that he likes, as their chasing their tales [*sic*], playing Ring a ring a Rosie, keeping food for their Mummy and Daddy, and kindness from anyone. When foxes are heroes he resents anything being done to them by guns, men, dogs. If dogs were heroes he would I'm sure be against foxes. I think some time I'll type out a few of their adventures and you can add the illustrations to make a book.

Wind has been blowing steadily again with rain, mostly S/W and S winds and very heavily. I'll have to wait awhile before I can use the boat. But I must get out or I'll become very soft indeed. I haven't been out but for one evening since I came back.

I don't see why Leonard can't come 15th–18th. I can look after him if you're not here. Anyhow I'm sure he can amuse himself a little if left alone but he could always walk with me, so please ask him to bring heavy boots and a waterproof.

There is no hurry about my errands. You can take your time about them. A morning in a taxi would finish them all if you felt well enough.

It's hard times on your sculpture I know.[156] But I suppose you know how important it is to have your mind at ease and your body relaxed. That's your job now as it has always been. Father Murphy wants you to visit the show he is going to put on for a frank criticism.[157] You could 'phone him in Rathmines. Have you sufficient picture wire in the house?

Best love,
Ernie

Please ask Bewleys to post on a few boxes of shortbread.

Letter to James Johnson Sweeney[158]

[*Burrishoole Lodge,*
Newport, Co. Mayo]
14 December 1939

[*James Johnson Sweeney,*
120 East End Avenue,
New York]

Dear Mr Sweeney,

Thank you very much for the copies of *Transition* which you kindly sent me. I thought I had replied but I find I had not.

Some time I hope to finish a book on Irish sculpture;[159] if the sun would show itself more frequently here it would make the work easier.

Kindest regards to Mrs Sweeney.[160]

Sincerely yours,
Ernie O'Malley

NO. 123 EOM PAPERS NYU
Letter to HHOM

Burrishoole [*Lodge,*
Newport, Co. Mayo]
29 January 1940

[*Helen O'Malley,*
Dublin]

Dear Helen,

Thanks for your letter. I'm glad you're in a house you like and that you are pleased with Cunningham;[161] he is the important part of your trouble and if you like him it makes you more confident. Now you can relax and take your ease until he decides that you can come back. I'm sorry I didn't know Dessie[162] was coming down or I would have asked him to come out. I am in bed to-day, cold, and the car won't start. I can't use my hand and Michael doesn't know the necessary sharp snap in the swing.[163]

McIntyre[164] is going on well. He fixed the pump. The temporary piece of wood used by Martin had got into the action. Pump will need a new board behind it to hold the heavy nuts. I will order it from Clearys. Michael I will not use after to-day but I will ask him to give his half days at 11/– per week, that is at the rate of 3/6 a day, the regular rate, I believe. You might ask Roisin's[165] brother what are the regular rates of pay for labourers in Co. Dublin and Midlands and in the West.

Hay is 5/– per cwt in Westport and as we have one cock we can then wait if you and others think the price will fall. India Meal is going up in price so I will buy a few sacks for the hens and the phantom cow. Unekas[166] is gone up out of all sense and I think boiled India Meal will do. As you are near to experts perhaps you had better find out about

Manures: for land

Food: for feed, poultry, cow, calf, pigs.

Then we could order it in bulk or at any rate compare prices ...

I meant to tell Michael on Saturday that that would be his last day but forgot but I told him today. McIntyre said he wasn't much help after the first day. To-morrow McIntyre will look up Philbin across the water and ask him to do a few days a week for us. It's hardly worth having anyone to come to do the chores: coal, cinders, pump. There is not a half day's work in that and unless you can think up work for men to do here I am not going to have a man employed here to scratch his backside. That is what the work of Martin and Michael has amounted to for the past two months save when you gave them a specific task. The result is that their will to work is broken and they are useless.

The girls will have to take turns at the pump whenever there is no man here, for we won't be able to get anyone for the few chores alone. Will you please consider this matter in your mind? A man could come every second day for the present if I can get one but the pumping meantime will have to be done by the house, or the fire will not be used in the kitchen on the intervening day.

I heard an interesting broadcast tonight by Don and young Dillon on a First Night at the Abbey. They were in the Foyer and back stage, Don did the back-stage work whilst young Dillon collared a few people. Perhaps that was rehearsed but it didn't seem to be rehearsed: Michael Scott,[167] Keating,[168] and David Sears,[169] Collins[170] (editor of *Dublin Opinion*).

Please see Des O'Connor[171] or Maureen Halligan[172] and find out the number of people who are willing to attend the Joos[173] [sic] class and the price they are willing to pay. You might inspect the proposed premises also.

About 3 weeks ago the PO in Rathmines sent on a form asking for 1/6 or some such sum in case we wanted to renew our address[174] for another year. Could you please phone them about it?

I think that you might have Lehane[175] return to us the material by post. I am not going to have him make suits again for he did not forward me pieces for repair and I need them as all my suits made by him are for rough country work.

I am thinking of sending you eggs. The hens are laying again, six eggs for past day and as I eat only an odd one you might as well have the benefit of them. I'll ask Nanna to collect them for you and butter them on the outside.

I am in bed again today so can do more writing. It's beginning to snow here now but I don't think it will continue. McIntyre is working away by himself. He suggested sending over Philbin to see me, a fine boy, and a worker. He might not be able to come every day but even if he came every second day it would suit: his farm is beside the water so that we could call upon him in an emergency. I showed McIntyre my 1600 map with MacPhilbin marked on it beside the castle of 'Borace'.

If you run across Stella[176] could you please ask her for the good book on beekeeping.[177] It's published by the English Bee Keepers Association or some such organisation. She gave me the name of it but it is gone with the envelope on which I jotted it down.

I hope the photos are doing well and that you have made a complete selection of them. Can I give you any assistance? It is just as well to get them printed while you can personally supervise them.

The cabbages are odourously rotting. Michael says that they are no good after Christmas. Nanna will begin to dig some of them up tomorrow as they are only using up ground. Snowdrops are out in clumps and in two or three days all of them will be out.

Take a good rest now while you can. There is no need for you to be here. The house runs alright and you haven't anything to do with the garden for a month or so.

With best love,

Ernie

NO. 124 EOM PAPERS NYU
Letter to HHOM

[Burrishoole Lodge,
Newport, Co. Mayo]
30 January 1940

[Helen O'Malley,
Swiss Hotel,
Fitzwilliam Square, Dublin]

Dearest Helen,

I was interrupted yesterday by Nanny having to go to the post. I have been making out the cost by a cow per day. It requires:

10 lbs. Bran and Meal mixed Bran = 12/– per cwt				
2 Stone Turnips	Meal	13/– per cwt		
2 Stone Hay	Hay	£5.0.0 per ton		
	Turnips	30/ per ton		
Meal per day	£0.1.0		Cost of cow	£30
Hay per day	0.1.3		Cost of cow house	£16
Turnips per day	0.4½			£46
Rent for field 5/ per week	0.8½			
	3.4 per day			
Cost of housing cow in new house if we stay for 2 years			5¼ per day	
Cost of cow giving it six years of life			1¾	
			4.0 per day	

Deduction for butter made
  ” for buttermilk   ?
  ” for calves   ?
  ” for manure   ?

Thus the cow will cost you 4/1 per day up to May = £6.0.0 per month not including wages of whomever looks after her. By next year you can have your own turnips. You won't save much, as you won't have your own hay.

A cow is therefore an expensive luxury when you haven't hay and turnips and you can't grow bran or India meal: you can save by selling a calf but even if you get £5 for a calf it would only be half of what the cow costs you per month.

Whilst you are in Dublin you might work out the cost of your bees and hens in a similar way.

This is what I meant to write to you about but I received quotations from Chambers[178] about the cost of feeding stuffs. If the cow has to remain being fed as I have outlined until May she will eat in that time

4 cwt of Bran
4 cwt of Meal   in three months
1 1/20 tons of hay
1 1/20 tons of turnips

Therefore we would need at least 1) ½ ton of Bran, 2) ½ ton of Meal, 3) at least 2½ tons of hay, 4) 2½ tons of turnips. I don't know where we can store 3) and 4) just now but perhaps you might inquire about such costs on Bran and Meal when in Dublin ...

———————

NO. 125 TRINITY COLLEGE DUBLIN MS 81171/1: LETTER 5/5
Letter to Thomas MacGreevy

Burrishoole Lodge,
Newport, Co. Mayo
31 January 1940

[Thomas MacGreevy,
London, England]

Dear Tom,

How are you? And what are you doing now? Jack Yeats gave me your address when I was last in Dublin c/o of some bank or other, but I searched endlessly for that address later but couldn't find it. Then at Christmas I had the bright idea of writing to Lennox Robinson, who later sent your address on to me. I have a photograph of Irish sculpture[179] for you to send. Then I injured my hand over three weeks ago and only yesterday could I write and I am getting this off before my hand gives out again.

Helen and I often talk of you here and wonder what you are up to, whether you are doing something you want to do or whether you are miserable because your mind cannot be properly used. I think that is the greatest misery. Anyhow I know you can see an odd exhibition of painting in London or can visit the National Gallery; then I begin to feel sympathy for myself who cannot do that down here in Mayo.

I had a few grand evenings with Jack Yeats when in Dublin. He's a grand fellow. Once I remember he talked of painting, it must have been a year ago or more, a very interesting technical and philosophical talk. I have asked Seamus O'Sullivan if a bibliography could be prepared for the 'Dublin Magazine' on the books he has helped to illustrate. I know of a few but I feel there must be many of them including early plays.

I have been reading Honore de Balzac steadily because I couldn't use my pen. Here in winter it seems easy to read him. He has a soft spot for military men, also his short passages about their prowess shows the latent sense of military pride which every Frenchman has. And the real passion very often is not love but revenge. *Cousin Bette* balances love and revenge fairly well. He is very unlike our present writers who cut down quickly or suggest the character in few enough strokes. I suppose Balzac was more like Holbein who had the ultimate conception in finish back in his brain unlike say Dufy who has no sense of continuous finish but conceives quickly and rapidly on a primary impression. Each, I suppose, is a different genre almost.

This year, rather last year, there was a show of contemporary painting in Clare Street by a new art shop – Longford. Amongst the artists were Derain, Kisling, Braque, L'Hote, Vlaminck, Gris, Dufy, Dietz, Bonnard, Gleizes and a few English: Gorther, Weirson, Lichert.[180]

Not of very great quality but interesting: for me the most interesting part of it was the people I met there.

Then Nora McGuinness had a show which I did not see but I saw some of the work that she was sending in. She has grown a good deal since she went to America: and I like her. Mainie Jellett[181] who gave a very good talk during the exhibition in Contemporary had a show as well, but it was not good. It's like Æ's poetry; there is some essential human passion and warmth left out. In her case there is the definite sense that a man is needed. Jack Yeats had a show:[182] I saw a good number of his pictures before they were hung. He told me that the pictures had been as well hung as they had ever been in any show of his. That also I missed. Nano Reid,[183] who showed some promise, had a show also but she needs the same stimulus as I have suggested for another painter. This judgment is of course in terms of things Irish, yet there were fine exhibitions worth going to see in the space of five weeks.

Have you been doing any translation? If you are translating a man whom you like well it is not so onerous. I was translating Rilke's *Letters to a Young Poet* from the French until I heard that Auden was to do it in America so I stopped.[184] Can you give me the names of any good French modern novels or books to read as I am lazy enough about French unless the book is very good; also a life of Balzac. I don't know if there is one in English; if so I have never come across it.

This letter actually is a thought from Helen and I to show that we remember and think of you and to wish we had you for a chat around one of our turf fires. War is far away from us here yet we feel what other peoples are going through at the moment; and we sense that we will be pulled in somehow when it reaches the general stage.

Affectionately,
Ernie

NO. 126 EOM PAPERS NYU
Letter to HHOM

[Burrishoole Lodge,
Newport, Co. Mayo]
2 February 1940

[Helen O'Malley,
Swiss Hotel,
Harcourt Street, Dublin]

Dear Helen,

Enclosed please find answer to ad.[185]

Can you find if lentils can be bought in Dublin; perhaps from Andrews & Co.[186] If so you might order a decent amount. We could do with more Stilton in jars.[187] If they put it up in a smaller jar it would be better. Anyhow we need 2 jars.

No Camembert or what they call Roquefort came this month so far that is in January.

Please order

1½ lb. of Ridgeways Fine Darjeeling

¼ lb. of Ridgeways Pure China Tea

¼ lb. of Ridgeways Her Majesty's Blend[188]

Then please look through this list and see if there is any special blend of China tea or of Ceylon that you want to try for yourself.

With love,
Ernie

Letter to Eithne Golden[189]

Burrishoole Lodge,
Newport, Co. Mayo
7 March 1940

[Eithne Golden,
New York]

Dear Eithne,

Thanks very much for your letter. I am glad to have as much information about you and my friends as you kindly give me. I hope you can come over soon. I injured my hand in January and it hasn't set properly. It isn't broken, though, but things haven't gone back properly, so I hope it won't interfere with my rowing in the bay. I row a good deal, though I'm not supposed to row at all, and I use the lug sail on days a decent boatsman would stay in by his fire and say the Rosary. So I want you more than ever here. I have a good deal of history, stories and miscellaneous material which I have collected from people around this Bay.[190] I have been busy for the last two months whilst my hand was bad. It's my right hand. I learned to drive perfectly with my left but at times writing is hard. Your mother would laugh over some of the stories. I want you to see this material and help me to put it in order. Perhaps then when I have taught you the technique you may be able to gather stories and material in your spare time, if you ever have any, for there are people of Irish birth in every State in your country. There is any amount of good material there which should eventually be used to supplement the Folklore Commission[191] here. It should be used as a repository for creative work, for myth is universal and always topical in application. The Irish Folklore Commission has done great work here in collecting its material. By this I think it has the most important collections, possibly, in Europe.

So you are needed here. First because I come and go in strength. I have to fight through the winter. Indeed I often think of living for a few years in Mexico, and I think I would have gone there if the war hadn't come in between. Also you could use my books for yourself and keep your hand in writing. I will send you your return fare if you can arrange to come. Please see Denis.[192] He's Secretary in Washington. Tell him you are a friend of mine and have a chat with him. He's a good lad, a good poet first of all, so therefore a practical consul. I'll write to him myself anyhow. Then send me on word at once as to how you propose to come and I'll let you have the money.

I'm more than surprised about what you write of the Modern Museum.[193] I should imagine that you had availed yourself of the Galleries on 57th St, Pierre Matisse,[194] the Down Town Gallery[195] and others. Also the 'Museum of Living Art'[196] in New York is in Washington Square. While you have the chance you certainly should visit the Metropolitan,[197] Spanish Museum[198] and others. It is only by seeing that you can eventually train yourself, that is if the feeling of the quality of the pictures isn't inherent in you. And keep at it. Your countrymen are too

---

much impressed by momentary trends in art as in business, but keep at it and don't neglect the Metropolitan. I can quite see Theodora's[199] eyes when you mention the external qualities of Picasso, but Theo could be very helpful to you. She has a clear, dispassionate approach to painting and her *judgment* would be sound. She can help you if you want her to and she may throw an odd brick at your emotions but that is to the good. I was very glad to hear of her. That's the first news anyone has written of her for years.

I hope your mother[200] is well again. She is a great soul. I wish she could come here too. I remember most her essential goodness – kindness, her very decent humanity and idealism and her love of books. And Marianna,[201] practical good hands mixed with her sense of the spirit. Mostly I want you to come to Ireland so that you can see it realistically. Over there you see it ideally. This is a hard, cruel and bitter country, but its faults are balanced by its virtues of humanity, kindliness and faith. Warped of course by too much failure, yet attempting everything at the one time when it has but some measure of freedom. You had best see it on the ground and in the country. Here you have clay in your boots and salt water on your hands: in the city you might see it intellectually or around too many drawing-room fires.

Maria,[202] I wrote to in San Antonio, a long letter a year ago, but no reply. But I'll drop her a note. I was upset when she didn't come over as I was planning to go to the islands in the West with herself and Dorothy.[203] Also Helen was in America and the house in Dublin was at their disposal. And so they didn't come and I felt as if I had passed through New Mexico on my way to Old Mexico and hadn't called in to see people in Taos or in Santa Fe.

I can understand your mother's wanting to go back to Taos. I feel the same about Dublin from here. Here you make your own life, particularly your intellectual life, for intelligence is suspect. You have to be very self-supporting to live in the Irish countryside, I mean intellectually self-supporting. There is no art, no library worth a small curse, no one who writes or paints near to you: very few people who read. That is different from your New Mexico. But I expect that your equipment must be eventually so that you can live in New Mexico, so this is the time to tank up.

I must write to Dee.[204] I would write to Terence[205] if you would kindly forward me his address. This censorship puts a mental check on writing. I don't like people to read my letters, naturally, though I have been trained as well as any to keep my mind to myself on paper. One person I want you to look up. Will you please do so and at once: Rebecca Citkowitz,[206] 100 Van Cortland Park South. If necessary take a subway train out to them and have a chat with her. She's my best friend in New York and she could quietly teach you a great deal. I haven't heard from her and I don't know how she is. I wanted her to come over here for a while and I am still anxious to have her here. Her brother, Israel,[207] a composer, and a fine lad, was teaching in the Juilliard School of Music,[208] and you might like to meet him. But Rebecca I like best, her mother and her father I have ever affectionate memories of their kindness and understanding of their two creatively-inclined children. It worried me greatly not to hear from Rebecca. I felt something had happened to her or to the family and I want my mind to be at rest. So that it is the first thing for you to see to and if you would be so kind send me a night letter about them and then write.

About your music. I have a few volumes of Bach, Scarlatti, 4 volumes of Haydn, 12 volumes Mozart, 22 volumes of Beethoven, 5 of Brahms, a few of Chopin and Franck, four of Sibelius, a few volumes of Debussy and odd lots of Strauss, Rimsky-Korsakoff, Schubert, Wagner. All orchestral music, a good deal of Oriental music, and a thorough selection of Irish vocal music in Irish. That itself, the Irish vocal, is a revelation. If you can notate you would be of extra use here as I could have you take down old unrecorded songs, especially in the bad weather.

About your clothes. You will want woollens all over, strong and stout. Here, you need wool against rain and cold wind, even in summer. So don't think you can wear flimsy American summer clothes here. You need some of them but you can be prepared for feeling the damp cold. Helen knows what it is by this. She was delighted when she knew that you might come and as you know you are as close to us as anyone so we don't see why there should be any difficulty about coming here. I can guarantee you financially, so there can be no difficulty raised in that respect. Denis Devlin will advise and help you anyhow, so please ring him up and make an appointment. I have a room for you on the ground floor with a Nora McGuinness and a Jean Lurcat, the other two walls filled with books, many rugs as good as Indian on your floor and curtains homespun in the mountains here. The rugs made here in Co. Mayo and the whole room designed and furnished in this country.

I am in a hurry for this to reach you, so I won't delay in finishing it. Please, my affectionate love to Theo, my dubious love to Maria, owing to her Anglisization, my love to your mother and Deirdre.

With my love,
Ernie

I have not heard again from the lady[209] to whom you gave my notebooks so I expect you have them yourself now.

4 July 1940

Please look at this date. I was expecting a letter from you all along in reply to mine but as you see mine has not been sent. I have had a few moves to Dublin and elsewhere since 7 March 1940. Will you please excuse me. Searching today for an address I came across this in the back of a portfolio.

Now, I'm glad that you didn't come over. Our tenure of life is short enough now. We are expecting the British to come in or the Germans or both simultaneously. That is the price of neutrality. I joined up but they haven't taken me so far and I doubt if they will.[210] The Regular Army runs things in its own way and I expect it does not want to be bothered with us ex-soldiers, though I think that when it's invasion time it will be glad enough to have us here.

Frankly, I don't see any chance of our survival as what we were, so I'm glad I had these last few years here, especially the last 2 years in Clew Bay. There are many things I would like to write you but I haven't much time now as the boat is due. You seem to stress safety, as all your people do. We have never been 'safe' here, yet we have survived: and in our own small way have made a contribution. And if we have to die we're content enough to die not as individuals but as a group. That's why we prefer to stay here and to meet what comes. Will you please give my love to your mother, Deirdre, Marianna, and Terence. If anything happens to me I will see that you get some of my books.

With my best love,
Ernie

I would like that Rebecca pass on my affectionate regards to Harold Clurman[211] and Paul Strand.

NO. 128 EOM PAPERS NYU
Letter to HHOM

[Burrishoole Lodge,
Newport, Co. Mayo]
22 July 1940

[Helen O'Malley,
Leinster Nursing Home,[212]
26 Upper Pembroke Street, Dublin]

Dear Helen,

I hope you are feeling somewhat better though I know you should be feeling worse. But the days are passing now and you should have nine days and not nine months to go.

Cathal is in bed with a cold. He was to write to you today; perhaps he will be able to write tomorrow. He is demanding attention, wants 'Cornelius', Barbar[213] seems to fade out now. The scene in the burning house has impressed his imagination. The air-raid shelter[214] is another deep impression. John[215] has made a good job of it but has neglected to make the entrance at right angles. It is dry and people can sit down inside.

Cathal, as I told Kevin,[216] has been talking to John who has told him the shelter is protection against German bombers. Yesterday Cathal asked me were the Germans coming in airplanes.

I said 'They might or the English might come.'

C. Isn't Andreas[217] German?

E. Yes, he is.

C. Are the Germans bad?

E. No worse than the English at times. The Germans are fighting the English.

C. Did the English do something to the Germans?

E. They did, a long time ago, 1918.

C. The English are bad. Andreas is good. Is his daddy good?

Andreas is evidently the link that keeps Cathal neutral and sane. Please tell Frau Hempel[218] that Cathal inquires often for Andreas and is curious to know more about the rest of the family.

Kevin has distemper, so says John. He got it suddenly this morning. Strangely enough two days ago I was going to ask about his diet and write as well to Father Sweetman[219] as I thought I would look after it when John went. Kevin is very sick and miserable.

The hay rick began to steam last night. I called John out. He said the top should be loosened. He loosened the top which was very hot, covered in taut firm with water proof covers. Today I went up for Michael. He came with another boy, said the top should not have been touched. John said also it should not have been touched. But I held him to what he said last night when he advised and helped me. I repeated his advice before him to Michael. He had nothing to say. No moral courage. He wants to show that the boss did the wrong thing, but not John.

The cow broke in to Duffy's field. Duffy came down to complain. I did not see him, but Nora came up to tell me. On Saturday I advised Nora to hobble the red cow. On Sunday I told her how to do it as young Gibbons had told me. Now, at 9 p.m. tonight, after a complaint John and she are gone up to hobble the cow. That is two days, Sunday, Monday.

Could you please forward me your keys as I may have a few people coming this week and I might have to use the silver. Dorothy is cheerful again. John is cutting hedges and is trimming the lawn.

Today was dry as from noon was and warm. I was able to get out in my boat but I could not make any headway against the wind which was due West further than the point of Rosgiblin.

I went to visit the O'Malleys when in Galway. They live in an ugly end of the 18th century house surrounded in back with small woods, a stream running near house; in front an opening of water then open sea and the Clare hills. Five acres of garden to look after with three workmen who help also on the farm. Mrs O'Malley,[220] a sister of Dr Jim Ryan sells the produce.

The family fine looking; one girl, beautiful in a special Irish way is studying architecture. They all play tennis on their own hard court and enjoy a healthy life. They are grown up, the youngest about sixteen, three girls and a boy at home.[221] I intend to visit them again when I am next in Galway. The garden produces peaches, figs, grapes. I was given the first ripe peach of the season as a special favour. Mrs O'Malley is the gardener and she will be anxious to compare notes with you. She is to send me a book on preserving vegetables. By the way, she says the Department[222] have a special book on the feeding of fowl quite a big one. Perhaps your nurse could get it and you might then read and forward it.

Yesterday the two cocks fought. I found the white one with blood on its comb and back whilst a favourite hen picked at it. Now, for one half of the day the brown hens will be shut in the high fencing; later they will be allowed out by themselves. This eliminates the chance of the cocks fighting. Bricriu[223] and the calf have now learned to go round by the sea shore and down the lawn. This was given me as a complaint that John and Duffy had to drive them back early in the morning. I pointed out that he could rehang the gate, which I did myself.

Sorry: I have to dash for the post. Rain here a great deal: and cold.

With best love,
Ernie

NO. 129 EOM PAPERS NYU
Letter to HHOM[224]

[Burrishoole Lodge,
Newport, Co. Mayo]
24 July 1940

Helen O'Malley,
Leinster Nursing Home,
[26 Upper] Pembroke St, Dublin

Dear Mammy,

I'm very sorry that she went, and she is very lonely for me I think. I'd like to go to Dublin in the morning so I would. Tell her to come back (when?) to-day (how) in surprise – on the train or in the car. I'd like to go down to see Mamma and then come back with Mamma and John.

Bricriu bit me. Didn't Bricriu kick Nanna? He's very naughty, and he kicked Nanna two times, one and two, and bit Nanna too in the arm, I think. I don't like him at all 'cause he's bold and I don't want to mind Bricriu 'cause he's bold. The calf kicked me, gave me a good kick and the calf is very good now. And the cow went out on the main road, the white cow and the red cow went out, I think, and Nora might have drove them back with a stick. The red cow had bad milk, the white cow has good milk I think. The hens are good (all of them?) Yes all of them. (They don't fight.) The cockerels fight with each other and the cockerels were bold to fight. (What did that do?) The old cockerel fights with the white cockerel and the white cockerel got blood on the head.

The sickens (chickens) are all right.

The boat's alright, my boat is alright and your boat.

Nora is alright, going on with the cows.

Dorothy is alright. Dorothy had a cold once but she better now.

Nanna is alright. Nanna had no cold. She is coughing, I think she has a cold. That might be all about Nanna. Tell her about my rocking horse – she's alright.

John is alright too. And John is telling me stories about Jimmy. John don't tell me about Jimmy where he lives. The rabbit had eaten all my garden and daddy you should shoot all the rabbits so you should and put a bit of wire 'round the center and then nobody tramp in my garden. My garden the calf has been walking on it and the donkey.

John's garden is quite well and the other garden when the nice potatoes is quite well.

The air-raid shelter is going on quite well and it's nice inside and a whole lot of sicks (sticks) put up on top, and a whole lot of pieces of wood put near the ladder and that will be all.

MacIntyre[225] is alright. (How do you know?) I know quite well. (When did you see him?) I never saw him only once a long time ago then he took you out.

Sean Brennan is now going on quite well. (Why?) Cause he's a big boy.

May Brennan is going on quite well. When you was away and I was over there I saw her with Nanna. (Do you like her?) Yes, but I'm going over to her.

Mike is going on with the hay and Martin.

The bees are going on. I know I seed them. The other bees hive alright in the drawing room.

The hammock is soaking wet, tell Mamma the hammock is soaking wet.

(What about the baby?) Say please Mamma would you bring the baby. I'll spank the baby if he wouldn't talk to me and I'll send him away to Dublin and he wouldn't come back. Tell Mamma that I love the baby and I'd like my drink of milk now. I'm very hungry and do you know I'd like my drink of milk now.

Please Mummy I like you very much and that all now.

Cathal

NO. 130 EOM PAPERS NYU
Letter to HHOM

Burrishoole [Lodge,
Newport, Co. Mayo]
5 August 1940

[Helen O'Malley,
Leinster Nursing Home,
26 Upper Pembroke Street, Dublin]

Dearest Helen,

It's too bad that you have to wait any longer. I'm sure you're thoroughly tired of all this waiting. I thought midwifery men could be more accurate, but evidently they cannot. I'm glad you are able to be up and about a little. It's hard enough to stay in bed save you can read or have people come in to see you.

The garden looks very nice now: the lower garden bright, high in colour, the center and upper garden also. I have not been to inspect the lower garden yet, the vegetable part, but I don't like to butt in on that as John seems to spend a good deal of time trimming hedges and cutting grass. I expect you know what he's supposed to do at vegetables.

I asked Nanna to have the turf brought in by Walsh.[226] He was to have brought it today but has not done so. I wanted to have John started on it so that he could begin the wiring of Brennan's pasture.

Molly Egan[227] was here yesterday. She brought the Gill's solicitor[228] and Josie Gill. They all ate in the boathouse and then came up to see us. None of them had the moral courage to demand tea later when I wanted to see them although they all said they wanted tea when she was out of the room.

Cathal is looking well. He has had baths when I was away but the weather looks not good just now. It's uncertain. There's no rain but I don't know if it will hold up.

Mother was getting on the Achill bus[229] when I was getting off. She had been here for a day or so. She reheated some of the jam. I had no time to talk to her. I will probably go out there by bus to-morrow with Cathal, then I can ask Stella[230] and Maria back with me. They could spend the night here if they wished.

I had a good passage by boat from Tullamore by canal[231] to the Shannon and then to Limerick. I met Johnny and Bea[232] there. Johnny tried to dissuade me from going by boat. It looked dirty which it was and unseamanlike. However, we had fine weather and good luck. We arrived in Westport at 5.45 last evening. As usual I am rushing for the post. I enjoyed very much having Sean[233] here. Male conversation is good I must say and we were out in the boat a good deal for the 3 days he was here. He was badly in love with someone so had to leave. I wish you were back here. The place is lonely without you. I intend to pick up the car shortly before the end of the week to visit Carna.[234]

> With best love,
> Ernie

By the way, could you get the August *Studio*?[235] It has a special French number and it might deal with painting. I would like if you could order the Yeats bibliography from Wally at Yale. It costs $1 I think. But please do so while any are left.

NO. 131 EOM PAPERS NYU
Letter to HHOM

Burrishoole [Lodge,
Newport, Co. Mayo]
19 August 1940

Helen O'Malley,
Leinster Nursing Home,
26 Upr Pembroke St, Dublin

Dearest Helen,

Thanks for your letter. I'm glad to hear you are getting on so well and that the baby is well.[236] If you decide when the christening should be I will go up. Has

Father Murphy[237] returned yet? If not Fr Traynor[238] would do. He lives at the Presbytery, Sandymount; maybe Don MacDonagh could give you his address and telephone number. Failing either of these two Fr O'Malley[239] would do.

I went to Achill on Thursday and remained until this morning. Monday, I remained with Mother for one night and spent the rest with Miss O'Flaherty in Dooagh. I met the Currans[240] there, Eileen Devlin[241] and they were all asking for you.

What have you decided about Cathal? Will he remain on until you come down or when do you think he should come down? That I suppose depends upon the date for Baptism. I meant to leave an order in Woolworths for a daily order of ice cream for you but I forgot. Perhaps you could have the nurse do this by phone or have her give the order to some shop near by to send up Woolworth cream.

With best love
Ernie

NO. 132 EOM PAPERS NYU
Letter to HHOM

*[Burrishoole Lodge,
Newport, Co. Mayo]
26 September 1940*

*[Helen O'Malley,
Dublin]*

Dear Helen,

I hope you have settled down to Dublin by this and that you have been able to see a few good plays …

Heavy clouds these days making the mountains stand out in relief, slate blue and mauve-blue, a fair amount of rain but not much wind. A fox tried to get Ferdia, the drake, last night but did not overturn the pen. I will have him moved to a hen-house for safety …

The Bell arrived. It is a good first number but naturally less of a documentary than the editor should by his introduction intend. I thought the Flann O'Brien article one of the best, Farrell's was distinctly poor, almost unreadable: the poetry was not improved by the rejection of Don MacDonagh's. I hope *The Bell* can continue but its continuance is dependent on all of us making an effort.

I hope you can see the Hempels before you leave. I don't think Cathal ever wrote that letter to thank Andreas for the boat.[242] He didn't remember sending it when I asked him yesterday as we were racing the two small boats in the inner bay. I was looking over the book *Die Minnefinger*.[243] A great number of cheerful figures with a Gothic smile, determined to be happy …

With love,
Ernie

Letter to HHOM

[*Dublin*]
10 December 1940

[Helen O'Malley,
Burrishoole Lodge,
Newport, Co. Mayo]

Dear Helen,

These pens hard to get so hang on to a few if you wish. Sent on some stocking, they're not good but best I would buy up on advice. If gun-metal were good I may be able to get some more.

Could you please look up the Russian shelf for Architbastoff[244] (not spelt properly), *A Russian Schoolboy* etc. There are 2 books of his on the shelf and I want their names and the no. of pages in each and what each starts as a chapter and ends with for it is in 3 volumes in the 'World Classics' and I don't know whether I have it in 2 volumes or not.

Do you want any books or anything? I really should move out of this place. It is much too expensive and I cut down on food, then go on a bust and spend more than I should. Please look up Chambers[245] and see that you get the 2 monthly copies of *The Bell* as he would never think of sending them out. I will possibly stay here for Mrs Salkeld's[246] play; would you like to come up for it, I am now a member of the Drama League.[247]

Love,
Ernie

Letter to HHOM

[Burrishoole Lodge,
Newport, Co. Mayo]
1 May 1941

Helen O'Malley,
Standard Hotel,
Harcourt Street, Dublin

1. Brass cleats; Beeswax.
2. Tow Hemp for boat for caulking seams.
3. Price of a few blocks (through which ropes run on sails).
4. Few batteries for Ever Ready (Reg. Design 830777).
5. Fountain pen from W. Bros. Suffolk St[248] You know the shop, ask him to send some on on approval at once and I will pick out a suitable one.
6. Diary. A good diary rather like the Brown & Nolan one so that I can

keep daily notes. If it had two pages to the day it would be all the better.

7. Some hops for making honey wine.

8. Pencils.

Dearest Helen,

I hope you are having a rest, the above list will serve to lessen it. Today, a beautiful day warm and kind. Tom and Michael went to McIntyre's and I went with them, making them pick stone for 3 hours first then it will be rolled: they then proceed to the Castle Field.

I had to shoot the blackbird as there was no way out of it. Caught a mouse in upstairs cupboard and set another trap, and found another just now, but I can find only 2 traps in the house. Hens are wired off so that they can't touch the flowers save they go through the back gate and up the side passage through the white gates, yet all of these open today and one hen near the flowers. One duckling dead. Julia then confesses that she knows nothing about ducks, about time for her to tell us that. Quinn[249] will bring over the other ducklings any day so if you don't have the pamphlet[250] forwarded I won't be responsible for them …

Love,

Ernie

NO. 135 EOM PAPERS NYU
Letter to HHOM

Burrishoole [Lodge,
Newport, Co. Mayo]
8 May 1941

[Helen O'Malley,
Standard Hotel,
Harcourt Street, Dublin]

Dear Helen,

I hope you are well. I was waiting to hear from you before I wrote as I did not know how long you would be in Dublin. I hope all your friends are well. Can you please see about Jack Hanlon's picture at the Contemporary Gallery.[251]

Sail Cloth: Have you bought it? The width is usually 32′ and I would need about 16 yards of this allowing me a little for repairs, 18 yards would be best.

Net twine: Light for sewing sails.

Sail needles: 4 or 5.

Ball of twine for whipping rope.

Yacht Manilla:[252] as I told you.

Catalogues from Green's of the Penguin Books and any spare catalogues he has, especially the Gollancz.[253]

A copy of Edgar Snow's *Scorched Earth* you might borrow from Roisin as it is dear to buy and I don't know if it is good.

Please order from Green's:

> John Strachey: *Post D.*
> Capt. Cyril Falls: *The Nature of Modern War.*
> Langdon-Davis: *Home Guard Training Manual.*

Also I want to get on loan from Roisin:

> P. Turnbull: *Black Barbary.*
> G. Ward Price: *The Foreign Legion.*

Any good personal book she has on the war in Spain.

Green's may say they have no catalogues but make them order them as it should be their business to supply good customers with catalogues even if they themselves may have to pay a measly penny for each catalogue.

I presume your garden is alright. You left me without instructions with regard to it. Weather has been very dry as you know. There is no hurry about your coming home, but if you want anything done in your garden you had better write to Tom or Michael.

P/S Some hops for my bee wine.

> With love,
> Ernie

NO. 136 EOM PAPERS NYU
Letter to HHOM

> *[Burrishoole Lodge,*
> *Newport, Co. Mayo]*
> *23 June 1941*

Helen O'Malley,
Standard Hotel,[254]
Harcourt St, Dublin

Dearest Helen,

I hope you are very well and that Cathal is enjoying his holiday in Dublin. I don't seem to remember that Dublin exists being so long ago from it in train of thought. However, please give my best regards to Nora[255] if you see her. I heard she was to go down to the Oughterard[256] side to take a cottage: perhaps she has done so. Will you please tell me the dates of mother's arrival and of Kevin's arrival as I want to know how I stand as regard these dates.

I wrote the enclosed (A)[257] on Saturday outside of the PO in Westport but in my hurry posted the second sheet.

I want to know *exactly* how this barometer works – the red and black as I can't read it and I want to read it for the cutting of hay.

McKenna & Verduns[258] on the Quays below the 'Independent' House you can try first. I have often bought before from them but never by name, always on the spot. If you fail there please try the other man whom you know, and if you don't understand anything please write and tell me. All this material is for a 3 ton open, strong working boat, so that the shopmen may know what the material is required for.

Cleats in brass if possible as the galvanised break off easily, yet I think galvanised wear better as brass tends to decompose.
A few sheaves, small and large, 4 or 5 shackles each of different size.
Drift bolt.
Rawl Plug No. 12 for boring holes in walls.
Quotation for Pulleys of varying sizes.
Thimbles: About 1 dozen of varying sizes.
Pal M for sewing sails.

Also I require about 1 oz. of icing glass as I want to make rhubarb wine and 6 lbs of loaf sugar, actually 12 lbs of loaf or 14 as I have a receipt for Beet Root and Currant Wines, one of which requires 3 lbs pressing sugar; also required:

Tartaric acid 1 oz.
Lump ginger 1 oz.
Lemon Essence small amount
Yeast 2½ oz.
Root Ginger 2 oz ...

The weather is keeping up fairly well; warm, not fairly well but really good. These last few days uncertain but the breeze S/W or nearly so. That is generally a sign of rain, today however the wind has gone South. There is nothing else to report that I can think of.

> With love,
> Ernie

Please don't worry if you can't get this sailing material as I think I may go up for it as soon as you come down but I would like to have what you can conveniently get.

Could you please send me on an angel cake? It's really the only cake I can eat and the consequences aren't too severe.

Can candles be bought in any bulk?

Letter to HHOM

Burrishoole [Lodge,
Newport, Co. Mayo]
23 August 1941

[Helen O'Malley,
Standard Hotel,
82 Harcourt Street, Dublin]

Dear Helen,

I hope you are well and that the furniture research is well on its way to sanity ...

Kelly phoned to say that he could not get a wind charger[259] and recommended a paraffin-driven lighting set, but as we don't get paraffin that won't work.

Brennans are yet working on the new house.

I saw sheep land today up at the lake. It's no good whatever for sheep. It would hardly feed light snipe for a year.

All well here. Étain knew me and talked away in her chair to me whilst I read and ate.

There seems to be a lot more, but I cannot think of anything.

I hope you get my telephone call about your key as I want it for the tea.

N.B. You owe the telephone company[260] £7.0.9 and you had best settle *at once* or they'll cut you off.

With best love,
Ernie

Letter to HHOM

[Stationery of] Standard Hotel,
[82 Harcourt Street,] Dublin
17 November 1941

Helen O'Malley,
Burrishoole Lodge,
Newport, Co. Mayo

Dearest Helen,

I hope you are feeling better by this and that the household is in working order. The weather has been wet here, and so I suppose it is doubly wet with you. I went around to see Mainie Jellett and she said she had not expected you to come that day as it was very wet. I also sent flowers to Miss Guinness,[261] and she wrote me a letter of thanks, so that is alright for a subsequent visit.

Very little done about my 'Quest for Carew'.[262] You should read that book in the Penguin series somewhere in my room and you would know what I am up against. I don't know how much longer I intend to stay: for a while if I get some information and if I don't I should do something on my own and get started on it. This thing takes a deal of time as I do not know the people I have to see and by the time I have made up my mind to see them I have lost a good deal of time. However, I have got to get moving one way or another. Tom McGreevy does not like the idea of my doing it at all. I know he is right for I should write of the origin of their family as an Irishman sees them, or in their Irish aspect. Covering the period of the old man means a good deal of time devoted to English influences: poets, painters, writers. It's hard enough to get hold of the Irish contacts. Anyhow that's my funeral, I expect.

If my presses are open could you please have the carpenter lower the shelves halfway. I mean, the lower presses in my room in which shelves are badly placed.

With best love,
Ernie

Your letters are in the drawer beneath. I had them today when I met you but I forgot I had them.

E.

I rang up Jelletts[263] but she won't be free until 8.30 this evening and then she can see you.

Ernie

NO. 139 EOM PAPERS NYU
Letter to HHOM

Burrishoole [Lodge,
Newport, Co. Mayo]
16 January 1942

*[Helen O'Malley,
25 Upper Pembroke Street,[264] Dublin]*

Dearest Helen,

I hope you are very well and that you are taking life easy. I suppose the flat is very nearly ready now, but I hope you didn't use the rubber substitute for covering. In the long run I expect tweed you will find best, both aesthetically and otherwise ...

I searched but couldn't find the radio key you mentioned. I tried all drawers in your desk, but I couldn't open the two lower big drawers. Mice ate holes in two of my coats whilst I was away but one can be patched though there is no material that I know of for my bog suit,[265] to repair it. I am slowly trying to get my room in order but it is yet like an avalanche.

The new press in the dining room looks nice, a welcome relief to the Butter junk in the flat, in looks anyhow. The gramophone was broken at Christmas, the spring gone. Julia has sent it on I now learn. That would be a sad loss if we were without a gramophone here. If you will again look for the key of the radio.

Men are working at the house as yet doing the inside. Hughes is waiting for a fine day to get at the roof, and MacIntyre is on the doors and window covers. It will take him about 2 weeks. The tractor hasn't come yet; it is waiting for a fine day. Stairs carpet needs to be put down so I think I will switch the men to that on tomorrow.

Cathal and Étain are well. Étain walks, but the weather has been very wet since I came so that I couldn't see them out of doors.

Time for post.

With love,
Ernie

NO. 140 EOM PAPERS NYU
Letter to HHOM

Burrishoole [Lodge,
Newport, Co. Mayo]
28 January 1942

[Helen O'Malley,
25 Upper Pembroke Street, Dublin]

Dear Helen,

Thanks for your letter of 23 January received here Wednesday morning. I'm glad to hear you are feeling better and I hope you are enjoying yourself.

About Julia you can please yourself and see her when you get home but she won't come back until you return. If she was kind to you whilst you were sick that is the least she might have done for you. I find her a pleasant, lazy slut especially when you are away.

Could you please settle with Lehane[266] and Fox[267] the tobacconist. Perhaps he could give you cigarettes sent after. I owe Fox £2.11.3 up to Dec. 18 but I owe more now. Lehane comes to over £17.0.0. I was told by the bank that I was considerably overdrawn – £50 – so I will have to pay you back[268] by installments. I have paid a Lipton bill of over £20, but I yet owe Carey Ltd. Thrashing is going on. This is the third day. The rain has interfered and also the softness of the ground the first day. The barley has been good as a yield, the wheat very poor. Winter wheat did not work out well. That might be due to the drought or to the cold nature of this land …

With love,
Ernie

Who has your petrol coupons? Do you get them every month?

Letter (EOM copy) to Sylvia Laithwaite[269]

Burrishoole Lodge,
Newport, Co. Mayo
[early February 1942]

[Sister Malachi, OP,
Grand Rapids, Michigan]

Dear Sylvia,

Your letter of Septuagesima Sunday[270] reached me and it was very welcome. Since then I have tried hard to get time to sit and think properly in order to reply. Imagine Gilbert[271] and I being rivals in ill-fame! Yet I have written you letters. One went with a box of Irish books a long time ago with a letter enclosed to which I received no reply. A long letter some time after the war began in which I have my views in detail and other particulars. No reply.

You don't seem to know that we now live in Co. Mayo. I found a house on the sea in November 1938, on a tidal river perhaps is better, but always there is sea in the bay in front. We have been here ever since save for a trip to Corsica and another to Paris.[272] I suppose I had best begin with the house and neighbourhood first as you don't seem to have received any of my letters or at least I will give you the benefit of the doubt.

The house was built about 1830 on the site of a house held by the O'Malleys. The former house was burnt by the Yeos[273] in 1798 as Colonel Austin O'Malley[274] with his brother accompanied by tenants and friends had fought with the French in 1798. Colonel Austin escaped to France, his brother was hanged. Colonel Austin is mentioned in *The Last Invasion of Ireland* by Richard Hayes and in the *Memories of Myles Byrne*. The house has two small piers and is on one side, the front, eight yards from the water: on the East thirty yards. Croagh Patrick[275] faces it; around the headland are islands and the Bay itself. There is a garden attached of about 3/4 of an acre in which Helen produces everything from Indian corn to artichokes.

We have two cows 'Strawberry' and 'Ruadh', a heifer calf of Strawberry's called 'Bawneen', a horse as yet unnamed, a donkey 'Bricriu', pedigree duck, Pekins, the drake Ferdiah, the duchesses Fionnuala and other names. Three breeds of hens in scientific houses, two bee hives looked after by myself, a dog given to us with a dubious name, 'Hitler': the latter is the touchstone, however, of opinion in this part of the parish as reactions to the name disclose the owners' beliefs or opinions. A dairy built of wood, painted blue, and moveable, equipped with separator, the last in from Sweden, and butter making apparatus. Helen has made a poem of the dairy which can be moved in four parts to an island if the worst happens.

I have a dug out shelter fully equipped, and a boat 'The Blunderbuss', a small lug-sail which goes about the bay in all weathers. I had hoped to have a bigger boat by this but I have not come across one. Luckily, from the beginning I would not use a petrol engine in the boat as I knew war was coming. I learned again to row long distances out to the farthest islands although rowing is strictly forbidden to me.[276]

Then I was sure of being ready to depend on the oars in all weathers. Now, there is no petrol, none for me at any rate, as the car is stored away, save once in a long while.

This year we rented land for food, and to-day there are nine acres ploughed for crops. We have got to put in some turnips as I by luck found seed. Seed as you may know is nearly impossible to obtain, especially vegetable seed. You know Ireland and the West, the general mentality. Hence supervision all the time. The result is we have no time for anything but land. By the end of this year, please God, we on this land, hope to be self-contained save for tea and certain luxuries.

Helen is very much a part of the landscape now. Useful with hands she can design, partially build, do interior decorating and so Irish material, suitably designed, has a large show in the house. But as you know the lack of initiative means that decisions and supervisings are quadrupled. That aspect is more than hard for an American, and as a result the time for thinking or for creative work has been so cut down for her that she has produced a small placque (can't spell it) and a head, as yet uncast.[277]

However, in the country living as we do you can understand cause and effect. Very few things can be taken for granted – water has to be carried from over a quarter of a mile away for drinking and be pumped for the household. Light means candles. Now, paraffin, which we use, becomes instead of six gallons a week less than a gallon. Soon there won't by any, or about half a gallon a month. It would be interesting to have eight people to support light on that amount. Food has to be brought from ten miles away, from Westport: other necessaries in proportion. Rio Chiquita[278] was nearer in every way to a source of supply. On the positive side there is health and an understanding of rural problems, yet health is easier to guard in a city during our winters.

Étain has two teeth. She is very fat; Helen thinks she is an O'Malley. Cathal seems to be a Hooker. Cathal's accent is a thing to wonder at as his nurse is a Connemara native speaker; not terribly interested in parting with her Irish and the local men have the local accent strong as home-made butter.

I have not been able to go to Dublin since the end of November so you can understand how the war has isolated even the counties in this province: and I don't now know when I will be able to get there. Helen and I have to go there every now and then to meet people who speak our own language. Here, nobody is interested in creative work: indeed I am the only one she knows in Ireland as equally interested as herself in painting and sculpture.[279] Her water colours are very good[280] indeed but she has not painted since she came to Ireland. I have nobody to speak the language of books, literature or criticism. One is driven back in on oneself too much. The County Library is in a room in the old courthouse in Castlebar, two rooms in fact, electric light on all day, books heaped on the floor ten thick, six feet high and no chance of the committee ever buying a new book which one would need, or keeping one which had any creative tendencies. I have often thought of you, when I looked on the books there: you would have made it part of the life of the county and a centre to co-relate their interests and imaginations with their natures.

The immediate family next in order of age: Cecil[281] in London, a surgeon,

Harley St, hit in hand by bomb splinters, house blown up. Sweetie[282] removed to South Africa as a kind of a companion, but trying to resume nursing again and to get back to England. Paddy[283] in the Bank, very interested in tactics instead of his devoted golf: out most nights on manoeuvres of some kind. Kathleen[284] nursing in Dublin, yet at home at times. Kevin,[285] physician attached to Mater Staff: scientifically detached, careful, thorough. Brendan[286] in some British unit in England. Dessie[287] first officer in an Auxilliary cruiser, torpedoed twice, injured in face, out at sea, I think now. I don't hear from Cecil, Brendan, Sweetie, Dessie, but I hear of them at intervals. Father[288] getting old, his health comes and goes; keeps his own council. Mother mostly at Glengarriff where her rheumatism gets some relief: last Summer she spent in Achill,[289] and to-day she sent beautifully knitted gloves for Helen and two pairs of three coloured socks for Cathal …

NO. 142 EOM PAPERS NYU
Letter to HHOM

Burrishoole [Lodge,]
Newport, Co. Mayo
4 July 1942

[Helen O'Malley,
25 Upper Pembroke Street, Dublin]

Dear Helen,

I hope you are well. I notice that Teresa is drawing £6 per month. Are you going to continue to do this? You will have to arrange with her for the two children at £36 and £72 = £108 and much too dear. £50 a year is quite sufficient for her. Tommy drew £40 a year with food.

Please see that the drawers in the desk are locked and that the store cupboard with wine is locked while she is there and that Radiogramme cannot be used for Records.

I am enclosing Customs Labels. One of the maple sugars had boiled over the top leaving half behind it; one of the others had a quarter of its contents gone. Winter evidently is the time to send maple sugar, but I'm sure you will be glad to have it. Unfortunately I have mislaid the key of the tea press and so I can't send you the Earl Grey, but I'll search the Guest Room cupboard for a box to-day and will send it up with Cathal.

Thank you for your letters.

Jams so far	
Gooseberry:	111 lb.
Strawberry:	19 lb.
Black Currant:	35 lb.
Red Currant: not finished – about	9 lb.
	165 lb.

I will do some more strawberry, red currant and black currant next week when the fruit ripens. We put whiskey in instead of wax to preserve them. Jam moulds because it is cold. I suppose you know this: and I don't know what the solution is in a house like this.

I do not know if this is how you wanted the jam apportioned. The preserving pot has not as yet arrived. We had to use saucepans which discoloured one lot of gooseberry jam.

Sorry; have to rush for post.

Love,
Ernie

I mentioned locking up because Teresa breaks all known rules.

NO. 143 EOM PAPERS NYU
Letter to HHOM

Burrishoole Lodge,
Newport, Co. Mayo
10 July 1942

[Helen O'Malley,
25 Upper Pembroke Street, Dublin]

Dear Helen,

It has been very hard on you to have to wait so long,[290] but I hope you can read whilst you are waiting. At the worst you are kept from rushing around frittering your nerves. Cathal should be company for you. What do you intend to do with him?

T... is a sly lynx as I have always told you but her faults have been minor ones. She never carries out a rule. I had to forbid her the bathroom. She had again been washing clothes there frequently and using the hot water when water was scarce. The reservoir dried. There was a little water left in the bathroom but I found her slipping in and out there frequently. At last I definitely forbid everyone the bathroom including Cathal. Will you please instruct her to wash Cathal in hot water in the morning and carry hot water in the evening up for his bath. She uses towels in the schoolroom. I find dirty towels stuck into drawers below them. By the time she returns please make out a list of her duties and I'll check on them. ...

I received your letter of 2 July and the pouch. It was very kind of you to send it. The letter was put in the hall by one of the girls and I did not come across it till to-day.

Butter supply is now 3 lbs. per week. I began to investigate to-day. I think Jane is being casual about the milk. I have taken the dairy key from her and give it to her for separating purposes only. It is therefore locked during the day so that she can't give milk to her brother and the workmen here. No record was kept as you know and therefore there is no check. The same with the eggs.

The nurse seems a very nice, pleasant kind of a girl. Bridie reported that you do not seem pleased with her work as laundress. To me she seems a decent girl, less cute than the locals.

I would not pay Teresa whilst she is on holidays. For goodness sake settle the salary before she comes back here.

With love,
Ernie

Will you please settle with K[291] for the rugs and I'll settle with you later.

NO. 144 EOM PAPERS NYU
Letter to Cathal O'Malley

Burrishoole Lodge,
Newport, Co. Mayo
10 July 1942

[Cathal O'Malley,
25 Upper Pembroke Street, Dublin]

Dear Cathal,

I hope you are very well. I am very sorry I couldn't be present for your birthday, but I'm sure you had a good time. I hope you didn't have a tummy ache. Etain has a new friend, Ted-ee, whom she brings to bed and talks to when she is with him alone. She brushes his hair, and I'm sure would give him a bath if she could.

Daisy is well. She has four puppies to look after. Their toes and noses are still pink. She is out hunting the rabbits whenever she gets a chance.

Blossom[292] got cross yesterday. John Connolly was working her, and he did not treat her properly so that she is getting a bit obstinate. Peter had to beat her yesterday, but she will be alright again in a week or so.

The Sea Horse[293] has had a few sails down to Rosgiblin[294] where we are working on fences and back. One day I brought Tommy, John Hughes and Michael with me. It was a very rough day so I took them for ballast to prevent the old *Sea Horse* going over with the wind. John Hughes took off his cap and said his prayers. Yesterday Michael was so slow letting down the main sail that it swung with the wind and sent me overboard. If I had the cabin boy[295] with me that would not have happened.

I saw Bawneen yesterday. The flies have her pestered. Maire Ruadb was out there also in Rosgiblin waiting to calf. The bull, Flann,[296] looks well but a little sad. I think he would sooner be out with Bawneen for she licks his nose. Are there any Molonies in Dublin; don't tell anyone the secret.

With best love,
Ernie

Letter to Kathleen Malley

Burrishoole Lodge,
[Newport,] Co. Mayo
19 July 1942

[Kathleen Malley,
St Kevin's,
7 Iona Drive,[297] *Drumcondra, Dublin]*

Dear Kathleen,

Thank you very much for the cigarettes. I have been smoking more lately as a result of the supply;[298] especially when I have anything to do with bees. But there's nothing to replace the pipe and unfortunately my pipe tobacco is hard to obtain.

I hope Cathal won't be a bother to you. He'll talk all day if you let him, and he's good company but I don't want too much attention paid to him or he will get out of hand.

Étain is looking well. She is not as fat as she used to be, and I think that is better for her. The new 'nurse' is a nice girl, bright cheerful and clean herself. Étain and she are great friends. They take long walks together. Would you please have Cathal's feet seen to whilst he is up there. Kevin could recommend someone. Teresa never carries out his exercises and as a result his feet are hopeless for walking.

We have had plenty of rain here. Every day it comes down. I hear you are all looking for rain above in Dublin. You can have our rain for the asking. I'm sorry I couldn't get up to see Cecil and his bride,[299] but the work must be done here by someone, or at least, overseen by someone.

July has been a bad month these past few years so I expect it will be bad until the end of the season. However, on land when working the weather doesn't matter as much. I hope you find the Army[300] as attractive as ever.

With love,
Ernie

Letter to HHOM

Burrishoole [Lodge,
Newport, Co. Mayo]
21 July 1942

Helen O'Malley,
26 Upr Pembroke St, Dublin

Dearest Helen,

I hope you are getting better and that you are taking things quietly and that you like the baby. You have had a hard time waiting and now you'll have to rest.

I am sending on the farming book to Roisin and the *Myths and Legends* to you. I expect that is what you want.

Étain is very well. The new nurse is very nice indeed, very cheerful, healthy and willing. She helped in the last jam making and at the preserves. Maureen Buckley left before the jam making began, but I carried out her instructions. Then Mrs Burke came on Sunday, and we all helped to make about thirty pounds of black currant jam.

So far:

Gooseberry	111½	
Strawberry	19½	
Black Currant	68½	
Red Currant Jelly	5	
Black Currant Preserve	15¼	= 219¾

I intend to make some Gooseberry and Raspberry Preserve.

> With best love,
> Ernie

NO. 147 EOM PAPERS NYU
Letter (EOM draft) to Robert Herbert[301]

Burrishoole [Lodge,
Newport, Co. Mayo]
1 December 1942

[Robert Herbert,
Limerick City Librarian, Limerick]

Dear Bob,

I have sent you on the books you kindly lent me on compost and silage. The silage book was good but badly written and its information hard to extract. That and Western inertia explain my long delay, but I had to reread three times to be quite sure. Thank you very much for letting me have them. The other books sent to the nursing home have never appeared.[302] I wish you would let me know their names, and I will have them ordered for you.

The thrashing is finished now. There is a bad local machine owned by Michael Kilroy's son[303] and a good machine also owned by his son. The good machine does not come this side of Newport. The result is that all cereal crops are imperfectly cleaned and unsuitable for seed. Next year I will keep what I can to feed cattle and grow the minimum of wheat, enough for our needs for I want to have thrashed cereals if necessary.

Today we have been thrown about in the salt water by cattle which we were attempting to swim to an island. Very cold the water was and we failed for this morning ...

Letter to John Raleigh

> Burrishoole Lodge,
> Newport, Co. Mayo
> *21 December 1942*

[John Raleigh,
Kilbane House,
Castletroy, Co. Limerick]

Dear Johnny,

Thanks very much to you and Bea for the magnificent ham which you kindly sent us. My great regret is that I am not in Dublin to pick a book for Peggy for her birthday has come and Christmas is here, and I have failed her. But I have been kept busy on the land. I have now about 54 acres to fence, drain, till and manage, and it seems a whole time job til the land is in some kind of order. I had hoped to pay you a visit, and so had Helen, but I'm afraid now we can't see our way together. We have not had a cook for 3 months past, the governess who looked after Cathal has left and so the children are on her hands.

However I feel sure that early in the New Year I can get to Limerick. I have got my ploughing to do as the plough has not as yet turned up.

With love to you both, to Peggy, to the girls and John.

> Ernie[304]

Letter to John Raleigh

> 4D, 25 Upr Pembroke St, Dublin
> *[9 November 1943]*

[John Raleigh,
Kilbane House,
Castletroy, Co. Limerick]

Dear Johnny,

I have a letter here in answer to an advert I put in the papers, from N Naughton, Chapel View, Adare, Co. Limerick, applying for the position of working steward. He states he can plough and do all farm work and that at present he works 100 acres for a widow but has no house. The letter sounds like the man we interviewed previously.

Could you ask Rochfort[305] to get in touch with him and when you have forwarded him my letter then find what he would come for. He did not state age or number of children. We give as perquisites some turf and firewood, 2 pints of milk per day and potatoes.

Can you let me know result as soon as possible as I am here trying to interview people but their prices are sky-high.

I hope Bea and all the children are well. Helen wishes to be kindly remembered to you.

Ever yours,
Ernie

Letter (EOM copy) to N. Naughton

4D, 25 Upper Pembroke St, Dublin
9 November 1943

[N. Naughton,
Chapel View,
Adare, Co. Limerick]

Dear Sir,

I received your letter.

There is a good house[306] with running water, separate scullery, separate lavatory, range, and hot press upstairs. House consists of kitchen, scullery, bathroom, downstairs room, bedroom with two additional rooms which may have to be used for men living in.

About 90 acres[307] of land, 13/14 acres ploughed last year. Five cows to be milked, 2 horses and a pony for work, some stock including calves, bullocks and heifers, 23 beasts. Land fair, requires working.

Sincerely yours,
E. O'Malley

Letter to John Raleigh

Burrishoole Lodge,
Newport, Co. Mayo
31 January 1944

[John Raleigh,
Kilbane House,
Castletroy, Co. Limerick]

Dear Johnny,

I hope you and Bea and all the family are very well. Helen told me to write you to thank you for the very nice ham which you sent us at Christmas. Please excuse my rudeness in not doing so. We enjoyed the ham very much indeed.

When I was in Dublin looking for men[308] I met Liam O'Regan:[309] indeed I was up to Dublin with him that day I left you. In the end about Dec. 10th he solemnly

---

promised Helen and I to work here. I was giving him a good salary, more than I could afford – £3 per week. He was to stay here for a limited time about six months and the agreement to stay longer was to be settled mutually. I then left Dublin contented as I had already engaged another pretty good man at £2 per week. O'Regan was to have come on Dec. 27th. He did not do so, nor did he reply to my letter of Dec. 18th. I sent him a telegram to which he did not reply but he wrote me a letter stating he was to meet Mrs Hastings in Dublin but that he was not going to go back to her as he would have his clothes packed to come here. I did not hear from him again until January 7th in which he stated that he was back again with Mrs Hastings and was 'sorry the inconvenience he caused me.' I did not reply to him.

When I met him in Dublin I advised him to return to Mrs Hastings as I thought he suited the place and her. He was definite he did not want to return. I met him at least twice a week and often three times a week when there; and at last when I saw he had made up his mind definitely to have no more to do with Mrs Hastings I began to look for work for him and eventually asked him to come to me. That is the little story of Liam and I. His honour is not his strongest point.

Hayes then looked up a man for me. I was to meet him this week in Limerick but I broke my leg on the 21st and am back here in a plaster cast and will not be able to move around properly for six weeks, so would you kindly see that he gets his train for Westport. He can get the Achill bus at the train and if he sits near the door if it is not crowded the conductor can let him off at the Gate Lodge where I will have someone to meet him. I am sorry to trouble you again and I was looking forward to a day in Limerick. Why don't you come up here sometime. You'll be buried long enough? Helen and the children are in Dublin. She's in trouble again. Her nurse and girl were to leave to-day to get ready for England. The bed doesn't suit me now as I was looking forward to getting the land ready for spring. Please give my love to Bee and the children. I hope Rochford, Martin Maguire, O'Reilly and your other friends are well.

Ever yours,
Ernie

P.S. The man Cummins is due in on Thursday evening and I told him to get in touch with you, thinking that then I would be there also.

Letter to HHOM

> Burrishoole [Lodge,
> Newport, Co. Mayo]
> *1 May 1944*

[Helen O'Malley,
25 Upper Pembroke Street, Dublin]

Dear Helen,

I am forwarding you bills which came recently. Also I am returning your agreement. I expect you are aware that we will now have to supply turf to the farm house and the gate house, 40 carts when turf, if not available on our bog will cost 30/1 per cart, a matter of £60 per year for two men. I would not give more than 12 carts per year and that from our own bog. It should be at our discretion to give more. Firing could be included, but with our consent as we would need to point out what trees or branches should be cut.

Will you please look up my red farm book and a black notebook 'Farm Administration', both of which I must have left in Dublin.

If both gardener and Tom require a garden, I would like to know where it will be. Every inch near the house is wanted for cows or for crops for them. Rosgiblin or Carrowkeel, they can have with pleasure; but that I'm sure they will not want.

> With love,
> Ernie

I have received Income Tax Return form. Am I responsible for children: or will I enter them on my list?[310]

Letter to HHOM

> Burrishoole [Lodge,
> Newport, Co. Mayo]
> *8 May 1944*

[Helen O'Malley,
26 Upper Pembroke Street, Dublin]

Dear Helen,

Thanks for your letter and for the lemon. I cannot leave here nor have I any intention of leaving until my leg is alright which may be yet some months from now. I know Americans believe in ceremony and they try to make memories for children and husbands but memory works of its own accord; it can't be organised, no more than you yourself can. So if Cathal is disappointed, it is because you have led him to expect something: a good sickening feed of ice cream can settle the matter, anyhow.

Kelly put in the basin; it is a smaller basin than the other, but it works; so far we have been unable to pump water as the well is dry and will be empty for another few weeks or more. Cormac is very well now and Étain is fat and blooming. I am sorry to hear that Cathal is sick again ...

> With love,
> Ernie

I wonder could you see Joe Griffin[311] of Supplies at Ballsbridge, Dublin. He used to be in charge of Beet Sugar, and he could put you in touch with the proper person to send this letter to. The silage was excellent this year; indeed cattle are getting nothing else now. Joe was my Director of Intelligence once; he escaped from the Four Courts with me. He will do anything he can to help; and also it would be well for you to have someone there whom you could go to.

> Ernie

NO. 154 EOM PAPERS NYU
Letter to HHOM

> *Burrishoole Lodge,*
> *Newport, Co. Mayo*
> *13 May 1944*

Helen O'Malley,
15 Whitebeam Ave,[312]
Clonskea, Dublin

Dear Helen,

I received your long letter to-day, 13 May 1944. Thank you very much for the trouble you have taken. The law, as I suspected, is more interested in observing the rule of law than the spirit of it. Surely, it is better to use rotten wheat than to use seed rye.

I see that Tom comes on Monday. I will arrange to get the room ready. It will be a very heavy expense for he will cost us £4.5.0 a week up until August. As for a plot I don't know where he can have one. Every inch of ground I need in Brennan's field and in Brennan's triangle.[313] He would have to take Hogan's field or go to Carrowkeel. However, that remains to be settled. One thing you will have to insist on that if he gets a plot he does not sell any of the produce, for I expect he will require manure. I can give him some manure for himself, but certainly none for sales purposes. That has to be thought over as we are always short of manure here. Presently I am starving cows and bullocks to keep them in their houses for the sake of manure.

Have you been to the Academy?[314] Could you tell me anything about it?

Cathal was very rude to use that special notebook. Please ask him to write me an explanation and an apology. He saw my name and he crossed it out. I must insist that whether he is dead or alive he respects the books in your room. If you cannot assure me of that, have the books sent on here. But see that he never enters that room unless you are there or with your permission. He is an undisciplined, whiny pup from my point of view, and whatever way he grows up he will have to grow up to respect my books but particularly papers written on, or notebooks.

The children are all very well.

With love,
Ernie

PART IV

Post-Emergency Life,
1945–1950

By late 1944 the isolation in Mayo had made a great impact on the personal rela-
tionship between EOM and HHOM. By then, even he wished for the company
provided by the literary and artistic community in Dublin. HHOM had initially
leased a studio in Dublin, to make her sculpture, and then decided to lease a house
in Clonskeagh to bring the children to Dublin for their education. EOM launched
into his interviews of artists and wrote the introduction to the first major exhibi-
tion of the works of Jack B. Yeats in Dublin in June 1945, in addition to other
critical articles and essays. EOM became books editor of The Bell *in 1947, at*
the request of Peadar O'Donnell, who took over as editor from Sean O'Faolain.
Throughout this period to 1950 there was a backdrop of unsettling domestic rela-
tions that found HHOM on long trips to America and EOM on regular visits to
London for Bell *business. His increased productivity was due in part to his need*
to raise funds for his own support as the royalties from his book had stopped. He
even had to sell some of his library from time to time.

In 1948 Cathal and Cormac contracted primary tuberculosis and were con-
fined to bed for six months. EOM became chief caretaker while HHOM was not
readily available. In late 1948 HHOM suddenly decided to give up the lease on
the Dublin house and so EOM retreated to Burrishoole Lodge with the children,
and once again home-tutored them until they could return to school. EOM had
decided that Cathal should learn Irish before going to Ampleforth College in
England. Cathal was dispatched to the Irish-speaking Ring College in Waterford.
Etain was sent as well, but Cormac was too young. EOM also started to interview

former comrades about the civil war so that he could revise his own draft memoir for that period, but the interviews expanded to cover the nationalist activities of his comrades from 1912 on. This work blossomed into a six-year project during which he interviewed over 450 comrades and made a significant recording of the Volunteer views on the independence movement.

Autobiographical Statement[1]

I met Helen Hooker in Greenwich, Connecticut, in her own house[2] in June 1933. I was brought by a friend of hers, Maraquita Villard, daughter or niece of an old liberal, Villard[3] of *The Nation*.

After dinner the Hooker family and I talked. Mr Hooker[4] took exception to some remarks I made about the American Indians, also I think an oblique remark of mine on the negro question. Hooker was the organiser of the Hooker Electro-Chemical Co. He had built the organization and the factories with his brains and some of his wife's money.[5] She was a Ferry, and was said to be related to William the Conqueror. She was quiet, agreeable; a pleasant, wealthy woman concerned with society, flowers and money.

Hooker was dynamic, restless and dogmatic. I could sense they were hostile to Ireland, the Irish and Catholicism, for the Irish were not in social circles, and when they were they conveniently forgot that they have Irish names. Catholics, with rare exceptions, were not represented in the Hooker social groups.

Helen brought me down to see her studio,[6] talked a great deal about sculpture and seemed to be interested in the fact that I knew about sculpture and painting. At that time I thought her insistent on showing every piece of sculpture she had made as some of it I considered unfinished. Later, I was told by Helen that her father forbade me the house. 'I was a dangerous man, a revolutionary', he said.

Mr Hooker has three[7] daughters. That irked him, but it pleased Mrs Hooker; she was afraid of boys. Young men were seldom invited to the house which was a 'dry' house as Hooker did not approve of drink. He was a Baptist. Mrs Hooker was a Christian Scientist. Hooker did not like Mrs Hooker's Christian Science. He once burned her books on the subject.

Helen had no religion; some vague notion of making an altar in the woods when young; a feeling for Greece where she had been for a year under a man called Kanellos.[8] I met Kanellos and his wife[9] in New York. I considered him completely romantic, a show off and a fairly bad artist. He had all the qualities I did not like, but which the lay mind attached to the real artist. He had, I know, made use of Helen for her money, had a sexual interest in her but in return gave her a feeling for Greece.

Mr Hooker wanted his daughters to win. At times he behaved as if Helen were a boy. He had her coached by tennis instructors and as time went on his ambition was for her to represent America in tennis.[10] She had drawn with or beaten Helen Wills[11] at one time. This intensive training and its publicity both pleased and annoyed Helen. She wanted to be a sculptor. Her father's intensity directed her to success in tennis. 'You must always play to win,' he had often told her.

Helen felt a sense of frustration. She had a stammer. Her inclination was towards a creative life, but a creative life with the background of social protection; and its judgment of social values. She spent about three hours daily in dressing and preparing for going out.

Her sister, Barbara had had a few 'break downs'. Later Barbara was placed in a private mental asylum. Mrs Hooker was nervous about Helen. Helen had no idea of the nature of money, no sense of time, no knowledge of having anything to do with a house save to stay there as a guest. Mrs Hooker knew that Helen had always overstepped her allowance, but hoped I would be able to keep accounts.

A sister, Blanchette, was married to John D. Rockefeller 3rd.[12] Blanchette had to behave as a princess would in a minor European capitol. Everything was planned and precise. Every move studied and weighed. Johnny and Blanchette did not know what to make of me, but Johnny did his best to put me at ease by asking questions on Irish production.

Adelaide was then unmarried. She married John Marquand,[13] a divorcée who had two or three grown children. Marquand was a best seller. His books were filmed. There had been doubts about Marquand at first but he passed all the jumps, social and economic, for he was deemed a gentleman, and he made a very respectable income. Adelaide was very doubtful and sceptical about me. I was not an American. It was an insult in her eyes for a Hooker to marry a European, but particularly an Irishman and a Catholic. Adelaide was almost 'half-baked' in her knowledge about the arts. She was interested in music and thought she might become an opera singer. Her figure was evidently the only real contribution to that ideal.

I had first heard of Helen when I was in New Mexico, in 1933. A friend of mine, Dr Lyght,[14] a good type of American liberal told me that a friend of hers, Dr Gantt[15] and a young society girl had stayed for a night or two in Rio Chiquita near Taos. The girl could not make up her mind to marry Gantt. They slept together and Gantt had hoped to marry her before they reached the coast. Helen was the society girl. She had met Gantt who had undertaken the first American translation of Pavlov's 'Conditioned Reflexes' in Russia[16] where they had become attached to each other. Gantt was not looked upon with much favour by the Hooker family for among other things, he had no money.

Helen, I found later, had no real idea of men. She had been sheltered by her family. She had no brother, and her mother was afraid of young men. Her mother was also afraid of Helen's philandering. She told me Helen was nervous and high strung, that she was very indiscreet. Mrs Hooker I found friendly, but puzzled about me. I had no money. I had come to America to rough it, and though I had met intellectuals and wealthy people, my heart was in Ireland. I thought, however, that Ireland would suit Helen. The country had no purely materialistic values, there was a sense of personality which could jump class distinctions, life was not either so thoroughly arranged as with the Hookers nor would Helen – except with certain Anglo-Irish families – find an equal sense of the importance of her name.

The Hookers were very proud of their position. What it was I could never exactly find out save that socially and financially they belonged to the 'upper crust'. They took themselves very seriously. No one of them had any sense of humour. I evidently passed the test of social amenity, and I met some of Helen's friends whom I liked. The Hookers sent a scout to England and to Ireland to check up on my antecedents. The scout, an elderly woman of 65, a Mrs Sheridan,[17] had been the children's companion. She had once been a singer. She was a strange mixture of sentimentality and spurious knowledge of poetry, but she was an antidote to the social American outlook on the artist who was a person never to be taken seriously save as an amusing appendage at a dinner table or as an old master, but also someone to acknowledge if he succeeded financially.

I had a cousin, Sir Gilbert Laithwaite,[18] who had been private secretary to Curzon,[19] or whoever tried to settle the Indian question at the expense of the Indians. Sir Gilbert evidently showed some sign of respectability. He was interested in Ming Ware, a good judge of claret and I expect he wore a silk hat in bed.

My financial prospects were bad, I must say. I had managed to exist between 1928 and 1935 in the USA, in Mexico and South America. I had wandered about assessing the USA as I felt it would take an important part in world affairs. The Irish civil war had killed the influence of the Irish vote for it was then split. Also the development of the Irish Free State conserved the energies of the home Irish in facing reality and responsibility. No longer was Ireland or the Irish Question a problem for official America. I had learned what happened to the Irish in America – a race of coolies who explored the frontier, built railways, supplied surplus labour and a sense of humour and bragadaccio. The Irish had supplied teachers, policemen, politicians, a gregarious sense and values in human relationships. But the Irish in America or the Americans, even those friendly to Ireland, knew nothing about the reality of Irish life. I mixed mostly with Americans, and I learned a good deal from them and from the Mexicans; but that knowledge was not a financial asset.

I had been badly wounded in 1922, in jail until 1924. I was expected by surgeons never to be able to walk properly again. In 1925 I had travelled through Europe on foot mostly for two years. I did medicine again in 1926–28 but had failed my second exam.

I had been promised a pension for service in Ireland. It amounted to two hundred fifty-nine pounds.[20] That service pension was confirmed before I left America, and I became engaged to Helen. At least we both thought we were engaged but of that neither of us was sure.

Helen and Adelaide, were brought by their mother to Japan, China and Manchuria, mainly to shake off an Irish phobia on Helen's part. Helen arrived in Ireland in 1935.[21] She met my people. I could not get married in Ireland as Helen had not been baptized, even. The process would take some time. Adelaide was willing to wait in London but for a short time only. I went to London, found I could be married for five pounds. That was in September.[22]

I returned to Dublin and enrolled as a medical student. Helen had little money. We began with butter boxes for furniture.

My only prospect had been my book which been rejected by about fifteen American publishers. I had never been given a reader's comment with the rejections but one publisher, Hal Smith, suggested that, in his case, rejection was due to lack of sexual interest. The book was accepted at once by a reader for Rich and Cowan.

1935–1937. I studied medicine but did not sit for an exam. I worked hard but Helen had to substitute a round of engagements in the New York fashion for a few dinner parties and theatre goings. Anyhow she was having a baby. She was upset and sick regularly. It was decided by a Dublin specialist that she should have a Caesarian operation.[23] She was badly cut up as a result as the doctor did not pay proper attention to her for the two weeks previous to her delivery. Cathal was born in 1936.[24]

Helen's lack of a time sense made me late in the university for lunch was never ready when I arrived and as I had to return each evening for dissections it was easier to eat in the bad college restaurant.

I was involved in a libel action as a result of the book: *On Another Man's Wound* published in October 1936. The case was tried in 1937.[25] Helen was not pleased with my solicitor. She seemed anxious for me to settle out of court, but I had to stand over what I had honestly remembered and had sincerely written. Also I knew that a series of libel actions could result. All through the case Helen upset me. I knew there was little chance, if any, of winning the case. I found it hard to obtain evidence. People who could verify facts and incidents in talk were reluctant to appear in court. Yet I could not persuade Helen to leave me alone. She was more concerned about her father's name being involved than she was with my determination to fight.

I lost the case. Six hundred pounds damages was assessed against me and the Three Candles Press.[26] The Three Candles Press had printed the book. I had prevailed upon the English publishers to have the book printed in Ireland. The Three Candles Press were also the Irish distributors and had made a considerable amount of money on the book. Now they refused to pay any money. I decided then to allow O'Doherty to send in the bailiffs. Helen was opposed to this. She evidently told her father who offered to pay the costs. I refused his offer. I knew that the house had been rented in Helen's name, that no one could know my books and effects from her possessions; and that if her goods were taken she could take legal action. She said she would state that books and possessions were my property if asked. She was hostile to my refusing to settle. Also she was again concerned about the Hooker and Rockefeller names being involved. The bailiffs were put in possession. Helen objected strongly. I borrowed money and paid off four hundred pounds. The Three Candles Press paid two hundred pounds.

I was unable to sit for my medical exams. I found it difficult to write. We moved to Mayo spending a year in Old Head Lodge[27] near the sea, probably in 1938.[28]

The only friction I remember then was in 1937. I worked late at night or I read in bed. Helen objected so strongly to my reading in bed that I moved into a bedroom downstairs.

I rented a house, Burrishoole Lodge, Newport, Co. Mayo.[29] Helen had always wanted to continue her sculpture, but she was anemic after Cathal. I brought her round Ireland on a study of sculpture from the 8th to the 12th century. She and I took photographs of detail.[30] I had intended to work on sculpture from the 12th to the 17th century. It was unknown even to scholars and archaeologists: a good deal of it was not even recorded. I slowly built up knowledge, visited remote graveyards by myself or with Helen to study detail and position of figures for architecture. This study continued from 1937 for a number of years.

Helen began to improve Burrishoole. I tried to prevent her over-elaborate improvements, but she was restless. After two years I advised her to buy Burrishoole, otherwise the rent would be increased out of all proportion. Burrishoole then had seven acres of arable land, but she rented a few further acres – about six, I think.

Helen's mother came over before the European War began. I did not want Mrs Hooker to come for I felt that war would break out in the autumn. By this time Mr Hooker had died.[31] Helen went to the USA[32] to arrange about her inheritance. As a result she bought Burrishoole for two thousand pounds. It included the Lodge, and a farm house. Later she bought the gate lodge and three acres of land.

Mrs Hooker was very alarmed when war broke out. She wanted to return to the USA at once. She was nervous. Nothing could be satisfactorily accomplished by phone it seemed. Helen thought that I should use my influence with de Valera[33] and his ministers to get her mother out of Ireland. At one time an American destroyer was suggested; at another time a British warship. Helen came up to Dublin. I had not procured a destroyer, nor had I seen de Valera. The situation at Burrishoole had been tense; now in Dublin it became hysterical. She was annoyingly upsetting in Kevin's flat when he and my brother, Brendan, were present. I tried to calm her down on several occasions, but she seemed convinced that I was unable to get her mother out of Ireland. I said I would not go back to Burrishoole when badgered under such conditions as, though Mrs Hooker might be important in the USA, here in Ireland she would have to accept the same conditions as other people. I asked Helen to explain the position to her mother. She did not explain, I found out later. Mrs Hooker came to Dublin. She was frigidly polite.

Adelaide had come to Ireland with John Marquand prior to their marriage.[34] I was asked by Adelaide to meet Marquand and herself in Dublin. At that time I was walking in Co. Galway on my way to the Aran Islands.[35] I stayed a few days with Liam and Barbara Redmond[36] in a house on Aran. Adelaide, who had been hostile previously, was now anything but pleasant to Helen. She looked at a head Helen had made of me in the USA. 'I can see he is mad,' she said. 'His face plainly suggests that.'

Helen began to build in Burrishoole – outhouses, a studio she wanted; she decorated and renovated. I tried to keep her within reasonable limits of effort, but failed. She is incapable of organised decision. She talks and talks about a detail. The result is good as design, but by that time everyone is worn out, including Helen. She has no capacity to let go of work. The normal tendency is to work until one knows that the mind is becoming stale; at least this is the creative approach. A few people can work when they are tired; often they achieve remarkable results. But a continuous effort when tired exhausts. Helen was only too often completely exhausted, and I was only too often completely tired of being deluged with all her problems at night. I tried to explain to her that with an Irishman the sense of beauty is too often in his mind. Therefore he tries to have his mind accurate and to live in it. The danger of accuracy I knew was pedantry. Americans, like Helen, evidently cannot exist without continuous change. They try to perfect completely their surroundings: but the cost in mental strain, worry and nerve shredding seemed to me to be too great.

I was working on the Elizabethan period.[37] After close on two years work I met Sean O'Faolain who was doing a book on Hugh O'Neill.[38] I spoke to him about the project, and as he was willing to sign a contract and as he needed the money, I did not proceed with the book. Instead, I worked on the Spanish Armada and its effect on the Irish chiefs.

We were considerably isolated in Burrishoole – a trip to France and to Corsica,[39] frequent journeys to study sculpture, but no organised society. I did not play cards nor did I play golf; neither did I fish nor shoot. That was against me socially. Also I avoided being bored if I can help it. I am impatient by nature, and I can put up with a great deal of solitude at times. We had no wealthy friends. I had made an arrangement with Helen that she would tell me whenever she was going to invite anyone to stay so that we could agree with reason.

Once a Miss Walsh arrived to stay. I decided to take a sudden holiday. I drove the car away unsure of where I would go. I went to Galway, took a boat for the Aran Islands. I stayed there for two weeks content because again I was writing.

Helen was anxious to farm. She rented land across the river which we ploughed.[40] I tried to keep her away from land as it meant trouble on account of fences, but she was determined to build up a 'model' farm in Burrishoole. By this time – about 1940 – Etain was born.[41] Farm buildings continued being put up until about 1943. They must have cost six thousand pounds.

In 1939, when Helen was carrying Etain a neighbour, Willie Walsh,[42] threatened to hit her. He said he would drive her out of Burrishoole. Helen had intended to buy land in the peninsula of Burrishoole.[43] I decided to buy the land as the onus of possession would then come on me. Also tenants had for years come to the house. They wanted Helen to buy land. I bought land by degrees. I fenced the land, built up banks and sea fences: – in all thirty acres of land, but as the fences had been destroyed for close on nineteen years,[44] it required a good deal of work.

Walsh and his brother[45] were abusive to Helen, myself and the men. They drove cattle and sheep on the land, broke down gates and there was a heavy menace. Also they were careful to work the safe side of the law. They threatened to shoot me often. Willie and Sean were violent. They had sudden white tempers. I had no intention of appealing to law or to police. I was studying hard at the farm, and I meant to hold the land which had been O'Malley land from early times. The house had been burned in 1798, the land confiscated, the brothers[46] who had lived there had been hanged, killed or exiled.

Helen was fearful, but after four years I won out. Eighty percent of the people were then on my side, but previously no one had ever given me any help.

Helen complained that I would not discuss farming matters with her. I did discuss a little of farming but not the minute detail she required. Anyhow she knew nothing of farming. Nor could she remember any of the complexities of farming.

She did not read. But she was interested in talking about farming to her Dublin friends and to acquaintances. I did the field work day after day in all weathers. I was often too tired at night to talk. Physically I was not fit. But there was a war on. I felt that our unit should produce food. There was a tuberculin-tested herd,[47] a bull on the land and the beginning of a herd of pedigree cattle.

I was able to make decisions about the land as I had some money. I owed for the land I purchased about one thousand pounds[48] but that loan I knew could be repaid in time. Whilst I was paying off for the libel action I could not make decisions which involved money; now I was able to.

In Dublin I had tried to dance[49] with Helen. I had seldom danced. Helen was impatient with the result. Also she had no sense of continuity. She would not hold to any discipline for a length of time. We tried reading aloud to each other. Helen had a stutter which was gradually improving until she was free of it. But she would not read in return as she said she was a bad reader. She had a good French accent but a poor vocabulary. She began to teach me the good accent but got tired of the work. I played music to her as I had a collection of records. She had no real understanding of music, but she was interested.

She suffered from isolation for she did not read. That drove her back on me for company but a good deal of my time was spent in study. And this made her dissatisfied.

I collected folklore around the Bay for over a year[50] but that was necessarily by myself. The 'woman of the house' would not consider me a stranger but Helen would be a social event. Consequently much of the folklore had to be collected by myself. That took me away until four or five in the morning for story telling begins about ten or eleven and lasts well into morning.

There was trouble about money. Helen never willingly paid a bill. I had asked at first as a matter of pride and face-saving that as I had little money and as I was buying off the libel action and later paying off for land that she placed some money to my account so that I could pay off bills addressed to me. This she did not accede to until about 1944 when she placed money to my account in the bank to pay labour and expenses.

Helen was friendly with the people and easier to approach than I was although she did not understand character or the many devious ways of the Irish nation. When she began to revert against its indirections and secrecy she became unduly suspicious. She suspected people whom she would formerly have been charmed with for their way of speech or for their easy way of life.

I tried to get her to keep accounts. I kept accounts but as Helen controlled expenditures, I could not budget. I asked her continually to employ an accountant as she was continually overdrawing. She borrowed money from me very often. This continual uncertainty about money was not good. Helen had a good income, and, by Irish standards, was a wealthy woman, but she was always in need of money. 'I love to buy things,' she often said and she was very content even when there had been friction if I came with her on a spending expedition.

Helen bought about twenty-six acres of land[51] across the river from the house. This helped, but the land proposition was never an economic entity. I had decided rightly or wrongly that the children should be brought up in the country. In Burrishoole they had sea and land. As the children grew up they would have the reality of land and a tradition of folk belief and of folk imagination which they could later discard: but it would be imbibed not from books but from people.

Helen was a society girl who at first was satisfied. I had become more laconic. I could never discuss any matter endlessly. When I had finished a point it was either cleared up or I failed to settle it, but I was not interested in a continual restatement. I had great difficulties with the farm but I did not complain. I concealed my difficulties from Helen for she was apt to misinterpret things or to talk about them to the men. Also I had not enough patience to listen to her troubles with servants, or the slow waste of time that goes on in Ireland before anything is accomplished. Helen was used to efficiency: good servants, good advice, experts around each corner.

I know nothing about investments. That was a matter for her American advisers, but she was accustomed to men who could handle finance to their own and to their women's satisfaction. Also in her eyes I was not either in the public eye nor was I producing books. I was farming a small portion of poor land in an isolated district.

Helen had built a studio in Burrishoole. She did a head, 'Island Woman', and a head of Delia Murphy[52] here, and some studies.

1943: October. A head, 'Island Woman', exhibited by Helen[53]
1944: Portrait of Liam Redmond Portrait of Eithne Dunne[54]

One year Helen had been away for some time I used the studio to store oats, wheat and feeding stuffs as the rats had eaten through all the other storehouses. Helen said I did this deliberately later although she had not been working in the studio for some time. One point I found disconcerting. When ever a point had been cleared up as I thought and I had either explained or taken the blame for it, I expected the matter to be closed. But when Helen became tense she again played variations on the theme.

The children Cathal and Etain had to go to school. Cathal went first to the local National School.[55] That was not a success. I tutored him for a time then there was a governess who, I found, beat him.

Helen inspected a house in Dublin or a series of houses. She had begun to know Liam Redmond. The house was two doors away from his house.[56]

Redmond was in the Abbey Theatre. Salaries then were poor and inadequate. A number of young players decided to leave the Abbey: Jerry Healy,[57] Eithne Dunne, Liam Redmond.

There had been friction about sleeping together I know. Helen's idea was that if there was trouble it could always be settled by sleeping. If I had a row with Helen I would find it hard to make love to her. It would have to wait until the right mood came, in peace. I had a dislike of 'post mortems'. Helen liked them. After a situation had been settled Helen would again bring it and previous situations to mind in subsequent troubles. This reiteration left me with a hopeless feeling. I thought and felt that life together had not been satisfactory and that I could not see a future. Also I thought the main thing to be solved was a future. I had little patience with Helen on these occasions. Many a time I asked her to leave my room.

My farm record books cover from 1941 to September 1944.

Helen told me at the end of September that she would not stay on the land any longer and that she intended to spend at least three years on sculpture, nor was she going to bother much about the children.

Cathal was then eight, Etain four and Cormac two. Cathal was then at school in Dublin.[58] The children, Cormac and Etain, were usually with me in Burrishoole.

I said that I was also fed up with land. It had injured my heart as Helen knew. I broke my right leg at the farm, and it took a good time to heal. Helen was away at the time. In March I went to Limerick to open the County Limerick Library Art Exhibition, went on to Dublin and then back to Mayo. I said I would leave the farm in future to Helen, that she could supervise it. Everything was in running order but it needed careful supervision. I had been a farm labourer, I felt, and it was time also for me to learn to write. I left Burrishoole, I think a few days later and came to Dublin. In July, August and September of this year Helen had been in Dublin working at sculpture or immersed in the theatre.[59]

October.[60] Helen was busy with Redmond about this time and with other players. She consulted me about a proposed new theatre.[61] Her work was in sculpture, I thought. Only by continuous work would she learn discipline, but the theatre was something outside her life save in the field of design. I advised her to keep to sculpture and leave the theatre to theatre people.

She wanted me to act on a board to read plays. The board as far as I remember consisted of actors. This I pointed out was a mistake. I had never liked actors. They were too extrovert, given to too much acting off stage. They had usually an exaggerated idea of their own importance and they were a closed circle in interests. They tended to develop a tension that was unsuitable to Helen.

I read three plays. One was by Redmond, *The Rocks of Bawn*.[62] It was a very bad play. Helen was very enthusiastic about it. She felt it was 'a really wonderful play'. She was to do sets for it. I did not like then to say exactly what I thought of the play for she would construe my criticism as due either to jealousy or lack of interest. I told her it might be written as a good play but did not suggest that the writer be not Redmond. *The Dark Stranger*[63] I told her would be a draw, but it needed a good deal of revision and good, hard writing. The third play was of no use. I advised Helen not to have *The Rocks of Bawn* produced.

Letter to Roger McHugh

15 *Whitebeam Ave,*
Clonskeagh, [Dublin]
23 *April 1945*

[Roger McHugh, MA,[64]
'Rose Cottage',
Ballybrack, Co. Dublin]

Dear Roger,

I had to wait until I could borrow a copy of the book to check on paragraphs needed.[65] Certainly, I give consent. It can't do school children any great harm. I don't know what biographical details you need; so you will have to be specific. I hope your wife[66] is well. She looked happy and charming the evening I saw her at your play.[67] I'm sorry it had not a longer run. I'm sure it would hold a house in Cork and the provinces.

Sincerely yours,
Ernan O'Malley

Letter to Etain O'Malley[68]

[Stationery of] Thriplow Farm,
Thriplow, Cambridge, [England]
2 *August 1945*

Etain O'Malley,
Burrishoole Lodge,
Newport, Co. Mayo

Dear Etain,

I promised to send you a [envelope with stamp] so, here it is. I went by a big [steamer boat] then by [train engine with carriage]. I saw your uncle [head of man] and a little [girl] and [boy] Kevin. [Boy] This is a better picture of Kevin.

I saw [two paintings] by your friend Jack Yeats.

Today I saw a big number of small [three cats] and [dog].

Love
Ernie

EOM's letter to his daughter, Etain O'Malley, dated 2 May 1945. Source: EOM Papers NYU.

Letter to HHOM

15 Whitebeam Ave,
Clonskeagh, Dublin
10 October 1945

[Helen O'Malley,
Zacheus Mead Lane,
Greenwich, Connecticut]

Dear Helen,

I received your telegram about the death of John T. Hughes[69] for which thanks, also a notification about your leaving USA on Nov. 21st. As you know, there is no hurry about your return. Everything is going smoothly, bills are being paid by degrees and you should be able to start with a clear slate again. You have now, I expect, ample time for your sculpture. The annoyances of farm, children and houses are eliminated and personally I think that as you feel yourself free you should now settle down to your work and stay as long as it suits you. I find no difficulty in doing what very little routine is to be done in connection with both houses. I have learned to simplify life when I was on my own and I intend to live it that way.

Roisin Walsh rang up Burrishoole, also later asked for an appointment with me to find out how the children were. She met mother[70] on the street and said she wondered whether they had clothes and boots. In Burrishoole she rang up Nanna,[71] and then wrote to her. I don't understand that procedure. I expect you do as formerly you seemed willing to broadcast your troubles around this echoing gallery of Dublin. Now, as is our agreement when you left, I said I would reply to any letters you wrote using the same time lag as you used yourself. I have replied on or about August 9th to two letters of yours. If you want any further information I will reply through the post direct to you, but I am not going to be interviewed by any of your friends nor am I willing to allow them to deal direct with servants. That may be an Irish point of view, but it is a definite one. When you had control I did not interfere as regards children save to prevent them being involved in what was then a pretty emotional and histrionic mess and in that attitude I felt justified.

I have not seen any of your friends lately so I don't know how they are. All the children are well, healthy and happy, so no one can expect more. Margaret, Cecil's wife, was over here for 10 days, but I was laid up. I saw her once, however; Bobs[72] was here and came to see me. The Players[73] are in London making good money on a movie, a bad one, but it is money. I thought you were also in London when I did not hear from you as I thought it time they should keep a job for you. Their pay is a mere £50 a week and that might have helped you. Kevin is well. I don't see much of him. He is busy and on his holidays; he fishes in Connemara.

Kathleen hasn't been too well, and I expect a rest will do her some good. I have just rung her up now, and I think she is going over to stay with Sweetie in Leeds.

I had a list of records to ask you to get as some are unobtainable here but I didn't forward them. I would be glad if you don't mind if you would forward me a list of books in the Modern Library which I think now comes through Random House. Bobs gave me her copy of a new issue of *Crime and Punishment*, an edition which I liked. Also I was looking for a complete Tolstoy for someone here. Perhaps you could find one in America as England prints only a limited number of books.

I hope you are taking it easy and that your mother and sisters are well. I hope Blanchette is as beautiful as ever and as kind and that Adelaide has worn down her will to some kind of acceptance and cooperation. And I hope you are doing your sculpture to your satisfaction. A few times here you remarked that I was jealous of your work. I'm afraid that is not true. I wish I was jealous about good writing which would be more in my line, but I am too full of admiration for any snatch of really good writing rather than racked by any jealousy which on the one hand might make me produce. Anyhow, you have your now care-free opportunity to do what you please but maybe you prefer to be a Greenwich lady and reactionary. That, I expect, has its advantages also.

Love,
Ernie

There are some letters here for you. Will I forward them? I had to open some letters but they were merely long overdue bills some of which I paid, so I expect it is legitimate to open what I think is a bill.

NO. 159 TATE GALLERY ARCHIVES (8726.3.11), LONDON
Letter to Sir John Rothenstein[74]

[15 Whitebeam Avenue,
Clonskeagh, Dublin]
26 October 1945

[John Rothenstein, Director,
Tate Gallery,
London, England]

Dear John,

This is to inform you officially that you have been adopted into this family. It consists presently of a Bobs Walston or Crompton or Boston,[75] as the case may be, and a boy called Cathal aged 9, and myself. There is an external representative in America called Helen; she doesn't know she is an external representative as yet.

As a member of this family you have the right to the use of a house in Dublin at any time and one in Mayo on the sea,[76] to the use of a boat which varies in size. Family members have the natural right to say exactly what they think of each other and to talk as long as the turf lasts. As some are naturally contrary and difficult, as I am given to understand, and the other members must defend him or her against undue onslaughts whether minded or not.

I understand that a meeting has been arranged here for December 6th.[77] Bobs says you people don't bear wool any longer but it would be rather nice if for ceremonial purposes you did dress yourself in it, and shillelaghs are not even necessary, indeed nobody seems to know how to spell it.

Bobs Walston, Crompton or Boston, as the case may be, says you are a regular guy and that is more than enough recommendation. You can, of course, use this place to meet people in and if there's any one you particularly want to meet kindly tell me in advance. I don't know any stuffed shirts much but Bobs is making me broadminded about them so I will probably have a collection ready for you. I understand you are due for Paris in the spring; is the family included?

Very sincerely yours,
Ernie O'Malley

Bobs will translate this for you or so she thinks.

No. 160 UCDA P106/1428(13)
Letter to Irish Pensions Board Regarding Madge Coughlan[78]

Burrishoole Lodge,
Newport, Co. Mayo
10 December 1945

To Whom It May Concern,

Madge Coughlan was attached to Command Intelligence Department, Northern and Eastern Command. I had direct contact with her through Sheila Humphreys; sometimes information was sent on directly to me, but more often it came through the Director Intelligence Command.[79]

Madge Coughlan had a day and night pass to Government Buildings, then the headquarters of the Provisional Government.[80] Due to her friendliness with the staff of the Minister, she was present when any of his friends or colleagues dropped into his office. She could overhear telephone conversations about cabinet and routine matters, proposed plans for movements of troops, and what was very important, she was able to give a good psychological appreciation of the various members of the Provisional Government and officers with whom she came in contact. She could witness their methods of publicity as remarks or speeches, extracts from captured documents, where often changed in her presence to suit the propaganda taste of Eimear O'Duffy,[81] then attached to Publicity.

She risked her life continuously as there was no doubt in my mind as to what would have happen to her if her activities were discovered. As time went on women became more suspect and were rounded up; young boys and members of our ASU were murdered on the streets or their bodies left in lonely places in the Dublin suburbs. She was definitely suspect a few times due to our Department of Publicity issuing her information directly rather than changing its terms. This was always a great danger to workers such as she, as Publicity never seemed to understand that a person's life was at stake, or that their usefulness would be lessened or destroyed by the perfidious habit of trying to make scoops. Her intelligence saved her from this definite focusing of suspicion and after a brief time she was again of use.

She brought out original documents as well as memorised précis of their contents; the documents were then quickly replaced. I must add that often her information was not passed on quickly enough to me or the Director of Intelligence, and often when it was passed on, I could not prevail on troops in our Command to act promptly and daringly. Once I was given immediate notice of a proposal to move all interned prisoners held by the PG to the Seychelles and was really sorry afterwards when I became a prisoner that we were not sent there.

She supplied me with information about movements of Ministers of the PG. It was my intention at the time to kidnap a few of them. Later, when I had the intention of storming Leinster House, and the Provisional Government Buildings, she was able to provide a very adequate staff officer's plan of the buildings.[82]

I would recommend her highly for whatever rank the Board would think necessary. She was one of our most important links, indeed the most important direct link with the enemy government mentality and activity. She was intelligent, daring, highly trained, as she had received her training from the very competent hands of Florrie O'Donoghue[83] who at one time in the Tan War was in charge of Intelligence for the First Southern Division. There is no question about the risks she daily ran, or no question of what a loss she would have been if anything, by reason of our ignorance, pointed too closely to her as a source.

As is often the case with our best applicants, she may not be able to make a good case for herself, as it may be difficult for her now that some of her contacts on our side are dead, to prove her services. To those not conversant with our subterranean activities, it may also be difficult to do credit to their statements or to understand their then importance.

I would like, if the Board think it necessary, to appear on behalf of Madge Coughlan, and also to claim special rank for her.

Sincerely yours,

...

Letter to HHOM

15 Whitebeam Ave,
Clonskeagh, [Dublin]
10 December 1945

[Helen O'Malley,
Zacheus Mead Lane,
Greenwich, Connecticut]

Dear Helen,

Thank you for your letter. I am glad you are enjoying yourself moving around, meeting your friends and doing as you want to do. It is nice to see your friends again after long absence. I had thought you might settle down to what you consider is your best sculpture, but evidently you have not worked at it. It's a good thing to see your own country with fresh eyes and get away from this one, which, at best, is a state of mind. To meet people who understand and appreciate you is a help and those I know you can find in America.

The children are well. I spent a week with them not so long ago. I find it hard to get boots for them as boots are not now available here:[84] but maybe strong shoes will serve for the present. I tried to get a bicycle for Cathal, but I failed, and I am passing on his bicycle to Étain. Tomorrow I shop with Cathal, but what he requires I cannot find either, a train with tracks and equipment. Such trains are not now to be bought. He seems very philosophical about it. The other two I have provided for, but so far I have been unable to find the case with Christmas decorations. You took it last year and since then nobody can find it.

I met Roisin Walsh the other day for lunch. She had asked me a number of times, so I went at last. She talked about you and her libraries, but I expect you correspond with her though she didn't mention that you had done so. I meet some of your friends from time to time and they ask about you. I don't see many of them as I don't move around much. Mother said you had asked for Sylvia's[85] address so I expect you have seen her by this. I hope you get out of Hollywood what is of use to you for whatever you need it for. Some of your activities are a source of mystery to me, but you naturally are the best judge of what you want and what you intend to do with it. I suppose you will join the Players in London where that kind of experience will be useful to them unless you intend to do something with movies here.

Bobs Walston I have seen a few times. She and Cathal got on well, but Cathal gets on well with everyone. He is strong and well. I don't know about his schooling but I expect that takes care of itself. I expect he learns something from me, what I don't know, bad and good I should think. Anyhow, I read to him.[86] He likes that. We have nearly finished Don Quixote, a very long book, close on 1,000 pages. He likes it, I am glad to say. Next week he is due for examinations which were always an ordeal to me.

Your bills continue to come in just as I thought they had all been cleared off

Vets	£31	
Land Rates	£47	The rate collector who was quite decent about it said he had seen you before you left, in April.
McCormack	£26	Due for two years or so.
Sundries	£50	
	£153	

The rates I will pay off at once; the others can wait a while. I hope that is all outstanding, but I am sure there are bills in J.J. O'Malley's and in some of the Westport shops. Anyhow in January they should all be settled.

I expect you will spend Christmas with your mother in New York as I think she stays there for the winter. I will be with the children. I am bringing down what toys Étain and Cormac have asked me to bring them, so I hope they will be content. They are easily pleased I must say and their wants are few enough. Please kindly remember me to all the members of your family for Christmas. I am sure you have made your own decisions by this with their help. I hope you stay as long as you want to and learn what you are anxious to learn as this country has been dull enough for you.

Love,
Ernie

NO. 162 ESTATE OF JAMES JOHNSON SWEENEY
Letter to James Johnson Sweeney[87]

15 Whitebeam Ave,
Clonskeagh, Dublin
18 January 1946

[James Johnson Sweeney,
Museum of Modern Art,
New York]

Dear Mr Sweeney,

I several times had the intention of writing to you, but the inclination passed. Helen said she met you in New York and that you proposed an American exhibition in Ireland. There are two groups here, 'The Friends of the National Collections'[88] who have bought some contemporary paintings, mostly French, and have presented them to the Municipal Gallery here. The Roualt was refused by the Gallery and was them sent on loan to Maynooth College.[89] The Friends to me have a faint hang-over air of patronage and uplift further notions, but also they have a few good workers. The other group, 'The Living Art Committee',[90] is all workers. They have succeeded for the past three years in putting on a show of representational and abstract work which would have been turned down by the Academy.[91] French and English painters now contribute yearly.

I suggest that any group here to put on a foreign show be built around this Living Art Committee. As in the Yeats Exhibition,[92] we could add names of people who will not work or help but whose names seem to have an importance to the outside world.

Helen says you are very well informed of affairs in Ireland. I hesitate then to cover ground which you already know, but anyhow I must make the position clear to you as I see it. This government as a whole has no understanding of or feeling for creative work; nor is it inclined to consult people of vitality. That is unfortunate. Generally they get their ideas through the School of Art[93] a reactionary (not politically) close minded group of workers. The Curator of the Municipal Gallery has a conventional academic approach but really knows nothing about art. Furlong,[94] of the National Gallery, does know but as he is poorly paid and hankers for titled ladies at London pre-War tea parties, is inclined to just sit down and keep quiet. This is good civil service procedure, I understand.

There is no gallery here available save the Municipal and some rooms in the School of Art. The National Gallery, which would be most suitable, had never in my memory had an exhibition. I remember in all two exhibitions in the Municipal. One is not allowed to charge for admission or, I believe, even to sell a catalogue of an exhibition without special legislation. There is no government grant for exhibitions.

I led up to the position slowly but so far all I have been given to look forward to is that the School of Art might be available for an exhibition in August and that if a grant were needed the Dáil would have to pass an act specially. The Living Art crowd said they had some money in hand and are willing to use it for an exhibition. As far then as I am concerned, I can say that a working group can be organised, a committee for show purposes built around them. The College of Art[95] possibly available for August which is the Horse Show month and brings a crowd to Dublin, but so far no answer from the Minister for Education.[96]

I wonder if you could forward me a list of books still available at the Museum. Helen was a member but dropped membership some 5 years ago. Good books on art are extremely difficult to get here and I try as hard as I can to get any I can see so that I can use and lend them to people interested. Is it possible to be put on the mailing list of the Museum so that I can be kept in touch with what you are doing. So far I know of you in two publications, *Negro Art*, which I liked well, and *Plastic Redirections*, excellent.[97]

I have two days ago been asked by Denis Devlin of the Irish Legation, Washington, about a Yeats show. W.O'D. Pierce[98] in the War Department and James Whyte[99] who runs a picture gallery in Washington wish to form a committee in Washington and then set up committees in other cities. Do you know of them and are they really in touch with people who are vital and who would help? I have to see Yeats about the matter as I do not know what he would require, a Loan exhibition or an exhibition for sale. I would personally prefer the former as most of his pictures, his good pictures, are in private hands the greater number of them, 80% I should think, in Ireland and of these 75% to 85% of that in the hands of Irishmen as against Anglo-Irish men. Anyhow his later work from 1925 on is very little known in the USA. I doubt if he had sold five of his 1931–1945 paintings there.

A Yeats show for sale is coming off in London in February.[100] I am trying to get to London for it, but the invitation to go to their country must now come from them or one is not allowed out. The Director[101] of the Tate was over here and seems willing to send shows over here. He mentioned the American exhibition and a French one; maybe I can fix up something with him.

Do you know the Director of the Pennyslvania Museum?[102] I am not even sure of his name, McElhenny.[103] Irish, I am told with a castle at Glenbeigh.[104] You know it and him, I expect. I would like to meet him if he comes over here this summer. Any chance of your coming over with your wife and children. I heard a lot about you both.

It would be a good thing if our Tourist Board[105] here would wake up and deal with cultural implications – prehistory artifacts, bronze, sculpture to the 17th century, illuminations viewed from the aesthetic standpoint and not the archaeological historical purely as they unfortunately are. They keep no contact with the USA or Europe. This year we will be flooded out with curried colonels and the most died-in-the wood conservative British who are fast buying up any property there is here.

Very sincerely yours,
Earnan O'Malley

NO. 163 EOM PAPERS NYU
Letter to HHOM

[Stationery of] Thriplow Farm,
Thriplow, Cambridge, [England,][106]
[with address] c/o Cecil [Malley]
Wednesday, 14 February 1946

Mrs Helen Hooker O'Malley,
15 Whitbeam Ave,
Clonskeagh, Dublin, Ireland

Dear Helen,

I hope you are building, painting, planning, steam-heating a studio and a few other activities. I had a quiet crossing, sea calm through which I slept peacefully, food got through alright but the train was late. Margaret was glad to see me and has been very kind. They have a nice house, nice from the view of good rooms in which to hang pictures spacious and comfortable. Not your kind of a house and not mine; tiles, bare floors but I miss the warmth of rugs, tweed curtains and the sense of texture.

The children I have not seen much of as I have been in bed in the morning. Kevin[107] is lively, alert makng friends with me on the question of motor cars. The girl is shy has not come any nearer to me and we are on hiding-behind-her-mother's-skirts terms.

I saw Bobs as you can gather from the notepaper. She looked tired as if she had been up all night. Harry also looked tired but today he looks an undergraduate; he works very hard and all the time.

I was in the Tate but the Tate is like an underground as it has been bombed out. Pictures are crowded in the few rooms I have seen several feet deep as in my room. I saw the Yeats show[108] before the opening: some of the pictures were very good, some not as interesting but a Yeats collection often grows on one as one lives around or sees more of it. One excellent painting looked like a Renoir[109] ... I saw the Paul Klee show. I liked it a good deal, meant nothing to me but who meant something was illuminating about people who since 1920 have tried whether to imitate Klee or Klee and Chagall or Klee and Chirico, and there are many who have consciously or unconsciously been influenced by them.

I hope everything is well. Please give my love to the children.

Ernie

NO. 164 EOM PAPERS NYU
Letter to HHOM

c/o Cecil [Malley, London]
16 March 1946

[Helen O'Malley,
15 Whitebeam Avenue,
Clonskeagh, Dublin]

Dear Helen,

I hope everything goes well with you. Cathal wrote that you had gone to Burrishoole perhaps for planting, painting, sculpture or to change the curtains or your bedroom. The weather has been bad here ever since I arrived except for two or three days. Now, it should be spring judging by the tree buds, but it is raining just as in Mayo.

In painting I haven't see much, about 5 Gainsborough oil sketches and two large paintings called sketches. They were exciting. Whenever Constable worked in terms of the Academy he overworked boiling the juice away. Two large sketches 5' x 5' have no relation to the finished picture and yet he did not consider his unfinished work as aesthetically satisfying. Ensor, a Belgian, I saw. He was not good. He had been brought over specially by the Arts Council. A little of what the French call 'quality' emerges, but out of about 80 or 90 oils and sketches, I would have picked 5 interesting works. Paul Klee, I saw an exhibition of about 70 from Swiss collection. That was really good. For if one follows Klee one follows a trend which was 10 or 15 or 25 years later exploited by people with a heavier coat of paint but with little to say. I felt that a Klee show was 'required seeing' for all young painters and for art critics. In him the development of certain aspects and approaches can be traced. Picasso, carefully chosen. Braque, a little Matisse, Klee,

Rouault, Chirico, perhaps Chagall and maybe a Daumier, Rousseau in an exhibition would adequately cover painting from 1905 to 1938.

Sculpture at Victoria & Albert from Westminister. Roumbert bronzes were good, a few and about 5 of the carved figures. Critics here seemed to me to rave about the exhibition and I looked at them blankly, then asked questions. I found they had no standard and simply did not understand sculpture: certainly they did not understand it as I do. Then I began to question myself wondering if it were pure egoism on my part, but I don't think that is correct. I may have value that I can't explain but they are real despite that inability.

I expect you have caught up with the theatre again and that you are doing what you want to do about it. I hadn't Michael Clarke's address or I would have seen him but Sunny[110] didn't write to me before I left as she said she would so I didn't follow the matter any further. Michael had a habit of talking down to me about the theatre and about art in general. He may see a play as an actor does but he certainly does not see it as I see it. It is difficult to go to the theatre unless you book ahead for weeks and I don't know how long I was going to remain or when at any point I was going to leave. I have visited a number of people and have stayed in their houses. I have seen more of Harry and Bobs as I know them best at least I knew Bobs, but as I saw more of Harry, I liked him and now understand him. People have been very nice to me and kind. Cecil[111] has been mystified at times by my sudden disappearances, but then I am roaming the world again and if I could get to France you would in time hear of me in Alaska.

A sailing ticket, I find, is very hard to obtain as people are now booked up for summer. This I should have looked up when I arrived, but I thought I could walk into a booking office and obtain one on the spot. I could I suppose get an air passage. That I must find out. I thought I had written you previously but maybe I hadn't done so, and so I'll end.

Love,
Ernie

NO. 165 EOM PAPERS NYU
Letter to Cathal O'Malley

c/o [Cecil] Malley, [London, England]
16 March 1946

[Cathal O'Malley,
15 Whitebeam Avenue,
Clonskeagh, Dublin]

Dear Cathal,

Thank you for the letter which you kindly sent me. I am enclosing stamps which I have collected from various sources. Yesterday I began to think of things for our boat:[112] rubber mattresses, oil skins, but so far all I have been able to find is an oilskin. You remember how hard the seats are to sleep on but perhaps you don't remember as the sleeping-out was exciting. The next day I always found myself tired because one or another slat seemed to get on or close to a wound so I thought it a good idea if I could find a few mattresses which could be blown up when required.

I expected the boat will need a coat of paint. The engine as you know from being a second engineer needs to be decarbonised and thoroughly overhauled. When I go back I will see Sweeny, the garage man at Achill Sound, have him come to take the engine away and work on it. He is by far the best man within or not within distance from us. Cecil thinks I should buy a new Kelvin engine run on paraffin as it is easy to start and easy to run, but, unfortunately, I had not the sense to bring the boat and engine dimensions with me, but I can send them on here later.

I have not see any books which might suit you. I have a good deal of reading to make up for with you so I hope you will come in to me every evening. Very often you did not. You know I seldom ask you to come in for me to read to you for if you really want it you should ask: otherwise I feel you have something that you regard as more important to do and I do not intend to force any reading on you unless you want it yourself.

I hope you are kind to Étain and that at times she can join your gang, not always of course as a boy cannot always allow a sister to share his play or games. I expect that Cormac will be able to talk and to tell stories when I return.

Love,
Ernie

NO. 166 EOM PAPERS NYU
Letter to Etain O'Malley

[c/o Cecil Malley, London, England]
16 March 1946

[Etain O'Malley,
15 Whitebeam Avenue,
Clonskeagh, Dublin]

Dear Etain,

How are your dolls? I hope they have been behaving and that the doctor does not have to come with his bag. Do you remember the last time the doctor with the black moustache and the strange clothes he came to visit you at Burrishoole? You told me about him, that he had found Candles and Batteries in the doll's stomach. It was a good thing he called in time. In England I have met a very good Dolls' Doctor. I have asked him to fly over to Ireland to inspect the Dolls of Dublin, maybe he will be there soon. He said that carrot tops well marked up are very good if they have a bad cold. I hope you and Cormac are going to school every day and that you don't fight with him too much about bricks or in the building of houses. Give Cormac my love and keep some for yourself.

Love,
Ernie

Letter to HHOM

[*Burrishoole Lodge,*
Newport, Co. Mayo]
10 July 1946

[*Helen O'Malley,*
15 Whitebeam Avenue,
Clonskeagh, Dublin]

Dear Helen,

Thank you for letter and cheese which you kindly sent, and for the presents. Cathal is very excited about all of them. I met Molly Gill[113] last Sunday. I invited her out for lunch. She could not come, but said she might come out in the evening …

I am glad you are working and enjoying yourself in peace without any disturbance. You should be able to get a good deal of work done before the end of summer.

The children are well. As you say I disturbed your staff last year, I am being more than careful indoors which, indeed, I was last year. Nanna runs the house. I don't inquire about bills so I expect that makes for satisfaction, and they get on well, I expect, amongst themselves. Last year I did not interfere save on the question of undue expense. I made no personal complaint at any time save to try to get kitchen and adjoining food rooms cleaned up. Nanna has always been kind and satisfactory, and I really don't think I make any demands on her. I never ask for anything; if she puts it on the table it is welcome. As for the outdoor staff there is no interference on my part. They live their own lives, do their work, and I expect they are happy and contented. Pat works away by himself. I do not intend to take Cathal out in the boat so he can live his own life also. I have talked to the men about him and to him as regards the men. If he carries on as you said he had been behaving in Dublin I cannot be held responsible. I have not had much contact or influence with or on him this year. Last year beyond trying to discipline him at sea and to make him useful in a house, both of which may have later had repercussions, as a boy naturally likes to be with a man more than with women.

Just now the jersey with letter enclosed has come by bus from Westport; thank you for sending them on. The weather is holding at present.

Love,
Ernie

Letter to HHOM

[*Burrishoole Lodge,*
Newport, Co. Mayo]
16 July 1946

[*Helen O'Malley,*
15 Whitebeam Avenue,
Clonskeagh, Dublin]

Dear Helen,

Thanks for your letter. I received the sweater (Aran), rosin and maps alright: thank you for sending them. I am glad you have settled down to work and are feeling at ease about it. I did not send the young girl on; she is to leave tomorrow, but she is too inexperienced to get a taxi by herself and have all arrangements at your end. Could you not have someone meet her? If you cannot arrange that then she had best come up with me as I would like to go to the ballet[114] on the 23rd and I may leave here on the 22nd.

I asked Kilroy[115] to forward bills to Dublin, and I am enclosing Molloy's[116] bill. I told Nanna about the moths here. Could you kindly forward some tea as I came down here without any. Also I would like a pound of coffee from Bewley's.

Have you got two O'Casey books, his autobiographies, in Dublin? I saw one in your room, *Pictures in the Hallway*; maybe, however, the second one is in my room.

Burrishoole is quiet and peaceful. The children enjoy themselves and the girls seem content but they may have another story for you. Kindly remember me to Kurt Joos [*sic*]. The theater must be pretty well booked out. I intend to come back here on the 24th.

Love,
Ernic

No. 169 EOM Papers NYU
Letter to Blanche Ferry Hooker

15 Whitebeam Ave,
Clonskeagh, Dublin
8 August 1946

Mrs Elon Huntington Hooker,
Chelmsford, Zacheus Mead Lane,
Greenwich, Conn., USA

Dear Mrs Hooker,

Helen told me this week when I returned from Donegal that you intended to come in September. I hope you will be able to manage this journey for we would all like to have you with us. The children have changed a good deal since last you saw them and Cormac you have not seen. Etain talks of sailing to America to see you as if America were the other side of the Bay from us.

Helen is working hard in her studio which is very nice as a working place and is a receiving place for her many friends. As the children and myself have been away since July she has had no family distraction to interfere with her work. By the time you arrive she will have a good deal of work ready. Her recent head of Joos[117] [sic] was good and a Frank O'Connor cast is excellent.

Burrishoole repainted is very attractive and I am sure you will like it there. I will certainly do all I can to make your stay a happy one.

With love,
Ernie

NO. 170 EOM PAPERS NYU
Letter to Blanche Ferry Hooker

Burrishoole Lodge,
Newport, Co. Mayo
17 September 1946

Mrs Elon Ferry Hooker,
Zacheus Mead Lane,
Greenwich, Connecticut, USA

Dear Mrs Hooker,

Thank you for your letter of September 10th which I received yesterday when I returned from Achill. There I met Buzz Crompton[118] who told me about meeting you when in America. Bobs was there in Achill with her children[119] and as the children left for England both have come to visit me.

I did not thank you for the socks which you kindly sent me. My intention was there but I put it off which is no way of answering a gift, so please excuse me. Also I received a long letter from you, a letter both kind and considerate which I read carefully and agreed with.

Helen is in London now and may remain there some weeks she said to study theatre interests there. She had also the intention of going to America as Eithne Dunne,[120] her actress friend, is due to go there in a few days and I expect Helen thought she might be able to help Eithne or to see her theatre friends again. Also she was to meet Mr Gilchrist in London, and was to make certain decisions which she did not tell me of, but which I think I know. Mr Gilchrist was a fine type of American and I liked him. I feel that Helen is in very competent hands, that he has listened to her and had understood her and that his decisions which also I sense are for the best as he knows how to protect her. His son I liked also, and had out in the Bay with Cathal. He and Cathal were very good friends. He was extremely kind and understanding with Cathal who in return grew very fond of him. I would have liked them to have stayed a little longer in Burrishoole which was quiet and peaceful, but Helen had arranged a series of visits and entertainment for them in Dublin.

Cathal is now in school as you probably know.[121] Helen and I went out to see him one evening when I was last in Dublin, some days ago. Cathal looked happy and at ease. That is, I think, the main thing as far as he is concerned. The principal's wife, Mrs Murphy, was a fine motherly understanding woman. Cathal's approach to her was interesting and satisfactory. I think the school will work out alright. It will do its part if Cathal does his part in return.

Cormac is strong and cheery but had been in bed here before he left Burrishoole for about ten days. He gets a kind of bronchial cold which he finds hard to get rid of. Stella, the nurse, was very kind to him. Helen did not think she was efficient, but there is an efficiency of the heart which makes up for much of the impractical, and Stella supplied that necessary nourishment. She has gone now. Nanna[122] will now be the nurse. Nanna is a very good housekeeper and indispensable, but somewhat too dominant as far as a young child is concerned.

Etain is quick, lively, talkative and very much a small girl. She gets on well with Cormac, but Cathal and she carry on what seems to be natural, a minor war of dominance and resistance. Cathal of course needed a boy of his own age in Burrishoole this year but that could not be arranged as Nanna was in Dublin with Helen and as Helen thought that a boy could not come here whilst Nanna was not here it made life somewhat more monotonous for Cathal. Next year I hope Cathal can have companionship of his own age, that is if Burrishoole yet remains with Helen. Anyhow that could be arranged if the family took a house in the West for a month.

It seems strange that you have not seen either Étain or Cormac, but then war has made a gap, a long gap in all lives. They talk of you, especially Étain who when out sailing with me, always wanted to go 'to Merica to see grandma Hooker'. I think you would like them both. I cannot say that they are any better or worse than other children, but I feel they are not spoiled or petted and that despite everything in the relationship of Helen and myself that the children make up for everything.

Helen's studio has been a big success. It is really a small flat in which she can work, entertain or sleep. She has been working hard and to her satisfaction, but it would be better to turn energy into one direction, for the time being that of sculpture. Decorative arts and theatre are absorbing and, while time, work; for a combination of all one needs concentration, organisation, energy, enthusiasm. Helen certainly lacks the first two save when on one aspect of work at a given time. Burrishoole is very beautiful now. It has been raining hard for days in this worst summer for 30 years. We are trying even now to cut oats and I hope we can get the crop in, but even now there are five acres of hay uncut, two months later than the ordinary time for cutting hay. Helen has decorated the inside with paint so that it reflects more light these days. The Gate Lodge is a fine piece of work and could be sold at any time, but I feel it would be easier to sell than to rent as it is not suitable for people who would come to the seaside for a month; however, it would suit fishermen who would want to use the lakes nearby.[123]

Annie, an island girl, looks after this house now. I find her excellent. I know all her family and I like all of them. Helen and Nanna complain a great deal about her and expect her to be efficient in directions which are difficult for her. She has limitations certainly much less of them that I have and her good points are so very good that she is a good person to be with.

Helen intends to stay with Buzz and Bobs in London so that she can now hear firsthand about you and the Cromptons. I liked Buzz. He is kind and gentle and I like Bobs. She has been very kind and helpful to me in England. Harry Walston I saw a fair amount of in Cambridge. He does not talk much on anything but he is a good friend. He is now in charge of the English zone in Germany for agriculture.[124]

Sometimes I don't write because my writing is so difficult to read and I expect I withdraw somewhat from letters because Helen does not answer letters, but on the rare occasions, I write I like it. Now that Helen has a typewriter to transmit messages it will solve her difficulties about spelling badly but no one minds bad spelling, I think.

Very affectionately,
Ernie

NO. 171 EOM PAPERS NYU
Letter to HHOM

Burrishoole Lodge,
Newport, [Co. Mayo]
11 October 1946

Mrs Helen Hooker O'Malley,
6 St James St, London SW1, England

Dear Helen,

I hope you have settled down in London and that you are working to your satisfaction. You are probably on movies by this, I expect.[125] Did you see the Irish exhibition and what did you think of it? It seems that some pictures belonging either to you or myself are there as I had a request from London about using some of mine for illustrations.

The children left this morning. That was a great surprise to have them. I was glad they were here for the Stations[126] and sorry you were not here. I am sure you would have like it. Mrs Quinn,[127] Mrs Burke, Nanna worked hard. The men I found even gathering the dead leaves from off the avenue. Pat Clark even put turf mould in a circle around the young apple tree, west of the house on the front lawn. Tom took stones off the grass on the avenue and placed them on the wall. Annie and Pat painted the larder under the stairs a gleaming white. Indeed, I have never seen the place look as clean taken all around. We had about 35 people for breakfast. I gave the men and women – anyone who could take it – a glass of port. All seemed to have liked the morning especially the Canon who said that my contribution was unheard of in the parish. I understood you paid dues at Easter: if that is so then everything is correct. I owe him for a few back years which I must square up. I kept the money in my press for a long time: every fair day in Newport when I was there at least on two occasion I went to his house but he was out, on others I had the money but drink and company kept me away.

The weather is beautiful now. The glass higher than at any time in the Summer.[128] My boat is under my window. I look forward to sailing but when I am any length away from the boat I am afraid to start again as I have too many frights at sea, but once I get started I don't mind about them. I am sorry you didn't sail this year as there was the good weather. There has been no sailing weather since.

Hay is in the barn save the rough haying Rossgiblin and in Brennan's field. I had to get some bullocks to eat down the Rossgiblin grass as otherwise there was no way of getting rid of it. All oats and wheat stacked; considerable loss of oats in Carrowkeel as the weather would not allow it to be gathered when it was ripe. Potatoes not much good as they have had no time to ripen with sun; carrots, parsnips in Carrowkeel practically do not exist, cabbage there poor, mangles in Clarke's garden rather hopeless. Silage, the summer crop, not too good as it was not earth covered when cut; the remainder of autumn silage should be finished in about 3 days, when potatoes begin to be dug. I have in purported to be 30 carts of turf but was really about 20, I understand judging by the lorry loads. Clonskeagh needs turf. I told Nanna to tell you as she has the address of the man who brought me good turf but as he needs to be paid instantly I did not order it until things on this end had been settled for.

You have 6 cows, about 3 too many as some are drying off.[129] They can be left out this winter when they dry to save hay and silage and they can't be sold now dry save at a big loss. Cattle are down, likely I think to stay down until March, so it's no good trying to get rid of heifers. I don't know your ultimate intentions about this place but never more than 4 cows are needed as if they were any good as milkers 3 would be enough. I have sent off about the young bull for permission to keep him if the Department[130] sends a man soon. It would be better to have him adjudged soon so that we would not have to give him so much milk; on the other hand the mere fact of having to look after him hopefully gives a good start to the beast.

Pat Clarke keeps the lawns well. He cuts, trims hedges. He certainly means well. He worked well with the others at harvest and at silage.

Josie Gill and Nora called yesterday with Moya Gill whose boyfriend was married a few days ago. They were asking for you. Cormac's cough has lasted too long. I saw Kevin about it the night before I left town. He suggested that an X-Ray be taken. I have asked Nanna to see Dr Shaw about it. You should see about letting the Gate Lodge when you have the chance as English people will probably be prepared to pay a better price for it but as I see it, it is useful for fishing only. Kelly[131] has not as yet put in the lavatory. I spoke to him about it two weeks ago but since he has made no move.

Do you require any food? I am sure butter could be sent on from Moran's shop[132] and maybe other things from Liptons? I hope you can work in London and that you are taking things easily; if you can now do that. It's a good thing to be ambitious for it's an antidote to others' lack of it, but sometimes ambition is not better than the lack of it for even success in some ways cannot hide a failure in others and vice versa. However, you know your own way best, but take it easy.

With love,
Ernie

P.S. I sent you on Lipton's account with Bobs. I have paid the two previous months July–August. Will Liptons send you on the bill only in future and me the book. Annie whom I paid 3 months wages in July which were then stated to be arrears now says I paid her up to the 1st of September so she is owed from that date. Will I pay her in future as long as I remain here?

NO. 172 EOM PAPERS NYU
Letter to HHOM

6 St James St, London SW1
6 November 1946

[Helen O'Malley,
15 Whitebeam Avenue,
Clonskeagh, Dublin]

Dear Helen,

This is to confirm my telephone conversation with you yesterday morning when it was agreed that I see you and Seebohm Rowntree[133] on November 13th. I am to find out from Brown's Hotel[134] on the evening of the 12th about your arrival, and you are to get in touch with Seebohm Rowntree and let me know as soon as possible when we are to meet. It seems simpler to me that you send on the date and time of meeting, and if necessary a telegram when you start from the airport, but already I know from you that you start at 3 p.m. on the 12th. I also know that you realize the importance of this meeting so I cannot think of anything which would postpone that plan.

The items essentially to be discussed by both of us are:

(1) duration of custody of children by us individually.
(2) agreed on arrangements for schooling of the children.

Will you please have your ideas of the above and anything else you consider necessary, ready for discussion.

With love,
Ernie

Letter to HHOM

6 St James St, London SW1, [England]
3 December 1946

Mrs Helen Hooker O'Malley,
15 Whitebeam Avenue,
Clonskeagh, Dublin, Ireland

Dear Helen,

I'm sorry to break your telegraphic instructions[135] by writing direct, but I do not know either Overend's[136] initials or his address, and I have some bills here about turf which I would like to put you right about.

With love,
Ernie

Letter to Thomas Gilchrist[137]

c/o 6 St James Street,
London SW1, [England][138]
9 January 1947

Mr Thomas B. Gilchrist,
[Bleakley, Platt, Gilchrist & Waber,]
14 Wall Street, New York 5, NY, USA

Dear Mr Gilchrist,

Thank you for your letter of December 10th which I received. I have been in bed for some time with a severe form of influenza, and, as I was alone, I could not get any typing done. Also I was reluctant to write because I have not written to Helen's family about her nor have I spoken about her to other people. Writing them would have involved my stating what brought me to London, which was to meet Helen and see that her talk here and in Ireland cease,[139] or arrange some settlement that would make her feel easier. A mutual agreement between Helen and I was broken by her. I was instructed by telegram to name my solicitor and in future deal only through her solicitor. That I took to mean that if I could not communicate with Helen. I could not enter her houses and so I remained on in London.

I find I have little to add to my telegram save that the children will remain in Ireland. When they are in Ireland, Helen is often not with them, and so it can be arranged that she or I be with them.

This address is not easy to find me at times as I am in other places in London, but usually I call or 'phone weekly to see if any letters are there for me.

I have a much longer letter written but it will take some time to type, and I do not know if it is advisable to send it.[140]

Sincerely yours,
Ernie O'Malley

Letter to Blanche Ferry Hooker

c/o 6 St James St,
London SW1, [England]
9 January 1947

[Mrs Elon Hooker,
Greenwich, Connecticut, USA]

Dear Mrs Hooker,

Thank you for your letter of December 9th. I was informed by Mr Gilchrist that Helen was in America to settle up amongst other things about her return to London. I regret that I could not comply with the request to send over the three children. Cathal, as you know, is behind hand with his schooling and although there would be, I expect, better schools in America yet there did not seem sufficient justification for his leaving for a few months to again return to his old system of schooling.

I am sorry that Helen was not with the children for Christmas, but owing to Helen's most recent communication, neither was I.[141] That, to say the least of it, is unfortunate.

Helen needs a rest. I had suggested to her in October that she take things easy and rest. Also I wrote to Kevin about her and suggested that he write to you about her going to America, but I do not know if he did write. I hope Helen can now take a rest with you.

Affectionately,
Ernie

NO. 176 EOM PAPERS NYU
Unsent letter to Thomas Gilchrist[142]

[London]
January 1947

[Mr Thomas B. Gilchrist,
Bleakley, Platt, Gilchrist & Waber,
14 Wall Street, New York 5]

Dear Mr Gilchrist,

Thank you for your letter of December 11th which I received. I have been here sick with a perfidious kind of influenza and I have been waiting until it was somewhat over before I wrote to you.

I did not wish the children to go to America because I thought they should remain together for the present. They are all three at school. Cormac could leave but the other two should continue, especially Cathal who is far behind in his work. I see no use in one going as Etain would then be lonely. I am sure Helen missed the children at Christmas, but so did I miss them.

When you were in Ireland the question of my remaining in Burrishoole was brought up. It had already been agreed between Helen and myself that I stay there and help to run the farm, but she in your presence said that I had not previously agreed to that. Anyhow I remained on until the end of October, hoping the children would come down for Christmas. Helen did not reply to a long letter I wrote her about the farm and turf supplies for the winter, but as I have been accustomed to Helen not replying to letters, it seemed usual enough yet under the circumstances as she had often talked of expenses mounting. I would have been thankful for a reply. I had already heard that Helen was looking out for a flat in England as she intended to remain there for some time. Also I heard that I was involved with at least three names in London, that I had driven Helen out of Burrishoole and out of Clonskeagh, and that in each place I had installed somebody else. At first I did not pay attention to the rumours. They had already been circulated in Dublin by Helen, with additions about our personal relationships which were, to say the least of it, untrue. Previously for some years I had not contradicted any of these reports nor had I ever spoken on Helen or our personal relationships to anyone. That was I thought a matter for ourselves. Nor had I involved Helen by talk with any of her groups, although she once stated to me that I had said in public that she was living with Liam Redmond. Even if she had been as I told her, I would not have spoken about it save to herself. I decided in October that this talk would have to cease. My brother, Kevin, had already listened to Helen as a dinner party in London with some of his friends whom Helen scarcely knew. I rang Helen up, said that I would meet her with a friend of her choice. I suggested Liam Redmond as they have known each other for several years and Helen has always listened to him for advice. She suggested Seebohm Rowntree, and I agreed. I asked if she was agreeable to discuss separation. She said she was. I thought that as she had often spoken of separation before that her mind would be eased and that living at peace with herself she would have no further cause to make life by talk impossible for me to live in Ireland, and eventually for herself.

I brought Mrs Walston[143] with me as she had been most deeply involved in Helen's talk. Helen had already seen Seebohm Rowntree and had with him agreed to a separation. I asked her if she wanted a separation and she said she did. Mr Rowntree later asked me if I agreed to a separation and I replied 'Yes'. He said that he also was of the opinion having (previously) talked to Helen at some length.

It was agreed that I meet Helen in London in two weeks time with Seebohm Rowntree and that the question of the children would come up not for definite decision but for discussion as we both agreed that the details concerning a decision be settled as between friends and then ratified without recourse to law. Also it was agreed that friendly relations be kept between Helen and I, no matter what was the eventual result. I asked that Helen take notice of her loose talk in London and in Dublin in which I was involved with three women, Catherine Walston, Barbara Rothschild[144] and Libby Eden and that it must cease. Helen denied talk until Catherine Walston quoted witnesses and offered to introduce them.

Seebohm Rowntree had to leave then. Catherine Walston and Helen continued their conversation which I had already heard through my brother, Kevin, and other sources. In the end we parted, Helen to return as she said she was going to Ireland in less than three weeks. Later I received a telegram: 'All negotiations must in future be between solicitors. Please inform me of the name of your solicitor'. That telegram came on November 8th. Since that date, as I had no intention of having a solicitor, according to our agreement I have had no communication from nor have I written to Helen.

Later from America, I had a telephone call from you to say that Helen was in the USA, would remain there for Christmas and would be thankful to have the three children sent over ...

NO. 177 EOM PAPERS NYU; ESTATE OF JOHN V. KELLEHER
Letter to Professor John V. Kelleher[145]

Achill Island, Co. Mayo
8 March 1947

John Kelleher,
37 Lanark Drive, Westwood, Mass., USA

Dear John,

Thank you very much for your letter of January 24 which was forwarded to England where I was supposed to be and back again to Ireland where I was. Finally it reached me in Achill on March 1st. I had flu and we were snow bound heavily. I expect that February 1947 will be spoken of in the West as 'the year of the Big Snow'.

I motored up to Dublin with your sleeping bags[146] on the evening before you had to leave Dublin, but the car broke down and I spent the night and a good part of next day on the road. Finally, when I reached the Club you had left and your plane had set out from Shannon before I could get in touch with you. I certainly am delighted to be able to keep the sleeping bags as they make sailing more a permanent idea for me. Thank you very much.

I did not know that it was you who had sent on the Melville and the Matthiessen. I have dipped into Matthiessen but as soon as I get back to Dublin I will read it. Thank you very much for sending them on to me. Perhaps your name was on the outside, but I think they had them repacked at Burrishoole for they reached me in England. I gave a broadcast over the Third Programme on 'The Tradition of the Arts in Mexico', and I have to do another on Irish sculpture.[147] I find it difficult to talk about such a vast subject in 1,000 words. The result is that I practically write a book first, then compress the juice of it working and reworking. The proper way, I understand, is to have a small knowledge of the subject, quietly expand by a fireside and make a subject pleasant, interesting and loose for listeners. I wrote about neutrality in Ireland for a French paper and a small article on Co. Mayo for an English magazine.[148] Again there was the difficulty to write about my county in a thousand words, when I always thought I should have written a book on it. The French were pleasant, being pleasant was also associated with 4,000 words and good pay for this part of the world. I met a great number of people, but at times I was despondent enough as I was not turning out sufficient work to justify my existence. However, it was good to get away to a place where people work and where there is a stimulus to work. Now that I am back here in Achill looking out at Clare Island with Inish Turk in the distance all that restless patchy life has disappeared; and yet I know that if I stayed for another month I would get bored because minds here in this large island are too placid.

I like the books on your list, except my own. I wish I had done a good job on it because when I reread bits it seems cryptic when it could have been more expansive. I find it hard to think of books but I have my own book catalogues, and I will read them down just now.

A. E.E. Cummings[149]	*The Enormous Room*
A. Jones, Henry Festing	*Diversions in Sicily*
A. Gissing, George	*Beside the Ionian Sea*
A. Flandlam*	*Viva Mexico*
A. Tomlinson [H.M.]*	*The Sea and the Jungle*
A. Stark, Freya	(*The Southern Gates of Arabia*)
	(*A Winter in Arabia*) I can't remember which
	(*The Valley of the Assassins*) was the best
Douglas, Norman	*Fountains in the Sand; Together*
Lucas, F.L.	**The Decline and Fall of the Romantic Ideal*
Knight, G. Wilson	*The Olive and the Sword: a Study of*
	Shakespeare's End)
Wilson, J. Dover	**The Essential Shakespeare*
A. Hudson, W.H.	**Far Away and Long Ago*
Quennell, Peter	*Byron: the Years of Fame; Byron in Italy*
Edited: Maurice, Sir J.F.	(*The Diary of Sir John Moore*)
Forman, Maurice Buxton	*The Letters of John Keats*
Sterne	**A Sentimental Journey*
A. Hillary, Richard	**The Last Enemy*
Jones, E.H.	*The Road to En-Dor* (story of an escape in the 1914–1918 war)
A. Prestley, J.B.	*Midnight in the Desert*
A. Sullivan, J.W.N.	*But for the Grace of God*
Burrows, George	*Wild Wales*
Pickthall, Marmaduke	(*Oriental Encounters*)
Kinglake, A.W.	**Eothen*
Power, Eileen	**Mediaeval People*
Synge, J.M.	*The Aran Islands*
West, Rebecca	*Black Lamb and Grey Falcon*
Yeats, W.B.	Autobiographies

Dodds, E.R.	Journal and Letters of Stephen MacKenna
(Fortescue, Sir J. edited	*Memories of Sergeant Bourgogne*)
(Allen, W.E.D.	*Anglo-Irish Guerilla War in Abyssinia*)
(Swinton, Maj Gen	*The Defence of Duffers Drift*) written under another name
(Xenophon	*Anabasis*)
A. Read, Herbert	*Annals of Innocence and Inexperience*
	Cavendish Life of Cardinal Wolsley (this I found a good contemporary account)

As I wrote out this list I was trying to remember first of all was it correct, then was it worth while. I have put a '*' in front of the books I would now stand by, '( )' round some which you might read yourself. 'A.' in front means autobiographical material.

Freya Stark has the cast of thought in her work. She has written 5 or 6 books some of which I have not entered here, but I think you may find her interesting. I have bracketed Gissing and Jones. Jones was in Sicily with Samuel Butler, and, as far as I remember, he writes well. The Gissing book is the only outlet Gissing had to be cheerful. I am not sure of 'Fountains in the Sand' but 'Together' is a good story with a skeptical, ironic twist. *The Essential Shakespeare*, I liked well at the time. Quennell makes Byron interesting, attractive and real. The Keats letters are the core of Keats, but they may be difficult for students.

Hillary was a young airman, but also a writer and it is a good book. *Sword of Bone* by Anthony Rhodes also I liked well as it dealt with the present war. So far as I know they were the two best books I have read on that episode in history. *The Road to En-Dor* is like a Chinese puzzle. I feel you might like it personally. It is dedicated to the pathologist of the Mater Hospital in Dublin.

I seem to remember that I liked *Wild Wales* but it might be boring for Americans. 'The Bible in Spain' seems to me to be an elaborate lie but it's a good lie well told; either that or Spaniards can be less excited by their Church than one would think. John Sommerfield has written a little book on the Spanish War *Volunteer in Spain*, which I consider a good soldier's book. Rebecca West may annoy you, but I liked the first volume for a kind of enthusiastic examination of a strange people. She is a Kerry woman.

I would like to write more about these books, or of others, but maybe my romantic feeling of strangeness runs away with me. I am afraid that I will have to send some of my books to England to be housed by a friend of mine who promises to return them to Ireland when I die. I have had a difficult task to keep the ones I need, and yet be fair to the person who will store them and maybe want to buy some. I have had some trouble with Helen for some years due to what might be called incompatibility and to her associationship with the theatre which makes life dull for her unless she is in the company of actors and actresses. All of this could eventually be reconciled, but her people are beginning to move now because I have refused to discuss matters which can only be properly settled by the two people really concerned, Helen and I. Unfortunately, I don't own a house of any kind although Helen has 5 here as I had them all in her name.[150] I am telling you this because I consider you one of the few people I would care to talk to about my situation, and also I had hoped you could be in Burrishoole again shortly. However, I have now a loan of a house in Achill for as long as I wish to have it. It is small, but I could move in a working library and it would always be available for you, your wife and family and friends for a visit for the last visit was your first. My boat is in Island Mór in the Bay at anchor, looked after by my good friend, Josie Gill. Thus, on this coast, there is a house, a boat and books, whatever happens.

This evening I had intended to work hard on fairy stories, but my material is notebooks on the civil war period and stories I put down as I talked to men.[151] You would like them, but I must again get this civil war down in writing. About half is finished but needs reworking and is in script and when you have read this far you will somewhat understand what my script is like. I have not done any work on this since you left although it should have been finished by Christmas. But I left for England in October and that broke up the writing. Now I must again get back to Burrishoole to look for my other folklore notebooks.

Eimear O'Duffy's[152] first book was *The Wasted Island*. It dealt with the 1916 fight and events leading up to it, particularly with the Count Plunkett's[153] family. O'Duffy was on the GHQ Staff of the Irish Volunteers.[154] He wrote very good articles in the *Irish Volunteer*[155] on a guerilla approach to fight and they were sound enough as they expanded material in official British Army textbooks. I will send you on a list of his other works, some of which I have not read. *The Wasted Island* was a novel.

A College Chorus was, I think, a collection of poems from the *National Student*, perhaps not his own poems. *Printers Errors*,[156] I have on my list but I forget what it was about. I remember O'Duffy as a student. He was doing medicine in Cecilia Street, a dental student, I think.[157] The 1916 fight put him somewhat out of gear as he strongly supported Owen MacNeill.[158] I will dig up information about him when I get to Dublin. I will also look up Gerald O'Donovan.[159]

This is a rambling disjointed letter, but I am in a rambling way of life again. Maybe I settled down for too long a spell but I expect I am entitled to my own mistakes, and to my in wrong doing; maybe complacency needs a good shake up every now and then. I will write to you again as soon as I get the material you need. In the meantime kindly remember me to your wife and to all the people, your friends whom I hear you talk of to me. I had it in my mind to send you a few things connected with perhaps the Civil War handbills or some such thing which would at least be original, and as soon as I can locate them, I'll send them on.

Very sincerely yours,
Ernie O'Malley

The best address for me for the present is: c/o O'Rahilly,[160] Mooreen, Clondalkin, Co. Dublin. Sorry. This should have gone off. Received your photos,[161] thanks. Will write again on 21 March 1947.

Draft letter to Thomas Gilchrist

Achill, [Co. Mayo]
[c. mid March 1947]

[Mr Thomas B. Gilchrist,
Bleakley, Platt, Gilchrist & Waber,
14 Wall Street, New York 5]

Dear Mr Gilchrist,

Thank you for your two letters, one of January which I have now with me and one of January 27th. I am sorry for this long delay and wish to apologise for it. Letters had been forwarded from London to the North of England again returned to London, forwarded to Oxford then back to Dublin. At last I received them in Mayo. Snow storms here have cut us off for about two and a half weeks almost. All telephones are out of order, roads until two days ago are impassable save for short distances.

Helen, I found, when I returned, had been in London for a time. I will ask her when I meet her if she has any information about my returns.[162] In the meantime perhaps you would be so good as to file a return for me. I have no documentary information about the amount of Hooker stock[163] in my name, how much has accumulated or what dividend I am to receive yearly. As I have not the necessary dollars at present nor a likelihood that I will have them in the future I suggest that you sell some of the stock to pay for the taxes or sell the stock in its entirety …

———————

Letter to Cathal O'Malley

15 Whitebeam Ave,
Clonskeagh, [Dublin]
16 March 1947

[Cathal O'Malley,
St Gerard's School,[164]
Bray, Co. Wicklow]

Dear Cathal,

Thank you very much for your letter of February 23rd which I received when I returned from the West. I left for Burrishoole, rather for Old Head on the 20th, went on to Achill and returned to Burrishoole, where I was snowed up for a week. Pat Clarke cooked for me as I was sick for a while and in bed. Luckily the hens were laying or I would have had to cook Pat, or he would have had to cook me. I don't know which of us would have been tougher.

Then as soon as the first bus was able to dig its way through the snow from Achill I went back there again. One day I was out in a boat. We went out towards

Clare Island then around by Achill Beg Island then up against the current to the Sound, at Achill bridge. Later I was able to take the bus back to Keel.

There were no trains running, but at last I was able to get a seat in a motor car which brought me back to Dublin. Étain and Cormac are getting better. They sit in bed together during the day in Nanna's room, and they get on very well together. I have to tell each of them a separate story every day for Cormac's story does not suit Étain. Nanna is getting better also. She hopes she will be soon out of bed.

Mrs Byrne was anxious to see you. Maybe you can be soon allowed out to visit her. I will find out tomorrow from the doctor if it is safe for you to come home and if so I hope you will be able to come this week-end. Étain is collecting stamps and so is Cormac, but I hear that you have a very good collection now. Can you come in on Sunday next?

My love to you,
Ernie

NO. 180 TRINITY COLLEGE, DUBLIN MS 4639/2295
Letter to Seamus O'Sullivan

[Stationery of] The Irish Academy of Letters,[165]
Dublin
21 March 1947

Seamus O'Sullivan, Esq.,
[2 Morehampton Road, Dublin]

Dear Sir,

There will be a meeting of the Academy of Letters (Council Meeting) on FRIDAY 28th inst., at 5:30 p.m. in the Abbey Theatre.

Yours faithfully
The Irish Academy of Letters
Ernest O'Malley, Hon. Secretary

Letter to Thomas Gilchrist

15 Whitebeam Ave,
Clonskeagh, Dublin
22 March 1947

[Mr Thomas B. Gilchrist,
14 Wall Street, New York 5]

Dear Mr Gilchrist,

Thank you for your letter of March 14th. As far as I can recollect there was some trouble periodically about this stock, but I am not sure of the details. Can you please tell me the actual value of the stock the amount of the yearly dividends, and the total money I owe in taxes? I can wait until you come over before I sell the stock, and as soon as I find out what I owe I can see a bank manager about advancing me money.

Helen has been in London since some time in January. Miss Dinneen,[166] who seemed from your letter an important asset to have over here, has had a nervous breakdown. How long she has been in bed before I arrived from London, I do not know. She had had to look after Miss O'Shea who has been in bed for close on three weeks. The children have been in bed with whooping-cough for five weeks. Miss O'Shea has been up for the past two days as have the children. As I have not heard from Helen, I do not know about her movements or her proposed movements, but I am sure I can meet you as soon as you arrive.

Sincerely yours,
Ernie O'Malley

Letter to Seamus O'Sullivan

[Stationery of] The Irish Academy of Letters,
Dublin
10 April 1947

[Seamus O'Sullivan, Esq.,
2 Morehampton Road, Dublin]

Dear Sir,

I should be obliged if you would sign enclosed Form and return at your earliest convenience.

An Extraordinary General Meeting of the Academy is necessary as Bernard Shaw refuses to be President. He has written saying he is too old.

Yours faithfully,
The Irish Academy of Letters
Ernest O'Malley, Hon. Secretary

Letter to Cathal O'Malley

Burrishoole Lodge,
Newport, Co. Mayo
21 September 1947

[Cathal O'Malley,
Glenstal Abbey School,[167]
Murroe, Co. Limerick]

Dear Cathal,

I suppose that by this you have settled down at school. Are you lonely or are there any boys you already know there? Anyhow, tell me how you are and how you like your school.

I have not heard from Étain or Cormac, but I sent them letters yesterday. I do not know where they now are but I expect they may be at their grandmother's house.[168] I hope you will write to them and to the people who were kind to you in America.

I was out in the boat the other day. She sails well with the new mast but needs a few alterations so that as soon as I get to Island Mór, I will have Josie[169] settle her properly. These last few days have been too windy to go to sea. Anyhow there is the harvest to be brought in: now it is nearly all in the haggard. I met Pat Quinn[170] yesterday. He was on the road with a cart of turf bringing home to his island. He has a long journey indeed from his bog for he can only bring the one cart in the day. He was asking for you. He is to bring over some sheep in his boat so I expect that by Easter we will have a few lambs, but ewes are hard to get now.

Please tell me if you want anything. Winnie[171] is here. Perhaps she could bake you a cake or whatever you most need.

With my love,
Ernie

Letter to Professor John V. Kelleher

Burrishoole Lodge,
Newport, Co. Mayo
22 October 1947

[Mr John V. Kelleher,
37 Lanark Drive,
Westwood, Massachusetts, USA]

Dear John,

I have a number of half-begun letters to you which are now of no use either to you or to myself. I heard of you indirectly from Stan Stewart[172] with whom I stayed a night when I was around with the BBC[173] keeping them in contact with people making the world easier for them. Then again I met Joe Sweeney[174] whom I liked for his own sake; doubly because he was a friend of yours.

I have been involved with *The Bell* endeavouring to build up a book-review section.[175] I find the work difficult. Reviewers are hard to find, good books are scarce, and English publishers don't care much whether they send books or not. I made a visit to England where I tried to get in to publishing houses to talk. I succeeded in some cases and as a result books are now sent on to me, but in a number of others I failed. Could you review Molly Colum's book for me, *Life and the Dream*; about 1,000 words. I borrowed a copy of it. I will order a copy for you. If you would like to do so I would be grateful as you could, I feel, do both sides of the Irish and the American life. Padraic[176] seems to have been largely side-stepped even as a human being. As I know you won't reply by letter maybe you could send me a night letter. Mary seems ill at ease in this Ireland of ours so uneasy that she ceased to write about it after 1922. However, it is my country and whether it builds up to a pre-conceived idea or not, it is a place to live in, and also to work in. Not that I can talk about work as I have not done anything about the Civil War[177] since I last saw you. I received a letter, thanks to you, from the Harvard University Press.[178] I have now bought a type-writer but *The Bell* takes a deal of reading before I send out books and a correspondence monthly with the office which loses reviews and books or forgets that material is already in galley-proof.

I have read a good book of Clarence H. Haring on *The Spanish Empire* in America. Is he belonging to your institution? It is a scholarly piece or work. I am forwarding you a copy of Don MacDonagh's poems, *The Hungry Grass*. I had a copy of his *Happy as Larry*, for you but I think Helen must have taken it away. At present there is a great dearth of writing: even for *The Bell* it is rare to find a short story that will suit.

Can you make out a list of books on Joyce written in America? Helen is over there. I especially asked her to find out about such books but she will probably forget it. The list would include a number of periodicals. I now have:

- a book on *Finnegans Wake* by two Americans, whose names I forget.
- a recently published book here by Faber, but not a good book.
- *Our Examination*, 1929
- Frank Budgen: *James Joyce*, 1934
- Harry Levine
- Louis Goeding: *James Joyce*, 1933
- Charles Duff: *James Joyce and the Plain Reader*, 1932
- S. Foster Damon: *Odyssey in Dublin*, Hound and Horn, Fall, 1929
- Bernard Bandler II: *Joyce's Exiles*, Hound and Horn, Jan. 1933[179]

I had others but as I lent them I can consider them missing.

Now, if you could send me on the list I can let Helen have it, for she will not return until December with the children. At least she says she will not, but I expect it depends on what plays can keep her in New York.

I have a few books in mind for you, searched the Dublin shops but failed. I'll be up there towards the end of November when I will have a good look again. What do you particularly want? There are some Cuala Press for you in Dublin, but I left in a hurry as Helen was in such a 5 days rush before leaving that I caught on some of her whirling forget-fulness. This in a hurry now. I have been working on Irish sculpture in my mind and through journals for the past 5 days as a result of looking at Eric Sexton's book *Irish Crosses* – a beautifully printed book, but not to me a good one. I will write to you next week. I find I have not been writing to people for the past few years and as I have to keep up an extensive correspondence on account of *The Bell*, I am now going to please myself about other correspondents.

Ever yours,
Ernie O'Malley

NO. 185 EOM PAPERS NYU
Letter to Cathal O'Malley

15 Whitebeam Ave,
Clonskeagh, [Dublin]
5 December 1947

[Cathal O'Malley,
Glenstal Abbey School,
Murroe, Co. Limerick]

Dear Cathal,

Thank you for your letter which I received when I was in Burrishoole. Étain, Cormac and Nanna have come back from the United States, of North America, as we used to say in Mexico. They look well. Étain has an American accent. She is fun to listen to especially if you tempt her to say words which you know will have an American inflection. Please write to the two of them as they are anxious to know how you are.

I met Peggy Woods[180] to-day. She said Joanna was looking forward to seeing you so I hope you can visit there at Christmas. Joanna will go to Belgium to school next year. I had your school report which I consider a good report as you are new to the school. The main thing is that you are happy there, the application can come next. I was sorry I was not able to see any of your teachers when I was there, but maybe if you return some other time early in the day I may be able to talk to them. Please write Nanna at once. Tell her when your holidays begin so that she can arrange for you to come here. I am leaving tomorrow, but I will be back before Christmas. Your mechano set is in John Raleigh's. Please collect it before you return. I have a book which you may read sometime about the Portugese adventurers in the 15th and 16th centuries. It is a good book, like all early reports of travels, as in Hakluyt's, which you looked through in Burrishoole for the Spaniards, and the other volumes of discovery in New Spain which I have shown you.

I hope you are content and happy.

With much love,
Ernie

Ernie O'Malley climbing in the Pyrenees, winter 1926
(Photographer unknown; source: COM Papers)

Ernie O'Malley driving Helen Golden's car from California to New Mexico, September
1929 *(Photographer Helen Golden; source: COM Papers)*

Ernie O'Malley in Carmel, California,
May 1929 (*Photographer: Edward Weston;
source: CCP, University of Arizona*)

Left to right: Ella Young, Eithne Gold
and Marianna Howe at Ranchos de Taos,
New Mexico, 1934 (*Photographer: Helen
Golden; source: COM Papers*)

Helen Hooker with her sculpted fawn,
New York City, July 1930 (*Photographer:
de Witt Ward; source: COM Papers*)

Helen Hooker, New York City, 1930
(*Photographer unknown; source:
COM Papers*)

Ernie O'Malley at Acoma Indian pueblo, New Mexico, 1930
(Photographer: Helen Golden; source: COM Papers)

Ernie O'Malley in the Yaddo Foundation Class of September 1932, Saratoga
Springs, New York *(Photographer: unknown; source: Yaddo Foundation;
COM Papers)*

Helen Hooker and Ernie O'Malley, New York City, 1934 *(Photographer: Helen H. O'Malley [née Hooker]; source: COM Papers)*

Ernie O'Malley and his brother, Dr Kevin Malley, at Kilteel, Co. Kilkenny, 1937 *(Photographer: Helen H. O'Malley; source: COM Papers)*

Helen H. O'Malley, 1937 *(Photographer: Ernie O'Malley; source: COM Papers)*

Catherine (Bobs) and Harry Walston, Burrishoole Lodge, March 1939 *(Photographer: Helen H. O'Malley; source: COM Papers)*

Ernie O'Malley at gravestones of Diarmuid and Grania, Louisburgh, Co. Mayo, 1938 *(Photographer: Helen H. O'Malley; source: COM Papers)*

Left to right: Cathal O'Malley, nurse and Ernie O'Malley, Burrishoole Lodge, 1939 *(Photographer: Helen H. O'Malley; source: COM Papers)*

Ernie O'Malley in beekeeping gear, Burrishoole Lodge, during the Emergency, 1942
(Photographer: Helen H. O'Malley; source: COM Papers)

Leased lands, overlooking Burrishooole Abbey, Burrishoole Lodge, 1942
(Photographer: Helen H. O'Malley; source: COM Papers)

Threshing of wheat, Burrishoole Lodge, 1942 *(Photographer: Helen H. O'Malley; source: COM Papers)*

Left to right: Etain, Cathal and Cormac O'Malley, Burrishoole Lodge, 1945 *(Photographer: Helen H. O'Malley; source: COM Papers)*

Left to right: Cathal, Etain, Helen, Ernie and Cormac O'Malley, Clonskeagh, Dublin, 1946 *(Photographer unknown; source: COM Papers)*

Jack B. Yeats *(left)* and Ernie O'Malley, at an art exhibition in Dublin, 1947 *(Photographer: unknown, published in Capuchin Annual, 1948; source: COM Papers)*

During the filming of *The Quiet Man*, June 1951:
back row, left to right: Ernie O'Malley, Maureen O'Hara, Tom Maguire;
front row, left to right: John Wayne, Metta Stern, John Ford
*(Photographer unknown, taken with Maureen O'Hara's camera;
source: COM Papers)*

Ernie and Cormac O'Malley, Burrishoole Lodge, with guard dog, August 1951
(*Photographer:* The Irish Press; *source: COM Papers*)

Cormac and Ernie O'Malley, Galway Races,
July 1954 (*Photographer:* The Irish Press;
source: COM Papers)

Ernie and Cormac O'Malley, Kilmurvey,
Inishmore, Aran Islands, August 1954
(*Photographer: Jean McGrail; source:
COM Papers*)

John Ford *(left)* and Ernie O'Malley, after filming, Co. Clare, May 1956
(Photographer: The Irish Press; *source: COM Papers)*

John Ford *(with cricket bat)* and Ernie O'Malley *(back, second from right)* on location in Co. Clare, May 1956 *(Photographer:* The Irish Press; *source: COM Papers)*

Left to right: Cabinet ministers Seán Lemass, Eamon de Valera and Frank Aiken attending Ernie O'Malley's state funeral procession in Howth, Co. Dublin, 27 March 1957 *(Photographer:* The Irish Press; *source: COM Papers)*

Funeral oration by Sean Moylan, TD, at Ernie O'Malley's graveside, Glasnevin Cemetery, Dublin, 27 March 1957 *(Photographer:* The Irish Press; *source: COM Papers)*

Letter to Cathal O'Malley

15 Whitebeam Ave,
Clonskeagh, Dublin
6 February 1948

[Cathal O'Malley,
Glenstal Abbey School,
Murroe, Co. Limerick]

Dear Cathal,

Thank you for your letter. It would be no harm if you always added the date on which you write. I will get your mother's address from Nanna for you. Have you any idea of when your school breaks up for the Easter holidays as your mother might be back in Ireland by that date.

Cormac has become stronger, but the illness took a deal of his strength away. He, Étain, Cecilia[181] and I went to the pantomine in the Queens. It was a very good pantomine, in which the audience joined. There was a large cat which came down to shake hands during the interval, and a magician who made pigeons disappear. Étain was very impressed with this magic, but Cormac liked the cat best ...

Étain and Cormac said they would write to you at the end of this week, so I hope they will. They have written a few letters to America, but they have yet to write to their Auntie Adelaide.

There was a great storm in the West. Luckily my boat was in the shed and the *St Brendan* in the boathouse. Philben's boat was carried up on to Murray's land.

McIntyre's boat was smashed as were all the boats belonging to Pat Quinn. I hope you are settling down. If you want anything, please, write to me.

With love,
Ernie

Letter to Cathal O'Malley

15 Whitebeam Ave,
Clonskeagh, Dublin
5 March 1948

[Cathal O'Malley,
Glenstal Abbey School,
Murroe, Co. Limerick]

Dear Cathal,

Thank you for your letter. Your school breaks up very late indeed; wasn't it the 27th, you said? I think Étain's school closes on the 15th March.

Johnny Raleigh was here recently. He said he would go out to see you or take you to his home for a weekend so if he does I hope you will have a good time with John.[182] Also you should get your mechano set: sorry, I now remember that you did get it by post although as far as I can see you kept to the one design.

Cormac and I are in bed with flu. He has a light and I have had a heavy attack, but the last two days my door has been open so that he can talk to me. He has been painting[183] for the last week and so has Étain but not to the same extent. School, I am afraid is ruining their sense of values for they are impressed by bad religious art. Now they don't like the later Jack Yeats, but they think his earlier drawings his best work. Are you painting at school or using chalks?

Cormac has been talking about his soul. He says it is in his stomach. Étain seems to spend most of her time learning the Catechism for she has to make her First Confession next week. She is getting very prim and proper, and I felt relieved when she danced into my room last night as a ballet dancer.

Do you want anything and have you any plans for Easter? I believe your mother intends to go to America, perhaps from London.

With love,
Ernie

NO. 188 EOM PAPERS NYU; ESTATE OF JOHN V. KELLEHER
Letter to Professor John V. Kelleher

Burrishoole Lodge,
Newport, Co. Mayo
9 March 1948

Mr John V. Kelleher,
37 Lanark Drive,
Westwood, Mass., USA

Dear John,

I had already begun a letter to you but flu got me down badly: then I took Cormac off to Skerries[184] to stay with a friend of mine thinking, as we were both sick, we might as well see if a coastal town would kill or cure us. It cured Cormac, but it damn near killed me. I didn't finish my letter but when I returned I found your letter here from Burrishoole. I am glad you liked the books: indeed I thought they had not turned up. Also I forgot to thank you for the Morley[185] book. There was no indication of your name in it. Before she left here a girl called Kitty, who is Liam O'Flaherty's[186] girl, said she would send me that book. I tried to get her address several times but no-one here knew of it, nor did many know of her surname. So now a belated thanks for it.

I was thinking of you 10 days ago when last on my feet. I saw a collection of Irish books in Hanna's:[187] some I would have bought for you as they were old, but then I did not know if you had them or not.

In Skerries I went out to drink with two airmen belonging to the Irish line[188] and with friends of mine. The airmen were English, very dull and inclined to be superior until we debauched, then deshirted them. The Irish lines have 4 Irish pilots and 80 English. 80 who have served in the British army: most of them hostile in mind or of English birth. When we returned home to Skerries we found five Irish army officers drinking stout in the front room of the house having put their host to bed. We had a very fine morning with them. They all seemed anxious to march on the North and at the same time be proud of their constitutional position serving 26 Counties.[189] However they thoroughly disliked their inefficient general staff who are kept because they are 'yes' men.

Here the Clann[190] was expected to win 30 seats. That is what they themselves hoped for. The Coalition[191] may do some good. It should help to break down the political hatred of the civil war. All the cabinet can now visit each other's houses and engage in some kind of social intercourse. Again Costello[192] who is a safe kind of a man, may be induced by MacBride[193] and Lavery,[194] his Attorney-General, to be interested in civil liberties. There were many abuses of which there was no notice taken by Dáil or Senate. MacBride in this could develop a national feeling, for previously he was concerned with defending IRA prisoners! Also, through his mother[195] he will probably help a reformation in the prison system. The third point is that if a younger crowd get into politics a man may be judged on his merits in the year of 1947 and not those of 1916 or 1922. That again would be a change for the better. But I see no one in this cabinet interested in art, literature, or the things of the mind which lead to planning for time. Fianna Fáil[196] is trying to detach adherents of the Clann by pointing out that the Clann has joined an alliance with Fine Gael,[197] the old spatters of walls in the early dawn.

I was trying to go to America recently. One reason was to help to start an Irish book centre in New York for distribution, but the books written for Irish publishers are poor stuff. I had a strange interview with a man in the Consulate. At the end I felt that I had been trying to both pick his pocket and had been caught. I do not know if you can help me.

Ostensibly, for quickness in dispatch, I was going to my relations in America.[198] I was asked if they would write to guarantee that I would be invited and not be short of money. They are in no way friendly to me so I said I could not ask them. I suggested, as I had an American wife, who had money in America, that that should suffice. They requested a declaration from her. Helen has been in London for the past 3 months. I wrote to her, talked to her on the phone, but my feeling is that she will stall and so hold me up indefinitely. I would like to be in the U.S. in early or middle April. Now could you give me an invitation to go there and cover whatever snags there are? I actually have some money in the U.S. so I need not worry my relatives, but until I fix a few things, and not until I get there, can I admit I have money. Please be as frank as you wish about this request.

The editor of *The Bell*, Peadar[199] has a peculiar conscience. He is a bad judge of literature and a bad man to suggest articles. He should never have permitted Kavanagh to publish the article on Frank,[200] especially as Frank was writing a very interesting article for that number on his experiences as a director of the Abbey.

Peadar O'Donnell was sorry when the article appeared in print, but sorry because people objected to it, not for its appearance. At present *The Bell* is being run without money for contributions.[201] It will close down this month for six months, I believe. Not since October have I received the galleys of reviews. Even then the editor did not take my selection of reviews, but made a choice of his own. Since October I have sent out books, but any review which came in has not been sent on to me. I neither know what the review is like or what is going to be inserted until I buy a copy of the magazine. However, I thought it best to stand by a boat in difficulties, when an editor did not understand what real liberty of the subject meant. Maybe I could help *The Bell* in America. The editor was refused permission by the U.S. Govt. for entry into the U.S.[202]

The witch-hunt is on, I see.[203] I expect it will continue. We hear less of war in Europe than you do in the U.S. I have been in London in December. There was no feeling then of impending war. No one in Europe is able to make war at present. The balance of power is with Russia. The balance of cultural strength is with France but France is too weak politically to be a spear-head. Outside of France there is no core in Europe. I have been reading hard around the 3rd, 4th, 5th, 6th centuries in Europe as a background to influence on early Christian art.[204] The parallel is not the same, I know, but it is an opposite parallel.

The clergy here preach about communism from the altar, but it seems to me that the pressure is being directed by the U.S. and that it does not come from Europe. There is no feeling of tension: maybe a sense of inevitability about the Prague episode[205] but little more. Russia will, it is thought, surround herself by buffer states. Most of the pro-war party whom I meet do not give one human damn for human liberty in any form. The Irish bishops were called to Rome and have been given their brief.

This is a disjointed letter but then I am also disjointed in bed trying to kill a temperature with whiskey and aspirin: or alternatively with lemon juice. The children are very well. In a week we go down to Burrishoole for the Easter holidays. This winter has been wet and stormy with us but no snow, so your adventures would have silenced us to immediate myth and story. Kindly remember me to the family. If I don't see you this Spring in the U.S. then maybe I will see you soon in Burrishoole.

Remind me to tell you about the goat in Skerries.

Affectionately,
Ernie

BROKEN LANDSCAPES

Letter to Professor John V. Kelleher

Burrishoole Lodge,
Newport, Co. Mayo
7 April 1948

Mr John V. Kelleher,
37 Lanark Drive,
Westwood, Mass., USA

Dear John,

Thank you very much for your letter and your enclosed letter. It reached Burrishoole, but I was away and no-one could be sure of where I was. In fact I was in Limerick. Not until I returned over a week later did I receive your letter. I have been in Burrishoole with the children, then Helen arrived from London where she has been for three months, on her way to the U.S.

I have to fulfil a schedule of necessities including permission from Helen for me to leave Ireland. That I do not understand as she can leave without my permission. Anyhow I will see the U.S. Consulate on the 8th: then I will know if they will allow me to go, and when I can leave.

You would have liked my last expedition. I took Cormac, Étain and the nurse, Nanna, down by car from Dublin. Helen had taken the petrol coupon-book and insurance to London, but I thought the children would have their first run to the West in a car. Petrol, as usual, was supplied me to start with by a Tan-war friend in a garage. I showed the children a clough at Tyrrels' Pass,[206] the old King John's Castle[207] at Athlone, built in John's reign and a few abbeys. They badly needed the freedom of Burrishoole as they are cramped in Dublin, and had been sick during the winter. They went wild for some time. The light boat had been painted a brilliant red and white and lay there frightening the salmon as they passed up.

Then I decided to go to Limerick to bring Cathal back. He is at school with the Benedictines there. On my way across by Leenane and the Maam Valley where the Joyces[208] settled I reached Galway, thinking I would have a night's hard drinking, but my best friend's wife just then had a baby[209] and he seemed somewhat reluctant to drink, so off I went to Limerick. Unfortunately, on the way a friend of mine at Old Head Alec Wallace said 'You have last year's tax on that car. If you're stopped you will get 3 months at least.' But I was on my way so I couldn't turn back for a sensible man like him.

In Limerick next day the new Gallery[210] was opened by his Grace of Limerick. He mentioned that 'the Church had always patronized the arts', but I failed to see anything of said patronage, save a rotten portrait[211] painted by Sean Keating from a photograph. Anyhow the gallery is now open. The pictures are bad, possibly 10 of them good, but Bob Herbert is custodian and is amenable to advice.

There was a bar upstairs, tea downstairs. Later in the night we returned to the upstairs bar which was in the reference library and remained until all whiskey was finished. Stan[212] we saw earlier in the evening, for I tried to take his pants off him in the bar of the Glentworth[213] for not appearing at the opening. Stan's trousers were a heavy pauper-grey which pinned him to earth.

Bob and I drank for 3 days: and in between times we talked of books working in the Library. Bob, Cathal and I equipped with one camera[214] and 6 bottles of whiskey, purloined by me in the noble city of Limerick, set off on Good Friday for Burrishoole. We went to Ennis Friary, Dysert O'Dea, Killinaboy, Kilfenora, Kilcreely on the sea shore near Lahinch, a little church above the spa in the Burren,[215] finally up over the ... Pass[216] into Gort. It was a beautiful day, warm dry and lark-singing. Bob and I drank away. Bob of course had to photograph for me as I discovered in Limerick that my camera would not work. We talked of you as we drank. I expect you know Clare: with me it is a second country. I love the people there especially in North Clare. I feel an affection for the land. The Burren strikes something in my heart and mind as does desert and bog. That indeed was a good day. Whiskey, my sculpture with Bob very interested, Cathal taking it all in slowly. There's a great view from the top of the Ceonke Pass looking towards Kinvara.[217] Bob, I think, discovered that it is of no use to be nervous with me when I freewheel down hills or charge up or down a road. Also at times there was slight tension on my part whenever I passed a guard.[218]

I saw a fine Christ in the porch of a modern church north of the Spa. It had been taken from an old church last year. I have been many times in this county, as apart from the Tan war, to photograph.[219] Here was a fine piece of expressionistic work indeed. Clare is rich in sculpture, as our richness goes. The light was good. I hope Bob has been able to improve on my earlier work. We were too tired in fact to drink after our meal.

Next day off to Kilmacduragh. Bob is a hopeless map reader. I know this country, but I forget turns. Kilmacduragh is beside a peaceful, murky lake spotted with seagulls and wild fowl. Later up along the edge of the Burren mountains up the pass to Corcomroe in its valley of limestone. There we photographed, waited for light to swing on the figures on capitals and drank. The drink was good as was the sun. We slept, on limestone, waking again to watch the light come on to the noblest figure in Irish personal sculpture: O'Brien buried there 1276 I think. Once I was to do a book on Connaught. Frank a book on Munster, Sean O'Faolain on Leinster, but I had annexed Clare as it is of Connaught by nature and by old thought and government. Frank objected to this, but I meant to include it anyhow.

Back down the pass to Kinvara, a great town of whitewash and unspoilt houses, to Dromacoo Church, then to Galway. I showed Bob my favourite pubs, and sculpture inside churches. I decided to go home across the mountains for my friend now had mumps.[220] My stay in Galway has always been dotted with his drinks, and I felt woe begone for Galway is the most friendly and the most Irish large town I know. Bob was pleased and very surprised at the friendly feeling here. I changed my mind when I spoke to Mrs Lydon[221] at her pub.

The County Club[222] could put me up as I am a member, but Rose who could not find room did find room for Bob. Cathal being 11½ could not enter the Club. I christened him under a glass of brandy in the bar. Then as Sir James Esmond[223] he was given a bed as well as the freedom of the Club of which I am a member. You can always stay there if I recommend you.

We drank late in the next morning with Duignan[224] of the University who is now building up a group of students. He is defeated by Connaught, we felt. He feels nothing can be done. That is a futile attitude. You can do a good deal and it requires 5 times as much will and energy as it does in any other part of the world outside of the tropics. I then decided I would do an article on Galway scuplture for Bob's periodical,[225] for Duignan felt it would take years for him to photograph Galway which is more coherent than any city of its size. Excellent drink there, better whiskey than Limerick, a good turf smell of the unwashed Connemara men. A University that something could be done with if there were people who fought enough for it.

Next morning we visited a few churches for sculpture. Then off to Tuam. An art exhibition was to open there at 12:30. I listened to His Grace[226] of Tuam read from his notes. A kindly, rather futile little man. And a rotten hanging of pictures. Nun's school with the gutless content of painting inspired by book illustrations, the good sound colour from technical schools. All in a mess of bad light, bad hanging, bad display. It is unhappy, for a few of us would arrange an exhibition and set a standard. However, now that I have a few people whom I know there, a little underhand work might produce results. Bob and I made one friend apart from a girl with breasts like a Galway shur-cock, and that was old Costello.[227] He is about 75, a gamey old bird who knows his part of the county well. His wife, English, has made that fine book on Connaught songs in Irish and is English. He came with us to the Protestant Cathedral.[228] The chancel arch is a beauty, early 12th, I think. Bob got some of the figure decoration. The old man talked and talked. We were cold, hungry and a little tired from hearty drinking. No one asked us to have a cup of tay, but the old boy kept on impartially relating pre- and post Reformation information.

The market cross[229] is ready to shed one of its panels. The Board of Works won't work. Even Costello can't get anything done. Yet I'm sure if I attended a service in the Protestant Cathedral a few of the townspeople would meet to denounce me. No meeting for the Cross. To-morrow I'll see what I can do in Dublin. The old boy has lovely Irish, a house half a museum, and a wide interest. If we had had a few drinks in we would have felt better: but as soon as he left us I went to the car which was parked slap up against a Protestant wall to make the Guards sure of its respectability; and we drank deep to Tuam.

This seems now a kind of diary. God help you, but I'm in a train where people are trying to be little bog-tussacks all to themselves. They are all women and respectable. Cormac and Étain have been wild since I left home. They are painting every day so I was met with very exciting watercolours. The weather became colder: some snow on the mountains. Helen came back. Bob and I drank hard until he had to leave me, which reminds me that you had very little to drink at Burrishoole. We pulled out the small billiard table. I made Etain a bar-maid,

Cormac a pot-boy. That was bad for we were plied with drink very fast as the 3 children drank orangeade quickly, and we had to keep company, to the terror of the green sword suffering from a deadly noise of overexcited bulls trying to play leapfrog.

Pat was talking about you 'a very nice man, very nice indeed and I hope he'll come soon again for your sake and for company's sake'. The other day he said 'I'm shallow about that now': meaning he knew little about it. I bought 5 bullocks on Monday. I have 3 ewes: 1 with 2 lambs, 1 with one, one with none. As Etain says it's like 'rithmitic. Also I have a pedigree cow the last of my original stock.

I see a hawk from its red sheen on wing outside in the bay. Stan looks well. He is his usual, charming self. When we left he was due for Kilkenny the following day so I expect he'll write you about it: but the proper way to see sculpture is with sun and plenty of whiskey.

Affectionately,
Ernie

NO. 190 EOM PAPERS NYU
Letter to Cathal O'Malley

15 Whitebeam Ave,
Clonskeagh, [Dublin]
29 April 1948

[Cathal O'Malley,
Glenstal Abbey School,
Murroe, Co. Limerick]

Dear Cathal,

Thank you for your letter. I enclose you a book of stamps. You get your holiday on Saturday May 15th and you have to return on May 17th; is that correct? I wish the car was in working order for then I could meet the train but it is, the car, here derelict. There is some licence which your mother has in America.

Anyhow I will send you your fare, so please say what train you can leave by.

Cormac has a puppy which he has called 'Wagger'. He wants to have it christened in the bird font. It is a very nice pup, but goodness knows if it will survive here. We have had a swing put up since last you were here. Now they can do 'monkey tricks', on it. Étain makes her first Holy Communion on the 9th. Her Auntie Sweetie will be there. Uncle Brendan and I hope Kevin, and Auntie Kay. Mrs Byrne asks for you as often as I call in, so please thank her whenever next she writes to you.

If you send me on word that you will be definitely here on Sunday 16th I can have a party ready for you that evening but you should send on a list of boys and girls you would like to have. I hope you will include young MacDonagh[230] this time. If there is anything you need please don't hesitate to write. You remember I read to you the *Anabasis* of Xenophon, the march of the 10,000 in Asia Minor on their way to Greece. Now there is a translation by a man called Rouse, so I will get it for you.

With love,
Ernie

NO. 191 EOM PAPERS NYU
Letter to Cathal O'Malley

15 Whitebeam Ave,
Clonskeagh, Dublin
11 May 1948

[Cathal O'Malley,
Glenstal Abbey School,
Murroe, Co. Limerick]

Dear Cathal,

Thank you for your letter. I am enclosing a cheque for your fare and I will meet you at the station.

Étain's Holy Communion went off very well. Your Aunties Ita, Sweetie and Kathleen were there and your friend Mrs Byrne. Later they came out for breakfast, but not Mrs Byrne.

I intend to bring you to the zoo on Sunday and I will invite young MacDonagh and perhaps young Salkeld[231] as well as Étain and Cormac. We can eat our lunch there as I am a member. Anyhow I will ask these two in advance as it seems a good thing to do on a fine day.

That is good the practice in rowing, for you will need that in Burrishoole, I hope.

The puppy is doing well. He is a little troublesome in certain respects, but he gives a great deal of pleasure to Étain and Cormac. Whang Ho and Sung[232] are here also. They were very thin and ill, as they had not been fed in Burrishoole, but I think they will recover slowly.

Your Auntie Kathleen, Sweetie, Ita, Harry and Mrs Byrne send you their love. If you can think of anything you would like to do whilst you are here please let me know as soon as you receive this letter.

With love,
Ernie

Letter (EOM copy) to Marion Malley Gargan-Daly

15 Whitebeam Ave,
Clonskeagh, Dublin
7 July 1948

[Mrs James P. Gargan-Daly,[233]
Leeds, England]

Dear Sweetie,

I hope you and Jim[234] are very well. Kathleen I was talking to yesterday. She is very cheerful in her difficulties but now her children have some infection. I was about to send Étain to her for a week, so that Étain would have children to play with. Helen objects to this as she wanted to take Étain away to Aran where she intends to remain for some weeks with the Redmonds. That I could not permit as Helen involved herself too much with Liam Redmond.

Cormac and Cathal are well. They are really very good for it is hard for a small lad like Cormac to stay in bed. We have now a nurse[235] from Templehill and a young governess of 21. She is good company for Étain and for Cormac, but she has to yet learn how to handle Cathal who does not like too many women around him. They are both in the front room downstairs where they eat and sleep. Winnie is in the Fever Hospital, Clonskeagh. I am trying to get her moved to a sanatorium, but she may have to wait some months. She will have to remain some time in bed as she has a cavity, I think.

It would be a relief if Helen would go away for a while, for as long as Redmond is two doors away she is a cause of trouble, though his wife and children are in Aran. Things don't get any better, I must say. I had intended to take the children away this summer though it would be hard on them to live my way, but I feel since Helen will not look after them, and as she has become more involved with Redmond[236] she will spend more time in London. She will sell Burrishoole this month, I think, and she plans to buy a house in England.[237]

If you drop in to the Yeats Exhibition[238] in Temple Newson House would you please send me two catalogues. I had very much hoped to have had you in the house, but things were bad just then.

With love,
Ernie

30/8/48. F/G : Frank Gallagher 40

Bob Brennan See for Foreign affairs
The O'Loughlin and the Clune negotiations.

Paddy Little : must have seen Smuts in South Africa
Ethne O'Byrne :
The Smuts order in Farnham's house. The American
correspondents who came to ask is the general in? the
girl says there is no general here and this is her
nights off :
June : Smuts. supposes the to slick for words. Dev
saw his elections. F read a book on him and
he was known as Slim Jannie (in a book on Gen Botha
It was assumed that he was doing a double shuffle. Smuts
had already let down his people & he never shows
us how near he has succeeded. At the crisis he
published a private letter he had written to Dev & this was
typical of him.

2. Did Dev know of Collins's meetings with Craig and
were there reports.
. a movement in the I.R.B & and Dev as President
(August 1919) He has certain members of the Republic
there got was to put the heads certain president. Then F/G
heard discussions in the Dáil as they took him to be
an I.R.B man.

EOM's interview with Frank Gallagher, 30 August 1948, as part of EOM Military Interviews for the Tan and Civil Wars. Source: UCDA P17b/86, p. 40.

Letter to Frank Gallagher

Burrishoole Lodge,
Newport, Co. Mayo
31 December 1948

[Frank Gallagher,
Sutton Cross, Howth, Co. Dublin]

Dear Frank,

I hope you and Cecilia and the girls are very well and that your seat in the sun in the Custom's House[239] has less ants in it by this. It's cold today, and we are all in bed, not because it is cold but because we all have colds, and also we are expecting turf.

Cathal and Cormac seem alright now although Cormac, the youngest, does not look too well these days. I brought Étain back as she was at a day school near Killiney.[240] Here, I have the young nurse who is the cook, a bad cook but a good heart so we live on good heart. Helen has an elderly female,[241] a half-lady in possession and as she cooks for the men who work here, it makes for an awkwardness and prevents me from cooking. There was an attempt to drive me out of Burrishoole by solicitors' letters[242] until I replied: since then there has been no further attempt. I am cataloguing my books with the help of Cormac mostly. It has been a long job as there are a great deal of books, but the most difficult is yet to come: to reduce the books which I now think I need again by half. I must be bad at arithmetic. So far I have no time to write, yet I get caught as I begin to read books which I think are important and that takes up time.

Yesterday I came across this in a book, *African Portraits*.[243] 'He bought the Irish members of the English Parliament'. He, being Cecil Rhodes.[244] Do you know anything of this? I have never liked the Parliamentary Party,[245] but I gave them mostly credit for ignorance in relation to a top-hatted lack of civilisation.

I have to write a play to-morrow for the children ever since I began 3 days ago to talk in an Abbey brogue[246] there had been a demand for a play. We have a band here. Cormac conducts on a tree stump. Cathal has a guitar, Étain a drum and penny whistle and Cormac my trumpet, which I sound when coming in from sea in my boat. A most difficult din is made by the combination.

Étain is slightly deaf in either ear. I must bring her up for an operation in January: removal of tonsils or some such matter first. I intend to send them to Ring[247] as soon as the boys are able to go, but that may be after Easter. In the meantime I must finish 'the booking', as Cormac calls it, remove books, then decide whether to move to that cottage in Achill. It has an open hearth; the kitchen is warm, but fires hardly work in the other three rooms so I think I had best go into winter quarters here, provided the nurse does not leave. I had the loan of a car[248] but it cracked up as I was on my way to Dublin, outside of Limerick when I went to bring Etain home. Now I must put a new engine into it.

I heard that you wrote an article on Erskine.[249] Have you got a copy of it, as I would like to have it. Here, a strange timeless world. I don't read papers. I have no wireless. Each week I go out to Mass at 8 in a trap. That is as much as I see of the outside world, which I expect is yet there. I have been reading Frank O'Connor's *Michael Collins*.[250] It is a strange medley of information and misinformation. Collins had colour but lent less to fighting Ireland than O'Connor thinks but then he wants to create a realistic legend or rather to back up a legend. It is a pity that there have not been a few other biographies written. One of Griffith[251] is needed. I must cease now as post time has come.

Thank you very much Frank for being so kind and helpful about the civil war[252] and my own particular civil war and thank Celia for her kindness. I have been reading of her yesterday in *The Jangle of Keys*[253] or whatever it was.

Affectionately,
Ernie

NO. 194 NLI MS 18353(14)
Letter to Frank Gallagher

Burrishoole Lodge,
Newport, Co. Mayo
February 1949

[Frank Gallagher,
Sutton Cross, Howth, Co. Dublin]

Dear Frank,

Thank you for your letter and your paper cutting which arrived here later. It was good to see such two names in print Erskine and John T.[254] and to feel that they wear well with the years.

Later in the same book I found the reference. Evidently Cecil gave £10,000 to the Irish Parliamentary Fund,[255] but whether they helped him or not in his African adventures, I doubt. Rhodes is even supposed to have said to Parnell, when he said, owing to his divorce, the priests were against him, 'Can't you square the Pope?' I cannot find the second Irish Party reference in this book.

There is nothing much to report from this part of the earth. It is like the Basques and their history. They have no written history. When questioned they say 'We are like good women: we have no history.' I am afraid I cannot answer like the Basques, but we lead a quietly enclosed life. Every 3 weeks or so we see someone; then we go back to the enclosed life.

About 3 weeks ago we all went to see *Hamlet* in Castlebar[256] at a matinee given by friends of ours from Dublin. That was a big event, especially the ghost. Once *Hamlet* was forbidden in Japan about 1938 in the city of Osaka. It 'was injurious to public morals', the police decided, partly because of the evil doings of royalty and the deviation from respectability of Hamlet's thoughts.

I have been rereading Coyle's *Evidence on Conditions in Ireland*.[257] It is a formidable book. Poor Ginnell[258] was rather obstreperous. It is surprising what good evidence was really obtained.

I am reading *Moby Dick* at night. It sounds fine when read aloud although it is not an easy book for 6½, 8½, 12½, but they all like it. There is a wonderful rhetoric in the prose, and a great deal of humour as can be judged by laughter before bedtime here. There is a sense of eternity in each chapter.

I hope the girls are very well. I suppose they cannot use a boat now nor play tennis. I have a small billiard table, but the children are not as yet strong enough, but there is a gambling game which is attended by Indians, cowboys and other boisterous frontier people at times.

> Love to you and Celia,
> Ernie

NO. 195 EOM PAPERS NYU
Postcard of The Custom House, Dublin, to Etain O'Malley

> [Dublin]
> 10 May 1949

Étain O'Malley,
Burrishoole Lodge,
Newport, Co. Mayo

Dear Étain,

I suppose you are climbing trees and swimming by this. I hope you take the boat gently. Cathal can row lightly now.

> With love,
> Ernie

NO. 196 EOM PAPERS NYU
Letter to Thomas Gilchrist[259]

> Burrishoole Lodge,
> Newport, Co. Mayo
> 10 January 1950

[Mr Thomas B. Gilchrist,
Bleakely, Gilchrist & Baker,
14 Wall Street, New York]

Dear Mr Gilchrist,

Thank you for being so kind as to send sweets to the children. The enclosed cards have been very much delayed for I was laid up. First, then I had books to number consecutively with the children's help and then as we gave the nurse a week's holidays, we had to cook.

I would definitely like to know your position with regard to the children and exactly what it involves on your side and on my side. It is for this reason as you have a guardianship,[260] but to that extent I do not know that I write the remainder of this letter.

Cormac remains at home for I teach him. He looks very strong now and has become fat, but maybe that is from eating porridge. He has to wear glasses but his teeth are sound.

Étain's last year was more momentous. Tonsils and adenoids removed on account of deafness, an operation, rushed to hospital for appendicitis, but any how I was expecting it and a surgeon was ready to operate at any time. Two tearing of stitches, teeth not too good about 4 refills. She is again suffering from deafness and had to sit in a front seat at school. I will take her perhaps at Easter to have her again seen to. She now wears glasses.

Cathal has bad teeth, about refilled as soon as he was strong enough to visit a dentist. He wears glasses permanently. (He had grown very tall.) Here the children use candles mostly for large lamps are dangerous for them unless an adult is always present. School suits them. They both like it. Food is simple and so is the school standard.

All the children help in the housework as we do everything independent of the resident staff with Nurse, so they cook, wash-up, look after their beds, bring in turf, etc. Since you were here[261] we have not used (a) vegetables from the garden, (b) eggs from the hens, but we have used milk. Anyhow Cathal now takes tea at school, so he is given tea at home.

I have not as yet paid Mrs O'Malley the money which was brought up by her for payment in your presence. That was, as you may remember, for food purchased on a single account, that of Mrs O'Malley's for 2 1/2 months. That payment, which is quite small anyhow, can wait now until after Easter of 1950, for a year is her time for paying local bills.

In September I was informed from a source, which I should rely on, that Mrs O'Malley had borrowed £500 from Mrs Sheridan[262] in London on the plea that she had just spent that sum on clothes for the children. Mrs O'Malley did buy some clothes for them in April when she was in Burrishoole but I had to equip them before they left for school in September. In November Mrs O'Malley sent clothes to the two children in Ring. I instructed the children not to use them. A supply of clothes cannot be left to individual caprice. I am, I take it, responsible for the children when Mrs O'Malley does not belong to the family unit. Previously, in winter of 1948, I had put Etain to school in Killiney, outside of Dublin, as a day girl. She stayed with a friend of mine.[263] Mrs O'Malley visited Etain and took her out shopping. I forwarded a checque for the clothes purchased, but in the case of the November, 1949, clothes, I could not afford that amount of money. Therefore I had the clothes put by until I could personally return them.

One item about your Burrishoole visit is slightly ironic. The nurse was brow-beaten about broken china, wedding present china, about which the nurse had no responsibility. All this while the cook, in Mrs O'Malley's employment, was drunk in bed. She had been drunk for four successive days, and the cook went on periodical bursts. I did not bring the matter up as the cook was not in my employment, therefore I had no control, nor had I with regard to Miss Dinneen[264] or Pat Clarke,[265] as since the day I arrived in October 1948.

I take it that this letter to you is a personal letter.

Sincerely yours,
E. O'Malley

NO. 197 EOM PAPERS NYU; ESTATE OF JOHN V. KELLEHER
Letter to Professor John V. Kelleher

Burrishoole Lodge,
Newport, Co. Mayo
30 January 1950

Mr John V. Kelleher,
37 Lanark Drive, Westwood, Mass., USA

Dear John,

Thank you for your letter of December 28 which I received about January 8th and for your lists[266] enclosed. I have been busy ever since for the last few days in bed when I returned trying to catalogue books, get them to Dublin and endeavouring to have a catalogue typed. In between I looked at the lists you sent me, and I could make nothing much of them for they required time and particularly good eyesight. Also the typing of mine done on this paper was by Herbert of Limerick, and he did not mention often enough when a book was printed, as well, a number of books selected by the Librarian's assistants are not by the people they think they are written by for example:

Davies, Sir John: *A True History of Why*[267]... 1650
The State of the Town of Newry 1725

The underneath book has nothing to do with Davies, but was always so inferred by your scriptesses of the library. Herbert should have put '?' or author unknown, or have drawn a blank line as he had an elaborate card index of mine for each entry.

The sale[268] is not until April 23rd, which I think is the date of the Rising, so my rush which was to have everything ready by mid January was not necessary I found out on the last week of January. People have no money until April anyway,[269] and, besides, that, money is now very short. The Yeats books sold well, but the art books and special presses did not at all realise what I once paid for them.

I am in bed as I have overdone it for my heart has been giving me trouble.[270] Now, I have a broken pair of glasses and flu, so that my rest in bed which meant refilling notebooks does not look too rosy. I have no Dublin house, by the way, for Helen closed on the lease of that[271] whilst the children were sick, and I have no other house but as Cathal and Étain are at Ring Irish College, it means I have only 2 of us to place, Cormac and I, and that is easier. This address will work until you ever hear to the contrary. Indeed, unless process of law begins,[272] I intend to be here until September as I must recatalogue English and European books before I move. I hope you can all come here on a visit. I rechecked the Saint Brendan last year as I had intended to sail for at least a month with the children, but I have to be away a good deal gathering materials so we had little sailing. This year we intend to stay out for at least two weeks at one go, sleeping aboard, or on island land and cooking in the lea of islands, peopled by fierce whites; for we are on the side of tinted races, which I expect is romantic temperament at work, as Frank[273] would say.

---

13 February 1950

My throat became very septic so I was laid up longer than I thought I would be, and today I received my glasses. I have a number of pamphlets which I have not put in with the other books as Harvard wanted them. To whom shall I now write to in Harvard stating the price? One thing I would like you to bring me, and I can settle for it when I see you is: a Parker 49[274] or whatever the number is. I had two of them. Both disappeared, the last one when I was in Dublin. They are useful to me for taking down notes as a man talks to me,[275] as they do not need refills as quickly as other pens.

For goodness sake don't forget that this country is chilly to the American born, especially the women, so either get your women folk to cut up family blankets for underclothes or make them all, the day they arrive, get heavy woolies – otherwise discontent and a grouse about climate ... Somewhere I have notes for you about Eimear O'Duffy and Gerald O'Donovan,[276] but where they now are I cannot discover. This house has been turned upside down many times: and the Dublin house suffered like a Blitz, for anything I left behind there was distributed I know not where by Helen.

As soon as I am in good form I have to write up my notes on the folklore of 1920–24,[277] then I can revert to the damn books again. I expect to be in Dublin sometime about April, so if I know where you are I hope I can see you and the family. Thank you, John, for being so kind about the books and please excuse my extreme preoccupation with the Irish Library[278] and my illness.

Affectionately,
Ernie O'Malley[279]

Why *The Bible in Ireland*[280] and not the two books Aseneth[281] published in America? Perhaps they are out of print.

PART V

Decline, 1950–1957

In March 1950 HHOM, who had effectively been living apart from the family, decided to take (or 'kidnap', as it was referred to) Cathal and Etain from Ring College to New York. The move had a devastating impact on EOM as he felt he had been unable to protect even his own children. He made sure that it would not happen to Cormac, keeping the child under close surveillance in terms of those who knew where he was and what he was doing. He immediately arranged for Cormac to go to a private school in Dublin and in 1956 he went on to attend Ampleforth College in York as previously planned. A further setback for EOM was HHOM's legal actions to evict him and Cormac from Burrishoole, but her legal efforts in Ireland collapsed. HHOM established residence in Colorado, and filed for a divorce from EOM that was granted in 1952.

Twice during his last six years, EOM had the chance to meet up with and work as a technical assistant to his friend, film director John Ford, first in 1951 on The Quiet Man *and again in 1956 on* The Rising of the Moon. *Most of those years, however, EOM was concerned with his deteriorating heart condition. He suffered an initial setback in 1952 and a significant heart attack in spring 1953 that laid him up in hospital for six months, plus a further few months of recuperation with friends in Dublin and with the Walston family in Cambridge, England. Thereafter he spent each winter in Cambridge where he was well taken care of, albeit isolated from his friends, books and working papers. Given his condition, he had to move from his beloved Burrishoole to a small flat in Dublin in mid 1954. Considering his financial position, and lack of support from HHOM for Cormac, he had to arrange to sell all of his land and many of his prized books, but never any of his paintings. As a substitute for sending Cormac to Ring College to learn Irish, EOM took him each summer from 1954 to 1956 to the Aran Islands.*

Due to his health, EOM could not circulate among his old friends. He took pleasure in renewing his friendship with Paul Strand, who had moved to Paris in 1950, and he and Cormac went to visit there each spring, 1954 to 1956. On Aran he met another American sculptor, Jean McGrail, with whom he corresponded in 1955 and 1956. By late 1956 his body started to fail. He moved from hospital in Dublin to Cambridge for his last Christmas and then returned to die in Dublin in March 1957. The Fianna Fáil party had just been elected prior to his death, and his former military subordinates, who were now cabinet ministers, made sure that their former assistant chief of staff received a state funeral, with the president, taoiseach and many of the cabinet at his graveside.

Draft letter to Sammy Somerville-Large[1]

> Burrishoole Lodge,
> Newport, Co. Mayo
> 6 May 1950

[Mrs L.B. Somerville-Large,
Brooklawn, Palmerstown, Co. Dublin]

Dear Sammy:

I am very sorry that I was not able to have a longer talk with you, but when I am in Dublin I work very hard, and I have no time to see anyone. Then, on account of my situation of having to watch two fronts for years, Cormac and on the other hand, Étain and Cathal, my movements were uncertain and necessarily unknown even to my friends.

Today I was informed by a solicitor[2] that I would have to remove my effects at once from Burrishoole, but I fight a delaying action here until I withdraw of my own volition or through Court pressure, and as far as I can judge public opinion in my own country is very much against Court pressure.

Now I have a few pictures[3] …

Letter to the Irish Pension Board regarding Mrs Marion Tobin

> Burrishoole Lodge,
> Newport, Co. Mayo
> 14 May 1950

To all whom it may concern,

I first met Mrs Marion Tobin in May, I think, of 1920. Sean Treacy,[4] Seamus Robinson[5] and I cycled to her house in Tincurry after an attack on the barracks of Hollyford.[6] Seamus was burned and so was I. We had been refused shelter by a senior officer of the Cahir Battalion, but Mrs Tobin took us in willingly, for she had previously sheltered Breen,[7] Robinson and Treacy. From that time onward I used her house as a headquarters for the Cahir and Clonmel, and afterwards the towards Rosegreen battalions. She carried my dispatches to the local Battalion, and at times to Mitchelstown, Co. Cork. She drove myself, and people who were working with me, to East Limerick, to North Cork and Rosegreen. She met me at times by appointment.

At times Robinson, Treacy, Breen and I used her house when we were experimenting with incendiary mixtures and with explosives. It was from her house we set off the night in which we were to burn Rehill Rifle Range,[8] and it was there later, when we had avoided the British round-up, that Sean Treacy and I came back, though at different times.

Here, in Tincurry, I trained a second group of officers and men, some time in August of 1920. Sean Treacy was there with them. I had intended them to be the core of a Flying Column for South Tipperary. I had come back from East Limerick to train this nucleus. We trained there all day for nearly a week.

Mrs Tobin had arms to dump from time to time, and to look after. Whenever I, or anyone else who meant to fight if surrounded, stayed in her house, she knew of our preparedness to fight, and she assisted us.

When I was appointed O/C Second Southern Division[9] I stayed there also, and in spite of numerous raids on her house for me personally, I was always welcome, and I stayed in the remains of the house after the British had blown it up.

During the Truce[10] a Divisional Council was held there at which Eoin O'Duffy[11] was present. The house was frequently used by officers whom I had in training in the Camp at Galtee Castle,[12] and there I held local Battalion Councils.

In the Civil War I came to the house to get news of the holding of an Executive meeting. Joe O'Connor[13] of Dublin was with me, and Mrs Tobin was able to direct me to the place appointed. As usual, she had special information entrusted to her and she was always able to direct our officers and men to where senior officers were.

I have great pleasure in giving this testimonial. I would be very pleased to appear before the Board to give evidence for Mrs Tobin.

Sincerely yours,
Ernie O'Malley

NO. 200 EOM PAPERS NYU; ESTATE OF JOHN V. KELLEHER
Letter to Professor John V. Kelleher

Burrishoole [Lodge,
Newport, Co. Mayo]
16 May 1950

Mr John V. Kelleher,
14 Priory Avenue, Stillorgan, Dublin

Dear John,

Here is the Harvard list[14] if it is of any use to you for the auction. I wasn't very sure of it; and anyhow some of the books were made up into lots already; but a few listed may be single. I forgot about it until just now. If it is not of use you might please return to me, for it is an interesting curio.

I hope all the family are well. A&S[15] have made a complete balls of the auction.

Ever yours,
Ernie

Letter to Liam Manahan[16]

> Burrishoole Lodge,
> Newport, Co. Mayo
> 19 May 1950

[Liam Manahan,
23 Royal Terrace West, Dalkey, Co. Dublin]

Dear Liam,

Thank you very much for meeting me and for talking to me. I had not time to take notes on your typed account.[17] I have been dodging a 'process' server[18] and trying to straighten out my book auction. I did not straighten out the book situation for the catalogue was an insult, but I did, I think, get some people to attend. I was served yesterday by 'guile with a summons for the High Court, so I suppose things will begin to move now so that I can be evicted. I hope to be able to see you when I am next in town.

> Very sincerely yours,
> Ernie O'Malley

NO. 202 PRIVATE COLLECTION – DUBLIN
Telegram to Tom O'Reilly[19]

> [Burrishoole Lodge,]
> Newport, [Co.] Mayo
> 28 June 1950

T. O'Reilly,
78 Gracepark Road, [Drumcondra,] Dublin

DID NOT KNOW DINNER[20] WAS ON. PLEASE GET TICKET AT YOUR TABLE AND REPLY.

> ERNIE O'MALLEY

NO. 203 EOM PAPERS NYU
Postcard of 'Old Houses, Holborn' to Cormac O'Malley

[Summer 1950]

Cormac O'Malley,
Burrishoole Lodge,
Newport, Co. Mayo

Dear Cormac,

I wish I was in Mayo and not in this hot, stuffy city. I am going to see some good paintings to-day. I met Louis MacNeice.[21] He sent you his love and did you remember the bold baby Bimbi[22] belonging to Heidi MacNeice[23] who stayed with us and Louis MacNeice, the poet. Now she is a big, nice girl of 6 and sends you a kiss.

With love,
Ernie

NO. 204 EOM PAPERS NYU
Postcard of Market Place, Tralee, to Cormac O'Malley

Tralee, Ireland
26 September 1950

Cormac O'Malley,
Burrishoole Lodge,
Newport, Co. Mayo

Nice and warm. I leave to-day to make my fortune.[24] Ask Nurse.

Love,
Ernie

Letter to Liam Manahan

[Burrishoole Lodge,
Newport, Co. Mayo]
5 November 1950

[Liam Manahan,
23 Royal Terrace West,
Dalkey, Co. Dublin]

Dear Liam,

Thank you very much for being so kind as to forward me the typed notes. I have been trying to rewrite some of my Cork notes before I go there again and so I am bringing your notes down with me to work on. I should be in Cork on Friday next as I would like to get as much as I can down before the year ends. In December I hope to be in Dublin in or about the 5th or 6th. I will look you up when I get there.

Very sincerely yours,
Ernie O'Malley

Letter to Liam Manahan

Burrishoole Lodge,
Newport, Co. Mayo
5 December 1950

[Liam Manahan,
23 Royal Terrace West,
Dalkey, Co. Dublin]

Dear Liam,

I have finished your typed script notes for I left them behind me when I again went South and West, and I will send them on to you to-morrow. I did not go into East Limerick, but I intend to go back there before Spring.

I should be in Dublin on Monday 11th. Would that evening be suitable for you as I could go out to see you after tea. I came across your track in a few places in Cork, O'Sullivan,[25] Paddy Coughlan[26] and I met people who wished to be remembered to you.

Sincerely yours,
Ernie O'Malley

Letter to Michael Sheehy[27]

Burrishoole Lodge,
Newport, Co. Mayo
3 June 1951

Michael Sheehy,
Rhode, Co. Offaly

Dear Michael,

I hope you and herself[28] and the children are very well. I am sorry about that Connemara pony.[29] First, Paddy O'Malley, vet, is unreliable. He goes on a course of drink which is stopped only by nervous exhaustion and from experience, he has no word.[30] Then George O'Malley means well, but he has no word either. So there you are, and I have no one else who could look up such a horse save I might get in touch with the Kings of Westport, cattle dealers and their word is good with me.

I saw Jack Comer on my way up to my last trial.[31] Indeed he came up and he sat beside me while it was on. The upshot was that the counsel arranged with the judge that Mrs O'Malley could come back without fear of Habeas Corpus.[32] The solicitors fussed so much over the wording for 3 weeks that I enclosed a note for her to sign that she would make no attempt to take Cormac while she was in Ireland. Now that was over two months ago, and I have not been given her signature about Cormac so in two weeks' time I will withdraw this offer for it makes me too nervous about him being taken, and she obviously does not want to come back.

I have been writing away, recopying notes ever since I last saw you save for 3 months in the winter when double pneumonia, flu and my heart began to see what they could make of me, and they didn't leave much, but I have taken days off for the past 5 days, and I have been lying out in the sun, mostly sleeping.

Will you come this way this year? If so I hope you'll stay and not carry out that hit and run effort of yours last year. I have had numerous enquiries about you as I moved about. How do you like your new job and are you yet housed in Mullingar and are B's hens doing well now, or has she declared war on them with knife and hatchet. Nurse has written to someone she knows in Connemara so maybe that will have some results.

Affectionately,
Ernie[33]

Letter to Dr Martin Brennan[34]

> [Burrishoole Lodge,]
> Newport, Co. Mayo
> 19 November 1951

[Dr Martin Brennan,
Banada, Tourlestrane, Co. Sligo]

Dear Maurteen,

I am now in Borrisoleigh, County Tipp, at the butt of the mountains, working. Thank you very much for your kind hospitality to me and that of your charming wife's. I am tired, and I find little chance to write until I get back to Burrishoole, but when I am out on the road I keep going until I drop. I saw Tom Duignan[35] later and Jim Hunt[36] but have to return some other time to connect bits and scraps. Please don't forget about the ballads and songs. If you know of any will you please try to get them recorded for people will do things for you which they would not do for me.

> Very sincerely yours,
> Ernie O'Malley

Sorry: This – I didn't post until today 25/11 and I am leaving Limerick for Limerick County.

Draft letter to George[37] …

> [Burrishoole Lodge,
> Newport, Co. Mayo]
> 19 December 1951

Mr George …

Dear George,

I had written to you but I wrote at my usual pace and the writing was illegible. What I really want is any details I can get about the Brigade and the Column, and the subsequent action of the men who were on the Column.

(a) About Liam:[38] How was he wounded in the Wesleyan? Where was the meeting held the night before; what was the feeling of the men just at the time of the disarmament?

(b) Were the officers out on the street the night of the smashing up of Fermoy? Where were you that night or did you see any of the smashing going on?

(c) Lucas:[39] Was there a housekeeper in the fishing lodge? Did Lucas or the other officers eat a meal there? I stopped with you when Lucas had to surrender his revolver to you …

(d) Had you any conversations with Lucas? The details of your fight with Lucas?

(e) Did you go on to the house where he was kept a prisoner?

Ned. If you have your ½" map you might indicate the spots to which you and Liam retreated that day.

(f) Escape of Dinny Daly. Did he cut the bar of his cell in Fermoy?

(g) Mallon: Did he go in to Lombardstown that night and remain there for a while to defend it. Any details about the column, hours he stayed on and our intentions? The areas we stayed in must have been safe for there was no attempt to round us up.

(h) Bde Hd Qrs. Any memories of the successive places Liam and you retired to.

NO. 210 ESTATE OF JAMES JOHNSON SWEENEY AND EOM PAPERS NYU
Note and Christmas Card to James Johnson Sweeney[40]

[December 1951]

[James Johnson Sweeney,
120 East End Avenue,
New York]

Cormac has been in bed for a while, so we look after each other. I do not suppose we can receive any worse raps in 1952 than in 1951.

With love from Cormac and Ernie

NO. 211 TRINITY COLLEGE, DUBLIN MS 4641/25691
Note and Christmas Card[41] *to Seamus O'Sullivan*

Burrishoole Lodge,
Newport, Co. Mayo
28 January 1952

Dr Seamus O'Sullivan,
2 Morehampton Road, Dublin

Dear Seamus,

Thank you very much indeed for the two books of O'Grady's.[42] I have been reading them at intervals and I find them very interesting. I have been looking for a painting of Cormac's to send you but though I have searched my rooms I cannot find one, and this has delayed my letter.

It has been bitterly cold here so I hope it has been easier in Dublin. Will you please kindly remember me to Stella.[43]

Sincerely yours, PTO
Ernie O'Malley

                                               6 February 1952

Dear Seamus,

    I have found Cormac's painting and I enclose it. I have not been able to use my right hand for close on a week, and it's not good I'm sorry to say.

                       Very sincerely yours,

                       Ernie

NO. 212 PRIVATE COLLECTION – NEW YORK
Letter to Rebecca Citkowitz Liber[44]

                       Burrishoole Lodge,
                Newport, Co. Mayo, Ireland
               Good Friday, 11 April 1952

[Mrs Armour Liber,
Bronx, New York]

Dear Rebecca,

    I have received your 31 March (some lines), #21 27 March on 5 April,[45] #22 31 March on 5 April, 28 March (1/4 page) on 8 April (non airmail) and a large parcel with everything you mentioned on the index inside it including the Joyce book[46] which was very interesting. Now I have all the coffee you kindly sent me even unto the third generation of coffee which I keep in a tin in my room upstairs waiting until I unearth a coffee grinder. For two years I have used coffee broken with a hammer for the annual Noyk dinner at Burrishoole, but I have hopes. Also I have kept some pecan nuts which Cormac and I will use this Easter Sunday beneath red lighted candles. He has been in bed since I brought him back on 4 April with a bad cold although he got up twice. Once to drive Liam O'Flaherty to Achill where we stayed the night leaving next morning as O'F was too rabid about this country, its reaction, its deadness, its supineness and he kept hammering at the truce until I could have pushed him into the rolling waves coming in from the Clare Island direction to Keem Strand.[47] That morning before we left he was charming but then he was flat in bed.

    The rate collector pressed for the money[48] and I was in an eddy of doubt for I could not work. Then a car drove up with two men in it. One of them said he was Barrett from Ballina, the income tax collector. I owed 2 years tax on the house and lands, he said. He came inside, sat down and I told him about the rates. 'I am only an official,' he said. 'Well, I am a human being,' I replied 'and that is an important thing to me.' In the end he didn't want to seize either furniture or the car but expressed concern for I was like a caretaker, living in one room, cooking there. The other man had been brought up near my house in Dublin, and he knew my brother Paddy. They left me feeling that there were two nice human beings.

    Some days later I went to Roscommon to see a serving army officer about his Tan war memory, but he had gone to Dublin without informing me by telegraph. In

Roscommon I saw an income tax collector who had fought against us in the civil war and was a friend of mine. He told me to see a TD and Co. Councillor[49] combined in Castlebar so off I went. The TD I knew. He was a Fianna Fáil representative. He was kind, helpful and promised to see the County Manager on Monday morning and asked me then to come in to see him on Monday evening. On Monday I found that the TD lived in our old house in Castlebar, and I went through it to find out the room I had once held up a visitor with a horse pistol shouting 'surrender' which I had learned from *Morte D'Arthur*.[50] Two hours later father found the guest trembling in the parlour while I kept guard on my captive. And I looked for the 4 seasons painted on the ceiling in oil on the drawing room ceiling, but now covered over. We saw the County Manager[51] who was then friendly, under pressure. He was to drop the rate injunction on me, proceed in USA against HHO'M for rates and as the TD (Dáil member) is a solicitor, I asked for publicity there. If that fails the Co. Council may switch on to me again. Rates= £90 =$270 a little more in fact. Total rates = £105 = $315. Income tax = for two years £140 = $420 roughly. This year as rates have increased I should be liable for £130 rates $390 on exchange rates and income tax is based I think on the valuation.

I borrowed money from a friend. I bought 9 + 4 cattle = 13 in all = £468 and I have to buy about a further 20 cattle but all this money I can now raise. This is an experimental year so I am keeping accounts but it is extremely difficult to manage cattle by myself with a bad hand. Luckily I know about their management but they need a daily visit. That would confine me to remaining forever in Burrishoole. Up to this I had depended on George O'Malley to sell and buy for me. I didn't trust him. I knew he was mean but his wife was decent. The family always helped me in an emergency. George, however, took in 4 or 5 cattle in Rosgibblin without permission maybe for months when I am away and when I am here. About 2 weeks ago I arranged for a man to buy 4 cattle which I had kept over the winter and were on the land. Then George was to buy 4 cattle for me, put them back on the land for when you sell you must buy to use up grass. He was given a good bargain of 5 cattle. He went into Westport Fair, sold the 5 at £20 profit, never said a word to me and did not give back the money. I had after a week's interval to go to him for the money. He said nothing about not putting back the 4 beasts on the land. I used to get a whisky bottle of 2 pints of milk from his wife every 2 or 3 days, but I have not gone to the house since. So I exist on condensed milk. That transaction upset me more than rates or income tax because as I needed mental loyalty in a wife, I need loyalty from people nearby about land.

MacIntyre who comes from Acres in Carrowkeel is a handy man who has a good head. He was repairing the roof 2 days ago. He said from on top as I was talking to him.

'Is it true that you have to borrow money to buy cattle?'

'Yes, Pat, it is.'

'Well, I could lend you money for I have over £400 invested and you can buy cattle with it any time.'

I went to thank a County Councillor in Westport who had seen the County

Manager before I had seen him but the CM[52] gave him no satisfaction.

'Do you find James Joyce difficult?' he said. He left rates alone to talk of Joyce.

Thank you for the Marquand article. I would like to write to Marquand, but it could look prejudiced. Marquand was the official apologist for the Hookers in my case. He wrote in an interview that Liam Redmond, actor, was a family friend and that he was the children's godfather. Liam Redmond is agnostic, and he stood as godfather for Cormac because HHO'M demanded it. Catholics have each a godfather and godmother who are supposed to look after their spiritual welfare if the parents die and even when they are alive. That was to explain Redmond who was interviewed in Belfast while he waited for the special plane[53] with HHO'M which was to bring them to France. He stayed about a week in Paris then went to Marseilles. He had been HHO'M's adviser and Adelaide also who had always been hostile to me whenever HHO'M visited the USA. Is there any chance of such information being of use.

I had Zuey's biography of Balzac[54] but it must either be dumped or now lost, and I would be glad to have a copy of it as I have all Balzac here in a not too good translation yet it gives the sense. I got another cheap edition of the Nally poems since so please keep the one. I will also get Wyndham Lewis[55] for it has been long on my list. I keep a bibliography of about sixty pages so as to keep up to date in books to read or look for second hand. Last year I lost my notebook somewhere and I had to begin another, but as I had stored up my notes before I had half filled the first big notebook I was at a loss about many reference books. I am sorry about the Yeats exhibition.[56] It was held in 1951. James Johnson Sweeney sent me an article recently he had written on Yeats. It was mostly quotation from Jack's books but I must read it again. No, I know nothing about letters to the New Yorker about articles as I do not ever see that magazine. Could you send me on one which had such corrections? I would be delighted to write a letter about Marquand. Helen was supposed to be the heroine of one book which I have not read: *BF's Daughter*.[57] She was at his place for some months the previous year and I expect he took consistent copy. I must think about him but unfortunately I have little factual evidence save that he did make a statement about Liam Redmond.

My rheumatic arthritis holds badly. It gives me continual trouble, but every now and then when I visit Dublin the lad in charge of the Rheumatic Clinic looks after me. He gives me injections but said I should hold it to the fire every night for 20 minutes which I do a few times a week. My car runs on 2 cylinders as I do. I have been promised a day's work or 2 on it free by a mechanic when next I go to Dublin. I am glad Armour is better and that he is back to his work. The new drugs must make observation especially interesting. I will translate O'Brien's card and return it to you. I thought Cormac and I might go over to him for a few days this Easter but Cormac has been in bed here, and when he is better he will have to clean the house room by room, cut and bring up seaweed for fruit trees,[58] clean up patches of broken branches among trees, cut down growing blackberry brambles and in general work on the place. Luckily he is always willing to work. He has to return by the 22nd, and I have some articles to finish and 2 to write[59] before the end of May that means field work. I will move cattle to Carrowkeel tomorrow perhaps for MacIntyre could keep an eye on them. Phiblin however had 3 asses in there all winter without my permission, and I have to declare war on him and then make peace. Both of which I think I have done. I saw his son made him take out the animals and then made peace. The biggest troubles are Brennans, the Railway woods,[60] the avenue, and Rosgibblin. On the first three Sean and Willie Walsh poach land whenever my back is turned, but it means only about 5 acres: in Rosgibblin George O'Malley can drive his cattle in over his fences, or around and through the sea fences. I must get fencing down in Rosgibblin, but it is impossible to get men for a day's work though I have been promised 2 on Easter Sunday. Thus I have 3 fronts to hold. I cannot by myself put out trespassing cattle as I need a second helper to round them up. That is another difficulty. The use of grass is another problem, but as I know what the land can do in each section I know when to change beasts from land to land.

I have not any *Partisan Review*[61] previous to … concerning Joyce, so if you can lay hands of any of them will you please tell me. Rebecca[62] was born in County Kerry and is of mixed blood although you would not suspect that. I think she mentions it in *Black (something) and Grey Falcon*.[63] Otherwise, like Joyce Carey and many another good writer, they are claimed as English. Honor Tracy[64] is another horse-faced Irishwoman who did work on *The Bell* before my time. I expect that is true enough. Courtesy is elaborate here in its ease not in its ceremony. The Irish on the other hand forget too easily as they are all too human. Think of the man i/c of Intelligence in the Dublin District during the Tan War, missed on Bloody Sunday and at many a race meeting then, now a race horse owner kindly settled in Kildare Co. That always was our trouble. People forgive until the English, the major historical enemy, repeats his treachery or insults again. The importance of face is very strong, but there is no obligation to revenge. I don't know what 'obligation' and 'revenge' mean. I must try to get hold of her book. She wrote for the Sunday papers on Ireland and was superficial as she could only point out what annoyed her and had no sense of the fundamental tempo of life here. Ireland annoys all of us for we are a family too close to each other and too unsparing. We believe in perfection, a quality of sainthood and that often makes life difficult yet the people among whom I live excuse all faults save one or two.

I wish I knew the number of my letter. Could you please renumber the recent ones I did not remember and then tell me the number of this so that I can start accurately from the next letter?

Have you any sample of an Irish letter to the *New Yorker* that I could see how many words and what kind of material is used? Kelleher did not come near me on his last long visit with his wife and children. His wife was a bad pain, his children ill mannered pups, so he made a mistake by bringing them with him for otherwise we might have taken his affectionate and reminiscent views of them when he was by himself. He was very scarifying about Irish life when he was here. I think his views were very much coloured by Frank O'Connor who reads his personal problem that of living here first with another man's wife whom he deserted, and now he's living with another girl. It has warped him, and I am sorry, but there is no latitude in the relationship of bourgeois people here to that although any creative workers would be his friends. Also during the War he worked for a British Intelligence service thinly disguised, when we were neutral. That I thought contemptuous. Love to both of you. Cormac has a painting for you.

Earnán

12 April 1952

Received yours 7 April unnumbered, with Marquand article which I cannot make out in a rush as pages are not numbered and it does not run in sequence.[65]

NO. 213 EOM PAPERS NYU
Letter to HHOM

Dublin,
28 May 1952

Mrs H. O'Malley,
6 Adria Hotel,
Queensgate, London SW7, England

Dear Helen,

I received your letter of May 2nd, Copy 3. I cannot go to England as you suggest for many reasons. If it suits you to meet me in Dublin on Tuesday, June 3rd, I can be there. I would be there on Monday, June 2nd, but it is a Bank Holiday and there would be no place I could think of to meet you, but if that day suits you best then you can send word. You can fix day and date and place by sending a wire to A.J. Woods, Piper Hill, Sandyford, Co. Dublin.[66] You can put whatever name you wish on it.

Nobody will know you are here beyond say some of the Special Branch men who watch entries and exits, but they will take no notice when they know you are permitted entry and exit. The period of your stay will, I presume, be only for so long as you wish to discuss matters with me about the family. I hope this suits as otherwise I will be tied up for almost the remainder of the year.[67]

Sincerely yours,
E. O'Malley

Letter to To Whom It May Concern, regarding HHOM

[Dublin]
28 May 1952

To whom it may concern,

This is to allow Mrs O'Malley permission to enter Ireland on June 2nd or 3rd, and to leave Ireland on June ... during which period she discusses matters relative to the family.

Signed,
Ernie O'Malley
28 May 1952

Letter to HHOM

Burrishoole Lodge,
Newport, Co. Mayo
28 June 1952

Mrs H. O'Malley,
6 Adria Hotel,
Queensgate, London SW7, England

Dear Helen,

I will be up about 2.30 on Wednesday, July 2nd and if the car holds out, I'll take some food on the way with friends so that I can be ready to see houses with you at once. Thank you for seeing to Cormac's teeth.

Please do not expect social events. I am writing and I must finish what I have promised to write.[68] I must write in my spare time in Dublin and if I do not I will return here all the sooner. You are freer than I am so you are better able to do what you want to.

Before you left I asked you to write to Cathal's doctor for a check up on him. I hope you have done this and I presume I should have a check up on Étain also. I want a complete report on Cathal with X-Rays of bones in regard to rickets and whatever other disease you think he has. He seemed to be an invalid according to yourself.

Ever yours,
Ernie O'Malley

Draft Letters to HHOM

[Burrishoole Lodge,
Newport, Co. Mayo]

c.7 August 1952

I received your letter of July 30th pm August for which thanks. As far as Cormac's birthday was concerned, it was simple. We have learned to live our lives without frills, Cormac and I trusting in each to help the other. I expect you read my account of what happened.

As you know my family have had nothing to do with me ever since you took two children away[69] so I do not see why their opinion becomes important or understanding. I appreciate some of your difficulties,[70] but you can certainly at the same time be looked after through your money so that the physical side of life which confronts us is eliminated. It seems to me that you have no control of your own finances. Firstly, because even with a considerable income, you are in debt. Secondly, there is a trust fund,[71] I presume, as a result of your debts to guard the remainder of your property. Thirdly, you have no control over the two children who are in the United States as you say your family 'may not be willing to let me take the children from America'. This is the first time you have mentioned this predicament, so it appears as if you talked to me as if you were free to move the children and actually you are not free. Why did you make tentative arrangements about bringing them over here? I would like to know specifically what control you have over the lives of these two children otherwise I do not see how any further discussion can proceed about a house or about the children.

I received your letter of July 30th on August, for which thanks. Cormac's birthday was simple enough. We received your parcels later.

From your letter it appears:

1. That you have no control over the two children who are in America. This is the first time you have stated 'my family may not be willing to let me take the children from America.' Who exactly constitute your 'family'?
2. You can not withdraw your American money. That I understand. Mainly I think because you who have a considerable income are generally in debt. You are in debt now to your mother and to Mrs Rockefeller.[72]
3. I do not accept Gilchrist's statement about my money which you have already told me is in your name in the 5th Avenue Bank, not being available until Feb 27, 1953. It was held pending the withdrawal of your furniture in Burrishoole. I have agreed to you withdrawing furniture from Burrishoole provided this money be handed over to some one I trust in America. I presume that you can settle this matter with your own Supreme Court[73] as it was you who forced seizure of that money.

In Dublin it was agreed:

a. That the children write to each other.

b. That Etain be sent to school in Ireland.
c. That Burrishoole be sold in our joint names.
d. That my money in America be returned prior to sale of Burrishoole, as a sale meant removal of furniture.
e. That a home be purchased in Dublin, be inspected and agreed on.
f. That you and I live with the children.[74] There is no barrier from my church which does not recognize divorce in this matter. You are divorced and you wanted a remarriage. That cannot take place as long as I am a Catholic. On the other hand you can annul your divorce.
g. You stated that Cathal was an invalid and that he would have to remain in America in a warm climate. I asked you on three different occasions for a report on Cathal's health with X-Ray plates and sufficient information for a doctor here to tell me what was wrong. I asked you on June 19, July 2nd and on July 26th. Now it appears you telephone Gilchrist who is an attorney who, as you say, adds to your difficulties when you might have first written to Dr Anderson. It is now over six weeks since I first spoke to you about Cathal. I do not see what your attorney has to do with your doctor when it concerns a child of ours.

I do not know what you mean by 'my constructive help'. You did not raise any doubts about it in your talks and I did not see how it has now become unconstructive.

You are aware that I am expected to pay rates on this land and that I prevented furniture from being seized this March. Also you stated that if Burrishoole were sold one third would be reserved for the purchase of a house, one third went to you and one third to me. Does that agreement yet hold?

Would you kindly put on paper what you consider was the agreement tentatively arrived at between us two.

NO. 217 EOM PAPERS NYU
Draft letter to Dan Nolan[75]

Burrishoole Lodge,
Newport, Co. Mayo
31 October 1952

[Dan Nolan,
c/o The Kerryman,
Tralee, Co. Kerry]

Dear Dan,
    I have now received portion of my manuscript in a mutilated condition, but you have not returned the plans which I had prepared to go with the articles.[76] You have indicated to me that it is your intention in lieu of using my material to

prepare parallel articles for publication, based, apparently, on the incidents which I have described; and it has come to my knowledge that you and your employees have approached people mentioned in my articles with proposals that they should supply you with material.

I must warn you that failure to return the missing portions of my manuscript and the missing plans will involve you in legal proceedings, and that if you persist in using information which you have acquired from my articles I must regard this as plagiarism and will be forced to go to the Courts for their protection.

Some of the manuscripts in their present condition are useless to me and it will be necessary to have them retyped. I propose to forward you the bill for this retyping.

Yours sincerely,
Earnan O'Malley

NO. 218 EOM PAPERS NYU
Letter to Francis MacManus[77]

Burrishoole Lodge,
Newport, Co. Mayo
13 November 1952

[Francis McManus,
Radio Éireann, Dublin]

Dear Francis,

I hope you and your work are well, that is the writing work. I spoke to Childers[78] on the phone, but he referred me to you. I have written 8 episodes. They took a long time to prepare as I wandered around a great deal to talk. They deal with the Tan War. The length of some may completely preclude your interest so I give the number of words so that it will save you time if they are too long.

The road to Carrowkennedy	[Co. Mayo]	15,000
Rearcross	[Co. Tipperary]	8,500
Rinneen	[Co. Clare]	7,130
Scramogue	[Co. Roscommon]	5,500
Hollyford	[Co. Tipperary]	5,900
Tourmakeady	[Co. Mayo]	5,200
Drangan	[Co. Tipperary]	5,400
Modreeny	[Co. Tipperary]	about 5,500[79]

Paddy Fallon said he could help me in dramatization if I went down to him for a while, but I am on the land watching bloody bullocks. Anyhow do you want to see these or not?

Sincerely yours,
Earnán O'Malley

Letter to Francis MacManus

Burrishoole Lodge,
Newport, Co. Mayo
20 November 1952

[*Francis McManus,*
Radio Éireann, Dublin]

Dear Francis,

Thank you for you letter of the 14th. Since then I have gone through the encounters about which I have written. The trouble is that I keep rewriting them. This lot took about eight months' work, though there is little to show for it. Two of them, Rinneen, and Carrowkennedy, could run as a kind of serial. In Rinneen this would cover the fight, which is of no importance, the retreat, which is important, and the destruction, which was the worst experience for the people in the entire Tan War, or as Childers called it in his brief phone talk with me 'The Anglo-Irish struggle'.

I have been rewriting 8 others, but if you, from reading the enclosed, think they might be of use, I could rewrite them in a length of 2,600 words for you. Also I have *A Life of Sean Connolly*[80] written. He belonged to Longford, and he it was who put Sean McKeown[81] on the map. He was killed in March of 1921. It runs to 50,000 words.

This year has been a series of catastrophes, which in their accumulative strength become funny. The reason I have these on hands is because Nolan of the *Kerryman* rewrote them. And I then refused their publication. He then went to the men mentioned and tried to get them to give him the information on which they once had given me, but I was able to prevent that. However, I think he will try to publish a garbled version in book form soon, so there is a certain urgency about these and another, which is being retyped, *Modreeny.*
Sincerely yours,
Ernie O'Malley

Note and Christmas Card to Armour/Rebecca Liber[82]

[*Burrishoole Lodge,*
Newport, Co. Mayo,
December 1952]

[*Mr and Mrs Armour Liber,*
The Bronx, New York]

... I am trying to write here. I received your letter ... your postcard, also your very nice box of Christmas presents. Cormac is well. The weather is bad. Rommel is well.[83] I am in despair as I write for my writing is worse than bad. I thought I would be finished by the end of the year but I think it will now be 2 January then I must get it typed. I understand it was to be published in serial as from 18 January. Thank you and Armour very much for all your kindness. I will write in the New Year.

Love to you both,
Ernie
With love,
Cormac and Ernie

NO. 221 EOM PAPERS NYU
Letter to Francis MacManus

Burrishoole Lodge,
Newport, Co. Mayo
7 January 1953

[Francis McManus,
Radio Éireann, Dublin]

Dear Francis,

Enclosed please find 4 episodes. The remaining 4 are being retyped. The amount of words is figured at the end of each episode.

1.	1919	Fermoy [Co. Cork]
2.	1920	Lucas [Capture of British army General Lucas in Co. Cork, 28 Jun 1920]
3.		Drangan [Co. Tipperary]
4.		Mallow [Co. Cork]
5.		Rinneen [Co. Clare]
6.	1921	Nad [Co. Cork]
7.		Modreeny [Co. Tipperary]
8.		Rathcoole [Co. Dublin]

They are numbered in point of time.

Sincerely yours,
Earnan O'Malley

Letter to John Raleigh

[Burrishoole Lodge,
Newport, Co. Mayo]
11 January 1953

[John Raleigh,
Kilbane House,
Castletroy, Limerick]

Dear Johnny,
    What about that dog?[84]
    ? ? ? ? ?

Ever yours,
Ernie

I hope Bea is well. I apologise for not writing to thank her for being so kind to me when I was there.
    I found more than enough snow in Cork.
    Are there no dogs in Clare, Una?[85] Maybe Mary[86] might find one in UCD. I'm sure Tierney[87] uses a few to bark at the students.

Letter to Francis MacManus

Burrishoole Lodge,
Newport, Co. Mayo
6 February 1953

[Francis McManus,
Radio Éireann, Dublin]

Dear Francis,
    I have written to Cormac's school as to the day he gets out for Easter so that I could find a day before he leaves Dublin; but I have had no reply. But I could go up after the high tides in March when I hope to do some sea fencing, say on Thursday, March 5th to be in Dublin and to be able to remain on Friday 6th or the 7th. Would that suit you?
    I have finished your book, thanks, and will post it back as soon as I can walk properly – a pier fell on my left leg and I have often felt better. I may have to get it x-rayed.
    The Press[88] was fussy. I told his nibs[89] I was offered £3.10.0 a thousand by the *Kerryman*. 'Oh no,' says he, 'We'll give you £15.15.0 an article,' but so far they have divided the 60,000 words into 12 and they pay me for 12. However, I am suggesting maps and sketches to the non- military mind as a help to understanding

of young readers and a help also maybe to spread the articles to reach 13. Thank you for your kindness when I was in the studio and Mervyn.[90]

Will you now kindly pass on dates to Mervyn for I began letter to you and I must post it for a man has suddenly appeared in the lawn.

Sincerely yours,
Earnan O'Malley

NO. 224 EOM PAPERS NYU
Letter to Mervyn Wall

Burrishoole Lodge,
Newport, Co. Mayo
12 February 1953

[Mervyn Wall,
Radio Éireann, Dublin]

Dear Mervyn,

Thank you very much for the 'Raids and Rallies'[91] 1 to 5 which you kindly forwarded to me. I will be then in Dublin on Thursday, March 5th, and I will turn up on Friday, March 6th at 11:30 a.m.

Sincerely yours,
Ernie O'Malley

NO. 225 EOM PAPERS NYU
Letter to Etain O'Malley

St Bricin's Hospital,
[Arbour Hill, Dublin]
24 March 1953

[Etain O'Malley,
55 East End Avenue,
New York]

Dearest Étain,

I'm glad you got the shamrock[92] and that it meant so much to you. I hope Nana[93] is well. I was talking about her to Mrs Burke one day on the road. Nana will talk to you about Ireland which is your country, your traditional warmth for song, music and story and your good memories of land and sea. For me all 3 children and I may have had some tough times, but we had good times here too with sail, music, song and story. The *St Brendan* wasn't injured. She sailed well last year.

I see where Ford[94] is going to be mixed up with another film this year here, and I must get in touch with him again. He's around the West at present, and I'm sorry

I cannot see him for I know he would give me a job and would also pick Cormac out for something. He is a good friend of mine and a very fine Irishman so it is a pleasure to work with John Wayne[95] or the others who have been trained into respect of the people by Ford.

My leg is alright now. It's my body that gives the trouble. Kevin wants me to leave the West and to take a place in Dublin. That's easily said. First, I have not the money. It takes a lot to raise the rates and taxes for Burrishoole, but it is a good place for Cathal[96] to come back to wander around and for us two to sail in. That makes up for trying to be a servant and cook for the rest of the year.

Una Joyce I hear regularly from. She has been in Dungarvan for a year, and she had a few talks with the Fear Mór[97] which the Fear Mór did not like. Your mother sent him on either £100 or £150, so she told me. The nurse has been always very kind to us, but it was as well for her to get away because I couldn't pay her. But she is with a nice family there, and she knows some of my friends as well. I am sure Cormac won't like Dublin for the holidays for he feels freer in Burrishoole, but maybe he will be able to see some of An Tostal[98] competitions in Dublin. Alec at Old Head will have a special curragh race[99] on April 19th, and the winning curragh races will be along the Liffey in Dublin. Alec always talks of you and Cormac with affection. Have you any Irish books to read? ...

NO. 226 EOM PAPERS NYU
Letter to Michael Sheehy

St Bricin's Hospital,
Arbour Hill, [Dublin]
13 April 1953

[Michael Sheehy,
Rhode, Co. Offaly]

Dear Michael,

Your card at Christmas was in my bag which I had been rooting through here. I hope I replied to it. I knew I was ill 7 weeks ago as I could not eat my own food so I left Burrishoole trying to get into Bricain's [*sic*]. I was held up for weeks so I worked in the National Library and then took to bed in a house[100] where everyone was out all day. By the time I got in here there was not much left of me. Heart bad. Some kind of blood infection, but Kevin looks after me, so here they simply carry out tests. A close thing evidently and Kevin does not know the future. He has been talking about my leaving Burrishoole, but Burrishoole though rates are very heavy yet I cover them and it helps to keep Cormac at school. Cormac on his holidays now was with an uncle[101] of his, and one day he slipped behind during a visit to say 'No books in the house – what will I do?' so I wrote to Mr Pembrey[102] of Green's to send him books. He works hard and is on an under-11 Rugby team. I have been working hard so I have not left Burrishoole save to make a sudden raid on the South for information; and on Longford. No 'phone now. Costs too much.

I wrote some articles for *The Kerryman* booklet, but as he had the impertinence to change them and to put in 'action stations' etc. which came from World War 2, I withdrew them and they'll come in *Sunday Press*.[103] I must add more, and they'd make a book eventually.

Cecil suffers from money instead of fighting it. It will eat him up in the end which is a pity.

Ever yours,
Ernie

Dear Biddens:[104]

Cormac looks fine and straight. He works hard at school which is what I never did. I am tired of bed, but it's necessary. I want to get hold of my pen again for there's work to do. I hope all the family are very well. It's a long time since I saw you, which is sad.

Affectionately,
Ernie

NO. 227 EOM PAPERS NYU
Letter to Francis MacManus

St Bricin's Hospital,
Arbour Hill, [Dublin]
16 April 1953

[Francis McManus,
Radio Éireann, Dublin]

Dear Francis,

Thank you for your letter. I myself feel better for the past few days, but I expect it will be a good time before I get out of here.

I have replied to McGrath.[105] I told him I would have to check on his situation through a surviving battalion officer. That is my custom. Publicity wakes up Rip Van Winkles. The old lads seem to have been pleased for a number of them wrote to me. I was worried that my voice might have failed.

Sincerely yours,
Ernie O'Malley

Letter to Etain O'Malley

St Bricin's Hospital,
Arbour Hill, Dublin
1 May 1953

[Etain O'Malley,
55 East End Avenue,
New York]

Dearest Étain,

Here I am yet in bed. I expect it will be a while before I can stand on the floor, but I am getting better. The trouble is that when I am sick in Burrishoole I cannot stay in bed for as I am cook I must look after the fire and the food, so that I get run down at times. Have you a typewriter now? I have a good deal of stuff to be typed, but I do not use my typewriter much.

I wish you could tell me the subjects at your school so that I could judge of your standard of education. In America it varies very much. I can't imagine what kind of a life you lead now. Cormac and I when at home use the rowing boat or the *Saint Brendan*. He is a good man in a bad sea. Once he saved me when I went overboard. Do you remember the time I went overboard, or the day you fell out of the *Seagull*? I play music and ballads or shanties, and I read books to him. Part of growing up is being by oneself in a place you love, so he learns to observe and think his own thoughts in the quiet of the country. He paints away when he feels like it and that is good for him as he says things in paint he cannot express in any other way. At school he works well, but he is not overburdened by too many subjects.

Mrs Byrne asks for you always whenever I see her. Indeed she has sent me in baskets of fruit and she should not do that, but she has always been kind to us. Winnie[106] came in to see me the other day. She looks very well, and she was asking kindly about you, but I had not much to tell her. Uncle Kevin was asking for you. I gave him your last letter to read. He read it many times and looked sad. I have not seen much of him for years for I am seldom in Dublin now save to bring up Cormac and carry him home.

Our good dog, a well-bred German police dog, was lost for he strayed away, or was suddenly, maybe, picked up and shoved into a car. I was supposed to enter him at dog shows, but I was only interested in him because he was a friend and you could hear him miles away at night when anyone came near the place. Also when all kinds of legal 'gentlemen' were trying to serve me with processes, his sudden rush and bark were both very useful. He was also a good sailor.

Josie Gill, Pat Quinn always ask for you when we land on the islands and Alec Wallace at Old Head Hotel. There was a curragh races there last month. A few times Cormac and I went out to Achill where now they catch the basking shark,[107] 9 tons weight and a lot of smell.

I hope you will send a small note to Cormac every now and then for we talk of you together. Have you any time to read books by yourself and if you have what kind of books do you read? I was reading R.L. Stevenson to Cormac last holidays, but I read *Treasure Island* myself here in bed with great pleasure.

With my best love,
Ernie

———————

NO. 229 EOM PAPERS NYU
Letter to Cathal O'Malley

St Bricin's Hospital,
Arbour Hill, Dublin
2 May 1953

Cathal O'Malley,
Millbrook School,[108]
Millbrook, New York

Dear Cathal,

Thank you for your letter from the island[109] but please put a date on letter for it helps. I am sorry for the delay but my condition became more serious[110] so that I could not write to you. Also I have forgotten events and names during the past two years, but I suppose I will remember them as I get better. It looks now as if I will have to remain in bed for a good while longer. That is a drawback for by keeping cattle on the land I am able to send Cormac to school. Recently while I was here the Rate Collector was to raid the house and seize anything he could. I was worried for fear he might take my papers and my notebooks, and only as I had not money to pay him which was due for two years on the houses, I was able to put him off until I was able to stand on my feet.

I did not get a reply from Étain to my letter, but she asked me not to blame her for not writing. Indeed, I do not but when everyone else thinks you won't last long it's nice to have a letter. I will enclose a letter for her in your envelope for now I do not know where she is.[111]

I would like to know about your work at school. What course are you taking, and how do you do at your exams? I hope by this there is more concentration on a few subjects in your school for that habit of knowing a little bit about everything seemed to be popular when I was in the USA.

Have you got a copy of the talk you delivered, for if it is available I would like to read it?

Burrishoole is the same. A good place in which to bring up children I found and yet find even though Cormac is alone. The islanders are as friendly as ever. Pat Quinn is failing, but he has the same kind welcome for us whenever we land: and he always asks for the absent two. Cormac is a very reliable man in a boat even in a bad sea. Josie Gill has come on to the mainland close to Westport, for his wife and children wanted to be near the town though Josie didn't, and the eldest boy is on the island now, alone.

I could look up some books for you on Ireland and get them for you when I get out of this hospital, if I felt you wanted them. What books did you consult when you delivered your talk?

I wish I had a behind of ample proportions. I get needles stuck into me four times a day: often the dose clogs and it means another needle. However the dose helps. I hope now I will be out before the end of May.

I hope you are well. You seem to enjoy yourself at school. Please be kind to Étain and thank you for writing to Cormac. He works hard at school and at home he does his housework and cooking kindly and graciously. I am sure you have a good collection of records now.

With love,
Ernie

NO. 230 EOM PAPERS NYU
Letter to Michael Noyk

St Bricin's Hospital,
[Arbour Hill,] Dublin
4 July 1953

[Michael Noyk, LLB, Solicitor,
12–14 College Green, Dublin]

Dear Michael,

I received your letter of July 3rd and Messrs. Goodbody's[112] enclosures. It seems to be a waste of time for Mrs O'Malley to continue to send unnecessary letters through her solicitors. I have written to Davis,[113] but it seems to me that Mrs O'Malley holds that money,[114] and will hold it. Cormac has money of his own[115] as has each of the children. I understand Cormac's money was to have been used for his schooling. However, it is in Mrs O'Malley's possession, and I expect she will hold it until Cormac is also in her possession.

I do not wish Dr Kevin to be involved in any family matters nor have I at any time asked him to act as an intermediary nor does he wish to be so used.

My answer then to Messrs. Goodbody is:

1. Mr Davis can communicate with me.
2. I have not yet seen Dr Malley.

I hope you are feeling well. I suppose you are now preparing for Galway.[116] Paddy Lenihan called in to see me here one day. I find it difficult to walk and it takes more time than I could have imagined for my legs to become legs.

Sincerely yours,
Ernie

Letter to Paul Strand

Burrishoole Lodge,
Newport, Co. Mayo
[Actual address: St Bricin's Hospital,
Dublin]
19 July 1953

[Paul Strand,
98 blvd August Balanguy,
Paris 13e, France]

Dear Paul,

Thank you for your letter of July 1st which was delayed at the Newport Post Office. I am very glad indeed to hear from you for I often wondered where you were. I will leave the hospital by the end of the month for I am tired of it, and I expect I will have to take things easy for a while but that is not easy for I run Burrishoole by myself, and when Cormac is home for the holidays, we cook together and we sail in the Bay.

I hope Hazel[117] is well, and I am glad you are both happy. I often remember the light in New Mexico and the effect it had on foreground and shadows. Two days ago a friend of mine took me out through the Dublin Mountains in a car.[118] You remember we once drove across them[119] and I burned a piece of turf for you. Since then some of the plantations have grown up, but I was busy taking photographs with my eyes for memory, and I returned with a bunch of fine heather. I am shaky on my legs, and I expect it will take time for me to get really strong. Cormac is now eleven. We have a good time together, and he learns from the sea and the countryside and sometimes from myself. I wish you could both come to Burrishoole for I think you would like it. I hope I can be able to remain there this winter.

As I write your book[120] came. Thank you very much indeed. Now I can take France to bed with me.

Affectionately always,
Ernie

Letter to John David O'Dowd[121]

> St Bricin's Hospital,
> [Arbour Hill,] Dublin
> 19 July 1953

[John David O'Dowd,
Fallduff Lodge,
Louisburgh, Co. Mayo]

A Cara,[122]

Thank you for the nice letter you sent to me in June. I expect to leave here by the end of this month, rather I should say that I will be leaving here by that time. I am shaky on my legs, but it is a question of time now by lengthening my stay out of bed. Hospital was alright for while I was really bad, but for some months past I have been tired of bed and that also affects my reading. I really want to get hold of my papers which unfortunately are not here and to do a bit of work. Writing is hard unless you keep it up continually, and now after this lapse, I must start again to learn.

I was brought out in a car through the mountains a few days ago. It was a fine evening, and I had a grand time. The Dublin and Wicklow mountains are rugged enough, the views back towards the city are very varied and interesting and the hills deep in ferns and growth of young plantations. I brought back what is now a jig full of heather ...

This week the art critics[123] meet in Dublin. I was one of two people who were yearly invited to France from this country but this year when I could meet the cost by leaving my bed at intervals I was not invited. I would like to see the *Playboy* for I expect the playing of this in Dublin will be good. The Abbey has fallen away considerably as the players now go to the movie studios[124] and they are judged in the hysterical money pattern even when they act on the open stage ...

> Ever yours,
> Earnan O'Malley

Draft letter to Dan Stephenson[125]

[*Dublin, mid August 1953*]

[Daniel F. Stephenson, PC, MIAA,
Managing Director,
James H. North & Co., Surveyors,
Dublin]

Dear Dan,

I am sorry I was unable to see you when in Dublin. I was in St Bricain's [*sic*] for treatment, but when I came out you were on holidays. I wrote acknowledging the letter I received from you, but I know a talk with you would be much the easier way of settling my mind about this land question.[126]

Helen bought Burrishoole in her name. With it went 44.909 acres. This I have had to make up from a duplicate map as I have never seen the original deed. There seems to be some trouble about getting a copy of it.[127]

Of this 44.909 there are 12 acres which could be used. The rest is bog, 3 acres, a peninsula of 15.136 called Duntrusk,[128] entirely useless, the rest bad wood. Accordingly she rented land so that we could have grass and food for cows. Land rented is just 8¼ acres. When tillage becomes necessary land rented became 15½ acres.

To make tillage I had to have men, machinery and horses. I employed three men. As rents for tillage land here increased I advised Helen to buy some land. She bought 20 acres from Michael Murray.[129] Of this 2 acres is supposed to be island actually less now by reason of the sea. 2 acres bank and about five acres rushes and untrained bog, of it 20 acres are workable, but, it is across the Burrishoole River and so tillage is a problem.

We have tubercular tested cows and heifers. This means they cannot graze on any land where there are other cattle nor can they touch them. That again means a waste in land lay out. The cows were infected by the local bulls, so I raised a bull of my own and keep him for the tested animals and for them alone. That means further land use for the bull …

Letter to Liam Manahan

> [*Newton Hall,*[130]
> *nr Cambridge, England*]
> *3 September 1953*

[*Liam Manahan,*
23 Royal Terrace West,
Dalkey, Co. Dublin]

Dear Liam,

Please accept my apologies for not writing to thank you for your kindnesses to me while I was in hospital. The real reason was that I had to leave the hospital by August 1st. I knew I was not well enough as I needed some one to look after me for a few months. Cormac and I went to Burrishoole and when I returned from trying to light fires and clean up that large house and put my papers in order, I was examined by Kevin who said I had done damage to my heart again and that I would have to rest for some time. I came to friends[131] in England with Cormac, but I had trouble in both lungs perhaps from a cold and for weeks I could not breathe save with pain. That now is practically gone away, but I expect I have to be careful of colds or exposure until I get stronger. That is a difficult task as I am not accustomed to regard myself as an invalid.

I have been asked to remain on here and I will probably remain, but Cormac will go across to school. I have not yet received word as to when he should be back in school. I have written to Fr Stanley[132] fearing that he may have forwarded his letter to Burrishoole, but I did not notify the Newport PO where I was so letters have not been sent on to me. The trouble again was that I did not want my address to be known as Mrs O'Malley was in England.[133]

> *9 September 1953*

Cormac leaves for school to-morrow. Some of my friends[134] will go across with him. He is glad to get back to school as it is a good home for him. I think it will be a slow process for me as I take hardly any exercise now, but I am able to work everyday at my notes trying to put them into better shape for reading so that they could be of use in case anything happens to me, and as I work I can build up some material for further stories about operations.[135] Somehow I must get back to East Limerick when you are in that vicinity for I have a very sparse record from that area and I am anxious to get at the truth.

Mrs O'Malley is in England with Etain, and Cormac and I have met them.[136] Etain has an American accent; she has forgotten all her Irish except the grace before meals, and she is behind hand as a student due to her bad American schooling. I refuse to allow Mrs O'Malley to enter Ireland[137] until I am well again whenever that may be, as a bad heart is incapable of meeting her problems. Please do not mention the fact to others that I am in England and please kindly remember me to Mrs Manahan[138] and the children.

Very sincerely yours,

Ernie O'Malley

Letter to Maighread Murphy[139]

[Stationery of] Newton Hall,
Newton, Nr Cambridge, [England]
9 September 1953

[Mrs Seamus Murphy,
6 Wellesley Terrace, Cork]

My dear Maigread,

Thank you for your letter. I was at Burrishoole for over a week, and when I came back to Dublin, Kevin said that I had overdone it and that I was not to walk unless I had to. The avenue to Burrishoole is over half a mile in length and as I had then to take a bus to Newport or Westport and return, the walking was too much, but Cormac got my breakfast and helped me to try to keep at bay invading moths.

I have been here since, I think, August 5th with Cormac. Tomorrow he returns to school, and I remain on here. One of my troubles is that I have not all my notebooks here or I would get ready for a few broadcasts,[140] but I am as usual rewriting my old notebooks into presentable form and out of that I hope to get some material.

I am sorry Seamus[141] and Tom Barry are on edge. Tom is Tom, and it is hard to find a way round him, but I hope the monument[142] will please Seamus for if it does, it will please another generation who will be pleased to know that a good artist was given a poor hand to make us proud of our death aesthetically. I wish him luck.

I hope you are well and Orla[143] and Bebhinn.[144] I would feel better if I knew the next step about Burrishoole. I was uneasy while I was there for fear the County Council should move against me. If I can remain on here for a few months I will go to Burrishoole, get my books packed, remove them, dump them, and try to get a flat in Dublin and I would love to go down to Cork if I was feeling well. Thank you very much for coming to see me in the hospital.

With my love,

Ernie

Letter to Paul Strand

> *[Stationery of] Newton Hall,*
> *Newton, Nr Cambridge, [England]*
> *7 November 1953*
> *Yours 6 August 1953*

[Paul Strand,
98 blvd August Balanguy,
Paris 13e, France]

Dear Paul,

A long time between the sending of this letter and my reply. I left Burrishoole on the 7th of August with Cormac, for England. I did not leave my address with the Post Office in Newport as I knew Cormac would return to school in Ireland in a month's time, and I did not wish to be thought to be out of the country when he was at school. The result has been that letters have been kept for me at the local post-office, until I had the post-office this week forward them to a Dublin address:[145] and so they reached me. Please excuse this very long delay.

I will be here until the middle of January when Cormac will return again to school, or I may wait until the beginning of February.

Burrishoole I went to mostly for Cormac's (CORMAC) sake as he is very fond of it, and also for my own. But when I saw Kevin at the end of 10 days, he said I had somewhat damaged my heart and that in future I was not to walk unless it was essential. I have friends here and as it is a large house with many servants, I can carry out a hospital way of life, by remaining in bed in the morning and going back again early in the night time. I have to see a specialist in London next week. I am unable to get rid of an ordinary cold and Kevin thinks a cold could again start of a line of infection. That seems like a life in wool. I am getting stronger, but it will take time to get somewhat hardy.

I liked your photographs very much, and I admire the carefulness with which you selected your people and your places. It would be fine if you could do an Irish book, and I would be very glad to help. There is, however, no Irish publisher who would produce a book at the cost of your book, £2.10.0, but then the proposition has not been placed before them. There are a few publishers here, but they are not big publishers. When I return to Ireland I can see some of them about the book.

I have been living in Burrishoole since 1938 I think.[146] It is on the edge of the sea in Clew Bay, and I was able to rear the three children to the sea and the land. Burrishoole Lodge is mine and it is not mine. It was given to me as a wedding present, but I put the purchase in Helen's name. *My Army Without Banners*[147] brought one libel action which took me some years to pay off, and I was determined then that I would not own property in my own name. That is why I transferred the place to Helen. She went off by herself for two years whilst I brought up the 3 children in Burrishoole. I had to teach the 3 of them, as CATHAL and CORMAC had primary tuberculosis,[148] and they had to remain in bed for over a year. I had little money, but I had fine books. I sold most of my valuable books there. I sent the two oldest, CATHAL and ETAIN, to school. But Helen pinched them from the school at the end of a year.[149] Then she took an action in the Irish High Court to remove her furniture and get possession of Burrishoole. Then another to put CORMAC and myself out of Burrishoole. The house was in her name and I had no evidence but Helen could not return to give evidence because I could have had her held until the children were returned to me. The case fell through. I would allow her to have the furniture if the children were sent home. I have been since in Burrishoole, but I sent Cormac away to school two years ago.[150] I would like to remain there if I was strong enough. Burrishoole has in ways been associated with our name since the 10th century, and I was anxious to bring the children up related to land and sea until they grew up.

Kevin, however, thinks I should not remain there by myself, that I should take a flat in Dublin. One reason I remained in the West was that it was cheaper to live there. Also Helen owes money, rates, on Burrishoole, which she promised to pay, but did not pay. The County Council was to take the furniture and my books last year while I was in hospital, but when I wrote to them, they said I could have until March of 1953, and even then they might wait another while.

You might as well have the background for the past few years though it has not been pleasant. My family was distressed at the publicity, and the talk prior to the actions in the High Court. As a result I avoided the family so that their hurt might soften. Kevin this year when I expected to die took charge of me in hospital and has been very kind. He lives in 57 Merrion Square, and he is a very good physician. I have a brother in London, throat and nose, Cecil, who they say is a very good surgeon and there is another brother, Brendan, on Tuberculosis in London. Both of them sat for exams in Ireland some years ago but their Gaelic was not good enough to please the examiners, so now they have to hold more lucrative posts in London. It's a funny world but it is an amusing world.

I cannot find a copy of *Army Without Banners*, or the English equivalent, *On Another Man's Wound*.[151] It is out of print. I had intended to have another edition printed, but I thought another book was more important. I did not rewrite the second book as I began to collect material on the 1916–1924 events,[152] and it is only recently I have rewritten a few of them. I had been writing for about 4 months when I became ill, but I had been to most small places in Munster and Connaught during these years, the last 5 years. I do not think there is a copy in Burrishoole, for my copies were borrowed, but I will search when I next get back. Hanna and Neale, bookseller, Nassau St might look out for a copy.

What have you done since the Mexican book? I should remember but since I was in hospital my memory suddenly fails. Does Hazel miss New Mexico? I miss it. Cormac and I often talk about it, as used the other two children. I enclose a photograph of Cormac but would you please return it. I have not another, but if I get a reproduction I will send you one. He is now 11 and some months. He works well at his school and he is a good sailor!

Johnny Raleigh talks of you whenever I go to Limerick. He is a good friend. Two of his daughters are married and there is a girl, Mary, a fine girl at the University.[153] Mary wants to be a writer, I think. Anyhow I hope Hazel and you can come to Ireland, but I would like it very much if Burrishoole were there so that you could use it as a base.

Affectionately to you and Hazel,
Ernie

Reading over this it seems that I am passing judgment on Helen, and it is not a habit of mine, but I was really trying to explain the difficulties about Burrishoole for Cormac, myself and my friends.

NO. 237 PAUL STRAND ARCHIVE, CCP, UNIVERSITY OF ARIZONA
Letter to Paul Strand

[Stationery of] Newton Hall,
Newton, Nr Cambridge, [England]
9 December 1953

[Paul Strand,
98 blvd August Balanguy,
Paris 13e, France]

Dear Paul,

Thank you for your letter of 20th. I was in bed for over a week, but now I am alright again, and I am in London.[154] Cormac will come over here on the 18th and will remain until January 13th when I will go back with him by sea and train. I hope you can come over before I leave. I can always come to London. The family have a house in St James St in which I can stay if the secretary who works there has notice; or I can remain in my brother's house. He is a throat and nose surgeon. I will return again, I think, before January 23rd. I had intended to clear out my books from Burrishoole, but that is a major undertaking for there must be over 4,000 of them and furniture for Cormac and myself. You see it is not possible for me to have a maid in Burrishoole for if I go away the maid would be by herself. The nurse, a hospital nurse, remained on for two years after Etain and Cathal were kidnapped, and she looked after Cormac and I, and cooked. When I was away, and I was away a good deal the second year, taking down experiences of the Tan War from men all over Ireland, the nurse could get a woman from nearby to remain with her until I came back. I do not like the thought of moving from Burrishoole, as a city is no place for a child who has been used to a home on the sea edge. Helen promised to pay the rates due, but she does not keep a promise and threatens to go back on it. However she has paid £45 recently, or she told me she had paid such a sum. That will hold off the County Council for a while. She is in London with Etain. She rented a house in August I think, and I have seen herself and Etain a few times. She wants to return to Ireland, but I can have her arrested if she lands there because in Ireland the father is the guardian of the children, and as she knows she would be arrested, she is not anxious to enter. She wants to return to live with me, but I have had more than enough.

I am working on these notes, I have taken for the past 5 years.[155] When I was too disturbed I thought it better to collect the information, because in Ireland the men will tell me the truth about themselves. I take the notes at speed as fast as they talk, but again that had to be rewritten into notebooks. It is a long piece of work. So far I must have written out about 2¾ million words, and I have rewritten close on 2½ million in my other notebooks. It is material to use at some time.

I hope you will be able to interest the Bodley Head.[156] I know a Dominican[157] who attends some publishing house in London weekly and he may be able to suggest a firm for you to see. I have not heard about Ella Young for at least 9 years. She was attached to the University of California[158] there, but whether she is now alive I do not know. I remember Bill James,[159] and I am glad that Beck[160] is settled there. It is a good place to live near, Taos, and I was glad to find a country I could settle down in. The first time I ever met the Hooker family, old Hooker was arrogant and insulting about American Indians. I defended the Indians warmly and I pushed Hooker to the wall. He didn't like it, but I made him withdraw some remarks. Afterwards he said to the family whom I then met for the first time: 'That young man is dangerous; he is never to be invited to this house again'. He was not accustomed to be questioned about his words, yet he was not a bad old lad. I was in a libel action over the book, and he sent a wire stating that he would pay the £600 for which I was liable, but I borrowed the money, and I paid it back in five years. This time I will bring back the manuscript[161] from Ireland, and I will work on it here until the Spring. I would like to go to France in Spring with Cormac and maybe that can happen, for always I find France warm, friendly and interesting.

I am glad your Italian book[162] is finished, and I hope by this you have found a publisher. The book is *On Another Man's Wound*. It was published by Rich and Cowan, who were mean to me,[163] but they are no longer in business. Indeed, I have the copyright of the book myself now, and I would have looked for a publisher again only I thought it best to keep on working. I hadn't much luck with the book anyhow. I have searched some London shops, second-hand shops, but no available copies. The Walstons with whom I stay got their copy back from a friend the other day. It is *Army Without Banners* which I know was taken from me by Mrs Walston. She may lend it to you. Hazel and you, I am sure, could stay in Newton if you would wish to, but I would want to know the date of your arrival in England and when you would be free; but I think I would prefer to meet you in London. I am getting stronger, I know, yet I am not yet able to face a cold. I have to go to bed when I get one. I was in Oxford for a few days and then in bed. I am sorry for the long delay.

Affectionately to you and Hazel,
Ernie

Letter to John Ford

[Stationery of] Newton Hall,
Nr Cambridge, [England]
9 December 1953

[John Ford,
Los Angeles, California, USA]

Dear Jack,[164]

I am sorry for the long delay which I have explained to Meta Sterne,[165] and I am sorry for your trouble with your eyes.[166] There is not much of me left except my spirit, but I always think kindly of you for you helped me with regard to Cormac's schooling,[167] and I wished that you with some of the others could have spent a week in Burrishoole.[168]

With reference to Martin's[169] letter. You cannot recommend him, nor de Valera, nor myself, only such people as have known him in action can write about him, and they must give their evidence before the Commission. It means really that only his comrades or his immediate officers who have known him, or have seen him in action, can verify. I, who had to be responsible for the greater part of the 3 counties at the end of the Tan War,[170] can not give evidence about a man whom I consider to be a good man unless I was in control of him in action. Michael must know this, and if he does not he should. In these cases only people who were with him in his own area can verify.

I don't know of your plans, but I wish I could see you again for a while when you were not working; but I learned a good deal when I saw you at work. Cormac is at school near Dublin. That I do not like, but I can't help it. I would prefer him to be with me until he was 13, for I quietly teach him a good deal. He has worked hard, and last year he got first class honors in all subjects, and he is on his school team for Rugby. I am glad he is working as I told him he would have to use his brains. I will always remember your kindness for I wasn't worth a damn to you. I was glad to work with a crowd who had your spirit and outlook. Goodbye, Jack, and remember we would always be glad to have you *so that you could rest.* At least we could relax here. I wish Cormac were here for he has to paint you a Christmas card, but he will be over here for Christmas. He does not like it here, neither do I, but my friends are good people. Please kindly remember me to all the people I knew here in Ireland.

Very affectionately,
Ernie

Letter to Paul Strand

[Newton Hall,
Newton, nr Cambridge, England]
18 December 1953

[Paul Strand,
98 blvd August Balanguy,
Paris 13e, France]

Dear Paul,

Thank you for your letter. I was told by Father Thomas Gilbey[171] that the Harvill Press[172] might be of use for your purpose. He knows very well Mrs Harris who is in charge and says that if you mention his name she will be nice to you. With her works Mrs Villiers, whom he also knows. This is a small press but a good one. It is near Victoria Station.

> Happy Christmas to you both
> Affectionately,
> Ernie

I am on my way to London to meet Cormac tomorrow.[173]

Please don't mention to Helen if you meet Kevin. He is tired of the subject.

I will write again. I will see if you both can stay here for a day or so as there is room and you could look around Cambridge.[174]

Note[175] *to Jack B. Yeats with card by Cormac O'Malley*

[c. December 1953]

Cormac and I send you on our very affectionate regards and we hope that you are able to paint and walk about a little. Like you I now walk a little.

> Ernie O'Malley

Letter to Etain O'Malley

[c/o Paddy Malley,]
59 Seafield Road, Clontarf, Dublin
27 February 1954

[Etain O'Malley,
Sacred Heart Convent,
Tumbridge Wells, Sussex, England]

Dearest Étain,

Thank you for your letter of January 24th, which I received on February 26th. The Walstons were away from Newton, and I did not think anyone would write to me there as Burrishoole always finds me, but the best address really is: 59 Seafield Road, Clontarf.[176] Cormac's address is: Willow Park, Blackrock College, Blackrock, Co. Dublin. I will send him your address this evening for I had left it behind me with some papers and I was not sure whether you had suddenly gone to America again, or that you were in France.

I have been in bed for over 3 weeks. Kevin was afraid I might develop my old trouble, but it is hard to remain in bed when there is nobody to look after you until six in the evening. However, I survive, but I am not really as well as when I last saw you, but my fat is going away or rather has gone. Cormac and I were in Burrishoole lighting fires, cleaning moths from off our clothes, bringing in turf. Luckily we have the pram in which you were once moved around. That has been my safeguard for you can push the turf in it into my room now which formerly had been the school room. Cormac and I cooked and we slept on the floor in our sleeping sacs.[177] We worked away for days until I had to return Cormac to school.

One day in Bewleys a girl came over to talk to me but I knew that I knew her, but I could not place her. It was Hiley, Nurse Hyland, who once looked after yourself and Cormac. She looks thinner now. I had a letter from Una Joyce who was asking for you and for Cormac. She is yet in Dungarvan. Mrs Byrne always asks for you. Her husband has been ill. He has very bad arthritis and I thought, when I saw him some weeks ago, that he would not last very long.

I am glad you are at school away from ballet and the theatre. Your discipline begins with school work and should be continued in your reading. I know you hear many opinions on drama but our Irish one is that in poetic plays the actor is very unimportant for actors tend to think it is they and not the well-written play which is of importance. In Ireland of course there is a natural use of the spoken word and a turn of phrase which makes a sentence seem dramatic; but that is not so. It is our method of reading an emphasis, or of registering a feeling.

I hope you can now settle down to work. For if you get your teeth into work you will eventually find it more interesting. Cormac has settled down again, but he was for close on two weeks in bed. What can you read yourself for your own interest? I do not know how schools work, boarding schools I mean. I sent on Cormac a pile of books, but I do not know what he is reading.

With my love,

O X O X O

X Ernie X

O X O

NO. 242 EOM PAPERS NYU
Letter to Department of Defence

[Actual address: Newton Hall,
Newton, nr Cambridge, England]
c/o Hibernian Bank,
College Green, Dublin
1 March 1954

[Department of Defence,
Hospital Department, Dublin]

Dear Sir,

I received your D.P. 2760[178] of the 25th of January in February. Dr Kevin Malley had your communication. This was the first time I had been made aware that I was responsible for my treatment in St Bricin's, and I was surprised that I had not previously been informed that I owed money to the Department of Defence. That reticence I now understand was not the fault of the Department; but was due to some of my friends, who had decided not to worry me.[179] That worry now, however, is there for I could have been treated without charge in another hospital, had I known of the conditions necessary for admission to St Brican's.

The responsibility for the payment for my treatment in hospital rests on myself as I was the patient, and Dr Malley is in no way responsible. I have now to return to England for further treatment, and I am considering your communication.

Sincerely yours,

Ernie O'Malley

Letter to Maighread Murphy

[Stationery of] Newton Hall,
Newton Nr Cambridge, England
Tuesday [mid April 1954]

[Mrs Seamus Murphy,
6 Wellesley Terrace, Cork]

Dear Maigread,

Thank you for your letter of the 9th. I hope Seamus was not too worn down by the West Corks. Maybe I can go to Cork afterwards, but I am not sure for this reason.

I have 25 cattle in Burrishoole, over £1,100 borrowed money. I thought, as always happens, they would be sold in December, but now the lad wants me to buy some of his cattle. I know there is not enough grass for my cattle. But I found out that prices have been dropping in Ireland and so the lad was afraid to tell me, but was willing to risk losses in the cattle by keeping them on the land until May or June. 3 weeks ago I wrote and told him to sell all cattle *at once*, and to hell with the loss. Also County Council may seize them for Helen's rate, yet unpaid.

So as he did not reply I must go to Burrishoole, remain on there to sell the cattle. That is risky for me to remain in the West for I intended to have Cormac over, see a few friends and return to England. So that I do not know whether I will be in hospital care if I remain in Burrishoole. However, I'll arrange for the hospital before I leave Dublin.

I have a cold, a bad sign for I must be in bed with a cold. Thank you for writing as I have just time to reply. I'll write from Burrishoole.

I have been rewriting my notebooks into almost legible script but I cannot do much in the day. But I have worked whenever I was not laid up and I feel stronger, but I am supposed to go easy. I hope Seamus, Bebhinn, Orla and Sean[180] and my friends in Cork are well.

With my love,
Ernie

Letter to Maighread Murphy

Newton Hall,
Newton, Near Cambridge, [England]
7 June 1954

[Mrs Seamus Murphy,
6 Wellesley Terrace, Cork]

Dear Maigread,

Thank you for your letter of June 1st and for news of the family. I am sorry Bebhinn had such a year, but I am glad about Orla. Cormac, I found, has a low year at school being worst at English of any of his subjects, and his marks were low.

I know Malinmore and the area around there from the Tan War. It's certainly far enough away. I thought you might be on your way again to Sligo and I thought Cormac and I might get to see Sligo, but I find it hard to plan in advance for my planning depends on my condition. But Cormac must have his holidays. Now I am trying to see that Cormac gets to the country for a while as he gets his holidays on June 16th, but in the Irish way replies are long in coming. If I could have him in the country I would go over on the first of July, hunt for a flat in Dublin for 10 days, go to Burrishoole where anyhow my books must be packed, but not by me yet I must be there and shelving. Then I must have it removed and stored in Dublin. I go on to Aran[181] for 4 weeks of August with a boy[182] of this house, Cormac's age. I don't know how that will work out, but we would not have to cook. Then maybe I get back to Burrishoole for a week and then to England.

I have no place really now for I am unable to remain in Burrishoole by myself and I have no work room in Ireland where I can sit in to write or think.

Helen O'Malley has been threatening me with an occupation of Burrishoole with the two children she kidnapped. That is foolish for I could take away Etain at once as I am now the guardian. If the poor idiot would only wait until I die, I expect she could do what she wishes for I doubt that anyone will care a damn about Cormac or bring him up when I am gone. I have only one poor friend[183] who even wants to take him out of his school from time to time on a Sunday.

I told Kevin to write to you so I hope he does. The Moriarty lad in the Mater is from Kerry, but he was trained in Dublin so he is not a Cork graduate.

Please remember me to all your nice family, Seamus, Bebhinn and Orla and Sean. If I could get hold of a place in Dublin, I would buy some kind of a second hand car and be more at ease on the road again. Here I can work, but I am buried. Everyone is very kind to me, but I should look after Cormac more.

With my love,
Ernie

PLEASE DO NOT MENTION Burrishoole much to Kevin for he knows it does me injury, but on the other hand I must look after Cormac and if I work I should have my books around me.

Letter to Paul Strand

[Galway]
31 July 1954

[Paul Strand,
98 blvd August Balanguy,
Paris 13e, France]

Dear Paul,

Thank you for your letter. I was in Burrishoole when it arrived. Our weather has been what even we might call wet. Last Sunday was a fine day and there have been I think 2 days of unrain since I came over here. It has not made much difference to me, but it has interfered with Cormac's wanderings by boat and bicycle. I expect you have had a sample of our weather, and I hope you have been able to work at the people instead, until the sun comes out. In 1904 I found by talking to an elderly man that it was a bad year. There was no summer, so I expect this is a similar visitation, and I do not expect to see the sun.

I came to Dublin on the 1st of July, spent 11 days looking for a flat, but unfortunately I visited Kevin two days before I came on to Burrishoole by train. Kevin said my heart was bad, but I knew it was as I had no place to rest during the day except the Library,[184] and I had to walk a good deal for in tourist July the Dublin streets were thick with foreigners from England. My work then in Burrishoole was to get my books packed for transport and for sale. Cormac and I worked for about 10 days, from reasonably early until 11 o'clock at night. Then a friend of mine[185] came on the 22nd to pack the books and dismantle the book shelves. He had been a packer for a few years once, but he took his holidays to help me. His health is poor, and he has 12 days leave in the year, but he took off 8 days for my sake. We readied the furniture and books until at last we were, the three of us, so tired that I slept whenever I sat down. But the evacuation had to go on. I could not leave books and furniture in Burrishoole until next Spring. The County Council might seize the property on account of the rates due to them and again I might never be able again to screw my courage to the task. Many a good O'Malley lies across the water in the graveyard of the Dominican Abbey[186] in Burrishoole, and I felt I would have bones of my friends there for company if anything happened to me.

Everything went wrong then. The lorry which was to arrive did not arrive, but eventually a day was again fixed while my friend Chris was with me, and it arrived. The railway lorry which was to come on the same day did not come. In one lorry I was to place my books, but it was an open lorry open to the rain on a day of wild rain with a rushing wind. So we packed book shelves and eventually as the pile mounted odds and ends such as beds. The driver and Chris left under the influence of gin carrying half bottle with them in case they had to float the lorry in the rain storm. Since then, since that Tuesday morning, I have had no word. Maybe they did reach Dublin; maybe they didn't.

Then the railway lorry arrived, an 8-ton lorry on the ground empty, which reached so high that it could not come in under the arch; but at length it was able to reverse and to face down the avenue. Then the books went into its maw, then odds and ends until at length. I felt that between the two lorries, we have removed almost twice as much as the flat would hold. The following day I found that the railway lorry I had to pay for by the weight of the books, and that cost me over three times the amount which I had expected to pay. But what the first lorry will cost I do not yet know. Now, Paul, that has been my quiet country rest in Burrishoole. I would not say my heart is worth much, and I do not know how I can rest in Aran; I mean rest physically for it depends on my room, my bed room. However, Cormac can rest and I hope I will be able to work in my bed room.

Our Folklore Commission[187] has for at least five years paid at least one field worker in Western Scotland and recently they presented mimeographs[188] of the work done to Edinburgh University and persuaded that Univ to collect their own material. I think you are correct in your choice of Uist[189] for it would be more sympathetic. Until 1600 the Western Islands sent their soldiers to our West, especially to fight as hired soldiers for us. During the times of planting and reaping the Irish were inclined to borrow soldiers. In many ways the people would resemble our people, but now I think South Uist is more behind hand than any of our remote places here.

Two days ago an American family called in to the guest house which is close to Burrishoole. They wandered around in the rain. 'It is delicious this Irish rain', said one of the girls, 'it is good for the hair and wonderful for the complexion'! Never did I hear of such Americans. They come from Minnesota. Cormac has survived, and I am sure he is looking forward to Aran, but he had to leave his boat behind him, his small yacht. I apologise for not writing before this, but this is the first time I have had to write to you since I came back to Ireland, and I am now in the city of Galway waiting until tomorrow for the boat to Aran. I hope I may be able to write now when I get there.

Mrs O Flaherty Johnston
Kilmurvey House
Kilmurvey, Aran Islands
Co. Galway

I met Mrs Laura Sweeney but James is yet in New York. Laura is a fuss pot. She is slightly arrogant, expects too much and is now unpopular along this coast. She behaves somewhat as do the retired wealthy English. She has no tact, and is inconsiderate to poorer people. I write this because the bay side is O'Malley land for such a long time that I do not like to see people settle down here who do not regard the people as more important than anything else here. I hope herself is surviving rain, mist and cold and that you are able to keep your strength. Here I am now tearing up my roots somewhat.

> Affectionately to you both.
> Please write again, and I will rest,
> Ernie[190]

Letter to Laura Sweeney

[Stationery of] Newton Hall,
Newton, Nr Cambridge, [England]
8 August 1954

[Mrs James John Sweeney,
Raith, Carrowbeg,
Westport, Co. Mayo]

Dear Laura,

Thank you for your kind invitation. I will be at the church for the baptism.[192] I hope Anne is feeling somewhat better by this.

I saw Henry Moore[193] the other day since I spoke to you for John Rothenstein and his wife, who were here for the weekend, were over to see him, so I went as well. But always I would like to see Henry and his wife.[194] They are friendly and kind, and Henry himself is a delight to meet so I hope I will be able to see him again.

Sincerely yours,
Ernie O'Malley

NO. 247 NLI MS 21218
Letter to Frank Gallagher

Kilmurvey House,
Kilmurvey, Aran Islands, [Co. Galway]
17 August 1954

[Frank Gallagher,
'Glór na Mara', Greenfield Road,
Sutton, Co. Dublin]

Dear Frank,

I hope that you and Cecilia and the children are well. Thank you very much for the nice meal which I had, and pleasant company at your house. Cormac and I worked away in Burrishoole against all orders and advice, and Christy worked with us for he had to pack my books. Christy left worn out, but Cormac and I remained cleaning up until at length we tottered on to and from the Galway bus, and we reached Aran where we have no longer to cook, or look after a house. Aran, I find, a problem as the economy is so upset that I am endeavouring to put its facts together and its former way of life, but nothing I fear can be done here. There is little activity and an active people settle down in an unreason of lack of effort and of the training of hardship and sea. Cormac is blooming, but he misses his boat in Burrishoole. Here a curragh may put out for an hour twice a week; being seamen we miss the sea, although it is all around us. This house was full of people, and there is no work room for me, but I am making use of my bedroom which is also Cormac's and a boy[195] of his own age whom I have brought over from England.

Today has been wet, but we have had a good deal of sun, and there are warm spots among the limestone. As usual I forget that I am no longer a mountaineer, but with the help of Cormac's bicycle I can ride down hill and then leave him the bicycle to catch up with me. I expect you have now fairly good weather for it must be somewhere.

With many kind thoughts to you and Cecilia,
Ernie and Cormac

NO. 248 PAUL STRAND ARCHIVE, CCP, UNIVERSITY OF ARIZONA
Letter to Paul Strand

[Actual address: 52 Mespil House,
Sussex Road, Dublin]
[Reply address:] Newton Hall,
Newton, Near Cambridge, [England]
30 November 1954

[Paul Strand,
98 blvd August Balanguy,
Paris 13e, France]

Dear Paul,

Thank you for your letter of October 25th. This is a late reply from me who has had my mind in a dark room. I hope by this you are sure that your book will be out by Christmas and that your plates are developing to your satisfaction. It is good to see your work shaping slowly for there are so many drawbacks in photography between the country or people realized, photographed, developed and printed.

Here I have slept late until it has become a bad habit, and I have spent time cataloguing books intending to get rid of a good number, but at least I have now space in which to place them together. Cormac and I have each a room. He comes out now whenever he can, usually on Saturday night at 6 if he is not playing for his Rugby team. He writes his composition in Irish on Saturday night, and he returns on Monday morning early. He cooks my breakfast on Sunday and on Monday mornings, and he likes the flat. He has a key of his own now so that he can come in whenever he wishes to cook a meal. I think that he has improved with this week-end looking after. Sometimes he can come on a Wednesday if he is not playing for his team. I had forgotten about his Rugby position and when I asked him recently 'How long have you been on the team?' 'Oh, for the past five years'.

December. Now this has been delayed for a Christmas card which I had hoped Cormac would make ready, but he is working for his exams which will begin on the 12th of December, and so I must wait until he again comes out. I have had Sean

O'Sullivan make a drawing of him, and that was an upset. I found that Cormac had missed his best match of the year by attending on Sean, but he did not like to tell me as I had arranged for his sitting. Then on the following Saturday he had to play another match, but though I waited outside Sean's studio many times he did not come in for I wanted to postpone the engagement, and so Cormac again was present.

The weather is broken here. It is rather like our Western weather when it gets out of hand in winter: rain, wind storm, cold, but the Dubliners are resentful as they do not know under what conditions we farm, but I feel more at home here when the wind surges up against the window then smashes forward at the glass and the walls.

Maybe you are in Italy now. I hope everything is now satisfactory about the book and that both of you are satisfied with the plates. As for me I have little to report. I did not get work done. I had intended to write for the *New Yorker* about Aran basing the article on Synge who lived in the Middle Island, but it did not work out properly. Then I read a fair amount thinking of my province Connaught from which came the Plan of Campaign that broke the landlords, the Gaelic League, which again took up language and song, Yeats, Moore, Martyn, Lady Gregory on all who started the Irish Theatre. I had intended to write a few articles for the Radio but I became too interested in the subject for that meagre information. Connaught has always been looked upon as a backward province, but it really was the basis upon which the later fight was able to develop although it did not achieve much in the field with the English. Kevin whom I saw for the first time since I came here in June said my heart was enlarged and to go easy. As a result Cormac and I leave for England on the 17th of December. I will remain on until mid February, perhaps. January and February are really bad months in Ireland, but England for me is an icy land, no interest in ideas or in talk and too frustrated with its own sense of authority from top to bottom. Also I will not have my papers. However I am secure against bad colds which lay me in bed, and this flat is now ready for work in the Spring and for the meeting of people, as I saw but few this time. As well there are rooms here for you both if you ever come over. Cormac and I have two beds, but there is a bed due to me and I could raise another. Rooms are so small that a bed takes up the essential space from books. Now here is Cormac's key rattling in the door and it is December 8th the last day on which to post a letter to France. Our love to you both, and a pleasant Christmas.

Ernie

Letter to Jean McGrail[196]

Newton Hall,
Newton, Nr Cambridge, [England]
25 January 1955

Miss Jean McGrail,
410 Park Avenue, 9A,
New York, NY, USA

Dear Jean,

Thank you for your letter of January 16th, which I received on the 23rd, and for your previous letter in December which went on to Burrishoole, back to Dublin, passed me by in London, but was here when I came down. It was nice of you to forward the photographs as they reminded me of the fort[197] which disappeared, and of the dark haired girl who went away. On Inishmaan[198] I searched many times for 'Synge's Chair', which is near the cliff edge, but I did not find it. I was reluctant to bring a guide with me, but one day I walked quarter-way round the island and halted at last, tired, on the edge of the water, high above it. I sat down in a built up pile of stone and after a while, as I watched the seagulls dive, I realised that I was in Synge's chair. There he wrote at times.

The family are away now from the house, the wife in London to-day, the husband in Peru, the boys,[199] save one[200] at school and here I am in bed, writing. Beside me are Cuala Press notebooks: *Pilgrimage in the West* by Mario Rossi, which deals with Ireland and the West, my West; *The Love Songs of Connaught* by Douglas Hyde, a man also from the West; *Poems and Translations* (with a preface by W.B. Yeats, from the West) by John M. Synge, the first edition, not the Cuala edition, with a preface by Yeats; *The Kiltartan Poetry Book* by Lady Gregory, once from Coole in the West. Then I have a one inch map of my bay, Clew Bay, and a one inch map of the Aran Islands. As well there is a good share of a bottle of Powers which I brought over with me as a reserve in case I would wish to have a drink, or maybe later to brew my kind of punch instead of being led along gently by the easy and unlively taste of Scotch. I know if you read the 'New Yorker' only the taste of Scotch exists outside of Bourbon. Bourbon is a fine drink, but Scotch is effete.

I am sorry to say that when I reread what I had written so far, really to discover if my writing was in any way readable, I find 'my' three times. I don't possess the West although in a way it possesses me, but I use 'my' as a term of affection. Anyone who lives in a folklore area, no matter what his subsequent impingements is very much shaped by that background to living. That is why people from the West go quickly to pieces in America or in England when they accept the strange contemporary unrooted life. Only I think intellectually can intellectuals understandably live beyond the Shannon towards the Atlantic.

I took a flat[201] in Dublin for a year in last July although I knew I could not be in the city until September, but Burrishoole is difficult in winter for I have no car now. There are one, no two, buses a day, the nearest village[202] two miles away, but you have to wait for hours for the return bus. And as I am by myself in winter the food question is difficult at times unless one picks 'blue shells'[203] off the rocks and makes soup with them, fries them in butter, or finds a tin of sweet corn on a disused shelf.

Tell me, have you any plans for this year? I ask because all Americans I have met in Europe have plans about time. I never have a plan when I am in Mayo for I live my life as best I can, but when I am abroad in a foreign country, I expect I must have some kind of a plan else I would remain here. I think I may stay here until Easter then I hope to go to Paris where I can, amongst other things, look at pictures. Beside me also is *Vogue*[204] for January 1955. I have read through the 'Museum lover's guide to eating in Paris'. Canard à l'orange at Auberge Franc-Comtoise with maybe cul-de-veau[205] and Chateau-Chalon,[206] which would mean two solid plates for the one course and fondue comtoise[207] and a bottle of Chateau-Chalon, which is not an excellent wine, but would satisfy me *pour le soif*.[208] The English are so funny about wine. They have elevated Claret to first rank because its handling, care and bottling are more secure, better classified with a small change of error, whereas good Burgundy is an adventure to find for it is very often one's own choice.

I hope you have a *Vogue* for I am next on my way to Moulin a Vent,[209] which name I remember as good Beaune[210] to drink. Just a touch of faux filet au Saint-Amour[211] or maybe instead Ducollets for steak au poivre à le Fenelon. My French is terrible now like as if a parrot was reciting Basque poetry,[212] so I'll have to work at it. I have not been in France for six years. I sailed across from Southampton in my brother's boat,[213] but to my horror I was sea sick, so was he, in the end, but I was too shaken to even feel that I was in disgrace and when he and the British ex-naval officer went to sleep I was at the tiller and kept the boat on the only point I had heard them talk about for they had charts in the cabin. When one of them, awakened by mistake, he was furious. I, the unmentionable, had brought the boat to within sight of France, without their advice even.

I am looking at the one inch map by which I sail, but then I know most of the northern side of the Bay in the dark. Inishakillew was the island I left and it was between Inishturk and Illannaconney. I saw the first light, between Inishfish and Taash, the second, away north at Muckinish was the third, but you would need a map. When I get back I can send you a map.

I have the Francoise Henry booklet[214] here. I meant to get it bound for you, but I had not the time. Also, Daniel Corkery's *The Fortunes of the Irish Language*, which I bought to send to you. The book about the Western Islands is in the flat. I will post it when I return. Corkery wrote a strange unwieldy book about Synge, but his *Hidden Ireland* really does break new ground, which has not been much sown in since then. Paul Walsh,[215] now dead, was a fine scholar, but unfortunately he died when he was too young.

I had a thought of going to Inisheer, the most westerly of the islands in August, but I do not know now. Also I was thinking of sailing in the Bay in July, but now

I must have help aboard. It is late, I have a cold and it would be, I know, easier to talk to you, but thanks to Herbert Read[216] I have been able to write to you. I know Read slightly. He has a good mind and I would send you his book, but paper-covered Penguins are not allowed in to America[217]…

NO. 250 EOM PAPERS NYU
Postcard[218] to Jean McGrail

[25 January 1955]

One of Lane's pictures. The largest Renoir I know and a very fine picture. The English at least have the decency to hang more of them now.[219] There are several of them in two rooms. A very fine Degas …

Lady Gregory's husband[220] once gave this Gallery a number of pictures. I will, next time I go to London, send you a Velasquez, *The House of Martha*[221] (was out of print). Sir Hugh Lane was the son of Augusta Gregory's sister, next in age to her.

NO. 251 EOM PAPERS NYU
Letter to Jean McGrail

Newton Hall,
Newton, Nr Cambridge, England
20 February 1955

Miss Jean McGrail,
410 Park Avenue, 9A,
New York, USA

Dear Jean,

Thank you for your letter of February 6th which I received on February 14th. This is being written in Dublin. My friends[222] decided to fly to Dublin, but at the last moment I was invited to come over. They have been eating and drinking, and we leave Monday morning at 9 a.m. I wish to see the Yeats exhibition,[223] but now I cannot see it. We live in two worlds, my friends and myself. In Ireland which they think is a part of England, they meet people they regard as Irish, whereas I think they are either stage Irish or hostile. Arriving at 3:30 on Friday I met my friends on Friday evening, mostly writers. We talked and after that I can face good food and bad talk, I am sorry. This seems rude, but I cannot talk to the English except aristocratic English or writers, taxi drivers, Cockneys and some others; and here I am, Sunday evening, so please forgive me. There is an English stolidity which is very upsetting.

I do not know if I had thought of you on that Saturday as I do not know about time when I am in England. I have been working through Yeats' notebook, the *Cuala Press* editions, picking out aspects of Yeats which I refuse to accept. The early Yeats was influenced through Lady Gregory, accepting what information suited his disposition. The Irish background he needed and he made use of it, but later becoming interested in the 17th century Irish: Swift,[224] Berkeley,[225] and others. He hardened his mind and his poetry making this poetry his best, the later poetry; but as a human being he tended to become an Irishman founded in the 18th century, close to the Anglo-Irish who held their lands, their lands confiscated from our people, and their prejudice. As I reread his remarks I see how retrograde from the point of essential freedom he was. Lady Gregory might have helped him, but Yeats went his own Fascist way.

Unfortunately I have not my books, but I have some books which years ago I sent as a present to my host's wife, and she has preserved her leaning towards Ireland and her somewhat understanding of it. I have her reading through the books which I sent her. *Lady Gregory's Journal*,[226] which I once hastily read through, I am now rereading carefully; and I am sorry for that hasty first run through, for now I find many things which I had overlooked. It seems to me that her life will not be written by Lennox Robinson now. Her son's children have the original diary[227] and are determined not to allow it to be made use of. This information I was told before I came over here by a trustee of Lady Gregory's property. I think of you as I take notes on some of these books so I hope it was on a Saturday a thought came across.

25 February 1955

Ireland was a rush. Eating largely and somewhat drinking with no time for me to look at a bookshop ever or to visit the flat. I did escape for a while on Friday evening to meet some writers who drink in the Bodega[228] every Friday, but I had to return for a meal at the Red Bank.[229] Jack Yeats had an exhibition, and I arranged to see it at 8:00 a.m. on Monday as our plane left at 9:30 but our party decided to breakfast at the airport although I laughed when I told them they could not have breakfast there. Out they went to arrive at 8:20; and they had to wait on account of ice until 11: breakfast was at 10:30. That was the second Yeats exhibition which I have missed. My party is not interested in painting, save as an investment.

(I apologize I have repeated myself as I read the first page.) I have been in bed since Tuesday evening with my strange kind of temperature and cold. Since 1952 I have had no resistance to cold. The cold lasts sometimes with a temperature and I must remain in bed. That is why I come over here in winter to this kind of a manor house, sprinkled with servants from butler to lady's maid. I can get into bed, but I am in such a hurry to get out of bed that I carry a cold with me for long intervals. I took a risk in Dublin. I met Cormac. We went to the movies, but we had to wait over an hour in the cold outside on Saturday evening. I never wait to get into a movie, but in Dublin one books or can book on Sundays. I knew I would be laid up, but I was determined to see the picture, Walt Disney's picture of the desert,[230] and I know the desert. A fine picture it was. And so I have had to lie low until today when I am sitting up to write. I feel like the Comanche when they were rounded up with the Kiowas in 1874 and were shoved into their reservation in Oklahoma.[231] They were hunters who have had since to become farmers. I have always been so hardy that I cannot accept this reservation of mine, but I had overdone it somewhat in the winter of 1951 by sleeping out in the Cork Mountains,[232] but in a sleeping sack. If you could bring over some peyote[233] then I might adjust, as did the Indians. Did you ever read Aldous Huxley[234] on peyote? A good book that.

I intend to go to the South Island of Aran in August. I expect I may be in Burrishoole for a while in July but it depends. If I could get a second hand car cheaply I would like to wander somewhat. Anyhow I think I will stay at the Old Head Hotel for a week before the 30th of July. It is a good hotel on the South side of the Bay, Clew Bay and the owner[235] is a friend of mine. He is a very nice lad; and we have trouble about bills. Perhaps I could induce another friend of mine[236] who has removed from Island Mór to the mainland to sail my boat for a week or so before June 23rd; but that will have to wait, I expect.

Making plans is alright, but up to this I cannot obtain the correct address of an hotel in Paris[237] where 5 of us flew from here in 1954. Mrs Walston, my hostess, knows someone in Paris who has the correct address, which we have all forgotten, but she forgets to write when I remind her.

The Walstons are friends of mine. I introduced them to Ireland. She knows the Bay from the land point of view, and Ireland is an adventure for her children always as they are free there to run wild to cook and to work around a house.

I have been making a small booklet from Yeats, Lady Gregory and Synge and others to save me carrying books around. It is a waste of time when I have other work to do, but also since I was laid up in 1952, my memory is not good. Recently a number of Americans in Dublin for some years past,[238] have been writing about Irish writers. They seem to forget that there are no foundations here to provide money for students to work with: and also unfortunately our universities do not seem to encourage a thesis, say on O'Casey or Lennox Robinson, O'Flaherty, or Frank O'Connor. I was hoping that Taft[239] could give some scholarships here to Irish students for work on Irish material; instead, the students go to the USA. That helps them, of course, yet I wish a few of them could work here.

I have seen a few fine movies in England since I came over in London. Two of Cocteau's,[240] *Les Enfants Terribles*, *L'Eternal Retour* [sic] and de Seca's[241] *Umberto D*; a wonderful American film *The Southerner* directed by Renoir's son.[242]

Thank you very much for the photograph[243] which I keep near my bed.

With kindest regards,

Earnán

I have been told just now (2 of 5) that the lady's maid will go to Cambridge this morning and so I can give her my letter to post. What a deal of books have recently been written on Yeats, a few almost ignore him as a writer or as a poet. One trouble about the spate of American students is that as successive questors come the individual who has the information will be less liable to give it: I wish that these students would write for publication only, but most of them collect the material for degrees. I enjoy Yeats' prose although some of it has not been republished in subsequent editions. This hunt for the influence which determined Synge's idiom has led me so far afield that I am far out at sea. I feel sure that Hyde gave him the send off, not Lady Gregory, aided by Aran English. Why I mention the American students is that always they say why don't the Irish do research? Answer: no money; and no incentive from the universities here which is a lack. Of late there have been theses on Irish historical subjects, but there is a big field to be written on in the hidden Irish tradition.

NO. 252 EOM PAPERS NYU
Letter to Jean McGrail

Newton Hall,
Newton, Near Cambridge, England
16–17 March 1955

Miss Jean McGrail,
410 Park Avenue,
New York 22, NY, USA

Dear Jean,

Thank you for your letter which I received when I returned to-day from London. I was sorry that I had disobeyed two instincts: one, to write to you at once when I received the book *Contemporary Mexican Artists*[244] which was forwarded from Dublin; two, to send you from Dublin shamrock for St Patrick's day. I find my first instinct is invariably right yet I allowed it to be argued with and around, which is sad for you would have had a letter while you were in bed. The book was fine, but I am sorry only a few of the painters' wives were included. I wondered whom Jean Charlot[245] had married. The children were nice, but no woman. I remembered the girl he once lived with, but he hardly married her as he, from the end papers, does not illustrate any of her books. Isabela and Oliver Lederma are good to look at. It is an interesting book from the human point of view, and I was very pleased to have it. France, Spain, New Mexico, Mexico, Italy, are my second countries.

A pity my work on sculpture never appeared. Now it will not. Five years work: photographs good as I took them from the aesthetic view point alone. I had to put the work by unfinished in 1949, to finish it when I had made some money, but I have not found my good photographs since 1953 when I was close on a year in bed. I covered ground from 8th to 17th century and periods at the end of the 19th. Some of Francoise Henry's photographs in *La Sculpture Irlandaise* are bad, but some photographs she later has taken, as shown in that small booklet I sent you, are very good. There is great trouble in taking photographs in Ireland. Often I got up early in Burrishoole, motored 180 or 200 miles on our type of roads, and when I reached my objective it had begun to rain but always, or nearly always, I found that I had reached a beautiful place and as I know our history fairly well and saga literature, I could console myself with what I could remember in spite of the rain. Really it's stupid for me to say 'saga' literature. I mean Red Branch or Fionn Cycle as well as the stories. Western Iceland has a distinctive saga literature due, a few say, to Irish influence. Once I had hoped to learn Icelandic so as to go there, but de Largy,[246] who is head of the Folklore Commission, knows Icelandic, has made use of it; but now he has lost his strength. Anyhow, I know everywhere in most counties where there is a piece of sculpture but I should, I expect, train some of the younger people; but I have not found anyone interested.

To-day in London I heard sad news. Evie Hone is dead. She was the best glass worker in Western Europe. I had hoped that she would have been able to keep her strength, but early last year she was in a motor accident. I had told her about some of the figure sculptures from the 12th to the 15th century. She had been able to make drawings, and to feel this material in her glass work. She was a really good, intelligent, saintly woman; rare that mixture is. Unfortunately Irish Catholic priests are so art-hostile, due to the destruction of artistic instincts in Ireland for 400 to 500 years; yet it could have been recentred, the aesthetic instinct, if any of the successive Cabinets were interested, any one member, I mean. In a way there is little time for if you do your work it takes all of your time.

I felt badly about the Yeats exhibition. My giving up that pleasure meant sweet-damn-all to my companions and was mistaken politeness. During his last exhibition I was in hospital in 1953 and I could not then trace his painting for the past four years. Once I went to see him when I was in Dublin almost once each week. I am very fond of Jack: he is getting old and now he cannot last long. In London I went to Ebury Street where I visited a painter friend[247] of mine who loves Ireland. He lived on the far side of my Bay for some years in the summer and his paintings are of the country underneath the Reek and further west out towards the Killaries.

Can you read my writing? It is very bad. I go over it again to improve it for you, but often I am afraid I make it all the worse. I have been working on a word of yours; when you go to Scotland, but after a long tussle I find the beginning is J, so it must be June. I had hoped to meet a photographer who was to have been in Scotland this month. I thought I might go there to one of the islands for a few days, but now he may not come until the end of this month. His book on Scotland will be published next month. He is a fine photographer. Paul Strand. Have a look, please, at some of his photographs. Where? In the Metropolitan,[248] or look in the 42nd St Library[249] for his book on Mexico; and in another some of his work in New Mexico. Also I had hoped to meet him in Paris where he lives with his wife, but now he will not be there. Goodness me. That was one of the reasons I had intended to go to Paris. He could have helped me in many ways, mostly by just being there to talk to.

I am going to Paris. I finally decided that to-day as I had the name of a cheap hotel sent on from Paris, and I had arranged for a return passage by air which is as cheap as by train and sea. Then when I came back here I found Paul's letter telling me he had booked a room for me. In a way, now, I do not want to go, but I do wish to work hard on the contemporary painters. I really cannot afford to go, but I know I can sell something later. Not books this time. You know Henry's book is very expensive now. I saw it advertised in Ireland £29 or £39, but if you come to Ireland I will let you have my books to study while you are there. Now that's fair enough, I think. I wish though you could be in Paris. Maybe you could travel in spirit.

Nothing I think can be done about that fever. My brother,[250] one of them, is the best physician I know in Ireland. I am supposed to take life easily and to get into bed when I catch a cold. Now, what do you think of that? My lungs are perfect, a bullet wound on the edge of one, my heart somewhat shaky, not wholly holey (can't spell it) due to Aran either. There is an Irish specialist in London who can check on me before I go back. He gave me a detailed check last June before I went to Ireland, but his advice is the same. TAKE IT EASY AND DON'T GET TOO EXCITED.

I cannot say I kept this advice in London. The Walstons have a London flat in Albany, Piccadilly, a secluded avenue of houses, self-contained. Now what do I mean by that? Self secluded between Piccadilly and the street parallel to it to the North. I can use it when I go to London. On Monday I saw a Yugo-Slav exhibition of books as I had promised the Yugo-Slav minister who was a guest here last week end to look at the books and recommend some of them to London booksellers, the books on mediaeval sculpture and ornament. Then to inspect pictures of the West of Ireland. Finally a long walk to the only movie worth seeing in London, *Seven Samurai*.[251] It is supposed to be cruel, savage and beastly, but I must have seen other aspects of it for I liked it, and the music was not Oriental enough, I thought. Tuesday: walked the National Gallery picking out my friends, but the Spanish, Netherlands and early French rooms are now closed up for repairs. Then to the Victoria and Albert[252] where I walked what was left of my legs. A very beautiful room of sculpture, fabrics, ivories, Byzantine, Coptic, Carolingean, and Romanesque, after which I explored the 'Print Room' for reproductions of some ivories. Then to my painter friend to advise him about what 3 pictures to send to the Academy.[253] Then to a friend of his, a poet, for a drink. In Ebury St the painter lives. Four doors down was once George Moore's place.[254] I walked down to stroke with my hands the pillars of the front door, for no matter what they say George Moore was kindly to many people.

This letter grows, but then you are maybe yet in bed. I must get up early to catch a bus to Cambridge to reach the post. Even if you are not now ill my intentions are good. I leave on April 4th and I return to London on April 15th or 16th. I leave Newton on April 1st so that I can take life easy in London for a few days but this I doubt. Then I may return to Ireland May 1st

Then on Tuesday evening at 7 as I could not find a decent movie, I made a meal in the flat, got into bed, dosed myself heavily with Veganin[255] as I had a cold on the way up. On Wednesday, I went to an exhibition of French pictures. Mr Walston was thinking of buying a Rouault.[256] I saw the Rouault which he liked. It was just £3,500, somewhat larger than a Rouault I was trying to buy in Paris for £180, but I could not afford the extra £80. I saw a fine Juan Gris,[257] very dear indeed and an excellent Dufresne.[258] Also two really nice Vlamincks.[259] Are you interested in painting? Really cross your fingers, and truly. Well then I'll show you a Vlaminck I have lent in Dublin.[260] One of these Vlamincks costs £2,000. I think people with money should buy contemporary pictures in Paris, pictures painted by those who have not made their names. After a long spell in this Gallery, so that I could pass on some information, which is of no use unless a person loves painting, I went to two booksellers[261] and at 4 Mr Walston driving a good car, a Mercedes, which went across country near his farm where he inspected, the 80 acres of barley, sewn since Tuesday. Now I will get to bed as I am tired. I sent you a book about the West from London to-day, a letter of Maria Edgeworth which deals with Connemara.[262]

Earnan

And in my hurry I sent it letter post with a string around it. Sorry I have no time to go over the writing. I hope you are really better now.

Affectionately,
Earnan

NO. 253 EOM PAPERS NYU
Postcard to Jean McGrail

[London, England]
25 March 1955

Miss Jean McGrail,
410 Park Avenue,
New York 22, NY, USA

This postcard was one of the three of Shaw painted at Lady Gregory's House by John.[263] Shaw presented it to the Gallery here. I wish we had it in Dublin, but Shaw has always been courageous about Irish events in the newspapers, and he left us a good deal of money for scholarship when he died.[264]

So you can see the West is with me even in Cambridge.

I hope you are better now. All evening an Englishman,[265] a charming Tory, has been talking nonsense about Ireland and Western Scotland. As well he is an M.P. but I did not like to hurt him by replying.

Earnán

Postcard²⁶⁶ to Jean McGrail

> *[Hotel du Bac,*
> *rue du Bac,*
> *Paris, France]*
> *10 April 1955*

Miss Jean McGrail,
410 Park Avenue,
New York 22, NY, USA

Dear Jean,

I received your card in time for Easter Sunday. Another mystery. I found a statue of Montaigne²⁶⁷ who is a friend of mine and indeed I fell at his feet here as a series of cars rushed at me, but I do not run, so down I went. I came back again. No Statue, but on another street was a base of a statute without a statue. What do you think? Do you think our kind of fairies are here also?

Much waking, smoking, fair enough drinking and pictures by the collection of foot-sores. Near thrown out of the Romanesque fresco hall because I gurgled like a gold fish trying to revive after too much water in imitation of a French guide to a party of Germans. The French girl laughed, but the Germans were cross and that pleased me.

Earnán

Letter to Jean McGrail

> *52 Mespil House,*
> *Sussex Rd, Dublin*
> *9 May 1955*

Miss Jean McGrail,
410 Park Avenue,
New York 22, NY, USA

Dear Jean,

This is the day for your shawl, cold, blowy and nearly as bad as England, but maybe now you are in Scotland. Paris passed off alright, hard on my legs and easy on my affections, but this moving about is hard for concentration. Now again, after a week in Ireland, I go over to Newton to help in the election as my host is a candidate for the Labour Party.²⁶⁸ Before I left he said when I told him I would come back: 'if there is anything worse in relation to this constituency than being a Catholic it's your being an Irishman', but I would like to see if the English can break into talk.

Did you receive a letter I sent from Cambridge on 19 March because I did not receive any *acknowledgment*? Paris was cold enough. There were three warm days when it was delicious to sit with my back to Notre Dame in a sheltered place surrounded by trees in blossom. Unfortunately some of the interesting galleries, L'Orangerie and Jeu de Pomme,[269] were being repaired, but as I know the Left Bank one could always walk although sitting in the open could be a burden at times by reason of a blustery east wind. I would have liked to have gone down the river in a canal boat, but I did not know any boat owners.

I had a woman in to clean up this flat the other day. She said there were too many books and odd things around, pictures on the floor, but if she could move the surplus into one room, she would clean up. So, cleaning can wait until I return. Too many books.

Best wishes,
Earnán

NO. 256 EOM PAPERS NYU
Letter to HHOM

[52 Mespil House,
Sussex Road, Dublin]
9 May 1955

[Mrs Helen Hooker O'Malley,
55 East End Avenue,
New York 28]

Dear Helen,

Thank you for the tie which you kindly sent me for Christmas. Paddy[270] gave it to me recently. I had not seen him for a long time and I expect he had forgotten it was there. I do not see members of the family for I know you can always work the women your way, and Cormac has yet to grow up here. It was a nice tie, the colour as good as some of the homespun material here.

I had intended to write to you last year about a number of things from Burrishoole which I have in the flat. I thought, however, that you might react in a legal way for my removing of them, and as I did not want to be involved in worry I thought it better to wait until the fine weather came when I am then better in health. I was afraid they might get stolen from Burrishoole or that the fabrics would be destroyed by moths, as much of the woven materials and woolens had been eaten up.

Here there are:

2 large tables (coffin tables)
Persian rugs – 9 I think, but I could not climb over the debris
Floor carpets, 3 and undercarpets or carpet of seisal
Chairs 1111 in passage way, 1 in Cormac's room, 1 broken in kitchen = 6
Arm chair: 1 in Cormac's room

Curtains: a number, and some rugs. Other odds and ends

I had intended to place them in storage but then I thought it best to keep them away, moths. Yet last night I was told that it is bad for carpets to be rolled up. They all need cleaning. Now what will I do about it? I can place them in Armstrongs and Ridgely's if you wish or in the removalists on the Green.[271]

They have been in the flat for long over a year. The rooms are small. The billiard table we could make use of in my room which is larger, but I did not try to move it on weekends for Cormac and now I do not know if I brought the cues. Anyhow, the materials fill up the small space so that the rooms are unhandy, awkward and certainly no room to turn in.

I received money, which I think you forwarded to the bank in January 1954, but not until the end of the year, did I realize what the money meant. Thank you for sending it as I did not know who it belonged to I did not make use of it and as I was in debt, hospitals etc., I sold my Rossgiblin land at a big loss to come clean.

Sincerely yours,
Ernie O'Malley

NO. 257 EOM PAPERS NYU
Letter to Jean McGrail

[Stationery of] Gernetto,
Lesmo (Milano), [Italy,]
52 Mespil House,
Sussex Rd, Dublin
6 June 1955

Miss Jean McGrail,
410 Park Avenue,
New York 22, NY, USA

Dear Jean,

Thank you for your letter of 24 May and for the envelope of photographs[272] which I received as I was ready to take the plane for Milan; and I was very pleased to receive them both. I like three of them best: the girl with her head to one side, the kneeling child, the head between hands. How long have you been a sculptor? I notice the light on '4 Seasons' is not good. That means not as careful a photograph as in the case of the girl whom I like best, but then it is more of a personal piece of sculpture in feeling, the first one.

I am sorry to hear that you were so long in bed but now you're better and are alright again. Even in bed it is hard to read at times. The Blake house at Renvyle had a good ghost in it. I think W.B. Yeats writes of it, but I don't think Gogarty[273] had anything to do with it, although he turned the old house into a hotel.[274] I have been looking for Maxwell's (W.H.) *Wild Sports of the West of Ireland*[275] for you, but I cannot find a copy. Once I had eight copies but I gave them away. The book deals with country to the N/W from Burrishoole during the early 19th century, and, as I remember it, it was well written.

The Spring in England was bad, seldom a warm day; Paris was warm for about two days for sun sitting, but the streets were reasonably warm. I went to Ireland at the end of April to find the good weather there ended, and I returned to Newton mid May to cold gloom, rain, sleet until the end of May. Walston was the Labour candidate for Cambridgeshire and although he said no two things could be worse if I returned, being both an Irishman and a Catholic, yet I felt his contest was somewhat of a forlorn hope, and we are reasonably good at forlorn hopes, being used in our country to nothing else since 1599. There was not much sense of humour about their method of conducting an election, but it was humorous to me. The Conservatives were annoyed because Walston, who is a wealthy man and the best farmer in the County, was on the Labour side. I was generally given the option of going to visit the Tories, but in England you are not expected to ask the voter what way he intends to vote, and the following was my approach to the Tory landlord.

'Good morning. I am canvassing. Did you vote last time?'

'Yes.'

'Will you vote this time?

'Most certainly.'

'Then I hope you'll vote for Walston as he is a good farmer.'

'Who I vote for is no business of yours.'

'That I know; but are you ashamed to say what way you are going to vote? So long as you actually vote then you assume a certain responsibility.'

'You needn't tell me that. Where are you from?'

'I'm from Ireland.'

'From Ireland, eh: from what part?'

'From the West.'

'I mean from the North or from the South.'

'We don't recognise North or South, for that is none of our business, but we recognise Ireland and the provinces, so I am from the West. I live on the sea edge.'

'Then what do you mean by interfering in English politics?'

'Why I might ask have you been interfering in Ireland for over 700 years? Two weeks here cannot upset your nation.'

'By God, were we 700 years there?'

'A little more: up to 1922, you were 750 years exactly, and you're yet in Ulster for another 33 years.'

'Hm.'

'Now will you vote for Walston?'

'No I will not, but I'll see you to the gate, and good luck.'

The unexpected sometimes upsets the English; but it is sad to have to raise the Irish question.

As I was preparing to come to Ireland I was given a passage to Milan and off we set, 6 of us in all, rather 4 of us in advance to stay with a Marchese[276] in his palace. He was a nice lad, his grandfather was Catholic Irish so we were able to talk about his ancestors. One of the bed rooms was the same size as a small tennis court, so I suggested that we put up a net and allow one of our number, an ex-cabinet minister,[277] to play there. They were all tired as a result of the election, but no one was really interested in painting so there was no chance of my seeing Bergamo, Milan, but we went for a day to the lakes near Como. We seemed to drink wine from breakfast time, eat in a trattoria, lunch, sleep, and supper at 9 o'clock and get to bed at twelve. It was what the English call a 'gentleman's weekend' as it lasted until Thursday evening.

The Marchese's land has been broken up by the government, and he has not yet received the government bonds which he cannot sell. In Ireland, our hereditary titles disappeared when land was divided out of the control of the owners, and in 1691[278] the land was practically entirely confiscated. In 1924[279] onwards lands which the English had taken in the confiscations were bought at a very good price for redistribution. The poor English have had not sufficient time to be philosophical, but we have had time and a sense of humour.

This notepaper is important as it was the only piece of writing paper in that house in Lombardy.[280] I do not know the Scotch Islands save through history, folklore and a few books. Last year I was to have gone to the islands when Paul Strand was there, but I was not feeling hardy enough. He has made a wonderful series of photographs of Eriskay and I hope he can be present when the plates are being printed in England. He sent me his French book last year, *La France de Profil*, and I have just received his Italian book, *Un Paese*. Do you know his work? Some of it is in the Museum of Modern Art, books on Mexico which I now cannot find when I search my shelves, and a book on him by Nancy Newhall[281] in the M of Modern Art. Some years ago I brought him to Ireland, but he never came back to do his book.

I am glad you saw San Antonio. I liked that part of the world best but my country is Northern New Mexico, Northern Arizona, Southern Utah and my West Wyoming and Northern California with a little of Oregon and Washington on his previous travels. Texas I can leave out save for a few places for there are too many Texans in Texas. Are you from Northern California or not? Because I draw the line at Carmel where I had good friends: from that North is real but south of Carmel I will sell you cheaply. Once I spent a while in the Mohave[282] when it was in flower, and I can yet see the flowers shimmering in the heat and remember the light.

I must get back to work, but I will do anything but work, look at books, arrange a shelf, waste time by doing nothing. I am for Burrishoole in July. An empty house there from which I cleared many things but though there are beds I will bring my sleeping bags. I do not know what I will do if I cannot sail this year. Somehow my boat must be sailed although I know I must not handle ropes. Last year I looked out at the sea and the islands which I well know, but this year I felt rebellious about looking as I feel stronger. In August I go to Aran and I expect I will remain for a month, but my heart is in Clew Bay.

Your birthday must be close to May. Mine is in May and the trip to Milan was in a way a birthday present. I wish I could get this flat into order. Books everywhere, rooms too small, too many books and furniture which I must store: pictures on the floor. Maybe I will be able to get a sense of order into the place before I go away.

Montaigne. On his base alright. I wrote down his words 'Paris holds my heart from childhood. I am French only through this great city, the greatest of all, incomparable in variety, the glory of France and one of the noblest ornaments in the world.' But remind me please to tell you of my conversation with the chief superintendent in Euston Station about the fairies and the missing notice. I hope you will have a very nice time.

Affectionately,
Earnán

NO. 258 PAUL STRAND ARCHIVE, CCP, UNIVERSITY OF ARIZONA
Letter to Paul Strand

52 Mespil House,
Sussex Rd, Dublin
6 June 1955

[Paul Strand,
'La Breardiere', rue de Marainvilliers,
Orgeval, Seine-et-Oise, France]

Dear Paul,

I arrived here on Saturday, June 4th, and I was lucky to be able to sit down in Euston and to catch a train to Liverpool that night. I had been in England for two weeks during the general election, a cold two weeks both climatically and emotionally, but funny enough from my viewpoint. Then I was invited to Italy when the Walstons intended to recover from the election. We stayed for five and a half days in a Marchese's country seat and then flew back to England.

Your book, *Un Paese*, had arrived while I had been abroad, and I am trying to remember my Italian. It is a fine book close to a distinct, but how well the people photograph in their seriousness. That is a wonderful tribute to your approach to them that their sense of reality is so overpowering. The depth of the picture gives the faces a sculpturesque quality. I was delighted to be back in Italy, but we had not the fun of the unexpected and the casual which always was my way of life in that country. We had no contact with the people around us save through our eyes, and through their expression, yet I would like to go back again and your pictures emphasize my wish.

Cormac had measles while I was away, but he is alright again, getting ready for his school sports on Sunday next and for his examinations on the following week. He sends his love to Hazel and yourself and to our other friends in Paris.[283] He has been pole-jumping at his school and is now busy at tennis, but I wish he could learn to swim properly before he goes to the West again. Paris anyhow has made him aware of France and on Sunday I noticed he was searching among my shelves for books on Paris.

Kindest regards to Hazel and you and thank you very much, Paul, for your beautiful book.

Affectionately,
Ernie

NO. 259 EOM PAPERS NYU
Letter to Eithne Golden Sax

52 Mespil House,
Sussex Rd, Dublin
10 July 1955

Miss Eithne Golden,[284]
102 West 90th Street,
New York 24, NY, USA

My dear Eithne,

Thank you for your letter of April 27–June 26th which I received on July 4th. I am sorry Étain could not have given you my address but it has not changed since she was here with me 6 years ago but the children, save for one portion of a year 1953, I think, do not write. I suppose you know of my circumstances: if not, I will briefly outline them because unfortunately certain precautions as far as I am concerned must be observed.

(I am bad on dates now and I may not be pinned down in the history lesson, which is personal).

1. About 1948[285] Mrs Helen (Hooker) O'Malley kidnapped 2 children from an Irish speaking school in Waterford, Étain and Cathal.
2. I then saw a judge, published a decree in the paper[286] that they were unlawfully held, for at that time I did not know where they were.
3. 1948,[287] Mrs O'Malley took 3 actions in the Irish High Court against me, 1), for removal from Burrishoole House of what she said was her property (case held), 2), For the ejection from Burrishoole of myself and Cormac, who then would be less than 7, 3), another action again to get us out. All cases were held by the Irish judge thinking that the family might get together.
4. Mrs O'M. proceeds against me in America to obtain a divorce, having first withdrawn from a 5th Avenue Bank £2,000 belonging to me,[288] all the money I had, and which I had intended to attempt to educate the children with. I did not do anything about the divorce, but Cormac and I were in great difficulties here.[289]

In 1946 Cormac and Cathal had primary tuberculosis. Mrs O'Malley was renting a house in Dublin where we all were for Burrishoole was where the children

---

had been brought up and it was an O'Malley place. Mrs O'Malley withdrew the lease of the Dublin house and I had the 3 children on my hands, so I withdrew by rearguard action to Burrishoole with a nurse (hospital) who kindly enough began to act as cook. I then had to feed the children by selling my books, close on 2,000, including all my good Irish books. Everything went wrong, the sale was a disaster. But I sold all my Yeats and special books in Sotheby's in London, beginning by this a rise in the price of Yeats which has since continued.

In 1952 I was laid up with some disease. By this time my family was not speaking to me on account of Mrs H. O'M's publicity in the Courts, and as I was unconscious, a doctor was called in named Malley. He was an O'Malley born in Philadelphia and his people had been left behind in the North during the Irish Wars about 1590. I did not call in my brother[290] who was a specialist and who looked after me as a patient. Anyhow, to Malley's surprise, I did not die. Next year 1953 I got a sudden infection and I was walking around Dublin unconscious. I knew I was ill, but also I had work to do. For the 3½ previous years Cormac had been in a boarding school. No one was ever allowed to visit him for his protection, nor could he be allowed out. I then went through the country collecting material from my men of the period 1916–1924. It was hard work as I had often to sleep beside my car or in it during the winters to save money, although indeed I could have slept and did often in any house I came to. By this time I had 2 books[291] ready winter 1952, but I had trouble with an editor who changed a series of articles and in a way rewrote them. So I withdrew them and so far they have not been published or the other book. Both deal with what we call the Tan War. All this time I was collecting information for a book I had already written in New Mexico and New York – The Civil War 1922–1924, but I knew I would have to rewrite it properly. Family, becoming a farmer, and other things, having a wife mostly, threw me off my real work.

Then 1953. I had a bad heart infection. I was brought into a military hospital which treated Army people, and us lads who had fought against the British. I was dying for a long time, I was told; but actually I was thinking of some chapters to write. Well, I did not die, but ever afterwards I was told I must be very careful, lie up a lot, be well fed, be looked after. Now I knew the only order I could carry out properly would be that of lying up. In August 1953 I went to friends of mine in England and there I remained until January 1954, went back to Ireland with Cormac and to Burrishoole, sold some of my land there to raise money and then went back to England until June. That year I went back again to England, but now July 1955 I seem to be in good form, because of the heat maybe. The winters, October to March, are hard on me for if I get a cold it is the same as pneumonia to a lesser degree and I cannot go into a cold room, or I will catch cold. So that is a problem.

Mrs H. O'M. wished to live again with me from 1953 but I know I must not worry or I am finished, and she is an endless source of worry: no quietness, improvident, and a doer of something or other. With Étain you can eliminate the brackets, but to understand us you at least must know what has happened and know about the children.

Last month Mrs O'Malley came over to Ireland with the children to bring them around.[292] Cathal is now Charles Hooker O'Malley. Étain is Étain O'Malley in accordance with your programme. Cathal does not like Ireland now and enters Harvard[293] this year. Etain is to study dramatics. She wants to be an actor. Etain and I were old friends, she has a sense of humour, good intelligence, and is wild enough, but I had no long talk with her. My attitude was, let the children search me out if they wanted to establish a contact, for I realise on meeting them that I have one child, Cormac, whom I must bring up as an Irishman, and if his intelligence and integrity are of use, he could help this country. Americans keep in touch very much when they meet you, but in absence they lose touch. The Irish do not keep much in touch when you are away from this country, but you can always after years of absence begin where you left off.

Now, Eithne, can you come over here. I have a flat in Dublin. It has 4 rooms. For the past year and a half it is crowded with books and rubbish. Now that I am stronger, we, Cormac and I, can fix it into shape this year. One room (no bed, bedroom for Étain), one room Cormac, a room for me and the Etain room for you. There is a fireplace in my room, where I burn turf, but there are heaters in all rooms turned on if necessary at night, which by morning take away the chill. There is a kitchen with electric cooker, fridge, and then a bathroom. So you could be comfortable in cold weather. You can stay until you are fed up, but I can tell you anything you want to know about Ireland, as I know or can know anyone here. I might be of use. For years Cormac and I have had to cut ourselves off. No money to entertain. Reports about me spread womenwise,[294] but it is I who have to take the blame for anything going wrong in relation to a wife. This autumn Cormac and I will go out again to meet people again. Now he is growing up and he must grow up in the freedom of affection that is here.

About the time you were writing first to me and a few times subsequently I woke up in the night thinking I was in New Mexico and also thinking I was in an adobe house. I wandered through this flat talking aloud and did not turn on the electric light as there is no electric light in New Mexico. At last I found I was in this oblong-shaped flat and I was sad. I had been reading the books about New Mexico and Arizona written by the Federal Works Program people.[295] Badly written they were, but they had information so if you come across second hand copies, please let me know. And now your letter brings me back again. I really loved New Mexico deeply and I love it now, but I suppose Ireland whatever way it is is my destiny, less easy than the South West but here are my roots, my people and what I should write about. I had intended to do a book once on the hill towns of New Mexico: maybe by some miracle I might yet, but I have the material for a few books here in my notes. One on Clew Bay on which Burrishoole stands, and for which I have collected the folk lore, one on my wanderings from 1925–27, 1927–1936 and one on the folk lore of the West; but first I must get rid of the other books to be completed.

I had worked for 5 years on Irish sculpture. H. O'M. had helped. She took photographs and I did also: but when she left she took the photographs away with her and has several times tried to publish them. She worked as directed by me and she does not even know the names of many places where the sculpture comes from. It dates from about 700 to 1650: and it is really good, the sculpture. But sad to say since I was laid up in 1953 I cannot find my own reproductions. I have the negatives of mine; but I do not know how injured they are now. So there's another lost book.

I taught the 3 children for about a year when two of them were in bed.[296] Somewhat different from your training: but it included geography (which was of the University type), folk music (Irish) and sea shanties, music – classical, Beethoven, Mozart, early church music, Haydn, from my records as well as my hated subject maths. It was very nice of you to remember my schooling, which goodness knows I found very difficult to carry out with you three: but I wish I had been able to continue the training.

Please kindly send my love to Deirdre and Terence. I knew, of course, how unorganized your life was and also I knew that after I had taught you for close on a year, I would have given you three your freedom. The discipline was strict, but then I would have made you forget the discipline and reintegrate it as your own personal sense of responsibility. This aspect I was able to carry out in Burrishoole. Cormac has the key to the flat since he was 12 and he can come and go when he likes. One thing, Eithne, I ask you is not to mention to Étain anything about our life, Cormac and my own, as Helen abstracts the information easily, and I do now know what harm she can do with it. I mean harm to Cormac.

I am sorry about your voice, but my brother, Cecil, is a throat and nose specialist ENT[297] and he might do something about your nodes. Can them, I expect. Anyhow, if you like 'She moves through the Fair', there are endless other beautiful songs here. I find that Mongolian music is close to Irish music. Once upon a time I did a series of talks on oriental music here, for Pueblo Indian music had given me a strange understanding of Oriental music and I found certain aspects of Irish music so close to Korean and Mongolian that an Irish dancer could dance to their tunes. I never pursued the subject for unfortunately H. O'M. took the records away. Etain speaks Irish, so does Cathal, as they were at an Irish-speaking school. My poor Cormac I do not know about. He should speak his Irish so that it is a natural expression. But H.H. O'M. bought the head[298] of the Irish College, and so I will not now send Cormac to an Irish College: but if you come I'll bring you to the Aran Islands where most people speak Irish.

Now, Eithne, I can't correct this letter. My writing is bad. I have a bad right hand: but do come and stay here. After all, I wandered around in America without any security: but things happened: and one of the nicest things was your family, for I had been kicked out by my family because I believed in freedom, not freedom for my people, but as the Irish see it, freedom for all people. Thank you for writing. Poor Sylvia,[299] always she said blamed me for H.H.O'M. going away, but I had little to do with it, although I accept full responsibility: and so I have not written to Sylvia about what has happened to me. But maybe I will someday.

Now, please, my love to Deirdre and Terence. I am glad they are settled and I seem to know so many aspects of them. And my love to yourself. Come here and this is your house: my books are here built up again somewhat and really I know everyone in Ireland, especially if I have an added reason for going out to talk to anyone I wish to talk to.

With my love and affection,
Ernie

My best address is: 91 Iveragh Rd., Gaeltacht Park, Whitehall, Dublin as Chris Smith is a true friend of mine and he always forwards letters. This place has 150 flats and I seldom leave my address when I go away. (Finished on 12th July the Orange day in our Ulster to celebrate the time a Pope was on the side of the Orangemen.[300])

NO. 260 PAUL STRAND ARCHIVE, CCP, UNIVERSITY OF ARIZONA
Letter to Paul Strand

[Actual address: Inisheer,
Aran Islands, Co. Galway]
52 Mespil House,
Sussex Rd, Dublin
3 August 1955

Paul Strand,
'La Breardiere',
Rue de Marainvilliers,
Orgeval, Seine-et-Oise, France

Dear Paul,

Thank you for your letter. I hope that you and Hazel are well and that now she will feel more content when she thinks about her country house. This holidays I sent Cormac away to a friend[301] of mine thinking that he might learn a little French for she was French, and then later about the 14th of July I met him in Burrishoole. By that time he was able to cook omelettes and to make pancakes but the open turf fire was a difficult heat for him to prove his culinary skill – our Primus[302] was out of order so we had to use the open turf-fire.

About the end of June Helen O'Malley suddenly appeared with Etain and Cathal. She had taken her divorce some 3 years ago, but she had never sent me the divorce papers. I met her and the children, but as Cormac was away he remained away. She had numerous parties in Dublin with her friends and my friends, but I did not join them. Until her divorce was published in the Dublin papers,[303] I would not meet her in public as people would think the family was together again and that misconception might be dangerous for Cormac. The children were grown up nicely enough, as wealthy children, and Ireland was a dim background to them. Cathal goes to Harvard in the autumn and Étain goes to some dramatic school.[304] Helen wanted to remarry me, but I had had enough uncertainty and the break up of a family. I went to Burrishoole with them, said I would hand it over and she could do what she wished with it. She was to return to America to marry someone or other[305] as I wouldn't remarry her, and I wished her luck.

Then I was upset as I thought I was not doing my best to help the two children, but I could see no way out of it. Worry I must avoid as much as I can and life with Helen would mean endless worry and little touch with the two children. Also the fact that I saw them meant that for them their lives and values were now American of a certain type, and I felt I could not do anything for them.

The weather has been warm for this past month. There has been no rain, and from our point of weather it is unusual, able to suit any American. As it is unusual for us to have dry, warm weather, we throw everything aside except the pleasure of the warmth. Burrishoole, we cleaned out as well as we were able, cut out seaways to the piers for it is an old rule that the ways to the piers must be kept clear in case seamen in trouble ever wish to land.

Here now we are on the South Island of Aran, Inisheer. The sea is Mediterranean blue, the weather warm, and we sleep in the sun during the daytime. Cormac at last is glad to have someone else to cook for him. There is great peace in Aran and good sleeping. The people are easygoing enough, and they have amenities which help them to produce money, but the winter is hard when the bad weather sets in. Towards the end of the month we return to Burrishoole to clear out all our sea gear in the hope that my boat may be made ready for Cormac next year, and then if I have some one who could sail it I could use it at sea.

Turf comes in here daily in boats from 25 miles distant.[306] It is dear this year, and the land people are not willing to accept what they formerly accepted, dried rock fish in exchange for the turf. The islanders were offered bogs[307] on the mainland, but they seemed unwilling to work them there.

Anyhow we are content. Cormac hopes to be able to catch from the rock edges, and we intend to explore the shores for shell fish, but the island has deep water around most of it. Please give our love to Hazel who must be full of interest about her new house and garden.

What is Marie's[308] name? Cormac had her address with many others in his notebook, but when he sent his coat to be washed at school, the notebook did not come back. She sent him a postcard from the desert and he wishes to reply.

Affectionately,

Ernie

Letter to HHOM

52 *Mespil House,*
Sussex Rd, Dublin
1 September 1955

Mrs Helen Hooker O'Malley,
Hotel Metropolitan,
Rue Cambo,
Paris 1, France

Dear Helen,

I received your letter of July 25 last night, August 31st when I came back to the flat. The guanitor – superintendent although given addresses, Burrishoole for instance, did not forward any of my letters. I told Étain and Cathal that my most reliable address for forwarding stuff is 91 Iveragh Rd, Gaeltacht Park, Whitehall, Dublin, and so letters are forwarded from there, but no information is ever given there about me.

I thought you said you would come back with Étain to go down to Burrishoole neighborhood again about July 7th, but when I didn't hear from you Cormac stayed where he was until July 20th,[309] came to Burrishoole, left there July 30th. We went off for close on a month together so that there could be cooking done for us. We came back to Burrishoole, packed up much of our things, brought all out boat gear away and we dumped it Wednesday morning and then came up by train.[310] We had plenty of sun. Cormac learned some Irish for now I can't send him to a purely Irish-speaking school and I had good sun as had Cormac.

So the only time in which you could have seen a little of Cormac would have been July 25–30 or August 26–31st He returns to school on the 6th.[311] Anyhow I didn't see much of the children, but then I am not possessive, and they have grown up in a medium that has little to do with us here.

Now I have asked for the divorce proceedings and the result.[312] You were willing to give enough publicity to Cormac and I by High Court proceedings and you will have to face that bit of print for if you do not send it through the solicitor, I will have it published in the Irish papers when next you land. Then people will know the situation and Cormac will be safer. That is essential.

To see Cormac you have to make arrangements ahead with me[;] that is the holidays for us [and] as I have told you we plan our holidays ahead and being people with little money we keep our arranged programmes. The key I have here with me.[313] You can get it when you need it but not through a solicitor.

I am sorry for this long delay; the fortunes of war, as I might say, but the superintendent said he did not get my letter. I have again overdone it by too much climbing of stairs and carrying at Burrishoole so I will have to rest.

Ever yours,
Ernie

Letter to HHOM

52 *Mespil House, [Sussex Road, Dublin]*
3 *September 1955*

Mrs Helen Hooker O'Malley,
Lansdowne Hotel,[314] [Dublin]

Dear Helen,

Thank you for your letter of 2 September 1955. I received a letter from you dated July 25th I think, when I returned here on late Wednesday. The gainitor or janitor (can't spell it) was to have forwarded my letters but although I wrote him my address he said he did not receive any letter from me. I posted you a letter to Paris on July 20th.

Presently I am laid up. Head feeble enough. I did too much packing in Burrishoole and went up and down too much at the end. So I must lie in bed until I rest. Tomorrow, Sunday, I must see a friend of mine with a family somewhat out of town and this appointment I must keep. I will come back by bus in the evening and I can be at the Shelbourne at 7 having first rested here for an hour. I will bring Cormac and you bring whom you like, Mr Roelofs[315] or any others. If that is agreed to you need not reply. I can bring you the Burrishoole key. We did not clear out all, but we did a good deal and I am somewhat broke.

As I told you I have a short time to live. I require peace of some kind and I must avoid worry. Somehow Cormac and I will manage. Burrishoole was very beautiful. I know and it shakes our minds but runs down my heart from work. It has a sense of roots in an O'Malley sense.

Now you are an ant by nature. You must keep on doing things and when you do them the doing is the only thing that matters. Your activities must be always floodlighted. Sculpture could keep you quiet when you were away, but you did not like the country even to work at sculpture. You have too many wants and no sense of sacrifice to swap for what might be of real importance in your wants. You are, and I often told you this, an incipient pioneer. You need a forest to keep on cutting down and then you devote a certain time to your creative urge. People who really want to write or paint or do sculpture can live almost any place, provided that they are given time to work and reflect.

And so you must live your own life and I must live my life, a very much quieter life than I had ever hoped to live. Life with you could kill me quickly. You married the wrong person so I hope you can settle down now and do your work. I am writing this for I do not want you to keep on being disappointed. You broke up the family group, one half by your taking away Cathal, [who] was already directed into your channels, and so it must rest without any ill feeling, or attempts to talk to other people about the situation. This happens to be my country and it is here one son of mine must be brought up.

Ever yours,
Ernie

Letter to HHOM

52 Mespil House,
Sussex Rd, Dublin
5 September 1955

Mrs Helen Hooker O'Malley,
c/o Chase Manhattan Bank,[316]
44 Rue Cambron,
Paris, France

Dear Helen,

Thank you for the nice party;[317] both Cormac and I enjoyed it very much. It was unfortunate that I was tired or I would have seen more of the Presbyterian astronomer in the end. And it was nice to meet Dick and to talk to him after you had spoken about him.

I am sorry about your letter being held over in 52[318] for that did not give you any chance to see us. Also tonight when I came out of a movie *The Keys of the Kingdom*[319] Cormac said that he had not told you that I did not know you were outside in the car on Sunday. He was cooking the breakfast while I went into the bathroom, when I began to clean up after his bath. Only when he came out did he say you were outside in the car and when I saw the car I sent him out: but as breakfast was finished by me I had to call him in to eat.

You know my letter to Paris in answer to your delayed letter only showed my fear that Cormac would be stolen. It is ridiculous for that fear to persist, but it does. About Cormac meeting Étain. I do not want you to be more in debt but if it is possible Cormac and I could go out to the airport to meet her as that would save her time so please reply at once. It is unfortunate that the children do not meet, but I think in the future it would be more satisfactory if they and you would write to me of any such plans, for Cormac and I also have to plan ahead for the holidays and we have to keep the plans once they mean the booking of rooms.

You talked about Burrishoole at the dinner and about Chambers.[320] However I do not know what you intend to do, but if you want any help then please ask my advice: or I will not give help if you act on Chambers's advice and then consult me in the end having made decisions which I would think are unfortunate.

Also please do not hold up Cormac's money for I must continue at times to borrow money to pay schooling. This year he was to go to Ampleforth[321] in September, but as outstanding amounts up to August had not been refunded to me then I did not desire to risk the Ampleforth venture which would be expensive, £100 each term, and his to and from railway and boat fares.

Cormac will reply to your letters if you write a normal letter, not a love letter showing how much you always loved him and how you are separated. I do not moan to the other two children, but when they were taken away, part of my life never recovered and I was never again able to teach Cormac music, play it to him, and, only recently I began to read books to him. So if you can write a chatty letter he will be glad to answer it. I stayed in bed until this evening and now I think I am alright again. We have almost cleaned up the place but yet it is upset. If Cormac knows you do not leave until the 12th he will write.

Affectionately,
Ernie

NO. 264 EOM PAPERS NYU
Letter to Jean McGrail

52 Mespil House,
Sussex Rd, Dublin
6 September 1955

Miss Jean McGrail,
410 Park Avenue,
New York 22, NY, USA

Dear Jean,

I received your letter of July 31st on August 2nd when I returned here. I had sent my address to the 'ganitor' or janitor or whatever he is called, but as I could not spell 'ganitor' as we do not use the word, I addressed it 'superintendent'. He says he did not receive any letter from me. I expected a letter; then I thought you did not say much in your previous note save that you were in Montawk[322] and that the future as regards travel was indefinite. Then as I felt I would not see you for a long time I intended to ask you for a photograph.

I had a wonderful holiday in Inisheer. The sun of course was in the main responsible, but the people themselves were an added attraction. They were simple and unspoilt. The children I thought beautiful at times and as wild as rabbits as regards strangers. The young boys had a sense of lightness but there were few girls and if there were they stayed indoors. Sitting down, sleeping in the sun and attempting to read. I wish you have been there this time for you would not have needed a shawl but could have gone around in your lightest clothes.

No rain except the first night I landed when a fog came as I wandered towards the south shore with a painter[323] who was looking for rabbits. He lost his way in the mist though he had been coming to Aran for 30 years. There was another slash of rain another night at 9.30, but then I was indoors reading *Don Quixote*, marking my copy which I have since mislaid. Even yet the weather is warm in Dublin.

I will have to do something about the Aran steamboat.[324] They will not allow me to buy a drink on board when the curraghs come to the steamer. How really can you say goodbye to people who have been kind except by means of a drink. When going away we went to Kilronan and when I talked to the captain, he said I could not have more than half an hour. I wanted to see Jim O'Brien,[325] the doctor, get a drink, take some tea for there was not tea between the islands on the boat. I met Jim O'Brien, had a drink with him and then as I was slowly on the way down a woman came out and said 'Your tea is ready,' and when I began to go into the house an American who is at Oxford came in. We took the tea in a hurry, the siren went before the tea came in. We had a mile to go in ten minutes.

Anyhow there was a horse and car outside. I unloosed the rope, but the American pulled hard on the other rope which was tied to a gate. When I loosed it I tried to make the old shambles of a horse move and just when he was moving a man about a half mile down, rushed from a pub and tried to stop the horse. He was in a great rage. 'Where are you going? What are you doing?' 'Going to sea and trying to drive this apology for a horse!'

His anger went as he recognised me so off we pelted. The blessed captain had taken off the gangplank and was being held up by a few women from Inisheer. And so we caught the boat.

Now what are you going to do? It's September. And I haven't talked to you for a year. So please write and if you don't mind send me a photograph especially if you can train it to talk and I'll answer it back.

Affectionately,

Earnan

NO. 265 ESTATE OF JAMES JOHNSON SWEENEY
Letter to James Johnson Sweeney[326]

52 Mespil House,

Sussex Rd, Dublin

7 September 1955

[James John Sweeney,
120 East End Avenue,
New York]

Dear James,

Thank you and Laura very much for the nice visit we had with you. I have been in bed – too much packing in Burrishoole I expect for I had intended to write to you. Yesterday, I met Michael Scott and as my former attempt to start a committee to give an exhibition of Evie Hone's work had not been acted on, we then decided to form a committee. When we get going we can ask the Government to give us a spacious wall for the exhibition, perhaps the State Room in Dublin Castle. But first I think we should find out what pictures are available and what pictures, drawings or glass in England can be sent on loan. Your name was suggested as a member of the committee, and we would be very pleased if you would accept. I intend to see C.P. Curran tonight.

There are a considerable number of large cartoons, of monotypes and sketches which are available outside of those owned by people in Ireland, and I think that with the exception of glass, her most important contribution, we could present a fair outline of her life's work.

I had a book for you as I was sending books to friends before I left Burrishoole, but Cormac packed it in a case by mistake. Have you a copy of it: *Letters from the Irish Highlands*, 1835. It was written by a Blake and the writer's house was that which Oliver Gogarty later turned into a hotel.[327]

Sincerely yours,
Ernie O'Malley

NO. 266 EOM PAPERS NYU
Letter to Patricia McHugh

52 *Mespil House,*
[Sussex Road, Dublin]
Thursday ? [22 September 1955]

Mrs Patricia McHugh,
Glenart, Grove Avenue,
Blackrock, Dublin

Dear Patsy,

Thank you for your telephone call. I found the ballet nice enough Monday.[328] I go tonight and to matinee Saturday with Cormac, then to dinner and tonight's performance with Kevin. Cormac really likes the ballet. Also I must bring him to the Abbey on Saturday evenings as I have not been to the Abbey for about 4 years.

It is lovely the weather. Terrible in the Library.[329] Yesterday I wished I could meet you and go off to the mountains. But you have your house and I have the pen.

Now about Tuesday. What time please, Patricia? Coming from the ballet, Cormac and I danced up Grafton Street afterwards. It's wonderful how it lightens your heart, floats your feet and releases your mind. The décor itself is an example for children of the good elements of design and gives an approach to painting. A poor sparse audience at Wednesday matinee and it was hard on myself and I presume the ballet company!

Affectionately,
Earnan

Draft letter to The Editor, The Sunday Press

[Newton Hall,
Newton, nr Cambridge, England]
Late October 1955

[The Editor,[330]
The Sunday Press,
Burgh Quay, Dublin]

Dear Sir,

I notice that in Florry O'Donoghue's[331] serial in your issue of October 18, his remark 'Dr O'Hagan[332] had an interview with Ernie O'Malley in Dublin at which some proposals were put forward' become corrected in words under a photograph of mine to 'Ernie O'Malley ... put forward proposals ...' I presume that your captions are not edited by the writer of the story.

I met[333] Monsignor O'Hagan in Dublin and on the last day on which I met him he was to meet Dick Mulcahy[334] on that same day. I had no proposal to place before the Monsignor. Already when I first met Monsignor O'Hagan, I had written to the Chief of Staff[335] informing him of the Monsignor's intentions of meeting members of the Provisional Government,[336] and I asked Lynch's permission to again meet this intermediary. I had already written to Mountjoy to Liam Mellows,[337] who had been Quartermaster General, and to Rory O'Connor,[338] who had been Director of Engineering, pointing out that their ranks had been filled in the Headquarters Staff and that the Army Council alone could deal with a political situation.

There had been previous experience since July of some of our officers, mostly senior officers, unfortunately who had met Provisional Government officers without authority from our General Head Quarters. Their talks had been used against us by our opponents who had consistently allowed their officers to meet our officers hoping to find a weak link in our fighting spirit. Such meetings helped to increase insecurity and uncertainty amongst certain sections of the Republican Army who understood that talks between officers from opposing sides were genuine.

I suggested that Monsignor O'Hagan tell Dick Mulcahy these words: 'Call off your Murder Gang'[339] – I was referring to the shooting of prisoners in our particular command at the time, the Northern and Eastern Command[340]...

52 Mespil House,
Sussex Rd, Dublin
8 December 1955

[Paul Strand,
'La Breardiere', rue de Marainvilliers,
Orgeval, Seine-et-Oise, France]

Dear Paul,

I hope you and Hazel are very well. Cormac is here just now as the 8th is a feast day.[341] He is baking pancakes as I write. He works hard at school and does well there at exams, but as I was never good at examinations, I don't know what it means, and he plays his Rugby well.

I would have written to you over 5 weeks ago, but I waited for a reply to a letter of mine about South Uist. The British intend to make a rocket station of it, and they will clear out the islanders. This I learned through our Folklore Institute for they have gathered the folklore of the Western Islands, have paid the collectors, and have then handed over their material to the eastern Scots in Edinburgh. So I was hoping to get in touch with the Oxford University Press. There is a good Irishman there, and they, if the Rocket business is imminent, might do your book at Oxford. So that explains the delay.

I have been working in the Library to find out what happened in 1920 and 1921 here. I am tired out, I have to stand all day in the newspaper room, peer, hold my notebook in my hands to write, but now I have done a year and 2 months. It's slow work, but I have been glad to do it. Then I will have to do 1918, 1919 and up to March 1920. Then I will know the relationship of people to events. Just now I am at a low ebb, heart bad, trying to stop from work but having wound myself up to a high pitch so as to get this hard labour over me. I find it difficult to slow down again. It makes me realize how a business man pretends he lives by shutting off contact except with business. In this country, one gaol is used by prisoners for newspapers, or through newspapers for prisoners. They work on from 1750 in some of our bound newspapers, and, as a result, the work has helped them and made them become of use.

What about your book? Are you shut off again? They were really wonderful those Scottish photographs. I hope you can get them printed as it would relieve your mind, and help you in other work.

I have been publishing some episodes in a Sunday paper here, and I will be glad when they are over. So far I have received two solicitors' letters, but have managed to stave off trouble. When you have to deal with people who do not read much, are very proud and have never seen their background in print it means trouble. At the weekend I am nervous about the following Sunday, but I intend to finish the work, and if I am under fire it is alright so long as the ammunition does not come in solicitor form.

Weather mild now. Indeed since July it has been lovely and the mildness makes ease for the winter. I suppose we have the other side of the year February–March to come yet. A city is strange enough to me as you are unrelated to earth, sky or sea. Houses and people, well as long as there are people.

During what we call 'The Emergency', World War 2, two police were questioning a German. When they heard he had been married for 6 years, but had no children they felt sorry for him, 'Yes my wife, she is insupportable', said the German. 'I know what he means', said one of the Guards, 'she is unbearable'. 'That's not the word', said the Sergeant 'but it's close enough'. What the man intended to tell us was that she's impregnable.

With love to you both,
Ernie

NO. 269 EOM PAPERS NYU
Letter to Michael Sheehy

52 Mespil House,
Sussex Rd, Dublin
11 December 1955

[Michael Sheehy,
Rhode, Co. Offaly]

Dear Michael,

This is a bad time for me to write as I am in bed trying to keep quiet and not do anything; but I put off your letter as I thought I would be strong enough these days. I had a nice letter from you when I got out of Bricain's [*sic*]. That was in 1953. I replied to it in England, but I had no addresses with me, and my memory has been hopeless ever since I was laid up. I addressed the letter I think to Welsh Island for I think I knew Welsh Island when I was in Offaly in 1918.[342] The letter was returned to me. I wrote another address, but this also was sent back. It was only this week when I turned over an old notebook that I found your address.

I remained in England from I think August of 1953 until January 1954 when I found that I owed money for my 6 months in Bricain's. I had to come back to sell cattle which had been in Burrishoole for over a year. I lost £400 to £450 on the cattle as I had been cheated by a friend of mine near to Burrishoole, but as I was done up by the journey I returned to my English friends in Cambridge and got back to bed. Then I returned about March 1954, sold what land I had bought in Burrishoole, 30 acres and cleared my debt.[343] I spent two months in Ireland in Summer with Cormac in Burrishoole, but as Cormac had too much work there, and I was unable to help sufficiently, we went to Aran where we boarded.[344] I returned to England later in the year, and I remained until close to Easter 1955 when I went to Paris with Cormac to get him accustomed to the Left Bank, the French sense of life, painting and the importance of French. I then went back to Cambridge, but

I came over in the end of June, sent Cormac for 3 weeks in Ireland to a French friend[345] of mine in Ireland who taught him to cook omelettes and pancakes and variations on domestic cooking which I had been teaching him for years. He came to Burrishoole with me in mid July, then to Aran Inisheer for August. I remained on here then as I have been trying to work in the National Library until I cracked. I did get through a great deal of work before I had to get back to bed about 3 weeks ago. I get up at intervals for a theatre or cinema, but unfortunately work has to cease. That is what makes it hard. Now Cormac is here for Christmas. I took a flat in Dublin early last year so as to be near him and since Sept. 12 months he comes out every week end. We cook for each other and talk somewhat.

How is Biddens? I hope she has not had to get back to hens again. And how are the children. Please tell me about them: and about yourself.

Cormac works well at school and I think he now knows how to work, or he will in a year's time if he keeps up this pressure. I feel that if he then continues he will know how to use his time until he can go to a University. Anyhow he is very kind here. He washes, cooks, sweeps and looks after me on weekends for then I am very close to being flattened out before I face the next week.

I have, I am afraid, no touch with anyone now as I have no time much left, and unless I can see people they do not see me. I have no 'phone nor have I a car. Flat is too expensive.

When you have time please reply, and maybe I will be able to see you some time if you ever come to town.

It is sad that Cormac cannot meet your 'tree climbers'.[346]

It is quite late now, but Cormac promised to wake me and to bring this out to the late post.

Kindest regards to you, Biddens and the children and a nice family Christmas.

Ernie O'Malley

Christmas Card³⁴⁷ to Jean McGrail

[Newton Hall,
Newton, nr Cambridge, England
December 1955]

[Jean McGrail,
New York]

         'The Connaught Toast'
         Health and long life to you
         The woman of your choice to you
         Land without rent to you
         And death in Erin.

This toast from my old province. It's a Jack Yeats drawing. We have two privileges, as my grandmother often told me, the men, anyhow: permission to poke the fire and to speak twice.

I received a very battered and torn coloured picture of Ranchos de Taos.³⁴⁸ I lived very close to it once, and I felt I might have lived there, but my own people called too much and back I came. It is difficult to live in another country save you can serve it with heart and blood.

A Happy Christmas, Jean.

                Very affectionately,
                Earnan

Letter to Chester C. Davis³⁴⁹

52 Mespil House,
Sussex Rd, Dublin
29 December 1955

[Mr Chester Davis,
Simpson Thatcher & Bartlett,
120 Broadway, New York]

Dear Mr Davis,

Thank you for your letter of December 14th and for the cheque³⁵⁰ which you kindly forwarded. I now send you the year's list which you can check with the other lists I have forwarded. Already I think I sent you a bill for some items purchased between January 1955 and June 1955 but I cannot now find the notebook. Part of my heart trouble is that I forget a great many things and as I work harder than I normally should as if I were hardy and then when the crash comes forget everything almost until I am well again. Presently I have been laid up for 3 weeks. Cormac also is in bed this week and I look after him, but next week I must start again to work.

In this list I include (page 1) Cormac's 14 days at home this month, which should be deducted and his pocket money for 4 weeks of December.

The account there is Page 1	£126.19.0	
	128. 2.10	School
Page 2	91. 0.6	Travel
	74. 9. 9 ,,	
Page 3	16.15.7	Clothes, etc.
	21.15.1	
	27. 9.1	
	486.11.10	
Deductions from Page 1	11. 0. 0	
	475.11.10	

For the three items marked X I have no available bill. The dentist's bill I can have repeated next week, but the two Aran bills are on the wings of the wind. Aran people are not interested in receipts but as they like Cormac and myself they might send on their receipted accounts.

I had intended to buy a good gramophone for Cormac. My gramaphone was destroyed 3 years ago and although I have a big number of classical records they are now warped. I gave Cormac a radio set last year, but I have not a radio here. His is a portable set. He makes use of it – perhaps too much use as it takes from his reading. Now I can buy him a good gramophone and some long playing records and teach him about music as he listens.

Sincerely yours,
Ernie O'Malley

(1)   1955

Painting materials – Brushes – Paints – Sketching Paper	£5.0.0
Repairs to boat – Burrishoole – Painting job	5.10.0
Bicycle repairs, lamps, etc.	4.10.0
Laundry when he came from school and before he returns	
– 1954/55 Christmas returned 20/1 –	
3 weeks 195	0.12.0
General clean	0.10.0
1955 Easter, clean before	0.10.0
Summer clean up when he came out	0.15.0
before he returns to school	0.15.0
2 weeks at home	0.8.0
Food sent to school 4/. per week 31 weeks	6.4.0
Pocket money 5/0 per week 52 weeks	13.0.0
31 week ends from school, 62 days	46.10.0
At home Christmas 1954/1955, 20 days, returned 20/1/55	15.0.0

Summer at home – 15 days		11.5.0
Christmas at home 1955 – 14 days 18/12 – 31/12/55		10.10.0
(X) Dentist (can't find bill but will ask for another)		6.0.0
		126.19.0
School 7/2		60.6.4
25/6		8.12.6
15/9		53.11.0
Laundry		2.10.0
		3.3.0
		128.2.10

Another school bill came. I can't find it. Another to come early in January for incidental expenses – autumn – winter term.

(2) Holidays: Paris – Dublin		53.10.6
Spring Brought £20 with me in francs		10.0.0
Changed £57 in francs		27.10.0
		91.0.6
Summer: To Derry – Derry Westport		
Westport Belmullet (one month)		5.0.9
Board and teaching		30.6.6
Burrishoole Galway: Hotel, food, boat		
Galway – Aran		6.1.0
(X) Aran board, nearly a month		20.0.0
Lobsters		
Small boat – Curraghs for him – laundry		7.0.0
Aran – Burrishoole, hotel, food, etc.		2.3.6
Burrishoole Dublin		3.18.0
		74.9.9

I cannot now find accounts for clothes from 1/1/55 to the 7/6/55, but I know I bought some clothes.

(3)	7/6	Elvery's[351] Tennis Racket	2.17.0
	11/5	Our Boys Socks	0.11.0
		Handkerchiefs	0.6.6
		Brush	0.9.6
		Corduroy Trousers	2.19.6
		Gym Shoes	0.9.0
		Sponge Bag Face Cloth	0.5.9
		Buttons	0.3.6
	12/7	Overcoat (oil skin)	2.2.0
		Southwester hat	0.7.11
	12/7	Waterproof cloth coat	5.4.11
		Braces	0.12.6
		Belt	0.6.6
			16.15.7

6/9	Fountain pen		1.14.3
7/9	Braces		0.12.6
	Belt		0.6.6
25/10	Second hand books for school		0.12.6
	Dictionary		0.15.0
	Clothing, Switzers		12.10.9
	Batteries (wireless)		0.15.7
31/10	Fountain pen		1.12.6
18/10	Shoes light		2.13.9
27/10	Books		0.10.6
29/10	Bicycle oil		0.2.9
31/10	Tennis Table Bat		0.7.10
	Bicycle Lock		0.3.6
			21.15.11

(3–A)

17/11/55	Switzers	Wellingtons	1.17.1
		Pyjamas	3.10.0
		Winter pants (underclothes)	3.15.0
Ordered 22/11, paid 22/12 –		Kingstons[352] Suit	4.5.0
		Trousers (long)	1.12.0
		Pants (leather)	3.0.0
		Dressing gown	5.5.0
(X) Aran knitted sweater from Aran – came in October.			4.5.0
			27.9.1

NO. 272 EOM PAPERS NYU
Letter to Jean McGrail

52 Mespil House,
Sussex Rd, Dublin
12 February 1956

Miss Jean McGrail,
Excelsior Hotel Gallia,
Milano, Italy

Dear Jean,

Thank you kindly for your letter. Back in Italy in the cold. Please tell me of your intended movement so that I can work on my memory. I know all Italy, but it was a long time ago, when I was in love with *painting* as I am yet. I walked through all of North Italy also. Have you been to Bergamo? If you tell me of your plans then I can read my books on North Italy and keep more awake about the places you stop at, and also refresh my memory.

I am glad you like snow. I sing when snow falls and I walk round singing when snow is on the ground. I found also the Pueblo Indians sing when snow comes so I expect, as the Mexicans say, we Irish must have arrived in the American continent a very long time ago.

Isn't it strange? There I was in the palace outside Milan where nobody was interested in painting, and I spent a pleasant time eating and drinking, but my heart was sore that I did not see any painting or sculpture. The English are the devil to travel with. That's not true. I mean the English who do not bother about creative work. Yet I found their conversation dull enough as compared with people's talk in this country, but then as they say, we have nothing to do but talk.

This year there were a few plays here, *Waiting for Godot*,[353] Jean Anhouil's *The Lark*, a good rendition of the *Beaux Strategem*. The Abbey has lost its vitality, but there are smaller groups who are working hard and well. Two days ago I saw a composite exhibition of 30 years of painting as exhibited by a gallery here.[354] There were a few bits of sculpture by Oisin Kelly[355] and Hilary Heron,[356] which would have interested you. Very few sculptors in Ireland, very few painters, very few anything, indeed. Yet Sam Beckett is Irish, and he is regarded as being important in France as he writes in French. He is an aloof man whom I like a good deal, interested in painting and in music, but not much of a talker save, I expect, in Paris.

To-morrow the French ballet company[357] will be here for two weeks, so I intend to see as much as I can of them. Few people like the Japanese because they thought them too static, and I think the music was difficult. I liked their quietude and their music, but then I had been well trained by the American Indians to listen.

I had a card from you from Ranchos. It was a battered card. At the time I was reading D.H. Lawrence and the plateau was vivid enough in my mind. Why do you keep going away from America – to Italy, Japan, Italy. Northern New Mexico is a great country I found, satisfying and much to teach. Anyhow I could always go to Italy. Once I spent a year walking through it. I noticed that one of Lawrence's earlier books suddenly became alive, *The Lost Girl*,[358] where he brought the girl to Italy, and I think that affection lingered, but Lawrence too often turned against the country he loved, but later turned again to it.

Now goodbye. I am trying to work hard but I have had a continuous cold for six weeks or longer and it lays me up. I should not be here in winter. Please write now.

Affectionately,

Earnan

One thing, please take note of any books on early Italian sculpture pre-Romanesque, Romanesque with names of publishers, as they are hard to find. I have a few and I will let you have the names.

Letter to Jean McGrail

c/o P. Strand,
La Briardière,
Montamet-Orgeval,
Seine-et-Oise, France
5 March 1956

Miss Jean McGrail,
Grand Hotel,
Roma, Italia

Dear Jean,

I am somewhat nearer as you can see, some hundreds of miles, but my efficiency evaporated when it came to travel. I realized when I was in Paris that my
letter to you rests on my mantelpiece in Dublin over a compressed turf fire. At any
rate you have kept in touch with the cold, although you may have had a few warm
days a week ago. Then I was able to sit in the sun outdoors. Again came down
with the cold.

Duffle coats are fashionable now in Paris, but blue grey handsome more attractive than khaki: the children dressing more like American children on the south
bank, pants, bright shirts, knitted hatlets to the photograph you have when you are
both in this kit. At once I feel lively, walking more, resting less. Yet it is no use to
come from damp cold to damp cold. Please enclose a small piece of sun when you
write: open your envelope, let the sun drop in for a while and I will let it out again.
To-day out in the country with friends I can sit at ease. An hotel is to me an hotel,
never the sense of ease of a house. I was reading a small book on the American civil
war, hoping to finish it before I returned. John Ford is helping to make 3 small Irish
pictures.[359] Lord Killanin is a kind of producer, but Ford is the real producer. They
were to have told me, Killanin and Scott,[360] the architect, but they didn't. Then Ford
arrives, puffs and blows, offers me a job, which I refuse as I had engaged a room
in a French hotel and there were friends outside Paris who expected me to stay for
awhile. So there you are. Ford annoyed. I who badly need the money, quite indifferent. I work, I suppose, for myself, but if you hire me, you give me some little
time: only twice in the year would I be absent, Spring in Paris: summer in West of
Ireland. And so I'll never make enough to leave Ireland for warmth. I think I will
not again go to France except in late Spring when it is warm or late autumn.

Winter wears me down. This year I had made arrangements for an exhibition
of Evie Hone's work for 1957 in the Aula Maxima in the University.[361] The Aula
granted for 2 months, cartoons 40 feet high of Eton Windows and other large
cartoons available or ready to borrow, 5 full windows to be taken out of Irish
churches: gouache, oil, drawings of Irish sculpture, small glass panels, all within
our reaches. Then the Arts Council begins to pound. I was the Chairman, Scotts
– Michael and Pat,[362] two fine architects on the committee for the arrangements
and décor. Now, blast them; they want to include other glass which is not good,

Clarke[363] and others, but that is only an attempt to block. Glass costs close on £400 a window to install in an exhibition room. They were to grant us £2,000 and we were to raise £2,000. Now they will not give us the money unless we put in what I consider bad glass, bad drawings. Evie's cartoons were actually art works. She is the only glass worker I know of who made cartoons with infinite care until they were creative works. On the aeroplane I met the president[364] of the Arts Council. He suggested a book on Irish glass instead. 'So take 5 years', I said, 'maybe with another Arts Council.' And what I didn't add – 'with only two people who are someway interested in art as a living thing like life and love'. So goodbye the exhibition.[365]

Sorry to write about it, but Evie Hone was the best glass worker in Western Europe. Her importance will increase in time, but it takes time to have an Arts Council which has vitality and another thing, it was my idea not theirs and then millstones began to grind. However the Committee was good, but it was not a working committee. I would have had to change it into sub-committees of workers later on. It was good to meet people as a group whose judgment was sound and who hoped for success.

This ink doesn't work, or my pen. It drags and drags. Perhaps that is well. If I write freely no one could read my scratches. I am trying to write slowly. Tell me this. How about your sculpture? Do you sketch when abroad or handle any material? This cold weather with a good stove on hand would occupy you. Now it hails outside. Great shoots in this lovely house, but I expected snow two days ago in Paris and my expectations were not met with my approval. Is it cold in Rome and what are you doing? If you knew the trattorias to which the country people go on fair days or business days and followed them, you could drink good Falernian around Rome, but I'm afraid you couldn't go by yourself. You should go to Sicily if you can for the Spring. Once I walked through Sicily in Spring. It was warm. I liked the Sicilians and they were very nice to me.

To-day I wear an Aran sweater which arrived the day before I left Ireland. I made the girl, I think she is a Joyce, knit a rolled collar on it. I feel beautifully warm as I write. This is the first time I have worn the new sweater. What did you do with your black shawl? Have you got it in Rome?

Oh dear. Letter writing is a strange form of communication. I would prefer to sit and talk to you, but unless you use your fairy power it is not so easy. Two days ago I met my brother[366] on the street in Paris. He was to have stayed for a week, but as I was thinking hard of him he appeared ready to leave next day. He seemed depressed and I suggested drink. We went to one of his bars, 'Chez Harry',[367] began on Irish whiskey and then he wanted Pernod. Pernod means nothing to me in effect, but I like the taste of easy-going 'Anis'. I brought him back to his hotel. The Pernod has some effect on him, it seems.

Have you read any of the Gregory letters?[368] A bad book I am afraid. Too much left out. I had a copy for you. Please note any books on Romanesque Sculpture, if you have time in Paris, name of editor, writer or publisher and please note Italian price …

Letter to Etain O'Malley

52 Mespil House,
Sussex Rd, Dublin
13 March 1956

Étain O'Malley,[369]
The Madeira School,
Fairfax Co., Virginia, USA

Dearest Étain,

Thank you for your letter. Any sign of Spring in Virginia? To-day here was a kind of a Spring day and I was excited by the nice air, by the bare trees in Stephen's Green and a kind of warmth in the air. Last week Cormac said to me 'what happens in Spring'? He had to write a composition so I brought him again back to Burrishoole to think over birds, ploughing, potatoes. Even St Patrick's Day, the 17th, is the symbol of a Pagan spring day which was then used for ceremonial. Even yet the girls get new dresses for Patrick's Day: with us at Burrishoole sea weed had to be gathered, and potatoes planted by that day. The Pagan Spring Festival began.

This was a difficult winter here. I held on as best I could on account of Cormac, but several times I nearly became a headstone. I don't want a Celtic Cross. I wish to have a good slab of granite over me, and face me to the East, towards the old British, for you were once buried in Ireland facing your enemies. Indeed they are no longer my enemies. Each man finds his enemies in himself. I had hoped to get away to the Sun but that seems insoluble as Cormac has to be brought up. Now he can type as he has been copying a series of exercises during the winter. I was hoping he could type some of my manuscripts for here they lie in the meantime. I was asked by the architects in the University[370] to lecture on Irish sculpture. I was very ill, but as I was worried about the lecture, having promised it, I worked in the night time getting out of bed every now and then to take a note. The young architects cheered me for a long time. I felt sorry for them for they told me they had nobody to talk to them about the things they were interested in. I wish I could organise lectures for them.

I am glad you are interested in history. It is a hard, long road, but maybe you have the guts. I don't know what America has done to you but scholarship is best if you are a scholar and have been trained to a method of work.

I had a very bad January, mid-January to the end of February, and I did not feel I could write to you. However, Spring is round about. Someday Cormac and I must take a bus and go away from here to the mountains if we can get a bus.

With my love X X XO XO,
Ernie

What kind is the country near you?

Letter to Jean McGrail

52 *Mespil House,*
Sussex Rd, Dublin
27 *May 1956*

Miss Jean McGrail,
410 *Park Avenue,*
New York 22, NY, USA

Dear Jean,

I had best get this letter off now, this 27th of May. I received two letters, both of them held up as I did not leave my address with the janitor before I left Dublin. Then since I returned I somehow could not write. I was upset about a few things including my writing, and I felt such a damn fool that I began again to work in the Library. That left me tired at nights, too tired to write letters, as I thought. That is no excuse, however, as there is always time to write letters, so please forgive the stupidity.

I went off at once to Ford as soon as I had tried to tidy up my papers. That meant work in Limerick city and in Kilkee, beside the western sea. I was Ford's assistant, I understand. I like Ford. He is difficult to work with and fun at times as he has a cyclonic temper, but as he carries all the burden of thought, he can stand inefficiency patiently enough before he explodes. In that he is like my former self, who learned to take life easier. My function, among others, seemed to be to get him up in the morning, stay by him until he was on the set, smooth him down and break the storm if it threatened to break. He is a fine worker, but as he works almost by intuition you never know what he intends to do, what he wants to do and so you cannot help him as you would if he would open his grim mouth. I find that difficult to be intuitive about intuition. Also I expect being too proud, I find it hard to be bawled out when I am not in error. It seems futile at times, and I stiffen and feel as if I could have thrown him under the railway engine. That happened once. I clicked my heels sharply to attention, turned around, walked away for about 100 yards. Then I thought: 'Don't be a damn fool, he's worried; go back.' Back I went. 'I'm sorry, my temper is bad.' 'So is mine,' he said, 'but I expect people to take it.' 'As you know I don't at times.' He does everything from A to Z, and it must be agony for him to work with stupid or inefficient people, to find that he cannot put over sufficiently well what he intends the words should convey. I hope the three short movies will be a success as they will be the first Irish movies.[371]

What are you going to do now for an apartment. It is very difficult to find a place which suits and is convenient to parts of town as your one was. I think you had better take an apartment in Dublin, while they are still to be had. Mine is alright in winter perhaps: cold but a fire keeps my work room comfortable; but in warm weather it is too warm betimes, and then cold at other intervals. The truth is I miss the country, the sea near by and above all the sense of walking out from the house to the sea or to the woods. I had better forget about the country, I think, and begin to work, but from now on I get restless.

Yesterday, remembering you, I went to see an exhibition of sculpture in the Municipal Gallery.[372] It was well I did as it closed to-day. Angela Antrim,[373] Irene Broe,[374] John Haugh,[375] Trevor Cox,[376] Oisin Kelly,[377] Desmond Broe:[378] these pleased me. There were no photographs in the Catalogue so it would not be of any use to you. This is a yearly exhibition and in time it will improve. Angela Antrim is the Countess of Antrim. I must call to see some of them as I have not talked to a sculptor for some time now.

Have you Mary Carbery's *The Farm by Loug Gur*, published 1937. If you haven't, I will send it to you. It is a good book, well written. Maybe you will like it as much as I liked it. Is there any book you particularly wish to have? I think you should have read *Poets and Dreamers* by Lady Gregory. I like it, but maybe because it deals with Raftery[379] and people in my province, Connaught. Even so, I know it is a good book. I can send it to you if you would read it.

The end of April from 13th to 30th was fine weather. We saved in all close on two weeks while working due to good weather. In Limerick the fire brigade had to be brought out to make rain and on the last night when the Spanish Arch at Galway had to be repeated in Kilkee it began to rain at 8 in the evening. That was miraculous, the dry spell, and I became very sun burned and red from the sun, which has now turned to brown.

This month has been good also. A few days ago hail, but on the 26th rich, warm sun. Maybe that is our summer, but we have hopes for later on. I had best stop now as I should post this letter to-night. There is a special post box not so far away which takes letters at 11.30 P.M. It is the only post box in Dublin I think which keeps late hours. It is used by the specialists[380] in and around Fitzwilliam Square. So goodbye now. I hope you find a place to suit you, but that is always a difficult proposition.

Affectionately,

Earnán

I meant to tell you what the Limerick woman said to me but I will next time.

52 *Mespil House,*
Sussex Rd, Dublin
12 June 1956

Miss Jean McGrail,
410 Park Avenue,
New York 22, NY, USA

My dear Jean,[381]

Thank you for your letter. I was waiting for the photographs to arrive before I wrote to you but writing often is like poetry. You remember a line of W.B. Yeats: 'Anything can keep me from this craft of verse'.[382] First then I did not reply promptly to the Secretary of the Institute of Sculptors, Ireland.[383] Then I had not an envelope to suit his photographs. That of course meant that I would stop work earlier and buy a special envelope. Then the photographs from my point of view were an insult. I am sorry that a sculptor, who is the secretary, should be so ignorant as to send me such a reject. Next I was worried about the Olmecs around Veracruz as I was puzzling over Mexican sculpture. I had remembered the wrong name, for though I was thinking in terms of the Olmecs who were evidently Mayans, what I was really worrying about was the Totomacs. Have you ever seen any Totomac sculpture? Well even if you have look again. Maybe in the New York Museum or whatever it is. Here I have to look for a catalogue of my own concerning art books to find out what I am writing about. I find the word is Metropolitan. It shows what my memory is like now.

I expect due perhaps to too much poring over newspapers in the Library, searching for an aspect of truth with regard to certain years, but also an excuse for not writing. Perhaps when I finish in the evening there is also a debate as to whether I will work for myself or not or whether I will first lie down to read. If I read I will fall asleep and if I sleep I will persuade myself I am too tired to cook. So you can see letters are difficult enough to write. Anyhow as this question brings up the question of the Totomacs, please, see if there is any work of theirs in the Metropolitan, and if not you will find some, perhaps, if and when you go to Harvard in the Fogg[384] and if there isn't any please ask Sylvanus Morley[385] why there isn't any. Of course he will say they are not Mayans, I expect.

I have been reading a book by Eric Thompson[386] on the Mayans and to me it seems a sensible book. I wish he had included a few more maps and had regrouped his city states. Sculpture is as good a way as any of dating architecture, but there are very few Mayan carvings that interest me, and as they are lightly cut they need extra care in their photographing. I am sorry I did not wander around Vera Cruz when I was in Mexico for the Totomacs had grace, ease and a sense of the aesthetics but I do not think much of their work has been discussed.

I read what I consider a good book by Alan Gheerbrant, *The Impossible Adventure*. That is the correct way to voyage in unexplored and hostile territories, without arms, but with Mozart records. Reading it in the evening certainly made me postpone cooking for myself. I find it difficult to bother too much about food in the summer time. Winter is a more settled period, but then a more difficult one on account of the cold and the draughts. Now again it is cold. I have been waiting for a fine day to sit in St Stephens' Green in a deck chair. On the 1st of June I sat there in the morning facing the circle of flowers. I do not think I know as lovely a series of flower beds, and as I tried to read a book I made a vow that I would sit there again the next fine day, but when the next good day came I said 'I'll work first and go there in the evening.' But I continued to work putting up the excuse that it was always difficult to find a place in the evening. That is true enough. The correct way to get a seat is to appear at 10 o'clock and again at 2.30 when some of the office girls who must rush their meal sink into a chair for close on an hour.

Limerick, I almost forgot. We had been making rain there by using the fire brigade to hose the Castle built by King John.[387] I was getting the crowd who were praying to move but without looking at the camera. During a halt I had a chat with a group of Limerick women. 'It's a great wonder this, the making of rain,' said one, 'and I'm glad to be in it.' 'I'm sure you could make trouble yourself,' I said to one of them, a fine hardy looking woman. 'Indeed and I could *agradh*,[388] come in here under my shawl.' The remark of the little girl at Kilkee railway station. The children were sitting on top of the wall. Every now and again they burst into talk, although whenever I came down – put my fingers on my lips, they kept quiet. During one stretch of talk Ford came down. 'Oh keep quiet,' he ordered in a loud voice. The children laughed but continued to talk. 'KEEP QUIE TE,' I SAID. The children were frozen by the shout. One girl of about 9 said, 'I think you are very rude,' and the others laughed suddenly.

A House in the Cevennes by Jeanne Saleil I read in the St Stephens' Green. Well written, with all the understanding of people with whom one lives and understands.

Affectionately,
Earnan

NO. 277 EOM PAPERS NYU
Letter to HHOM

52 Mespil House,
Sussex Rd, Dublin
10 July 1956

Mrs Hooker O'Malley,
115 East 67th Street,
New York 21, NY, USA

Dear Helen,
    We don't live here, but we use up the notepaper when we can.[389] I found a letter in the bank when I went there on July 9th. It had been posted on May 20th but I

had forgotten to tell the bank to forward my letters. People in the letter would like to know if Burrishoole is for sale or if it could be 'let' on a long repairing lease. They are interested in the fishing. I do not intend to reply to them as I have nothing to say, but I can send you on their address.

Summer is almost here; not quite as it is cold now and I keep up my fire.

There is a matter you could settle; that is, of course, if you wish to; but you may have your own reasons for not signing. Mr Davis was anxious that you should sign for monies spent on Cormac a few times a year. I did not ask him to make this arrangement, but I think his reason was that 'he' knows I have not money. So do you. The money sent for Cormac, I take it, is Cormac's money. Banks here do not lend money. At least my bank does not. There is a slow financial crash looming and we are getting it here. As my last account was not forwarded here some of it dealing with last year, I did not send on any other accounts.

I intend to revise by the end of this month Cormac's expenditure and I will cut it down as drastically as I can. I have already cut mine since Easter.

I hope you are well and that you are enjoying life. We, as we say, in Ireland, are alright.

Affectionately,
Ernie

NO. 278 EOM PAPERS NYU
Letter to Chester Davis

52 Mespil House,
Sussex Rd, Dublin
27 July 1956

[Mr Chester Davis,
Simpson Thatcher & Bartlett,
New York]

Dear Mr Davis,

I am forwarding an account note of monies used up to April 30, 1956. I have not had a reply from you since January 12th, 1956. You then said you had received my letter of December 29th, 1955. Indeed at times I thought you had not received that letter, but I found your letter of January 12th a few days ago.

Some weeks ago I wrote to Mrs O'Malley telling her I thought she should forward money more regularly and that as I had already cut down on my expenses I would have to do the same with Cormac's note expenses, but I am reluctant to do that. Also I mentioned that she may have a reason for not forwarding the money and that I am unaware of the reason. It is not a subject I care to write about.

If I do not hear from you by August 9th, will you kindly hold over a reply until you again hear from me. Could you kindly return wireless licence. I was fined because I had not registered Cormac's receiving set which was run on electric batteries and which, I thought, was a toy, although an expensive toy.

I have not the bill for Hotel de Lutece for 4th until the 17th.[390] It is somewhere among my papers but my papers pile up or I burn them at intervals. Although we stayed with friends for a while we kept our hotel rooms.

Your last letter was torn open when I received it so I intend to register my letters with accounts in future.

Sincerely yours,
Ernest O'Malley

NO. 279 EOM PAPERS NYU
Letter to Michael Sheehy

Mater Private Hospital, Room 24,
30 Eccles Street, [Dublin]
20 September 1956

[Michael Sheehy,
Rhode, Co. Offaly]

Dear Michael,

I hope the family is very well and that Biddens has not got back to chickens again. In August some date about 13th the janitor left in a note to say a 'Jimmy Sheehy' had called and would call about 12 the following day. Cormac and I went out early, but we came in about 11 a.m. I wondered who the 'Jimmy' was. Later Cormac said it might be yourself. Was it? If you ever come again drop a note into 52. At about 2 that day we caught a train for Galway.

I have been laid up for close on a month: heart bad, a new phase of it. It's hard to look after oneself when the heart is bad. I should be out in a week. If you ever come to Dublin please look me up, I may have to go to England when I get out.

Ever yours,
Ernie O'Malley

Letter to Paul Strand

[Actual address: Mater Private Hospital, Room 24,
30 Eccles Street, Dublin]
52 Mespil House,
Sussex Rd, Dublin
26 September 1956

[Paul Strand,
'La Breardiere',
rue de Marainvilliers,
Orgeval, Seine-et-Oise, France]

Dear Paul,

I hope you and Hazel are very well, and that she has reduced the garden to its proper degree of order, although I am sure your summer was bad, especially for you and your camera. I was not well for a considerable time dating from the middle of May. I missed Cormac, and as I, for his safety, had cut myself off, I did not see people, and my treadmill work in the Library uses up my time and energy. It is really too difficult as I do not take off sufficient time to cook properly, and as I am by myself cooking is not much fun. However, I may grow up with regard to work and cooking.

Despite rain and storm threats Cormac and I went off to Aran in August. As usual we were able to trap sun, and we both became burned. Cormac does not lie out in the sun nor does he search for it. He seldom went out in a curragh, but I know he enjoyed it. We stayed in a house run by a widow. The double bed evidently thought it was a replica of the Alps, yet, we slept and in the end knowing I was very cold, she put a few fires in the dining room for me. Cormac was picking up Irish from a group of island boys. Our food was uneventful, but the people are nice, and we like them. Our room had three nails on the back of a door for clothes, but using it as I would a prison cell we found everything adequate.

The remoteness from a sense of time and from the passage of time is the most extraordinary thing about Aran. It is sad to see a people wither away when the fish leave them, or when they depend too much upon government subsidies. Most of the young people leave the islands.

When I returned I found the flat flooded, kitchen, bathroom the passage and two and a half rooms. The upstairs tenants had thrown tealeaves into the sinks and as they became clogged water flooded up into the bath, handbasin and sink. The janitor helped to get rid of the water, but rugs and carpets had to be put outside. Some books were damaged and paintings left on the floor wetted. Cormac worked away, but I expect I got a cold, then flu. Kevin had left for Stockholm to preside at a heart conference the day my heart began to give trouble as I could not breathe, but Cormac saw a Greek doctor married to an Irish actress whom I met with John Ford on the Irish film.[391] They brought me away to their house, and after two weeks I phoned Kevin's doctor on the heart clinic. He insisted on my coming to hospital at once. The heart rhythm is irregular. I have to take something regularly to slow down the heart and will probably have to continue taking a drug. Kevin does not return until the 9th October as he has to go to Madrid. I am in Kevin's hospital, the 'Mater Misericordiae'. Everyone is very kind to me. As soon as I took the drug my laboured breathing ceased, and here I am in bed beginning to work to day at some of my notebooks after a week in steady luxury: meals without effort as with Hazel. I wrote to Mrs Walston to know if I could go over to lie up, but she will be here on October 1st, so I can have a talk with her.

Cormac went over[392] on September 20th, and he left his love with me for Hazel and yourself. He works hard enough when in the flat. I was packing up some books, or rather he was packing up some books for sale, but I expect I did shift too many of them. He has grown a good deal.

That is my story, Paul, sorry for the personal explanation. I expect I will have to be careful when I get out of this place.

> With love to you and Hazel and good luck to the garden,
> Ernie

Kindly remember me to the family on the hill, to Barbara and to Marion.[393]

NO. 281 EOM PAPERS NYU
Letter to Jean McGrail

[52 Mespil House,
Sussex Road, Dublin]
16 October 1956

[Miss Jean McGrail,
410 Park Avenue,
New York 22]

My dear Jean,

Thank you very much for your two letters. I lay in hospital and I kept quiet, but when I came out I caught a cold at once and unless my brother[394] takes me out to his flat I cannot eat.

I go to England on Saturday and then I will lie up for some time as they will keep me in bed. I am sorry for this poor note but I will write when I settle down in Newton where I was previously.

I think I was fool enough to help to pack some books which I wanted to sell and though Cormac did all the work I am sure I did more than I should have done. I was threatened with hospital last night by my brother if I did not remain in bed here.

I sympathise with your removal of things. They just grow and when one wants to get rid of them, one of them fatuous and all as they seem in memory seems to be as important as the thing really worth while. Now when my books are packed the shop wishes to examine them so I hope he has X-ray eyes. They will now have to remain, I am afraid, until I return.

I will write as soon as I have settled into an English bed. Thank you very much for writing.

Very affectionately,
Earnan

NO. 282 EOM PAPERS NYU
Letter to Jean McGrail

[Stationery of] Newton Hall,
Newton, Nr Cambridge, [England]
4 November 1956

Miss Jean McGrail,
1 Sutton Place South, 6D,
New York 22, NY, USA

Dear Jean,

Thank you for your letter which came here. I can see the new flat, the sense of hopelessness of ever being able to get done what you want done, and the accumulations piling up. In a way people should change their rooms say once every four years, move around their paintings at least once a year, and get rid of what might be considered unimportant material about every two years. You should see my flat. Books which should have been sold over 8 years ago suddenly turned up without explanation. I thought they had been sold. Then another pile in cardboard boxes when I was exhausted listing the first lots. I expect it was that work which injured my heart. And in the end when a man did come from a shop to examine the books, he wanted to empty them over the floors and tables, whereas they had been packed so that he could take them to his shop and inspect them there. And so the books remain until I return.

I hope by this you have settled down in New York with the climate of energy [and] your unstinted energy work is not a problem. My books have to make my rooms, but there are too many of them for the size of the flat, and now far too many paintings. Had you anything of our bad summer and the bad western European summer? It produced a bad harvest and a starving need of sun.

This is an empty house. All the children away at school, the elders in Bermuda and France. And so I am between two stools. I know the staff well but their cooking is 'cook to death', which might have been alright for cannibals and this I doubt very much. The butler thinks he is in charge, the kitchen staff cook only when the family is home, cook properly I mean, but I am finding my way slowly as the old staff know me and like me. It's a funny situation but Mr Walston returns to-morrow and then food will improve.

I have not been out of bed since I came here. It is cold, the heat, steam-heat, has not been turned on so I am not inclined to walk along my corridor to visit other empty rooms. I read and I know I am improving for now I can drop the *Cosmopolitan* magazine and read a book. I think I will keep quiet for another month or so until Mrs Walston comes home for I feel I must keep quiet in bed. I brought over a pile of work to begin on but that must wait for another week or so.

The Marchese Patrizi called suddenly. He had left his son, aged 19, at Cambridge. He had just returned from North America where he had been delighted at the frankness of Americans as compared with Europeans: It is a good thing to be free from fear of oneself, as are most Europeans. Now I must end as it is Sunday and the chief maid will, I hope, post this. I hope your mother feels better and that the flat seems more liveable ok as is, but I would not like to have been there these past few weeks.

Affectionately yours,
Earnán

NO. 283 EOM PAPERS NYU
Letter to Cathal O'Malley

c/o K. Malley, Esq. M.D.,
57 Merrion Sq, Dublin
14 February 1957

Please excuse this delay.
[Cathal O'Malley,
Harvard University,
Cambridge, Massachusetts, USA]

Dear Cathal,

Thank you for your letter and for your book, both of which arrived when I was in a Dublin hospital. I had read a good deal of MacLeish[395] and I have his earlier works which I intended to sell if I get fit enough to go to the flat and get help to lie in bed there while someone looks after me, and someone helps with the books. Kevin will not allow me to stay in the flat by myself. I cannot afford a maid so it seems I must sell as many books as I can and put the others someplace else. If you remember I did that when we left Whitebeam.[396] My books are yet in one house, but a good number have disappeared.

I should be soon out of hospital then I will be under a nurse's care for 3 weeks or so. Maybe if I feel better I may get Winnie to stay with me in the flat for a few weeks until books are got rid of, yet as a student I need a lot of books. Kevin is very kind and thorough, but I do not get any stronger.

MacLeish is indeed easy to read so I have had a very enjoyable time going through this book.

I do not know what Iveragh address you made use of: Christopher Smith, 91 Iveragh Rd, Gaeltacht Park, Whitehall, Dublin. Christy is an old and a poor friend of mine and I have often been there for weeks at a time ill 5 or 6 years ago for both himself and his wife go out to work every day.

Marion O'Rahilly and Eoghain have just been in to see me. They seem to be very busy for they left in a few minutes.

I am sure the variety show[397] will give you a good deal of fun and bring you to less known places. We don't seem now to produce playwrights. I didn't think much of Brendan Behan's play.[398] It would have needed a good deal more of work on it. The English don't know what to make of us half the time because they are so confused and dulled by the fact that for several hundred years they thought we were English.

With love,
Ernie

Afterword
On Republican Reading

DAVID LLOYD

Jack B. Yeats' haunting painting, *The Funeral of Harry Boland* (1922), is unusual in his oeuvre. Its uncharacteristic quality is not due to its explicitly political theme, commemorating the funeral of the anti-Treaty republican who was murdered by Free State forces while seeking to escape arrest, for it belongs among a number of such paintings, sympathetic to Irish nationalism and to the republican struggle, which Yeats produced throughout his life.[1] It is, rather, unusual for its formal qualities. Yeats' paintings are generally composed around a strong triangle converging at a vanishing point away from the picture plane, occasionally with such triangles overlapping one another. *The Funeral of Harry Boland*, however, is marked by a line of vertical forms – mourners, gravestones, trees – that virtually bisects the painting horizontally, and these elements are united by the lower portion of a round tower that amplifies the vertical thrust of the painting and dominates the centre. Separated from it by the line of mourners, and balancing it as the visual centre of the painting, is the wreath-covered grave of Boland that forms a visually peculiar horizontal void among the standing mourners. It succeeds in emphasizing the isolation of a figure generally identified as Kevin O'Higgins, Free State Minister of Justice, from the other mourners, and also interrupts what might otherwise have been the left side of a dark triangle running from the black-clad mourners centre-left through a small group of similarly dark figures on the far side of the grave and then culminating in the tree-shadowed upright of an obelisk or monument to the right of the round tower. At this point, that dark line might have met the corresponding line running from O'Higgins through another group of dark mourners, completing the visual triangle that should unify the composition. It is as if the absence of Boland in death prevents the completion of his commemoration, making a rupture of memorial and leaving a void at the heart of the work. That void, indeed, in a kind of visual pun, is re-echoed through the hollow forms of the wreaths laid on the grave and borne by the mourners who face the viewer.

The presence of the Free State's first Minister of Justice, who presided over the executions carried out as reprisals for republican actions during the civil war, and who was therefore responsible for the elimination of many of the movement's foremost leaders and intellectuals, may suggest that this void constitutes a challenge to the legitimacy of the state that his legally sanctioned violence was designed to establish. The moment of commemoration fails to represent the consolidation of the new state, laying to rest the conflicts out of which it was forged, but shelters instead an absence at its core. As Nicholas Allen has argued in his recent *Modernism, Ireland and Civil War,* the persistent failure of the republic to be realized remains as a kind of absent centre in Irish culture even as the surviving figures who had stood most clearly for it either withdrew much of their commitment or felt themselves marginalized in the culturally conservative Free State. Yet, politically and institutionally marginalized as they may have been, or may have felt themselves to be, republican intellectuals and artists maintained a constant critique of the state. Far from being the atavistic and backward-looking caricature of recent revisionist writings, republican thinking was often associated with the most aesthetically advanced and culturally progressive work of post-independence Ireland and with the ongoing project of decolonization. Yeats, the leading and probably the most restlessly experimental of twentieth-century Irish painters, may be one prime instance of this tendency, such that Samuel Beckett, in his review of MacGreevy's book, foregrounded Yeats' commonalities with the great European painters even as he balked at MacGreevy's specifically spiritual and expressive version of nationalism.

Certainly Ernie O'Malley, a friend of all three of the above, may be considered among an extensive group of internationalist, socially and culturally critical republicans who contributed to the shaping of experimental, cosmopolitan, and decolonizing cultures at the margins of official Ireland. The letters and papers collected in this volume provide an extraordinary wealth of first-hand information about O'Malley's post-independence life and attitudes. Wounded badly at the time of his arrest in Dublin, O'Malley would be one of the last republican prisoners to be released. After a brief – and, given their political attitudes, doubtless uneasy – convalescence at his parents' home, and against the advice of doctors who believed he would never walk properly again, he departed to the Pyrenees for a walking tour and then spent an extended time on mostly borrowed funds in Rome and travelling in Italy, Spain and France. In a sense, this determination to push himself and to overcome his potential disability, is of a piece with the highly self-disciplined and disciplinarian IRA officer that the memoirs and civil war papers reveal. Not less of a piece with that self-discipline is O'Malley's lifelong, systematic autodidacticism in art history, music and literature. Already in prison, he compiled and sent out lists of books, begged for gramophone records and art catalogues and sought at the same time to engage his fellow prisoners with his readings. In Italy and in Paris, he devoted hours to self-education in art history, developing a rich and erudite understanding of visual art that was, as his later writings on Yeats and le Brocquy and his essays and broadcasts on Mexican art all reveal, a technically informed and not merely amateur connoisseurship. After a frustrating tour of the United States seeking to raise funds for de Valera's *The Irish Press* (a paper O'Malley hoped, perhaps over-optimistically, would further an independent, decolonized public opinion in Ireland), he spent several years in New Mexico, Mexico, and around New York and New England, where he befriended numerous artists and writers in the bohemian sub-cultures of Taos, Yaddo and the Group Theatre workshop. Among those he encountered, some of whom would become lifelong friends, were photographers Paul Strand and Edward Weston, Hart Crane, Clifford Odets, Lee Strasburg and Georgia O'Keefe. In Ireland, after his return, his friends included Liam O'Flaherty, Denis Devlin, the painters Evie Hone, Nano Reid, Mainie Jellett and Louis le Brocquy, in addition to MacGreevy, Yeats and Beckett. His letters and notebooks furnish the record of his generally ethically and aesthetically demanding responsiveness to a remarkable range of artists and art forms, from Mexican art to Asian music, from old Irish sculpture to contemporary theatre. This responsiveness, on account of the format of these mostly private remarks, is singularly woven together with his judgments on individuals and on politics and society, as well as with the often desolating daily history of a crumbling marriage and with the efforts of a committed father to maintain his relationship with his children. They also reveal an intense engagement with art and artists that is part of what O'Malley himself would probably have understood as the foundations of his own spiritual self-culture.

The link O'Malley makes between spiritual culture and decolonization – or its truncation – is never very fully theorized. But it is a constant of his writings from the time of his imprisonment, when he had cause to reflect on the failure of the republican project of a total decolonization of Ireland. That project, which involved both political sovereignty and the liberation of Irish cultural attitudes from their continuing subservience to English values as to British domination, was the ideal for which republicans fought and for which partition and the oath to the crown were vital obstacles in distinct registers. O'Malley's own adherence to a left-wing interpretation of this struggle, which clearly embraced a spectrum of ideological positions, is everywhere evident. It is evident in his description at several points of the Irish revolution as being one 'between exploiters and exploited';[2] in his consistent anti-fascism and support for republican Spain; in his respect for indigenous peoples in New Mexico and Mexico; in his association in the United States with left-wing cultural movements like the Group Theatre; and in his sympathy with the down-and-out, unemployed and striking men during the Depression that he experienced first-hand in his American sojourn. However, the scepticism that he shows at every juncture towards what he regards as the 'cliches' and 'isms' of political organizations challenges the reader to assemble some consistent sense of O'Malley's post-independence politics.[3]

This is particularly so since the term 'spiritual' has become so vexed a hostage to revisionist interpretations of republicanism in Ireland, a code word for narrowness, callous idealism, reactionary Catholicism and backward-looking identity politics. Indeed, there has been little work in Irish historiography to compare with that of, for instance, Rey Ileto on the Philippines, which could illuminate imaginatively what 'spirituality' might actually represent in terms of the ways in which anti-colonial popular movements lay hold of and transform for radical purposes the available religious rhetorics. Recognizing the kind of division between the spiritual and the material that Partha Chatterjee has explored as an essential – and deeply gender-coded – aspect of nationalism, revisionist historians are unable to acknowledge that it recurs as a no less essential aspect of the division of spheres in the liberal state. Consequently, they have proved unable to read as fundamentally political a terminology expressed as spiritual. They can only read the recourse of republicans in the prisons to a language of spirituality as a recursion to the institutional Catholicism that would come to dominate the Free State and to which, on the contrary, it may be deeply opposed.[4] In O'Malley's case, though he was a practising Catholic, his Catholicism was hardly narrow or exclusive and served rather to connect him, if the evidence of his papers is sound, with a rich European and Latin American intellectual context than to isolate him in a conservative Irish state.

It is in the context of his imprisonment that O'Malley begins to reflect in a sustained way on the failure of republicanism and in this context that he begins to place his emphasis on what he recurrently terms the 'spiritual' aspect of the struggle. That this has little to do with spirituality in the New Age sense, and equally little to do with organized religion, is quite clear. His concern is with the failure to move beyond immediate, pragmatic political or military goals and to engage with the question of nationality, by which he seems to mean precisely the problem of decolonization understood as the realization of cultural difference. If the problem of colonization, as so many theorists of decolonization have argued, is the assimilation of the cultural norms and mores of the colonizer, together with an implicit assumption of their superiority, then the process of decolonization necessarily involves a cultural – or spiritual – declaration of independence and its actualization. For O'Malley, the Treaty represented not only a succumbing to British state terror – to Lloyd George's threat of 'immediate and terrible war' – but the consequence of a failure to develop a decolonized sense of national culture. Writing to Sheila [Sighle] Humphreys, fellow republican prisoner, in the wake of the failed hunger strike of 1923, O'Malley sketches a critique of the superficial national sentiment ('enthusiasm') that the republican struggle engendered and an assessment of the need for a more thorough decolonization:

> Previously I have pointed out that our traditions are wrong and that we foster them knowingly or without thought. We are and have been slaves and so have the slave mind. The open fighting of 1920–1921 and some of the fighting of 1922–1923 has helped somewhat to eradicate slavish defects, but at heart we are still slaves and have slaves' meannesses and lack of moral qualities. It is inevitable. All enslaved nations have ever been the same. ...

I'm afraid it will take a big length of time to make up for the personal loss of the [19]'16 group. [Patrick] Pearse and his group set out to minister to the spiritual side of the nation. They were replaced by [Michael] Collins and [Richard] Mulcahy neither of whom, from what I could see of them during the 1918–21 fighting, were spiritual; they had genius for work though. For years these men directed and in the end, attempted to direct a guerilla war – a most demoralising form of the most demoralising kind of war. If at the same time they had directed effort to keep the national soul up to the proper pitch of spirituality and not of enthusiasm all would have been well.[5]

We await, even yet, an objective assessment of Pearse's understanding of Irish decolonization. Clear from the bulk of O'Malley's writings, however, is that he stands, not for the spirit of blood sacrifice and fanatical spiritual nationalism that he has come to represent, but rather for a republicanism vested in the popular ownership of land and resources and a decolonization predicated on undoing the 'slave mind' inculcated by British education and media. This is what O'Malley describes as 'the right of a people to its own soil so long as that people would not accept domination'.[6] Despite over a century of nationalist organization and propaganda, the resistance to domination, as O'Malley seems to see it in his reflections, was forged in the struggle rather than pre-existing it as a fully theorized body of principle or analysis. At this late stage of republican discussions of their failure in the Curragh internment camp, 'all they seemed to have in common was that they resisted economic, social and clerical pressure together'.[7]

Yet that very triad of qualities belies the notion that the decolonizing process could ever be either solely military or solely 'spiritual'; the problem was rather that the different aspects of that process were out of kilter: 'Driving force was there, but no vision or attempt at economic solution. There was an economic root to the fight, though many on our side would not better their position by a result in our favour. Freedom comes religious, political, economic. We were at the political stage. We had not the faculty for thinking things through sufficiently.'[8] O'Malley proceeds to quote George Russell (Æ), half-hearted proponent of nationalism, who speculated that the Irish fought for freedom 'because they feel in themselves a genius which had not yet been manifested in a civilization, as Greek, Roman and Egyptian in the past have externalized their genius in a society with a culture, arts, and sciences peculiar to themselves. Ireland, through Sinn Féin, is fighting for freedom to manifest the Irish genius.'[9]

It is, of course, all too easy at this juncture to critique such notions of genius and spirit as a legacy of romanticism that would inevitably culminate in fascism or blood-and-soil nationalism. Yet it is not a language peculiar to Irish, or even to major European state-nationalisms, but one that Irish nationalists hold in common with, for example, W.E.B. Du Bois in *The Souls of Black Folks* or Indian nationalists like Sri Aurobindo. It is, indeed, their common legacy from the German romanticism of Herder and von Humboldt. While it could furnish the ground for a deeply reactionary cultural politics, it could also, as the instances of Æ and Du Bois suggest, subtend the claim to the rights of small nations or oppressed peoples and assert the specific contributions of diverse cultures. If it can lead to Heidegger, it can lead no less to the cultural anthropology of a Boas or the linguistics of Sapir and Whorf; it can lead no less to the language of decolonization that refuses to admit that the only conceivable course is that of assimilation to the dominant power. In the latter case, there is no contradiction between a deep investment in the cultural or aesthetic specificity of a particular people or region and a comprehensive cosmopolitanism, one grounded not in the idea of advanced civilizations but in a radical equivalence of diverse cultural modes. It anticipates what we might now think of as a kind of cultural ecologics that insists on the necessity of cultural as of biological diversity. O'Malley's career, with his travels, his reading and his writings, make clear that in the wake of republican defeat his overall project is to further his own self-education as a means to a certain kind of exemplary cultural decolonization in a Irish context.

It is surely as a result of discussions in the jails that O'Malley determines that his future work on behalf of the republican movement would be neither military (of which he was probably no longer physically capable) nor practically political (work for which he had little inclination or aptitude), but cultural. Writing to Mabel Fitzgerald from Kilmainham in December 1923, he claims that, being physically unfit, he wishes 'to place at my country's service what training I can by reading, and think[ing]'.[10] This determination follows an exhaustingly long list of books that he has read while in jail or intends to read and queries about other things with which he should be acquainted. The list is characteristic of many of his letters, both during his post-civil-war imprisonment and throughout the rest of his life. O'Malley was a relentless autodidact and constantly sought advice from an extraordinary range of acquaintances as to reading that he should undertake in literature or art history or music that he should hear. Given what was available to him before he had mastered languages other than English, and under the circumstances of books lent by friends, the lists he enumerates tend to be dominated by English literature, from Shakespeare to Shaw, Galsworthy and Wells, even as he follows an extensive curriculum in the Anglo-Irish literature that he had started to read after 1916.

In recent times, O'Malley's love of English literature has come to betoken the possibility of reconciliation, as if culture were the site of a rapprochement without decolonization, a *détente* that bridges domination with understanding. Declan Kiberd concludes *Irish Classics* with the following fable regarding Patrick Mayhew, then British Secretary of State for Northern Ireland:

> One day as this [peace] process was beginning to take shape, Mayhew read the prison letters of Ernie O'Malley, an IRA veteran of the War of Independence. He found in them to his amazement an unambiguous celebration of the masterpieces of English literature. This confirmed – even if Mayhew might not have so phrased it himself – those postcolonial theories which held that nationalism was doomed to frustration by the myth of its own singularity: only by contact with the art of other peoples could anything approaching a national culture be born. O'Malley clearly revered English literature as deeply as many of the great Anglo-Irish writers had

admired Gaelic culture. What struck Patrick Mayhew most was an account of how the wounded IRA man, as he lay waiting for first aid during a long gun battle, took comfort from his pocket edition of the sonnets of Shakespeare. On the basis of that strange epiphany he concluded – rightly as it turned out – that a meaningful peace process between ancient enemies might yet be possible. Irish, or British, or both.[11]

It is a fable that appeals to – and records – a certain cultural narcissism. It is, accordingly, hopelessly partial. It is not simply that the conclusion implied, the continued partition of Ireland, is one that O'Malley could scarcely have regarded as the grounds for a 'meaningful peace process'. It also drastically simplifies both O'Malley's attitude to English culture and the place of English literature in the larger scheme of his reading and thought. Throughout his life he took rather more seriously than this anecdote implies the need for nationalist culture to have 'contact with the art of other peoples'. What is perhaps most striking, in watching not only O'Malley's efforts to reach beyond the 'prison-house' of English in the jails, but moreover his process of self-education throughout his life, is the urgency of his need for perspectives beyond those that English education imposed on Irish colonial culture – and, indeed, that persisted through Irish school and university curricula long after independence.[12] With a certain self-satisfaction, perhaps, the eye of a Mayhew, or of biographer Richard English, arrests itself at the litany of English literature to which O'Malley has access and in which he systematically immerses himself.[13] A nice parablepsy occludes his equal interest in French, Russian and American writing, his insistence on teaching himself Greek, Latin and Spanish, even while in jail, and, in particular, his lifelong reaching over the dismal wedge of England to the richer intellectual and artistic culture of the continent and beyond. 'France, Spain, New Mexico, Mexico, Italy, are my second countries,' he writes to an American friend in 1955.[14]

What is at once fascinating and instructive in following the evidence of O'Malley's reading, as in following his interest in art history, is less its anglo-centrism than its breadth and resolute modernity. Accustomed as we are to the insistence that republicanism is and has always been a backward-looking and anti-cosmopolitan movement, insular and repressive, it is a peculiar thing to find O'Malley as a young man engaged in guerilla warfare reading Blake and Villon by the roadside or discovering Tagore, Dostoevski and Melville while in jail. Though Tagore and Dostoevski (like Turgenev, Chekhov and Tolstoy, whom he also reads) may represent instances of alternative modernity of immense value for a republican intellectual in a culture whose achievements were all too often evaluated in relation to English canons, Melville, and in particular *Moby Dick*, remained a touchstone throughout his life. He read *Moby Dick* aloud and passed it around in both Kilmainham and the Curragh, and a late letter in the present volume depicts him reading it, accompanied by much laughter, to his young children. *Moby Dick* perhaps represents the republican allegory *par excellence*, with its heterotopic vision of a community of differences, its various struggles for both co-operation and against dominance, with its ambiguous pursuit of an ambiguous object. Certainly O'Malley interprets it thus in *The Singing Flame*:

> *Moby Dick* was a favourite. I had copies of it sent in to me for the men. I had re-read it many times, now I knew some of it by heart. Was not the white whale the whale of empire which devoured us, or was it the ideal of freedom, which would make *brus* of us until we could improve the harpoon of a social system that would bring it alongside.[15]

Not accidentally, O'Malley's circulation of this complex work is at one with his faith in the possibility of 'spiritual' work in the jails, confirming his belief that '[t] he feeling of the men was instinctively for what was good in subject matter'. His own self-pedagogy, and his apparent indifference to institutional academic sanction throughout his life, might be seen as an unspoken commitment to that principle.

Shakespeare, of course, appears, but not always with either the solemnity or the pre-eminence Kiberd's anecdote would seem to accord him. Typical is an interlude in O'Malley's account of the siege of the republican-occupied Four Courts by Free State troops in *The Singing Flame*:

> My leather portmanteau had been cut and torn, my clothes and books damaged. I picked up some of my books from a shelf. Baudelaire, two *al fresco* prints, Tintoretto and Piero della Francesca, a portfolio of drawings. There were two bullet holes through a copy of Vasari's *Lives of the Italian painters*. Authors had been drilled and torn out of all proportion to the number of books. 'Bad luck to them, anyhow,' I said in the direction of a piece of artillery gone through a Synge illustrated by Jack Yeats. 'They mustn't like books or anything to do with books' ... Cuchulainn had suffered most of all ... I turned over another undamaged volume of Vasari, and sitting on my bed read his remarks on Andrea del Sarto ... A volume of Montaigne had escaped shell and bullet. He would have been a good man to have here with us; he could have joined our philosophic discussions under the dome. I put him in my pocket where he lay beside a thin copy of Shakespeare's Sonnets which I had been reading last night. Beneath a red plush chair I found my bright yellow boots, untouched; a terrible colour to wear.[16]

Much like the Bible and Shakespeare on the desert island, the Sonnets in a military tunic pocket is a cliché of military reminiscence from the First World War to the Malvinas. O'Malley gently ironizes it here, pairing the Sonnets with a tasteless pair of boots. Synge and Yeats, and of course Cúchulainn, one might expect in a republican's canon, but the accompaniment of Baudelaire, Vasari and Montaigne comes as a considerable surprise on first reading this passage. Is this republican reading? The sceptic and the biographer of the Renaissance, the epitomes of an inaugural moment of modernity and of the questioning rather than dogmatic possibilities of European Catholic culture, appear alongside the dark angel of urban modernity even as another modern city is being reduced to rubble, not by Haussmanization but by government shelling.

The episode, like O'Malley's engagement in the next decade with American modernists, reminds us that republicanism is not, as Kiberd characterizes nationalism, 'another in the long line of attempts to cope with modernity',[17] but is itself an agent and an effect of modernity. O'Malley's intellectual career suggests a stake not in the modernization of Ireland, understood in accord with capitalist modernization internationally, but in an alternative modernity that seeks to assert its differ-

AFTERWORD: ON REPUBLICAN READING

ence. Despite O'Malley's highly prized self-discipline, his intellectual formation was haphazard and irregular and often conditioned by the contingencies of his encounters and by the resources available to him in rural Mayo where he settled after the mid 1930s. Nonetheless, reading through his assembled papers and published writings, one can discern the outlines of a consistently held set of principles that conjoin his interest in the art of Western Europe with both his enduring concern for Irish art and his interests in culture further afield. Within these contexts, he grasps both Ireland's 'incongruity' and its affiliations. The Anglo-Irish War was 'a clash between two mentalities, two trends in direction, and two philosophies of life',[18] differences that were never seen by O'Malley in essentialist terms, but – as they also were viewed by James Connolly – as specific characteristics determined by Ireland's anomalous history.[19] As O'Malley put it in an article for *Architectural Digest*:

> Ireland is a country difficult to assess, for the ordinary measuring stick may not give the best results. ...
>
> Her people carry into the modern world some qualities which belong to another age and which may appear incongruous. Either by accident or design the Irish have avoided some incidents in world history which have helped to shape the European scene: Roman occupation, the Renaissance, the Industrial Revolution and in recent times, the last world war and conscription. Lack of a sense of centralized authority [that?] might have come from the Romans; instead it came very much later in time, through the British. Explicit participation in the Renaissance can be dimly sensed in a study of poetry in Irish, but aspects of the medieval mind can be more easily seen in every day use. ...
>
> We speak English but, with mouths shaped from long centuries of a native language, our pronunciation and lack of stress is different. English with us has also a different intuitional and psychological value as it represents a completely different consciousness and tradition.[20]

Ireland is both part of and anomalous to the European Catholic cultural and philosophical world. But its anomaly is not understood simply as backwardness in relation to some perceived norm, but as a set of alternative resources the Irish 'carry into the modern world'. For O'Malley and other republican intellectuals, these resources are not hindrances to be overcome in order to modernize, but potentialities to be unfolded in their own terms.

It is perhaps for this reason that O'Malley's encounters with Indians in New Mexico, with whom he worked in 1930 while employed in rebuilding Dorothy Brett's cabin near Taos, and with the indigenous and *mestizo* peoples of Mexico, remained so important to him. Initially he understands colonial relations in Mexico by analogy with Ireland. 'This is of course an Indian country though it has been ruled by whites and maztitos [*sic*],' he remarks, 'it's the problem of mixing Gaelic and Anglo-Irish and solving the problems of both ...'[21] He accordingly retains his impatience with the white tourist or anthropologist in New Mexico, 'who goes out there to escape humanity or to become interested in ceremonies, dance or legend of the Indians and who does not care a damn for the actual spoliation of the Indians or Mexicans there.'[22] His later essay for *The Bell*, 'The Background of the Arts in Mexico', maintains a similar perspective and insists on the same connections.

'Mexico', it opens, 'is of interest to Ireland because for over three centuries it has been subject to foreign domination and for close on a century and a half it has been struggling to integrate itself.'[23] The essay ends with a more extended reflection on the similarity between the position of the Irish and the Mexican Indian:

> The burden bearer, the Indian, in passive despair and apathy threw [off] all consciousness of contact with his oppressors although in remote regions he could preserve his enduring bodily strength and his way of life. His culture had been destroyed and despised, monuments of his race had been heaped over with earth or split by forest growth and the Indian was not even vaguely aware of the contribution of his race to world history.
>
> In some such manner the Irish of the 18th century had been isolated from and unaware of their achievements in the past. They had withdrawn from the conscious life of their conquerors as if they were living in another dimension. The plastic arts were not even a dim memory. Literature was a survival of the tongue, history was kept alive by folklore memory alone. Criticism in the creative sense had neither material to work on nor educated people to work with.[24]

O'Malley continues to make some unexpected remarks that distinguish the situation of Mexican from that of Irish art:

> Mexican pre-conquest art has an advantage over Irish material in that the former has little history associated with the objects unearthed or already in position. This lack of history can help when objects are looked at for their own sake and as an end in themselves. They have then less to do with factual information or with literary association, but demand more attention from the eye and a more sympathetic perception of form and design.[25]

In Ireland, on the contrary, 'history is used as a compensation for a vanished past for which there has been no critical understanding as a result of the lack of continuity in the tradition of scholarship'.[26] Such remarks may seem odd, coming as they do from one who devoted his life to the study of Irish and Western European art history and who has just demonstrated considerable mastery of Mexican art and history. On consideration, however, it is of a piece with the praise he gives to the French archaeologist Françoise Henry for her rich 'aesthetic approach'.[27] He opposes this approach to the 'museum outlook', 'with its emphasis on catalogues and dates, superseded sensitive understanding'.[28] He promotes a vivid juxtaposition of the contemporary and the 'primitive', not a pure and abstract aesthetic apprehension of the object: 'Now that contemporary art has paid more attention to feeling, to basic rhythm and design, it has helped our age to understand and appraise primitive art work.'[29] In a peculiar, almost chiasmatic way, the interest of modernism in the 'basic' elements of 'primitive' art, comes to reveal the 'modern' cosmopolitanism of a supposedly primitive culture. With its 'native aptitude for seizing on an idea and altering its character',[30] Irish art is characterized by its capacity for 'meeting waves of foreign influences, absorbing them or possibly rejecting them, for centuries, though never scorning them'.[31] The aesthetic sense that O'Malley espouses becomes a capacity for grasping the distinctive in Irish (or Mexican) art precisely by the juxtaposition of what is contemporary with what is past, what is foreign with what is local, through comparison and differentiation alike. It is, in effect, a refusal of what Walter Benjamin termed historicism, that insistence on the continuity of history or tradition thorough 'empty homogeneous time',[32] a refusal that is perhaps crucial to a culture whose experience of history has been that of rupture rather than continuity and for whom the artefacts of often jarringly disparate traditions are often violently pressed into alignment.

Something of this appears in O'Malley's description of the energy and clash of Mexican Baroque, with its confluence of Spanish and Indian elements: 'Line was broken at every possible angle to form recessions, and facades became as richly exuberant as interiors whilst Indian craftsmen elaborated their designs in a maze of carved or sculptured detail.'[33] On the other hand, the achievement of Diego Rivera and especially of Jose Clemente Orozco, whose frescoes O'Malley preferred, was to have brought the Indian into representation, absorbing the 'high purpose' of folk art that had survived colonization and was 'invariably aesthetically satisfying'.[34] Part of that achievement is to have 'drawn on the sculptured faces of his countrymen', faces that 'were unlike the academic Greco-Roman European tradition'.[35] In the Irish context, in his various writings on Jack B. Yeats and Louis le Brocquy in particular, it is on the effects of landscape and light that his attention falls as much as on both artists' interest in the portrayal of Irish popular culture. Landscape becomes almost an allegory for the clashes of colonial culture, throwing up 'improbable colour combinations', 'subtle, unrelated colour which is not easily seen as pattern, but develops in a strange orchestration'.[36] The consequent 'strongly dramatic sense' demands a rupture with academic convention[37] just as it fails to furnish '[t]he sense of formal composition and defined pattern met with in French landscape and elsewhere'.[38]

In both Yeats and le Brocquy, O'Malley also discerns a tendency towards the representation of the outsider – the circus clown, the tramp, the rogue, the prisoner[39] – that are the human correlative to the unconventionality, in painterly terms, of the Irish landscape. They are also indices of the survival of a republican mentality, as they were for MacGreevy in his book on Yeats, and of a persistent resistance to domination. Le Brocquy's paintings of tinkers of this period draw O'Malley's attention for this reason:

> Their aloofness, intractability, and fierce independence interested le Brocquy. They are, he could see, outside of the closely organized life of the parish unit, looked on with mistrust and suspicion, but generally treated with the tolerance given in the country to groups outside of its parish life. They become the symbol of the individual as opposed to organized, settled society, and to the growing power-control of the State; a symbol, also, of the distressed and dispossessed people of Europe wandering, unlike the tinkers, without hope of changing their condition by individual effort. For the creative worker they could represent the artist who deals in the unexpected and the unrecognized, and who suffuses with meaning familiar things against the inanition of their too facile and unmeaning acceptance.[40]

The layered enfolding here of the aesthetic and the political judgment lodged in the particular work of a given artist is typical of O'Malley's reflections on art. So also is the movement from the local condition and observation to the recognition of a wider historical situation to which Ireland has a distinct relation. At the very moment that his acquaintance Samuel Beckett is writing back to Ireland from Normandy, promising 'a vision and sense of a time-honoured conception of humanity in ruins, and perhaps even an inkling of the terms in which our condition is to be thought again',[41] O'Malley is writing out from Ireland with a parallel vision of the legacies of dispossession and displacement that bring the Irish experience of the past into conjunction with Europe's devastated present. Indeed, both in art and culture, O'Malley grasps Irish neutrality and the 'Emergency' less as confining Ireland to a stultifying isolation than as an opportunity to fall back on itself and discover independent and distinctive resources. His perceptions, unelaborated but none the less intense, draw the traditions of Irish republicanism into alignment with the philosophical critique of the nation state and of governmental modernity that has stemmed from Hannah Arendt's concern with the post-war displaced peoples in *The Origins of Totalitarianism* to the work of Giorgio Agamben on the fate of the Roma and other minorities in the contemporary period.[42] It also foreshadows a later republican solidarity with the Palestinians, displaced from their own historical lands by a Zionist settler state.

But what is crucial to O'Malley's arriving at such networks of relation and solidarity is precisely the imbrication of the aesthetic and the political. If, as Philip Pettit has argued, the European republican political tradition, of which the Irish one forms part, has emphasized not the liberal concept of freedom in the form of non-interference, but the understanding of freedom as non-domination, there follows from that principle the primacy of cultural independence.[43] Just as much as the individual, cultures require freedom from domination in order to realize their own potentialities as distinctive ecologies of human historical experience. The demand is as much aesthetic as it is political or social: every culture takes its formation from specific historical and geographic factors that have shaped it, and the function of political freedom is to allow for the unfolding of the aesthetic possibilities, in the broadest sense, that a culture implies. It is for this reason that the logic of republicanism has tended to be anti-capitalist: O'Malley's discomfort with the homogenizing tendencies of urban American society, as he saw them, is not untypical. But it is also why republicanism has tended to remain illegible to Marxism, insistent as Western Marxist analysis has tended to be on industrialization and modernization as pre-conditions for revolutionary struggle.

The Irish republican tradition, which grew out of the conditions of primitive accumulation in eighteenth- and nineteenth-century Ireland and was articulated through the Fenians, Connolly and the left republicans, among them O'Malley, always affirmed other possibilities than the destructive passage through industrialization and modernization for the radical transformation of the colonial order. O'Malley discovered as a guerilla fighter among the Irish people the latent persistence of recalcitrance to colonial domination that could flare up into open resistance according to its own peculiar rhythm or tempo. He sought to articulate this perception in his writing and thinking as a post-revolutionary intellectual, in the form of a lifelong meditation on the specificity of Irish cultural possibilities and on their disjunctive relation to other cultures, most notably those of Catholic Europe and of Mexico.

If the patterns of his thought are at times hard to decipher, it is not only because of the disparate and fugitive nature of most of the writings collected here, but largely on account of the fact that, in no way an institutionalized or formally trained intellectual, O'Malley inhabited the republican tradition more than he reflected upon it.[44] In many ways, he embodied its principles, with the unfortunate consequence that all too often, in the wake of the defeat of republicanism in the civil war, his own individual disdain for subservience stands in for any larger reflection on the *collective* conditions for furthering decolonization. The political and aesthetic principles he did embody in his own individual way were by no means unique to O'Malley, nor are they unique to the Irish context. One finds resonances everywhere not only with Connolly or Fintan Lalor, for example, but with Hugh MacDiarmid in Scotland or David Jones in Wales, in their appeal to specifically Celtic cultural formations, and, more remotely, with the writings of anti-colonial intellectuals like Amilcar Cabral or Ngugi Wa Thiong'o. Precisely at a moment when a restructuring of the global order promises a more violent imposition of domination under the cover of modernization and liberal democracy, and in which the forces that defy the renewed injustices of accumulation are mostly dispersed and localized, the resources of such traditions of culturally differentiated and ecologically distinct resistance still have much to teach us.

APPENDIX I

Critical Works by Ernie O'Malley

(IN CHRONOLOGICAL ORDER)

1. Book review of Françoise Henry's *Irish Art in the early Christian Period* in *The Bell*, I:1 (Dublin, October 1940).

2. 'Introduction' in *Jack B. Yeats National Loan Exhibition Catalogue*, National College of Art and Design (Dublin, June–July 1945).

3. Book review of Thomas MacGreevy's *Appreciation and Interpretation of Jack B. Yeats* in *The Bell*, IX:4 (Dublin, January 1946).

4. 'Louis le Brocquy' in *Horizon*, XIV:79 (London, July 1946).

5. 'County of Mayo' in *Holiday* (London, 28 October 1946).

6. 'The State of Painting in Ireland' lecture at Limerick City Library (autumn 1946).

7. 'Renaissance' in *La France Libre*, XIII:74 (London, December 1946–January 1947).

8. 'Traditions of Mexican Art' in BBC *The Listener* (London, 23 January 1947).

9. 'Painting: The School of London' in *The Bell*, XIV:3 (Dublin, July 1947).

10. 'Ireland' in *Architectural Digest*, XVII:7 (London, July 1947).

11. 'The Background of the Arts in Mexico' in *The Bell*, XIV:5 (Dublin, August 1947).

No. *1. Book review of Françoise Henry's* Irish Art in the early Christian Period *in* The Bell, I:*1 (Dublin, October 1940), 85–7*

IRISH ART IN THE EARLY CHRISTIAN PERIOD
Françoise Henry. With 80 collotype plates and 55 illustrations. (Methuen, 25s.)

Next to scholarship and detachment one of the most important assets of the modern archeologist is the aesthetic approach. The museum outlook, with its emphasis on catalogues and dates, superseded sensitive understanding. Now that contemporary art has paid more attention to feeling, to basic rhythm and design, it has helped our age to understand and appraise primitive art-work.

Mlle. Françoise Henry, who has given us the first really comprehensive and intelligent study of early Christian art that we possess, is rich in this virtue. In everything that she considers, the laborious scientific analysis of influences at work, and the evolution of influences to create a style is always guided by a feeling and an understanding of the creative effort under examination. Her attitude to the beautiful slabs from Duvillaun and Inishkea are cases in point. If one adds that she has also a sound practical knowledge of the technique of craftwork and of circumambient history, it will be evident that she is unusually well equipped for her task.

Any one problem in this field will show how essential it is that a worker should possess not merely two or three of these qualities, but all of them – scholarship, detachment, aesthetic feeling, a practical knowledge of craftwork, a knowledge of the social and political background. Take the problem of dating. Dating is essential to any discussion of schools of thought and of influences. Only the worker who combines scholarly caution and artistic sensibility ever fully realises how tentative and suggestive at best any dating can be, seeing that early forms and methods will constantly persist side by side with more highly-developed prototypes; so that incased jambs as in VIth century megalithic doors can be found in XIIth century Clonfert: and XVIth century sculpture may include work which, by feeling and execution, might have come out of the XIIth century. To this tentative fixing of dates Mlle. Henry devotes a good deal of space.

In the main the book deals with architecture, metal-work, illumination, and sculpture, from the VIIth to the Xth century; but we see, almost at once, at the end of the Iron Age in fact, that the native craftsman has achieved not only a vigorous and refined technique, a sound basis for later work, but developed what seems to be a native aptitude for seizing on an idea and altering its character.

This is exciting: and almost thematic. We observe how the native Greek geometric patterns change here to a divergent spirit more nearly resembling plant growth. The essentially plastic is reduced to two dimensional linear pattern. Naturalistic motives are distorted and re-embodied. Asymmetry becomes endemic. There is an unwillingness to use natural forms. As time goes on we see this involved restlessness become more and more opposed to clear statement. Its obscurity tends to draw attention to one particular part, to the detriment of the all-over design. The early fiercely insistent strength develops its own excesses. Dynamic drive is endangered by its strength of fantasy. The classical mould of conquering Rome, with its logic and discipline, did not control this barbaric fantasy, or the sense of freedom in the craftworker.

In the VIth century Irish isolation is penetrated by Saxon, Gaulish, Spanish, and other influences. By the VIIth century influences from the known Christian world are being felt and sifted. But, again, one notes how Pictish realistic animal art had no direct influence on Ireland. A cross from Banagher, and a fragment from Clonmacnoise, corresponds in animal treatment with Scottish crosses from Pictish territory, and they have a feeling for rhythmic line that is almost Chinese. By the VIIIth century metal-work designs transferred to stone crosses cover the entire surface in phantasies of movement. Next comes the Byzantine feeling for dividing a space into panels. By Monasterboice and its kindred group the feeling for space is refined, and the figures have now achieved a third dimension. In all this, and especially in her analysis of the work of individual artists in the crowning achievement of the Book of Kells, Mlle. Henry is most refreshing; although the chapter in which she offers an interpretive synthesis of the Irish mind in its conscious creative evolution is probably the most interesting chapter in her book.

One closes it with a feeling that one has seen men, across the centuries, solving creative problems, meeting waves of foreign influences, absorbing them or possibly rejecting them, for centuries, though never scorning them. But one feels above all that, at their peak, they were at harmony with the finest artists of the outside world.

No. 2. *'Introduction' in* Jack B. Yeats National Loan Exhibition Catalogue, *National College of Art and Design (Dublin, June–July 1945)*[1]

Jack B. Yeats spent his boyhood in Sligo town, a small port on the Atlantic edge. Sligo is flanked in a half circle by mountains which show a wild inland cliff scenery shaped to fantastic form; small lakes, then strong outbursts of rock carry the other flank to the sea. The sea brought the outside world to the doors of a small town in a casual mention of foreign cities, strange words and wild doings; it made for wonder and mystery later seen if only as a gloss on piracy. From the land side came the country people to shop, shy and awkward in the foreign life of a town, but fierce and intractable when following their realistic land calling at fairs and markets. Family life for them centred around the oldest of man's allegiances, the hearth, woven with memoried legend; their land work built as much on folklore as on the hard reality of uneconomic holdings.

The town presented a knowledge of character and incident, the vagaries of personalities with oddities even to the daft accepted as part of its world. It would be an open book like any other Irish town, whose inhabitants are mainly interested in motive and intention of others, in knitting daily events in a conversational form to be related before evening as direct and indirect implication threaded by affection, malice or envy.

Here then is his native town he could see people who were not accepted in a conventional setting. They bore much the same relationship to the tightened security of bourgeois respectability, ringed by experience which it fears to enlarge, as the artist does that to life; and with them the unexpected was always in the offing. The sailor, a transitory form who came on shore for drink and company after the indifference of ocean, forgetful of hardship in his now remembrance of outland ways and customs, to light the imagination of stay-at-homes. Tinkers with the wildness of life in the open and their utterly untamed fierceness who fought after a feed of porter in a whoop of song. Countrymen, freed for a few days in the year from the greedy tyranny of land, wander through their favourite pubs to meet neighbours and relations, ridding themselves of hard-earned money in a spacious generosity; at ease in gestured extravagance with a background of their own song. Outside in the street a ballad singer to relate past and present in a long string of verse, sure of heightened talk and soothing drink before the night came.

When the circus arrived its flamboyant posters exalted grace and beauty to ballet level, a band renowned for noise shook the side walls whilst brightly costumed performers wound through the streets. At night, clowns in their tragic way acted the scapegoat, slapped their fellows, made fun of themselves in simulated awkwardness, often to emerge from the chrysalis, as grace. The clown related his humor to the tragic sense of life inherent in his audience, through outsiders, as in the clown, might see only uncaring lightheartedness. Circus music, colour, baroque gesture, essentially sweep the mind, free the heart, but relate nomadic tent existence to settlement, leaving an aching sense of unfulfilment and nostalgia behind.

Jack Yeats would be moulded too by the physical nature of his province, Connacht. Great roaring winds sweep in from the Atlantic to drench the land with spray, soften the intention, weaken the will and perseverance. Cloud forms drift slowly in threat or, when storm has ceased, model to a painter's delight land forms below. Sky bulks large to give a sense of infinite distance and mystery mixed with tragic desolation. This spaciousness of sky is the most noticeable feature of the Western scene; it is, at times, as if the land were a prelude to the atmosphere above. Swirling cloud makes for a Turneresque dramatic effect, difficult to register, shot as it is with daffodil, duck-egg green and improbable colour combinations. Land can become sogged with persistent rain; it is then more than ever a burden and a heart-breaking task to work, or to brood a melancholy in the mind. With shafted light after the rain comes a lyrical mood in which tender greens vibrate in tones, whins crash with yellow glory and atmosphere is radiant.

The shifting scene is temperamental and induces mood. It is a hard country to paint as it presents problems of subtle, unrelated colour which is not easily seen as pattern, but develops in a strange orchestration. This subtlety and its opposite, and strongly dramatic sense, must be the despair of academic painters whose minds have been trained to accept the conventional impression, but whose eye may fail to record the sudden unexpected impact. Memory must play its part, for painting hours are episodic, broken by rain or rebellious wind. The sense of man is present in enclosures of light-filigreed stone walls which map land hunger, or in unobtrusive cottages, dwarfed by mountain and hill to an almost tragic insignificance.

Beyond the Shannon in a train the West can be sensed; in a spate of talk, an expansion of interest which breaks down impersonal aloofness to introduce the co-operative sharing of a sense of life, an immediate hint of vitality and a degree of wonder which rounds a mediaeval quality of mind. People have charm, time is judged as a convenience not as a burden, talk is an expression in a form of entertainment which interests to free the imagination and give a sense of ease. Subtlety of mind, easily directed to cunning in land or business, is now judged as diplomatic adroitness. Above all is a sense of wildness and freedom, an untamed naturalness, the unexpected even in a phrase, a feeling of equality through an understanding of the natural dignity of man.

Jack Yeats experienced some such quality of life in Connacht and he has since interpreted it. With a hawk's swift eye he has seen this panorama as material, and his sensitive psychological understanding of it has fused its meaning in his spirit. The visual world has been absorbed, selected and re-created slowly with innocent freshness in terms of emotional colour. He can capture the intensity of his feeling which has viewed an aspect of as simple a pleasure of life as the interior of a circus tent. The circus is a boy's delight but also a man's, if his emotions have not been smothered by what is known as discretion, or by the death of the heart.

There is a genuine interest and affection in his work for the incidents portrayed. They grow out of love and a profound sensibility of what to some are outlandish ways with a certain colourful appeal. The outward form of life has changed since he has grown up but the fundamental attitude of mind remains. Practical people often find life in the West hard; as indeed it is when progress is viewed philosophically in relation to eternity; but artists whose energy is turned to observation see the relationship of people to each other, to events and to their environment.

In his earlier work he is a draughtsman who stresses illustrative content directing it in a vital sense of line to a personal idiom. Later, in water colour he uses water colour with this same illustrative content not as a medium but as flat colour tones to give vitality to his drawings. It was, I think, a lucky chance when he found a number of his early water colours destroyed by damp. This accident made him think more in terms of oil and he began to experiment. Then continued a long period in which definition became gradually more colourful and his essential bent, that of a colourist, more emphatic. By the year 1921 he had reached the limits of his expression in this manner.

When the artist reaches his spiritual limit in any one method of expression he follows either of two ways. He continues to reproduce his impressions in a manner he has outgrown until the individual painting is no longer a problem for the sum total of what constitutes his being, but is related to hand and eye alone; or he experiments until he has created a new way of approach to his problem. Jack Yeats found his world in a greater feeling for the emotional use of paint, as it were, escaped its mould to become an end in itself. It is hard to explain a change in direction, but one of the factors may have been the heightened sensibility which could result from the tension of life during the struggle for freedom in Ireland then, and the new note of intensity felt by a sensitive observer.

As he enlarged his experience as a painter, he also enlarged his vision. His work no longer dealt with his perception of countrymen in relaxation or at ease in a folk-lore tradition. His figures now enter a subjective world in which they are related to the loneliness of the individual soul, the vague lack of pattern in living with its sense of inherent tragedy, brooding nostalgia, associated with time as well as variations on the freer moments as of old. Visionary worlds of Tir-na-nOg, California, palaces, are opened to us with persuasive paint, and all action is subordinated to thought. Aspects of Dublin workers are searched for inherent character or nobility. Anna Liffey gets its due tribute from one who has the Dubliner's realisation of its significance; reflective mood floods people and furniture in light-splashed rooms; or light itself is the subtly dramatic force. He had always a strong sense of man in relation to the impersonality of the Irish scene; isolated figures never dominate the landscape, but they are now more related to it in symbolical significance which increases their stature to bulk in the mind. One departure of his was completely new in Irish painting, the depiction of national events. The memory of the dead makes for a tragic understanding in Ireland. It evokes a feeling of dead generations who served or have died for a common cause, their struggle echoed in each generation. *The Batchelor's Walk*[2] incident is shown as a simple, but hieratic incident of a flower-girl who casts a flower outside a doorway where men might have been shot down. There is restrained dignity and grace in the movement of her hand and a tenderness that evokes a sense of pity.

He has used the funeral or burial as a symbol. The death of a man who has suffered in the national fight has often been one of the few public tributes that a people could give to one whom some of them recognised only in death. A sense of ceremonial, which had seemed to disappear from consciousness, would emerge and an impressive ordered intensity show understanding and devotion. The memory of the dead has changed its meaning when seen as a political artifice, or has become outworn in verbal misuse, but in Jack Yeats' pictures it holds an eternal significance.

For over twenty years he has been painting in this new manner. For a time he worked in philosophic isolation amongst an indifferent audience who resent an artist's new direction in implementing his vision. This has always been the attitude of a world of punditry, which, becoming complacent, does not risk disturbance except in terms of what it regards as its own interpretation of creative work. A true artist's vision is directed by a keener mental and physical eye, trained selective capacity, contemplative detachment, and inventive technical sense, which is used to rebuild the microcosm architecturally, descriptively, or emotionally. Gradually, however, people came to recognise his genius and originality, his unusual color sense and his absolute integrity. Of late he has himself been the major factor in the training of our eyes to understand what is indeed a school in itself, his quality of mind in paint.

In Ireland the visual sense is not strongly developed in terms of creative painting, but there is a fine feeling for colour, well expressed in small towns where white-wash is mixed with paint powder to give house fronts a fascinating texture of tender pastel shades. Irish atmosphere softens and blends the clash that might have ensued from the individuality of the owners in selection of colour. There is, as well, a peculiar unliterary affection of landscape, but the manner of looking at paint is too often determined, not by this corrective, based as it is on evasive colour and the inherent structural sense of line and form in bare mountain, but by thinking of other paintings. Due to the destruction of the arts by conquest there is but one continuous tradition, the literary tradition; we are enclined to see paint in a literary way as if the implied title should continue as a story on the canvas.

In Jack Yeats we have a painter who is as much concerned with what he has to say in paint as with his manner of saying it. He brings a fresh experience to each canvas he paints; his individual work can not be judged in terms of previous work but in the individual canvas one looks at. That demands alertness of mind and an unprejudiced, innocent eye. He is a romantic painter who through memory has made notes all his life of material which has stirred him by its emotional significance. Those notes may remain unused for years but they have been sifted in his consciousness. When he calls on them he can recollect his original impressions, organise his perceptions through an enlargement of that experience, and create a work of art.

With him colour is an emotional force and his method of using it varies in regard to its substance as pigment and as texture. He may create homogeneous surface with his brush, improvise an absorbing study in chiaroscuro, or use the priming of the canvas to aid luminosity of light and shade. At times, impatient with the brush to communicate his feeling for the richness and charm of pigment and his sheer joy of its expressive power, he employs the palette knife to give swiftness and vigour to the immediacy of his emotion. Seemingly unrelated colours directed by this urgency create an orchestration due to his unerring taste in colour harmony; and in a form of evocative magic, make a direct impact on the mind. Even a casual glance at a small collection of his work shows how inexhaustible is his colour invention. As he experiments in technique he reaches a point in mastery where his handling of knife or brush seems to be by instinct.

In this exhibition as his development is studied from his earlier stages to his more subjective and symbolical work, his steady growth can be seen. The new Ireland, still fluid politically and socially, has found in Jack Yeats a painter of major rank, whose vision is used to make us aware of inherent characteristics, psychological directives and eternal verities.

In return for this understanding of us it is pleasant to realise that Irish art lovers should, over the years, have made it possible to bring together a collection of his pictures that show his development in its completeness, and thus bring about the present tribute from the whole nation.

No. 3. Book review of Thomas MacGreevy's Appreciation and Interpretation of Jack B. Yeats *in* The Bell, *IX:4 (Dublin, January 1946)*[3]

A Painter of His People
It seems strange that Thomas MacGreevy's book is the first work to be published on the paintings of Jack Yeats: delayed for eight years it is now more than ever important. Articles even have been sparse, published as they have been in magazines not easy of reach. Yeats's full stature as the most important painter this country has yet produced is now recognised, but it is well to have that understanding clinched in print.

This year the National Loan Exhibition has made a large public familiar with his development as a painter: to some it has given for the first time an opportunity to study his work closely and to judge it, as it should be judged, in terms of paint. Yeats is so poorly represented in the public galleries of the city where his most important work has been, and is being painted, that a student cannot, when it suits him, study a few consecutive good examples but must wait for an occasional exhibition. This book, well written and deeply felt, fulfils a definite want. Its illustrations give an idea of the painter's earlier work, in which this interest is replaced by colour as a means of organisation, can only be hinted at and the reproduction used to supplement direct, intense vision.

The writer stresses the relationship of Yeats to the people. 'It is through him that after centuries of repression had brought them down to zero in all the arts, the under-dog, conquered people of Ireland came for the first time to a measure of self-expression in the modern art of painting.' During this century people here, who are not reading people, have begun to see themselves on the stage and in print for the first time in their history. The seeing has occasioned resentment, distorted pride, acceptance or understanding. In paint also a tradition of seeing and of understanding has yet to be established as there is no national painting tradition. Our National Gallery, a very good gallery, which should be the corrective, has never been really part of us. It is indeed an institution. We have not as yet learned to co-operate with institutions, nor they with us. And so the English colonial tradition (of academic painting), more hidebound than its mother tradition, is the standard by which most onlookers have learned to judge a work of art.

Thomas MacGreevy mentions painters who might have been able to influence Yeats – Constable, Daumier, Millet[4] – the former in landscape, the two latter in an approach to subject matter. Constable has been one of the basic elements in vital English painting. His influence can be felt to-day on some contemporary Englishmen but his contribution to Yeats would be difficult to discern. Daumier is closer in thought, spirit and in his understanding of and sympathy with the under-dog and with men of goodwill. In Daumier's case also it is difficult to trace influences: both evolved their own style in the process of thinking in paint. Miller may have had some effect, but to one reared as Yeats was reared, in the West, with his access to people whom he later painted, there would be no need for an emphasis or direction from another painter who was interested in the relation of people to land.

To Irish landscape Yeats has brought a fresh vision and a creative palette. Ireland is an Atlantic outpost, and, as an outpost, it meets strong wind, cloud, reflected light. It takes more than its share of rain, and its soft atmosphere blends, what in drier climates might be colour crudities. Into this Irish effect of light, which even when seen is difficult to believe, the painter builds and relates his humanities, based on his understanding of the Anglo-Irish as well as of the people, to fit into the imaginative and seeming extravagance of colour values.

'I think he has struck a new balance between the landscape and the figure ... With Jack Yeats, the landscape is as real as the figures. It has its own character, as they have theirs. It is impersonal ... the sense of the impersonal is an enrichment of the personal, a new element added to the humanity of the figures.' That is well said, and to prove his contention the writer searches at length for correspondences amongst some of the masters of European painting. The Irish landscape is aloof, detached, seemingly unrelated to man. Yet this relation of the impersonal to the personal can be found in certain Irishmen as between their impersonal mind and their personal heart.

Thomas MacGreevy traces Yeats's later development in which he seems to be preoccupied with colour and movement rather than with form. Movement he is always miraculously sure of, but as he develops it is more significantly simple in the means expressed. His horses, for instance, are a blend of imagination, under-standing and delight: their gleaming flanks, eagerness in effort and conscious well-being echo subtly in this land of good horses. Poetry and imagination in a mythological reassessment create a sense of wonder in *A Race in Hy-Brazil*,[5] a painting which unconsciously relates him to the *Fauves*,[6] and to a more significant canvas than that of a Dufy.[7]

Space is given by the writer to an interpretation of *In Memory of Boucicault and Bianconi*,[8] to *Helen*,[9] one of his largest works, and to *The Blood of Abel*,[10] which, when shown, provoked comment and inquiry.

Dublin is lucky to have had presented to it one of his finest works, *Low Tide*,[11] also made mention of. It hangs in the Municipal Gallery[12] in a room of contem-porary European painting. It certainly steals the honours from that selection. His development, as the writer points out, is primarily that of a colourist, who surprises, enchants and disturbs, with his economy of means, sureness of touch, and that sense of inevitability which makes his paint induce one to study and study again a canvas, which to a casual observer, may seem a *fortuitous improvisation*.

No. 4. *'Louis le Brocquy' in* Horizon, *XIV:79 (London, July 1946)*,[13] 33–7, signed Earnán O'Malley

Louis le Brocquy, who is now twenty-nine, has had no formal Art School training, nor had he, until he was twenty years of age, more than an intelligent interest in painting. One day, when studying reproductions of Rembrandt and of Manet, he suddenly realized that painting was a vital process and that it concerned himself. It was as if a door to a hidden world had been suddenly swung open: what had formerly been latent meaning and a pleasant preoccupation now became understanding combined with feeling and imaginative perception. This sudden flash of illumination decided his direction, and from that day onwards he became in essence a painter.

Le Brocquy's earlier work shows the influence of Manet, Velasquez, and Goya; then came an interest in Dégas, Whistler, and in a use of Oriental line. The ever-present danger of preoccupation with the incidentals of representing reality made him seek other methods. Jack Yeats helped him by his imaginative conception, symbolic interpretation, and by the sheer poetic implication of his paint. Through simplification le Brocquy learned economy of means and the use of suggestion. His handling of broader masses was replaced by an interest in planes. His colour became more subdued as a study of form led to a new sense of its organization and a different feeling for line.

During the war, Ireland, cut off from outside activity, was driven back to her sea boundary. Economically the country had to become self-supporting and in this attempt a new strength and assurance was created, reflected by an added interest in painting and in music. For painters, this shutting away of the outside world tended to dim foreign impact. For years there had been the abstract influence of Glieze[14] and Lhôte[15] at work through their pupils, as well as an understanding of present-day European painters. As nineteenth-century and contemporary work is very poorly represented in Irish galleries, students have had to depend on visits to Europe for analysis, understanding and stimulation. The need for the steady influence of good examples of creative work, which can meet prejudice or change it to acceptance or understanding, was most felt during the war. Indeed, until generosity enriches this deeply felt want, people and painters here will remain isolated from first-class minds expressing contemporary ideas in terms of paint. But one result of this withdrawal was that artists had more time to assess themselves and to develop their own personal contribution. Some, for the first time, discovered the influences and creative possibilities of their own landscape; le Brocquy was amongst these.

Irish landscape reflects the remoteness of this country from the industrial revolution. In this it echoes an attitude of the Irish mind, which has also been separated from Roman centralization, and somewhat from the Renaissance and the result of the Reformation. There is a dual quality in the landscape which can induce a merging or a withdrawal. From one aspect results an aloof, impersonal sense of remoteness or of hostility to Man, in which hills tower in imaginative height over small holdings and well-divided fields. At times it seems an undiscovered land which Man has yet to explore. With such an aspect there can be no sentimentality, and as a result there is no sentimental attachment. Louis le Brocquy wandered through Connemara, a gaunt, ragged district of mountain form, freckled lakes, broken bouldered slopes bedazzled with light and serrated with an edge of sea. The sense of formal composition and defined pattern met with in French landscape and elsewhere is seldom seen here. Harsh light, which strongly emphasizes form and structure, is absent also. Instead is an untamed country lacking in pattern, whose informality makes it easier for people and their world to dovetail and create a mood, and whose elusive colours merge and orchestrate in atmospheric softness. For le Brocquy, as for others, the land was an absorbing challenge, which for a time replaced continental conceptions of paintcraft, and demanded expression in a personal idiom.

Famine Cottages, Connemara, shows his feeling for this land as an emotional concept of colour and form. White-walled cottages, abandoned in the great famine of 1848, indefinite now in reduced form as hollow wind-worn shells, slowly sink back into the soil from which they have come. Pink hills relieve the contrast of upright house fragments, islands are suggested in indefinite distance, and amber seaweed mist echoes colour and symbolizes the sea edge with the dependence of people on it as an alternative source of livelihood. Shawled women jut out of darker paint passages in the foreground as if they were worn stone shapes. An inverted tarred curragh overhanging a path seems an earth shape of bridge with flowing water, and a muffled green landscape threads in and out through the variegated colour planes of white wall shadows.

In his oils le Brocquy draws first in charcoal, which is then fixed, and paint is scumbled over the preliminary priming to make it as translucent as possible. He feels his way in colour, which is put on in transparent layers and emphasized by brush stroke or finger rubbing. The thin layers are a reaction to his former thicker use of the medium, and an attempt to break down the opacity of oil. He draws his brush sideways or across the fleck paint on the surface as an aid in creating textural richness. The transparent priming achieves the same effect as gesso, and the scumbling creates a movement in this underlying paint. The total effect is a richly luminous surface, broken up and livened by this method and again helped towards unity by the fusion of these transparent areas. Every part of the composition now functions equally. From 1942 le Brocquy experimented with form and avoided emphatic colour. In his series of 'Classic Themes' he used the human bodies purely as an exercise in form in an architectural way. Legs become pillars, knees and arms seem to emphasize weight and stress, and the body is distorted as a sense of supporting mass is built up. The colour is confined to somber green-grey, and the total effect is severely gaunt.

Condemned Man is a later work, and in it he shows a desire to get rid of this undue severity. There is now no attempt to show things as what they look like, but a desire to show them as they are. This oil is a mental as distinct from a visual idea of a gaol, and it has a particular interest in a country where gaol was a natural place in which to meet friends or to say goodbye. Broken interrelated planes, and the precision of all that surrounds the prisoner, make for a feeling of space. Ponderous weight of wall is indicated into which the occupant is dovetailed; behind him a window, normally expected to give light, casts the dark shadow of oppression and hopelessness over part of his face. The prison wall is cut across to show him in stylized impersonal awkwardness as a cipher. The monotony of dull wall is brightened by a blue book held in his hand, and by two small blue-and-white flowers which symbolize beauty, and, viewed in another way, an image of desire, a woman's face. A lantern-eyed cat, the only free being in the gaol, prowls beyond an iron door which leads to further cells, but yet moves carefully. High up, silhouetted against light beyond the envelopment of wall, is a small beckoning figure, the sense of freedom.

In 1945 le Brocquy, whilst in the midlands near Tullamore, became interested in tinkers, who are peculiar to this country, and in no way related to gypsies. They may have in them a basis of the wandering scholar and craftsman, and their language, the Shelta,[16] has a word use in Irish, but largely they are the once-dispossessed people of confiscations wandering without security of land through the countryside. By trade they are tinsmiths and horse jobbers, beggars in a wheedling monotonous and patterned chant in towns, but in the country they induce hospitality by the involved drama of their conversational skill. Their doctoring of horses, by which, for a short time during a fair, a broken-winded, limping animal becomes a glistening, high-stepping edition of a bloodhorse, results in enviable or reluctant folklore amongst settled landsmen. They are lithe and hardy, sharp in feature, and capable of sudden calls on endurance from their uncertain way of life in a difficult climate. With them primitive emotions are easily aroused and expressed; their women drink and fight as readily as their men, and bear children without halting the day's journey.

Their aloofness, intractability, and fierce independence interested le Brocquy. They are, he could see, outside of the closely organized life of the parish unit, looked on with mistrust and suspicion, but generally treated with the tolerance given in the country to groups outside of its parish life. They become a symbol of the individual as opposed to organized, settled society, and to the growing power-control of the State; a symbol, also, of the distressed and dispossessed people of Europe wandering, unlike the tinkers, without hope of changing their condition by individual effort. For the creative worker they could represent the artist who deals in the unexpected and the unrecognized, and who suffuses with meaning familiar things against the inanition of their too facile and unmeaning acceptance.

In le Brocquy's latest work, again studies of tinkers, he shows them grouped in their family unit enjoying Springtime, watching a sick child, or clustered around a fire.

Le Brocquy's notebook supplies him with quick sketches, which later become watercolours and oils. His Indian-ink line from imaginative memory is backed by scumbled wax on which he creates movement, as if the line floated with independent existence in front of its background. The line may change in process as the mood dictates, but it must always be consciously felt as it gropes its way. There is a danger in such use of line. It may lose its first deeply felt impression or, by simplification and distortion in the service of design, it may become mentally laboured. Used in oil, this line may by emphasis detract from apparent simplicity. In his watercolours, as in the manner of Henry Moore,[17] he rubs wax over colour, then adds another colour layer. Each tone now, as well as fusing visually, keeps its own identity. This creates a superimposed movement within a small area, and adds to the total impression of vitality. Monotonous surface is broken up, and colour subtlety is increased. By these means the artist aims at a strength of texture which he opposes in counterpoint to what might otherwise become a hard isolation of line.

The oil, *Making the Twig Sign*, is pervaded by a sense of ritual and mystery. The moon, a symbol of wonder, intuition and the unknown, floods soft green light over the head and back of the standing tinker and across the country in the background. A tinker bends forward on his knees completely absorbed in his almost sacerdotal task of holding two sticks which he crosses on the ground. Opposite to him a kneeling woman with flaming wind-careless hair, holding a similar stick in her hand, is ecstatically withdrawn by the ceremony. Her light blouse and patch-coloured dress oppose the darkly luminous tones of the man's clothes. A child, uniting kneeling man and woman, watches eagerly, whilst on the right a lean-jawed woman, isolated by treatment of strong light which surrounds her, lifts her face in apprehension. Along the mountainside the figure of a woman rests as if tradition, watching and guiding in a spirit of reverie, were present. Diverging paths lead up to houses, in front of which is a lyrical mood of tender green landscape, a contrast in settled possession and quiet beauty to this isolated, stark intensity, of inherited mystery.

No. 5. 'County of Mayo' in Holiday *(London, 28 October 1946), signed Earnán O'Malley*

County Mayo is in the extreme north west of Connaught. To the east lies a lime stone plain unequally bounded by a group of large lakes; beyond which bogland and harder rock reach to the sea, save for a limestone strip opening on Clew Bay. Mountain and bog cover than half of Mayo's surface, while sea, breaking west and north, indents a resistant coast from the Killaries to Killala Bay.

The most interesting part of the country is the sea edge and its background, which can best be seen either from a boat or on a height. Mweelrea, gray bald mountain top, the highest point in Connaught, is 2686 feet, rising from sea level, but its effect on the sight and mind cannot be explained by practical measurement, for its towering bulk is echoed by all the ranges within sight. From its tip, sinuous bare slopes are seen, distant and near-by, and, if there be wind, its force in breath stopping and backbending can be understood.

Close by on the land side are the projecting shoulders of the Sheeffry Hills, and Ben Gorm; further away rises Maumtrasna with surprising echelon of cliff in its valleys, and the Partry mountains fringing Lough Mask. In between these heights are glens, which open or close suddenly as surrounding slopes are gentle or abrupt, and lakes which need a patient foot. Doo Lough at the foot of Mweelrea is over hung by mountain; velvety green clashes with cold out-thrusts of knarled schist, whilst Ben

Gorm adds a fantastic background of duplicated triangles. Lough Nafooey, best approached through the Galway mountains, is an unexpected, peaceful delight.

Southward, the narrow fjord of Killary Harbour eats ten miles inland. Once a river valley scored out by ice, it has deep water for a fleet, but its mouth is narrow and often difficult. Away to the east beyond undulating bogland, subtly mysterious in blended colour, are the cones of Croagh Patrick, Nephin, across Clew Bay, Nephin Beg and Croaghaun in Achill.

The bareness and austerity of the hills withdraws them from human contact, yet small white-washed houses contact remoteness and emphasize the struggle with land. People eager for the relaxation of good talk can rise suddenly out of bog depth or come down from hill height. Curve and outline satisfy the mind while changing colour makes them close to the heart. Trees find difficulty in growing near the spray-drenched coast save in shelter, when fuschia can become tree high and rhododendron a spreading menace. In the open, trees curve away from the wind or their branches keep to leeward.

Below, are wide strands edged with the thin streak of the West Road, close to the sea. This is a country of story tellers whose memoried tradition keeps alive aspects of a forgotten or unrecorded past. Out to sea, low lying Inishbofin, hilly Inishturk with a sacred island, Caher, whose soil keeps away rats, a sperm whale's head, on its lea. Clare Island, on guard at the mouth of Clew Bay, with the extended spiny ridge of Knockmore looks a mainland mountain.

Prevailing winds are westerly. They bring Atlantic strength and rain when clouds meet the hills. Sky, in the west, expands in a prolonged sense of space which at times demands more attention than either sea or land. Cloud shapes change quickly, move swiftly and form mould landscape beneath. Light is the western artist. Light can be cautious, subtly pervading or bold, but seldom harsh; a vast Atlantic mirror reflects this ever changing light, concentrates or diffuses it. The protecting layer of moist air softens and harmonises unusual effects of colour, which combined with clouds show a mixture of gentleness and fierceness characteristic of the race. A day near the sea can begin with flamingo works – through ducks' egg green, gentian, primrose yellow to a final saffron, salmon pink and speckled gold, with intermediate tints throughout. On gray days colour seeps from land to sky in the same extended range. As pure landscape the West has no equal, yet it creates problems that artistically are seldom solved. Cloud, light, hill, bog and sea tear at the heart, free the imagination but anchor this land in memory.

Clew Bay with its surrounding mountain coast and islands facing westwards, is best seen from a boat. They are weathered to corvette shape, hump-backed as whales, or have their exposed ends out off sharply to form perpendicular marl cliffs. Squalls tear down from the mountains to make sailing difficult and dangerous, but even in difficulties these islands and hills have an unexpected quality of changing shape and varying mood. Individual mountains such as Croagh Patrick with its geometrical certitude, dominate range cohesion, yet their outlines coalesce in a natural composition of curve and distance. Seawards, beyond Clare Island, Atlantic rollers make boat work less uncertain. Here, in spring, the sharp triangular sail of a basking shark's fin breaks the water, seals lift their curious heads and gannets move slowly on their wide winged sweep.

Achill Island stands out in cliff, strand, and mountain strength. It has the cleanness and heady force in wind and sea peculiar to western islands, and their sense of another world. Keem Bay to the westward is a cove of startled surprise in a stark mountain siding, its water green against sand depth. Croaghaun overhead it, a cliff edge of close to 2000 feet, and from its flanks, whilst watching the cascading leaps of wild goats, the islands, coast and mountains to the Northeast can be picked out. Duvillaun, the Iniskeas, Inisglora, were used by monks from about the seventh century. On Inisglora the bewitched children of Lir[18] took human shape; here they were buried. Within living memory sails were dipped when boats passed Inisglora as was the custom off Caher.

Inland, a welter of bog leads to the long cliff edges of the Nephin Beg Range. Here the bog has a desolate strength and spaciousness. This almost unpeopled level, with the forty mile sickle curve of mountains to the east shielding a lake-riddled upland, creates an isolation and aloofness that induces contemplative withdrawal. The northern coast has little shelter from the wild sea which cuts away at its interesting cliff face, yet in early winter the mildness of the air brings arctic gulls skuas related to the great auk and roseate terns. The land in this part of Erris and Tirawley, where strange customs and traditions are kept in tenacious memory, is the most remote in Ireland.

No. 6. 'The State of Painting in Ireland' lecture at Limerick City Library (autumn 1946)[19]

Painting was a product not marketable outside of the country as few Irish artists had previously given either joint or single exhibitions in England. These artists were unknown in England save for those who had worked there. Isolation now for some painters meant a new attitude to the Irish scene and to the Irish landscape. Previously painters had gone abroad to study, to work and to keep in touch with contemporary ideas and practice in paint. Travel was especially necessary as the work of contemporary painters is lacking save in private collections and in the works presented to the Municipal Gallery in Dublin. Now some painters for the first time and others have freshly thought about their own landscape. They looked at it with curious rather aloof eyes and found that as landscape it was subtle, evasive and technically difficult to paint. The all pervading light which floods in from the Western coast created an orchestra of diffused colour which may merge slowly or change rapidly. Light effects are toned by an atmospheric softness to luminous pearly results and cloud forms rapid in movement change land values as they pass overhead. Even in Dublin there had been a difference in atmospheric colour during the war. Turf smoke had made the air purer and cleaner and room interiors were more strongly steeped in soft persistent light.

The rediscovery of landscape made a change in the handling of paint in an attempt to solve its problems. In addition painters were unable to visit the continent or to study European painting in London galleries. That lack of stimulation helped some to shed or to be more fully conscious of what was often an undue influence. It made them concentrate more on their own innate contribution.

French influence had slowly reached Ireland, not through the academic and conventional school of art but through individual understanding of perception. The academic pupils of the conventional school were not aware of contemporary trends and ideas. Academic painting was, with slight variation, a product of the English school. As well there had been the influence of Velázquez and Goya as seen through the watering down at a distance.

For some years before the First World War there had been in Dublin a collection of good French painting among which was *Les Parapluies* by Renoir. These pictures were on loan until a proper gallery was built for them by the city. This was the Sir Hugh Lane Collection. In an acrimonious dispute with the city, Lane sent the pictures on loan to the National Gallery in London, and in his will he left them to that gallery. Subsequently he signed an unwitnessed codicil to his will by which the pictures were to be given to Dublin, but before this will could be legalized, he was drowned on the *Lusitania*.[20] The pictures had not been long enough in Dublin to influence students as they later influenced a generation of English painters.

Knowledge then of the most important contribution to later European painting, the French School, was singularly lacking. The history of art was not taught to students nor did they, or indeed artists, study and work from paintings in the National Gallery which is one of the best small galleries in Europe. Study in the gallery would have at least given an immediate first hand sense of values and a standard of comparison. Pupils of Gleizes and of Lhote brought back from France the abstract colour conceptions of the former and the hard discipline of Cubism.

Mainie Jellett, a pupil of both French men, linked up their abstract colour with earlier Irish abstract design in metalwork and in illumination. Gleizes had so great an influence on her that it retarded her own creative ability. Slowly she was breaking free from his influence when she died. Mainie Jellett was a discriminating influence and eager to make contemporary painting known to both the public and the painters and was always willing to help. Rouault had somewhat influenced another pupil of Gleizes and Lhote, Evie Hone. Gleizes was too rigorously abstract, too dominant as a teacher and it was difficult with him to avoid undue influence. The restraint and discipline of Cubism suited her clarity of mind as did its emphasis on selective colour and on the structural basis of composition have affected her subsequent work as did its emphasis. She developed her knowledge of form and of distortion to give coherence to expression. Most of all she felt, as others have felt that she was at ease with the people who thought creative art was important and who respected and loved it. Later she discovered her real talent which is that of a worker in stained glass and for close on ten years she had slowly built up a reputation until now she is possibly the most important artist in that medium in Western Europe. Recently she has finished six large windows for a chapel in Tullobeag College.[21] Her importance as an influence can be seen when her work with its structural strength of rich colour is compared with the facile line weakness of commercial church glass.

It is rare now to find an artist who can create religious art of this unique quality without either rhetoric or sentimentality. Nano Reid, having had an academic training in Ireland later became interested in Egyptian sculpture while studying at the Chelsea Polytech.[22] The economy and simplicity of this sculpture disturbed her realistic sense of value which had placed more emphasis on mechanical dexterity than on thought. Her next most important influence was the work in gouache of Marie Howet[23] a Belgian artist who had lived for a while by the sea in Western Ireland. Her sensitive eye and subtly delicate palette had combined in a new interpretation of this landscape. Marie Howett had for the first time made Reid interested in the fugitive certainty of watercolour. Reid has since refined her mental processes and her colour sense and as a colourist shapes form with a touch of magic known by the pure colourist. She recreates a composition by extracting each primary core and by ignoring all accidental inessentials.

One of the difficulties about painting in Ireland was that not many people were interested in art and that there were few commercial galleries. The National Gallery seldom ever has used its walls for a loan exhibition and apart from its own fine collection; it has no contact with the outside world. The Municipal Gallery which includes the work of many living artists is conservative. It seldom gives an exhibition and subsequently the world of thought and of experiment and of vitality in paint is shut out. This seeming lack of interest may be due to the fact that since the reconstruction of Charlemont House[24] for its collection some years before the war, it has been unable to purchase pictures and will not be able to purchase them until the heavy building debt is paid off. Official galleries have been and are of little use to the students or to the painters who wish to see the present day world of art or the influences which have shaped it.

During the recent war there has been an exception to this exclusion. The School of Art which yearly hangs pictures selected by the Royal Hibernian Academy has opened its gallery to other exhibitions amongst which is the selection of pictures organised through the governing body of the Gaelic League[25] by Irish artists. So far its selective taste has not been sufficiently rigorous. For the past twenty years the gallery owned by the Dublin Painters[26] has shown the work of experimental painters; of those who differed from the academicians.

The Dublin Painters have also been responsible for Irish Exhibition of Living Art which has been represented by three successive exhibitions until 1946 in the School of Art. The first opening included academic painters who have not since sent in canvases. In the more recent shows works by Henry Moore, Graham Sutherland[27] and David Jones.[28] In 1945 Edward Pignon[29] and Charles Walch[30] were exhibited for the first time in Dublin. The organisers of Living Art have taste, knowledge and sympathy and they are energetic workers. The result of their efforts has shocked or has interested the public and yearly there has been an added interest, an added incentive for a visit to the gallery. The failure of Living Art to be granted the School of Art last year raises an interesting problem as there is now no gallery in Dublin which is sufficiently large to be used by them or in which a loan exhibition from abroad can be shown.

The Friends of the National Collection have helped to develop interest by buying pictures which they present to the Municipal Gallery. A painting by Rouald was refused by the Municipal, but by a clever and amusing contradiction the picture *Christ Mocked* was accepted on loan by the Catholic University of Maynooth. The Friends, as they are called, organised in 1944 an exhibition of Continental art[31] from Irish galleries and from Irish private collections which include painting from Monet to the present day. There were great gaps in continuity but many of the Fauves were well represented. The pictures provoked controversy and delighted interest.

It has been thirty years, apart from the Hugh Lane Collection, since the post Impressionists had first been seen in the old Municipal Gallery.

Another important showing was that of the retrospective work of Jack Yeats in June 1945. It included a working stretch of fifty years during which his change in development from interest in flamboyant character and dramatic realisation to poetic and symbolic interpretation could be fully studied from the one hundred and eighty works shown. The exhibition was a national tribute. The paintings came from Irish galleries and from Irish houses and the public were able to study, look at his while their eyes remembered Continental paintings. Indeed some of his canvases had a quality comparable to the reputable work of the School of Paris.[32] His essential poetry and vitality, the evocative nuances of his suggestive and implied colour and his progressive changes in method created a standard judgment for onlookers. This exhibition had an important result as it helped many to understand aspects of good painting and it helped realise that since the end of the eighteenth century there has been no monied class with taste and until now there was little here of that political or economic security which fosters appreciation. Newspapers treated of practical matters such as the speed of greyhounds and hearses, murder and surgical improvisations or the involuted pride of our distorted history. Writing and its criticism assumed some small importance but art has little space. The lack of intrinsic worth of art criticism here affects the public, the artist and the quality of writing. During the war there was a slight improvement.

No. 7. *'Renaissance' in* La France Libre, *XIII:74 (London, December 1946–January 1947), 138–43, signed Ernest O'Malley*[33]

Ireland, for a long time, longer that other nations care to remember, has been a mental concept to its own people. Held by an outside power which claimed a legal right to its continued occupation as part of an empire, it could only exist as an independent country in the minds of those Irish who refused to surrender or to submit. For centuries there had been a condition of muffled war in which the people lived their own life apart from that of the conquerers whose right to rule was never accepted. From 1916 onwards there began a resistance movement which gradually organised the resources of the people, and which was, indeed, the first effective resistance in contemporary Europe. In 1922, by a majority of four in the formerly outlawed Dáil or Parliament, a treaty with England was accepted. As a result Ireland was divided into two: the Irish Free State, or the Twenty Six Counties, and the Government of Northern Ireland, or the Six Counties.

The immediate response to the Treaty was unrest followed by civil war. Civil war split the comradeship of united effort, weakened the nation by bitterness and harsh memory, and made people doubt intention and motive. Formerly the country had been divided into those who held Ireland for the British, the Anglo-Irish and Scots in the North, and those who believed in or had worked for independence. Now came another cleavage between those who accepted a measure of freedom and those who refused to accept that measure.

One immediate result of this strife was a new understanding and an unromantic realisation of ourselves as a people. At one time it had been easy to blame the British for our faults and easy to interpret them in terms of conditions forced on us by historical necessity; now, some learned to analyse cause and effect, to blame themselves and to face the evil necessity of power. Later, some of the separatist opposition in the civil war became the government. They helped to change the Free State status to a greater measure of freedom, substituting a name *Éire*, an ancient name for the entire country. The word 'Ireland' then has two meanings. It may have a geographical implication, or it may be used, as it is by most people there, as if the country were undivided.

The civil war added complications to an already very complicated pattern. During successive conquests and confiscations, Ireland had been divided into those who owned and controlled the country, the English, and those who had little or no property and influence, the Irish. The English in Ireland were known as the Anglo-Irish only when their allegiance was given to England and when their interests and mentality were hostile to Ireland. When they contributed in any way towards freedom, they were immediately accepted and regarded with affection. Some of them had laid the basis for the understanding of political freedom, yet in all movements of revolt it had been the people themselves who supplied the motive power.

The Anglo-Irish, essentially a garrison, had built around them a focus of Irish who accepted and who worked with them. The two races since the Reformation had an additional barrier as the Anglo-Irish were Protestant, the Irish Catholic. Suspicion, hatred, contempt and class-interest kept the two peoples apart, yet the amenities of life could make both share at times a tolerant acceptance of each other. Both peoples by the end of the nineteenth century spoke the same language, but with a very important different psychological and intuitive understanding of it, and of each other.

In this present century local administrative control was gradually passing to the Irish and as land had been partially redistributed by the breaking up of large estates, the hereditary influence and patronage of the Anglo-Irish was weakened. University education was now available to the middle classes and by scholarship to the poor.[34] In politics the Anglo-Irish sided with any party who wished to make a closer contact with the Empire. Slowly barriers are being broken down but cross-currents of memory and frustration can perpetuate old feuds when a political conviction could be a matter of life or death. Compromise, the English way of political life, has had seldom to face such an aspect in decision.

During the war the Twenty Six Counties remained neutral. Neutrality was then more than anything else, an expression of nationality and a determination to enforce that attitude in spite of adjacent and distant pressure. Even in the Six Counties the delicate nature of the relationship between a minority who believed in an united Ireland and the majority who had always announced their loyalty to the British Empire, was given due consideration. Conscription was not imposed on the Six Counties. Factories to aid [the] war effort were built there and additional troops moved in for training and for defence. In the Twenty Six Counties new and women joined the British army or its essential services. Irish workers built aerodromes or tilled British soil. The proportion of soldiers from the neutral area was greater than that from the Six Counties.

In the Twenty Six Counties the regular army was greatly increased. A Volunteer force to assist the regulars was built up until its number reached 150,000. As the German advance through Europe continued, Ireland became a possible landing ground for an attack on England. The British were anxious to occupy a number of defended posts and naval bases which had been handed over to the Irish before war broker out.[35] These ports had been involved in an ultimate financial settlement, and had been heavily paid for. They were, I think, the last link in a chain of reparation by which the undue taxation of Ireland, since the beginning of the nineteenth century, had at last been compensated for. The ports were then a symbol of reparation and of good will but it would have been an undue demand that a bitter past could be eliminated from immediate memory by such a symbol.

There was as well the fear of internal complications if the ports had been handed over. There was an underground secret organisation, the Irish Republican Army, the IRA, which refused to accept Partition or any connection with the British Government. The IRA had once been the striking force of the resistance movement, but it had then been actively supported by the people and by its underground government. Now it acted without this background or social cohesion. Both governments in Ireland had attempted to suppress the IRA. They had made it ineffective, but it was always a potential menace and it could excite sympathy.

British troops or landing parties might have been sniped at or attacked by the IRA. Bridgeheads could then have been pushed in further for security and punitive action might have been taken, or the Government might try to round up the attackers. Sympathy for men who fight against the British is latent in Ireland and that sympathy would be shown by some to men who needed shelter even though their hosts might not agree with their beliefs. There was then a real fear that a minor civil war might develop.

The great bulk of the population were more interested in the question of the partition of Ireland than they were in the general European situation, which itself did not seem to be clear to many peoples until their own country was invaded. The partition question can always be raised by a political party or used at elections, but being a question difficult of solution no practical means have been suggested to end it. To the Irish mind [a] portion of Irish territory was already occupied by foreign troops and the continuation of a government in the North meant a diversion of nationalistic energy which could be emotionally tapped by a political party, either as a real problem or as a temporary political expedient.

Neutrality was accepted by the people; it was very largely accepted by the men who fought abroad for the British. There was a small majority of Imperialists who were more loyal to the vicissitudes of the British Empire in difficulties and less interested in the moral issue of fighting Nazism. Some of the Anglo-Irish had always been more aggressively loyal than the British themselves, and as they had developed a class distinction by ownership of confiscated land, they were often more illiberal than their British prototype. In war they had always served the British and had suffered heavily in casualty lists. On the other hand there were people in Ireland, stirred especially by the Spanish war which was the real prelude to the latest fight, but who remained neutral.

Since the civil war there had been an amount of doubt and apathy amongst the younger generation who had had to listen to the recrimination and apathy of the older generation. As a result the youth were skeptical about the deeds, supposed or real, of their elders for they had seen them exploit their past when life was uncertain and the ultimate issue doubtful. They had watched some of the older people change and become soft, content to remind themselves of their former integrity and idealism as they made use of them for political or economic purposes.

Neutrality helped to change this cynical pessimism, and out of neutrality grew a new loyalty to a country that needed service. Younger sons of Imperialists served in the ranks of the Volunteer Defence Force with the sons of separatists. Men who had fought against each other in the bitter civil war met again as comrades, or served on committees and as war ravaged Europe memories of our own struggle were softened and made gentle. The healing of the aching sores resulting from the civil war were for some the most important result of neutrality.

There was an exception to this feeling of harmony. Since the civil war the two major parties which followed Cosgrave[36] and de Valera[37] were an extension into politics of that feud. They did not meet in a friendly way, or socially and war was carried on in isolation and bitterness without growth in understanding, especially by party leaders. During the war joint committees of the two parties met, but when the Emergency[38] was over each party would, it was felt, revert to their former political warfare. The anomaly about this attitude is that from the official government viewpoint the civil war is not supposed to have happened. In this hostile attitude politicians might have learned from men who had fought against each other in the field. Over the years they had met in friendship or with respect for each other, and the former affection, which unity had once given, was being steadily built up.

A political conviction in Ireland had often meant that one was willing to fight or to die for that conviction, or it might result in imprisonment or exile. Under the British and in the early years of the Irish Free State people of extreme belief were isolated, even physically. If one met an opponent one met not human values but an abstract inheritance of lack of compromise and unfriendliness in which human sympathy was ruled out. These feelings were in themselves hostile to the warm nature of the people who are naturally courteous, who respond at once to any sympathy or understanding and who can be quickly swayed by intuition in personal contact. Equally people who by experience have had to think in terms of their opponents would on meeting them become hostile at an intonation, or insincere in their expression. All of these undercurrents were now in this war enhanced by danger, or modified by it, to a form of equanimity.

Skilled propagandists endeavoured to prove to the outside world that Ireland was in sympathy with the Germans and that they were allowed to abuse neutrality. It is true that the IRA had been in touch with the Germans and has, I expect, been financed by them, but it was a case of one side making use of the other without any understanding or sympathy. The government interned a large number of suspect or overt IRA leaders and that reduced the danger of collaboration or cooperation. They did not intern sturdy Imperialists who were bitter partisans nor was any action taken against British espionage agents who were numerous enough. Neutrality was resented by the Imperialists who had always viewed Ireland as a subject country which in every war until this last war, had been compelled to conform to Imperial ruling.

In Ireland there has been an instinctive feeling of hostility to British politicians. Their motives are questioned and their sense of moral righteousness examined carefully, especially in war aims and in treaties. In recent years this feeling has become less conscious but it can be roused by deliberation or by stupidity. In the past the Irish were inclined to support the British enemy although there is a warning if sardonic proverb: 'the devil you know is better than the devil you don't know'. That support is now an unthinking reaction from the past when armed help and intervention was looked to from Spain, France and Italy. These countries naturally used Ireland as a pawn and a weak spot in their enemy's flank and Irish exiles guided or misguided their adopted countries in the reality of the home situation. The Irish sometimes deceived themselves by believing that foreign help came from undiluted sympathy and understanding. The Irish government which on the whole had friendly relations with Britain did play on anti-British latent feeling to keep defense energies, but it would have had equally played an anti-German feeling if it had been understood by the people.

Ireland is in essence remote from world affairs. Until the treaty of 1921 an amount of vital energy was spasmodically directed towards political freedom. For at least a century and a half Ireland's contact with the continent has been severed and a population which had no tangible creative exchange of thought, ideas or the arts could neither induce nor evoke a response that would make for understanding. Instinctive regard and affection there was for some countries: for France, Spain, Italy and for oppressed peoples, but this regard was viewed through an emotional under-standing which had no relation to subsequent political or intellectual life abroad. On the continent, in Latin countries, an Irishman or woman feels instinctively at home, especially in France. There is an immediate individual response because we can meet people there as human beings without any reciprocal feeling of distrust or suspicion.

In the last century the United States of America has been the new home for dispossessed Irish people, or for young blood intolerant of home conditions. The Irish in America, mainly if not entirely landsmen drifted to the cities and large towns. Their gregarious nature made them feel more secure when they were close together almost as former parish or county units in their new strange world where work and ambition could produce practical results. This gregariousness and their instinctive understanding of local politics made them ready to exploit themselves in politics and to be exploited by politicians. There is hardly a parish in Ireland, particularly in poorer districts, which had not a large number of its inhabitants in America. They or their children return home for a visit or they sometimes settle down again. Their knowledge of America is often restricted to the wanderings of friends, the people they work for and the power of city politicians. Real knowledge of America seems to be lacking in Ireland. Irish contacts are mainly nationalistic and one sided from the home end and are concerned with people of Irish descent and with Irish American politics. Within the past three decades, however, there has been an interest in the Irish theatre and in Irish writers and that had provided a growing basis for understanding.

To those exiles the Irish at home looked for support and for money in every effort for independence. People who in distress and in bitterness had left their country helped those who by striving for freedom hoped to change political and economic conditions. In America the Irish, deeply suspicious of England, watched any move which might damage heir new country. The Irish vote was a powerful vote and had to be considered by American politicians, especially in war time. As a result America had to be careful of Irish feeling in the First World War. The Irish civil war split this cohesion and subsequent political development in Ireland reduced its necessity and importance. In this was an attempt by America to extract territorial concessions was refused.

As the war went on Ireland became more isolated and in-driven. The policy of two successive governments had already enhanced this isolation by insistence on compulsory Irish in schools and for public appointments, and by the teaching of history. History, as taught, was more concerned with Ireland as a unit in itself rather than as a part of the European fringe. History was a glorification instead of a critical detached assessment. Irish, it was felt, was a building basis for national awareness, which would give psychological understanding to expression and hidden meaning and help to develop consciousness which had never been expressed in English. Whatever the sincerity of the motives involved, the results were inclined to travesty the intention.

The difficulty about the reintroduction of Irish was that there was no literary language on which to base it, and no aesthetic. Irish was a spoken language,

---

preserved in remote parts where life was practically uneconomic. There a vitality, interest and meaning was preserved in a classless cohesion. Speech was an instrument, rich, varied and packed with good imagery. Poetry was known not only by the poets, but by the entire community, who listened with pleasurable understanding and fervour, and memorised with joy. These districts had preserved the mediaeval mind, enhanced by an intellectual interest which through lack of opportunity was not able to develop further. Values there were difficult to access, difficult to transmit.

On the outside of this fringe a new middle class was being built up slowly. It was hostile in its interests and values to the fringe, unsure of itself, puritanical, unaware of the arts. Proper economic security would have helped the fringe to radiate outwards its good qualities and a good educational system would perhaps have aided the rest of the country in understanding contemporary economic and esthetic ideas, and in grafting them on to what was sound in the fringe. The new Irish-speaking movement then went back to a folklore tradition which it did not thoroughly understand. It ignored the few good contemporary writers of Irish who were unable to live by their work and driven by purpose it made of Irish a grammarian boy.

Ireland is thus isolated in many ways. In addition it is geographically an island without a seaman's tradition, or a carrying trade of its own. Politically, it holds a suppressed people who did not reach a measure of freedom until 1922. Economically, it has been a land mainly concerned with agriculture and its products, having England as its chief market. Culturally, through destruction of the arts and the non development of others, it had a broken tradition. The arts are largely kept alive by individuals and all cultural contacts with Europe is maintained by individuals. Neutrality was then a serious problem as an attempt had to be made to balance agriculture with industry, to replace coal with turf for factory power and heat, to increase tillage without artificial fertilizers and to reorganize transport. There was the problem of conflicting loyalties and of inexperience through lack of technical training, but the country solved its problems in its own way.

No. 8. 'Traditions of Mexican Art' in BBC The Listener *(London, 23 January 1947), 145–6.[39] It was aired on the BBC Third Programme[40] on Thursday, 2 January 1947*

My first real experience of Mexico was in San Luis Potosi[41] when I had come by road, or rather by a hypothetical road, across the northern desert. I was confused by facial types and at first, as is common enough, attracted by a superficial quality of romanticism in the colour and pattern of the land and its people. Faces were unlike the academic Greco-Roman European tradition. The mixture of Spanish and Indian had produced a race which varied between the two, but the basis was mainly Indian. As well there was the pure Indian, slender in hand and feet, lithe in muscle, resilient and capable of extreme endurance. There were more people of pure Indian blood in Mexico, I found, than in all the Americas combined.

The Indian and the mixed race in Mexico had more elaborate emphasis in facial structure, in forehead, eyes, cheekbones and chin. They were essentially plastic, disturbing in their values, save to a sculptor. Their faces provoked a memory, but a memory of the sculpture of successive races which had occupied this land and which I had formerly seen in photographs; memories of Olmec, Huaxtec, Totonac, Zapotec, Mixtec, Mayan, Tarascan, Toltec and Aztec sculpture, more or less in their order of origin.

The dark golden brown of the Indian fulfilled the same effect as that of colour in Mayan and Toltec decorative sculpture. These old races had painted background and raised surface to emphasize the decorative effect and to avoid the overcrowding result of detail. Like the sculpture, these faces had a monumental effect. They could be enlarged without loss of values in light and shade. The rich gold of flesh and its varying tones enhanced the hollows and put a soft emphasis on projections. Here, then, in the flesh was a plastic and a decorative sense which had echoed through all their history.

It could be seen in a Tarascan brown earthenware figure, in a piece of Olmec jade which shapes a head from Vera Cruz, or in the Aztec head of an eagle knight, in hand-worked andesite, now in the museum of Mexico City. In the market square Indians and Mestizos[42] squatted all day in formal quietness in front of their wares, or carried on an animated, prolonged bargaining. Their pottery, sombreros, woven stuffs, fruit or flowers were neatly arranged in pattern. Small oranges were piled in small pyramids, flowers and vegetables arranged in simple decorative designs. Their pottery was well shaped, well proportioned, and always correct in aesthetic appeal. They had worked to please themselves and their utensils were made to be used. Time was not of value, but their own value was the result of time in good workmanship. The women wore rebozos[43] or shawls, the men sarapes.[44] The colours were restrained and subtle, again against a background of flesh colour which pulled the whole effect together as in good painting. In the evening I saw women and men trotting home under heavy loads, some with a few flowers in their hands for the altar of their household saint.

Here, then, was a folk tradition which was enriched in memory as I wandered through Mexico. It had strength, interest and vitality. In colour, form and design it was invariably aesthetically satisfying. This tradition of craftsmanship has affected the conscious artist and the popular hand-worker in Mexico. At times, especially in the nineteenth and the early twentieth centuries when taste was florid or banal, folk art kept its high purpose. In a time of resurgence, from 1910 to 1922 it was drawn on for inspiration by the conscious artist. Clemente Orozco[45] had used the popular woodcut to aid his feeling for social satire and for expression. Siqueiros[46] had drawn on the sculptured features of his countrymen to give his figures plastic strength. Diego Rivera[47] had used the bright colours of decorated pottery, or the weaver's strength in all-over design. Others had studied, as well, retablos, small pictures of miraculous invention, found in churches, and the large scale decorations or pulquerios or puls, as an aid to descriptive work on walls.

On my way southwards, I saw many influences at work in the churches I visited. Mexican churches are massively built. Building material is always to be found, labour was easily exploited, and earth-quakes possibly influenced the accent of solidity. Building stone varies from honey colour to red volcanic stone in Mexico City, green in Oaxaca and the blue-grey of limestone in the plains of Yucatan. In the distance the coloured tiles of domes flash in the hard, clear atmosphere, an atmosphere which extends the range of sight. The coloured octagonal domes warm the superstructure. They replace the emphasis of the discrete or elaborate stone carving or the coloured stucco of the facades.

Architectural styles brought over from Spain: Plateresque, with its resemblance to the work of the silversmith, Baroque and Churrigueresque, these were here amplified and accentuated. Baroque by its implied movement of interrupted line and its decorative tendency replaced static elements. Carved and painted stucco, or coloured wood made church interiors a blaze of controlled colour. Decoration became more elaborate and involved as Baroque developed its Churrigueresque form. Line was broken at every possible angle to form recessions, and facades became as richly exuberant as interiors, whilst Indian craftsmen elaborated their designs in a maze of carved or sculptured detail. Predecessors of the Indians had similarly coloured stucco or had covered their sculpture with bright colours. The Mayans had carved stucco ten centuries earlier in their numerous cities in Yucatan, and they had then coloured the stucco. From Teotihuacan southwards, through Mitla and back to Yucatan greens, blues, and crimsons had been used on decorative sculpture, and extravagance had led also, as in the churches, to over-emphasis and weakness.

By the time I had seen the church of Santa Rosa in Queretaro, La Valenciana and the sanctuary of Ocotlán, my eyes had been accustomed to a rich profusion. The side altars of Santa Rosa reach to the roof in curving spirals, in which carved heads and figures join the mounting flame of decoration. Gold leaf had first been added to the wood, then greens and reds mixed with transparent varnish had been placed over the gold leaf. The resultant colour had a jewel-like intensity of glowing light. Ocotlán with its gleaming white front edged with glazed scarlet brick on the lower half of its towers was peculiarly an Indian achievement, and one of the most beautiful churches in Mexico.

In Cholula, which had once been an important pre-Conquest religious centre, there is now a spate of churches. One Easter I entered a small church. Inside it altar pillars were now tree trunks, and golden branches wove their way around carvings of fruit, angels and seraphs in lacquered blue, green, ruby and purple, harsh and astringent, but beautiful. Hanging from the branches were live parrots in cages, and oranges covered with silver and gold paper to represent the moon and sun. A few Indians were strolling about in quiet possession. One of them played on a chirimia, an Indian flute which made a thin sound of successive notes. This was a church proudly shown by the Indians as one of their possessions.

The valley of Mexico has always been a centre of activity. It is on a high plateau of over 7,000 feet, surrounded by mountains with snow-topped peaks of beyond 18,000 feet. The air is live and fresh, and induces energy. Around the city of Mexico are a number of temples and pyramids, and amongst them, Teotihuacan. This was a religious centre built to plan in a space of four miles by two. The pyramid of the Sun is eighty feet lower than the highest Egyptian pyramid. It rises in five steps with a wide staircase on the west. Close to the pyramid of the Moon is the temple of Quetzalcoatl, god of life, of the wind and of the morning. There are found four tiers of sculptured, snake-like monsters which had once been coloured. The sculpture suits its recessed height. The lightly woven, massive pattern was meant to be seen at a distance. It lacks the energy and grace of good Mayan work. Instead it has strength and vigour, as had the later Aztec sculpture, but none of its sometimes stylised simplicity. Experts differ in the date of this city as between 1000 B.C. and the third Christian century.

In such religious centres from the Mayan cities to Monte Albán and Mitla, up to this valley, different cultures used a calendar based on astronomical observations. Mayan civilization of what is known as the Old Empire dates from the first century. Between the fourth and the eighth century many cities were built. Mayans had no knowledge of the true arch. Their buildings of cut stone are usually one story high and are long and narrow. Their sculpture is monumental in conception, and, at the same time, pays minute attention to detail. Mayans were particularly interested in low-relief, in the sureness, purity and subtlety of line, and the deft use of perspective such cutting requires. At Palenque and a few other places, they have beaten the Assyrians and Egyptians in this low-relief. Their extant work shows that Mayan artists were subtle and sophisticated, graceful and sensitive, and that in an extreme form they had the Indian attributes of equilibrium, repose and religious feeling. In Yucatan today, Mayans have the grace of body, strongly rounded heads, aquiline noses and pure cut features of their ancestors as we know them in cut limestone and in fresco.

Mexico City is the storm centre of this land of mixed races and of tragedy. Now it is integrating an indigenous cultural unity. Inspired by revolutionary zeal, painters made the history of their country and its struggles live on the walls of public buildings in fresco and encaustic. They studied the way of life of their people, their customs and legends. Some were influenced by the school of Paris, or by study in Spain, others by the descriptive monumental work of the Italian Renaissance. Painters carried on this battle for indigenous expression aided by the Minister for Education, Vasconcelos, and the anthropologist, Gamio.[48] Painters contributed to a system of education based on native art, and through them open-air schools of painting and sculpture were opened. Walls continued to be covered even with implied criticism of the Revolution, and some frescoes were mutilated. Siquerios, Rivera, Orozco, and Mérida[49] experimented until at last true fresco was again established as the best medium. Siquerios, Orozco and others had at times to leave the country for their own safety, but the expression in paint continued and yet continues as a vital interest amongst the older and the many younger artists. Contemporary plastic expression in sculpture is singularly absent.

No. 9. 'Painting: The School of London' in The Bell, *XIV:3 (Dublin, July 1947), signed Earnán O'Malley[50]*

The exhibition of drawings, paintings and sculpture at the Waddington Gallery[51] during portion of March and April is the first comprehensive showing[52] in Dublin of contemporary English work. The new gallery in which the work was on view is a credit to the architect, Robinson,[53] first name, and to Victor Waddington's judgment. Both direct and indirect lighting are excellent. The technical difficulties of the problem are not apparent so that thought and skill are made to seem easy and natural. The result is that the onlooker can see without strain and the artist's work is flattered as it should be. That neglected Cinderella, sculpture, has at least been given a good light in which to shows its three dimensions.

The size of the gallery means that other group exhibitions can be shown and the numbers of works to be viewed should give the public ample materials to form judgment. The catalogue was well printed, but it would help if the date on which a work was completed was inserted, particularly in the case of an artist not previously seen here. There are two advantages in the catalogues of Irish dealers as compared with their English prototypes; the catalogues is free and the price of the exhibit is unequivocally stated in print.

In all thirty-two artists are represented. Living Art[54] in 1944 and 1945 has shown an Irish public the work on nineteen British artists, nine of whom are not see in the new gallery. Living Art has set a high standard even though war made selection on the artists' part difficult. The introduction of younger painters, Colquhoun, MacBryde, Kessell, Agar,[55] Collins gives us an opportunity of testing judgment, and is particularly of interest to our younger artists. The majority of the painters represented have been working for a considerable time. Hodgkins, Smith, Artmstrong, Hitchens, Spencer, Murray, Nicholson and Lowry[56] in order of age, have their youngest date at 56. Moore, Tunnard, Piper, Sutherland, Richards, Burra, Hillyer[57] are in the next group, and Hillyer is 42. To a public which may be somewhat unaware of the development of these artists, it is necessary to emphasise their continuous search for expression and the influences which have impinged on their work.

Adler, Kokoschka, Topolski and Gotlib[58] though included have nothing to do with English painting, but they now work in London as exiles. French influence is strong in the native born English. The Continentals add individual contribution and their link with the school of Paris. Topolski is not successful as an oil painter. He lacks both the feeling for oil, the subtlety of its use, and in addition, the creative surprise of paint. He is a brilliant Pole whose flamboyant and suggestive line is well known through reproduction in England and in American periodicals and through his war sketches. The swift impression of Augustus John[59] in beery proclivity and attitude and his loosely spread strength is an excellent drawing. Kokoschka and Gotlib, both Austrian, are disappointing. Kokoschka has had a great influence on German expressionism after the First World War. His angular emphasis, his exaggeration of feature and line to overload spiritual qualities, and his emphatic brush stroke afterwards gave way to a tightly woven sense of fine colour which is or about 1924 loosens in his later important landscapes to an impressionistic vision. Gotlib had much of Bonnard[60] and of impressionistic techniques in him, but his colour is hotter and less interesting. His juxtaposed colour areas do not illustrate recession and contrast, nor as surface quality do they help the design. Ivor Hitchins might be studied to illustrate these points. His colour in a modified Matisse[61] handling is fresh, clean and interesting. It slowly creates design and recession in its abstract and carefully thought out relationship, in landscape. In *Piano Player* colour contract is more strongly emphasised and there is added form in his oil. *Poppies and Black Jug* is essentially lyrical in feeling and in the use of delicate economy. Adler's colour and his preoccupation with texture make his approach personal but not satisfying. His *Sitting Woman*, which has its own charm, is too reminiscent of Picasso's adventures in the analysis of form.

Mervyn Peake[62] is a draughtsman whose sense of the grotesque is his drawings has not the advantage of distortion to hold the unit together, and therefore comes into the class of illustration. His oil is a well-handled and striking piece of direct painting. Colquhoun's Irish types show the Scotsman's technical mastery of his medium and his first strength. Previously he used an archetype in hid drawings based, it seems to me, on Assyrian relief. But during this recent Irish visit character and vivacity were included in his formal pattern. His oil is good. It has a solid sense of the quality of paint and a feeling of vitality. Vitality also can be sensed in another of this countrymen, MacBryde, whose *Singing Man*, steeped in haunting evocation has the abstract quality of a mask reinforced by carefully thought out tonal relationship. Murray, another Scotsman, is considerably older in years. He is a fine colourist. In 'Boy with a Hoop' colour is broken up into recessive shafts, balance, as in stained glass, is achieved by alternate dark and light areas in opposition. His *Dancer* has an amusing connotation as it might be a saintly apotheosis. *The Clinic* again shows his lively colour sense and the carefully organised balance of his composition. It has an El Greco tinge which I may read into it in admiration.

El Greco has been introduced as a note by Matthew Smith, but none of his paintings give one an idea of Smith's ability, or if they are recent, of his strength. He has always been limited to a small subject range in which he has worked out his emotional and harmonious colour schemes. For him, strongly influences by Matisse, Derain and the *Fauves*,[63] we have here in Ireland to consult an illustrated Penguin as well as visit Charlemount House. The Penguin would be necessary also to interpret the work of Burra or of Sutherland, or we would have to work our memories back to their loans to Living Art, especially to Sutherland's 'Red Landscape.' Sutherland is an important original artist who has gone back to seldom used natural form from which he has built a world to mirror the greater universe. His experiments with colour washes and technique have also influenced his contemporaries and younger painters. Frances Hodgkins[64] is the senior painter of this exhibition. She is now close on 77 but she paints with youthful eyes. At the London retrospective exhibition of her work this year her surprising later development could be seen. Her best work is in waterolour. They have a poetic sense which suffuses her farmhouses and landscapes with a quality of natural magic. In her oils here the flat pattern is too apparent, unrelieved by full colour, which does not do her justice.

Henry Moore and John Piper have a good showing of sound work. Moore is not interested in the representation of natural appearance. He seeks for a symbol to express the stone or the conception in line. Pin-headed figures deliberately avoid any undue emphasis on the accepted academic standard of reality, but in their worm ending they may relate to the earth, or, even though not meant to do so, stir a curiosity which may make us come back again to study the form. Moore finds the hollow, with its significance of cave and womb, as interesting as the solid, and its working shapes as difficult to present. This counterbalance of concave and convex is again seen in his drawings which have always a sculptural quality, unlike those of Barbara Hepworth.[65] During the war he had to keep his imagination busy with pen and pencil, as stone was difficult to have quarried and impossible to have moved from a distance. His shelter records, one of which is shown, took the moment in time which the good artist seizes upon; his figures are petrified and isolated in time, but inter-related in a communion of dead and living matter. His bronze shows his sculptural method. His frequent monumental sense which begins as an organised concept in his mind has no relation in its flowering to the eventual size of such a group of small figures. Some bronzes were begun as models for stone but stone under his hand in his methods of direct cutting takes a slightly different form. The bronze, like the stone, is asymmetrical, meant to be seen from different angles and related in its worked on shapes to weathering in nature or stone smoothed by water action.

John Piper has already had a one man show in Dublin, as had Epstein.[66] Consequently there is more knowledge of their work here. Piper is in the Romantic tradition of English landscape. His influences have been the early water colour painters as well as Blake, Samuel Palmer, with his sepia effects of swarthy illumination and graphic ability, and Constable. He has a sense of dramatic lighting which is aided by his strange combination of materials. In oil the roughness of paint is a starting point from which to evolve a kind of sullen luminosity in a use of transparent glazes. The war with its drain of circumstances and destruction made casual inconsequence, which was a surrealist virtue, an ordinary event. Destruction brought him back again to architecture, this time to architectural fragments, which with their disjointed edge and cavernous interiors in telescoped time, made his avoid his feeling for nostalgic decay. His previous contacts with Braque and Helion interested him in abstract painting. This elimination of subject-matter made him concentrate on a limited range of colour-relationships which, aided perhaps by his persistent interest in stained glass, strengthened his subsequent use of colour. His technical experiments are related to those of Graham Sutherland. The country freest from a literary conception and from industrial dullness, Wales, may have influenced them both and, in Piper's case, has lessened his dramatic external heightening.

Stanley Spencer takes us back to the main English tradition, the precision of line and the interest in meticulous detail, but in him there is a freshness of the perception of ordinary things which links him to primitive feeling. *Caulking* may have grown out of his war series of workers in shipyards on the Clyde when he related manner to materials with man as the dramatic element. *The Beatitudes* shows a mood which varys [*sic*] between religion and sex. Here is a sardonically humorous aside with the artist's personal portrait as the sly commentator.

A sense of humour is too often lacking in creative work. Murray supplies a little. Topolski in his drawings, Barbara Hepworth unconsciously, when his *Abthos* in white marble was frequently reached for as an ash tray.

Lowry's painting is quite undramatic. Sometimes, as in *The Arrest*, it over-stresses the social content which is present more subtly in *The Mill Pond*. His is a simple statement of elongated perpendiculars and horizontals supported by a clever arrangement of curve, with clear zones of paint each of which has a precise value. Hillier has pushed an able surrealist technique beyond its bounds so that its colour and precision brings it to the point of illustration. Eileen Agar's imaginative use of colour in *Venus* is let loose. Translucent viridian and green on a paper base almost gives an impression of green coloured ink wash. The effect is brilliant and interesting as in her use of texture in *Landscape*. John Armstrong[67] has three oils. In each he uses a different and unrelated technique. A mosaic pattern is one, a flat and exceeding[ly] decorative surface is another, when his animals looks like a patterned rendition of Chinese bronzes, and the third, a clearly outlined study of inclined planes which work against an inflated human. It is difficult to understand his real direction from these examples, but of his competence there is no doubt.

Tunnard is a sincere and interesting painter and a fine colourist. His colour scheme is subtle and relates to this earlier experience as a textile designer. But his use of colour has a basis of Paul Klee in its organization as space and in its texture. Interpenetrated planes bring the eye and the mind in a play of lines surcharged with a symbolism of abstract shapes which deal, with war precision instruments on land and sea and which amplify his sense of distance. Sea enters largely into his awareness for he has worked in Cornwall.

Mary Kessel's oil creates a feeling of spring in its veiled colour and invokes a mood of mystery which suggests more than those the carefully defined. Mary Kriskna's subtle sense of line is expressed in one drawing which approaches the work in the Altamira caves, but she has fused so nearly with the Eastern technique that she had lost her own quality. Dora Gordine,[68] a Russian, is at her best in *Ballerina*, with its careful use of surface. This is the most interesting bronze, apart from the Moore, in its refined sense of form, as opposed to the strength, force and sensual energy of the Epsteins.

English painting began with a linear bent, but the destruction of painting and frescoes after the Reformation was so thorough that it is now impossible to find what was the strength and direction of the indigenous trend. The import of successive Germans swamped native effort and it was not until Hogarth's time that there was recovery, or indeed until the imaginative line of Blake set a standard. Constable should have been the basis of an important school but empire-building and capitalism and the security of academic formalism helped to retard interest, and destroyed taste. The Pre-Raphaelites tried to stem the flow of bad taste but they were too literary and too anemic to refresh good tradition. Impressionism hovered around but not until some years after the end of the First World War did an accumulation of French influence break through an insular front. By the beginning of the Second World War successive facets of the school of Paris from Fauvism, Cubism to Surrealism in a reorientation of form and colour had been absorbed or digested. The last war made use of the conscious artist. It brought him in touch again with an immediate public, gave him a sense of unity with his fellow-man and confronted him with a problem of recording devastation and activity. That lull threw the English back on their own heritage which they systematically explored. What their new direction will be is difficult to say, as it is with the French School, but an approach to representation based on the experiments of the school of Paris is a present trend. The dominant painters, with the exception of Stanley Spencer, have a basis in cubism, abstraction, surrealism, or use Klee's phantasy or Picasso's many contributions as a departure.

No. 10. 'Ireland' in Architectural Digest, XVII:7 (London, July 1947), 172–4, signed Earnán O'Malley

Introductory Article for a series of Articles on 'Ireland'
Ireland is a country difficult to assess, for the ordinary measuring stick may not give the best results. Engaged in a struggle for freedom, Ireland was not related to the world of government or of decision, and not until our time was she able to accept responsibility for her own activities.

Her people carry into the modern world some qualities which belong to another age and which may appear incongruous. Either by accident or by design the Irish have avoided some incidents in world history which have helped to shape the European scene: Roman occupation, the Renaissance, the Industrial Revolution and in recent times, the last world war and conscription. Lack of a sense of centralised authority might have come from the Romans; instead it came very much later in time, through the British. Explicit participation in the Renaissance can be dimly sensed in a study of poetry in Irish, but aspects of the mediæval mind can be more easily seen in everyday use. The Reformation came through colonies planted by James the First, and by contrast is reflected from that source, and from later colonies, as an incipient Puritanism on to the old religion, which was again influenced by Jansenism.[70]

We speak English but, with mouths shaped from long centuries of a native language, our pronunciation and lack of stress is different. English with us has also a different intuitional and psychological value as it represents a completely different consciousness and tradition. That is often forgotten by the stranger who may assume that because English is spoken there is only the barrier of what is called a brogue between us and others who speak the same language.

Scandinavians, Normans, English, Scots have been with us for a considerable time as overlords and their blood has mingled. Naturally we know something of their psychology and mentality even though such knowledge, in its most pronounced way, is revealed as if an unhappy wife uncovered facets of her husband which varied between sound intuition and distortion. Our climate shapes our temperament as it has changed the temperament of invaders so that when we speak of the English we confound them with a different race, the Anglo-Irish, who like ourselves see things largely as black or white.

Ireland has neither been industrialised nor mechanised. Although a beginning has been made both to build up industry and to supply electricity from water power, lack of mineral wealth determines the nature of industrial enterprise. During the war Ireland was thrown back on its own resources. The policy of self-sufficiency evolved a new assurance which has repercussions, from an increased interest in painting to a fashionable use of the once scorned home-spun material and fabrics.

City and urban populations, with the exception of Dublin, are small and the countryside gives no impression of being over-built. To the south of Dublin, within easy walking distance, there is a mountain area which is more remote and unpeopled than many distant parts, where the sense of man is usually present in the most unexpected places. People have never taken kindly to town life save where the English have been long established; yet even in such towns of Leinster and Munster, which are very different to their Connaught prototypes, there is less of an established order than one would expect. The dominance of the countryman is easily felt in Ireland and his mentality is persistent.

People have an air of leisure. They seem willing to take time off to talk even when they are business people, perhaps because business is not more important than an interest in people, or because living itself is important. A middle class has not been built up until this century and even now it is not firmly rooted enough to make class distinctions, for the natural dignity of man is more important than any subdivision. This sense of human dignity assists the most out-of-the-way countryman in putting a stranger at ease and in a sympathetic sharing of his sense of life. This helps conversation, makes for immediate response or adds additional variety to the day's round. In some towns, in the west particularly, small shops seem to be kept mainly for the purpose of conversation, although there is a steady sense of huxtering as well. A shopkeeper who is usually curious and interested can extract information in an oblique manner which has an element of sleight of hand. If greed for information is uppermost, however, the facile threads of conversation woof may be replaced by a sharp battery of objective questions. One result of talk is that very little happens unknown to others, news spreads in mysterious byways, ideas and plots are talked out instead of being written in creative form.

Until recently politics in Ireland meant that you wished the country to have complete or partial freedom, or that you were content with British rule. At times, that political interest could suddenly become a matter of life or death, as it became during and after the First World War when what would now be called a resistance or underground movement gathered strength. Expediency, class interest or belief in freedom could swing some people from one side to the other, creating in a community, where one was expected to take sides, somewhat the same situation as developed in France during the last war. A political movement in Ireland was really a smothered war which at times was more intense than a major war would be with other peoples. Action grew out of personal responsibility and individual effort rather than as an organised service of authority and a symbol which relieved the individuals from personal responsibility. The sense of expediency or of compromise, which are commonplace in English politics, are not easy to apply to such fundamental issues.

Life has a slower rhythm in Ireland than in industrialised countries. The use of turf, for instance, is a necessary adjunct to most small farmers rather than an industry, although there are government-controlled bogs which use machinery. Turf varies in calorific value according to the nature of the bog and the depth of the cutting. It takes up excessive space in transport, loses material in successive handlings, but since the beginning of the last war it has become the main source of heat and, in some instances, of power. Its absorbent nature is often made use of when sold as fuel to carry an additional weight of water. Turf as well is a pleasant symbol of hospitality in the country of storytelling and talk in the long winter evenings when the hearth becomes the centre of the house.

Machinery, save for cutting hay and corn, is seldom used on small land divisions which vary from 15 to 30 acres. In good land such a holding is barely economic, but with poor land, sons and daughters formerly emigrated to America, or go now to England and Scotland for seasonal work or permanently. The money sent home helps to balance the meagre budget. New land divisions meant new slated and cemented houses which are serviceable but ugly compared with the thatched house. A large number of houses are built by the farmers themselves but when local authorities carry out planned buildings, a sense of utility is invariably more important than the æsthetic possibility.

The thatched house was built of stone, whitewashed in some districts three times a year. Recession, distortions and assymetrical boldness gave a special quality to the building where shadows and contours were played on with affectionate impress of hand. Farm buildings or extensions were added in a series of separate units which duplicated forms and repercussed shapes which on rising ground were particularly satisfying to the eye.

Irish towns have seldom any sense of continuity, whilst Irish villages are a collection of farm buildings thrown together by chance. They cannot compare with the English regional use of wood and variety of coloured stone nor with its steady architectural tradition. There is, however, on the outside of buildings, the use of colour in delicate pastel shades which becomes more emphasised in the west. Western light softens and blends, reconciles incongruities and reiterates colour combinations which are as incredible in sky as they are on house fronts.

The two-storied house is a town affair, or, if it is in the country, indicates a rise in social importance. It belongs to the schoolteacher or priest, but it seldom fits properly into the landscape. Again, it is the thatched house which blends with less sharply defined gable and less angular roof.

Another tradition in building, that of the Georgian house, with its economy, precision and restrained elegance, shows in some Dublin squares a use of gaily-coloured porticos which echo the spring colour of shrubs close by, or relieve a wintry starkness. The two traditions with variations seem to contain a sense of indigenous architecture but neither have been sufficiently developed in the imagination of architects.

There is a lack of continuity in the arts in Ireland. Religious architecture is fragmentary, as buildings were given to seculars or to the new church in Elizabeth's time. Ancient cathedrals and churches now in the custody of the Church of Ireland have been restored or rebuilt out of sympathy with the original conception, but in Kilkenny, Killaloe, Galway, Kilfenora, and Clonfert, tombs, altars, doorways and windows retain the flavour of the middle ages. There is an important tradition in sculpture from the eighth to the sixteenth century, to be seen in ruined churches or in isolated freestanding crosses. In certain areas stone cutters carved fine grave stones from the close of the eighteenth century to the first quarter of the nineteenth. The eighteenth-century flavour lingers in Dublin squares or in squalid slums, in cities like Limerick, in unexpected corners of towns, and in isolated country houses.

The literary tradition persisted longest as it was kept in memory mainly through poetry, but not until the beginning of this century did the novel or the drama express contemporary life. It was difficult for a people not accustomed to creative work to see themselves in print or on the stage. The sudden realisation was not at first accepted, as the absence of the steadying influence of a printed creative tradition had made people glorify themselves or explain away their faults, and had made them less amenable to the writer's intuition and understanding.

In Ireland, painting has never developed from the illuminated manuscript stage. The new tradition in the early eighteenth century was that of the British school, and an academic variation of the school persists. During the war, Irish artists were cut off from the Continent and from exhibitions of contemporary outside painting. Thrown back more thoroughly on their own resources they were able to digest experience and revalue influences. A new interest in art produced numerous exhibitions and stimulated the painters. The most important painter is Jack B. Yeats, whose stature is European and whose reputation is spreading slowly. Evie Hone, an important worker in stained glass, is known best through her glass but also by oils and gouaches. There are a number of other painters, Le Brocquy, Nano Reid, Norah McGuinness, Judy Kelly,[71] O'Neill,[72] who are affecting a larger public.[73] Painting, indeed, has for the time being replaced creative writing as an expression.

In this land of broken tradition there is a continuous folk-lore tradition which relies on memory to carry the flotsam of centuries. It persists in ballads, songs and remembered poetry, but contains stories from heroic cycles and the hidden life of the people when there was no other method of expressing that life. In Irish speaking districts this tradition is a living one where poetry is shared and understood by the community and where people use memory and improvisation as well as song and dance to provide their own entertainment. As there was no printing press for Irish the tradition came over when the country became more English speaking. Fresh-ness and a deft sense of words, feeling for a phrase and conversational ease, all of these are carried into writing. The memory tradition accepts heroic figures as if present to-day. It telescopes time, its imaginative perception turns what may have once been defeat into a tale or song of individual prowess and as its allusions are generally understood it replaces the written word of other countries.

No. 11. 'The Background of the Arts in Mexico' in The Bell, XIV:5 (Dublin, August 1947), 59–69, signed Earnán O'Malley

Mexico is of interest to Ireland because for over three centuries it has been subject to foreign domination and for close on a century and a half has been struggling to integrate itself. Apart, however, from its political and economic interest Mexico has made and is now making an important contribution to art history. Successive cultures have been given names by archaeologists and historians, but the early his-tory of the country is ambiguous. From the conquest, which took place in 1519, onwards, Mexican pre-conquest and post-conquest history has been a Spanish interpretation as practically all Mexican manuscripts were destroyed by the con-querors and the remnants can only give a rough outline of a few areas. In addition, the absence of any indigenous written language made the pictograph writing for-merly in use, a very unreliable method of preserving history for posterity. History, therefore, has been learned through archaeology, folklore and anthropology, and of these three, archaeology has produced the most important results.

The main pre-conquest trend in the arts was plastic, expressed by pottery, small figures in terra-cotta or stone, free-standing sculpture, or by decorative sculpture as related to architecture. Religion was the chief basis of Mexican art. Important buildings and even cities were planned as religious centres where a priesthood took astronomical observations, which were used for agricultural purposes and on which a planned economy was built up. Mathematics and astronomy made Mayan chronology extremely accurate, as accurate as that of Pope Gregory the Third a thousand years later, and the mathematical bent of mind induced an intellec-tual use of line. From central Mexico southwards cities were built: – Teotihuacan, Cholula, Tenochtitlan, Mitla, Monte Alban, until Yucatan is reached. These cities are associated with the names of the races who worked in the district, Toltecs, Aztecs, Mixtecs, and Mayans.

Mayan civilization, which lasted for over twelve hundred years, came to its secondary flowering in Yucatan. Numerous well-planned, well-organised cities were built and art evidently took advantage of periods of peace; then for some, as yet, unexplained cause, which may be associated with faulty agricultural methods, the Empire melted away. Mayan growth, peak and decadence, can now be seen through sculpture which, in the outlines of development follows a scheme peculiar to all great cultures. Every five years a sculptured pillar or stelae on which date symbols were carved was raised to mark time. It was difficult for an artist to make use of such date hieroglyphics for his own purposes but the problem was solved and the result was a time record which has aesthetic value in abstract design.

Depth of cutting to enhance light and shade, relationship to other symbols, balance to emphasize design over the total stone surface had to be considered by the artist. Figures of priests busy in ceremony were incised with a perfect sense of graceful line and a delicate understanding of perspective. In the main this sculpture has a monumental quality and is static and serene, yet the habit of over elaborating detail is a potential danger which is often uncontrolled. At times the writhing shapes and elaborate ceremonial plumage on stone remind the onlooker of the persistent and less organised jungle, ever a danger, to be controlled in the interest of man, but which now covers what were once gleaming cities. In Chichen-Itza there are twelve figures of the Chac-Mool, a reclining God who rests on his elbows with feet drawn up beneath bent knees and head turned at right angles to the body. This unusual torsion of the head must have been difficult to relate to the resting body when first thought of by the artist, without straining the unity of the idea, and as is usual with Mayan work the figure is not completely free from the block. Simply conceived in formal dignity the Chac-Mool has the sense of the quality o stone, a spacious massiveness and the directness of statement of a conception creatively felt and realised.

Both the relief in cut stone and its background is coloured as was the custom throughout Mexico. Reds, blues, yellows, and scarlets were used and later, under Toltec influence, the colour scheme was enlarged. Stucco, used as a facing to stone, was carved and shaped in low relief and then painted, so that in effect there was a mixture of painting and sculpture. The light in Mexico is hard and bright, the atmosphere is clear and objects can be seen sharply outlined at great distances. The gleaming colour of the buildings in the limestone planes of Yucatan must have been a delight to the approaching traveller. In Ireland, on the contrary, the atmosphere softens and blends colours, eliminates sharp edges and limits the range of vision.

Frescoes cover walls and portion of walls in San Juan Teotihuacan, Mitla, and in Yucatan. Those of Chichen-Itza date from the twelfth century and are very freely handled. By the use of very thin coats of lime and successive paint, texture and colour are given additional interest. A landscape in the Temple of the Tigers is suggested in the manner of Raoul Dufy with a few, seemingly careless brush strokes. The technique is complicated but the result is a simplified statement of movement in battle. The architectural problem was difficult to solve as rooms were low and the fresco had to be seen from the position of people seated on the ground. Perspective is arranged by making receding figures progressively larger in scale, yet to the onlooker all figures seem to be of the same size.

The old Mayan Empire, which came to an end about the eighth century, is probably the most interesting contribution of a cultural unit that America has produced in art. The new Empire, as it has been called, or perhaps the renaissance of the old Empire, was founded by clearing the jungles of Yucatan. The difficulty of creating a civilization in this soil and climate may be judged by the present day difficulties even of communication, for the peninsula can be approached by air and by sea easier than by land. Here, architecture is the most important manifestation of the new revival, and sculpture as applied to buildings replaces the detached sculpture of the older period.

Mayan civilization was maintained without the horse, or other beast of burden, without cow, sheep, or pig. Metals in use were copper and a natural bronze, but stone implements carried out whatever quarrying, cutting, and carving was needed. The wheel, or the potter's wheel had not been invented nor had the principle of the true arch been worked out. The only cereal was maize, or Indian corn, which, luckily, could be stored for long periods. There were no rivers, and a water supply meant a steady search for natural wells, or the cutting of artificial reservoirs.

Along the east coast in the State of Vera Cruz, the Huaxtec and Totonac cultures developed. The Huaxtec is the more ancient – but dating civilization is difficult in Mexico. There has been little of Huaxtec sculpture unearthed up to the present but what there is of it makes one hope for more. Their sculptors were interested in economy of means, in simple planes, and in stark and fascinating juxtaposition of line and curve. Distortion was used for emphasis or it fits quietly into the pattern of the flow of stone. Totonac sculpture has the refinement and perfection of the best Mayan work. Its decorative sense is apparent in an ease of line which functions simply and sincerely, and if Totonac work has to be summed up, imaginative grace would perhaps suggest it. As sometimes happens when emotion is stimulated to a happy glow one wishes to talk to the artist who has created the work, about stars and sea or about small things which gave him pleasure. Totonacs used basalt, and other stone which was extremely difficult to cut and work, but their technical skill is shown in every object made by them.

Tarascons came from the central Pacific Coast. They introduced a very different element into Mexican life. Mayans, Toltecs, and Aztecs were primarily interested in their Gods, and their work is a ceremonial interpretation of their religious beliefs and particularly with the Aztecs of the grim and fearsome presence of death and evil. Tarascons were potters whose brown earthenware shows their interest in the human qualities of joy, humour, and satire. Their plastic sense is seldom strained to produce a given result. Their work has great freedom and sensitivity and a disconcerting feeling that they are making an easy play or a pun of their own well-thought-out and well-planned effort. They play with lines and curves, elongate and shorten limbs and feature, always, however, with a complete sense of balance in relation to the finished unit.

The Valley of Mexico has always been the chief prize of the conqueror and the natural centre of the country. A high plateau of over 7,000 feet is ringed by mountains whose slopes were once forest-covered. The mountain barrier is never lower than 10,000 feet and the passes were easy to guard. Lakes below preserved the water supply and the land was suitable enough for agriculture, but could not supply a large population. The climate is temperate, which is unusual in this country of extremes, and the dry air and live atmosphere prevent lassitude. It is difficult for us in our moist, will-softening climate where morning rising or concentrated work is a resultant menace, to understand the energy and forcefulness that result from living in places like Mexico City, New York, or Rome.

In the valley a civilization that had established itself before the birth of Christ built cities, amongst which were Cholula and Teotihuacan. One pyramid in either city is of greater bulk than the Egyptian pyramid of Cheops, and the building lines are more interesting. Mexicans shape pyramids as a series of recessive planes with sculptured areas close to the base. Teotihuacan has oblong lengths of alternate geometrical and rounded projecting forms separated by flat intervals of carving, all of which are encased in a stone frame. The frame and its contents are repeated on four successive steps. The angular Gods relieved by the round and the encasing frames, form when seen at a distance a design which in the original must have looked a great decorative mosaic, whilst the receding planes cut the clear sky in a contrasting perpendicular sharpness.

The Aztecs first arrived in the valley in 1324 as roving hunting tribes but by 1519 when the Spaniards intruded, a great Empire had been built up which reached northwards to the desert and southwards to Guatemala. The Aztec religion made use of the blood sacrifice to give strength to their Lord, the Sun, or otherwise with its loss of vigour, life on earth would cease. As their priesthood gained authority and decided on matters of state, what had once been a symbol came an obsession. The newcomers were the most energetic people of their time in this land. They had a strong administrative sense and they were fierce in war. They formed a hegemony of peoples who surrounded the valley, but they were the spearhead and eventually the autocratic overlords. The Spaniards when they came were able to use weak links in the chain of dependant or oppressed peoples.

Aztecs inherited the Toltec tradition of the valley in decoration, design, and architecture. They carved obsidian, which is black volcanic glass, obdurate jade and andesite, as if they wished to show their conquest of the difficulties of these fine materials. Aztec monumental sculpture shows their love of naturalistic detail which was used as a decorative *motif* in the mystical representation of Gods. They had none of the Mayan sophistication or subtle skill, as they were more vigorous workers who attacked artistic problems in a simpler and broader, but in a not less creative way. Their sculpture has vitality, directness and an inherent sense of form which has impressed contemporary sculptors and painters.

The Spaniards, who were accustomed to their own fine architecture, were amazed at Aztec buildings, the beauty of their gardens, and their personal splendour. Bernard Diaz del Castillo wrote of the city in the lake, Tenochtitlan which held over a quarter of a million people and its satellites: 'When we saw so many cities and villages built in the water and other towns and dry land on the level causeway towards Mexico we said it was similar to the enchantments in the legends of Amandis, due to the great towers and temples and buildings arising out of the water, all built of masonry and our soldiers even asked if the cities that we saw were a dream.' The lake building rested on a springy base of volcanic ash which has been a problem for architects until reinforced steel eased stress. Tenochtitlan, however, save for a small corner, was destroyed street by street in merciless attack.

Spaniards had come from a Spain which had in 1492 completely reconquered their country from the Moors. The Conquistadores brought a tireless energy and a more ruthless warfare than was the Indian custom. Soon Mexico was divided into great estates, the Indians became slaves with a mark of their owner, and later of numerous subsequent owners, burnt into their faces. A few Friars after the conquest tried to protect the Indians, notably Bartolome del las Casas and others of his Franciscan Order, but though they fought hard and gained some hearing in Spain, they fought against clerical and lay interest. The manuscripts were burnt in many centres, especially in Yucatan, where Father Landa, who was responsible, at least took extracts which give information about Mayan cultures.

The Spaniards built fortresses and Gothic churches which could be defended. Building stone which varied in texture and in colour was plentiful, easy to obtain and in itself became an important part of the decorative scheme. The Conqueror had found, as in the Inca Empire of Peru, a people of a settled, organised way of life, many of whom were accustomed to city administration. The Mexican nobles had a ceremonial splendour and a sense of luxury which had awed the Spaniards, and as a result there were numbers of well-trained craftsmen who could weave and embroider, paint portraits on cotton, work precious metal into intricate design, construct mosaic in precious stones and mould richly painted pottery. In some areas there was a knowledge and a feeling for poetry which would not be appreciated by the Conquerors.

As soon as they had subdued the native peoples, the Spaniards built palaces and churches on a more elaborate scale. The designs came from Spain but Indian craftsmen continued their ancient tradition so that gods and old motives were worked into church ornament. Indians were found to be able to carve from a drawing and to memorize detail which as often successively changed in the working.

The first architectural style from Spain was plateresque, which was named after the relationship of its ornament to the meticulously rich hand work of the Silversmiths. Plateresque was followed by Baroque with its implied movement and interest in sculpture. Richness of complicated detail, the decorative use of colour on wood or on carved and polished stucco, and relief in stone, all of these fitted into the new architectural ideas. Brilliantly carved altar pieces in successive storeys climbed to the ceiling in a controlled maze of sculpture and of architectural invention. Glazed, multi-coloured tiles formed contrasting bands or mosaics on the octagonal domes of churches, and the tiled dome became a Mexican feature. Buildings became massive to withstand earthquake, and supporting towers on the flanks of the facades added strength and a plain surface which could alternate with glazed brick stucco and decorative stone areas.

The development of Baroque, the Churrigueresque, tested native craftsmen to the extreme of effort. The swirling baroque curve is emphasised, the broken line becomes a necessity and sculpture with a moving rhythm absorbs the function of architecture. This fantastic use of wooden carving, bright with gold and enamel lacquer creates a dreamlike colour impression as the figures in decoration mount and interweave roofwards to be again echoed in the vaults of the dome. Here again, as with the older cultures, the potential danger of over-elaborate ornament can be found when the creative effort weakens.

Fresco had at first been used on the walls of Churches by Indian workmen who had been taught to use European models by the Friars, but when paintings and artists were imported from Spain fresco was replaced by huge areas of canvas. Spain had been influenced by Flemish painters who had worked in Italy or been subject to Italianate ideas, and painting in New Spain shows a similar trend as well as the persistence of a more purely Spanish tradition. Painting seems to have lost its vitality when it reached Mexico as there are few outstanding colonial masters, and no native tradition sufficiently strong to correct the imitation of removed European standards.

The Colonial contribution then was architecture, decorative interiors and facades. A native plateresque style developed, Baroque and Churrigueresque became almost indigenous, and they created a number of buildings which surpass anything to be seen in Europe in this manner. San Augustin Alcolman, the Sanctuary of Ocotlan, San Sebastian of Taxco and Santa Clara in Queratero are probably the finest Churches built, two of them more Indian in expression and more elaborate in coloured wood and stucco. The Colony had a price to pay for conquest as had the Mother Country. As the Colony developed mine owners extracted enormous wealth from silver and gold. The share of the bullion sent to Spain helped to make the King and his interested friends more independent of their people and autocratic, more ambitious, and finally contributed to the fall of Spanish power. In the Colony, neglect of agriculture and land erosion through the cutting down of forests for smelting, resulted in worn out soil. Restrictions on trade and commerce by Spain destroyed initiative and industry and made for revolt.

The burden bearer, the Indian, in passive despair and apathy threw all consciousness of contact with his oppressors although in remote regions he could preserve his enduring bodily strength and his way of life. His culture had been destroyed and despised, monuments of his race has been heaped over with earth or split by forest growth and the Indian was not even vaguely aware of the contribution of his race to world history.

In some such manner the Irish of the 18th century have been isolated from and unaware of their achievements in the past. They had withdrawn from the conscious life of their conquerors as if they were living in another dimension. The plastic arts were not even a dim memory. Literature was a survival of the tongue, history was kept alive by folklore memory alone. Criticism in the creative sense had neither material to work on nor educated people to work with.

Mexican pre-conquest art has an advantage over Irish material in that the former has little history associated with the objects unearthed or already in position. This lack of history can help when objects are looked at for their own sake and as an end in themselves. They have then less to do with factual information or with literary association, but demand more attention from the eye and a more sympathetic perception of form and design. Most people, however, would prefer to associate extraneous information with a piece of sculpture or a painting, and although what it rings may stimulate interest it is of much less importance than the necessary effort of contemplation to understand or to see the material freshly.

In Ireland history is used as a compensation for a vanished past for which there has been no critical understanding as a result of the lack of continuity in the tradition of scholarship; or it is a source of undue pride in superficial knowledge. It is easier to talk of a tradition than to know and to analyse it, or even while talking to be unaware of its living existence. Ireland has had both a literary and a plastic tradition. Native literature has had some kind of continuity but the absence of printing has retarded development in many branches, and even yet the assessment of the literature demands critical interpretation. Decorative and illuminative Art is scattered in Museums through Europe but free standing sculpture is to be seen in the open air. Decorative sculpture is fragmentary but it reaches to beyond the medieval period. Sculpture is a definite and important heritage which should be a source of true pride to our imagination and to our eyes, and a challenge to creative inspiration.

APPENDIX II

Malley and Hooker Family Relationships

1. MALLEY FAMILY

Luke Malley (Castlebar, Co. Mayo) and Marion Kearney Malley (Castlerea, Co. Roscommon) married on 29 October 1894 in Dublin. They had eleven children:

Francis [Frank] Luke Malley (1895–1921)

Ernest [Ernie/Earnán] Bernard [O'] Malley (1987–1957)

Marion [Sweetie] Malley 1898–1948)

Albert [Bert] Patrick Victor Malley (1899–1925)

Cecil Patrick Malley (1902–1981)

Charles [O'] Malley (1904–1922)

John Parick [Paddy] Malley (1905–1964)

Luke Kevin Malley (1907–1985)

Kathleen [Kaye] Mary Malley (1910–1987)

Brendan Joseph Malley (1912–1982)

Desmond [Dessie] Francis O'Malley (1918–2004)

2. HOOKER FAMILY

Elon Huntington Hooker (Rochester, New York) and Blanche Ferry (Detroit, Michigan) married on 25 January 1901 in Detroit, Michigan. They had four children:

Barbara Ferry Hooker (1901–1991)

Adelaide Ferry Hooker (1903–1963)

Helen Huntington Hooker (1905–1993)

Blanchette Ferry Hooker (1909–1992)

List of Works by or about Ernie O'Malley

BOOKS BY ERNIE O'MALLEY

On Another Man's Wound (London: Richard & Cowan, 1936; Dublin: Anvil Books, 1979, 2002).

The Singing Flame (Dublin: Anvil Books, 1978).

Raids and Rallies (Dublin: Anvil Books, 1982; Cork: Mercier Press, 2011).

Rising-Out: Sean Connolly of Longford, 1890–1921 (Dublin: UCD Press, 2007).

BOOKS BASED ON LETTERS BY ERNIE O'MALLEY

Prisoners: The Civil War Letters of Ernie O'Malley, eds Richard English and Cormac O'Malley (Dublin: Poolbeg, 1991).

'No Surrender Here!' The Civil War Papers of Ernie O'Malley, 1922–1924, eds Cormac K.H. O'Malley and Anne Dolan (Dublin: The Lilliput Press, 2007).

CRITICAL WORKS BY ERNIE O'MALLEY DELIVERED OR PUBLISHED NOT INCLUDED IN APPENDIX I.

Radio Éireann talk by Ernie O'Malley, 'My Favorite Gramaphone Records: Music from Japan to Tunis', 18 February 1947.

The Bell, XV:6 (Dublin, March 1948), edited by Earnán O'Malley: books reviewed by Ernie O'Malley, *The Fixed Wheel* by Graham Greene; and Padraic Fallon.

POETRY PUBLISHED BY ERNIE O'MALLEY

Poetry magazine, January 1935, 192–4 (4 poems) and March 1936, pp. 304–5 (2 poems).

Dublin Magazine, October–December 1936 (2 poems).

BIOGRAPHY OF ERNIE O'MALLEY

Richard English, *Ernie O'Malley: IRA Intellectual* (Oxford: Clarendon Press, 1998).

Abbreviations

AARIR	American Association for the Recognition of the Irish Republic
COM	Cormac K.H. O'Malley
C/S	Chief of Staff
EOM	Ernie O'Malley
F/S	Free State
GHQ	General Headquarters
GPO	General Post Office, Dublin
HAG	John O'Hagan Papers, Irish College, Rome
HH	Helen Hooker (prior to September 1935)
HHOM	Helen Hooker O'Malley
IRA	Irish Republican Army
LA	Los Angeles
MP	Member of Parliament
NYC	New York City
QMG	Quartermaster General
SF	San Francisco
TD	Teachta Dála (parliamentary representative)
UCD	University College Dublin
UCDA	University College Dublin Archives, often with particular reference to the Ernie O'Malley Papers lodged there in 1974 by COM as UCDA P17a/ (documents) and UCDA P17b/ (interviews with survivors of War of Indepence and civil war)

Notes

Introduction: Nicholas Allen, *Ernie O'Malley's Afterlife*

1. For discussion of this read Anne Dolan, 'The Papers in Context' in *'No Surrender Here!' The Civil War Papers of Ernie O'Malley, 1922–1924*, eds Cormac K.H. O'Malley and Anne Dolan (Dublin, 2007), p. xliii.
2. English's biography is a mine of material information whose rich resource is limited by its situation in a late-century Irish historiographical frame that has no place for an imaginative response to the cultural dimensions of republicanism. For all the brilliance of English's empirical assembly, the biography is split into five parts that never constitute a whole. Read Richard English, *Ernie O'Malley: IRA Intellectual* (Oxford, 1998).
3. Dolan, 'The Papers in Context' in O'Malley and Dolan, *'No Surrender Here!'*, p. xliii.
4. First published in 1940, *The Bell* was edited initially by Sean O'Faolain and then by Peadar O'Donnell. Both were anti-Treaty in the civil war and whatever their subsequent, and divergent, convictions, both retained connections to the artistic cultures that grew in part from republican military defeat.
5. Letter from EOM to Dorothy Brett (11 March 1930), see Letter No. 41.
6. Ernie O'Malley, *The Singing Flame* (Dublin, 1978), pp. 124–7.
7. EOM, application to Irish Pension Board (*c.* June 1934), see Letter No. 2.
8. See for example EOM's letter to Molly Childers of 17 November 1923 when he writes of his enduring fascination for Albrecht Dürer. O'Malley and Dolan, *'No Surrender Here!'*, p. 401.
9. Letter from EOM to Harriet Monroe (10 January 1935), see Letter No. 69.
10. EOM's diary (13 October 1928), see Letter No. 28. For an account of Irish republicans in New York City during this period, see Brian Hanley, 'Irish Republicans in Inter-War New York' in *Irish Journal of American Studies* (2008).
11. Letter from EOM to Merriam Golden (early May 1930), see Letter No. 42.
12. *Ibid.*
13. Letter from EOM to Dorothy Brett (11 March 1930), see Letter No. 41.
14. *Ibid.*
15. Letter from EOM to Harriet Monroe (10 January 1935), see Letter No. 69.

16. Letter from EOM to Merriam Golden (18 January 1931), see Letter No. 46.

17. Hart Crane's *The Bridge* (1930) is a rhapsody to the American landscape, most notably in the passages on the Brooklyn Bridge and the natural wonder that is Cape Hatteras. The sequence resonates with the lyrical passages of EOM's *On Another Man's Wound*. Given Crane's homosexuality it is provocative to think further of the homosocial relations between O'Malley and his men in the revolutionary war.

18. Ernie O 'Malley, *On Another Man's Wound* (London, 1937; Dublin, 1979; Dublin, 2002), pp. 207–8. References herein are to the 2002 Anvil edition.

19. Letter from EOM to Merriam Golden (19 January 1931), see Letter No. 46.

20. The script of EOM's broadcast was published as 'Traditions of Mexican Art' in *The Listener* (London, 23 January 1947), 145–6. See Appendix 1, No. 8.

21. See 'Processional', *Motley*, April 1932, 8.

22. Autobiographical statement (July to September 1950), see No. 155.

23. *Ibid.*

24. Letter from EOM to Helen Hooker (17 December 1933), see Letter No. 61.

25. Letter from EOM to John Raleigh (4 June 1935), see Letter No. 75.

26. *The Irish Press* (17 November 1937).

27. *Ibid.*

28. Letter from EOM to Helen Hooker O'Malley (6 April 1938), see Letter No. 96.

29. O'Malley, *On Another Man's Wound*, p. 238.

30. Letter from EOM to Thomas MacGreevy (1 May 1939), see Letter No. 108.

31. Hilary Pyle, *Jack B. Yeats. A Catalogue Raisonné of the Oil Paintings*, vol. I (London 1992), p. 451.

32. Ernie O'Malley, 'Introduction', *Jack B. Yeats National Loan Exhibition Catalogue*, held at the National College of Art, Dublin (June–July 1945). See Appendix 1, No. 2.

33. *Ibid.*

34. Ernie O'Malley, 'Louis LeBrocquy', *Horizon*, XIV:79 (London, July 1946). See Appendix 1, No. 4.

35. *Ibid.*

36. O'Malley, *On Another Man's Wound*, p. 151.

37. *Ibid.* p. 153.

38. Letter from EOM to Eithne Golden (29 May 1938), see Letter No. 97.

39. Letter from EOM to John Kelleher (7 April 1948), see Letter No. 189.

40. *Ibid.*

41. EOM, diary for May 1948. See EOM Papers NYU.

42. Letter from EOM to Rebecca Citkowitz Liber (11 April 1952), see Letter No. 212.

43. Letter from EOM to Jean McGrail (6 June 1955), see Letter No. 257.

44. This funeral was itself the moment when a young Cormac O'Malley first realized that his father was a presence beyond the family. A lifetime of work has gone into Cormac's own persistent maintenance of his father's archive and legacy, for which we are all in his debt.

45. My argument proceeds in part from observations made in Gregory Dobbins' essay, 'Connolly, the Archive, and Method', *interventions*, X:1 (2008), 48–66.

Prologue: *A Volunteer's Experience*

1. Taken from EOM's draft of his typed application.
2. Richard Mulcahy (1886–1971), deputy chief of staff; chief of staff in March 1919.
3. Michael Collins (1890–1922), revolutionary and politician, killed in the Irish civil war. See Ernie O'Malley, *On Another Man's Wound* (Dublin, 2002 edn), p. 84.
4. *Ibid.* pp. 98, 101–3.
5. EOM's description of his activities in Donegal in the *Irish Press* serial and book publication of *On Another Man's Wound* led to his losing a libel case brought by Joseph O'Doherty, a Volunteer who refused to take part in a raid. EOM suggested O'Doherty's excuse was his family. O'Doherty, a Fianna Fáil deputy by the time of the libel case in November 1937, argued that his possible capture would have had a negative political effect as he was then a Dáil representative. See O'Malley, *On Another Man's Wound*, p. 126 and *The Irish Press* (17 November 1937).
6. This combined the area of the 1st, 2nd and 3rd Southern Divisions created in reaction to introduction of martial law.
7. O'Malley, *On Another Man's Wound*, pp. 303–12.
8. On 10 July 1922; see *'No Surrender Here!' The Civil War Papers of Ernie O'Malley, 1922–4*, eds Cormac K.H. O'Malley and Anne Dolan (Dublin, 2007), p. 45.
9. EOM's arrest in the home of the Humphreys family was reported in *The Irish Times* (6 November 1922): 'One soldier of the national Army was killed, a prominent leader of the Republicans was seriously wounded, and two women were slightly injured when national troops went to search 36 Ailesbury Road, Dublin, last Saturday morning', p. 7; see O'Malley and Dolan, *'No Surrender Here!'*, pp. 325–8.
10. St Bricin's Military Hospital, Arbour Hill, Dublin.
11. EOM was released in July 1924.
12. The Irish White Cross was created in 1921 as a vehicle to distribute funds raised by the American Committee for Relief in Ireland. Those in need could apply. In light of his medical condition, EOM had applied for money to help him recover, using it to support himself as he walked through southern Europe trying to regain his health.
13. Gearóid O'Sullivan was adjutant general, GHQ staff, during the War of Independence, and went pro-Treaty.
14. O'Malley, *On Another Man's Wound*, pp. 98–100.
15. Diarmuid Lynch initially had been the officer commanding EOM's F Company, 4th Battalion, North Dublin and then became the Sinn Féin director of food control. See O'Malley and Dolan, *'No Surrender Here!'*, p. liii.
16. Co. Offaly.
17. O'Malley, *On Another Man's Wound*, p. 90.
18. *Ibid.* pp. 98–103.
19. Cathal Brugha (1874–1922), republican, chief of staff of IRA to March 1919, elected TD in 1918, minister of defence, went anti-Treaty, killed in civil war.
20. O'Malley, *On Another Man's Wound*, p. 113. Three Brennan brothers were involved in the Clare Brigade: Padraig, Michael and Austin. Michael had been appointed to succeed Padraig on orders from GHQ.
21. Padraig Pearse's St Ita's girls' school was established after St Enda's boys' school in Cullenwood House. Michael Collins had a dug-out built on the property and EOM worked in an office there. O'Malley, *On Another Man's Wound*, pp. 112, 126.
22. *Ibid.* pp. 129–30.

23. Seán Treacy (1895–1920), a leader with the 3rd Tipperary Brigade; see ballad commemorating him. *Ibid.* p. 226.

24. Séamus Robinson (1890–1961), officer commanding 3rd Tipperary Brigade, vice-officer commanding for 2nd Southern Division under EOM, a TD in 1921, anti-Treaty.

25. *Ibid.* pp. 168–73.

26. *Ibid.* p. 178.

27. *Ibid.* pp. 193, 195–8.

28. *Ibid.* pp. 202–4.

29. Jerry Kiely joined the Irish Volunteers and then the IRA and was a member of the 4th Battalion, 3rd Tipperary Brigade; assisted EOM in his organizing activities in Co. Tipperary and subsequently when fighting with the 2nd Southern Division; anti-Treaty in the civil war; killed in action in early April 1923. EOM has a warm memorial to Kiely in O'Malley and Dolan, '*No Surrender Here!*', p. 371.

30. The Kilmichael ambush took place in Co. Cork on 28 November 1920. An IRA detachment under the command of Tom Barry killed seventeen British Auxiliars.

31. Frank Teeling was captured and condemned to death but he escaped with EOM. O'Malley, *On Another Man's Wound*, pp. 298–312.

32. Simon Donnelly was a member of the IRA and escaped with EOM. *Ibid.*

33. The former IRA split into two camps: those following Michael Collins and the National Army and the anti-Treaty republicans under Liam Lynch as chief of staff.

34. The Four Courts had been occupied by an anti-Treaty garrison since April 1922; a bombardment began by government troops on 28 June, resulting in the destruction of centuries of public records.

35. The name given to the pro-Treaty government by dissidents who did not recognize its authority.

36. Seán Lemass (1899–1971), republican, politician and taoiseach from 1959 to 1966. They escaped from Jameson Distillery where those who had surrendered in the Four Courts were placed temporarily pending transfer to proper jails.

37. April 1923.

38. In fact, July 1924.

39. Seán Russell (1893–1940), republican and IRA chief of staff during the bombing campaign in Britain in 1939. Sympathetic to German intervention in Ireland, he travelled to Berlin in May 1940 and died in a U-boat off the Ireland's Atlantic coast in that August.

40. Taken from EOM's draft of his typed application.

41. The deltoid muscle is in the shoulder; the latissimus dorsi is on the trunk, behind the arm.

Part I: European Travel, 1924–1926, and Ireland, 1926–1928

1. Madge Clifford (1895–1982) from Tralee was secretary to Austin Stack in the department of home affairs from 1918–22. She was anti-Treaty and was in the Four Courts during the attack and knew EOM there; later was his assistant from June to his capture in November 1922. See Note 91 to Letter No. 23.

2. Frank Aiken (1898–1983), officer commanding 4th Northern Division under EOM

during the civil war and later chief of staff after the death of Liam Lynch in April 1923. Aiken brought about the ceasefire that ended the fighting. See Note 2 to Letter No. 28.

3. P.J. Ruttledge, had been appointed in August 1923 by President Eamon de Valera as acting president in anticipation of his own arrest.

4. Seán Lemass.

5. Miss Áine O'Rahilly, sister of The O'Rahilly, who was shot at the General Post Office during Easter Week, 1916. EOM had mistakenly shot her in his fight to avoid capture in November 1922.

6. Possibly Austin Stack. Madge Clifford worked as his secretary.

7. Tom Derrig, anti-Treaty republican, had been adjutant to EOM in his role as commanding officer of Northern and Eastern Divisions, and was later adjutant general on GHQ staff until his capture in 1923.

8. Eileen McGrane, later McCarville, had been in Cumann na mBan in the War of Independence and civil wars, was appointed a member of staff at UCD English department in the early 1920s, and was a good friend. EOM had stayed and worked occasionally in her Dawson Street flat during 1920. See Ernie O'Malley, *On Another Man's Wound* (Dublin, 2002 edn), p. 149, where Michael Collins also left materials and all his and Collins' materials had been caught in a raid on 31 December 1920.

9. Usually written as Humphreys. Sighle, usually referred to by EOM as Sheila (1899–1994), was the daughter of Dr David Humphreys and Mary Ellen (Nell) Humphreys, née O'Rahilly, and a sister of The O'Rahilly and Áine. As a young Volunteer, EOM's company had been inspected by Nell Humphreys in 1917. See O'Malley, *On Another Man's Wound*, p. 61. It was in her home that EOM was captured in November 1922, and Sighle, her mother and aunt, Miss O'Rahilly, were also arrested.

10. Dick Humphreys, son of Ellen.

11. 36 Ailesbury Road was Ellen Humphreys' home.

12. EOM remained in Dublin working for Sinn Féin until he took off for Europe in February 1925.

13. EOM had met Johnny Raleigh in Limerick *c.*1920 in connection with the IRA. They travelled to London during the Truce to purchase arms for the 2nd Southern Division in November 1921. EOM borrowed money from Raleigh during his European travels from 1925 to 1926 and they remained lifelong friends. EOM became godfather to Raleigh's daughter, Peggy. There is a note to an unidentified correspondent on the reverse side of this letter that reads, 'Please forward to Johnny Raleigh and obliged, I hope you are very well.' This individual is presumably the O'Sullivan referred to at the end of the letter.

14. Gertrude Crowe, one of EOM's republican connections in Limerick.

15. Madge Daly was from a Limerick family of longstanding Fenian sympathies who also were anti-Treaty. Her brother, Edward or 'Ned', was executed in 1916. Her sister, Kathleen Daly (1878–1972), married Tom Clarke, who was also executed in 1916. Madge was a member of Cumann na mBan. See Sinéad McCoole, *Guns and Chiffon* (Dublin, 1997), *passim*.

16. Mgr John Hagan (1873–1930), sometimes called O'Hagan in the Irish form, was Rector of the Pontificio Collegio Irlandese or Irish College in Rome, and had visited Ireland during September 1922 to try to reconcile the fighting factions. In that capacity he met EOM and other senior military and political leaders; see *'No Surrender Here!' The Civil War Letters of Ernie O'Malley, 1922–1924*, eds Cormac K.H. O'Malley

and Anne Dolan (Dublin, 2007), pp. 205, 215, 245. Hagan had an extensive network of Irish correspondents of all persuasions, including Seán T. O'Kelly and Eamon de Valera. Notwithstanding his personal, more independent views, Hagan, as Rector of the Irish College, had supported the Irish bishops during the civil war and was, effectively, anti-republican, pro-Treaty and pro the provisional government. See *Seán MacBride, That Day's Struggle, A Memoir, 1904–1951*, ed. Caitriona Lawlor (Dublin, 2005), p. 88. Vera Orschel, as archivist at the Irish College, Rome, has catalogued the Hagan correspondence up to 1930.

17. The meeting was on 22 September 1922.

18. See O'Malley and Dolan, *'No Surrender Here!'*, p. 443; EOM met Fr Morrissey on 28 November 1923, just after EOM ended his 41-day hunger strike in Kilmainham Gaol, Dublin.

19. Frances (Frank) Brady was the sister of Kay Brady. Their father, James Brady (*c.*1880–1944) was a successful Belfast Catholic linen manufacturer, whose father had come from Manchester and was a friend of Charles Stewart Parnell. Brady had strong republican sympathies. Their brother Gerard, known as Bobby, was ordained a priest on 29 November 1925 in Rome and their sister, Blathnaid, Beatrice or Bee, was professed a nun in the Carmelite order on the same day. EOM met up with Frank and Kay in Florence and Rome in November and December 1925.

20. In late June, Hagan was going to Ireland on a pilgrimage with Archbishop Daniel Mannix (1864–1963), as he reported in his letter to de Valera.

21. Fr Peter E. Magennis was the first Irish Superior of the Calced Carmelites and was known as 'the General'. He was a close friend of Liam Mellows (1892–1922), had been with him in New York in 1919 and was first president of the Friends of Irish Freedom when Mellows and de Valera were there, and in Rome was independent of the politics of the Irish College. See Lawlor, *Seán MacBride, That Day's Struggle, A Memoir*, pp. 88–9.

22. Robert Barton (1881–1975), a signatory of the Anglo-Irish Treaty, turned republican and was in Kilmainham Gaol with EOM.

23. Though Kathleen (Kay) Brady's family was from 2 St John's Park, Ormeau Road, Belfast, she lived in Dublin. Her sister Frances (Frank) later married Andy Cooney, chief of staff, IRA. EOM wrote to Kay and Frank while travelling. The James and Mary Brady family was strongly religious and republican. Letter from EOM to John Hagan (19 June 1925), see Letter No. 6. Prior to her return to Ireland, Kay stayed in Menton, France, where EOM wrote her this letter. Assistance on finding and preparing these Brady letters has been generously given by the late Michael MacEvilly, Dublin, and Dr Carlo Maria Pellizzi of the University of Pisa.

24. Mgr John Hagan.

25. Travel guidebook.

26. Fr C.F. Ronayne, St Albert's College, Rome, Assistant-General of the Calced Carmelites.

27. Mary (Molly) Childers (1887–1974), American-born, writer, nationalist and wife of Erskine Childers (1870–1922), writer and republican, executed during the civil war. EOM had corresponded with her extensively while in jail during the civil war, and those letters are included in *'No Surrender Here!'*.

28. Mgr Michael Curran from Dublin was a historian at the Irish College and became Rector in 1930.

29. EOM signed his letters to Kay as Cecil, in keeping with his false passport identity of

Cecil E. Symth-Howard. Letter from EOM to John Hagan (3 April 1925), see Letter No. 5. He maintained covert habits of signature and address throughout his long correspondence, learnt from his experience during the War of Independence.

30. Michelangelo.

31. Francis (Frank) Luke Malley (1895–1921), Dublin Fusiliers and later King's African Rifles, died in Dar es Salaam, British East Africa, and Albert (Bertie) Patrick Victor Malley (1899–1925), Connaught Rangers and later Nigerian Frontier Forces, died in Lagos, British West Africa.

32. EOM was interned in the Curragh Camp during the final stages of the civil war.

33. Molly Childers.

34. One of many Americans that EOM met in Rome.

35. Honor Murphy.

36. Fr C.F. Ronayne.

37. Gerard or Bobby Brady, Kay's brother, who had just been ordained in November 1925.

38. The Irish College, Rome, where Bobby Brady was located after his ordination.

39. 1 January 1926.

40. Possibly EOM's abbreviation of Michelangelo.

41. Matriculation, or entrance examination.

42. EOM humour: he did not serve in any foreign campaign.

43. Fr C.F. Ronayne.

44. Áine O'Rahilly.

45. Mrs Ellen (Nell) Humphreys, also a sister of The O'Rahilly.

46. Emmet Humphreys, son of Mrs Humphreys.

47. The quotation comes from lines taken from various crime stories in Edgar Wallace, *The Murder Book of J.G. Reeder* (1925). EOM continues to quote Wallace in this and the next letter.

48. John Addington Symonds, *Renaissance in Italy: The Revival of Learning* (1897), and subsequent volumes.

49. Reference to EOM's description of Emmet Humphreys in his letter to Kay Brady (6 January 1926), see Letter No. 11.

50. Possibly '*Qui lo sa*', 'Who knows?'

51. Money.

52. After his arrest in Kilkenny in 1920, EOM's feet were badly injured when his booted captors trampled them. 'My toes were crushed; some stamped hard with the full weight of their legs on instep and toes', O'Malley, *On Another Man's Wound*, p. 253.

53. Mgr John Hagan, Rector. EOM is referring to past circumstances of their respective civil war roles.

54. Kevin Malley.

55. *L'Illustration* was a weekly French newspaper famous for the early reproduction of photography.

56. The quotation is from Lucian's life of Demonax, a philosopher who lived in Athens in the first and second centuries after Christ.

57. Leopold Godowsky (1870–1938), concert pianist, composer and transcriber, particularly of Chopin, born in Sozly, Lithuania, and died in New York.

58. Ferdia is a central figure of *The Táin*, in which he is killed by his friend Cúchulain, champion of the Red Branch warriors of Ulster.

59. Kay and Frank Brady both lived in Dublin and maintained strong republican links

during development of factions within Sinn Féin in 1926 when de Valera split off to form the Fianna Fáil political party. Their good friend was Andy Cooney, who was chief of staff of the IRA at the time of this exchange of letters. Whether the possible coup refers to Ireland north or south is unclear.

60. Fr C.F. Ronayne.

61. Seán MacBride (1904–1988), son of John MacBride and Maud Gonne, married Catalana 'Kid' Bulfin (1900–1976) in Dublin in January 1926 while he was on the run. They then left to live in Paris where EOM stayed with them from time to time. Kid was anti-Treaty and was one of the typists in the Four Courts GHQ. EOM had met Major John MacBride, who was executed after the Easter Rising. 'I had known MacBride. He had been to our house a week before the Rising and had laughed when I told him I would soon join the British Army. He had patted my shoulder and said, "No you won't." ' O'Malley, *On Another Man's Wound*, p. 47.

62. Seán MacBride had been assistant director of organization on EOM's headquarters staff in the Four Courts, April–June 1922, where Kid Bulfin was a typist. He was later to become chief of staff of the IRA in the 1936 period.

63. Letter from EOM to John Raleigh (March 1925), see Letter No. 4.

64. Leopold Kearney, Irish Consular Delegation, Paris, subsequently Irish Ambassador to Spain.

65. Dr Bernadette Lynch, lived in Paris at 20 rue de la Paix.

66. La rue Faubourg St Honoré, Paris.

67. Fr P.E. Magennis.

68. Seán T. O'Kelly wrote to Hagan on 30 October 1926 that he had visited EOM at his home and that 'he is opposed personally to F[ianna] F[áil] but he favors it being given a chance by S[inn] F[éin] and the Army [IRA]. He has gone back to his medical studies and intends to give his spare time to Army work.' Irish College Rome Archives HAG 1/1926/506.

69. Mgr Michael Curran, Rector of Irish College after Mgr John Hagan died in 1930. See EOM's interview in UCDA P17b/117.

70. Dr Quinn and his wife, friends of Seán MacBride and John Hagan in Paris.

71. Seán and Kid MacBride. Letter from EOM to Kay Brady (4 March–26April 1926), see Letter No. 14.

72. Upon his return to Dublin EOM reverted to signing as 'Ernie' rather than 'Cecil', since he was now safely at home. Many of the books he carried with him while abroad had also been signed on the inside cover as 'Cecil'.

73. Frank Gallagher (1893–1962), republican, civil servant, author and future first editor of *The Irish Press* in 1931.

74. Estella (Stella) Solomons (1882–1968), artist. EOM had worn a belt given to him by Stella during the War of Independence. 'It had been given to me by a Dublin artist, Stella Solomons, wife of Seamus O'Sullivan, editor of *The Dublin Magazine*. It had belonged to her brother who had served in the British Army, and she had taken it from her house unknown to her people.' O'Malley, *On Another Man's Wound*, p. 354. When EOM was in prison they corresponded on art matters. See O'Malley and Dolan, '*No Surrender Here!*', pp. 439–40, 471.

75. Cecilia Gallagher, neé Saunders (1889–1962), from Cork, strong republican family, anti-Treaty, married Frank Gallagher in May 1922, was jailed during the civil war.

76. Relatives and supporters of those who served in the British army wore red poppies each year on 11 November to mark Armistice Day and later Remembrance Day.

This remembrance became a focus for republican protest after 1922. See Fearghal McGarry, 'Too Damned Tolerant: Republicans and Imperialism in the Irish Free State' in *Republicanism in Modern Ireland*, ed. Fearghal McGarry (Dublin, 2003).

77. Harold Speakman (1888–1928), author, in 1925 published his travels in Ireland.

78. Patrick Fleming had been anti-Treaty, officer commanding 3rd Eastern Division when captured, was in Mountjoy Jail with EOM, and then on hunger strike but was released; he was later appointed chief of staff of the IRA in 1947.

79. Seamus O'Sullivan was the pseudonym of James Sullivan Starkey (1879–1958), poet and editor of *The Dublin Magazine*, and married to Stella Solomons.

80. Patrick Malley, younger brother of EOM.

81. Kevin Malley, younger brother of EOM.

82. EOM had been active at UCD in reorganizing the republican clubs, trying to get them to continue to follow the traditional Sinn Féin line and not support the Fianna Fáil policy of agreeing to enter the Dáil.

83. Mae and Eva Tobin, daughters of Mrs Marion Tobin, of Tincurry, Co. Tipperary. EOM had established his headquarters for the 2nd Southern Division in her house during 1921, and as a result her home was burned down by the Black and Tans in May 1921.

84. Bob de Courcy had been divisional engineer for EOM's 2nd Southern Division, 1921, and was later with him on hunger strike with other republican prisoners in Kilmainham Gaol from October to November 1923. He was elected mayor of Limerick in October 1923.

85. For the Misses Daly see Note 15 to letter from EOM to John Raleigh (March 1925), Letter No. 5. The 'Blue Nuns' were the Catholic sisters of the Servants of the Immaculate Heart of Mary, so called because of the colour of their habits.

86. Frank Geary. The reference is probably to the small munitions factory established outside Limerick during the Truce between pro- and anti-Treaty factions.

87. EOM sometimes signed the Irish version of his name when signing letters or putting his name on books while in prison from 1922 to 1924, and sometimes in later years.

88. Gertrude Crowe from Limerick.

89. Kid MacBride's daughter, Anna, was born on 24 November 1926 in Paris.

90. Seoirse Plunkett, anti-Treaty republican in the Four Courts, later on hunger strike with EOM in Kilmainham Gaol, see O'Malley and Dolan, '*No Surrender Here!*'.

91. See Note 1 to letter from EOM to Madge Clifford (28 July 1924), Letter No. 3. Jack Comer from Co. Galway (1897–1974), anti-Treaty republican. He had gone to University College Galway and was involved in republican activities, was medical officer with the 3rd Southern Division, knew EOM during the War of Independence, was interned in the Curragh from March 1923–June 1924, where he acted as medical officer to his fellow prisoners, including EOM. On release he was initially debarred from holding a medical post but eventually received an appointment in Rathdowney, Co. Laois, in 1925.

92. Dr Bernadette Lynch, resident of Paris and friend of Seán MacBride and John Hagan. Note 65, letter from EOM to John Hagan (25 May 1926), see Letter No. 17.

93. Possibly a group of EOM's friends.

94. EOM wrote poems, limericks and other notes in his medical notebooks. See EOM Papers NYU.

95. In Seán T. O'Kelly's letter to Mgr John Hagan, he noted that he had caught up recently with EOM and that EOM was looking forward to seeing Hagan on his next visit. Irish College Rome Archives HAG/1/1927/241.

96. Note 9, letter from EOM to Madge Clifford (28 July 1924), see Letter No. 3. EOM addressed her as Sheila, not Sighle, Humphreys.

97. Whatever his reservations as expressed to Humphreys, EOM was reported as a leading figure at that year's twelfth anniversary of the Easter Rising in Limerick. 'Over 500 took part in a procession to St Lawrence Cemetery, Limerick. The rosary was recited at the Republican plot and at a meeting held subsequently, Mr E. O'Malley (Dublin) presided.' *Irish Independent* (9 April 1928).

98. Stella Hotel, Kilkee, Co. Clare.

99. Bea Raleigh.

100. EOM was susceptible to sunburn.

Part II: *Travel in the United States and Mexico, 1928–1935*

1. Columbus Day marks the anniversary of the arrival of Christopher Columbus in the Americas in 1492.

2. EOM and Frank Aiken (1898–1983), officer commanding the 4th Northern Division under EOM during the civil war and later chief of staff after the death of Liam Lynch. Aiken brought about the following ceasefire and supported de Valera's break with the Sinn Féin policy of non-participation in the parliamentary process in 1926, which EOM opposed. Aiken was later minister of defence in de Valera's government in 1932.

3. EOM landed in New York during Prohibition.

4. Matthew Garth Healy (1893–1954) was born to Irish parents in South Africa, from where he emigrated to Ireland in 1912, studying accountancy and joining the civil service. He was sent to New York in 1919 to head the office for the Irish Bonds, remaining as officer in charge of the bond drive to help the newly declared Irish Republic through to the 1935 repayment of the funds to the bondholders. Healy was also secretary to the American Promotion Committee for *The Irish Press*. He later served as vice-consul in New York, secretary of the Irish delegation in Washington DC and consul general in Chicago and later New York from 1947 to 1954.

5. Hotel McAlpin, 50 West 34th Street at Sixth Avenue, built in 1913, was then the largest hotel in New York.

6. Thomas J. Ford, editor of *The Irish World*, a left-leaning Irish-American newspaper founded by his father Patrick Ford, who was proprietor from 1870 to 1913.

7. Gotham Book Mart, 41 West 47th Street. In fact Frances Steloff (1887–1989) had established her famous literary bookstore elsewhere in 1920 and this was her third move.

8. D.H. Lawrence (1885–1930), writer. Letter from EOM to Dorothy Brett (11 March 1930), see Letter No. 41.

9. These were bonds were raised by Eamon de Valera and associates in America in support of a notional Irish republic during the War of Independence. Following legal disputes after the Irish civil war, the New York Supreme Court ordered the return to the American subscribers of the cash held on deposit for the bonds in 1927.

10. Patrick Nally, Riverside Drive, New York.

11. St Patrick's Cathedral, Fifth Avenue, between 50th and 51st Streets.

12. St Francis of Assisi Church, West 31st Street, New York. EOM attended the 12.15 pm

mass, the first afternoon mass to be celebrated in an American church.

13. Commonly known as Gaelic Park, this site was purchased by the Gaelic Athletic Association in the Bronx in 1926.

14. Sean Ryan was president of the Gaelic Athletic Association from 1928 to 1932.

15. Probably took the Sixth or Ninth Avenue 'elevated' subway. There were also elevated subways on Second and Third Avenues.

16. The Tailteann Games were a sporting and cultural festival organized in support of the newly independent state in Ireland. They were held in 1924, 1928 and 1932, and took their name from the ancient games originally held in honour of Queen Tailte.

17. There were two forts: Fort Washington and Forest Hill Fort and the latter had been made into Fort Tryon Park. George Washington's Continental Army was defeated here on 16 November 1776.

18. American football.

19. 225 Broadway, Room 3907, New York, the location of the office of *The Irish Press*.

20. EOM's geography is mistaken. By east and west he means the East River and the Hudson River to the west.

21. See Note 9 in Diary No. 28, when bond funds were to be identified and segregated for return to bond subsribers.

22. EOM referring to an airship or blimp.

23. Frank P. Walsh (1864–1939), born in St Louis, Missouri, lawyer and advocate of Irish and anti-imperialist causes, he attended the Paris Peace Conference, was involved in the Irish republican bond affairs from 1919 to 1913, chaired the Commission for Irish Independence, was appointed by President Woodrow Wilson to head the US Industrial Relations Commission and in this context was chairman of the American Promotion Committee for *The Irish Press*.

24. Alfred (Al) E. Smith (1873–1944), four-time governor of New York and presidential candidate for the Democratic Party in 1928. Smith was the first Roman Catholic and Irish-American to be a major party nominee.

25. Eugene O'Neill (1888–1953), Nobel Laureate in Literature and winner in 1928 of the Pulitzer Prize for *Strange Interlude* (1927). EOM may be referring here to a production of *Dynamo* (1928).

26. Peadar O'Donnell (1893–1986), republican and writer. EOM referring to O'Donnell's first book, *Islanders* (1928).

27. EOM's actual itinerary for the autumn differed from his proposed (UCDA P104/2626(2–4)) and kept him on the East Coast and out to Chicago as follows: New York/New Jersey, 12–13 October; Boston and around, 26 October–14 November; Connecticut, 16–23 November; Philadelphia, 25–9 November; Pittsburgh, 30 November–2 December; Cleveland, 3–8 December; Detroit, 9–10 December; Chicago, 12–19 December; Cincinatti, 20–2 December; Washington DC, 25 December; Baltimore, 26 December; New York City, 27–9 December. See UCDA P17b/167.

28. Aiken was fundraising for *The Irish Press* on the west coast while EOM worked on the east coast.

29. EOM wrote to de Valera on 5 November 1928. De Valera replied to EOM on 30 November 1928: 'I hope you are keeping in good health and that you do not find the work too strenuous. You will not, however, allow yourself to be disheartened by the difficulties which you are meeting. The thing to keep in mind constantly is that without a newspaper it will be impossible to make any real national progress in our generation.' UCDA P104/2638(2).

30. EOM continued to use terms of military association in his fundraising activities.

31. Major Michael A. Kelly (d. 1930), immigrated to America in 1900 and was highly successful in business. He fought in the First World War with the Third 'Shamrock' Battalion of the old Irish 69th Division and was known as 'Dynamite Mike'. He supported the Friends of Irish Freedom but subsequently went with the de Valera side.

32. AAIR or AARIR is The American Association for the Recognition of the Irish Republic. It was a national organization with its headquarters in Chicago and offices in many cities with the aim of influencing political opinion in Washington and elsewhere to recognize the Irish Republic, declared in 1919 after the opening of the Sinn Féin parliament in Dublin. EOM had a ten-page list of their various offices and would have called on many of them as he tried to secure funds for *The Irish Press*. The president at the time was Capt. Denis M. Malloy of Chicago, Illinois, 1st Vice-President J.J. Castellini of Chicago, Illinois, 2nd Vice-President P. Joseph Gillespie of New York, 3rd Vice-President, John J. Reilly of Philadelphia, Pennsylvania, 4th Vice-President Elizabeth Needham of Roxburg, Massachusetts, 5th Vice-President, John G. Murphy of Cleveland, Ohio, 6th Vice-President Capt W.H. McEnhill of Newark, New Jersey, and Secretary-Treasurer, William P. Lyndon of Chicago, Illinois.

33. Frank Aiken wrote in reply to EOM on 2 November 1928 with detailed notes on Fall River, Providence, Waterbury, Hartford, Philadelphia and Pittsburgh. Aiken ended by saying, 'You'll find the work pretty trying, but it's all in the game. "Tis in vain for soldiers to complain." ' This last is a quote from Wolfe Tone, cited by EOM in Ernie O'Malley, *The Singing Flame* (Dublin, 1978), p. 141, his memoir covering the period from the Truce through the end of the civil war.

34. Letter written on the stationery of the American Association for the Recognition of the Irish Republic, National Headquarters, 127 North Dearborn Street, Chicago.

35. John T. Hughes (1871–1945), an Irish-American lawyer and Irish republican sympathizer in Boston with whom EOM stayed during his visits to Boston; he was also a bibliophile, and so they talked much about books. EOM's actual itinerary for the three winter months differed from what he had proposed (UCDA P104/2634(6)) and kept him on the East Coast, to Chicago and then the West Coast as follows: Boston and Rhode Island, 7–31 January; New York and around, 1–27 February; Chicago 29 February; Butte, Montana, 3 March; Spokane, Washington, 5 March; Seattle, Washington, 6 March; Tacoma, Washington, Portland, Oregon, 13 March; San Francisco, California, 15 March; Sacramento, San Francisco, Monterey, April; Carmel, May; San Francisco, May; Carmel, May; Los Angeles, June; Santa Barbara, June; Los Angeles, June/July. This marks the end of EOM's work for *The Irish Press*. He subsequently travelled to Pasadena, San Diego, Los Angeles, August; Pasadena, September; Grand Canyon, 12–20 September; then to Santa Fe and Taos, New Mexico, October. UCDA P17b/167.

36. De Valera wrote to EOM with regard to *The Irish Press* on 15 December 1928: 'Your reports of November 17th and December 3rd to hand ... I am afraid the Organisation over there is gradually falling to pieces and after all one can hardly be surprised. Our friends over there have been more than generous and they have had a good deal of disappointment in the results here.' UCDA P104/2639(3).

37. EOM refers to *Days of Fear* (1928), which Gallagher published under the name David Hogan. In a letter of reply dated 26 March 1929 Gallagher wrote of the story 'The Challenge of the Sentry' that 'You figure (though of course not by name or by any identification except by little things we both know) in two of the stories, "Shadows in the Prison Yard" and "The Staring Sleep".' NLI MS 18353(14).

38. EOM writes regretfully in *On Another Man's Wound* of his limited diet when on the run from 1919 to 1921. Cabbage and bacon were particular familiars.

39. Bhang is the leaf and flower of the Cannabis sativa plant, chewed for sedative effect. It is usually drunk in a liquid preparation or smoked.

40. Mary (Molly) Childers.

41. Solomons illustrated D.L. Kelleher's *The Glamour of Dublin* (1928).

42. In a letter of 30 January 1929 to Frank Aiken, de Valera wrote of *The Irish Press* that ' ... a sum of £100 was passed at the Board meeting to cover EOM's personal allowances from January 1st'. UCDA P104/2644(1). Frank Aiken wrote to EOM on 12 February 1929 that 'a check for $584.50 I had received in a draft for one hundred pounds sent to you by Dev as a personal allowance for the period 1st January to 1st April'. UCDA P104/2632(5).

43. Aiken had written to EOM on 12 February 1929 that 'If possible I want you to be present at the mass meeting we are holding in New York on Sunday, 17th to protest DeV's arrest. We expect to do much good for the paper at it.' UCDA P104/2632(5). As suggested here, EOM preferred to keep his work for *The Irish Press* separate from any specific association with Fianna Fáil and the arrest of de Valera.

44. Probably Preston McKresson or McCresson, a sign painter and weaver based part-time in Santa Fe, whose wife, Helen, was trying to start up a shop in Carmel to sell Native American handicrafts, and EOM met them again in Santa Fe.

45. Ella Young (1867–1957), Irish poet, political activist and mystic. She had been friends with W.B. Yeats and taught at the University of California, Berkeley. By the fall of 1919 EOM had sought out and met Young in Taos and she gave him criticial comments on his poetry. She was a member of the Halcyon, California, community.

46. John Osborn Varian (1888–1934), poet, mystic, and a founding member of the Temple of the People, a theosophical community in Halcyon.

47. Samuel James Hume (1885–1962), stage designer, founder and director of Arts & Craft Theatre, Detroit. At Harvard took Professor George Pierce Baker's famous 47 Workshop, a laboratory for playwrights. He became director of Greek Theatre at the University of California, Berkeley, in the late 1920s.

48. This refers to a reduction in the subscription cost for *Irish Press* shares. This change in subscription caused the printing of a new prospectus, mentioned later.

49. This meeting is probably what was reported in the *Seattle Post Intelligencer* and *Seattle Times* of 8 March 1929, when he was quoted regarding his ambition 'to restore Ireland's interest in' the arts.

50. The Ancient Order of Hibernians was founded in New York in 1836 as an Irish-American fraternal, benevolent society with a national membership composed of Irishmen by birth or descent and who are Roman Catholic.

51. Probably the committee to create a memorial to honour Fr Peter C. Yorke (1864–1925), who was born in Galway, worked with Archbishop Riordan in San Francisco, was editor of *Monitor* and *Leader* newspapers, strong supporter of Irish independence and workers' rights including the Teamsters' Strike in 1901 and the railway strike of 1906, and associated with St Patrick's Church. The United Irish Society of San Francisco holds an annual commemorative event at the tomb of Fr Yorke in Holy Cross Cemetery on Palm Sunday.

52. Dublin Metropolitan Police.

53. EOM had not yet received Aiken's letter of 5 April 1929 in which Aiken had enclosed a cheque for $184.50 for EOM's expenses. Aiken recorded: 'We have now some

$131,000 in the bank ... I have told Dev that we will have done all we can here by end of April ... Please let me know what are your plans after we finish at the end of April. Do you intend staying in the U.S. for a couple of months ...' USDA P104/2633(9).

54. Probably Preston McKresson, whom EOM met in San Francisco. EOM diary (29 March 1929), see Letter No. 35.

55. Name unclear in the MS.

56. Edward Weston (1886–1958), photographer, who had lived in Mexico for several years.

57. José Clemente Orozco (1883–1949), writer, painter and muralist.

58. Diego Rivera (1886–1957), painter and muralist.

59. Louis Henri Jean Charlot (1898–1979), writer, painter and illustrator.

60. Maximo Pacheco (b. 1907), a Mexican-Indian muralist who worked with Diego Rivera.

61. Tina Modotti (1896–1942), photographer, actress and radical.

62. Manuel Martinez Pintao, born in Spain.

63. Manuel Rodriguez Lozano (1896–1971), artist, teacher and writer.

64. Francisco Goitia (1882–1969), artist.

65. Brett Weston (1911–1993), photographer.

66. Preston and Helen McCresson, who later moved to Santa Fe.

67. Robinson Jeffers (1887–1962), poet, then living in Carmel. His wife Una had Irish connections and they visited Ireland just several months after EOM visited them in Carmel.

68. Beryl Boynton, wife of the artist Ray Boynton, was a sculptor.

69. Isadora Duncan (1877–1927), dancer.

70. Ambrose Bierce (1842–1914), journalist, writer and satirist.

71. Ireland and Irish in the following abbreviation.

72. Ray Boynton (1883–1951), artist and fresco painter, later established the Boynton Studio in Santa Fe, NM.

73. Possibly Carmel or California.

74. Gottardo Piazzoni (1872–1945), artist.

75. Armand Hanson, watercolour painter, California.

76. Possibly Stedman Woods (1894–1983), artist.

77. Arthur Hill Gilbert (1894–1970), artist.

78. William Frederick Ritschel (1864–1949), artist.

79. William C. Watts (1869–1961), artist.

80. Edward Weston, photographer, married Flora Chandler in 1909. Their children included Chandler, Brett and Cole. Edward and Flora divorced; he then lived between Mexico, Los Angeles and Carmel, where he built his studio. Weston was the founder of a photographic movement known as Western strategic photography. EOM had met Weston in Carmel on 19 April and on a subsequent visit to Carmel in May Weston had photographed him.

81. Sonia Noskowiak was a photographer and Edward Weston's partner from 1929 to 1934.

82. James Marie Hopper (1876–1956), author, helped create Carmel as a literary and artistic colony in 1906.

83. Possibly Mr and Mrs Frederick Beckdolt, whose names come up in EOM's letters to Edward Weston.

84. Edward Weston referred to EOM as Sean and surprisingly EOM reciprocated.

85. This letter survived as a fragment copied in Sighle Humphreys' own handwriting and given to COM.

86. Probably his doctors suggested avoiding strenuous exercise due to the continuing effect of his wounds.

87. EOM was familiar with Tone's writings; see O'Malley, *On Another Man's Wound*, pp. 65–6.

88. Hon. Dorothy Brett (1883–1977), known as 'Brett', the daughter of Lord Esker, was an artist in London who went to Taos in 1923 with novelist D.H. Lawrence (1885–1930) and his wife, Frieda, at the invitation of Mabel Dodge Luhan. Luhan gave the Lawrences the Kiowa Ranch on Lobo Mountain, about twenty miles north of Taos, where they lived. Brett, who typed Lawrence's manuscripts, lived with them, but when they departed in 1924, she remained on and took care of the ranch. In early 1930 Frieda wrote to Brett that she wanted her off the ranch and then there was a partial reconciliation, but Lawrence died on 2 March. Since Brett was good friends with Bill and Rachel Hawk, owners of the nearby Del Monte ranch where she had often stayed, the Hawks rented Brett a place to build her own summer log cabin on Lobo Mountain. See Dorothy Brett, *Lawrence and Brett: A Friendship* (1933), p. 214. From there she could see the northern flank of Taos Mountain, the sacred mountain for the Taos Pueblo Indians. Brett continued to live in Kiowa until the two-storey cabin was completed, but had asked EOM to help supervise its construction by some local Taos Indians. Some of the logs were taken from the two huts that the Lawrences had originally lived in. Brett continued her art work in Taos, where COM visited her in 1965. Brett replied to EOM on 21 March saying she 'was glad to get your letter – it made me feel less desperate'. EOM Papers NYU.

89. Gertrude Light, MD, and a local GP in Taos, New Mexico.

90. Kiowa Ranch.

91. Frieda Lawrence (1879–1956), a German aristrocrat, was married to Ernest Weekley when she met D.H. Lawrence in 1912. They eloped and were married in July 1914 after her divorce.

92. EOM had lost three brothers. Frank Malley died in 1921 while serving with the British army's East African Rifles in Dar es Salaam. Charles O'Malley was killed by a sniper shot in Dublin on 3 July 1922, during the Irish civil war. Albert Malley, EOM's next-youngest brother died in 1925 while serving with the British army's Nigerian Frontier Forces in Lagos.

93. Helen Golden, née Merriam (1891–1944), actress and wife of Cork-born Shakespearian actor, Peter Golden. Peter had bad health and while in the process of moving his family to California, died on the train in Denver. Merriam Golden went to California in any case as planned. The Golden family assume that EOM first met Golden in Pasadena, where she was living with her three children, Terence, and twins, Eithne and Deirdre, through his Irish connections, given that he was working for *The Irish Press* at the time, in June 1929. EOM drove the Goldens to Taos in September 1929 and stayed a few months. When they returned in early spring 1930 they stayed at the Adams Auto Camp on the east side of the Pueblo Road, near the present post office. The Goldens then purchased an old house and undertook some renovations as it was a 150-year-old adobe house in the Rio Chiquito section of Talpa, about four miles south-east of Taos.

94. Miss Josephine (Joe) Doherty was an old Irish-American friend of the Golden family living in Pasadena. She had taken care of Terence and Deirdre when Merriam Golden went on her second trip to Taos in the winter of 1929–30. She took Mariana Howe and Eithne Golden on that trip. Miss Doherty moved along with the family to Taos in April 1930.

95. Josephine Doherty.

96. A.R. Orage (1873–1934), journalist, editor and intellectual.

97. John Esquameling (1645–1707), sometimes identified as Alexander Exquemelin, a French pirate who later became an author and wrote about sea travel.

98. Richard Hakluyt (*c*.1552–1616), British geographer and travel author, published ten volumes of his *Voyages* 1579–1600; was nephew of geographer of same name (1535–1591) who introduced him to travel.

99. Charles de Coster (1827–79) was a Belgian novelist who wrote *La Légende et les adventures héroiques, joyeuses, et glorieuses d'Ulenspiegel et de Lamme Goedzak au pays de Flandres et aileurs* (1866). 'Owlglass' is the English rendering of the central character, Ulenspiegel.

100. EOM wrote three chapters of what became *On Another Man's Wound* during his stay in Brett's cabin.

101. Terence, Eithne and Deirdre Golden. EOM referred to them as the 'Kick in the Pants Tribe'.

102. The Fianna Éireann was a training organization for adolescents. EOM was involved in their supervision from *c*. August 1916 to March 1918. His company included his younger brothers Cecil, Paddy and Charles. Members frequently graduated to the Irish Volunteers.

103. Walter Willard 'Spud' Johnson (1897–1968), writer, journalist and longtime fixture on the New Mexico literary scene. When Spud left for the winter in Carmel, he invited EOM to take care of his house in Taos, and so EOM lived there for a time before working on Brett's mountain cabin.

104. Nora Hellgren lived in California where EOM met her. She had been in Russia during the Revolution and had worked as an English-language secretary to Chicherin, the Bolshevik foreign minister. When EOM went to Mexico she provided a letter of introduction for him to Sergei Eisenstein during the production of the film *Thunder Over Mexico*.

105. Mariana Howe, cabinet maker, originally from Boston, moved with the Goldens to Taos from Pasadena in 1930.

106. EOM was supervising the construction of Dorothy Brett's cabin on Lobo Mountain.

107. Unclear in MS.

108. Frank Hoffman was a painter who did covers for *The Saturday Evening Post*. He lived with his wife, Hazel, close to the hills where the road to Raton goes into Taos Canyon.

109. Mariana Howe.

110. Spud Johnson.

111. Deirdre Golden.

112. The Chapmans had a house on Pueblo Road, Taos, the upper story of which was Brett's usual winter quarters.

113. Eileen McCarvill, née McGrane. The application was for a position in *The Irish Press*. Peadar O'Donnell had written to Frank Gallagher on 29 December 1930 're – Ernie O'Malley and his suitability for the Literary page of the new paper … The content of Ernie's mind qualifies him beyond all others for this feature of the new paper.'

114. The Dublin Horse Show is held the first week in August every year at the Royal Dublin Society. It is considered a social and an equestrian event.

115. The Criminal Intelligence Division, an armed force under control of the Ministry of Home Affairs during the civil war, and not the police.

116. Kevin Malley writing in regard of EOM's work as a fundraiser for *The Irish Press*.

117. Frank O'Connor (1903–1966), pen name of Michael O'Donovan, short-story writer, author, critic and one-time republican during the civil war.

118. A weekly commentary edited by George Russell from 1923 to 1930, fiercely supportive of the independent state. See Nicholas Allen, *George Russell (Æ) and the New Ireland, 1905–30* (Dublin, 2003).

119. Frank O'Connor, 'Guests of the Nation', *Atlantic Monthly* (January 1931). O'Connor's story tells of the execution of British soldiers held prisoner by Volunteers in retaliation for the execution of a prisoner. One of the final scenes of *On Another Man's Wound* details EOM's own involvement in the execution of captured British officers. See O'Malley, *On Another Man's Wound*, pp. 371–6.

120. EOM retained an anxiety regarding letters and their contents from the War of Independence. He may be referring here also to the difficulty of receiving post through secondary addresses.

121. The following matter was also enclosed with the letter of 27 May 1930: NLI MS 18353(14). In August–November 1930 EOM gave a series of Friday evening lectures on Irish poetry, drama and literature, including James Joyce, in El Zaguna, Santa Fe.

122. Written on three separate dates from 6 to 19 January 1931 at the start of his visit to Mexico.

123. Dorothy Newkirk Stewart (1891–1956) and Theodora Goddard, a New York painter. The journey to Mexico was essentially a painting expedition for Stewart and Goddard. EOM 'agreed to go along to protect us from bandits', said Goddard to COM. They drove to Mexico City in Stewart's lettuce-coloured Chevrolet, and returned the same way. EOM ultimately drove the same car to New York in June 1932.

124. Antonio (Tony) Mirabel was a Pueblo Indian whom EOM liked because of his militant feelings about the wrongs that had been done to his native people. Carl Gustav Jung visited Taos and had long talks with Tony. Manuel Lujan was some relation of Tony Luhan, husband of Mabel Dodge, and had helped the Goldens with the reconditioning of their house in 1930. He was active in Pueblo affairs and was three times the governor of the Taos Pueblo.

125. Anita Lopez. Merriam Golden bought her house from Anita's father, Remigio Archuleta. Anita did a lot of work for the Golden family. Her son Margaro Lopez was known as Margarito or Margo.

126. Lucinda Lopez, a daughter of Anita Lopez.

127. *Avion* is French for aeroplane; 'dic' is probably dictionary. The comment reflects on the poor condition of the Mexican roads at the time. Theodora Goddard told COM that EOM had told her that with the bumps in the Mexican roads, he could feel 'the bullets scraping together in my spine'.

128. Sylvia Laithwaite. She was EOM's first cousin on his mother's side, raised in England. She had met EOM in Cincinatti in 1928 and later went to Santa Fe and became a librarian there. She subsequently became a nun in the Dominican Order in around 1933.

129. Mabel Dodge Luhan (1879–1962) and Tony Luhan (*c.*1880s–1950s). See her memoir: Mabel Dodge Luhan, *Lorenzo in Taos* (1932). Tony Luhan was a Pueblo Indian from Taos. In Mexico City EOM and his companions stayed initially at a boarding house owned by the Gussmans.

130. Carleton Beals (1893–1979), journalist and author of *America South* (1937).

131. Mullingar was the Goldens' dog.

132. Mrs Ida Eastman, or Ida Rauh (1877–1970), actress, poet and director.

133. Dorothy Brett, *Lawrence and Brett: A Friendship* (1933).
134. Moisés Sáenz Garza was secretary of Public Education in Mexico in 1928. He was also a selector for Guggenheim Fellowships in that country. His works include a book describing a famous educational project designed to integrate indigenous peoples into the Mexican state. See Moisés Sáenz Garza, *Carapan: bosquejo de una experiencia* (1936).
135. Possibly David Alaro Siquerios (1896–1979), a pro-Stalinist mural artist.
136. *The Carmelite* was the local weekly newspaper in Carmel, California.
137. This letter survived as a fragment copied in Sighle Humphreys' own handwriting for COM.
138. Moisés Sáenz Garza wrote EOM a letter of introduction to Se or J.G. Nájera, Director of the Cultural Mexico and Rural Normal School on 12 May 1931, explaining O'Malley's expressed 'desire to go to Oaxtepec'.
139. EOM went on a 41-day hunger strike in October 1923 during the Irish civil war.
140. Popocateptl is a volancic mountain overlooking Mexico City.
141. Mary Josephine Cranny Plunkett (1858–1944), wife of Count George Noble Plunkett (1851–1948) and mother of seven children, including Joseph Mary Plunkett (1887–1916), executed for his role in the Easter Rising.
142. 'Who knows?'
143. EOM did not complete his university education.
144. Count George Noble Plunkett (1851–1948) had written on painting and early Irish Christian art. In 1921 de Valera made Plunkett a minister for fine arts outside of the cabinet. EOM spent time talking to him socially during the War of Independence.
145. All members of the Plunkett family. Eoin Plunkett had worked with EOM in the Irish Volunteers during the War of Independence.
146. EOM was still in Mexico when he wrote this letter with a New Mexico return address. In expectation of his return to New Mexico EOM gave a Santa Fe address. Kathleen O'Connell, secretary to de Valera, wrote to Garth Healy on 15 July 1931, indicating EOM's postal address in New Mexico courtesy of Sylvia Laithwaite, while EOM was actually living in Mexico. On 2 June 1931 Hart Crane wrote to Malcolm Crowley, 'I have my most pleasant literary moments with an Irish revolutionary, red haired friend of Liam O'Flaherty … the most quietly sincere and appreciative person, in many ways, whom I've ever met. It's a big regret that he's Dublin bound again after three years from home, in a few weeks, Ernest O'Malley by name. And we drink a lot together – look at frescoes – and agree.' See *Hart Crane: Complete Poems and Selected Letters*, ed. Langdon Hammer (New York, 2006).
147. Near to hand.
148. The bank used on behalf of *The Irish Press*.
149. Paul Strand (1890–1976), photographer and filmmaker, and his wife, Becky, spent May–September of 1932 in Taos, where EOM got to know him before leaving for New York.
150. Paul Strand wrote to EOM on 8 July 1932 that he had heard from Clifford Odets about EOM's visit to The Group Theatre in New York. Strand also made reference to Ted Stevenson, Mrs Ames of Yaddo, Helen Golden and Ella Young. He concluded with 'affectionate greetings … and best of luck'. EOM Papers NYU.
151. Hutchins Hapgood (1869–1944), journalist and anarchist. Hutchins and his wife, Neith Boyce, were friends of Mabel Dodge Luhan and spent time in Taos. *Taos: A Memory* (Alburquerque, 1992) was published after the death of their daughter,

Miriam Hapgood DeWitt (1906–1990), with references to EOM in 1929–32.

152. Yaddo Foundation, Saratoga Springs, New York.

153. Philip (Ted) Stevenson (1896–1965), author, playright, screenwriter, based in New York, literary friend of Paul Strand, visited Taos, referred to sometimes as 'Ted S.'

154. Elizabeth Ames (1885–1977), was appointed first executive director of the Yaddo Foundation in 1923.

155. The Group Theatre was founded in 1931 in New York by Harold Clurman, Cheryl Crawford and Lee Strasberg.

156. Lee Strasberg (1901–1984).

157. Harold Clurman (1901–1980).

158. Gerald Sykes (1903–1980s), novelist, literary critic; he later visited EOM in Ireland in 1939.

159. Strand had exhibited at An American Place in New York in April 1932. This gallery was opened by Alfred Stieglitz at 509 Madison Avenue in 1929.

160. The letter is postmarked 1 August 1932. EOM used this address knowing that mail would be forwarded.

161. Mariana Howe.

162. Mr and Mrs Flavio and Anita Lopez lived next door to the Goldens. Their children were Lucinda, Felinici, Ernesto and Margarito. Aurora was one of EOM's local pupils. Andres Maestas was another neighbour.

163. Ella Young.

164. Elizabeth Ames was the executive director of the Yaddo Foundation and its controlling spirit.

165. EOM's arrangement with Helen Golden was that he tutored in exchange for a room where he could write and board.

166. Letter from Mrs Ames, dated 9 August 1932, offering EOM a space at Yaddo from 15 August to 15 September. EOM Papers NYU.

167. These were First World War veterans and their families who demonstrated in Washington, DC, in the spring and summer of 1932 asking for cash payments in place of their 'Service Certificates', granted in 1924 and due to mature twenty years later.

168. The Amalgamated Union.

169. The overground mass transport that ran on Third Avenue, New York City.

170. Rebecca Strand, née Salsbury (1891–1968), Paul Strand's first wife. Her father was Nate Salsbury, the founder of the Buffalo Bill Touring Rodeo.

171. Dynamic symmetry was a theory of painting that Emil Bisttram taught to artists in Taos.

172. Conor (Connie) Neehan, Cork IRA, survived a 79-day hunger strike in 1920, anti-Treaty, emigrated to the US, acted as IRA Army Council representative. See *Survivors*, ed. Uinseann MacEoin (Dublin, 1980), pp. 234–58.

173. *The Irish Press*.

174. The letter was not mailed as EOM did not have Helen Hooker's (HH) home address in Greenwich.

175. Mariquita Serrano Villard, a New York artist friend of the Hooker sisters, had introduced EOM to the Hooker family. She was the niece of Oswald Garrison Villard (1872–1949), a significant newspaper owner in New York.

176. Mariquita Villard, later Mrs Henry Platov.

177. At the Chicago World's Fair, summer 1933.

178. Adelaide Hooker.

179. Nicolai Fechin (1881–1955), a Russian painter who arrived in Taos in 1927 with his wife Alexandra and daughter Eya to treat his tuberculosis condition. His Fechin House is now a museum in Taos.

180. Ernest L. Blumenschein (1874–1960), painter, and Mary Greene Blumenschein (1869–1958), painter. He founded the Taos Society of Artists. The Blumenschein home is now a museum in Taos.

181. Mary Parmele Hamlin (1871–1964), New York-based author and playright who lived in Taos in 1933.

182. Sylvia Laithwaite.

183. F/S is Free State; Dan McGrath was the Irish Free State Consul General in Chicago.

184. Joseph Campbell (1879–1944), poet and scholar.

185. Dorsha Hayes was an American dancer, writer and poet. Paul Hayes, her husband, came from Ireland and assisted as her manager.

186. Mary Heaton Vorse (1874–1966), suffragette, journalist and radical; she was at Yaddo with EOM in 1932.

187. Mabel Dodge Luhan had tried to organize a market in the Taos Plaza to sell items, but it did not last.

188. Rory, the Goldens' St Bernard dog.

189. Concerning Abyssinia, the Field Museum in conjunction with the *Chicago Daily News* had sent an expedition of five scientists there to collect specimens in 1926–7.

190. Scipio Africanus, the Roman general who defeated Hannibal in the Second Punic War.

191. EOM mentions his Taos friends dropping by: Dorothy Brett, Edward Bright and Miriam Hapgood Bright, Ernest and Mary Blumenschein, and Mary Hamlin. Pablo Esteban O'Higgins (1904–83), painter.

192. Possibly an edition of a poem by Vachel Lindsay (1879–1931), 'Alone in the Wind, on the Prairie'.

193. Dorothy Newkirk Stewart.

194. Maria Chabot (1913–2001), began the Indian markets on the Plaza in Santa Fe, New Mexico, and was a friend of Georgia O'Keeffe.

195. Helen Crowe, an Irish American librarian who worked at the Morgan Library, New York, and member of the Irish Progressive League.

196. The Civil Works Administration was launched as a relief programme in the winter of 1933–4. It provided funds to local authorities, mayors and governors for public projects such as road, bridge and school construction. It was stopped after several months. Many of the projects were later incorporated in 1935 into the Works Progress Administration.

197. The New York Public Library.

198. Hartford House, Young Men's Christian Association.

199. Art lectures for James Johnson Sweeney given at New York University as Fine Arts 68 on 'Tendencies in Modern Painting', a fifteen-lecture series open to public enrolment for $22 in the academic years 1933–4, 1934–5.

200. Padraic Colum (1881–1972), writer and folklorist, married in 1912 and moved to New York in 1914 for eight years. A member of the Irish Progressive League, he returned permanently to New York from Paris in 1933, where EOM met him.

201. Arthur Griffith (1872–1922), nationalist, journalist and president of the Dáil from January to August 1922.

202. Mary Colum (1884–1957), critic and writer best remembered for her memoir, *Life and the Dream* (1928). She was married to Padraic Colum.

203. The manuscript of *On Another Man's Wound*. Samuel Sloan of Harcourt, Brace & Company had written to EOM on 11 May 1933, also rejecting the manuscript.

204. Joseph Campbell restarted *The Irish Review* in 1934. This title was originally published as *A Monthly Magazine of Irish Literature, Art and Science* from 1912 to 1914. Its editors included Joseph Mary Plunkett and Thomas MacDonagh, both executed after the Easter Rising.

205. The Great Atlantic and Pacific Tea Company, started in 1858, and abbreviated eventually as 'A&P'.

206. A busboy clears the tables in a restaurant and is below a waiter, who would receive the tips.

207. Julius Meier-Graefe (1867–1935) was an art critic who published widely on Impressionism. His books included a biography of Van Gogh. See Kenworth Moffett, *Meier-Graefe as Art Critic* (Munich, 1973).

208. Fernandez's study, *André Gide*, was published in 1931.

209. The New York Public Library.

210. EOM met Edward Weeks (1898–1989) in Boston, when seeking advice about how to get his manuscript published. Weeks was editor of the *Atlantic Monthly* from 1938 to 1966.

211. Strand was working on *Redes*, released in English as *The Wave*, a film commissioned by the Mexican government.

212. *Men in White* was a satire of science fiction films directed by Richard Boleslanski in 1934.

213. Gerald Sykes.

214. Dr W. Horsely Gantt (1892–1980). HH had met him in St Petersburg, Russia, in 1928 when she was studying art with the modern Russian artist, Pavel Filonov (1883–1941), and they revived their friendship upon his return to the United States in 1930, but she never became engaged officially with parental consent.

215. Paul Rosenfeld (1890–1948), journalist, music critic and author of the autobiographical novel, *The Boy in the Sun* (1928).

216. Israel Citkovitz (1909–1974), composer. EOM met him at Yaddo and afterwards met his sister, Rebecca Citkowitz (later Liber), and continued corresponding with her into the 1950s. Rebecca typed many of EOM's poems and manuscripts while he was in New York and was most supportive of him in the 1950s.

217. HH did volunteer painting in Hartford House after EOM left.

218. What EOM probably meant to write was '*Is fia atá geallta*', meaning 'what is promised is a debt'.

219. Harriet Monroe, editor of *Poetry: A Magazine for Verse*. EOM sent some of his poems in early August 1934. They were stamped by the office on 8 August. A standard postcard was sent to him signed 'The Editors', asking him 'to send a brief "autobiography" for use in the literary notes … '. EOM Papers NYU.

220. Alice Corbin Henderson (1881–1949), poet and editor, married to William P. Henderson, had been associated with *Poetry* magazine.

221. Robert J. Flaherty (1884–1951), filmmaker. His *Man of Aran* (1934) is a fictional documentary of life off the west coast of Ireland. The film was released on 17 October 1934 and EOM had already seen it by 22 October 1934. Flaherty is sometimes referred to in the text as 'F.'.

222. The Viking Press.

223. Harold Clurman and Gerald Sykes.

224. EOM's poems were published in *Poetry* in January 1935 and again in March 1936.

225. Eduard Tissé (1897–1961), Russian actor and director of photography on Sergei Eisenstein's films. EOM met Tissé and Eisenstein in Mexico in 1931 on location making the film *Thunder Over Mexico*. The film was released on 15 November 1933 in New York.

226. Sergei Eisenstein (1898–1948), Russian film director and theorist.

227. After its run in Boston, *Gold Eagle Guy*, written by Melvin Levy, was performed in New York by The Group Theatre at the Morosco Theatre and opened on 28 November 1934.

228. EOM's poems were included in the January 1935 edition.

229. Thomas MacDonagh (1878–1916), republican, scholar, poet and playwright. His books include *Songs of Myself* (1910), *Lyrical Poems* (1913) and *Literature in Ireland: Studies Irish and Anglo-Irish* (1916), to which EOM refers. EOM knew MacDonagh's children, Donagh MacDonagh (1912–1968), a poet, playwright, songwriter and judge, and Barbara MacDonagh, who married Liam Redmond.

230. Vassos Kanellos (1887–1995) was a Greek dancer. Tanagra Kanellos refers to Charlotte Markham (1892–1937), his American dancer wife. They were also both exhibiting artists. HH had spent much of 1930 and 1931 dancing in Kanellos' Greek Chorodrama Academy in Athens.

231. COM found a letter of rejection from the Irish Pension Board dated November 1936 denying EOM's claim for coverage for his heart condition as they said it was not covered by the act. *'No Surrender Here!' The Civil War Papers of Ernie O'Malley, 1922–1924*, eds Cormac K.H. O'Malley and Anne Dolan (Dublin, 2007), p. 341.

232. The documentary evidence suggests EOM travelled in Spain to recuperate his health. The only suggestion discovered of radical activity occurs earlier in the allusions to Basque separatists; however, Seán MacBride refers to EOM and then-Paris resident Col Francesco Macia (1959–1933) of the Catalan army, Exercit Catala, and his attempted invasion of and insurrection in Spain in 1926. See *Seán MacBride, That Day's Struggle, A Memoir, 1904–1951*, ed. Caitriona Lawlor (Dublin, 2005), pp. 101–5.

233. There is no documentary proof of this travel though confirming stories have been relayed to COM.

234. Georgia O'Keeffe (1887–1986), artist and married to Alfred Stieglitz, the photographer. She first went to Taos in 1929 and stayed initially with Mabel Dodge Luhan.

235. Mary Cabot Wheelwright (1878–1958), founder in 1937 of the Wheelwright Museum of the American Indian in Santa Fe. Alcalde was north of Taos.

236. The Yeibishi was a curative Navajo tribal ceremonial dance performed after the first frost and about which EOM had written a poem.

237. Possibly the Poetry Society of America, founded in 1910.

238. Liam O'Flaherty's 'The Mountain Tavern' was first collected in *Red Barbara and Other Stories* (1928). No doubt the story appealed to EOM for its tragic rendering of a civil war engagement from a republican perspective.

239. Theatre in Action was an English theatrical group founded by Ewan MacCall (1915–1989) intending to develop a Marxist aesthetic of theatre.

240. ARTEF was an acronym for Arbeter Teater Farband, or Workers' Theatrical Alliance. It was founded in New York as a Yiddish collective in December 1925. It officially opened as the Artef Theatre Company with a production of *Baym Toyer* by Beynush Shteyman in December 1928.

241. Eva Le Gallienne (1899–1991), actress, producer and director.
242. *Stevedore*, a play by George Sklar and Paul Peters, was produced by the Theatre Union in Eva Le Gallienne's venue at Sixth Avenue and 14th Street, New York. The next play should be *Silors of CaHaro*.
243. Play by Israel Axenfield.
244. Michael Chekhov had trained in Moscow under Constantin Stanislavsky and Vladamir Nemirovich-Danchenko, then visited New York on tour in 1922 and started the Moscow Art Players.
245. Play by Marc Connelly, written in 1930, for which he won a Pultizer Prize for Drama in 1930.
246. Katharine Cornell (1893–1974), actress and later presenter of plays.
247. Unclear in the MS.
248. Brian Aherne (1902–86), actor, played Mercutio in *Romeo and Juliet* at the Martin Beck Theatre, December 1934.
249. *Life is Beautiful* (1933), dir. Vsevolod Pudovkin.
250. *Road to Life* (1931), dir. Nikolai Ekk; the first Soviet film with sound.
251. *Chapayev* (1934), dir. Georgy and Sergey Vasilyev.
252. Merriam Golden must have eventually found and shipped the notes to EOM in Ireland as EOM had them there; now in EOM Papers NYU.
253. *The Dial* was an American literary magazine, originally founded by the transcendentalists in 1840. Published irregularly, it became associated with modernism through its publication of Djuna Barnes, Hart Crane, Ezra Pound, W.B. Yeats, and many others from 1920 to its demise in 1929.
254. HH had already left New York for her trip to Japan with her mother, Blanche, and her sister, Adelaide, and they were to catch their ship with the Garden Club of America tour of Japanese gardens from San Francisco.
255. Photographs of EOM.
256. Reference to a lecture EOM probably gave at Harvard as part of a course by Fred Norris Robinson (1871–1996), Professor of Celtic Languages including Irish and Welsh. EOM had in his files a copy of the 1934–5 Harvard course catalogue. EOM Papers NYU. EOM's 1937 diary mentions his October meeting with Robinson in Dublin.
257. Mary O'Brien was personal secretary to Blanche Hooker for many years.
258. Harvard, Massachusetts, a town about thirty miles west of Boston.
259. Daffodils.
260. Charles A. Lindbergh (1902–1974), aviator, famous for the first solo transatlantic flight in 1927.
261. EOM went from Boston to New York by bus.
262. EOM and HH spent a weekend together in the Berkshire mountains in Massachusetts in early 1935.
263. Eunice Stoddard Smith Whittlesey (1906–2006) had been a school friend of HH's and was heavily involved in The Group Theatre under her stage name of Eunice Stoddard.
264. No items have been located.
265. The New York Workers' School was founded by the American Communist Party.

1. Bea Raleigh and her four Raleigh daughters, Peggy, Sheila, Mary and Oona. EOM was Peggy's godfather.
2. EOM was never proficient in Irish and wanted to improve his knowledge. He had translated poems from Irish while in the New York Public Library and found it laborious.
3. Probably the Irish Pension Board to adjudicate on EOM's wound claims or claims of others.
4. Con Moloney, from Tipperary, had been adjutant, Tipperary Brigade, was appointed as EOM's adjutant, Second Southern Division, 1921, and later was adjutant general, anti-Treaty headquarters, July 1922–April 1923.
5. Sean Moylan (1888–1957), republican, TD and government minister. Moylan was on the republican GHQ staff in July 1922. Moylan, then minister for agriculture, gave the graveside oration at EOM's funeral.
6. Mrs Marian Tobin lived in Tincurry House, Co. Tipperary, where EOM had established his headquarters for the Second Southern Division. She had two daughters, Mae and Eva Tobin. EOM and his Volunteers went there after their attack on Hollyford Barracks and he included a lyrical description of her house and gardens in *On Another Man's Wound* (Dublin, 2002 edn), pp. 173, 336.
7. EOM stayed with the Keane family from time to time, and they forwarded his mail to wherever he could next receive it.
8. Cobh, Co. Cork, was the deepwater port for ocean liners arriving from the Atlantic crossing.
9. The manuscript for *On Another Man's Wound*.
10. South-west.
11. Aran Islands.
12. Paddy Malley worked at the Hibernian Bank, College Green, Dublin.
13. The Irish Tourist Association, National Tourist Board, was founded in 1925 under the aegis of the Ministry for Industry and Finance. At that time, nine out of every ten tourists to Ireland were British, a fact EOM comments upon later with some irony.
14. The historical seat of the Diocese of Clonfert, Co. Galway, founded as a monastery by St Brendan in 563 AD.
15. Elon Huntington Hooker was father of HH (hereafter HHOM). He did not approve of EOM as a potential son-in-law. EOM's autobiographical statement, see No. 155.
16. Adelaide Hooker was present for the wedding.
17. EOM/HHOM moved into 229 Upper Rathmines Road, Rathmines, Dublin in late October.
18. Jim Moloney was brother of Con Moloney.
19. Tincurry House, home of Marian Tobin.
20. Refers to the intense lighting mechanism EOM/HHOM used on their photographic expeditions.
21. The Spring Show was held annually at the Royal Dublin Society, Ballsbridge, usually in March, and included a large agricultural exhibition as well as many other sections.
22. Frank Geary, McGlynn and John Grant were friends of EOM from Limerick; David Dundon of 26 High Street, Limerick had been in the Mid Limerick Brigade, went anti-Treaty and had written to EOM in 1936. See EOM Papers NYU, NLI MS 10973(17) and UCDA P17b/114.
23. The letter was forwarded to Mrs Victor Schaepperle, Hobart Avenue, Short Hills, New Jersey.

24. The letter was written in and mailed from Calvi, Corsica, France, while EOM and HHOM were on their delayed honeymoon after their first year of marriage, birth of their first child, his medical studies and book.

25. Eithne Golden wrote to EOM on 25 April 1936, see EOM Papers NYU. She had read a notice of publication under 'The New Irish Books' in the *New York Times* (29 March 1936). Actual publication of *On Another Man's Wound* did not occur until October that year and the American edition was in 1937.

26. Second year of medical school for the fifth time.

27. Cathal O'Malley was born on 10 July 1936.

28. The Cézanne retrospective exhibited at the Musée de l'Orangerie, Paris, 1936.

29. Published by Rich & Cowan, London.

30. EOM referring to a second-year university exam for his medical degree.

31. Liam Redmond married Barbara MacDonagh, daughter of Thomas MacDonagh, executed in 1916, and brother to Donagh MacDonagh, a good friend of EOM.

32. O'Malley, *On Another Man's Wound*, pp. 118–19.

33. Adelaide Hooker and her mother Blanche Hooker.

34. EOM, HHOM and Kevin Malley took photographs of early Irish monuments.

35. Arthur Kingsley Porter (1883–1933), historian and medievalist with a great knowledge of art, architecture and Romanesque sculpture, in which EOM was keenly interested and who owned Glenveagh Castle, Co. Donegal.

36. Kevin Malley had by this time become quite knowledgeable in the realm of archaeology.

37. In this context, a niche probably refers to a framing space for a reliquary.

38. Bea Raleigh was then pregnant with her fifth child, John Raleigh.

39. EOM's medical studies.

40. EOM had known both Madge Clifford and John 'Jack' Joseph Comer during the War of Independence and civil war period. See Letter No. 1. Upon his return from his American soujourn, the Comers asked EOM to be godfather to their son, Diarmuid, later known as Jerry, who was the youngest of their eight children.

41. Patrick Pearse (1879–1916), nationalist and revolutionary. March 5th is the end of the academic term.

42. Christopher (Todd) Andrews (1901–1985), republican and civil servant.

43. EOM was godfather to Diarmuid Comer.

44. Cathal O'Malley.

45. Desmond Ryan (1893–1964) was a student of Pearse's at St Enda's. He was disillusioned by the civil war and returned home to London. He was author of *Remembering Sion* (1934) and *Unique Dictator* (1936); the latter is probably what EOM referred to as 'your other book'.

46. Ryan wrote to EOM on 14 December 1936 to congratulate him on the publication of *On Another Man's Wound*. 'It nearly shattered the peace of this household, let me tell you, for I had two long sessions of five hours each, two nights running, with it, and more, and my wife called down curses on your head ... Perhaps I owe you an apology for describing you in *Remembering Sion* as a "gunman" in your meeting with Childers, but then I didn't know it was you! I was watching out for your book when writing on de Valera but it was all in type before yours came out.'

47. O'Connor's life of Collins was published as *The Big Fellow* (1937).

48. Françoise Henry lectured on 'Early Irish Enamels' to the Royal Society of Antiquaries of Ireland on Tuesday, 2 March 1937.

49. The following is EOM's wish-list miscellany included in the letter for HHOM.

50. Rebecca Citkowitz.
51. Harold Clurman of The Group Theatre.
52. Chicago's World's Fair, 1933, during which EOM worked in the Irish Free State Pavillion.
53. Rich & Cowan were EOM's publishers at 25 Soho Square, London, and he gave HHOM their address.
54. Presumably EOM is referring to his publishers' lawyer since Rich & Cowan were afraid of libel.
55. Winnie Comstock Bowman, Vassar College classmate (1925), singer and friend of Adelaide Hooker; married Dr Wilfred Venn Bowman in 1929 and lived in London.
56. Each number in the catalogue refers to a painting. They are (1) *Paysage*, André Derain, lent by Mr E.A. McGuire, (4) *Le Pays Devaste*, Maurice Vlaminck, lent by Miss S.H. Purser, (5) *St. Tropez*, Moise Kisling, lent by Miss S.H. Purser (14), *Water colour*, Max Pechstein, lent by Mr Joseph Hone, (16) *Water colour*, André Lhote, lent by Mr Justice Meredith, (17) *Drawing*, Raoul Dufy, lent by Mr Justice Meredith, (27) *Thames from Adelphi Terrace*, C.R.W. Nevinson, lent by Mr Dermod O'Brien PRHA, (35) *Painting*, Roger Bissière, lent by Mrs Leonard Kirkwood.
57. Norah McGuinness (1901–80), painter, (19) *Temple Street Dublin*, £10.10.0 (20) *The Customs House*, £12.10. These two paintings were purchased by either EOM or HHOM.
58. HHOM had been helpful in designing the interiors of several libraries for her good friend, Roisin Walsh, and these included the Pearse Street City Library Headquarters, as well as the Pembroke/Ballsbridge library, where Frank O'Connor was librarian, and the Howth library. Walsh was appointed Chief Librarian of Dublin City Library in 1931; the same year she hosted a meeting of the General Army Convention of the IRA at her Templeogue home.
59. Probably Dr Wilfred Venn Bowman and Winnie Comstock Bowman, the latter an American friend of HHOM.
60. William J. Free, Fruiterer, 147 Upper Rathmines Road, Rathmines, Dublin.
61. Elon Hooker was visiting Paris on business and intended to visit Dublin, but due to the illness of his brother Horace, who died in September, he returned home to New York; the letter was forwarded from Paris to his office at 60 East 42nd Street, New York.
62. Paddy Malley.
63. Cathal O'Malley.
64. Pádraic Ó Conaire (1882–1928), writer and journalist.
65. There were atrocities on both the government and republican sides in Kerry during the civil war. Most notorious were the killings at Ballyseedy in March 1923 when government troops were killed by a bomb, inciting reprisals that included the killing of eight republicans by binding them to a landmine.
66. Actually Eileen Comer, daughter of Jack and Madge Comer, who was aged five at the time and was named after Eileen McGrane MacCarville, her godmother.
67. Refers to EOM returning to medical studies twenty years after starting them and dealing with the libel – defamation – action taken against him in 1936, which he lost in November 1937.
68. Domenico Ghirlandaio (1449–1494), painter.
69. From Dublin to Liverpool.
70. EOM was seeking information on the number of books published and his international sales, including sales of the German edition of *On Another Man's Wound*,

published by Alfred Metzner as *Rebellen in Irland* (Berlin, 1937), for which he never received any royalties.

71. EOM collected picture postcards as additions to his art collection.

72. The Courtauld Institute of Art.

73. Item not traced but Andrew McDonnell of 6 Glenagard Road, Rathgar, had been officer commanding Dublin Brigade No. 2 in the civil war.

74. The letter was forwarded to Rancho de Taos, NM.

75. Boulavogue, Co.Wexford, was a centre of insurrection during the 1798 Rebellion. The rebels were organized in part by Fr John Murphy, who is remembered in the ballad 'Boulavogue'.

76. Elon Hooker died in Pasadena, California, on 10 May 1938, necessitating HHOM's return to Greenwich.

77. The Irish nurse employed to look after Cathal O'Malley.

78. Hibernian Bank.

79. Helen Merrill, née Helen Phelps Stokes, of Greenwich, Connecticut and New York, and close friend of HHOM.

80. Fr Michael Murphy (*c*.1900–1971) was parish priest in Rathmines, friends with the artistic and literary community, married Roger and Patsy McHugh as well as Michael and Sunny Clarke, and frequent visitor to EOM/HHOM social events.

81. May Keating, wife of the painter.

82. EOM referring to a painting by Alexandre Ganesco (1910–1979) they bought in Paris.

83. EOM gained a Diploma in European Painting at UCD in 1938.

84. Rebecca Citkowitz.

85. Byrne's Fruiterer & Florist, 35 South Anne Street, Dublin; Mr and Mrs Byrne were good friends of EOM.

86. A general election was held on 17 June 1938, closely following the previous year's election on 1 July 1937. Both resulted in Fianna Fáil parliamentary victories.

87. Wanamaker's Department Store, located at 770 Broadway in New York. The store had started in Philadelphia as one of the earliest quality department stores.

88. As part of a possible move away from Dublin, EOM and HHOM had planned to rent Old Head Lodge, a cottage overlooking the southern shore of Clew Bay in Louisburgh, Co. Mayo, thus leaving their Dublin house unoccupied.

89. The Mater Misericordiae University Hospital, Dublin.

90. HHOM planned the interior design of Dr Patrick and Eileen MacCarvill's house at Edenmore, Raheny.

91. Mrs Curtis was mother of HHOM's high-school friend in New York, Helen Pelham Curtis.

92. Xthenae Kanellos, a dancer and daughter of Vassos and Tanagra Kanellos; Tanagra had died in 1937.

93. International bookshop, Paris.

94. Abbaye de Saint Germain-des-Prés, Paris, founded in the sixth century. Saint-Germain-des-Prés Museum, Paris.

95. Henry was author of a number of books on early Ireland. EOM was referring to her *Irish Art in the early Christian Period* (1940). See his review: Appendix 1, No. 1.

96. Luke Malley, EOM's father.

97. Marion Malley, or 'the Ma', EOM's mother, had left for Biarritz, France.

98. Sean O'Faolain (1900–1991), writer, married Eileen Gould (1900–1988), an author of children's books, in 1929, and they lived in Killiney village, Dublin.

99. Richard Hayes (1902–1976), bibliographer, archivist and librarian of the National Library of Ireland from 1940.
100. Richard Hayes, *The Last Invasion of Ireland: When Connacht Rose* (1937).
101. Irish Academy of Letters. The Council was the executive committee for the Academy.
102. Sean O'Faolain, *King of the Beggars: A Life of Daniel O'Connell, the Irish Liberator, in a Study of the Rise of the Modern Irish Democracy (1775–1847)* (1938).
103. Newell's Ltd, Ladies' Outfitters, Grafton Street, Dublin.
104. Refers to the rented house in Louisburgh, Co. Mayo.
105. Mabel Dodge Luhan when EOM was living in Taos.
106. The Royal Society of Antiquaries of Ireland, of which EOM had been a member for several years.
107. National Library of Ireland.
108. John T. Hughes.
109. A cartoon from *The New Yorker* where a man says to a canary, 'Yeah, and that goes for you too!' EOM wrote underneath: 'No comment'.
110. Tobacco pouch.
111. Persons referred to include Mary O'Brien; Anna Johnson, a German-born member of the Hooker household staff; Blanchette and Adelaide Hooker; John Marquand.
112. Sarah (Belinda) MacDonald Sheridan (1864–1949), concert singer, companion to Hooker daughters, acompanying them on their European tours in the 1920s, and later companion for Mrs Hooker. She was also the grandmother of Catherine (Bobs) Walston.
113. Peggy, daughter of Johnny and Bea Raleigh, was EOM's godchild.
114. Oona Raleigh.
115. Burrishoole Lodge, Newport.
116. EOM meant to refer to Mary Raleigh; Major was the Raleigh family dog.
117. Exhibition of Venetian paintings and drawings held in aid of Lord Baldwin's fund for refugees at the Matthiesen, London, 23 February–6 April 1939.
118. HHOM's oldest sister, Barbara (Bobby) Hooker, had been hospitalized.
119. Foyle's Bookshop, Charing Cross, London, founded in 1903.
120. London bookshop from which EOM ordered books.
121. Andie McDonnell.
122. Thomas MacGreevy (1893–1967), poet, critic, and director of the National Gallery of Ireland from 1950 to 1963. His books include studies of T.S. Eliot and Jack Yeats. EOM had first met MacGreevy in 1920; see O'Malley, *On Another Man's Wound*, p. 238.
123. Eileen McCarvill, née McGrane.
124. There were two exhibitions including works by Camile Pissarro (1830–1903) in late 1938 at Arthur Tooth & Sons, 3–26 November, and Rosenberg & Heft Gallery, 16 November–24 December.
125. With permission from the Estate of James Johnson Sweeney. James Johnson Sweeney (1900–1986), curator, later director of paintings and scultpure at MOMA from 1935 to 1946, director, the Solomon R. Guggenheim Museum from 1952 to 1959 and director, Museum of Fine Arts, Houston, Texas. As editor of *transition* in Paris he had helped James Joyce publish *Work in Progess*, the basis for *Finnegans Wake* (1939).
126. Jack B. Yeats, *Death for Only One* (1938).
127. Ultimately MacGreevy's manuscript was published as *Jack B. Yeats: An Apprecia-tion and an Interpretation* (1945); EOM reviewed it in *The Bell*, January 1946, see Appendix 1, No. 2.
128. Houghton Mifflin published the American edition of *On Another Man's Wound* as

Army Without Banners in 1937.

129. Cecil Malley did not join in the end.

130. ARP was an acronym for Air Raid Precautions during the London Blitz.

131. Flann O'Brien was the best-known pseudonym of Brian O'Nolan (1911–1966), writer and satirist.

132. Forwarded to Portobello Nursing Home.

133. Lists not included.

134. *Suibhne Geilt* is the central character of *Buile Suibhne*, or *The Frenzy of Suibhne*. EOM refers here to J.G. O'Keeffe's 1913 translation, reissued in 1931 by the Dublin Stationery Office.

135. Bought on HHOM's travels, before marriage, in Greece and Russia.

136. EOM first met Lennox Robinson when he stayed in the playwright's flat the night of Bloody Sunday, 1920. This was also the first night EOM met Thomas MacGreevy. See O'Malley, *On Another Man's Wound*, p. 238.

137. Probably a reference to the *Irish Statesman*, edited by George Russell from 1923 to 1930 and to which O'Faolain contributed. O'Faolain became editor of *The Bell* in 1940. EOM was a contributor and books editor of *The Bell* under O'Faolain's successor, Peadar O'Donnell, 1947–8.

138. Frank Pakenham, Earl of Longford (1905–2001).

139. Burrishoole Lodge had effectively been stripped of its former large landholdings and had been reduced to the house, a meadow through which the drive passed, and several sections of wooded land. In order to farm, the O'Malleys leased arable land from neighbours, some of which they later bought.

140. Presumably Mr Gantley was the principal behind Gantley's shoemaker's store at 45 York Street, Dublin.

141. McCann, Verdun & Co. Limited, rope and sale manufacturers, 2 Burgh Quay, Dublin.

142. EOM substituted drawings instead of words and these have been placed in brackets in text. The man mentioned is Aodghain O'Rahilly; letter was enclosed with letter to HHOM of same date.

143. Victor Waddington (1906–1981), art gallery owner on St Anne's Street, Dublin, had many exhibitions of Jack B. Yeats.

144. Possibly the Contempory Picture Gallery, 133 Lower Baggot Street, Dublin.

145. In 1931 Jack B. Yeats sent thirty-seven paintings for exhibition and sale at the Ferargil Gallery and the Museum of Irish Art in the Barbizon Hotel, New York. The museum had been recently founded and was directed by Patrick Farrell. None were sold.

146. Dr Bethel Solomons, gynaecologist.

147. Eduard Hempel (1887–1972), German Ambassador, and his wife Eva.

148. Thomas J. Kiernan (1897–1967), diplomat, and Delia Murphy (1902–1971), singer.

149. Cecil Salkeld (1908–1969), painter.

150. Michael Henehan, assistant keeper of the National Museum of Ireland, who was keenly interested in folklore.

151. Helen Landreth (1892–1987), American author of *Dear Dark Head* (1936), visited EOM in Burrishoole and was doing research on Robert Emmet for her next book, *The Pursuit of Robert Emmett* (1948).

152. Possibly the culmination of activities undertaken by Helen Leventhal.

153. Delia Murphy, the singer and wife of Thomas J. Kiernan, director of broadcasting at Radio Éireann and later an Irish diplomat to the Holy See, Australia, West Germany, Canada and the United States.

154. M. Rowan & Co. Ltd, seed merchants, 51 Capel Street; Browne & Nolan, Publishers, Stationers, Booksellers, Colour, General Printers, 41 Nassau Street; and probably Maguire & Gatchell, plumbing, 10 Dawson Street, Dublin.

155. Georgette Kerrigan, French-born wife of Dr Sarsfield Kerrigan of Lifford, Co. Donegal.

156. HHOM had not worked on her sculpture much in these years, to her frustration.

157. Fr Michael Murphy, who was looking for HHOM's advice on hanging pictures.

158. Printed with permission of the Estate of James Johnson Sweeney. This note was written on EOM's Christmas card for 1939, which was a photograph of an early Irish Christian sculpture, but it may never have been posted.

159. The only remaining evidence of this project is the photographs that EOM took over several years.

160. Laura Sweeney.

161. John Francis Cunningham, Professor of Gynaecology, University College Dublin, with offices at 38 Fitzwilliam Square.

162. Desmond O'Malley, EOM's youngest brother, at that time serving in the British Merchant Marine.

163. Michael was a member of the farm staff; the snap refers to cranking the car engine to start.

164. Pat McIntyre, local boatman and carpenter.

165. Roisin Walsh, Dublin City Librarian.

166. Unclear, probably some sort of animal feed.

167. Michael Scott (1905–1989), architect. His landmark building is Busáras, Dublin.

168. Sean Keating (1889–1977), artist.

169. David Sears, playwright.

170. Tom Collins, formerly a civil servant and editor from 1926 with Charles Kelly of *Dublin Opinion*, a satirical magazine well known for its cartoons.

171. Des O'Connor, actor who later married Deirdre Halligan (1915–1989), one of the three Halligan sisters.

172. Maureen Halligan (1914–2008), who later married Ronnie Ibbs and moved to Texas, sister of Sunny Halligan (later Mrs Michael Clarke).

173. Kurt Jooss (1901–1979), German-born ballet dancer and choreographer.

174. To forward mail from their old Rathmines address to Newport, Co. Mayo.

175. Lehane & McGuirk, military, civil and sporting tailors, 27 Eustace Street, Dublin.

176. Stella Frost.

177. EOM kept bees to have honey and help with cultivation of flowers and fruit.

178. Merchant shop owned by Francis Chambers, Main Street, Newport, Co. Mayo.

179. In 1936 EOM and HHOM started photographing and writing about early Irish Christian monuments with the intention of publishing a book, which was never completed.

180. EOM owned paintings by Derain, Kisling, Vlaminck and Dufy.

181. Famous for her modernist works, including the cubist *Decoration* (1923), Jellett helped found the Irish Exhibition of Living Art in 1943. Jellett's talk was on 'The Influence of Contemporary French Painting', delivered in October 1939 as part of 'A Loan and Cross-Section Exhibition of Contemporary Paintings'. Louis MacNeice also delivered a lecture in this series.

182. Jack Yeats had a solo show in Jack Longford's Contemporary Picture Galleries, South Leinster Street, Dublin, in November 1939. Bruce Arnold, *Jack Yeats* (New Haven, 1998), p. 291.

183. Nano Reid (1905–1981), painter. Reid had an exhibition at the Gallery at 7 St Stephen's Green in November 1939.

184. No such translation appeared, though Auden refers to Rilke in the poem 'New Year Letter', written in 1940. It may be that EOM heard rumour of Auden's intentions through MacNeice, who delivered a lecture in the same series as Jellett, above.

185. Refers to responses to newspaper advertisements placed by HOM for domestic staff.

186. Andrews & Company, 20 Dame Street, Dublin.

187. English blue cheese sold in airtight jars for preservation.

188. These are all blends of fine tea; Her Majesty's Blend was designed to suit Queen Victoria's taste.

189. Formerly from Taos, NM; EOM was previously in correspondence with her. Golden was at this time working for the American State Department in Portugal.

190. Refers to EOM's private folklore studies around Clew Bay.

191. The Irish Folklore Commission collected materials from 1935 to 1971 under the leadership of James Hamilton Delargy. It was succeeded by the Department of Irish Folklore at University College Dublin.

192. Denis Devlin was at this time part of the Irish Legation in Washington DC.

193. The Museum of Modern Art was founded in New York in 1929.

194. Pierre Matisse (1900–1989) was the son of Henri Matisse and ran a modern art gallery in the Fuller Building, 41 East 57th Street, New York, from 1931 until his death.

195. The Downtown Gallery was founded by Edith Halpert and Berthe Kroll Goldsmith as Our Gallery in 1926, changing its name the following year. It was located in Greenwich Village and was important for its promotion of American Folk Art.

196. The Museum of Living Art was originally known as the Gallery of Living Art, changing its name in 1936. It was housed in New York University from 1926 to 1943 and its initial collection was given by the banking heir, A.E. Gallatin. Its paintings included Picasso's *Three Musicians* (1921) and Mondrian's *Composition in Blue and Yellow* (1932).

197. The Metropolitan Museum of Art was founded in 1870 in New York. It housed early works by Renoir and Matisse, as well as Dutch and Flemish masters.

198. The Hispanic Society of America Museum and Library was founded in 1904 in New York. The Museum building opened in 1908 and held regular exhibitions of Spanish art.

199. Theodora Goddard.

200. Helen Merriam Golden.

201. Mariana Howe.

202. Maria Chabot.

203. Dorothy Stewart.

204. Deirdre Golden.

205. Terence Golden.

206. Rebecca Citkowitz was a friend of EOM whom he had met in 1932 through her brother, Israel, who had been resident at the Yaddo Foundation at the same time as EOM. The address is in the Bronx.

207. Israel Citkowitz (1909–1974), pianist and composer.

208. The Juilliard was then located at 132 Claremont Avenue, New York, having changed its name from the New York Institute of Music in 1926. It is now located at Lincoln Center.

209. Sheila Barnet Brown, an executive at Random House publishers and a friend of Helen Merriman Golden. Brown corresponded with EOM, visited him in Burrishoole and met him in Dublin in 1948.

210. EOM was asked to give lectures in Cork on military tactics to the Irish Defence Forces.

211. Harold Clurman (1901–1980), theatre director, critic and a founder of The Group Theatre, New York.

212. HHOM went to this maternity nursing home to rest. Her first child had been delivered by Caesarean section. She was expecting her second child, Etain O'Malley, shortly.

213. Characters in the Barbar elephant book series for children.

214. An air-raid shelter was built close to the walls of the old castle on the grounds near the pier as there was no basement in the house.

215. John Connolly, farm help.

216. Dr Kevin Malley, brother of EOM.

217. Andreas Hempel, son of the German Ambassador to Ireland, Eduard Hempel.

218. Eva Hempel, wife of the German Ambassador.

219. Dom John Francis Sweetman, OSB, of Mount St Benedict, Gorey, Co. Wexford.

220. Mrs Christina O'Malley, née Ryan, wife of Professor Michael O'Malley, lived just outside Galway.

221. Children were Eithne, Sheila, Evelyn and Michael O'Malley.

222. Refers to the Department of Agriculture.

223. Family dog.

224. Taken down by EOM from Cathal O'Malley, 24 July, with EOM's questions in parenthesis.

225. Pat McIntyre, boatman and carpenter.

226. Willie Walsh was a close neighbour who lived off the long avenue to Burrishoole Lodge.

227. Molly Egan lived at Westport Quay.

228. Lorcan Gill, solicitor, Westport.

229. Marian Malley went to Achill for one month each summer for several years. There were three buses from the Westport railroad station to Achill each day, one each morning, noon and evening.

230. Probably Stella Frost (1890–1962), artist.

231. EOM brought his new boat cross-country by canal before sailing up the west coast to Clew Bay.

232. Johnny and Bea Raleigh.

233. Probably Sean O'Faolain.

234. Co. Galway.

235. Art magazine published in London.

236. Etain O'Malley.

237. Fr Michael Murphy. Mixed in the literary, theatrical and artistic set.

238. Fr Timothy Traynor. Mixed in the literary, theatrical and artistic set.

239. Probably the Newport parish priest.

240. Constantine (Con) Curran (1880–1972), friend of Joyce, art critic, writer, lawyer and Registrar of the High Court, Dublin. His wife, Helen Laird (1874–1957), was an Abbey Theatre actress and founder-member of the Irish National Theatre Society. The couple were famous for their Wednesday 'at homes', at one of which EOM records meeting Jack B. Yeats in August 1937.

241. Wife of Denis Devlin.

242. Referring to a present given to Cathal by Andreas Hempel.

243. Book by Hans Naumann (1886–1951), German literary historian and folklorist.

244. Sergei Aksakov (1791–1859), writer and friend of Gogol. *A Russian Schoolboy* was one of his several autobiographical volumes.

245. Francis Chambers, merchant and newspaper-shop owner, Main Street, Newport.
246. Blanaid Salkeld.
247. The Dublin Drama League was founded by Lennox Robinson in 1919. EOM was involved with several Dublin theatre companies, including the Drama League and his founding role in the Dramatic Society at UCD from 1926 to 1928. EOM also pursued his interest in theatre, while in New York, at The Group Theatre.
248. Waller Brothers, 20 Suffolk Street, Dublin.
249. Pat Quinn, Iniscuttle Island, Clew Bay.
250. Probably a Department of Agriculture pamphlet.
251. Fr Jack Hanlon (1913–1968), watercolourist. EOM possibly purchased his Hanlon painting from this exhibition.
252. Manilla rope has three strands and is made from natural fibre.
253. Victor Gollancz Ltd was a distinguished liberal English publishing house.
254. Forwarded to 'Parma', Howth Summit, Howth, the home of Dr Kevin Malley.
255. Norah McGuinness.
256. Oughterard, Co. Galway.
257. Referenced material is not included.
258. Refers to McCann, Verdun & Co.
259. To generate electricity.
260. At this time the Ministry of Posts and Telegraphs.
261. Could refer to May Guinness (1863–1955), a modern artist who influenced Mainie Jellett and Evie Hone.
262. Sir Peter Carew (1514–1575), Elizabethan colonist and adventurer.
263. Mainie Jellett and her family lived at 36 Fitzwilliam Square, Dublin, where she had her studio.
264. HHOM had leased a flat as her sculpture studio at No. 4D, 25 Upper Pembroke Street, Dublin.
265. EOM's tweed suit of dark colours, which he wore in Mayo.
266. Lehane & McGuirk, 27 Eustace Street, Dublin, merchant tailor.
267. James J. Fox & Co., 119 Grafton Street, Dublin, tobacco merchant.
268. Refers to the constant adjustment of accounts between EOM and HHOM.
269. Sylvia Laithwaite (1897–1984) was EOM's first cousin. Born in Dublin, while her English father worked at the GPO, she went later to Taos and then Santa Fe, New Mexico, and worked there as a librarian. Laithwaite joined the Dominican Order in Detroit.
270. Late January.
271. Gilbert Laithwaite (1894–1986), also EOM's first cousin and born in Dublin, was later to be knighted, and was the first British Ambassador to Ireland in 1949.
272. In 1936 and 1938 respectively.
273. Yeomen.
274. Austin O'Malley had lived in Burrishoole Lodge and escaped to France after he and his brother, Captain Joseph O'Malley, joined Humbert during the rebellion, and was hanged when he surrendered in Ballinamuck, Co. Longford.
275. Croagh Patrick is a mountain that rises on the south side of Clew Bay. It is named after St Patrick, where tradition holds that he fasted for forty days on its summit. It remains a site of pilgrimage.
276. Medically speaking, EOM was in poor condition and had been advised not to undertake strenuous exercise or activity such as rowing or even sailing by himself.

277. HHOM was anxious to resume her sculpture when she settled in Ireland. She built a modern studio with a northern skylight at Burrishoole.

278. The isolated village of Rio Chiquita, New Mexico, was easier to supply from Taos than Burrishoole was from Westport.

279. HHOM had long practised as an artist, working in drawing, painting, sculpture, dancing and photography. She collected many artworks during her extensive travels. Both HHOM and EOM had a broad understanding of the practical and academic aspects of art.

280. HHOM's principal painting medium had been watercolours in her travels in Greece, Russia and the USA.

281. Cecil Malley, was an eye, nose and throat specialist, then in London.

282. Marian Malley had trained as a nurse, like her mother.

283. Patrick Malley worked at Hibernian Bank, Dublin, and had volunteered for the Local Defence Force during the Emergency.

284. Kathleen Malley, the younger sister, also followed the Kearney-Malley family tradition for nursing, and joined the Irish Nursing Corps.

285. Kevin Malley was a physican at the Mater Hospital and had a private medical practice.

286. Brendan Malley was the third doctor in the family. Neither he nor Cecil did sufficiently well in their required Irish language exams and went to London to follow their medical careers.

287. Desmond O'Malley was the youngest and apart from EOM was the only brother formally to use the 'O' in his surname.

288. Luke Malley had retired from the Irish Land Commission by this time.

289. Marian Malley visited Achill for a month each summer.

290. For COM's birth, 20 July 1942.

291. Kathleen Malley.

292. Horse.

293. EOM's sailboat with a lug sail.

294. Land owned by EOM.

295. Refers to Cathal O'Malley, who often sailed with EOM.

296. The first name was a heifer's, the second a cow's and the third a bull's.

297. Luke and Marian Malley's family home, where Kathleen and Paddy Malley were still living; address had been changed to Drumcondra from Glasnevin.

298. Likely that Kathleen had sent EOM a supply of hard-to-get cigarettes.

299. Margaret Kilcommons Malley, originally from Glinsk, Co. Galway, was a nurse in London. She married Cecil Malley on 14 July 1942 in the Brompton Oratory, London.

300. Irish Army Nursing Corps.

301. Robert Herbert (1911–1957), Limerick City Librarian from 1938 until his death. He helped start the art collection there.

302. Herbert had sent some books to HHOM in Dublin. They did not arrive and EOM offered to replace them.

303. Paddy Kilroy, Newport. Michael Kilroy from Newport had been O/C West Mayo Brigade in the Tan war and 4th Western Division in the civil war, and had led the hunger strike in Mountjoy and Kilmainham, in which EOM had participated.

304. The letters slacken here during the war years as EOM and HHOM did not travel apart for any period of time between December 1942 and November 1943.

305. Friend of Johnny Raleigh who was helping EOM locate a superintendent for Burrishoole.

306. The superintendent's farmhouse.

307. Total size of the Burrishoole acreage, arable and non-arable.

308. To work on the farm.

309. Applicant for work on the farm at Burrishoole.

310. A reference to EOM's list of liabilities on his tax return.

311. Joe Griffin was Director of Intelligence on EOM's staff in the Four Courts during the civil war and escaped with EOM from government custody on 30 June 1922. See UCDA P17b/87.

312. HHOM had leased a new house in Clonskeagh, a suburb of Dublin, so that she and EOM could live there and let the children attend school in the Dublin area.

313. Small parcels of land purchased with the Gate House from Brennan and thereafter called after him.

314. Royal Hibernian Academy exhibition.

Part IV: Post-Emergency Life, 1945–1950

1. The following is an autobiographical statement through 1944 written by EOM, around the July–September 1950 period, and was probably prepared in order to give his solicitor, Michael Noyk, some background information on his relationship with HHOM and her family from the time he first met her in 1933.

2. HHOM's parents' house, 'Chelmsford', Zacheus Mead Lane, Greenwich, Conn.

3. Mariquita Villard. Oscar Garrison Villard (1872–1949), editor of *The Nation* from 1918 and a founder of the National Association for the Advancement of Colored People.

4. Elon Huntington Hooker was from Rochester, New York. He was a civil engineer and founded his own company to produce chemicals from passing electricity through a solution of salt and water.

5. Blanche Ferry Hooker was daughter of Dexter Mason Ferry of Detroit who had built a successful seed business, Ferry Morse Seed Company.

6. HHOM had her studio over the garage building.

7. There were four daughters but only the three unmarried daughers were present.

8. Vassos Kanellos: HHOM had spent about twelve months, 1930–1, dancing in Athens with his Greek Chorodrama Academy.

9. Thenagra, a dancer and the American-born wife of Vassos Kanellos.

10. HHOM gave up her tennis career after winning the American Under-Eighteen Singles Championship in 1923.

11. Helen Wills and HHOM were American Under-Eighteen Doubles Champions in 1922.

12. They were married in 1932; HHOM was her bridesmaid.

13. John P. Marquand (1893–1960), Pulitzer Prize-winning novelist for *The Late George Apley* (1938).

14. Dr Gertrude Light.

15. W. Horsely Gantt (1892–1980), psychophysiologist. Gantt was a student of Ivan P. Pavlov's in Russia in the 1920s. He spent his career from 1929 in Johns Hopkins University School of Medicine.

16. HHOM had lived with her sister Adelaide in St Petersburg and Moscow from October 1928 to March 1929, principally to study painting with Pavel Filonov, a leading modern Russian painter. While there she had met 'Vasily' Gantt.
17. Sarah 'Belinda' Sheridan.
18. Sir Gilbert Laithwaite (1894–1986), civil servant and diplomat. His mother was a sister of EOM's mother, Marian Kearney Malley.
19. George Nathaniel Curzon, 1st Marquess Curzon of Kedleston (1859–1925), Viceroy of India and Foreign Secretary.
20. EOM ultimately received a £259-service pension plus £130 in disability payments for his wounds.
21. In May–June 1935 Mrs Hooker took her two daughters to Japan with the Garden Club of America tour of Japan. After that tour the sisters travelled independently for two months through the rest of Japan, and then over to Korea and China. They reached London in early September.
22. EOM and HHOM were married on 25 September 1935 at the Oratory, London.
23. Bethel Solomons, gynaecologist, 42 Fitzwilliam Square, Dublin.
24. 10 July 1936.
25. The court case taken by Joseph O'Doherty was first reported in *The Irish Press* (17 November 1937).
26. The liability was split. £400 was awarded against EOM and £200 against the Irish publisher.
27. Louisburgh.
28. At Louisburgh, Co. Mayo, July, August and October, 1938.
29. Beginning November 1938.
30. Between them they took over 1000 photographs of early Irish Christian monuments. HHOM took additional images of the people and landscapes of the west of Ireland.
31. Elon Hooker died on 10 May 1938.
32. HHOM was in America from mid May to June 1938.
33. Eamon de Valera (1882–1975), politician and revolutionary. De Valera kept a high regard for EOM but they had no close personal relationship and EOM did not introduce HHOM to him socially. No doubt EOM did not like being asked to request favours.
34. Adelaide Hooker married Marquand in 1937.
35. EOM had always loved the isolation of the Aran Islands, Co. Galway. He went there on several occasions as a form of retreat.
36. Liam Redmond (1913–1989), actor, had married Barbara MacDonagh, the daughter of Thomas MacDonagh.
37. EOM made extensive private studies and notes on available Elizabethan papers and books.
38. Sean O'Faolain, *The Great O'Neill: A Biography of Hugh O'Neill, Earl of Tyrone, 1550–1616* (London, 1942).
39. To France in 1936 and Corsica in 1938.
40. Carrowkeel.
41. 8 August 1940.
42. A neighbouring small landowner.
43. Rossgiblin.
44. The owners of the neigbouring land had purchased it from the former Burrishoole Lodge estate, itself taken over by the Congested Districts Board.
45. Sean Walsh.

46. Austin and Joseph O'Malley. See Note 274 in Part III above.
47. This was apparently the first tuberculin-tested herd west of the Shannon.
48. The land was located in Rossgibblin.
49. HHOM had loved ballroom dancing in New York society.
50. Clew Bay, 1940.
51. At Carrowkeel.
52. Mrs Thomas J. Kiernan, a well-known folk singer.
53. The first Irish Exhibition of Living Art, which opened on 16 September 1943 at the National College of Art, Kildare Street, Dublin.
54. Eithne Dunne, Abbey Theatre actress and a founding member of the Players Theatre.
55. Derada National School.
56. 15 Whitebeam Avenue, Clonskeagh.
57. Jerry Healy, actor and a founding member of the Players Theatre, was married to the actress Eithne Dunne.
58. Xavier School, Donnybrook.
59. HHOM maintained a studio flat in Upper Pembroke Street that she used as a studio.
60. 1944.
61. Helen and a group of friends founded the Players Theatre in late 1944. The idea was to produce new Irish plays and to pay actors a wage of £1 per day so that they did not need to hold a second job to support their family.
62. Redmond's *Rocks of Bawn* was first performed by the Players Theatre at the Olympia Theatre in late April 1945. A review observed that 'Helen O'Malley's elaborate setting for this play fills the eye, and suggests that something better than what emerges inside it may begin to happen at any moment. But it never happens ... ', *The Irish Times* (24 April 1945).
63. This became the film *I See a Dark Stranger*, directed by Frank Launder and Sidney Gilliat, part of which was filmed in Wicklow, with Redmond's involvement as an actor. The story relates the relationship of an Irish girl with a German spy. See *The Irish Times* (16 June 1945).
64. Roger McHugh (1908–1987), scholar and playwright. The two met at UCD in 1926 and both worked to develop the UCD Dramatic Society. McHugh was appointed the first Professor of Anglo-Irish Literature and Drama at UCD in 1965.
65. McHugh wrote on 20 April requesting permission to quote from several passages of *On Another Man's Wound* in his forthcoming prose anthology for Brown & Nolan.
66. Patricia Kelly McHugh, originally from Dublin.
67. McHugh's historical play *Rossa* won the Abbey Theatre Award for an historical play in 1945.
68. EOM substituted drawings instead of words and these have been placed in brackets in text. EOM's family references were to his brother, Cecil Malley, and his children, Jacqueline and Kevin Malley.
69. EOM had stayed with him in Boston on several occasion during his travels from 1928 to 1935.
70. Marian Malley.
71. Bridget O'Shea.
72. Catherine (Bobs) Walston, married to English Labour politician, Harry Walston.
73. EOM is referring to the fact that several members of the Players Theatre were in London working on *I See a Dark Stranger*, then shooting at Denham Studios. *The Irish Times* (29 October 1945).

74. John Rothenstein (1901–1992), director of the Tate, London, from 1938 to 1964.
75. The Boston reference could be a clever combination of 'Bobs' and 'Crompton'.
76. Clonskeagh and Burrishoole Lodge respectively.
77. EOM was to give a dinner party in Dublin in order for Rothenstein to meet Jack Yeats.
78. Madge Coughlan had been anti-Treaty in the civil war, working within EOM's Northern & Eastern Division.
79. Michael Carolan was director of intelligence in EOM's Northern & Eastern Division during the civil war and later worked with anti-Treaty GHQ.
80. The name given to the first Free State government, regarded as provisional since republicans did not recognize its legitimacy. Abbreviated as 'PG' later in this letter.
81. Eimear O'Duffy (1893–1935), writer.
82. Leinster House, Kildare Street, Dublin, is still the seat of the Dáil.
83. Florence (Florrie) O'Donoghue (1895–1967), intelligence officer, Cork No. 1 Brigade in War of Independence. He was neutral in the civil war. See EOM's military interviews in UCDA P17b/95 and 96.
84. There was still a limited supply of consumer goods as a result of the war.
85. Sylvia Laithwaite.
86. EOM's notes reflect his readings for Cathal and Etain: *Don Quixote*, Joyce, *Arabian Nights*, *Hakluyt's Voyages*, *Scots Ballads*; for Cormac alone: *Gods and Fighting Men*, *Cuchullain of Muirthemne*, *Scots Ballads*, *The Cuchullain Saga*, *The Story of Burn Njal*, *The Crock of Gold*, *Gulliver's Travels*; and for all three: *The Odyssey*, *Anabasis*, *Moby Dick*, *The Lays of Marie de France*, *The Memories of Sergeant Burgoyne*, *Guadrum*, *Arthurian Legends*, Day-Lewis' *Poetry for You*.
87. Printed with the kind permission of the Estate of James Johnson Sweeney.
88. The Friends of the National Collections of Ireland was formed as a charitable group in 1924 to purchase and donate paintings.
89. Georges Roualt's *Christ and the Soldier* was offered to the Municipal Gallery of Modern Art in 1942, but was attacked by Sean Keating, among others. The Catholic hierarchy offered to house the painting in Maynooth College.
90. Reference to the committee that established the Irish Exhibition of Living Art in 1943.
91. The Royal Hibernian Academy.
92. The Jack B. Yeats National Loan Exhibition, 1945, for which EOM was a member of the Committee.
93. John F. Kelly was director.
94. George Furlong (1898–1987) was director of the National Gallery of Ireland from 1935 to 1950. Suitably, he returned to London after his tenure, having worked there previously in the National Gallery.
95. The National College of Art was formed from the Metropolitan School of Art in 1936.
96. Tomás Ó Deirg (1897–1956), TD, was Fianna Fáil minister for education from 1943 to 1948 and was formerly EOM's adjutant for his Northern and Eastern Division in the civil war.
97. James Johnson Sweeney, *African Negro Art* (1935); *Plastic Redirections in Twentieth Century Painting* (1934).
98. Watson O'Dell Pierce (1904–1991), author, involved in the art world; probably working temporarily with the War Department during the war.
99. James Whyte ran a bookstore in Washington that sold foreign-language books, maps

and modern art, and after 1939 Franz Bader persuaded him to hold monthly art exhibitions.

100. Sale held at the Wildenstein & Co. gallery, London, from 13 February to 9 March 1946.

101. John Rothenstein.

102. Originally founded as the Pennsylvania Museum and School of Industrial Art in 1876, and now known as the Philadelphia Museum of Art.

103. Henry McIlhenny (1910–1986) was curator of the decorative arts at the museum from 1935 to 1963; Fiske Kimball was then director of the museum.

104. McIlhenny bought the Glenveagh mansion, Co. Donegal, from his former art professor at Harvard, A. Kingsley Porter, in 1937.

105. Irish Tourist Association, National Tourist Bureau, forerunner of today's Fáilte Ireland.

106. EOM was staying with his brother, Cecil, and his family just outside London, but the letter was written on stationery from Thriplow Farm, Harry Walston's farm near Cambridge, where EOM often visited.

107. Kevin Malley, elder brother of Jacqueline, the girl referred to next.

108. Wildenstein & Co. Ltd, 147 New Bond Street, London, had a Jack Yeats exhibition from 13 February to 9 March, 1946. The sixteen paintings included *Two Travellers*, which was purchased by John Rothenstein, director of the Tate. EOM had introduced Rothenstein to Yeats in December 1945 in Dublin.

109. EOM also attended the Leicester Galleries in Leicester Square for their 'Winter Exhibition of painting, drawing and sculpture, February 1946', and the National Gallery exhibition of 'Paul Klee, 1879–1940'.

110. Suniva 'Sunny' Halligan Clarke.

111. Cecil Malley, his brother.

112. The three-ton *St Brendan*, moored at Burrishoole in Clew Bay.

113. Molly Gill Egan of Westport Quay.

114. Kurt Jooss' *The Green Table*, a dance drama, first performed by him in Paris in 1932, was produced at the Gaiety Theatre, Dublin.

115. Michael Kilroy, Newport.

116. Merchant from Westport.

117. A bust of Kurt Jooss, the German ballet-troup leader, was exhibited at the fourth Irish Exhibition of Living Art that year, as was the head of Frank O'Connor.

118. David (Buzz) Crompton, son of Lillian Crompton and grandson of Mrs Belinda Sheridan, former companion of Mrs Hooker. Buzz was brother to Catherine (Bobs) Crompton Walston and was living in England.

119. Anne, David, Oliver, and twins, Bill and Susan Walston.

120. An actress in the Players Theatre, 1944–5.

121. Cathal had started as a boarder in St Gerard's School, Bray, Co. Wicklow.

122. Bridget O'Shea.

123. Burrishoole River and Lough Furnance were well known for salmon fishing.

124. Given his academic background and significant farming experience, Harry Waltson was appointed as an agricultural advisor in the English-controlled zone of Germany.

125. HHOM had talked about getting American film executives interested in using Ireland as a film location.

126. This was a rural social event when the local parish priest performed the Stations of the Cross in a family home.

127. Mary Kate Gillespie Quinn of Glenhest, near Burrishoole, wife of Pat Joe Quinn of Inniskellew.
128. Refers to the barometer.
129. The cows were not supplying milk.
130. Department of Agriculture.
131. P.J. Kelly, builder, of Westport.
132. Shop closest to Burrishoole Lodge on the Newport–Achill road.
133. Benjamin Seebohm Rowntree (1871–1954), Quaker, reformer and industrialist.
134. Brown's Hotel, Mayfair, London.
135. Shortly after their London meeting with intermediaries in November, HHOM had informed EOM that all his future communications for her should be made only through solicitors.
136. George Overend was a partner in the solicitors firm of A. & L. Goodbody in Dublin, which had represented HHOM in Ireland since her arrival in 1935.
137. Thomas Gilchrist was HHOM's new lawyer in New York.
138. Address of convenience for EOM to collect post in London. It was in reality the residence of the Walston family.
139. This refers to rumours that HHOM had spread in London about EOM's extramarital conduct.
140. The draft letter is not included.
141. EOM felt that he could not be present in Burrishoole based on HHOM's instructions as owner of the house.
142. EOM noted on this item 'Letter to Gilchrist which I did not send'.
143. Catherine Walston.
144. Barbara Rothschild, neé Hutchinson (1911–1989), then recently divorced from Victor, 3rd Baron Rothschild (1910–1990).
145. John V. Kelleher (1916–2004) was researching Irish literature on a Guggenheim Fellowship. He was then teaching at Harvard University and would become a professor of Irish Studies in the Department of Celtic Languages and Literature. He visited EOM in Burrishoole while in Ireland. He was also COM's history tutor while COM wrote his thesis on modern Irish history in 1965 at Harvard.
146. John Kelleher had brought two sleeping bags for EOM from Rebecca Citkowitz Liber of New York.
147. EOM's BBC *Third Programme* was aired on 2 January and his essay was published in *The Listener* (23 January 1947), 145–6, see Appendix 1, No. 8; he never did the broadcast on Irish sculpture.
148. EOM's essay on neutrality was published as 'Renaissance' in *La France Libre*, XII:74 (December 1946/January 1947), 138–43, see Appendix 1, No. 7; 'The County of Mayo' was published in *Holiday* magazine (28 October 1946), see Appendix 1, No. 5. He did not mention his articles on 'Painting: The School of London' in *The Bell*, XIV:3 (July 1947), see Appendix 1, No. 9, nor 'The Background of the Arts in Mexico' in *The Bell*, XIV:5 (August 1947), 59–69, see Appendix 1, No. 11.
149. EOM wrote 'A' for autobiographical material, '*' for books he thought good and '( )' for books Kelleher might read himself.
150. These properties were Burrishoole Lodge, the Gate House, the Superintendent's House, and in Dublin the house in Clonskeagh and the studio flat.
151. As EOM conducted interviews on military actions during the 1916–24 period, he also took down folklore as he came across it, particularly in Co. Mayo.

152. Eimear O'Duffy (1893–1935), author, poet and playright, wrote *The Wasted Island*, published in 1920.
153. Count George Noble Plunkett (1851–1948), Irish nationalist, created Papal Count by Pope Leo XIII in 1877, curator of National Museum, joined Sinn Féin, went anti-Treaty; EOM refers to his discussions with him on art in *On Another Man's Wound*, and probably had an influence on EOM in that area.
154. The Irish Volunteers were formed in 1913 to defend Ireland after the Ulster Volunteers had been established in 1912 to protect the union of Great Britain and Ireland.
155. *The Irish Volunteer* was the official organ of the Irish Volunteers.
156. *Printed Errors* by Eimear O'Duffy.
157. As a student enrolled in what is now University College Dublin.
158. Eoin MacNeill (1867–1945), scholar and nationalist, co-founder of Gaelic League, editor of its *Gaelic Journal*, professor of early Irish history at UCD in 1908, chief of staff of the Irish Republican Brotherhood in Easter Week, Sinn Féin, and pro-Treaty.
159. Gerald O'Donovan (1871–1942), ordained as a priest but left priesthood to become a writer.
160. Aodghain O'Rahilly, son of Michael O'Rahilly, The O'Rahilly, who died at the GPO, 1916.
161. Photographs that John Kelleher had taken during his visit to Burrishoole.
162. Refers to annual tax returns.
163. This refers to shares in the Hooker Electrochemical Company that Mrs Blanche Hooker gave to EOM. These were retained in New York. EOM never received any benefit from them; they were ultimately seized by HHOM.
164. EOM planned to send Cathal to a series of Benedictine schools: St Gerard's in Bray, Co. Wicklow, Glenstal Abbey School, Co. Limerick, and Ampleforth College in York, but he never made it to the latter.
165. EOM writing on official stationery in his capacity as the organization's secretary.
166. Eily (Eileen) Dinneen (1905–1969), originally from Ballylanders, Co. Limerick, and with over twenty-five years of experience in America, was hired by HHOM to help run the O'Malley household. She was from a family with strong nationalist and cultural links as well as Mayo connections. Her father, Frank B. Dinneen (1862–1916), had been president and general secretary of the Gaelic Athletic Association (GAA), 1895–1901, and was involved in the purchase of Croke Park in Dublin. No doubt, HHOM thought that Eileen, as she was known to the O'Malleys, could help better organize the family, but she was perceived by EOM as being HHOM's ally.
167. Glenstal Abbey School is a Benedictine secondary school for boys near Limerick city.
168. Mrs Blanche Hooker.
169. Josie Gill.
170. Iniscuttle, Clew Bay.
171. Winnie Hyland.
172. Stan Stewart lived in Limerick.
173. EOM introduced and compered *Country Magazine* for BBC *Third Programme* with contributions from Seamus Ennis (tin whistle), Mrs Tierney, Tom Maxwell, Michael Cronin, Desmond Kernan, Charles Osborne, Bryan McMahon, Bill Thompson (tenor) and Albert Healy (accordion), which aired on 7 September.
174. Jack Sweeney, Lamont Library, Harvard University.
175. EOM worked as books editor, 1947–8, with Peadar O'Donnell, who succeeded Sean O'Faolain as general editor.

176. Padraic Colum (1881–1972), poet, novelist and playwright, husband to Mary/Molly Colum.
177. EOM interviewed civil war survivors so that he could edit his draft of what became his civil war memoir, *The Singing Flame.*
178. Thomas J. Wilson of Harvard University Press wrote to EOM on 11 August 1947, asking him about his Irish civil war book.
179. EOM had become interested in James Joyce. He created his own Compendium in several volumes of notebooks to better read and understand *Ulysses* and other Joyce works; see EOM Papers NYU.
180. Margaret 'Peggy' Woods was wife of the surgeon Robert R. Woods; they had three children: Joanna, Margaret and Robert.
181. Cecilia Gallagher.
182. John Raleigh, son of Johnny Raleigh.
183. In watercolours.
184. Skerries, Co. Dublin.
185. Possibly Christopher Morley (1890–1957).
186. Catherine (Kitty) Harding Taylor.
187. Fred Hanna, Ltd, Dublin, medical, scholastic and general booksellers, new and second-hand.
188. Aer Lingus.
189. Ireland did not become a republic until 1949.
190. Clann na Poblachta.
191. The Coalition included Clann na Poblachta, Fine Gael, Labour and Clann na Talmhan.
192. John A. Costello.
193. Seán MacBride.
194. Cecil Lavery (1894–1973).
195. Maud Gonne MacBride.
196. Party created by Eamon de Valera in 1926 when he lost a vote at the Sinn Féin convention hoping to approving their joining in the parliamentary political process.
197. Party founded from Cumann na nGaedheal, the representatives of pro-Treaty nationalist opinion.
198. Mrs Kearney Burton, EOM's aunt in Baltimore; Patrick and Joseph O'Malley, his uncle and first cousin in New York.
199. Peadar O'Donnell.
200. Frank O'Connor.
201. EOM wrote his book review of Graham Greene's eight short stories, *The Fixed Wheel* in *The Bell*, XV:6, 61–4, March 1948.
202. O'Donnell was refused a visa possibly due to his socialism and IRA activities; he had been a member of the Irish Brigade during the Spanish civil war.
203. Reference to the inquiries of Senator Joseph McCarthy (1908–1957).
204. EOM had had a long-standing interest in early Christian art in Ireland and photographed many sites.
205. Possibly the role of Russian and American influence in Czechoslovakia after the Second World War.
206. A clough is a stone structure; Tyrell's Pass, Co. Westmeath, was a battle site in 1590.
207. A castle built at the time of King John.
208. This part of Connemara is known as Joyce Country.
209. Stan and Mary Barry.

210. Limerick City Library Gallery, run by Robert Herbert; the date is 22 March 1948.
211. EOM never bought a painting by Sean Keating, whose style was more representational.
212. Stan Stewart.
213. Glentworth Hotel; this had been EOM's headquarters when he took over Limerick in March 1922.
214. To photograph early Christian monuments.
215. The Burren, Co. Clare, is a unique limestone landscape, known for its unusual flora.
216. MS unclear but should be a pass from the Burren towards Gort, Co. Galway.
217. Kinvara is a small village on Galway Bay.
218. Policeman or Garda.
219. EOM had photographed this area extensively with HHOM in 1936–8.
220. Cathal O'Malley.
221. Margaret Fox Lydon had a pub in Eyre Square, Galway.
222. The County Club, Eyre Square, Galway, where EOM was a member.
223. A fictitious name adopted for Cathal for the occasion, but in fact there was a Sir James Esmonde, the 7th Baronet of the Esmonde Baronetcy from Co. Wexford, and it is possible that EOM knew that name.
224. Professor Michael V. Duignan, co-author of the *Shell Guide to Ireland*.
225. *Thomond Archaeological Journal*, of which Robert Herbert was secretary and Stan Stewart was treasurer.
226. His Grace, the Most Revd Dr Walsh, Archbishop of Tuam, who opened the sixth Annual Exhibition in St Jarlath's College, Tuam.
227. Dr Joe Costello.
228. In Tuam.
229. Distinguished high cross in Tuam.
230. Breihne MacDonagh.
231. Possibly Beatrice Salkeld (1925–1993), who married Brendan Behan in 1955.
232. Two family cats.
233. Marian (Sweetie) Malley, EOM's sister, married Dr James Gargan-Daly in 1948 and died later that month in a plane crash in France.
234. Dr James P. Gargan-Daly, who also died in the crash.
235. Una Joyce from Carraroe, Co. Galway.
236. Work relating to a proposed production in England of plays by the Irish Players Theatre.
237. This remained an unfulfilled ambition as HHOM retained Burrishoole until 1981.
238. This exhibition is not listed in Hilary Pyle's *Jack B. Yeats: A Catalogue Raisonné of the Oil Paintings* (London, 1992).
239. The Custom House, Dublin.
240. Etain stayed with Sunny Halligan Clarke in Montone, Killiney, Co. Dublin.
241. Eileen Dinneen.
242. Refers to letters from HHOM's New York lawyers.
243. Stuart Cloete, *African Portraits* (1946).
244. Cecil John Rhodes (1853–1902).
245. Irish Parliamenty Party in the House of Commons.
246. The Irish country accent personified by the Abbey Theatre portrayal of rural Irish characters.
247. Ring College, Dungarvan, Co. Waterford, an all-Irish-speaking school. EOM had made plans in 1945 to send both Cathal and Cormac for one year to Ring to learn Irish before sending them off to Ampleforth College, York.

248. EOM had to give up his car due to financial pressure but occasionally borrowed one to get around the countryside to conduct his military interviews with the independence movement.

249. Erskine Childers. Frank Gallagher had worked with him on IRA publicity during the Tan and civil wars.

250. Frank O'Connor, *The Big Fellow* (1937).

251. Arthur Griffith (1872–1922), author, founder of Sinn Féin, and president of Dáil Éireann.

252. EOM interviewed Frank Gallagher; see UCDA P17b/31, 86 and 90.

253. By Frank Gallagher.

254. Erskine Childers, with whom Gallagher had worked in 1922, and John T. Hughes of Boston, with whom EOM had stayed during his American travels.

255. Cecil John Rhodes (1853–1902), English industrialist who made a fortune in South African mining.

256. Probably a production put on by one of the many small touring theatrical companies in rural Ireland.

257. Albert Coyle, report for the American Commission on Conditions in Ireland, 1920–1921, published by the US government, 1921.

258. Lawrence Ginnell (1854–1923), a Sinn Féin MP.

259. HHOM's American lawyer and trustee.

260. Guardianship in connection with HHOM's assets.

261. Refers to Gilchrist's August 1948 visit to Burrishoole.

262. Sarah 'Belinda' Sheridan, grandmother of Catherine Walston.

263. Sunny Halligan Clarke; Etain attended Holy Child Convent while there.

264. Eileen Dinneen.

265. Farm worker employed by HHOM.

266. Reading lists from Kelleher's Harvard courses on Irish history and literature.

267. Sir John Davies (1569–1626) did not write *A True History of Why* ... or *The State of the Town of Newry*.

268. Auction of EOM's books by Sothebys, London.

269. The date when taxes are due in Ireland and England.

270. Heart murmurs.

271. The Clonskeagh house lease was given up by HHOM in late 1948.

272. Reference to HHOM trying to evict EOM formally from Burrishoole, and she tried again in May.

273. Probably refers to Frank O'Connor.

274. EOM's favourite type of smooth-nibbed ink fountain pen.

275. In the course of EOM's military interviews.

276. Eimear Ultan O'Duffy (1893–1935), writer and political economist; Gerald O'Donovan (1871–1942), novelist.

277. Refers to writing up the military interviews of the Tan and civil wars. See UCDA P17b.

278. EOM's books and their sale.

279. In late March 1950 HHOM took Etain and Cathal O'Malley away from Ring College, without permission of either EOM or the headmaster, drove them to Belfast, hired a private plane to fly to France and thence to New York. The loss of his two children had a significant emotional impact on EOM, as these letters disclose. It also meant he became concerned that HHOM might try to 'kidnap' Cormac, who at the time was in

Burrishoole. EOM instituted habeas corpus proceedings in the High Court in Dublin against HHOM, demanding that she produce the two children to the court.

280. *The Bible in Ireland (Ireland's Welcome to the Stranger)* by Asenath Nicholson, neé Hatch (1792–1855), a Vermont lady who spent over four years in Ireland during the Famine years to observe, record, proselytize and give charitable aid.

281. Asenath Nicholson's American publications included *Excursion 1844–5*; *Ireland's Welcome to the Stranger*; and *Excursions through Ireland in 1844 & 1845 for the purpose of personally investigating the condition of the poor*; *Annals of the Famine in Ireland in 1847, 1848 and 1849* (1851).

V: Decline, 1950–1957

1. Beatrice 'Sammy' Sherlock married the surgeon Lionel Beecher Sommerville-Large. EOM met her on the Aran Islands in 1944 with the English artist Elizabeth Rivers. This is the first letter after the kidnap of Cathal and Etain by HHOM and reflects the actions being taken by HHOM through Irish solicitors.

2. Michael Noyk.

3. Page missing. In contemplating the security for his pictures and having to depart from Burrishoole, EOM asked several of his friends to take care of his remaining important paintings, those not loaned to Limerick City Library. Mrs Sommerville-Lodge cared for *Reverie* by Jack B. Yeats for many years. Subsequent to EOM's death she notified the family and returned the painting.

4. Seán Treacy from Tipperary was killed in March 1920 in the War of Independence.

5. Séamus Robinson (1890–1961) was second in command to EOM in Tipperary and was an anti-Treaty republican; see UCDA 17b/95, 99, 101.

6. Both locations in Co. Tipperary.

7. Dan Breen (1894–1969), revolutionary and TD.

8. Rehill Rifle Range in Rehill, Ballylooby, Cahir, Co. Tipperary.

9. In March 1921.

10. After 12 July 1921.

11. Eoin O'Duffy was a member of the IRA Executive during the civil war. See UCDA P17b/40, 42 and 46. See also P17b/96 and 105.

12. Galtee Castle was located on the slopes of the Galtee Mountains, near Carrigeen, Co. Tipperary.

13. Joe O'Connor was from Cork and a member of Dublin 3 Battalion. He was anti-Treaty; see UCDA 17b/96, 105.

14. List of EOM's books for sale not included.

15. Refers to auction of EOM's books by Sothebys, London, on 15 December 1949, in London.

16. Liam Manahan (1878–1965), originally from Limerick, was in the process of making a statement to the Bureau of Military History and had given EOM a copy of his draft statement, some of which EOM incorporated into his write-up on his interview with Manahan. See UCDA P17b/106, 117.

17. Early draft of statement given to Bureau of Military History.

18. In support of legal action in the High Court in Dublin initiated by HHOM to evict

EOM from her apparent property, Burrishoole Lodge. She had now left Ireland and returned to the United States, having kidnapped Cathal and Etain O'Malley from their school in late March.

19. Tom 'Skinner' O'Reilly was in 1st Dublin Brigade in June 1922 and was anti-Treaty.

20. This refers to the Annual Dinner of the Four Courts Headquarters Garrison, of which Tom 'Skinner' O'Reilly was the organizer for many years.

21. Louis MacNeice (1907–1963), poet, writer and broadcaster.

22. Corinna MacNeice, daughter of Louis and Hedli MacNeice, was born in 1943.

23. Hedli Anderson, a singer, married Louis MacNeice in 1942.

24. Probably on his way to the Tralee Races.

25. Unidentified; EOM interviewed several O'Sullivans in Cork.

26. See EOM interviews, UCDA P17b/111.

27. See EOM interviews, UCDA P17b/103.

28. Bridget 'Biddens' Sheehy.

29. Sheehy had asked EOM to identify a a good Connemara pony for sale. EOM tried his local friends Paddy O'Malley and George O'Malley, who knew about horses.

30. In the sense that his word cannot be taken on trust.

31. Reference to the court hearing in Dublin regarding HHOM's attempt to evict him from Burrishoole.

32. Immediately after the kidnapping of his children EOM had sought an order for their habeas corpus for HHOM to produce the two missing children, but it failed as it could not be served properly on HHOM.

33. EOM spent most of the summer of 1951 acting as technical adviser to John Ford on the making of the film *The Quiet Man*, based at Ashford Castle, Cong, but with shoots all around Connemara. EOM, and COM on occasion, would drive back and forth to Cong daily as needed. Una Joyce was still resident in Burrishoole and so cared for COM when he was not on the film site. Maureen O'Hara and others from the film group visited Burrishoole.

34. Martin 'Maurteen' Brennan (1901–1956), then a doctor in Sligo, and local politician; see UCDA P17b/133.

35. Tom Duignan, see UCDA P17b/133.

36. Jim Hunt, see UCDA P17b/133.

37. This draft is included to reflect how EOM collected military information during the process of his interviews, now at UCDA. The draft letter was probably intended for George Power of Fermoy, who, based on his interviews in the UCDA, was involved in the referenced actions. UCDA P17b/100, 123, 132.

38. Liam Lynch, former officer commanding, 1st Southern Division of the IRA and later chief of staff of the anti-Treaty republicans.

39. Refers to the capture of Brigadier General Cuthbert Henry Tyndall Lucas (1879–1958), commanding the British 18th Brigade, Shropshire Regiment, and of two officers, Col Danford of Royal Artillery and Col Tyrell of Royal Engineers, while fishing on the Blackwater near Fermoy, Co. Cork; EOM had stopped his interview at this point.

40. Printed with kind permission of the Estate of James Johnson Sweeney.

41. Christmas card with sailboat in foreground and mountains in the background, painted by COM.

42. Standish O'Grady (1846–1928), writer and antiquarian.

43. Estella Solomons.

44. Rebecca Citkowitz, now married to Dr Armour Liber.

45. EOM had a system for numbering his letters for extensive correspondence since his military days.

46. EOM had asked to be sent one of the latest American books on James Joyce.

47. Keem Strand is near the western end of Achill Island.

48. Anthony Chambers of Newport, looking to collect rates owed on land in possession of EOM and HHOM.

49. Michael Moran, TD, local county councillor and solicitor, living in the Malley family home, Elison Street, Castlebar, Co. Mayo.

50. Sir Thomas Malory's *Morte d'Arthur* was a fifteenth-century compilation of earlier romances connected to the legend of King Arthur.

51. Liam MacLachloinn.

52. County manager.

53. HHOM had hired a six-seater plane to fly with Cathal, Etain and Liam Redmond to Paris, but they landed in Le Havre due to engine trouble and continued by train to Paris, and thence to Marseille.

54. Honoré de Balzac (1799–1850).

55. Percy Wyndham Lewis (1882–1957), painter and writer.

56. Jack B. Yeats, A First Retrospective American Exhibition, initially organized by the Institute of Contemporary Art, Boston, and shown at the New York National Academy, 1951.

57. Blanche Ferry was HHOM's mother and the BF of the title; this novel was published by Little, Brown in 1946.

58. Seaweed is used to fertilize trees in the springtime.

59. EOM was researching and writing articles for what became *Raids and Rallies*.

60. Land along the railroad track at Burrishoole.

61. *The Partisan Review* was an American quarterly political and literary review published from 1934 to 2003.

62. Rebecca West (1892–1983), author.

63. *Black Lamb and Grey Falcon: A Journey through Yugoslavia.*

64. Honor Tracy is the pseudonym of Lilbush Wingfield (1913–1989).

65. Enclosed with this letter were three pages in an envelope marked 'Research on Sean Connolly, born Ballinalee 1890, Ernie's Questions for history to Brady 28 March 1952'. EOM was writing a biography of Sean Connolly at the time and wanted to ask questions of James J. Brady, formerly of Longford and then of 622 West 114th Street, New York. The questions related to Sean Connolly's activities during the War of Independence.

66. Tony Woods was an old friend of EOM and a comrade from the War of Independence and the civil war.

67. EOM intended to continue his military interviews.

68. EOM working on what would become *Raids and Rallies*, to be recorded in March 1953.

69. Cathal and Etain O'Malley.

70. Refers to HHOM's financial difficulties as well as problems in getting re-established in the United States with two children.

71. HHOM's mother had provided for certain funds to be placed in trust so that HHOM could not use the assets without prudent oversight of a responsible trustee.

72. Given the strictures imposed upon HHOM by the trustee, she borrowed money from her mother and younger sister.

73. EOM was implying that if HHOM wished to release funds she could get permission from the trial court in New York, known as the New York Supreme Court.

74. HHOM and EOM were to purchase a residence in Dublin to serve as a home base for all three children, two of whom would be going to day school there.

75. Dan Nolan, editor of *The Kerryman*, had offered to print a book based on EOM's military research and interviews on the War of Independence, under the title *Raids and Rallies*. EOM had typed and signed his copy of this letter for his own records.

76. Dan Nolan had edited and altered EOM's manuscript; in addition EOM had forwarded him maps and plans of military engagements, which were not returned.

77. Francis MacManus (1909–1965), novelist and broadcaster, was responsible for airing EOM's programme on the War of Independence military history on Radio Éireann.

78. Erskine Childers (1905–1974), Fianna Fáil politician, later president of Ireland, and son of Erskine and Molly Childers.

79. All these articles were published in *The Sunday Press* during 1955 to 1956 and later published in book form by Anvil Books as *Raids and Rallies* (1982) with the help of Dan Nolan and Frances-Mary Blake.

80. This was published later as Ernie O'Malley, *Rising-Out: Sean Connolly of Longford (1890–1921)*, ed. Cormac O'Malley (Dublin, 2007).

81. Usually written as Sean MacEoin.

82. Formerly Rebecca Citkowitz.

83. EOM's German Shepherd guard dog named after the 'desert fox', German Field Marshal General Erwin Rommel.

84. Rommel had disappeared and EOM needed a newly trained guard dog.

85. Oona Raleigh, later Linehan.

86. Mary Raleigh, later Kotsonouris.

87. Dr Michael Tierney (1894–1975), president of University College Dublin, formerly professor of Greek, and a founder of Fine Gael.

88. *The Sunday Press*, to which EOM had offered publication of the stories.

89. The editor was Col Matthew Feehan.

90. Mervyn Wall (1908–1997), novelist and playwright, formerly involved with the Players Theatre.

91. The typed manuscript for the radio broadcast that had been reviewed by Mervyn Wall at Radio Éireann.

92. EOM probably sent shamrock to Etain for St Patrick's Day.

93. Bridget O'Shea, who had been with the O'Malley family in Burrishoole in the early 1940s, was now with HHOM in New York to help with Etain.

94. John Ford (1894–1973), film director; EOM was contacted by Ford and EOM helped him as technical assistant on *The Rising of the Moon*, three short films made in Ireland in 1956.

95. John Wayne, alias for Marion Robert Morrison (1907–1979), actor and lead in *The Quiet Man*.

96. EOM meant Cormac.

97. Séamus Ó h-Eochadha, headmaster of Ring College.

98. Festival held in March and April that was first developed in 1953 to beautify Dublin and attract tourists earlier than the summer months.

99. Alec Wallace, the owner of Old Hotel in Louisburgh, was a good friend of EOM. The curragh was typically a working boat used widely along the west coast and is constructed on canvas attached to a light wooden frame, after which the canvas is

tarred for waterproofing. It was flexible and light, and used commonly for fishing and transport.

100. Home of Christy and Annie Smith in Whitehall, Dublin; Christy was an old comrade whom EOM also interviewed. See UCDA P17b/96, 98, 110.

101. COM stayed with Patrick Malley and his family in Clontarf for Easter and for part of the summer in Greystones for July family holidays while EOM was recovering in St Bricin's, March–August.

102. Pembrey owned and ran Greene & Co.'s bookshop, Clare Street, Dublin.

103. Refers first to Dan Nolan of *The Kerryman*. These articles were published in *The Sunday Press* from September 1955 to June 1956 as *Raids and Rallies* and was the paper's longest-running series until then.

104. Bridget Sheehy, Michael's wife.

105. John McGrath of Thurles, Co. Tipperary, had written to EOM to correct a fact from EOM's radio lecture of 6 April.

106. Winnie Abbey, former nurse in Clonskeagh, 1948.

107. The basking sharks caught off Achill could be over twenty feet long, longer than the curraghs.

108. Private boarding secondary school, north of New York City.

109. Cathal had visited the Marquand family in the Bahamas, probably over the Easter holidays.

110. Referring to EOM's heart condition.

111. Etain O'Malley was living in HHOM's New York apartment under supervision of Bridget O'Shea.

112. A. & L. Goodbody were HHOM's Irish solicitors. Their letter dated 1 July 1953 relayed a suggestion of making funds available to EOM for COM.

113. Chester Davis, HHOM's newly appointed New York lawyer and trustee, who had married one of her cousins.

114. Proceeds from the sale of stock owned by EOM.

115. HHOM's mother had established a small trust with funds to cover COM's education and general expenses.

116. The Galway Races are held in late July and early August.

117. Hazel Kingsbury (*c.*1900–1982), an American photographer who married Paul Strand (1890–1976) in 1951. They lived in Paris afterwards.

118. Probably with Kevin Malley.

119. Paul Strand visited EOM in August 1935 on his return from Russia to New York but never returned to make a book on Ireland.

120. Paul Strand's book of photographs on France, *La France de Proil* (1952).

121. John O'Dowd (1880–1969), a member of the IRB in Louisburgh, Co. Mayo. EOM met O'Dowd when he was recording folklore in west Mayo in the 1940s.

122. An Irish salutation meaning 'Dear Friend'.

123. *Association International des Critiques d'Art* (AICA). EOM had represented Ireland previously in France, as had Thomas MacGreevy and James Johnson Sweeney for the USA.

124. Many Abbey Theatre actors worked in London and Hollywood in this period.

125. Daniel Stevenson, surveyor and property dealer, son of Paddy Stevenson, an old republican friend of EOM.

126. EOM was trying to determine precisely the ownership and configuration of the different lots of land belonging to Burrishoole.

127. The deed was actually maintained by HHOM's solicitors, A. & L. Goodbody, of which EOM may not have been aware.

128. The Duntrusk land was a small peninsula with non-arable land sticking into Lough Furnace.

129. Michael Murray was a neighbour who had bought the Carrowkeel land from the Land Commission and later sold it to HHOM. His son Martin and daughter-in-law were most kind and helpful to EOM during these years.

130. Address of Harry and Catherine Walston's Cambridge farm where EOM spent long periods of time resting and recuperating between 1953 and early 1957.

131. The Walston family, Cambridge.

132. Fr Joseph Stanley from Clifden, Co. Galway, was headmaster of the boys' preparatory school, Willow Park, a junior school to Blackrock College, Dublin.

133. HHOM was living in London and attending to theatre projects while Etain O'Malley was placed in the Sacred Heart Convent in Tumbridge Wells, Sussex, England.

134. Refers to the journey from Cambridge to Dublin via London in order to resume school at Willow Park.

135. EOM referring to his War of Independence and civil war military interviews.

136. They had all met in late August, 1953.

137. EOM still refused to allow HHOM enter Ireland without his specific written permission for fear that she would kidnap COM.

138. Josephine Manahan, née O'Sullivan, and her children, Marianne, Joan and Kevin.

139. Maighread Murphy, née Higgins, from Youghal, Co. Cork; EOM misspelt her name.

140. Continuation of the broadcasts he gave earlier in 1953 for Radio Éireann.

141. Seamus Murphy (1907–1975), sculptor.

142. Probably Murphy's monument to the West Cork Brigade, completed in Bandon, Co. Cork, in 1953.

143. Maighread Murphy's younger daughter, Orla Murphy.

144. Maighread Murphy's older daughter, Bebhinn Murphy.

145. EOM usually had letters forwarded care of Christy Smith, 91 Iveragh Road, Whitehall, Dublin.

146. In November 1938 Burrishoole was first leased and was subsequently purchased.

147. The 1937 American edition of the English publication *On Another Man's Wound* (1936).

148. Both children were diagnosed with primary tuberculosis in mid 1948.

149. In late March 1950.

150. Boarding schools: 1950–2, Chapelizard Convent, Dublin; 1952–6, Willow Park, Blackrock College. EOM would not disclose names of schools, even to good friends.

151. The American edition was called *Army Without Banners* but due to the loss of the libel litigation in 1937 there were no further editions, and by 1953 it was difficult to find copies.

152. Reference to EOM's military interviews.

153. Peggy Raleigh Lawler; Oona Raleigh Linehan; Mary Raleigh (later Kotsonouris), then at UCD.

154. Staying at St James Street, the London residence of the Walston family.

155. His military interviews started in at least 1948 and there is evidence that he did some earlier interviews.

156. A small private English publisher.

157. Possibly Fr Thomas Gilby, OP.

158. Young was teaching at the University of California, Berkeley, but her papers are at UCLA.

159. EOM had known Paul Strand's first wife Rebecca Salsbury in Taos, New Mexico, in 1932. He would also have known Bill James, who later married Rebecca, at the same time.

160. Rebecca Strand, née Salsbury (1891–1968), Paul's first wife. Her father was Nate Salsbury, the founder of the Buffalo Bill Touring Rodeo.

161. The manuscript of his civil war book.

162. Paul Strand's new book on Italy, *Un Paese: Portrait of an Italian Village* (1953), photographs of the village of Luzzara taken in 1952.

163. EOM felt that Rich & Cowan Ltd had not properly publicized his book. They failed further to tell him that they had agreed on a German edition. He also remembered the excruciating editing process.

164. An intimate name for John Ford who signed his letters to Cormac as 'Uncle Jack'.

165. Meta Sterne, John Ford's indispensable secretary and script supervisor (Joseph McBride, *Searching for John Ford*, New York, 1971, p. 531), who wrote some of the communications to EOM.

166. Ford had bad eyesight.

167. Ford gave EOM some financial support.

168. Maureen O'Hara, the leading actress in *The Quiet Man*, did visit.

169. Martin Feeney was a cousin of John Ford and was applying for an IRA pension. Ford asked EOM to vouch for Feeney, which he could not.

170. When EOM was officer commanding, 2nd Southern Division (East/Mid Limerick, Tipperary and Kilkenny).

171. Fr Thomas Gilby, OP.

172. Small private London publisher, subsequently acquired by Random House.

173. COM was due to arrive in Euston Station after travelling from Dublin by boat and train for the holidays.

174. Paul and Hazel Strand visited EOM in January 1954. Strand inscribed his then most recent book 'To Ernie O'Malley with friendship and affection and in memory of a day together after long years', signed Paul Strand, Cambridge, January 1954.

175. National Gallery postcard of Duccio's *The Annunciation*. EOM and COM also sent cards in December 1955 and 1956, NGI Yeats Archives Par 45 (2)(51) and (3)(40).

176. Address for EOM's brother Patrick Malley.

177. Kelleher had brought over two sleeping bags from America in 1947. EOM and COM used to sleep out in them, either under the car or inside the car if there was rain, when travelling, thus avoiding the expense of a hotel.

178. Document not found in EOM papers.

179. Tony Woods and Kevin Malley paid the bill.

180. Sean Henricks, 1 Cork Brigade, see UCDA P17b/111, 117, 118.

181. Kilmurvey Guest House, Inishmore, Aran Islands, for the month of August, 1954.

182. William Walston, son of Catherine and Harry Walston.

183. Liam Manahan of Dalkey, Co. Dublin, who was the only friend allowed to take COM from school to visit the Manahan family occasionally on Saturdays.

184. National Library of Ireland.

185. Christy Smith, Dublin.

186. Burrishoole Abbey was originally a Dominican friary, built around 1470.

187. Irish Folklore Commission, based at UCD.

188. The use of a mimeograph was an inexpensive method of duplicating or printing documents.
189. Strand's book of photographs of South Uist was called *Tir a'Mhurain, The Outer Hebrides of Scotland* (1954), with text by Basil Davidson.
190. As of 1 August 1954, EOM rented a flat, 52 Mespil House, Sussex Road, Dublin.
191. Printed with kind persmission of the Estate of James Johnson Sweeney.
192. Baptism of Laura Sweeney's granddaughter, her daughter Anne Sweeney's first child.
193. Henry Moore (1898–1986), English artist and sculptor.
194. Irina Radetsky Moore (1907–1989), painter.
195. William Walston, son of Catherine and Harry Walston.
196. Jean McGrail (1919–2001), an American sculptor and travel writer, whom EOM met in Kilmurvey, on Inishmore, the largest of the Aran Islands, during August 1954. They corresponded regularly for his last two years but never met again.
197. Dun Aengus, a prehistoric stone fort on the cliffs above Kilmurvey.
198. The middle of the three Aran Islands.
199. David, Oliver and Bill Walston.
200. James Walston, the youngest member of the Walston family.
201. 52 Mespil Flats, Sussex Road, Dublin.
202. Newport, Co. Mayo.
203. Mussels.
204. Monthly fashion magazine published in several countries.
205. Auberge Franc-Comtoise located in the town of Villers le Lac, Franche-Comte, in the Jura region of France. The 'cul-de-veau' is veal.
206. Chateau-Chalon is a wine from the Burgundy area, not too far from the restaurant.
207. *Fondue comptoise* is a heated cheese course made with the local comte cheese from the Jura region.
208. 'As a drink'.
209. EOM was not correct as Moulin-à-Vent is not a Beaune but a Burgundy.
210. The Beaune wines are also Burgundy but are located further north.
211. A filet of sirloin from Saint-Amour, a town in the Jura area.
212. Refers to EOM's long-held knowledge of Basque culture and geography.
213. Cecil Malley kept his boat in Southampton.
214. Françoise Henry, *Art Irlandais* (1954), published for the Committee on Foreign Relations.
215. Fr Paul Walsh (1885–1941), priest and historian.
216. Herbert Edward Read (1893–1968), poet and critic.
217. End of letter is missing.
218. Written on a postcard from the National Gallery, London, with an image of Renoir's *Les Parapluies*, which EOM included with his letter of 25 January 1955.
219. The Hugh Lane Collection was retained by the Tate Gallery but it had not been shown on a regular basis. Since 1959 the Collection has been shared regularly between London and Dublin.
220. Sir William Harry Gregory (1817–1892), colonial administrator and landlord.
221. Diego Rodríquez de Silva y Velásquez (1599–1660), *Kitchen Scene in The House of Martha*.
222. Catherine and Harry Walston, with friends.
223. Exhibition of 'Oil Paintings', Victor Waddington Galleries, South Anne Street, Dublin, February 1955.

224. Jonathan Swift (1667–1745), satirist and cleric.

225. Bishop George Berkeley (1685–1753), cleric and philosopher.

226. *Lady Gregory's Journal, 1916–1930*, ed. Lennox Robinson (1947).

227. The children of Major William Robert Gregory (1881–1918).

228. Dublin bar.

229. Dublin restaurant, mentioned in Joyce's *Ulysses*.

230. *The Living Desert*, dir. James Algar (1953).

231. EOM paints a grim reference by comparison of his failing health and unfinished projects to the surrender by the Native American tribes of their traditional way of life.

232. In course of conducting his military interveiws.

233. Peyote is a hallucinogenic substance made from a form of cactus.

234. Aldous Huxley (1894–1963); probably referring to *Brave New World* (1932).

235. Alec Wallace.

236. Josie Gill moved to the desmesne of Lord Sligo near Westport.

237. Hôtel du Bac, rue du Bac, Left Bank.

238. Possibly John Kelleher and Richard Ellman amongst others.

239. William Howard Taft III (1915–91), US Ambassador to Ireland (1953–7).

240. Jean Cocteau (1889–1963), writer, painter and director of films including *Les Enfants Terribles* (1949) and *L'Éternel Retour* (1943).

241. *Umberto D.*, dir. Vitorrio de Seca (1952).

242. *The Southerner*, dir. Jean Renoir (1945).

243. McGrail had sent a photograph of herself to EOM.

244. Virginia Stewart, *Contemporary Mexican Artists* (California, 1951).

245. Louis Henri Jean Charlot (1898–1979) had lived in Mexico and eventually went to the United States in 1947.

246. James Hamilton Delargy (1899–1980), folklorist.

247. Probably David Rolt (1916–1985) an English artist who lived at 115 Ebury Street, and probably met him through the Walstons as he had often visited Newton Hall. Rolt did a pencil portrait of EOM at about this time.

248. Metropolitan Museum of Art.

249. New York Public Library.

250. Kevin Malley.

251. The Japanese film, *Seven Samurai*, was directed by Akira Kurosawa and released in 1954.

252. Victoria and Albert Museum.

253. Royal Academy of Art Annual Exhibition.

254. Probably David Rolt.

255. Veganin provided relief for headaches, rheumatic pain and other symptoms.

256. Georges Roualt (1871–1958), French artist.

257. Juan Gris (1887–1972), French artist.

258. Charles Dufresne (1876–1928), French artist.

259. Maurice de Vlaminck (1876–1958), French artist.

260. EOM had loaned his Vlaminck paintings to his brother, Kevin Malley.

261. We know from EOM's London invoices that for art books he often went to the premises of A. Zwemmer, 76–80 Charing Cross Road, and Bernard Quaritch Ltd, 11 Grafton Street, New Bond Street.

262. Maria Edgeworth (1768–1849) wrote on 8 March 1834 to Pakenham Edgeworth, giving a description of Connemara in twenty-seven pages. The letter is held in the National Library of Ireland and has been published variously.

263. Oil painting of George Bernard Shaw by Augustus John, in the Fitzwillam Museum, Cambridge.

264. George Bernard Shaw (1856–1950) left one-third of his estate each to the National Gallery of Ireland, the British Museum and the Royal Academy of Dramatic Art.

265. Rt. Hon. Richard R. Stokes (1897–1957), Labour MP for Ipswich, former minister of works (1950–51) and minister of materials (1951).

266. Photograph of a stone carving from the Cathedral at Autun, France, entitled *Réveil des Mage*s.

267. Possibly the statue in the *Thermes de Cluny* in Paris, with the words 'Paris à mon coeur' inscribed on the statue.

268. Harry Walston.

269. Le Musée de L'Orangerie and La Galerie Nationale du Jeu de Paume, Paris.

270. Patrick Malley, EOM's younger brother.

271. R. Strahan & Co. Ltd, 135 St Stephen's Green, Dublin, was used by HHOM for her removals.

272. Photographs of Jean MacGrail's own sculptural works.

273. Oliver St John Gogarty (1878–1957), physician, wit and writer.

274. Renvyle House Hotel, Renvyle, Co. Galway.

275. William Hamilton Maxwell, *Wild Sports of the West of Ireland* (1823).

276. Bernardo Marchese Patrizi Naro Montoro (1912–1971).

277. Rt. Hon. Richard R. Stokes, MP.

278. Following the defeat of King James II during the Williamite Wars.

279. The formation of the Irish Land Commission, which succeeded the Congested Districts Board.

280. The Marchese's house.

281. Nancy Newhall, *Time in New England* (1950).

282. Desert in the southwestern United States that extends into California, Utah, Nevada and Arizona.

283. These included Michele Guyard and Barbara Myers.

284. Eithne Golden had married Ernie Sax in 1954 and worked as a United Nations translator in New York.

285. Late March 1950.

286. The presiding judge was the president of the High Court, Justice George Gavan-Duffy (1882–1951). He died while the case was pending though it is understood that he had issued a reserved judgment dismissing HHOM's case against EOM and granting him costs. The decision was never issued officially, but the unofficial draft does exist.

287. Actually 1950.

288. This issue was raised by EOM with Thomas Gilchrist in earlier letters as it related to the shares of Hooker Electrochemical Company given to EOM by Mrs Blanche Hooker.

289. Reference to poor financial position of EOM; his pension was not adjusted adequately for inflation, in addition to his other financial problems.

290. Kevin Malley.

291. These manuscripts became the basis for the posthumous publications: *Raids and Rallies*, ed. Frances-Mary Blake (Dublin, 1982) and *Rising-Out: Sean Connolly of Longford, 1890–1921*, ed. Cormac K.H. O'Malley (Dublin, 2007).

292. HHOM visited Dublin with Cathal and Etain in June 1955.

293. Cathal entered Harvard College in September 1955 in the class of 1959.

294. EOM refers here to rumours HHOM had spread regarding EOM's relationships with

other women. He denied these and confronted HHOM about them in London in 1948.

295. There were several art-related programmes started under Franklin D. Roosevelt's New Deal including the Public Works of Art Project (1933–4) and Federal Art Project (1935–43).

296. In 1948.

297. Ears, nose and throat.

298. EOM alleged that HHOM had given An Fear Mór £150 to facilitate her taking of the children.

299. Sylvia Laithwaite, EOM's first cousin and a Dominican nun in America, previously referred to.

300. So named for Prince William of Orange who secured Protestant accession to the British crown after the defeat of King James II.

301. Georgette Kerrigan and Dr Sarsfield Kerrigan, Lifford, Co. Donegal.

302. Portable gas stove often used for camping trips or cooking in the bedroom in Burrishoole.

303. The divorce had been issued in Colorado in 1952 but was never published in the Irish newspapers.

304. Etain attended Madeira School, a private boarding school for girls in Fairfax County, Virginia; there she participated with keen interest in her school plays.

305. Richard Roelofs Jr (1898–1971), HHOM's future husband; they were married in 1956.

306. The turf boats came to Aran from mainland ports such as Carraroe in Connemara, Co. Galway.

307. Islanders were offered tubbery rights to cut turf on the mainland since there was none on Aran.

308. Probably COM's friend Anne Baudin to whom Hazel Strand had introduced him in Orgeval.

309. COM was staying with the family of Luke Duffy in Clooncagh, Strokestown, Co. Roscommon. Duffy had been a Volunteer and met EOM in 1918. Though Duffy was pro-Treaty EOM renewed their friendship in the 1950s as he was doing his military interviews. See UCDA P17b/107, 137.

310. EOM and COM had been in the Aran Islands, information which EOM did not share previously with HHOM. His equipment and boat, *St Brendan*, were left in the care of Josie Gill.

311. Willow Park, Blackrock College, Dublin; EOM was now willing to share the name of COM's school with HHOM as he had her undertaking that she would not 'kidnap' him.

312. HHOM initiated divorce proceedings in Colorado in 1951, after she had been resident there for the required one year. She was awarded a divorce and custody of Cathal and Etain in 1952.

313. Key to Burrishoole.

314. HHOM was staying here when she went to Dublin with Richard Roelofs Jr; probably hand-delivered.

315. Richard Roelofs Jr.

316. Forwarding address for HHOM as she was due to go to France; the letter was forwarded to New York.

317. Dinner at the Shelbourne Hotel on 4 September.

318. 52 Mespil Flats, Dublin.

319. *The Keys of the Kingdom*, dir. John Stahl (1944).

320. Anthony Chambers, Newport, Co. Mayo.

321. Ampleforth College, York, a Benedictine secondary school where both Cathal and COM were registered in 1945; in fact COM had been first accepted in 1945 for summer term 1956 and did attend as planned.

322. Long Island, New York.

323. Seán Keating (1889–1977), artist.

324. The *Dun Aengus* went from Galway to Kilronan, Inisheer, Inishmaan, Kilronan and back to Galway.

325. Dr James O'Brien was the local general practicioner for the three Aran islands.

326. Printed with kind permission of the Estate of James Johnson Sweeney.

327. Renvyle House, Renvyle, Co. Galway.

328. EOM had taken Patsy, wife of Roger McHugh, to the ballet, as he often did.

329. EOM at this time was going through each of the national and regional daily newspapers and making detailed notes on all the recorded events of the Tan and civil wars.

330. Col Matthew Feehan; this letter was not published and is only EOM's file copy.

331. Florence (Florrie) O'Donoghue (1894–1967) originally from Kerry, was intelligence officer of Cork No. 1 Brigade, and neutral during civil war, wrote *No Other Law* (1954) about Liam Lynch, see UCDA P17b/95, 96.

332. Mgr John Hagan, then Rector of the Irish College, Rome.

333. A second draft EOM letter expanded: 'I met Monsignor O'Hagan at his express wish, but there was no hint in his note to me that he had proposals to discuss. I informed him that I could not meet him officially without the consent of my Chief of Staff and that he could not discuss terms of agreement without the consent of the Army Council.'

334. Richard Mulcahy (1886–1971), revolutionary, soldier and politician, held responsible by many republicans for reprisal violence against them during the civil war.

335. Liam Lynch (1893–1923), republican and chief of staff of anti-Treaty forces to whom EOM reported.

336. Name given to the Free State government.

337. Liam Mellows (1892–1922), republican who surrendered in the Four Courts and was executed on 8 December 1922.

338. Rory O'Connor (c.1890–1922), republican who surrendered in the Four Courts and was executed on 8 December 1922.

339. The name given to the Free State Criminal Intelligence Division, members of which were accused of murdering republicans summarily.

340. EOM responded to other letters to the editor published in *The Sunday Press* on 13 and 27 November 1955, and 22 April and 8 May 1956.

341. Feast Day of the Immaculate Conception, a Holy Day of Obligation in the Roman Catholic Church.

342. EOM was sent to Offaly by Michael Collins to organize the Irish Volunteers.

343. His friends did not tell EOM that the St Bricin's Hospital bill had been paid off by Kevin Malley and Tony Woods. When he found out he felt obliged to repay them.

344. In 1955 they stayed on Inishmaan, the middle island.

345. Georgette Kerrigan, Lifford, Co. Donegal.

346. Michael Sheehy's children, including Peter Sheehy who was about the same age as COM.

347. Reprinted from a Cuala Press *Broadside* as a Christmas card.

348. The village near Taos where EOM had lived with the Golden family in the period from 1930 to 1932.

349. New counsel and trustee for HHOM in succession to Thomas Gilchrist; Davis was married to a cousin of HHOM.

350. Davis forwarded funds to EOM on behalf of HHOM for COM's maintenance.

351. Elvery Sports in the 1920s was at 2 Lower Abbey Street, Dublin (where Samuel Beckett's father bought his tennis rackets); the shop moved later to 20 Suffolk Street, Dublin.

352. Kingstons, O'Connell Street, Dublin, was a clothing merchant where EOM bought COM's clothes.

353. Samuel Beckett's *Waiting for Godot* was produced in Dublin by the Pike Theatre, beginning Friday, 28 October 1955.

354. The exhibition marked Victor Waddington's thirty years in Dublin as an art dealer, beginning with his first premises in South Anne Street. Waddington planned now to leave for England for health reasons. See *The Irish Times* (9 February 1956).

355. Oisín Kelly (1915–1981), sculptor.

356. Hilary Heron (1923–1976) sculptor.

357. The Olympia Theatre hosted a festival of French ballet beginning Monday, 13 February 1956. Its star was Ludmilla Tcherina, who was engaged for two weeks.

358. D.H. Lawrence, *The Lost Girl* (1920).

359. *The Rising of the Moon*, dir. John Ford (released to theatres in 1957), consisted of three short films and was produced in Ireland in 1956.

360. Michael Scott (1905–1989), architect.

361. University College Dublin.

362. Patrick Scott (b. 1921), artist.

363. Harry Clarke (1889–1931), illustrator and stained-glass artist.

364. Patrick Little (1884–1963), TD for Waterford.

365. An exhibition of Evie Hone's abstract paintings was held in the Dawson Gallery, Dublin, in April and May 1957.

366. Kevin Malley.

367. A well-known bar on the Right Bank, Paris.

368. Probably refers to Lennox Robinson's edition of *Lady Gregory's Journals 1916–1930* (1946).

369. Letter was forwarded to the family home, 115 East 67th Street, New York.

370. University College Dublin.

371. EOM referring possibly to the use of Irish actors as opposed to the casting of Ford's earlier Irish films, *The Informer* and *The Quiet Man*.

372. The Institute of the Sculptors of Ireland exhibition, which included a head of Jimmy O'Dea by Marshall Hutson.

373. Angela Christina Antrim (1911–1984), sculptor and illustrator.

374. Irene Broe (1923–1992), sculptor.

375. James (John) Haugh (b. 1922), sculptor and carver.

376. William Trevor Cox (b. 1928), sculptor, but better known as William Trevor, author.

377. Oisín Kelly (1915–1981), sculptor

378. Desmond Broe (1921–1968), sculptor.

379. Anthony Raftery (1784–1835), poet.

380. Refers to the medical consultants who kept practices on Fitzwilliam and Merrion Squares.

381. A note reads, 'Please put a bit of sellotape on your envelopes as two were torn, one opened in France, and I would like to read your letters to myself'.

382. EOM refers to the first line of W.B. Yeats' poem 'All Things Can Tempt Me': 'All things can tempt me from this craft of verse'.

383. The Institute of Sculptors of Ireland was formed in 1952 under the leadership of Peter Grant. It was disbanded in 1959.

384. The Fogg Art Museum, Harvard University, which EOM had visited previously.

385. Sylvanus Griswold Morley (1883–1948), archaeologist and Mayan specialist.

386. Sir John Eric Sidney Thompson (1898–1975), archaeologist who had worked under Morley.

387. King John of England's castle in Limerick was built between 1200 and 1210.

388. 'Love', a colloquial term of endearment.

389. Letter written on Shelbourne Hotel stationery.

390. The dates are in April; the friends mentioned later are Paul Strand and his wife.

391. Dr Dean Elefetry, Greek husband of Doreen Madden, who had a part in one of the shorts in *The Rising of the Moon*. They lived on Northumberland Road, Dublin.

392. To England to attend school at the Benedictine-run Ampleforth College, York.

393. Barbara Myers and Michelle Guyard, friends of Paul Strand who welcomed EOM in Paris.

394. Kevin Malley.

395. Archibald MacLeish (1892–1982), poet and writer.

396. 15 Whitebeam Avenue, Clonskeagh, the rented house in Dublin of the O'Malleys from 1944 to 1948.

397. Hasty Pudding Theatricals put on the the Hasty Pudding Club of which Cathal was a member. The annual show is put on in early spring and then goes on tour.

398. Brendan Behan, *The Quare Fellow* (1956).

Afterword: David Lloyd, *On Republican Reading*

1. Though later critics and biographers, such as Hilary Pyle and Bruce Arnold, tend to sidestep Jack B. Yeats' political affiliations, Thomas MacGreevy, his friend, and author of the first lengthy study of his work, discusses a number of political paintings all sympathetic to republican ideals, that includes this painting, and does so in an explicitly political context. See Thomas MacGreevy, *Jack B. Yeats: An Appreciation and an Interpretation* (Dublin, 1945), pp. 25–6, 37–8.

2. Ernie O'Malley, *On Another Man's Wound*, (Dublin, 2002) p. 353.

3. See for example O'Malley's letter to Paul Strand of 19 August 1932 about New York: 'Street corner meetings every night, men talking in cliches. It's stupid, a shirted crowd mostly, waiting eagerly for a few honest, direct words; instead they get isms. It's brutal and selfish. Why the hell aren't some men trained to talk now, speak out of their hearts?' See Letter No. 56. Elsewhere he laments the lack of 'sturdy independence' among the transients that he had been living with.

4. Richard English's biography is typical here. Despite acknowledging that 'O'Malley was not a fascist' (a wonderful instance of raising suspicion by denial), he proceeds to tie republicanism, and by implication O'Malley, to fascism: 'the early 1920s republican world which he had inhabited indisputably echoed many of the themes of continental fascism: the emphasis on sacrifice, the cult of youth, the celebration of militarism, the

anti-democratic slant, the desire for the rebirth of ancient culture'. Richard English, *Ernie O'Malley: IRA Intellectual* (Oxford, 1998), pp. 169–70. Evidently the same traits could be found among British imperialists of the same period, but at this point English conveniently abandons his emphasis on O'Malley's anglicized culture that he elsewhere pursues. For postcolonial work on spirituality and decolonization, see Reynaldo C. Ileto, *Pasyon and Revolution: Popular Movements in the Philippines, 1840–1910* (Manila, 1979), and Partha Chatterjee, 'The Nation and Its Women' in *The Nation and Its Fragments: Colonial and Postcolonial Histories* (Princeton, 1993), pp. 116–34. One might also invoke, among many others, Shahid Amin's brilliant work, *Event, Metaphor, Memory: Chairi Chaura, 1922–1992* (Berkeley, 1995), on the popular memory of one peculiarly violent moment in Indian nationalism and its connection to religious understandings of Gandhi.

5. Letter from EOM to Sheila Humphreys, 25 December 1923, in *'No Surrender Here!' The Civil War Papers of Ernie O'Malley, 1922–1924*, eds Cormac K.H. O'Malley and Anne Dolan (Dublin, 2007), p. 473. In a letter in the present collection, also to Sheila Humphreys, O'Malley remarks no less firmly, though less elaborately, that 'The spiritualistic interpretation of nationality is the only thing that matters and that no one save the '16 group ever seriously considered.' See Letter No. 26.

6. Ernie O'Malley, *The Singing Flame* (Dublin, 1992 edn), p. 286.

7. *Ibid.* p. 286.

8. *Ibid.*

9. *Ibid.* pp. 286–7.

10. O'Malley and Dolan, *'No Surrender Here!'*, p. 452.

11. Declan Kiberd, *Irish Classics* (London, 2001) p. 632.

12. In a late letter in the present volume, he laments to his American friend Jean McGrail the lack of intellectual support and research funding available to Irish students wishing to research Irish literature. Letter from EOM to Jean McGrail (20 February 1955). See Letter No. 251.

13. Richard English, *Ernie O'Malley: IRA Intellectual* (Oxford, 1998) pp. 114–21.

14. Letter from EOM to Jean McGrail (16 March 1955), see Letter No. 252. Despite having numerous English friends, O'Malley seems to maintain a sardonically amused relation to English culture as he witnessed it, joking about the ignorance of Tories on their country's relation to Ireland, or commenting ironically on the English feeding pigeons in Trafalgar Square while ignoring the treasures of their National Gallery.

15. O'Malley, *The Singing Flame*, p. 289. It is perhaps worth recalling how O'Malley's interest in *Moby Dick* anticipates scholarly interest in the text, given that Carl Van Doren's work on Melville appeared only in 1917, his *The American Novel* not till 1921, while D.H. Lawrence's *Studies in Classic American Literature* appeared in the early 1920s. F.O. Matthiessen's *American Renaissance* was not published till 1941. O'Malley was not alone in finding resources in *Moby Dick* for an alternative political culture, or a radical interpretation of modernity. C.L.R. James's *Mariners, Renegades, and Castaways: The Story of Herman Melville and the World we Live in* (1953) and Charles Olson's *Call Me Ishmael* (1947) are both very different counter-cultural or 'antithetical' appropriations of Melville.

16. O'Malley, *The Singing Flame*, p. 105.

17. Kiberd, *Irish Classics*, p. 631.

18. O'Malley, *On Another Man's Wound*, p. 353.

19. On Connolly's sense of Irish history and the specific characteristics of its culture, see

David Lloyd, 'Rethinking National Marxism' in *The Irish Times: Temporalities of Modernity* (Dublin, 2008), pp. 101–26.

20. Introductory article by EOM for a series of articles on Ireland, *Architectural Digest* (London, July 1947), see Appendix 1, No. 10. O'Malley's insistence on Ireland's lack of centralization seems to be a fundamental republican observation, one he shares, for example, with Countess Markievicz. See David Lloyd, 'Nationalism against the State', in *Ireland after History* (Cork, 1999), pp. 19–36.

21. Letter from EOM in Mexico to Sheila Humphreys (13 March 1931), see Letter No. 49.

22. Letter from EOM in New York to Eithne Golden (28 March 1935), see Letter No. 70.

23. Ernie O'Malley, 'The Background of the Arts in Mexico', *The Bell* XIV:5 (August 1947), See Appendix 1, No. 11.

24. *Ibid.*

25. *Ibid.*

26. *Ibid.*

27. Ernie O'Malley, review of Françoise Henry, *Irish Art in the Early Christian Period*, in *The Bell*, I:1 (October 1940), see Appendix 1, No. 1.

28. *Ibid.*

29. *Ibid.*

30. *Ibid.*

31. *Ibid.*

32. See Walter Benjamin, 'Theses on the Philosophy of History' in *Illuminations: Essays and Reflections*, ed. Hannah Arendt, trans. Harry Zohn (New York, 1969), pp. 262 and passim.

33. Ernie O'Malley, 'Traditions of Mexican Art', BBC *The Listener* (January 1947), pp. 145–6, see Appendix 1, No. 8.

34. *Ibid.*

35. *Ibid.* For comparison of Rivera and Orozco see letter from EOM to Merriam Golden (19 January 1931), see Letter No. 46.

36. Ernie O'Malley, 'Introduction', *Jack B. Yeats National Loan Exhibition Catalogue* (Dublin, 1945), see Appendix 1, No. 2.

37. *Ibid.*

38. Ernie O'Malley, 'Louis le Brocquy', *Horizon*, XIV:79 (London, July 1946), see Appendix 1, No. 4.

39. His discussion of le Brocquy's *Condemned Man*, a beautiful cubist-inspired canvas, is both precise and evocative, and understands it as of 'particular interest in a country where gaol was a natural place in which to meet friends or to say goodbye'.

40. *Ibid.*

41. Samuel Beckett, 'The Capital of the Ruins', radio script, 10 June 1946, in *As the Story Was Told: Uncollected and Late Prose* (London, 1990), pp. 27–8.

42. See Hannah Arendt, *The Origins of Totalitarianism* (1948; New York 1973 edn with added prefaces), pp. 267–302; Giorgio Agamben, 'Beyond Human Rights' in *Means Without End: Notes on Politics*, trans. Vincenzo Binetti and Cesare Casarino (Minneapolis, 2000), pp. 15–25.

43. Philip Pettit, *Republicanism: A Theory of Freedom and Government* (Oxford, 1999), Part 1: 'Republican Freedom', pp. 17–126.

44. It is possible to read the numerous references throughout O'Malley's letters, to the purchase of tweed for suits, the furnishings at Burrishoole Lodge, Co. Mayo, the

purchase of turf and other local produce, as a practical inhabitation of nationalist ideals of self-sufficiency and reliance on local resources, ideals that perhaps have regained their force for us in recent decades.

Appendix I: Critical Works

1. This essay was published as the introduction to the catalogue for the National Loan Exhibition that opened on 11 June 1945. During the opening speeches Taoiseach Eamon de Valera sat beside the artist, listening to the speakers, including EOM and Thomas MacGreevy. There were no footnotes in the original catalogue text.
2. Jack B. Yeats, *Bachelor's Walk: In Memory* (1915). The painting represents a flower-girl and a boy at the site of the killing of four people on 26 July 1914 by the King's Own Scottish Borderers following the landing of arms for the Irish Volunteers at Howth, Co. Dublin. Yeats visited Bachelor's Walk the day after.
3. EOM was working with *The Bell* and became book review editor there in 1947–8. These notes were not part of the original text.
4. John Constable (1776–1837), English artist; Honoré Daumier (1808–1879), French artist; Jean-François Millet (1814–1875), French artist.
5. See Hilary Pyle, *Jack B. Yeats, A Catalogue Raisonnée of the Oil Paintings* (London 1992), painting No. 503.
6. The *Fauves* included the French artists Henri Matisse (1869–1954) and André Derain (1880–1954) and believed in the use of intense colour. Their name, which means 'wild beasts', derived from a critic's reaction to the first showing of works in the Salon d'Automne of 1905.
7. Raoul Dufy (1877–1953), Fauvist painter.
8. Pyle, *Jack B. Yeats, A Catalogue Raisonnée*, painting No. 498.
9. *Ibid.*, painting No. 499.
10. *Tinker's Encampment: The Blood of Abel. Ibid.*, painting No. 516.
11. *Ibid.*, painting No. 54.
12. Dublin's Municipal Gallery of Modern Art was founded by the art collector Hugh Lane (1875–1915) in 1908 as the first public gallery of modern art in the world. After Lane's death on the *Lusitania* there was substantial controversy over the terms of his will, a codicil of which indicated his desire to leave a collection of thirty-nine continental paintings to Dublin, rather than London's National Gallery. Agreement was only reached on the matter in 1959. The Municipal is now known as The Hugh Lane Gallery.
13. These notes were not part of the original text. Illustrations reproduced in the article were: *Famine Cottages, Connemara* (1944), 50 cm x 75 cm, oil on greaseboard; *Travellers Making the Sign of Twigs* (1946), 40.5 cm x 53 cm, oils on board (detail); *Irish Travellers: In Fear of Cain* (1947), 31 cm x 51 cm, pen and watercolour; *Southern Window* (1939), 59 cm x 46 cm, wax-resin medium on sail cloth mounted on hardboard. All were from the collection of the Hugh Lane Municipal Gallery of Modern Art, Dublin.
14. Albert Gleizes (1881–1953), French artist.
15. André Lhote (1885–1962), French artist.
16. Shelta is a form of language spoken by Travellers.

17. Henry Moore (1898–1986), English artist and sculptor.
18. This note is not part of the original text. Legend has it that the children of Lir, Fionnuala, Aodh and twins Fiachra and Conn, were turned into swans by Lir's second wife, Aoife, and spent their third term of three hundred years on the lake of Inishglora, where they eventually returned to human form, died and were buried.
19. While researching in COM's files, Mary Cosgrove found EOM's notes and reconstructed his lecture, but these notes have been added.
20. The RMS *Lusitania* was an ocean liner sunk by a German torpedo off the coast of Co. Cork on 7 May 1915.
21. St Stanislaus College, Tullabeg, Co. Offaly.
22. The Chelsea Polytechnic, London, later called the Chelsea College of Science and Technology.
23. Marie Françoise Céline Howet (1897–1984), Belgian painter.
24. Charlemont House, Parnell Square, Dublin, purchased in 1927 by Dublin Corporation as site for the Municipal Gallery of Art.
25. On EOM's copy of the 1944 catalogue for the Oireachtas of Clár an Teasbántais Ealadan, he noted 'pictures in search of an Irish quality of mind, their failure to find it'. Some of the 157 paintings were also by Jack B. Yeats, Louis le Brocquy, and Basil Rakoczi.
26. The Dublin Painters' Gallery, St Stephen's Green, Dublin.
27. Graham Sutherland (1903–1980), English painter.
28. David Jones (1895–1974), English painter.
29. Édouard Pignon (1905–1993), French painter, designer, illustrator; Irish Exhibition of Living Art catalogue, 1945, No. 17.
30. Charles Walch (1898–1948), French artist; Irish Exhibition of Living Art catalogue, 1945, No. 58.
31. The Loan Exhibition of Modern Contemporary Paintings at the National College of Art, Kildare Street, held in August 1944.
32. These notes were not part of the original text. Referring to a group of artists not from France who worked in Paris between the two world wars.
33. These notes were not part of the original text. EOM wrote this article in English and it was translated into French for publication. It was the first in a series of articles about Ireland included in that issue that had been in part co-ordinated by EOM for Hamish Hamilton of London, the publisher of the French liberal magazine, *La France Libre*. In it EOM explains to a French audience the rationale for Irish neutrality during the Second World War and the historical and cultural background that resulted in such a decision by the Irish government at the time.
34. EOM had in fact won a Dublin City Corporation Scholarship in 1915 to University College Dublin, and probably could not otherwise have attended university.
35. In 1938 the de Valera government signed an Anglo-Irish Treaty covering defence, finance and trade pursuant to which the Irish Free State received back full authority over their own ports that had been restricted under the Anglo-Irish Treaty of 1921; in return the Irish paid £10 million.
36. William T. Cosgrove (1880–1965) was leader of the Cumann na nGaedheal party and elected prime minister of the Irish Free State from 1922 to 1932.
37. Eamon de Valera (1882–1975) was initially president of Sinn Féin, and then founder of the Fianna Fáil party in 1926, and in 1927 led his party into the Dáil as the principal opposition party, eventually becoming prime minister in 1932.

38. The Emergency in Ireland refers to the period of the Second World War when the Dáil approved the grant to the government of certain Emergency Powers for defence.

39. These notes are not part of the original text. The three illustrations published in *The Listener* were: a Totemec seated pelican in stone from Coatepec, Vera Cruz; a Mexican limestone Huaxtec statue of a goodess from Tampico, Tamaulipas; and the church of Nuestra Se or de Ocotlán, Tlaccala, *c*.1745.

40. The *Third Programme* was a radio broadcast begun in late 1946 with a cultural and intellectual focus.

41. In 1931; letter from EOM to Merriam Golden (6 January 1931), see Letter No. 46.

42. People with mixed European and indigenous blood.

43. Long rectangular shawl worn by women.

44. A type of shawl worn by men.

45. Jose Clemente Orozco (1883–1949), Mexican artist.

46. David Alfaro Siquerios (1896–1975), Mexican artist.

47. Diego Rivera (1886–1957), Mexican artist.

48. José Vasconcelos Calderon (1882–1959), Manuel Gamio (1883–1960).

49. Carlos Mérida (1891–1984), Mexican artist.

50. There were no footnotes in the original text.

51. 8 South Anne Street, Dublin, owned by Victor Waddington.

52. First exhibit in renovated gallery with thirty-two English artists. Some of the English artists had exhibited individually in the Irish Exhibition of Living Art in the following years: Edward Burra (1944), Jacob Epstein (1945), Ivon Hitchens (1945), Frances Hodgkins (1945), Henry Moore (1944–5), Ben Nicholson (1944), John Piper (1944–5), Matthew Smith (1944–5), Graham Sutherland (1944–5).

53. Robinson & Keefe, architects, 8 Merrion Square.

54. The Irish Exhibition of Living Art, organized by the Living Art Committee.

55. Robert Colquhoun (1914–1962), Robert MacBryde (1913–1966), Mary Kessell (1914–1978), and Eileen Agar (1899–1991).

56. Frances Mary Hodgkins (1869–1947), Matthew Arnold Bracy Smith (1879–1959), John Rutherford Armstrong (1893–1973), Ivon Hitchens (1893–1979), Stanley Spencer (1891–1959), Ben Nicholson (1894–1982), and Laurence Stephen Lowry (1887–1976).

57. Henry Spencer Moore (1898–1986), sculptor; John Samuel Tunnard (1900–1971), painter; John Egerton Christmas Piper (1903–1992), painter; Graham Vivian Sutherland (1903–1980), painter; Ceri Giraldus Richards (1903–1971), painter; Edward John Burra (1905–1976), painter; and Tristram Paul Hillier (1905–1983), painter.

58. Jankel Alder (1895–1949), Polish painter, Oscar Kokoschka (1886–1980), Austrian painter and graphic artist, Feliks Topolski (1907–1989), Polish painter and stage set designer and Henryk Gotlib (1890–1966), Polish painter.

59. Augustus John (1878–1961), Welsh painter.

60. Pierre Bonnard (1867–1947), French painter and printmaker.

61. Henri Matisse (1869–1954), French painter.

62. Mervyn Laurence Peake (1911–1968), painter and writer.

63. Henri Matisse and André Derain (1880–1954), French painters, were the principal Fauvist artists, based in Paris around 1905–7.

64. Frances Mary Hodgkins (1869–1947), English painter.

65. Barbara Hepworth (1903–1975), English sculptor.

66. Jacob Epstein (1880–1959), English sculptor.

67. John Rutherford Armstrong (1893–1973), English painter.
68. Dora Gordine (1895–1991), sculptor, born in Estonia.
69. There were no footnotes in the original article. At the article's beginning there is a large photo of a cottage with the caption: 'The photo shows a "developed" cottage in the country. The original one–room cottage has a thatched roof (half concealed by the peat stack in front of it); the added bedroom is roofed with slates of local stone; and the most recent addition – a second bedroom – has a corrugated iron roof. The "developed" Irish house is never more than one room in width, for it is considered unlucky to widen a house.'
70. A party in the Roman Catholic Church that held with Cornelius Jansen (d. 1638) that the human will was incapable in itself of goodness.
71. Judy Boland also known as Frances J. Kelly (1908–2002), artist.
72. Daniel O'Neill (1920–1974) Northern Irish artist.
73. There are two pictures on the opposing page, one entitled *Trinity College with, on the left, the Bank of Ireland*, and the other *The River Liffey and O'Connell Bridge. In the distance can be seen the dome of the Four Courts.*

Index

The following abbreviations are used throughout the index: COM for Cormac O'Malley; EOM for Ernie O'Malley; HHOM for Helen Hooker O'Malley. Page numbers in italics indicate pages with illustrations.

1798 Centenary xxiv, 150

Abbey, Winnie 268, 302, 373
Abbey Theatre 180, 224, 261, 270, 306, 324, 351, 360
Abthos (Hepworth) 419
Academy of Fine Arts, Mexico xix, 109
Achill 147, 162, 192, 193, 203, 210, 238, 241, 249–54, 270, 287, 302, 402, 403
Adler, Jankel 416
Æ *see* Russell, George
Aer Lingus 260–1
African Negro Art (Sweeney) 234
African Portraits (Cloete) 270
Agamben, Giorgio 386
Agar, Eileen 416, 419; *Landscape* 419; *Venus* 419
Aherne, Brian 113
Aiken, Frank xvi, xx, xxv, xxix, 7, 9, 45, 47–8, 49–50, 86, 122, 128, 153; EOM's letters to 51–3, 55–7, 58–9, 60–2, 93
air-raid shelter 188, 191, 201
Aksakov, Sergei 194
Algar, James: *The Living Desert* 328
Allen, Nicholas: *Modernism, Ireland and Civil War* 376

Allen, W.E.D.: *Anglo-Irish Guerilla War in Abyssinia* 251
Allno, Maximo 66
America xiii, xvi–xvii, xxiv, xix, 45–76, 87–116, 134, 150, 154, 186, 215, 217–19, 221, 241, 247, 249, 257, 261, 262, 263, 373, 377, 411; *see also* individual states and cities
America South (Beals) 137
American Association for the Recognition of the Irish Republic 53, 55, 61
American football 49
American Poetry Society 111
Ames, Elizabeth 87, 92; EOM's letters to 90–1
Ampleforth College 215, 277, 348
Anabasis (Xenophon) 30, 251, 267
anchors 174, 176
Ancient Order of Hibernians 61
André Gide (Fernandez) 101
Andrea del Sarto 382
Andrews, Christopher 'Todd' 135
Andrews & Co. 184
Anglo-Irish, the 407–8, 409, 421
Anglo-Irish Guerilla War in Abyssinia (Allen) 251

Anglo-Irish Treaty xii, 378, 407, 410
Anhouil, Jean: *The Lark* 360
animal feed 179–80, 181–2, 189, 207, 211, 224; *see also* hay; silage
animals *see* basking sharks; birds; cats; cattle; chickens; dogs; donkeys; ducks; horses; pigs; rabbits; sheep
Annaghdown 158
Annals of Innocence and Experience (Read) 251
Annals of the Four Masters 158
Annie (nurse) 151, 154, 156, 157, 161, 167, 202
Annie (staff member, Burrishoole) 242–3, 245
Antrim, Angela 365
Appian Way, Rome 24
Arabian Deserts (Doughty) 65
Aracoeli, Rome 14, 16
Aran Islands 124, 131, 221, 222, 268, 278, 319, 321, 322–3, 324, 325, 329, 331, 338, 343, 344–5, 349–50, 354, 355, 357, 370; *see also* Inisheer; Inishmaan; Kilmurvey; Kilronan
Aran Islands, The (Synge) 250, 324
Arboe 128
archaeology xix, 85, 109, 125, 131, 220, 235, 384, 390–1, 424
Architectural Digest 383, 420–4
architecture *see* buildings
Ardee 3
Arendt, Hannah: *The Origins of Totalitarianism* 386
Arizona 63, 130, 338, 342
Arles 131, 132
Armstrong, John Rutherford 416, 419
Army Without Banners (EOM) 129, 137, 310, 311, 313
Arp, Hans: *Concretion Humane* xxi, 169
Arrest, The (Lowry) 419
art xvi, xviii, xix, xxi–xxii, 14, 15, 16, 20, 30–32, 38, 64–5, 66, 70, 80, 130, 138, 152–3, 168, 183, 185–6, 233–5, 236–7, 260, 326, 327, 331, 332–3, 350, 359–60, 377, 382, 383–5, 391–401, 403–6, 412–20, 423, 424–30; *see also* exhibitions; galleries; paintings; sculpture
Art News xxi, 137, 153
ARTEF theatre group 112, 113

Arts, The 114
Arts Council of Ireland 361–2
Aspects of the Novel (Forster) 163
Association International des Critiques d'Art 306
At Swim-Two-Birds (O'Brien) xxi
Athenry 128
athletics 339
Athlone 263
Atlantic Monthly 75, 102, 106
Auden, W.H. 101, 166, 183
Augusteum, Rome 18, 27
Aurobindo, Sri 379
Autobiographies (Yeats) 250
Avignon 130
Awake and Sing (Odets) 113
Axenfield, Israel: *Recruits* 113
Aztec civilization 413, 415, 424, 426, 427

Bach, Johann Sebastian xx, 137, 139, 140, 141, 187
Bachelor's Walk (Yeats) 394
Balearic Islands 11
Ballerina (Gordine) 419
ballet 240, 351, 360
Ballymoe 3, 5
Ballytrain 3
Ballyvaughan 147
Ballyvourney 131
Balzac, Honoré de 183, 184, 289; *Cousin Bette* 183
Banagher 391
Bandler, Bernard: *Joyce's Exiles* 257
Bansha 127
Baptist church 217
Barcelona 8, 10–12, 33–4
barley 200
barometer 196, 244
Barry, Clarke 38
Barry, Stan 264
Barry, Tom 309
Barton, Robert 13
basking sharks 302
Basque separatism xvi, 109
Bathers, The (Cézanne) 130
Baudelaire, Charles 73, 382
Beals, Carleton 80–1; *America South* 137
Beatitudes, The (Spencer) 419

Beaux' Stratagem, The (Farquhar) 360
Beckdolt, Frederick 67, 83, 84
Beckett, Samuel xiv, xv, xxiii, 360, 376, 377, 386; *Waiting for Godot* 360
bee-keeping xx, 181, 182, 191, 201, 206
Beethoven, Ludwig van 28, 136, 139, 140, 141, 143, 187, 343
Beethoven (Schauffler) 139
Beethoven: His Spiritual Development (Sullivan) 139
Behan, Brendan xv; *The Quare Fellow* 374
Belfast 146, 289
Belgium 36, 109
Bell, The xiii, xxiv, 193, 194, 215, 257, 258, 261–2, 290, 383–4, 390–1, 396–7, 416–20, 424–30
Bellini, Giovanni 138
Ben Gorm 401–2
Benjamin, Walter 385
Bergamo 359
Berkeley, George 328
Berkeley 59–60, 107
Bernardo, Marchese Patrizi Naro Montoro 337–8, 373
Beside the Ionian Sea (Gissing) 250, 251
Bewleys 145, 178, 240, 316
BF's Daughter (Marquand) 289
Bible 70, 115
Bible in Ireland, The (Nicholson) 275
Bierce, Ambrose 66
billiards 18, 177, 265, 272, 336
birds xviii, 136, 138, 195, 266; *see also* chickens; ducks
Black Barbary (Turnbull) 196
Black Lamb and Grey Falcon (West) 250, 251, 290
Black Pit (play) 112
Blackwater Valley xviii
Blake, Frances-Mary xxviii
Blake, Henry: *Letters from the Irish Highlands* 351
Blake, William 418, 419
Blood of Abel, The (Yeats) 397
Bloody Sunday xxi, 290
Blumenschein, Ernest 63, 95, 98
Blumenschein, Mary 95, 98
Boas, Franz 138, 380; *The Mind of Primitive Man* 138

boat equipment 174, 176, 178, 194, 195, 196–7, 237–8, 345, 346
boating *see* curraghs; rowing; sailing
Bodley Head publishers 313
Boland, Judy 423
Bologna 34
bonds 47, 50
Bonnard, Pierre 183, 417
Book of Golden Deeds (Young) 28
Book of Kells 391
books xvii, xxi, 23, 26, 30, 33, 37–8, 40, 65, 68, 69, 70, 71, 73, 100–1, 111, 122, 125, 131–2, 137–8, 143, 151, 158–9, 163, 183, 187, 193, 194, 195–6, 202, 207, 212–13, 229, 232, 234, 238, 250–51, 252, 257–8, 260, 270–2, 274–5, 280, 281, 287, 289, 302–3, 304, 309, 311, 312, 316–17, 319, 320–1, 322, 325, 326, 327–8, 329–30, 332, 333, 335, 336–7, 339, 351, 365, 366–7, 371–2, 373, 376–7, 380–2
boots *see* shoes
Borris-in-Ossory 4
Borrisoleigh 285
Boston 54, 56–9, 66, 68, 102, 104–6, 107, 108, 109, 114–16, 117, 118, 158–9, 165
Boston Museum 118
Botticelli, Sandro 31
Boulavogue xxiv, 150
bourbon 325
Bowman, Wilfred Venn 143
Bowman, Winnie Comstock 140, 143
box compass 176
Boy with a Hoop (Murray) 417
Boynton, Beryl 65, 66
Boynton, Ray 66, 115, 152
Brady, Frances 'Frank' 8, 12, 13, 15, 16, 17, 18, 19, 21, 29, 31, 33
Brady, Gerard 'Bobby' 19, 20, 35
Brady, James 8
Brady, Kathleen 'Kay' 8; EOM's letters to 13–33
Brahms, Johannes 139, 141, 143, 187
brandy 265
Braque, Georges 183, 236, 418
Bray 242
Breen, Dan 279
Brennan, Austin 3

Brennan, Martin: EOM's letters to 285
Brennan, May 191
Brennan, Michael 3
Brennan, Padraig 3
Brennan, Sean 191
Brett, Dorothy xvii, 63, 72, 81, 83, 84, 89, 95, 98, 132, 148, 150, 383; EOM's letters to xvii, 69
Bridge, The (Crane) xviii
Bridgeport 55
Bridie (staff member) 167, 205
Bright, Edward 95, 98
Broadway, New York 47, 50, 112
Broe, Desmond 365
Broe, Irene 365
Brown, Sheila Barnet 187
Brown's Hotel, London 245
Brugha, Cathal 3
Buckley, Maureen 37, 207
Budgen, Frank: *James Joyce and the Making of Ulysses* 257
buildings xviii, xxiii, 47, 49–50, 77, 143, 221, 366, 414, 415, 416, 422–3, 427–9
Bulfin, Catalana 'Kid' 33, 36, 40
Bulletin of Historical Research 162
Bumpers (bookshop) xxi, 163
Bunyan, John 70
Burke, Mrs 207, 243, 299
Burra, Edward John 416, 417
Burren xxiv, 131, 264
Burrishoole xii, xiv, xv, xx, xxii, xxiv, xxv, 134, 160–70, 175–213, 215, 220–5, 228, 229, 230–1, 236, 239–45, 248, 253, 258, 260–6, 268, 270–5, 277, 279–81, 283–91, 292–9, 293–4, 299–300, 302, 303, 305, 307, 308, 309, 310–11, 312, 314, 316, 318, 319, 320–1, 322, 325–6, 329, 330, 335–6, 338, 340–1, 344–5, 346, 347, 354–5, 363, 368
Burrows, George: *Wild Wales* 250, 251
buses 46–7, 48, 97, 117–18, 192, 253–4, 322, 326, 363
But for the Grace of God (Sullivan) 250
Butler, Samuel 251; *The Way of all Flesh* 65
Butte City 60, 68
butter 201, 204, 244
Byrne, Mrs 254, 266, 267, 302, 316
Byrne, Myles: *Memoirs* 201

Byrne's Fruiterer and Florist 153, 160, 174
Byron, Lord 250, 251
Byron in Italy (Quennell) 250
Byron: The Years of Fame (Quennell) 250

cabbages 181, 244
Cabral, Amilcar 387
Caher 402, 403
Cahir 4, 279
Caledonia 146
Calendar of Judiciary Rolls 158
California xvii, 59–60, 63–8, 338; *see also* Berkeley; Butte City; Carmel; Hollywood; Los Angeles; Monterey; Oakland; Pasadena; Sacramento; San Diego; San Francisco
Cambridge xxv, 226–7, 235–6, 243, 277, 278, 308–15, 317–19, 325–33, 337, 352, 354–6, 372–3
Campbell, Joe 95, 100
Caracalla, Baths of, Rome 24
Carbery, Mary: *The Farm by Lough Gur* 365
cards 17, 222
Carew, George: *Manuscripts* 158
Carew, Sir Peter 198–9
Carlow 2, 4
Carmel xvii, 63, 64–6, 84, 109, 118, 338
Carmelite 83
Carna 192
carpentry 71, 96, 132
Carrowkeel 211, 212, 222, 223–4, 244, 288, 289–90, 307
Carrowkennedy 295, 296
cars xxiv, 9, 39, 47, 49, 51, 53, 66, 85, 87, 88, 98, 99, 154, 164, 168, 179, 192, 235, 249, 254, 263, 270, 289, 305, 306, 325, 333
Castle, The (Kafka) 111
Castlebar xi, xxv, 202, 271, 288
Catholicism xviii, 50, 116, 117, 217, 218, 289, 294, 331, 334, 337, 378, 407
cats 267
cattle xx, 170, 180, 181–2, 189, 190–1, 201, 205, 207, 209, 211, 212, 223, 244, 266, 288, 289–90, 295, 303, 307, 318, 354
Caulking (Spencer) 418–19
Cavendish, George: *Life of Cardinal Wolsey* 251

censorship 186

Cervantes, Miguel de: *Don Quixote* 232, 349

Cézanne, Paul xxi, 130, 165; *The Bathers* 130

Chabot, Maria 98, 186, 187

Chagall, Marc 237

Chambers, Anthony 348

Chambers shop 182, 194

champagne 28

Chanler, Ig 116, 117

Chanler, Maria 116–17

Chanler, Teddy 116

Chapayev (Vasilyev) 113

Charlot, Jean 64, 330

Chartres 131

Chatterjee, Partha 378

cheese 184, 239

Chekhov, Anton 117, 381

Chekhov, Michael 113

chewing gum 46

Chicago xix, 51, 55–6, 60, 68, 94–8, 109, 138

Chicago World's Fair xix, 94, 95–6, 102, 138, 163

Chichen Itza 425

chickens 170, 180, 182, 189–90, 195, 201, 284, 355, 369

Childers, Erskine (father) xxviii, 270–1

Childers, Erskine (son) xxviii, 295, 296

Childers, Molly xxviii, 15, 17, 57; EOM's letters to xxviii

children xiv, 14, 16, 24–5, 71, 349, 361, 367; *see also* O'Malley, Ernie: family life and children

children of Lir 403

Chimayo 87, 109

China 121, 166, 219; *see also* Peking

Chirico, Giorgio de 236, 237

Cholula 414, 424, 427

Chopin, Frédéric 140, 187

Christ Mocked (Rouault) 406

Christian Science 217

Christmas cards 286, 296–7, 314–15, 323, 356

churches xv, xxii, 14, 16, 48, 64, 125, 264, 265, 413–14, 423, 428, 429

Chronographical Description of West of H-Iar Connaught (O'Flaherty) 159

Cincinnati 55

cinema *see* films

Citkowitz, Israel 93, 103, 156, 186

Citkowitz, Rebecca 93, 138, 153, 156, 186–7, 188; EOM's letters to 287–91, 296–7

City Library Gallery, Limerick xxiv, 225, 263, 403

Civil War xii, xxiv, 1, 2, 4–5, 109, 134, 212, 219, 230–1, 252, 257, 271, 280, 288, 341, 352, 375–6, 407, 411

Clann na Poblachta 261

Clare xxiv, 2, 3, 4, 131, 264; *see also* Ballyvaughan; Ballyvourney; Burren; Corofin; Dysert O'Dea; Ennis; Ennistymon; Inagh; Kilcreely; Kilfenora; Kilkee; Killaloe; Kilmaboy; Lahinch; Lisdoonvarna; Rinneen

Clare Island 250, 254, 287, 402

Clarke, Harry 362

Clarke, Michael 237

Clarke, Pat 239, 243, 244, 253, 266, 273

Clarke, Suniva 'Sunny' 237, 273

classical music xx–xxi, 18, 26–8, 134, 136–7, 139, 140–1, 143, 187, 223, 343, 357

Cleveland 55, 56, 68

Clew Bay xiv, xxii, 131, 134, 187, 201, 223, 310, 325, 326, 329, 338, 342, 401, 402

Clifford, Madge *see* Comer, Madge Clifford

climbing xvi, xxvii, 19, 27, 84, 105, 106–7, 109, 124

Clinic, The (Murray) 417

Cloete, Stuart: *African Portraits* 270

Clonfert 125, 390, 423

Clonmacnoise 391

Clonmel 279

Clonskeagh 215, 226, 229, 233, 236–9, 274, 275, 340–1

clothing 21, 29–30, 32, 46, 48, 50, 70, 77, 125, 140, 142, 156, 159, 165, 170, 174, 177, 180, 187, 199, 240, 241, 248, 273, 358–9, 361, 362; *see also* shoes

clouds 72, 193, 392, 402

Clurman, Harold 88, 107, 138, 156, 188

Cobh 124, 130

Cocteau, Jean: *Les Enfants Terribles* 329; *L'Éternel Retour* 329

coffee 32, 240, 287
Coleridge, Samuel Taylor xvii, 70
College Chorus, A (O'Duffy) 252
Collins, Michael 2, 3, 100, 136, 271, 379
Collins, Tom 180
Colorado 277
Colquhoun, Robert 416, 417
Colum, Mary 100; *From These Roots*
    137; *Life and the Dream* 257
Colum, Padraic 100, 257
Columbus 88
Comer, Eileen 147
Comer, Jack 40, 135, 147, 284
Comer, Madge Clifford 40; EOM's letters
    to 9, 135, 147
communism 119, 262
concerts 18, 26–7, 28
Concretion Humane (Arp) xxi, 169
Condemned Man (le Brocquy) xxii,
    399–400
Cong 167, 168
Connaught 28, 157–9, 170, 264–5, 324,
    356, 365, 392–3, 421
Connecticut 55; *see also* Bridgeport;
    Greenwich; Hartford; New Haven
Connelly, Marc: *The Green Pastures* 113
Connemara 115, 122, 228, 398–9
Connolly, James 383, 386, 387
Connolly, John 188, 189, 190–2, 205
Connolly, Sean xxx, 296
Constable, John 236, 396, 418, 419
Contemporary Gallery, Dublin 195
Contemporary Mexican Artists (Stewart) 330
cooking 43, 145, 167, 253, 272, 273, 275,
    287, 300, 302, 304, 305, 312, 316, 323,
    344, 353, 355, 367, 370, 372
cooks 147, 208, 270, 273–4, 341
Cooney, Andy 7
Copeland, Aron 93
Corcomroe Abbey 131
Cork 2, 5, 134, 226, 279, 283, 298, 309,
    318, 329; *see also* Blackwater Valley;
    Cobh; Fermoy; Glengarriff; Mallow;
    Mitchelstown; Nad; Newmarket
Corkery, Daniel: *The Fortunes of the Irish
    Language* 326; *Hidden Ireland* 326
Cornell, Katharine 113
Corofin 131

Corsica 130, 201, 222
Cosgrave, William T. 409
Cosgrove, Mary xxix
Cosmopolitan magazine xxv, 373
Costello, Joe 265
Costello, John A. 261
Coughlan, Madge 230–1
Coughlan, Paddy 283
Country Women's Association xxiv–xxv
County Club, Galway 264–5
Courtauld Institute of Art 149
Cousin Bette (Balzac) 183
cows *see* cattle
Cox, Trevor 365
Coyle, Albert: *Evidence on Conditions in
    Ireland* 271–2
Crane, Hart xviii, xxi, 77, 78, 103, 105,
    108, 377; *The Bridge* xviii
Crime and Punishment (Dostoyevsky) 229
Crivelli, Carlo 31
Croagh Patrick 201, 402
Croaghaun 402, 403
Croce, Benedetto 163
Crompton, David 'Buzz' 241, 243
crops 200, 201, 207, 211, 212, 242, 244;
    see also barley; oats; wheat
Crowe, Gertrude 10, 39
Crowe, Helen 99, 100, 151
Cuala Press 258, 325, 328
Cubism 404, 420
cults 59
Cummings, E.E. xviii, 108; *The Enormous
    Room* 250
Cunningham, John Francis 179
Curragh Camp xvi, 2, 5, 7, 17, 379, 381
curraghs 300, 302, 322, 349, 370
Curran, Con 134, 174, 193, 350
Curran, Mgr Michael 15, 36, 40
Cutting of an Agate, The (Yeats) 163

dairy 201, 204
Daly, Dinny 286
Daly, Kathleen 39
Daly, Madge 10, 39
Daly, Tom 47
Damon, S. Foster: *Odyssey in Dublin* 257
dance music 38
Dancer (Murray) 417

dancing 17, 65–6, 223
Dark Stranger, The (play) 225
Daumier, Honoré 237, 396
Daunted, The (Smith) 70
Davis, Chester 304, 368; EOM's letters to
   356–9, 368–9
Days of Fear (Gallagher) 57
de Coster, Charles 70
de Courcy, Bob 39
De La Serra xxi, 152
De Quincey, Thomas xvii, 70
de Seca, Vittorio: *Umberto D* 329
de Valera, Eamon xvi, xxv, 45, 51, 60,
   62, 74, 122, 221, 314, 377, 409; EOM's
   letters to 86
Dead Christ (Michelangelo) 38
death xiv, xvii, 69, 394
Death for Only One (Yeats) xxi, 165
Debussy, Claude xxi, 137, 141, 187
Decline and Fall of the Romantic Ideal, The
   (Lucas) 250
decolonization 376–9, 380
Defence of Duffer's Drift, The (Swinton) 251
Defoe, Daniel 70
Degas, Edgar 327, 398
Deirdre (Stephens) 71
Deirdre (Synge) 71
Delargy, James Hamilton 331
Department of Defence: EOM's letters to 317
Derain, André 183, 417
Derrig, Tom 7, 9
Desiderio da Settignano 38
Detroit 55, 56, 59–60
Devenish Island 128
Devlin, Denis 36, 153, 185, 187, 234, 377
Devlin, Eileen 193
Dial 114
Diary of Sir John Moore, The (Maurice)
   250
Diaz del Castillo, Bernal 427
Dinneen, Eileen 255, 270, 274
Dinny, Rene 83
Diversions in Sicily (Jones) 250, 251
dogs 162, 167, 190, 201, 205, 266, 267,
   296–7, 302
Doherty, Josephine 'Joe' 70
Dolan, Anne: *'No Surrender Here!'* xi, xii,
   xiii, xxx

Don Quixote (Cervantes) 232, 349
Donaghmore 128
Donegal 2, 3, 123, 240
Donegal Fairy Tales (McManus) 28
donkeys 161, 191, 201, 290
Donne, John 100
Donnelly, Simon 4
Doo Lough 401
Dostoevsky, Fyodor 111, 381; *Crime and
   Punishment* 229
Doughty, Charles Montagu 70; *Arabian
   Deserts* 65
Douglas, Norman: *Fountains in the Sand*
   250; *Together* 250
Dowling, John 135
Downtown Gallery, New York 185
Dramatic Society, UCD 36
Drangan 4, 295, 297
drinking xv, xxiv, 80, 167, 244, 260–1,
   263–6, 320, 328, 334, 338, 349, 360,
   362; *see also* brandy; champagne; gin;
   Pernod; whiskey; wine
Drumcliff 128
Du Bois, W.E.B.: *The Souls of Black
   Folks* 379
Dublin: architecture 423; Cathal in 196,
   204, 211–13, 225, 232, 236, 344; COM
   in 267, 268, 300, 323, 328, 348, 353,
   355; during Civil War 4; during War of
   Independence 2–3, 297; EOM's death
   in xi; EOM in xii, xv, xxiv–xxv, 36–42,
   121–8, 134, 135–48, 150–60, 164, 165,
   170–4, 187, 194, 198–9, 202, 208–10,
   221, 223, 225, 226, 228–30, 232–5,
   249, 253–5, 258–60, 266–8, 277–8, 283,
   291–2, 307, 316–17, 320, 323–4, 325,
   327–8, 331, 334–51, 353–60, 363–72;
   Etain in 254, 259, 344, 348; HHOM in
   xii, 126, 128, 134, 168, 176–82, 188–93,
   194–8, 199–200, 202, 203–5, 206–7,
   210–13, 215, 221, 223, 224–5; and
   Jack B. Yeats 394; and painting 403–4;
   weather 36, 139, 140, 143, 148, 154,
   159, 174, 198, 324, 354, 365, 367; *see
   also* Killiney; Rathcoole; Skerries
Dublin Castle xvi, 2, 3, 4, 350
Dublin Drama League 194
Dublin Horse Show 74, 128, 146, 234

Dublin Magazine 134, 183
Dublin Mountains 305, 306, 421
Dublin Opinion 180
Dublin Painters' Gallery 405
Dublin Zoo 267
ducks 193, 195, 201
Duff, Charles: *James Joyce and the Plain Reader* 257
Dufresne, Charles 333
Dufy, Raoul 183, 397, 425
Duignan, Michael V. 265
Duignan, Tom 285
Dun Aengus 325
Duncan, D.S. 139, 140
Duncan, Dave 128
Duncan, Isadora 66
Dungarvan 300, 316
Dunne, Eithne 224, 241
Duvillaun 390, 403
Dyf, Marcel 152
Dynamic Symmetry 92
Dysert O'Dea xxiv, 128, 264

Easter Rising 1, 3, 108, 252, 274
Eastman, Ida 81
Eden, Libby 248
Edgeworth, Maria 333
Egan, Molly Gill 192, 239
eggs 180, 205, 273
Eisenstein, Sergei 77, 78, 107; *Thunder Over Mexico* 77
El Greco 152, 417
elections 36, 50, 153, 261, 334, 337, 339
Elefetry, Dean 370–1
Emergency *see* Second World War
emigration 54, 411
England xxv, 2, 3, 8, 152, 155, 215, 218, 249, 253, 257, 268, 325–33, 334, 337; *see also* Cambridge; Leeds; London; Oxford
English, Richard 381; *Ernie O'Malley: IRA Intellectual* xi, xii, xiii, xxix; *Prisoners: The Civil War Letters of Ernie O'Malley* xi, xxviii
Ennis xxiv, 131, 147, 264
Ennis, Seamus xxv
Enniscorthy 4
Enniskillen 128

Ennistymon 147
Enormous Room, The (Cummings) 250
Ensor, James 236
Eothen (Kinglake) 250
Epstein, Jacob 418, 419
Erickson, John R. 65
Ernie O'Malley: IRA Intellectual (English) xi, xii, xiii, xxix
Ernie O'Malley Story, The (O'Farrell) xxviii
Esquameling, John 70
Essential Shakespeare, The (Wilson) 250, 251
Evidence on Conditions in Ireland (Coyle) 271–2
exhibitions 130, 142, 161, 163, 165, 172, 183, 212, 233–5, 236–7, 243, 265, 268, 289, 327, 328, 331, 332–3, 350, 360, 361–2, 365, 405–6, 416; *see also* galleries

fairy tales 28
Fallon, Paddy 295
Falls, Cyril: *The Nature of Modern War* 196
Famine Cottages, Connemara (le Brocquy) xxii, 399
Far Away and Long Ago (Hudson) 250
farm buildings 221, 222
Farm by Lough Gur, The (Carbery) 365
farm machinery 200
farming xx, 54, 134, 170, 179–80, 181–2, 189–90, 198, 200, 201, 207–8, 211–12, 222–5, 244, 256, 289–90, 295, 303, 307, 318, 422
Farquhar, George: *The Beaux' Stratagem* 360
Farrell, Patrick 173
Fauvism 397, 417, 420
Fay, William 36
Fechin, Nicolai 95, 98
Feehan, Matthew 298, 352
Feeney, Martin 314
feminism 31
Fermoy 285–6, 297
Fernandez, Ramon: *André Gide* 101
Ferns 4
Ferrara 34

fertiliser 170–1, 212, 289

Fianna Éireann 71

Fianna Fáil xix, 54, 261

Field Museum, Chicago xix, 96–7

films xxv, 63, 102, 105–6, 113, 232, 243, 277, 328, 329, 332, 348, 355, 364, 367, 370

Fine Gael 261

Finnegans Wake (Joyce) 257

fishing 46, 64, 105, 222, 228, 242, 244, 345, 368, 370

Fitzgerald, Mabel: EOM's letters to 380

FitzSimon, Brigid xxviii

Flaherty, Robert J.: *Man of Aran* 105–6

Flandrau, Charles M.: *Viva Mexico* 250

Flaubert, Gustave 73

Fleming, Paddy 38

Florence xvi, 13, 18, 29, 38, 109

flowers 57, 64, 116, 153, 160, 161, 170, 181, 195, 338

Fogg Art Museum 366

folklore xv, xxiii, 134, 185, 223, 252, 275, 325, 342, 353, 391, 423–4

food 48, 49, 57, 80, 119, 136, 143, 170, 177, 178, 184, 197, 202, 208, 209, 223, 239, 244, 273, 326, 328, 338, 360; *see also* cooking; fruit; groceries; restaurants; vegetables

Ford, John xxv, xxix, 63, 277, 299–300, 361, 364, 367, 370; EOM's letters to 314; *The Informer* 63; *The Quiet Man* xxv, 277; *The Rising of the Moon* xxv, 277, 361, 364, 367, 370

Ford, Thomas J. 46

Foreign Legion, The (Ward Price) 196

Forster, E.M.: *Aspects of the Novel* 163; *A Passage to India* xxi, 163

Fortescue, Sir J.: *Memoirs of Sergeant Bourgogne* 251

Fortune 138

Fortunes of the Irish Language, The (Corkery) 326

Forum 100

Fountains in the Sand (Douglas) 250

Four Courts xii, xv, 2, 4, 5, 212

Fox & Co. (tobacconists) 200

Foyle's (bookshop) xxi, 163

Fra Filippo Lippi xvi, 31, 32

France xiv, xvi, xxi, 8, 12, 34–5, 36, 109, 130, 131, 132, 150, 155, 156, 201, 222, 262, 305, 313, 326, 330, 340, 360, 376, 381, 410–11; *see also* Arles; Avignon; Chartres; Le Havre; Marseille; Nice; Paris; Provence

Franck, César xxi, 28, 137, 140, 141, 187

Francois Villon (Wyndham-Lewis) 47

Frascati, Rome 28

Free, William J. 144, 160

French 12, 18, 28, 30, 99, 101, 132, 166, 183–4, 223, 326, 344, 345, 360

frescoes 64, 66, 80, 384, 415, 429

Friends of the National Collections of Ireland 233, 406

From These Roots (Colum) 137

Frost, Stella 174, 180, 192

fruit 189, 203–4

fuel *see* paraffin; petrol; turf

Funeral of Harry Boland, The 375

Furlong, George 234

Gaelic games xvii, 48, 147

Gaelic League 324, 405

Gaelic Park *see* Innisfail Park

Gainsborough, Thomas 236

Gallagher, Cecilia 37, 38, 57, 75, 270, 271, 322

Gallagher, Frank: *Days of Fear* 57; EOM's letters to 37–8, 41, 57, 74–6, 270–2, 322–3; *The Jangle of Keys* 271

Galerie Nationale du Jeu de Pomme 335

galleries xxi, xxiv, 25, 30–32, 149, 172, 183, 185, 195, 229, 233–5, 236–7, 263, 327, 332–3, 335, 360, 365, 396, 397, 403–4, 405–6, 416; *see also* exhibitions

Gallop, Rodney: *Portugal, a Book of Folk Ways* 140

Galsworthy, John 41

Galtee Castle 280

Galway 3, 5, 122, 123, 131, 147, 158, 189, 221, 222, 263, 264, 320–1, 369, 423; *see also* Annaghdown; Athenry; Ballymoe; Carna; Connemara; Gort; Headford; Kilmacduagh; Kinvara; Leenane; Maam Valley; Oughterard; Tuam

Galway races 304

Gamio, Manuel 415
Ganesco, Alexandre 152
Gantley (shoemaker) 170, 172
Gantt, W. Horsely 218
gardening 57, 116–17, 155, 160, 166–7,
    168, 181, 189, 191, 196, 201, 211,
    212, 244, 370; *see also* flowers; fruit;
    vegetables
Gargan-Daly, James 268
Gate Lodge, Burrishoole 242, 244
Geary, Frank 39, 128
Germany 36, 109, 166, 410
Gheerbrant, Alan: *The Impossible*
    Adventure 366–7
Gilbert, Arthur Hill 66
Gilbey, Fr Thomas 315
Gilchrist, Thomas 241, 247, 293, 294;
    EOM's letters to 246, 247–9, 253, 255,
    272–4
Gill, Josie 173, 244, 252, 256, 302,
    303, 329
Gill, Lorcan 192
Gill, Moya 244
Gill, Nora 244
Gilmore, George 129
gin 320
Ginnell, Lawrence 272
Giorgio de Castlefranco (Richter) 153
Giorgione 138, 153
Giotto xvi
Gissing, George: *Beside the Ionian Sea*
    250, 251
Gleizes, Albert 183, 398, 404
Glendalough 128
Glengarriff 203
Glenstal Abbey School 256, 258–60
Glentworth Hotel, Limerick 264
Goddard, Theodora 77, 80, 98, 99, 117,
    132, 152, 156, 186, 187
Godowsky, Leopold 28
Gogarty, Oliver St John 336, 351
Gogol, Nikolai 111; *The Inspector General*
    113; *The Marriage* 113
Goitia, Francisco 64
Gold Eagle Guy (Levy) 107, 113
Golden, Deirdre 71, 72, 79, 80, 81, 89,
    96, 99, 101, 132, 148, 150, 186, 187,
    188, 343

Golden, Eithne xxix, 71, 79, 80, 81,
    96, 101, 153; EOM's letters to 97–9,
    110–11, 130–2, 148, 150–1, 185–8,
    340–4
Golden, Helen Merriam xvii, 63, 87,
    148, 150, 186, 187, 188; EOM's letters
    to xvii, xix, 70–3, 79–81, 89, 95–6,
    99–101, 112–14
Golden, Terence 71, 79, 89, 96, 101, 132,
    148, 150, 186, 188, 343
Golding, Louis: *James Joyce* 257
golf 146, 222
Gonne, Maud 261
Goodbodys' solicitors 304
Goor, Frances 83
Gordine, Dora 419
Gort 264
Gotlib, Henryk 416, 417
Gould, Eileen 156
governesses 17, 208, 224, 268
Goya, Francisco 398, 404
Gozoli, Bonotzo 80
Grafton Street 37, 138, 351
Graham Brothers 174
gramophone records 38, 164, 165, 223,
    228–9, 343, 357, 376
gramophones 19, 162,165, 199–200, 357
Grand Canyon 63
Grant, John 128
Great Hunger, The (Kavanagh) xv
Great O'Neill, The (O'Faolain) 222
Greek literature 28, 99, 108–9
Green Pastures, The (Connelly) 113
Greene & Co. (bookshop) 300
Greenwich 93, 94, 134, 150, 217, 228–9
Gregory, Lady 324, 327, 328, 329, 330,
    333, 362; *The Kiltartan Poetry Book*
    325; *Poets and Dreamers* 365
Gregory, Sir William 327
Griffin, Joe 212
Griffith, Arthur 100, 271
Gris, Juan 183, 332–3
groceries 144–5, 177, 184, 377
Guanajuato 79
Guests of the Nation (O'Connor) xix, 75
Guilio Romano 14
Guinness, May 198
Guyard, Michelle 371

Hagan, Mgr John xxx, 8, 14, 15–16, 26–8, 352; EOM's letters to 11–13, 34–6, 40

Hakluyt, Richard: *Voyages* 70, 258

Hale, Philip L.: *Vermeer* 138

Halligan, Maureen 180

Hamlet (Shakespeare) xxv, 271

Hamlin, Mary 95, 98, 111

Hanlon, Jack 195

Hanna and Neale (bookshop) 260, 311

Hanson, Armand 66

Hapgood, Hutchins 87

Hapgood, Miriam 63, 95, 98

Hapgood, Neith Boyce 63

Happy as Larry (MacDonagh) 257

Haring, Clarence: *The Spanish Empire in America* xxiv, 257

Hart Crane (Horton) 137

Hartford 55

Hartford House, New York xix, 100, 102, 103, 108

Harvard 114–15, 116, 275, 280, 342, 344, 366

Harvard University Press 257

Harvill Press 315

Hasty Pudding Club 374

Haugh, John 365

hay 179, 181–2, 189, 196, 242, 244

Haydn, Joseph 187, 343

Hayes, Dorsha 95

Hayes, Paul 95

Hayes, Richard 156; *The Last Invasion of Ireland* 156, 201

Headford 131

Healy, Jerry 224

Healy, Matthew Garth 46, 53, 56, 59, 62, 86

Heidegger, Martin 380

Helen (Yeats) 397

Helion, Jean 418

Hellgren, Nora 71

Hempel, Andreas 188–9, 193

Hempel, Eduard 134, 174, 189, 193

Hempel, Eva 174, 189, 193

Henderson, Alice Corbin 105, 108

Henehan, Michael 174

Henricks, Sean 318, 319

Henry, Françoise 137, 155, 326, 384, 390–1; *Irish Art in the Early Christian Period* 390–1; *La Sculpture Irlandaise* 330

Henry, Paul xxi

hens *see* chickens

Hepworth, Barbara 418, 419

Herbert, Robert xxiv, 263–5, 274; EOM's letters to 207

Herder, Johann Gottfried von 379

Here's Ireland (Speakman) 37–8

Herodotus 30

Heron, Hilary 360

Hidden History (documentary) xxix

Hidden Ireland (Corkery) 326

Hidden Ireland (documentary) xxix

Hillary, Richard: *The Last Enemy* 250, 251

Hillier, Tristram 416, 419

Hispanic Society of America Museum 185

Hitchens, Ivon 416, 417

Hoboken 46

Hodgkins, Frances Mary 416, 417–18

Hoffman, Frank 72

Hogarth, William 419

Holbein, Hans 183

Holiday magazine 401–3

Hollyford 279, 295

Hollywood 232

Home Guard Training Manual (Langdon Davis) 196

Hone, Evie 173, 331, 350, 361–2, 377, 404–5, 423

honey wine 195, 196

Hooker, Adelaide xix, 93, 94, 96, 97, 115, 118, 121, 126, 131, 152, 154, 160, 218, 219, 221, 229, 259, 289

Hooker, Barbara 'Bobby' 117, 119, 154, 156, 160, 161, 162, 218

Hooker, Blanche Ferry 93, 121, 131, 146, 154, 156, 160, 217–18, 219, 221, 233, 293; EOM's letters to 240–3, 247

Hooker, Blanchette xix, 93, 115, 118, 119, 154, 160, 218, 229, 293

Hooker, Elon xix, 93, 134, 154, 156, 217, 221, 313; EOM's letters to 126, 146

Hooker O'Malley, Helen: in America xxiv, 134, 150, 186, 215, 221, 228–9, 232–3, 241, 247, 249, 257, 277; at Burrishoole xii, xiv, xx, 134, 166–8, 169, 170–1, 173–4, 194, 198–9, 201, 220–5, 236, 241, 242–3, 344–5; and classical music

xx–xxi, 137, 168, 223; death of father
134; described by EOM 132; divorce
277, 294, 340, 344, 346; in Dublin xii,
126, 128, 134, 168, 176–82, 188–93,
194–8, 199–200, 202, 203–5, 206–7,
210–13, 215, 221, 223, 224, 225, 236–7,
242, 344, 347; EOM's letters to xxix,
94, 96–7, 104, 114–19, 123–6, 136–46,
149, 151–60, 161–3, 167–8, 170–1,
173–4, 176–82, 184, 188–200, 203–5,
206–7, 211–13, 232–3, 235–7, 239–40,
243–6, 291, 292–4, 335–6, 346–9,
367–8; family background 217–19;
family life and children xv, xx, xxiv,
129, 130, 132, 133, 134, 192–3, 202,
204–5, 206–7, 208, 210, 211–13, 215,
220, 222, 224–5, 245–9, 268, 277, 289,
342, 344–9; and films 232, 243; finances
134, 142, 152, 155, 198, 200, 203, 211,
217, 218, 223, 224, 229, 232–3, 245,
273, 293–4, 304, 311, 312; garden tour
to Japan 121, 123, 126, 219; gardening
166–8, 169, 196, 201; health 156, 166,
168, 178, 179, 188, 200, 220, 247;
interior design 134, 166, 201, 221, 236;
kidnaps Cathal and Etain xxiv, 277,
311, 312, 340, 347; and Liam Redmond
248, 268, 289; in London 121, 126,
138–46, 161–3, 219, 241, 243–6, 253,
255, 263, 268, 291, 292, 308, 312; at
Louisburgh 134; maintenance payments
for COM 348, 356–9, 368; marriage
to EOM xi, xiv, xix–xx, 126, 217–25;
meets EOM, and courtship xix, 93,
96, 102–3, 217–19; painting 202, 236;
paintings, collecting 168, 177; religion
217, 219; remarriage 345; sculpture 96,
131, 134, 169, 178, 202, 215, 217, 220,
224, 225, 228, 236, 242, 342–3, 347;
separation from EOM 245–9, 251–2,
272–5, 293–4; tennis 217; and theatre
225, 237, 241, 251; wishes to live with
EOM again 313, 341, 344–5
Hopper, James Marie 67
hops 195, 196
Horizon magazine xxii, 397–401
horses 24, 31, 201, 205, 209, 284, 397
Horton, Philip xxi; *Hart Crane* 137

Houghton Mifflin 129, 165, 169
House in the Cevennes, A (Saleil) 367
Howe, Mariana 63, 71, 72, 79, 81, 89, 96,
98, 99, 100, 101, 132, 148, 150, 153,
186, 188
Howet, Marie 405
Huaxtec people 413, 426
Hudson, W.H.: *Far Away and Long Ago* 250
Hugh Lane collection 327, 404, 406
Hughes, John 200, 205
Hughes, John T. 56–7, 58, 112, 158–9,
228, 271
Hume, Sam 59–60
Humphreys, Dick 9
Humphreys, Ellen 'Nell' 9, 21
Humphreys, Emmet 21
Humphreys, Sighle xxix, 9, 230; EOM's
letters to 42, 68, 84–5, 378–9
hunger strike xvi, xxviii, 2, 5, 12, 84
Hungry Grass, The (MacDonagh) 257
Hunt, Jim 285
Huxley, Aldous 329
Hyde, Douglas, 330; *The Love Songs of
Connaught* 325
Hyland, Winnie 256, 316, 373

Iceland 331
Ileto, Rey 378
Illannaconney 326
Impossible Adventure, The (Gheerbrant)
366–7
In Memory of Boucicault and Bianconi
(Yeats) 397
Inagh 3
Independent, The 75
Indianapolis 87
Indians *see* Native Americans
Informer, The (Ford) 63
Inishbofin 402
Inisheer 326, 344–5, 349–50, 355
Inishfish 326
Inishglora 403
Inishmaan 325
Inishowen 2, 3
Inishturk 250, 326, 402
Iniskea Islands 155, 390, 403
Inistiogue 2, 4
Innisfail Park xvii, 48

Inspector General, The (Gogol) 113
Institute of Sculptors of Ireland 366
interior design 134, 166, 199–200, 221, 235
Irish Academy of Letters xxiv, 134, 156, 254, 255
Irish American Cultural Institute xxix
Irish Art in the Early Christian Period (Henry) 390–1
Irish Civil Defence Forces 134
Irish Classics (Kiberd) 380–1, 382
Irish Crosses (Sexton) 258
Irish Culture League 175
Irish Exhibition of Living Art 233–4, 405–6, 416
Irish Folklore Commission 185, 321, 331, 353
Irish Historical Society xxiv
Irish language 42, 54, 99, 102, 108–9, 112, 122, 160, 202, 215, 278, 308, 343, 346, 370, 411–12, 420
Irish music 187, 343
Irish National Theatre 324; *see also* Abbey Theatre
Irish Parliamentary Party 270, 271
Irish Press xiii, xvi–xvii, xx, xxix, 45, 53, 129, 377; *see also* O'Malley, Ernie: fundraising for the *Irish Press*
Irish Republican Army 7, 109, 127, 135, 261, 352, 408, 410
Irish Review 100
Irish Statesman 74–5, 170
Irish Times xvi
Irish Tourist Association 125, 235
Irish Volunteer 252
Irish Volunteers 2, 3, 36, 96, 109, 216, 252
Irish White Cross 2
Irish World 46, 54
Irving, Washington: *Knickerbocker's History of New York* 65
Island Mór 165, 168, 173, 252, 256, 329
Italian 14, 18, 28, 30, 339
Italy xiv, xvi, 8, 13–33, 109, 313, 324, 330, 337–9, 359–60, 376, 377, 410, 429; *see also* Bergamo; Bologna; Ferrara; Florence; Milan; Naples; Ravenna; Rome; Sicily; Siena; Tuscany; Venice

Jack B. Yeats (MacGreevy) 396–7

jam making 203–4, 207
James, Bill 313
James Joyce (Golding) 257
James Joyce: A Critical Introduction (Levin) 257
James Joyce and the Making of Ulysses (Budgen) 257
James Joyce and the Plain Reader (Duff) 257
Jameson's Distillery xvi
Jane (staff member) 204
Jangle of Keys, The (Gallagher) 271
Japan 121, 123, 125, 126, 219, 271, 360; *see also* Kyoto; Osaka
Jean-Christophe (Rolland) 65
Jeffers, Robinson 65
Jellett, Mainie 152, 173, 183, 198, 199, 377, 404
John, Augustus 333, 416
Johnson, Anna 160
Johnson, Walter Willard 'Spud' 63, 71, 72, 73, 132
Jones, David (Welsh academic) 387
Jones, David (English painter) 405
Jones, E.H.: *The Road to En-Dor* 250, 251
Jones, Henry Festing: *Diversions in Sicily* 250, 251
Jooss, Kurt 180, 240, 241
Joyce, James xv, 76, 83, 88, 109, 257, 287, 289, 290; *Finnegans Wake* 257; *Ulysses* xiv, 70, 76, 83
Joyce, Una 268, 300, 316
Joyce's Exiles (Bandler) 257
Juilliard School of Music, New York 186
Julia (staff member) 195, 200

Kafka, Franz: *The Castle* 111
Kanellos, Tanagra *see* Markham, Charlotte
Kanellos, Vassos 108, 155, 217
Kanellos, Xthenae 155
Kansas 88
Kathleen (staff member) 178
Kavanagh, Patrick xv, 261; *The Great Hunger* xv
Keane family 123–4
Kearney, Leopold 34
Keating, Mary 152
Keating, Sean xxiv, 180, 263, 349
Keats, John: *Letters* 250, 251

Keem Bay 287, 403
Kelleher, D.L. 57
Kelleher, John xxiv, 290; EOM's letters to xxiv, 249–52, 256–8, 260–6, 274–5, 280
Kelly, Michael A. 51
Kelly, Oisín 360, 365
Kelly, P.J. 244
Kerrigan, Georgette 176, 344, 355
Kerry 123, 147, 282, 290
Kerryman 294–5, 296, 298, 301
Kessell, Mary 416, 419
Keys of the Kingdom, The (Stahl) 348
Kiberd, Declan: *Irish Classics* 380–1, 382
kidnapping 277, 311, 312, 340, 347
Kiely, Jerry xviii, 4, 5
Kiernan, Thomas 174
Kilcreely xxiv, 264
Kildare 290
Kilfenora xxiv, 128, 264, 423
Kilkee 3, 43, 122, 160, 364, 365, 367
Kilkenny 2, 4, 109, 423
Killaloe 423
Killanin, Lord 361
Killary Harbour 402
Killiney 270, 273
Kilmaboy xxiv, 264
Kilmacduagh 128, 264
Kilmainham Gaol 2, 4, 7, 380, 381
Kilmichael ambush 4
Kilmurvey 322–3
Kilronan 349–50
Kilroy, Michael 240
Kilroy, Paddy 207
Kiltartan Poetry Book, The (Gregory) 325
King, Mae 39
King of the Beggars (O'Faolain) 156
Kinglake, A.W.: *Eothen* 250
Kingsbury, Hazel *see* Strand, Hazel
Kinvara 264
Kisling, Moise xxi, 152, 183
Kitchen Scene in the House of Martha (Velasquez) 327
Klee, Paul 236–7, 419, 420
Knickerbocker's History of New York (Irving) 65
Knight, G. Wilson: *The Olive and the Sword* 250
Knockmore 402

Knox, John 33
Kokoschka, Oscar 416–17
Korea 121
Kriskna, Mary 419
Kurosawa, Akira: *Seven Samurai* 332
Kyoto 123

La France de Profil (Strand) 305, 338
La France Libre 134, 406–12
Lady Gregory's Journal (Robinson) 328, 362
Lahinch xxiv, 264
Laird, Helen 193
Laithwaite, Sir Gilbert xix, 201, 219
Laithwaite, Sylvia 80, 86, 95, 97, 98, 232, 343; EOM's letters to 201–3
Lalor, Fintan 387
Landreth, Helen 168, 174
landscape xvii, xviii, xxii–xxiii, 30, 64, 130, 148, 165, 169, 176, 193, 305, 306, 385, 391–2, 395, 397, 398–9, 401–4
Landscape (Agar) 419
Lane, Sir Hugh 327, 404
Langdon Davis, John: *Home Guard Training Manual* 196
Lark, The (Anhouil) 360
Last Enemy, The (Hillary) 250, 251
Last Invasion of Ireland, The (Hayes) 156, 201
Lavery, Cecil 261
Lawrence, D.H. xiv, xvii, 47, 63, 69, 83, 132, 360; *The Lost Girl* 360; *The Plumed Serpent* xvii, 69; *Sons and Lovers* xvii, 69
Lawrence, Frieda 69
Lawrence, T.E.: *Wanderings in Arabia* 65
Lawson, J.: *Success Story* 113
lawyers *see* Davis, Chester; Gilchrist, Thomas; Goodbodys' solicitors; Noyk, Michael; Overend, George
le Brocquy, Louis xiv, xxi, xxii, 377, 385, 397–401, 423; *Condemned Man* xxii, 399–400; *Famine Cottages, Connemara* xxii, 399; *Making the Twig Sign* 401
Le Gallienne, Eva 112
Le Gallienne, Richard 73
Le Havre 130
Leadership of Giorgione, The (Phillips) 153

Lederma, Isabela 330
Lederma, Oliver 330
Lee, J.J. xii, xiii
Leeds 228
Leenane 131, 263
Lehane and McGuirk 177, 180, 200
Leinster House 231
Lemass, Seán xvi, xxv, 4, 9
Lenihan, Paddy 304
Les Enfants Terribles (Cocteau) 329
L'Éternel Retour (Cocteau) 329
Letter to a Young Poet (Rilke) 166, 183
Letters from the Irish Highlands (Blake) 351
Levin, Harry: *James Joyce: A Critical
    Introduction* 257
Levy, Melvin: *Gold Eagle Guy* 107, 113
Lewis, Samuel: *A Topographical Dictionary
    of Ireland* 158
Lhote, André 183, 398, 404
libel action xx, 134, 148, 150, 220, 223,
    310, 313
Liber, Armour 289; EOM's letters to
    296–7
Liber, Rebecca *see* Citkowitz, Rebecca
libraries xix, xx, xxi, 28, 93, 97, 98, 99,
    102, 105, 143, 158, 165, 300, 320, 351,
    353, 355, 364, 366, 370
Life Along the Potomac River (Williams)
    137
Life and Letters Today 143
Life and the Dream (Colum) 257
Life in the West of Ireland (Yeats) 169
Life is Beautiful (Pudovkin) 113
Life of Cardinal Wolsey (Cavendish) 251
Light, Gertrude 63, 69, 79, 96, 98, 99,
    101, 148, 218
Lilly (staff member) 145
Limerick xxiv, 2, 4, 5, 39, 109, 122,
    127, 192, 208, 210, 225, 263–4, 270,
    279, 280, 283, 285, 308, 311, 364,
    365, 367, 423
Lindbergh, Charles 117
Lipton's shop 200, 244–5
Lisdoonvarna 131
Lisvernane 127
Little, Con 36
Little, Patrick 362
Lives of the Italian Painters (Vasari) 382

livestock *see* cattle; pigs; sheep
Living Art Committee 233–4
Living Desert, The (Algar) 328
Lloyd, David xii, xiii
Lloyd George, David 378
Local Security Force 175
London 3, 8, 36, 39, 121, 126, 132, 138,
    143, 149, 158, 161–3, 183, 202–3, 215,
    219, 228, 232, 235–8, 241, 243–6, 248,
    253, 255, 262, 263, 268, 282, 311, 312,
    325, 327, 329, 331, 332–3, 416–20
Longford, Jack 183
Longford 3, 296, 301
Long Island xix, 46, 90
Lopez, Anita 79, 89, 99, 101
Lopez, Ernesto 89, 99, 101
Lopez, Felinici, 89, 99, 101
Lopez, Lucinda 79, 89, 99, 101
Lopez, Margo 79, 89, 99, 101
Lorenzo di Credi 31
Los Angeles 59, 63, 67–8
Lost Girl, The (Lawrence) 360
Lotto, Lorenzo 31, 138
Lough Corrib 158
Lough Mask 401
Lough Nafooey 402
Lough Neagh 128
Lough Reagh 157
Louisburgh 134, 160–1
Love Songs of Connaught, The (Hyde) 325
Low Tide (Yeats) xxii, 397
Lowell, Henry 105
Lowenthal, Helen 149
Lowry, Laurence Stephen 416, 419
Luca della Robbia 38
Lucas, Cuthbert 285–6, 297
Lucas, F.L.: *The Decline and Fall of the
    Romantic Ideal* 250
Luhan, Mabel Dodge 63, 80, 81, 83,
    132, 157
Luhan, Tony 63, 80, 83–4, 132
Lujan, Manuel 79
Lurcat, Jean xxi, 153, 187
Lusitania 404
Luzano, Manuel Rodriguez 64
Lydon, Margaret Fox 264
Lynch, Bernadette 35, 40
Lynch, Diarmuid 3

Lynch, Liam 2, 4, 285, 286, 352
Lynn 58

MacAlpine Hotel, New York 46
MacBride, Anna 40
MacBride, 'Kid' *see* Bulfin, Catalana 'Kid'
MacBride, Sean 33, 36, 261
McBrien, Peter 75
MacBryde, Robert 416, 417
McCarthy, Joseph 262
McCarthy, Mary 40
McCarthy, Minnie 61
McCartney, Peter xvi
McCarvill, Eileen 9, 74, 155, 163, 165–6
McCresson, Helen 65, 66, 83, 96, 132
McCresson, Preston 64, 65, 83, 96, 132
MacDiarmid, Hugh 387
MacDonagh, Barbara 131, 221
MacDonagh, Breihne 266, 267
MacDonagh, Don 164, 166, 174, 193;
    Happy as Larry 257; *The Hungry*
    Grass 257
MacDonagh, Thomas 108, 131
McDonnell, Andie 149, 163
MacEoin, Sean 296
McGahern, John xii, xv
McGilligan, Eileen 37
McGonigal, Maurice 172
McGrail, Jean xxix, 278; EOM's letters
    to 325–35, 336–9, 349–50, 359–62,
    364–7, 371–3
McGrane, Eileen *see* McCarvill, Eileen
McGrath, Dan 95
McGrath, John 301
MacGreevy, Thomas xxi, xxix, 199, 376,
    377, 385; EOM's letters to xxi, 163–4,
    165–6, 169–70, 182–4; *Jack B. Yeats*
    396–7
MacGuinness, Jim 135
McGuinness, Norah 142, 168, 174, 177,
    183, 187, 196, 423
MacGuinness, Sean 135
McHugh, Patricia: EOM's letters to 351
McHugh, Roger 36; EOM's letters to 226;
    Rossa 226
McIlhenny, Henry 235
McIntyre, Pat 179, 180, 191, 195, 200,
    259, 288, 289–90

MacKenna, Maureen 161
MacKenna, Stephen 251
MacKenzie, Compton 28
McKernin, Mae 70, 82
MacLachloinn, Liam 288
MacLeish, Archibald 373
Macmillan 100
MacManus, Francis: EOM's letters to
    295–6, 297, 298–9, 301
McManus, Seamus: *Donegal Fairy*
    Tales 28
MacNeice, Corinna 282
MacNeice, Hedli 282
MacNeice, Louis xxi–xxii, 282
MacNeill, Eoin 252
Maam Valley 263
Madden, Doreen 370–1
Madison Gardens, New York 50
Madison Square, New York 47
Madrid 152, 371
Maestas, Andres 89, 99, 101
Maeterlinck, Maurice 73
Magan, Manchan xxix
Magan, Ruan xxix
Magennis, Fr Peter 13, 35, 36
Majorca 11
Making the Twig Sign (le Brocquy) 401
Malley, Brendan 203, 266, 311
Malley, Cecil 126, 140, 142, 144, 149,
    155, 162, 165, 166, 202–3, 206, 237,
    238, 301, 311, 343
Malley, Jacqueline 235
Malley, Kathleen 126, 140, 155–6, 160,
    167–8, 203, 228, 266, 267, 268; EOM's
    letters to 206
Malley, Kevin (brother of EOM) 26, 38,
    74, 85, 122, 123, 128, 131, 143, 155,
    158, 188, 196, 203, 206, 228, 244, 247,
    248, 249, 266, 300, 302, 308, 310, 311,
    315, 316, 317, 319, 320, 324, 331, 341,
    351, 362, 370–1, 373
Malley, Kevin (son of Cecil) 235
Malley, Luke 155–6, 203
Malley, Margaret 228, 235
Malley, Marian 156, 174, 192, 193, 196,
    203, 228, 232
Malley, Marian 'Sweetie' 203, 228, 266,
    267; EOM's letters to 268

Malley, Patrick 38, 125, 142, 146, 203, 287, 300, 335
Mallow xv, 4, 297
Malory, Thomas: *Morte D'Arthur* xxv, 288
Malraux, André: *Man's Fate* 111
Man of Aran (Flaherty) 105
Man's Fate (Malraux) 111
Manahan, Josephine 309
Manahan, Liam 319; EOM's letters to 281, 283, 308–9
Manet, Edouard 398
Mantegna, Andrea 20
manure *see* fertiliser
maps 31, 67, 125, 162, 180, 240, 307, 325, 326
Marchand, Jean xxi, 152
Marin, John 63
Markham, Charlotte 108, 217
Marquand, John xix, 160, 218, 221, 289, 291; *BF's Daughter* 289
Marriage, The (Gogol) 113
Marseille xxi, 130, 289
Martin (staff member) 168, 180, 191
Martin, Colbert xxviii
Martyn, Edward 324
Marxism 386
Mary (staff member) 153, 155, 156, 157
Massachusetts 55; *see also* Boston; Harvard; Lynn; New Bedford; Norwood; Provincetown; Worcester
Mater Hospital 369–71
Matisse, Henri 236, 417
Matisse, Pierre 185
Matthiessen, F.O. 249
Maumtrasna 401
Mauritania 46
Maxwell, W.H.: *Wild Sports of the West of Ireland* 336–7
Mayan civilization 366, 413, 414, 415, 424–6, 428
Mayhew, Patrick 380–1
Maynooth College 233, 406
Mayo 49, 131, 157, 158, 215, 249–50, 253, 326, 401–3; *see also* Achill; Burrishoole; Carrowkeel; Carrowkennedy; Castlebar; Clew Bay; Cong; Inis Mór; Iniskea Islands; Louisburgh; Newport; Rossgiblin;

Tourmakeady; Westport
Mediaeval People (Power) 250
Meier-Graefe, Julius 101, 111
Mellows, Liam 352
Melville, Herman 249, 381; *Moby Dick* 65, 70, 272, 381–2
Memoirs of Sergeant Bourgogne (Fortescue) 251
Men in White (Boleslanski) 102
Mérida, Carlos 415
Merrill, Helen 152
Metropolitan Museum of Art, New York 185, 331, 338, 366
Mexico xiii, xvii–xix, 61, 64–5, 77–85, 103, 105, 107, 108, 109, 113–14, 150, 185, 186, 219, 330, 331, 338, 366, 377, 381, 383–5, 412–15, 424–30; *see also* Chichen Itza; Cholula; Guanajuato; Mexico City; Mitla; Monte Albán; Oaxaca; Palenque; Queretaro; San Luis Potosi; Tenochtitlan; Teotihuacan; Veracruz; Yucatan
Mexico City xviii, 79–85, 105, 109, 413, 414, 415, 427
Michael (staff member) 168, 174, 176, 179, 180, 181, 189, 191, 195, 196, 205
Michael Collins (O'Connor) 271
Michelangelo xvi, 16; *Dead Christ* 38
Middletown in Transition (Williams) 137
Midnight on the Desert (Priestley) 250
Milan 336, 337–9, 360
milk 145, 204–5, 273, 288
Mill Pond, The (Lowry) 419
Millet, Jean-François 396
Mind of Primitive Man, The (Boas) 138
Minnefinger, Die (Naumann) 193
Mino da Fiesole 38
Mirabel, Tony 79
Mitchelstown 5, 279
Mitla 414, 415, 424, 425
Mixtec people 413, 424
Moby Dick (Melville) 65, 70, 272, 381–2
modernism xii, xiv, xv, 382
Modernism, Ireland and Civil War (Allen) 376
Modigliani, Amedeo xxi, 117, 152
Modotti, Tina 64
Modreeny 295, 296, 297

Mohave desert 338
Molloy's (Westport) 240
Moloney, Con 123
Moloney, Jim 127
Monaghan 2, 3
Monasterboice 391
money *see* Hooker O'Malley, Helen:
   finances; O'Malley, Ernie: finances
Mongolia 121
Monroe, Harriet xvii–xviii; EOM's letters
   to xviii, 104–5, 108–10
Montaigne, Michel de 334, 339, 382
Monte Albán 415, 424
Monterey 66, 83
Moore, George 324, 332
Moore, Henry 322, 400, 405, 416,
   418, 419
Moore, Irina Radetsky 322
Moore, Sir John 150
Moran, Michael 288
Moran's shop 244
Morley, Sylvanus 366
Morrissey, Fr 12
Morte D'Arthur (Malory) xxv, 288
Moscow Art Theatre 113
Moscow Laugh (film) 113
Mount Lobo 63, 69–73
Mountain Tavern, The (O'Flaherty) 111
mountains *see* Ben Gorm; climbing; Croagh
   Patrick; Croaghaun; Dublin Mountains;
   Maumtrasna; Mweelrea; Nephin;
   Nephin Beg; Partry mountains; Pyrenees;
   Wicklow Mountains
Mountjoy Gaol 2, 4–5, 7, 352
movies *see* films
Moylan, Sean 123
Mozart, Wolfgang Amadeus xx, 28, 137,
   139, 140, 141, 187, 343, 366
Muckinish 326
Mulcahy, Richard 2, 3, 74, 352, 379
Mullingar 157–8, 284
Municipal Gallery, Dublin 233, 234, 365,
   397, 403, 405, 406
Murphy, Bebhinn 309, 318, 319
Murphy, Delia 174, 175, 176
Murphy, Honor 16, 18
Murphy, Maighread: EOM's letters to 309,
   318, 319

Murphy, Fr Michael 152, 155, 178, 193
Murphy, Orla 309, 318, 319
Murphy, P.A. 7
Murphy, Seamus 309, 318, 319
Murray, Michael 307
Musée de L'Orangerie 335
Museum of Living Art, New York 185
Museum of Modern Art, New York 185,
   233–5
museums xvi, xix, 30–1, 60, 96–7, 118,
   125, 155, 185, 235, 237, 332, 366
music *see* classical music; dance music;
   gramophone records; Irish music;
   Oriental music
mussels 326
Mussorgsky, Modest xxi, 137
Mweelrea 401
Myers, Barbara 371

Nad 297
Nally, Patrick 48, 51
Nancy (staff member) 143, 144–6
Nanna *see* O'Shea, Bridget
Naples 17
Nash, Harold 132
Nation, The 217
National College of Art, Dublin xxii, 234
National Gallery, London xxi, 149, 183,
   332, 404
National Gallery of Ireland 234, 396, 405
National Library, Dublin xxi, 28, 158,
   165, 300, 320, 351, 353, 355, 364,
   366, 370
Native Americans 71, 83, 85, 92, 109,
   110, 217, 313, 328–9, 360, 366, 377,
   383–5, 412–13, 428–9
Nature of Modern War, The (Falls) 196
Naumann, Hans: *Die Minnefinger* 193
Neehan, Conor 93
Nelligan, Dave 147
Nephin 402
Nephin Beg 402, 403
Netherlands 36, 109
neutrality 187, 249, 291, 386, 408,
   409, 410
New Bedford 58
New Haven 55
New Jersey 50, 53

New Mexico xvii, xviii, xix, 63, 69–76,
77, 83, 86–7, 90, 95, 103, 107, 109, 130,
131, 148, 150, 186, 218, 305, 311, 330,
331, 338, 341, 342, 360, 377, 381, 383;
see also Chimayo; Rio Chiquita; Santa
Fe; Talpa; Taos
New York xvi–xvii, xix, 46–53, 55, 56,
58–9, 63, 68, 81, 86, 87–94, 96–104,
106–14, 116–19, 124, 138, 150, 185–6,
217, 233, 261, 277, 341, 372, 377, 427
New York Public Library 93, 99, 102,
105, 331
New Yorker magazine 289, 290, 324, 325
Newark 53
Newberry Library, Chicago xix, 97, 98
Newhall, Nancy: *Time in New England* 338
Newmarket 4
Newport 161, 162, 168, 174, 176, 207,
244, 309
Ngugi Wa Thiong'o 387
Nice 15, 18, 40
Nicholson, Asenath: *The Bible in Ireland* 275
Nicholson, Ben 416
'No Surrender Here!' (eds O'Malley &
Dolan) xi, xii, xiii, xxx
Noah (play) 113
Noggle, Jenny 98
Nolan, Dan 296; EOM's letters to 294–5
Nora (staff member) 189, 190
Normandie 158
Norwood 58
Noskowiak, Sonia 66, 83, 84
Notre Dame 335
Noyk, Michael 279, 287; EOM's letters
to 304
nurses 140, 145–6, 151, 154, 156, 157,
161, 167, 202, 205, 206, 242, 270, 272,
273, 284, 312, 341; *see also* Abbey,
Winnie; Hyland, Winnie; Joyce, Una

O'Brien, Flann 167, 193; *At Swim-Two-
Birds* xxi
O'Brien, Jim 349
O'Brien, Mary 115, 117, 118, 119,
123–4, 160
O'Callaghan, Jerry xxix
O'Casey, Sean 240, 329; *Pictures in the
Hallway* 240

Ó Conaire, Isaac 147
Ó Conaire, Pádraic 147
O'Connell, Daniel 156
O'Connor, Des 180
O'Connor, Frank 74–5, 136, 160, 241,
261–2, 264, 275, 290, 329; *Guests of the
Nation* xix, 75; *Michael Collins* 271
O'Connor, Joe 280
O'Connor, M.J. 51, 53, 59
O'Connor, Matthew xxviii
O'Connor, Rory 352
O'Connor, Ulick xxviii
Ó Deirg, Tomás 234
O'Doherty, Joseph xx, 220
O'Donnell, Peadar 7, 51, 215, 261–2
O'Donoghue, Florrie 231, 352
O'Donovan, Gerald 252, 275
O'Dowd, John David: EOM's letters to 306
O'Duffy, Eimear 230, 252, 275; *A College
Chorus* 252; *Printed Errors* 252; *The
Wasted Island* 252
O'Duffy, Eoin xx, 280
O'Faolain, Sean xxi, 156, 170, 192, 215,
222, 264; *The Great O'Neill* 222; *King
of the Beggars* 156
O'Farrell, Padraic xxvii–xxviii; *The Ernie
O'Malley Story* xxviii
O'Flaherty, Liam 260, 287, 329, 377; *The
Mountain Tavern* 111
O'Flaherty, Roderic: *Chronographical
Description of West of H-Iar
Connaught* 159
O'Grady, Standish 286
O'Higgins, Kevin 375–6
O'Higgins, Pablo Esteban 98
Ó h-Eochadha, Séamus 300, 343
O'Keefe, Georgia 63, 93, 110, 111, 156,
157, 377
O'Kelly, Sean T. xxv
O'Loughlin, Peadar 131
O'Malley, Austin 201, 222
O'Malley, Brendan *see* Malley, Brendan
O'Malley, Cathal: in America xxiv, 150,
154, 294, 303–4, 343; birth xv, xx,
129, 130, 220; at Burrishoole 167–8,
176, 177, 178, 188–9, 190–1, 200, 239,
241–2, 344; childhood 132, 133, 135,
139, 143, 144, 146, 154, 156, 160, 161,

167–8, 176, 177, 178, 188–9, 190–1,
192, 196, 200, 202, 204, 206, 211–13,
224, 225, 229, 232, 236, 239, 241–2,
247, 263–5, 268, 273; in Dublin 196,
204, 211–13, 225, 232, 236, 242, 344;
education 134, 215, 224, 225, 232, 242,
247, 256, 258–60, 268, 273, 275, 303,
311, 342, 343, 344; EOM's letters to
171, 172, 205, 237–8, 253–4, 258–60,
266–7, 303–4, 373–4; health 188, 212,
215, 264, 270, 292, 294, 310, 340;
kidnapped by mother xxiv, 277, 311,
312, 340, 347; and music 270; reading
258, 267, 304; rowing 267, 272

O'Malley, Cecil *see* Malley, Cecil
O'Malley, Christina 189
O'Malley, Cormac: in America 258; Aran
Islands visits 278, 322–3, 343, 346,
354, 355, 370; athletics 339; and ballet
351; birth 134, 206–7; at Burrishoole
265–6, 273, 275, 289, 293, 302, 303,
305, 308, 309, 310, 311, 312, 316, 322,
344–5, 346, 363; childhood 212, 225,
233, 238, 241, 242, 244, 247, 254, 256,
259, 263, 265–6, 267, 268, 273, 275,
289, 293, 300, 302, 303, 305, 322–3,
344–5, 348–9; Christmas cards 286,
296–7, 314–15, 323; cooking 273,
304, 305, 316, 323, 344, 353, 355; in
Dublin 267, 268, 300, 323, 328, 348,
353, 355; education xxiv, xxv, 215, 260,
268, 273, 277–8, 300, 301, 302, 303,
304, 308, 311, 314, 319, 323, 339, 341,
343, 346, 348, 353, 355; in England
308, 309, 310, 312; EOM's fears of
kidnap 284, 341, 343, 344, 346, 348,
370; EOM's letters to 282; health 215,
242, 244, 254, 259, 260, 270, 286, 287,
289, 292, 296, 310, 316, 339, 340, 357;
maintenance payments from HHOM
348, 356–9, 368; and music 270, 357;
'No Surrender Here!' xi, xii, xiii, xxx;
painting 260, 265, 287, 291, 302, 315;
Paris visits 278, 354; *Prisoners: The
Civil War Letters of Ernie O'Malley* xi,
xxviii; reading 300, 317; religion 260;
rowing 302; rugby 300, 314, 323–4,
353; sailing 300, 302, 303, 305, 311,
345; swimming 339; tennis 339; and
theatre 351
O'Malley, Desmond 179, 203
O'Malley, Ernie: *Army Without Banners*
129, 137, 310, 311, 313; and art xiii,
xvi, xxi–xxii, 14, 15, 16, 20, 30–2, 38,
64–5, 66, 70, 80, 130, 138, 152–3,
168, 183, 185–6, 233–5, 236–7, 326,
327, 331, 332–3, 350, 359–60, 377,
382, 383–5, 391–401, 403–6, 412–20,
424–30; art studies 134, 152, 153, 158,
377; arthritis 287, 288; articles and
essays 134, 215, 249–50, 289, 324,
353, 383–4, 390–403, 416–30; auction
of books 274–5, 280, 281, 341; birth
xi; as books editor at *The Bell* xxiv,
215, 257, 258, 261–2; broken leg 210,
211, 225; at Burrishoole xii, xiv, xv, xx,
xxii, 134, 160–70, 175–208, 209–13,
215, 220–5, 230–1, 239–45, 248, 253,
256–8, 260–6, 270–5, 279–81, 283–91,
292–9, 300, 302, 303, 308, 309, 310–11,
316, 318, 319, 320–21, 322, 325–6,
329, 330, 340–1, 344–5, 346, 354–5,
363; capture of xvi, 2, 4, 5, 7, 376;
in the Civil War xii, xvi, 2, 4–5, 109,
136, 212, 230–1, 257, 280, 288, 352;
and classical music xx–xxi, 18, 26–8,
134, 136–7, 139, 140–1, 143, 187, 223,
343, 357; climbing xvi, xxvii, 19, 27,
84, 105, 106–7, 109, 124; clothing 21,
29–30, 32, 70, 125, 142, 159, 165, 170,
174, 180, 199, 240, 241, 413; cooking
80, 167, 287, 300, 302, 305, 312, 316,
367, 370; death xi, xxv, 278; deaths of
friends and family xiv, xvii, 69; diaries
and notebooks xxiii, xxiv–xxv, xxix,
xxx, 46–51, 59–60, 64–6, 65, 77, 82,
114, 134, 194–5, 212–13, 252, 289,
303, 306, 318, 353, 354, 371, 377;
divorce 277, 294, 340, 344, 346; does
not run for Dáil xix–xx, 122, 153;
drinking xv, xxiv, 80, 167, 244, 260–1,
263–6, 328, 334, 338, 349, 360, 362; in
Dublin xii, xv, xxiv–xxv, 36–42, 121–8,
134, 135–48, 150–60, 164, 165, 170–4,
187, 194, 198–9, 202, 208–10, 221,
223, 225, 226, 228–30, 232–5, 249,

253–5, 258–60, 266–8, 277–8, 283, 291–2, 307, 316–17, 320, 323–4, 325, 327–8, 331, 334–51, 353–60, 363–72; and early Irish sculpture 125, 131, 134, 179, 182, 202, 220–1, 258, 262, 264, 265, 330, 342–3, 361, 363, 390–1, 423, 430; education 17; *see also* medical studies; art studies; election canvassing 337, 339; in England xxv, 3, 8, 36, 121, 126, 215, 219, 235–8, 246–9, 257, 262, 282, 308–15, 317–19, 325–33, 337, 339, 341, 352, 354–6, 372–3; eviction court hearings 284, 340; family life and children xv, xx, xxiv, 129, 130, 132, 133, 134, 139, 143, 144–6, 154, 156–7, 160–61, 167–8, 171–2, 176, 177, 178, 188–9, 190–1, 192–3, 198, 200, 202, 204–5, 206, 208, 211–13, 215, 222, 224–5, 228, 229, 232–3, 237–9, 240–43, 245–9, 254, 256, 258–60, 263–5, 266–8, 270, 272–3, 274–5, 277, 279, 284, 292–4, 299–304, 310–13, 340–3, 344–9; farming xx, 134, 170, 179–80, 181–2, 189–90, 198, 200, 201, 207–8, 211–12, 222–5, 244, 256, 289–90, 295, 303, 307, 318; and films 277, 328, 329, 332, 348, 364, 367, 370; finances 10, 20, 32, 38, 39, 58, 74, 83, 85, 86, 88, 89, 90, 93, 98, 102–3, 125, 134, 142, 150, 187, 200, 212, 215, 218, 219, 220, 223, 224, 243–4, 253, 255, 261, 273, 277, 287–9, 293–4, 300, 303, 304, 310–11, 317, 332, 336, 340–1, 346, 354, 368–9; and folklore xv, xxiii, 134, 185, 223, 252, 275, 325, 342, 423–4; fundraising for the *Irish Press* xiii, xvi–xvii, xxix, 45, 47–8, 51–7, 58–62, 74, 377; health xxiv, xxv, 13–14, 15, 21, 25, 34, 56, 58, 74, 110, 112, 122, 165, 185, 202, 210, 246, 247, 249, 253, 260, 262, 270, 274, 275, 277, 278, 284, 286, 289, 299–306, 308, 310, 312, 316, 318, 320, 324, 328, 331, 341, 347, 355, 356–7, 369–74; heart condition 274, 277, 284, 300, 303, 308, 310, 320, 324, 341, 356, 369, 370–1; in hospital 2, 5, 299–306, 341, 369–71; hunger strike xvi, xxviii, 2, 5, 12, 84; injuries to feet xvi, 9, 21, 25, 34, 219,

376; injury to hand 182, 185; injury to leg 298, 300; internment xvi, 2, 4–5, 7, 109, 219, 378, 380–1; interrogation xvi, 4; interviews with republicans xv, xxiii–xxiv, xxx, 134, 216, 252, 269, 271, 281, 283–6, 287, 301, 308, 311, 312–13, 341; introduction to Jack B. Yeats exhibition 215, 391–5; lectures 76, 83, 97, 100, 103, 108–9, 114–15, 117, 134, 363, 403–6; libel action against xx, 134, 148, 150, 220, 223, 310, 313; in Local Security Force 175; at Louisburgh 134, 160–1, 220; marriage to HHOM xi, xiv, xix–xx, 126, 217–25; medical studies xvi, 36–42, 45, 109, 126, 129, 130, 131, 134, 135, 148, 219, 220; meets HHOM and courtship xix, 93, 96, 102–3, 217–19; *On Another Man's Wound* xii, xiv, xv, xviii, xix–xx, xxiii, xxiv, xxvii, 70, 79–80, 87, 90, 93, 100, 102, 106, 107, 109, 110, 112, 124, 129, 131, 136, 166, 219–20, 226, 311, 313, 341; painting jobs 84, 93, 96, 100, 102; paintings, collecting xxi, 152–3, 168, 177, 187, 195, 332–3; pension applications 1–5, 122, 123, 127, 219, 230–1; photography xxii, 27, 92, 128, 134, 147, 182, 220, 264, 342–3; poetry 75, 82, 105, 107, 112, 121, 134; radio xxv, 249, 256, 295–6, 297, 298–9, 324, 412–15; *Raids and Rallies* xxvii, 292, 294–6, 297, 298–9, 301, 341; reading xvii, xxi, 23, 26, 30, 33, 37–8, 40, 65, 68, 69, 70, 71, 73, 93, 100–1, 111, 112, 131, 134, 137–8, 143, 148, 151, 158, 163, 167, 183, 193, 194, 195–6, 220, 229, 232, 234, 238, 250–1, 252, 257–8, 260, 270–2, 274–5, 287, 289, 324, 325, 326, 327–8, 329–30, 365, 366–7, 373, 376–7, 380–2; republicanism xii, 377–82, 386–7; *Rising-Out: Sean Connolly of Longford* xxx, 296, 341; rowing 165, 167, 178, 185, 189, 201–2, 302; rumours of infidelity 248, 342; sailing xxii, 131, 134, 162, 169, 185, 205, 244, 249, 256, 275, 299, 300, 302, 303, 305, 326–7, 329, 338, 345; separation from HHOM

245–9, 251–2, 272–5, 293–4; shares in Hooker Electrochemical Company 253, 255; short stories 107, 121; *The Singing Flame* xxvii, 381–2; sketches 63, 82; smoking 15, 20, 31, 38, 71, 200, 206, 334; society memberships xxiv–xxv, 134, 156; stamp collecting 19, 26, 27; teaching 90; translation 93, 101, 109, 112, 166, 183; travel *see individual locations*; in the War of Independence xii, xv, xvi, xviii, xix, 2–5, 109, 127, 129, 280, 285–6, 295–6, 297, 319; wounding of xvi, 2, 4, 5, 25, 219, 376

O'Malley, Etain: in America xxiv, 258, 302–3, 343; and art 260, 265; birth 134, 192–3, 222; at Burrishoole 206, 207, 242, 265, 267, 272, 344–5; childhood 198, 200, 202, 205, 206, 207, 212, 224, 225, 232, 233, 241, 242, 247, 254, 256, 259, 263, 265–6, 267, 268, 272, 273; in Dublin 254, 259, 344, 348; education 215, 224, 247, 259, 260, 268, 270, 273, 275, 294, 302, 308, 311, 316, 342, 343, 344; EOM's letters to 226, 227, 238, 272, 299–300, 302–3, 316–17, 363; first communion 266, 267; health 254, 270, 273, 292; kidnapped by mother xxiv, 277, 311, 312, 340; in London 308, 312; and music 270; reading 302–3, 316–17; religion 260

O'Malley, Fr 176, 193
O'Malley, George 284, 288, 290
O'Malley, Helen *see* Hooker O'Malley, Helen
O'Malley, Jacqueline *see* Malley, Jacqueline
O'Malley, Joseph 222
O'Malley, Kathleen *see* Malley, Kathleen
O'Malley, Kevin *see* Malley, Kevin
O'Malley, Luke *see* Malley, Luke
O'Malley, Margaret *see* Malley, Margaret
O'Malley, Marian *see* Malley, Marian
O'Malley, Marian 'Sweetie' *see* Malley, Marian 'Sweetie'
O'Malley, Michael 189
O'Malley, Paddy 284
O'Malley, Patrick *see* Malley, Patrick
O'Malley, Thomas 158
O'Neill, Daniel 423

O'Neill, Eugene 50
O'Neill, Hugh 222
O'Rahilly, Áine 9, 22, 29
O'Rahilly, Marion 374
O'Regan, Liam 209–10
O'Reilly, Tom 'Skinner'; EOM's letters to 281
O'Shaughnessy, Frankie 157–8
O'Shea, Bridget, 'Nanna' 180, 181, 190, 192, 228, 239, 240, 242, 243, 244, 254, 255, 258, 259, 299
Ó Súilleabháin, Micheál xxix
O'Sullivan, Geróid 2, 135
O'Sullivan, Sean 323–4
O'Sullivan, Seamus 38, 40, 57, 183, 254, 255; EOM's letters to 286–7
Oakland 61
oarlocks 174, 176
oats 224, 242, 244
Oaxaca 414
Ocotlán sanctuary 414, 429
Odets, Cliff 113, 377; *Awake and Sing* 113; *Until the Day I Die* 113; *Waiting for Lefty* 113
Odyssey in Dublin (Damon) 257
Offaly 2, 3, 192, 354, 391, 400
Ohio 55, 88; *see also* Cincinnati; Cleveland; Columbus
Old Head Hotel, Mayo 263, 300, 302, 329
Old Junk (Tomlinson) 70
Olive and the Sword, The (Knight) 250
Olman, Arthur 59
Olmec civilization 366, 413
Omaha 115
On Another Man's Wound (EOM) xii, xiv, xv, xviii, xix–xx, xxiii, xxiv, xxvii, 70, 79–80, 87, 90, 93, 100, 102, 106, 107, 109, 110, 112, 124, 129, 131, 136, 166, 219–20, 226, 311, 313, 341
On Another Man's Wound, Scéal Ernie O'Malley (documentary) xxix
On Reading (Orage) 70, 73
Oola 4, 5
opera 26; *see also* classical music
Orage, A.R.: *On Reading* 70, 73; *Readers and Writers* 73
Oregon 60, 338
Oriental Encounters (Pickthall) 250

Oriental music 187, 332, 343, 360

Origins of Totalitarianism, The (Arendt) 386

Orlando (Woolf) 111

Orozco, José Clemente xviii, 64, 80, 385, 413, 415

Orschel, Vera xxx

Osaka 271

Ostia, Rome 18

Oughterard 196

Our Examination 257

Overend, George 246

Oxford 313

Oxford University Press 353

Pacheco, Maximo 64

Pacific Ocean 68

Paganism 363

paintings: collecting xxi, 152–3, 156, 157, 168, 177, 187, 195, 332–3; framing 166, 169, 177; *see also* art; exhibitions; galleries

Pakenham, Frank 170

Palenque 415

Palma Vecchio 31

Palmer, Samuel 418

pantomime 259

paraffin 171, 201, 238

Parapluies, Les (Renoir) 404

Paris xxi, 8, 34–5, 36, 130, 153, 155, 201, 278, 289, 326, 329, 331–2, 333, 334–5, 337, 339–40, 354, 360, 361–2, 377

Parnell, Charles Stewart 271

Partisan Review 290

partition 377, 381, 407, 409

Partry mountains 401

Pasadena 63, 109

Passage to India, A (Forster) xxi, 163

Pater, Walter 73

Pavlov, Ivan P. 218

Peake, Mervyn 417

Pearse, Patrick 135, 379

Peck, Martin 72

Peking 123, 124–5

Peloponnesian War, The (Thucydides) 30

Pellerin collection 165

pelota 130

Pennsylvania 55, 56

Pennsylvania Museum 235

pens 13, 37, 84–5, 125, 166, 194, 275, 362

pensions board: EOM's letters to 1–5, 122, 123, 127, 219, 230–1, 279–80

Pernod 362

Peru 325, 428

petrol xxiv, 171, 200, 201–2, 263

Pettit, Philip 386

peyote 329

Philadelphia 55, 56

Phillips, Duncan: *The Leadership of Giorgione* 153

photographs 24, 47, 65, 87, 94, 114, 115, 118, 125, 148, 150, 152, 310, 325, 330, 331, 336, 366

photography xxii, 27, 92, 103, 113–14, 128, 134, 147, 182, 220, 264, 305, 323, 342–3, 370

Piano Player (Hitchens) 417

Piazza Navona, Rome 19, 21

Piazzoni, Gottardo 66

Picasso, Pablo 186, 236, 417, 420

Pickthall, Marmaduke: *Oriental Encounters* 250

Pictures in the Hallway (O'Casey) 240

Pierce, Watson O'Dell 234

Piero della Francesca 382

Pignon, Edouard 405

pigs 161, 170, 180

Pilgrimage in the West (Rossi) 325

Pincio, Rome 24, 27

Pintao, Manuel Martinez 64

Piper, John 416, 418

Pissarro, Camile 163

Pittsburgh 55, 56

planes 117, 260–1, 331

Plastic Redirections (Sweeney) 234

Playboy of the Western World, The (Synge) 306

Players Theatre 225, 228, 232, 268

Plumed Serpent, The (Lawrence) xvii, 69

Plunkett, Eoin 85

Plunkett, Fiona 85

Plunkett, George Noble 85, 252

Plunkett, Mary: EOM's letters to 85

Plunkett, Seoirse 40, 85

Plutarch 30

Poems and Translations (Synge) 325
poetry 65, 100–1, 108–9, 125, 163, 183, 325, 328, 329–30, 412, 420, 423; EOM's 75, 82, 105, 107, 112, 121, 134
Poetry magazine 104–5, 107, 108, 112
Poets and Dreamers (Gregory) 365
Popocateptl 84
poppies, wearing of 37
Poppies and Black Jug (Hitchens) 417
Porter, Arthur Kingsley 131
Portland 60
Portugal, a Book of Folk Ways (Gallop) 140
Post D (Strachey) 196
postcards 32–3, 137, 149, 152, 153, 272, 282, 333, 334, 345
potatoes 49, 57, 162, 167, 191, 244, 363
Power, Eileen: *Mediaeval People* 250
Powys, John Cowper 70
Practical Criticism (Richards) 163
Prague 262
Priestley, J.B.: *Midnight on the Desert* 250
Principles of Literary Criticism (Richards) xxi, 163
Printed Errors (O'Duffy) 252
Prisoners: The Civil War Letters of Ernie O'Malley (eds English & O'Malley) xi, xxviii
prohibition 46
Proust, Marcel xxi, 137
Provence 130, 131, 132
Providence 56, 58, 62, 117
Provincetown 96, 109
Pyrenees xvi, 8, 106, 376

Quare Fellow, The (Behan) 374
Queen Mary 156
Quennell, Peter 251; *Byron in Italy* 250; *Byron: The Years of Fame* 250
Queretaro 414, 429
Quiet Man, The (Ford) xxv, 277
Quinn, Mary 243
Quinn, Paddy 47
Quinn, Pat 195, 256, 259, 302, 303

rabbits 100, 171–2, 190, 205
Race in Hy-Brazil, A (Yeats) 397
radio xxv, 165, 249, 256, 270, 295–6, 297, 298–9, 324, 357, 368–9, 412–15

Raftery, Anthony 365
Raids and Rallies (EOM) xxvii, 292, 294–6, 297, 298–9, 301, 341
Raleigh, Bea 43, 122, 123, 133, 160–1, 166, 167, 192, 208, 209, 298; EOM's letters to 128
Raleigh, John 160–1, 192, 258, 259–60, 311; EOM's letters to 10, 33–4, 39, 41, 43, 122–3, 128, 133, 166–7, 208–10, 298
Raleigh, John (son of John) 260
Raleigh, Mary 128, 161, 298, 311–12
Raleigh, Oona 128, 160, 161, 298
Raleigh, Peggy 122, 123, 128, 208; EOM's letters to 160–1
Raleigh, Sheila 128, 161
Raphael 16, 20, 31; *Transfiguration* 14
rates 287–9, 294, 303, 311, 312, 318, 320
Rathcoole 297
Ravenna 34
Razumovsky 141
Read, Herbert, 327; *Annals of Innocence and Experience* 251
Readers and Writers (Orage) 73
Rearcross 4, 5, 295
Recruits (Axenfield) 113
Red Landscape (Sutherland) 417
Redmond, Barbara *see* MacDonagh, Barbara
Redmond, Liam 131, 221, 224, 225, 248, 268, 289; *The Rocks of Bawn* 225
Reid, Nano 183, 377, 405, 423
religion 217, 219, 260, 289, 407, 424; *see also* Catholicism
Rembrandt 398
Remembering Sion (Ryan) 136
'Renaissance' (EOM) 134, 406–12
Renaissance in Italy, The (Symonds) 23
Renoir, Jean: *The Southerner* 329
Renoir, Pierre-Auguste 236, 327; *Les Parapluies* 404
Renvyle House 336, 351
republicanism xii, xiii, 375–82, 386–7
republicans, EOM's interviews with xv, xxiii–xxiv, xxx, 134, 216, 252, 269, 271, 281, 283–6, 287, 301, 308, 311, 312–13, 341
responsibility 22
restaurants 48, 119, 130, 326, 328, 338

Rheims Cathedral 38
Rhode Island 55, 56, 58, 62, 117
Rhodes, Anthony: *Sword of Bone* 251
Rhodes, Cecil 270, 271
rhubarb wine 197
Rich & Cowan 129, 131, 139, 140, 142,
    149, 219, 313
Richards, Ceri Giraldus 416
Richards, I.A.: *Practical Criticism* 163;
    Principles of Literary Criticism xxi, 163
Richter, George Martin: *Giorgio de
    Castlefranco* 153
Rilke, Rainer Maria: *Letter to a Young Poet*
    166, 183
Rimbaud, Arthur 101
Rimsky-Korsakov, Nikolai 187
Ring College 215, 270, 273, 275, 277,
    300, 343
Rinneen 295, 296, 297
Rio Chiquita 202, 218
Rising of the Moon, The (Ford) xxv, 277,
    361, 364, 367, 370
Rising-Out: Sean Connolly of Longford
    (EOM) xxx, 296, 341
Ritschel, William Frederick 66
Rivera, Diego xviii, 64, 80, 385, 413, 415
Road to En-Dor, The (Jones) 250, 251
Road to Life (Ekk) 113
Robinson, Lennox 170, 182, 329; *Lady
    Gregory's Journal* 328, 362
Robinson, Séamus 4, 279
Rockefeller, John D. III xix, 218
Rocks of Bawn, The (Redmond) 225
Roelofs, Richard 345, 347, 348
Rolland, Romain: *Jean-Christophe* 65
Rome xvi, 8, 13–29, 109, 362, 376, 427
Romeo and Juliet (Shakespeare) 113
Ronayne, Fr C.F. 14, 18, 21, 31, 35, 36
Roscommon 2, 287–8, 295
Rosegreen 279
Rosenfield, Paul 103
Rossa (McHugh) 226
Rossetti, Dante Gabriel 73
Rossgiblin 189, 205, 211, 222, 244, 288,
    290, 336
Rossi, Mario: *Pilgrimage in the West* 325
Rothenstein, Sir John 235, 322; EOM's
    letters to 229–30

Rothschild, Barbara 248
Roualt, Georges xxi, 152, 233, 237, 332,
    404, 406; *Christ Mocked* 406
Rousseau, Henri 237
rowing 165, 167, 178, 185, 189, 201–2,
    267, 272, 302
Rowntree, Benjamin Seebohm 245, 248
Royal Academy of Art 332
Royal Dublin Society xxiv
Royal Hibernian Academy 212, 233, 405
Royal Society of Antiquaries in Ireland
    xxiv, 137, 158
rugby 300, 314, 323–4, 353
Ruskin, John 16
Russell, George 183, 379
Russell, Sean 5
Russia xix, 83, 96, 98, 107, 121, 218, 262
Ruttledge, P.J. 9
Ryan, Desmond: EOM's letters to 136,
    175; *Remembering Sion* 136
Ryan, Sean 48

Sacramento 60, 61
saga literature 330–1
Saicha, The (Smith) 70
sail cloth 195
sailing xxii, 131, 134, 162, 169, 185, 205,
    244, 249, 256, 275, 299, 300, 302, 303,
    305, 311, 326–7, 329, 338, 345
Sailor of Kathare (play) 112
St Brendan (boat) 259, 275, 299, 302
St Bricin's Hospital 2, 5, 299–306, 317,
    341, 354
St Gerald's School, Bray 242
St Germaine-des-Prés Museum, Paris 155
St Ita's School 3
St Stephen's Green 363, 367
Saleil, Jeanne: *A House in the Cevennes* 367
Salkeld, Beatrice 267
Salkeld, Blanaid 194
Salkeld, Cecil 174
San Antonio 338
San Diego 63
San Francisco 58, 59, 60–2, 63, 68,
    109, 115
San Luis Potosi 81, 412
Santa Fe xviii, 70, 74–6, 83, 86, 105,
    109, 186

Santa Rose church 414
Sapir, Edward 380
Saratoga Springs 91–2, 95–6, 109
Saturday Review of Literature 51
Savonarola, Girolamo 31
Scarlatti, Domenico 187
Schauffler, Robert: *Beethoven* 139
Schreibman, Susan xxix
Schubert, Franz 137, 141, 187
Scorched Earth (Snow) 195
scotch 325
Scotland 321, 331, 333, 334, 338, 353, 387
Scott, Michael 180, 350, 361
Scott, Patrick 361
Scramogue 295
sculpture: early Irish 125, 131, 134, 179,
    182, 202, 220–1, 258, 262, 264, 265,
    330, 342–3, 361, 363, 390–1, 423, 430;
    exhibitions of 96–7, 237, 332, 360,
    361–2, 365, 416, 418, 419; HHOM's
    96, 134, 178, 215, 217, 220, 224, 225,
    228, 242, 347; Jean McGrail's 336;
    Mexican 366, 413, 424–7
Sculpture Irlandaise, La (Henry) 330
Sea and the Jungle, The (Tomlinson) 250
Sears, David 180
Seattle 45, 60
Second World War 134, 170, 185, 187–9,
    201, 202–3, 221, 223, 291, 301, 354,
    386, 398, 404, 408–10, 418, 420, 423
Sentimental Journey, A (Sterne) 250
Seven Samurai (Kurosawa) 332
Sexton, Eric: *Irish Crosses* 258
Shakespeare, William 33, 70, 115, 250,
    382; *Hamlet* xxv, 271; *Romeo and Juliet*
    113; *Sonnets* 100–1, 381, 382
Shanahan, Brian 48
Shaw, George Bernard 73, 255, 333
Sheeffry Hills 401
Sheehan, Mick 68
Sheehy, Bridget 'Biddens' 284, 355, 369;
    EOM's letters to 301
Sheehy, Michael: EOM's letters to 284,
    300–1, 354–5, 369
Sheehy-Skeffington, Owen 129
sheep 161, 167, 198, 256, 266
Sheridan, Belinda 126, 160, 161,
    218–19, 273

Sheridan, Niall 153
shoes 38, 114, 118, 140, 156, 159, 168,
    170, 172, 178, 232
short stories 107, 110–11, 121
Shorthorn Breeders' Association xxiv
Shostakovich, Dmitri 140
Sibelius, Jean 28, 140, 141, 187
Sicily xvi, 109, 251, 362
Siena 13
silage 207, 212, 244
Sinclair, Mary: *The Three Sisters* 111
Singing Flame, The (EOM) xxvii, 381–2
Singing Man (MacBryde) 417
Sinn Féin 7
Siqueros, David Alfaro 413, 415
Sistine Chapel, Rome 16
Sitting Woman (Hitchens) 417
Skerries 260–1, 262
Sligo 128, 319, 391–2
Smith, Al E. 50
Smith, Christy 300, 320, 322, 344, 373–4
Smith, Dana 70
Smith, Matthew 416, 417
smoking 15, 20, 31, 38, 71, 200, 206, 334
Snow, Edgar: *Scorched Earth* 195
Solomons, Bethel 173, 220
Solomons, Stella 37, 40, 57, 286
Somerville-Large, Sammy: EOM's letters
    to 279
Sommerfield, John: *Volunteer in Spain* 251
Sonnets (Shakespeare) 100–1, 381, 382
Sons and Lovers (Lawrence) xvii, 69
Souls of Black Folks, The (Du Bois) 379
South Africa 203
Southern Gates of Arabia, The (Stark) 250
Southerner, The (Renoir) 329
Spain xiv, xvi, 10–12, 33–4, 109, 111,
    124, 196, 330, 376, 381, 410, 414,
    415, 428–9; *see also* Balearic Islands;
    Barcelona; Madrid; Majorca
Spanish 11, 18, 28, 30, 71, 80, 111,
    151, 381
Spanish Civil War 129, 251, 377, 409
Spanish Empire in America, The (Haring)
    xxiv, 257
Speakman, Harold: *Here's Ireland* 37–8
Spencer, Stanley 416, 418–19, 420
Spender, Stephen 101

spirituality 377–8, 382

sport *see* American football; athletics; Gaelic games; golf; rugby; tennis

Spring Show, Dublin 128

Stack, Austin 7

Stahl, John: *The Keys of the Kingdom* 348

stamps 19, 26, 27, 237, 254, 266

Stanley, Fr Joseph 308

Stark, Freya 250, 251

Stein, Gertrude: *Three Lives* 138

Stella (nurse) 242

Steloff, Frances 47

Stephens, James 73; *Deirdre* 71

Stephens, Wallace xviii, 108

Stephenson, Dan: EOM's letters to 307

Sterne, Laurence xvii, 70; *A Sentimental Journey* 250

Sterne, Meta 314

Stevedore (Sklar and Peters) 112

Stevenson, Philip 'Ted' 87, 88, 90, 91, 105, 110

Stevenson, Robert Louis: *Treasure Island* 303

Stewart, Dorothy xvii, 77, 79, 80, 87, 96, 98, 132, 148, 151, 186; sketch of EOM 77

Stewart, Stan 256, 266

Stewart, Virginia: *Contemporary Mexican Artists* 330

Stieglitz, Alfred 93, 111, 156

Stoddard, Eunice 118

Stokes, Richard 333, 338

Strachey, John: *Post D* 196

Strand, Hazel 305, 311, 312, 313, 339, 340, 344, 353, 370, 371

Strand, Paul xxii, xxix, 87, 110, 126, 156, 188, 278, 331, 338, 377; EOM's letters to 87–9, 91–2, 102–3, 105–7, 305, 310–13, 315, 320–1, 323–4, 339–40, 344–5, 353–4, 370–1; *La France de Profil* 305, 338; *Un Paese: Portrait of an Italian Village* 313, 338, 339

Strand, Rebecca 63, 92, 313

Strasberg, Lee 87–8, 377

Stravinsky, Igor xxi, 137, 141

Strauss, Richard 140, 187

Studio 192

subways 46–7, 49, 92, 149

Success Story (Lawson) 113

Suibhne Geilt 168

Sullivan, J.W.N.: *Beethoven: His Spiritual Development* 139; *But for the Grace of God* 250

Sunday Press 298–9, 301; EOM's letters to 352

Surrealism 420

Sutherland, Graham 405, 416, 417

Sweeney, James Johnson 93, 289, 321; *African Negro Art* 234; EOM's letters to 164, 179, 233–5, 286, 350–1; *Plastic Redirections* 234

Sweeney, Joe 256–7

Sweeney, Laura 179, 321, 350; EOM's letters to 322

Sweetman, John Francis 189

Swift, Jonathan xvii, 70, 328

swimming 68, 95, 97, 340

Swinburne, Algernon Charles 73

Swinton, Sir Ernest Dunlop: *The Defence of Duffer's Drift* 251

Switzerland 34

Sword of Bone (Rhodes) 251

Sykes, Gerald 88, 93, 102, 105, 107

Symonds, John Addington: *The Renaissance in Italy* 23

Synge, J.M. 324, 326, 329, 330, 382; *The Aran Islands* 250, 324; *Deirdre* 71; *The Playboy of the Western World* 306; *Poems and Translations* 325

Synge's Chair, Aran Islands 325

Taash 326

table tennis 177

Tacoma 60

Taft, William 329

Tagore, Rabindranath 73, 381

Tailteann Games 48

Táin Bó Cúailnge 71, 73

Talpa 73

Tan War *see* War of Independence

Tannhäuser (Wagner) 26

Taos xvii, xviii, 63, 69–73, 87, 89, 92, 109, 110, 130, 186, 218, 313, 356, 360, 377, 383

Tarascan people 413, 426

Tate Gallery, London 229, 235, 236

Taylor, Kitty Harding 260
Tchaikovsky, Pyotr Ilyich xxi, 137, 141
tea 26, 32, 136, 145, 167, 184, 192, 198,
    201, 203, 240, 273, 349–50
Teeling, Frank 4, 217
tennis xvi, 177, 189, 217, 272, 338, 339
Tenochtitlan 424, 427–8
Teotihuacan 414, 415, 424, 425, 427
Teresa (staff member) 203, 204, 205, 206
Termona 128
Texas 338
theatre xxv, 50, 59–60, 80, 87–8, 107,
    112–13, 117, 134, 143, 180, 193, 194,
    224, 225, 226, 237, 241, 251, 259, 271,
    306, 316, 324, 351, 355, 360
Theatre in Action 112
Thomond Archaeological Journal 265
Thompson, Eric 366
Thoreau, Henry David 137
Three Candles Press 220
Three Lives (Stein) 138
Three Sisters, The (Sinclair) 111
threshing 200, 207
Thucydides: The Peloponnesian War 30
Thunder Over Mexico (Eisenstein) 77
Tierney, Michael 298
Time in New England (Newhall) 338
Tincurry 279–80
tinkers see Travellers
Tintoretto 138, 152, 153, 156, 382
Tipperary 2, 3–4, 109, 127, 279–80;
    see also Bansha; Borrisoleigh; Cahir;
    Clonmel; Drangan; Hollyford;
    Lisvernane; Modreeny; Rearcross;
    Rosegreen; Tincurry
Tipperary Men's Club, New York 52
Tissé, Eduard 77, 78, 107
Titian 20, 138
Tivoli, Rome 27, 28, 29
Tobin, Eva 39, 123
Tobin, Mae 39, 123
Tobin, Marian 123, 279
Together (Douglas) 250
Tolstoy, Leo 229, 381
Toltec people 413, 424, 425, 426, 427
tomatoes 167, 168
tombs 16, 31, 423
Tomlinson, H.M. 70; Old Junk 70; The

Sea and the Jungle 250
Tommy (staff member) 195, 196, 203,
    211, 212
Tone, Theobald Wolfe 68
Topographical Dictionary of Ireland
    (Lewis) 158
Topolski, Feliks 416, 419
Totonac people 366, 413, 426
Tourmakeady 295
Tracey, Sean 3, 5
tractors 200
Tracy, Honor 290
Tralee 282
Transfiguration (Raphael) 14
Transition 164, 179
translation 93, 99, 101, 109, 112, 151,
    166, 168, 183, 218
transport see buses; cars; planes; subways
Transportation Building, New York 49–50
Travellers 392, 400–1
Traynor, Fr Timothy 193
Treacy, Sean 279–80
Treasure Island (Stevenson) 303
trees 116–17, 118, 402
Trembling of the Veil (Yeats) 163
Triple Thinkers, The (Wilson) 137
Tuam 128, 158, 265
Tullamore 192, 400
Tullow 9
Tunnard, John 416, 419
turf 28, 166, 184, 192, 208, 211, 229,
    244, 246, 248, 256, 270, 305, 316, 342,
    345, 404, 422
Turnbull, Patrick: Black Barbary 196
Tuscany 29–33
typewriters 15, 117, 123–4, 243, 257, 302
typing 79, 82, 83, 93, 246, 274, 295, 297,
    302, 363
Tyrell's Pass 263
Tyrone 2, 3, 128

Uffizi gallery 31–2
Uist 321, 353
Ulysses (Joyce) xiv, 70, 76, 83
Umberto D (de Seca) 329
Un Paese: Portrait of an Italian Village
    (Strand) 313, 338, 339
United Arts Club xxiv

University College Dublin xvi, xxi, xxvi, 36, 105, 109, 298, 311–12, 361, 363
Until the Day I Die (Odets) 113
Utah 338

Valley of the Assassins, The (Stark) 250
Van Gogh, Vincent 101, 111
Varian, John O. 59
Vasari, Giorgio: *Lives of the Italian Painters* 382
Vasconcelos, Jose 415
Vatican 16
Vecchio, Palma 138
vegetables 162, 167, 170, 181, 189, 191, 201, 202, 244, 273, 363
Velasquez, Diego 398, 404; *Kitchen Scene in the House of Martha* 327
Venice 34
Venus (Agar) 419
Veracruz 366, 413, 426
Vermeer, Johannes 138
Vermeer (Hale) 138
Vernon's (rope and sail manufacturers) 171, 174
Veronese, Paolo 31, 138
Victoria and Albert Museum, London 237, 332
Viking Press 106, 107, 109, 110
Villard, Mariquita 93, 94, 119, 156, 217
Villard, Oscar Garrison 217
Virgile, Gladys 152, 155
Virginia 363
Viva Mexico (Flandrau) 250
Vivaldi, Antonio 28
Vivarini, Antonio 31
Vlaminck, Maurice de xxi, 152, 153, 183, 333
Vogue magazine 326
Volunteer in Spain (Sommerfield) 251
von Humboldt, Wilhelm 379
Vorse, Mary 95–6
Voyages (Hakluyt) 70, 258

Waddington, Victor 416
Waddington gallery 172, 416
Wagner, Richard 187; *Tannhäuser* 26
Waiting for Godot (Beckett) 360
Waiting for Lefty (Odets) 113

Walch, Charles 405
Waldorf Astoria, New York 47–8, 52
Wales 250, 251, 387, 418
Wall, Mervyn 299; EOM's letters to 299
Wall Street, New York 50–1
Wallace, Alec 263, 300, 302, 329
Wallace, Edgar 23, 24
Walsh, Frank P. 50
Walsh, Paul 326
Walsh, Roisin 143, 159, 174, 179, 195–6, 207, 228, 232
Walsh, Sean 222, 290
Walsh, Willie 192, 222, 290
Walston, Catherine 'Bobs' 228, 229–30, 232, 236, 237, 241, 243, 245, 248–9, 277, 308, 313, 316, 325, 327, 329, 332, 371, 373
Walston, Harry xxv, 236, 237, 243, 277, 308, 313, 316, 325, 327, 329, 332, 333, 334, 337, 372
Walston, William 319, 323
Wanderings in Arabia (Lawrence) 65
War of Independence xii, xv, xviii, xix, xxiv, 1–5, 81, 109, 127, 129, 280, 285–6, 287, 290, 295–6, 297, 314, 319, 341, 353, 383
Ward Price, George: *The Foreign Legion* 196
Washington DC 55, 234
Washington Heights, New York 49
Washington State 45, 60, 338
Wasted Island, The (O'Duffy) 252
Waterford 215; *see also* Dungarvan; Ring College
Watts, William C. 66
Way of all Flesh, The (Butler) 65
Wayne, John 300
weather: Aran Islands 131, 323, 345, 349, 370; California 67, 68; Cork 298; Dublin 36, 139, 140, 143, 148, 154, 159, 174, 198, 324, 354, 365, 367; England 236, 337; France 35, 335, 361, 362; Ireland generally 124, 275; Italy 19, 34, 35, 359–60; Mayo 147, 161, 162, 163, 165, 166, 167, 169, 176, 177, 189, 192, 195, 196, 206, 239, 242, 244, 249, 259, 265, 286, 296, 320, 345, 346, 402; New Mexico 72, 73, 110; New York 49

Weber, Carl Maria von 141
West, Rebecca 290; *Black Lamb and Grey Falcon* 250, 251, 290
Weston, Edward xxix, 64–5, 377; EOM's letters to 67, 83–4
Westmeath 3, 157–8, 263, 284
Westport 131, 147, 156, 161, 162, 163, 171, 173, 179, 192, 196, 201, 210, 233, 239, 284, 288, 303, 309
Wexford xxiv, 2, 4, 150
wheat 200, 207, 212, 224, 244
Wheelwright, Mary 110
whiskey xxiv, 22, 157, 204, 262, 263–4, 265, 266, 325
Whistler, James McNeill 398
Whorf, Benjamin Lee 380
Whyte, James 234
Wicklow 2, 4, 128, 148, 242
Wicklow Mountains 306
Wild Sports of the West of Ireland (Maxwell) 336–7
Wild Wales (Burrows) 250, 251
Wilde, Oscar 40, 73
Williams, William Carlos xxi; *Life Along the Potomac River* 137; *Middletown in Transition* 137
Willow Park school xxiv
Wills, Helen 217
Wilson, Edmund xxi; *The Triple Thinkers* 137
Wilson, J. Dover: *The Essential Shakespeare* 250, 251
wine 28, 32, 80, 119, 160, 195, 196, 197, 203, 326, 338, 362
Winter in Arabia, A (Stark) 250
Wood, Stanley 66
Woods, Joanna 258
Woods, Peggy 258

Woods, Tony 291
Woods, Violet 162
Woodstock 94, 96, 109
Woolf, Virginia: *Orlando* 111
Woolworth Building, New York 49, 50
Worcester 55, 58
Workers' School, New York 119
Wyndham-Lewis, D.B.: *Francois Villon* 47
Wyndham-Lewis, Percy 289
Wyoming 338

Xenophon: *Anabasis* 30, 251, 267

Yaddo Foundation xix, 87, 88, 90–2, 93, 109, 377
Yale Review xxi, 137
Yeats, Jack B. xiv, xxi–xxii, 134, 164, 165, 169, 173, 177, 182, 183, 192, 215, 226–7, 234–5, 236, 260, 268, 289, 327, 328, 331, 341, 356, 375–6, 377, 382, 385, 391–6, 398, 406, 423; *Bachelor's Walk* 394; *The Blood of Abel* 397; *Death for Only One* xxi, 165; EOM's letters to 315; *The Funeral of Harry Boland* 375–6; *Helen* 397; *In Memory of Boucicault and Bianconi* 397; *Life in the West of Ireland* 169; *Low Tide* xxii, 397; *A Race in Hy-Brazil* 397
Yeats, W.B. 73, 163, 169–70, 274, 324, 325, 327–8, 329–30, 336, 366; *Autobiographies* 250; *The Cutting of an Agate* 163; *Trembling of the Veil* 163
Young, Charlotte: *Book of Golden Deeds* 28
Young, Ella xvii, 59, 63, 75, 89, 98, 101, 102, 106, 107, 111, 132, 313
Yucatan 414, 415, 424, 425–6, 428

Zapotec civilization 413